Growing Up Gay in the South
Race, Gender,
and Journeys of the Spirit

"A WONDERFUL BOOK. . . . From one point of view, it is a stirring and, for me, disarming and revelatory look into the anguish that so many young gay people undergo in this society. This alone would make the book important. But, from another point of view, it is a wonderful portrayal of the way all kids grow up—the cliques that form, the sense of pecking order, the fear of being spurned, excluded by the kinds who form the 'in group' in junior high or high school; and this, I think has relevance to almost anyone. . . . So, in this sense, it is a book about conformity and independence on a larger scale than sexuality. . . . It is a critically essential novel about gay youth. But it is also an important portrait of the coming-of-age of all young people in this country. The secret anguish of adolescence has rarely been more meaningfully portrayed."
Jonathan Kozol, Educator and Award Winning Author of *Death at an Early Age* (National Book Award Winner), *Illiterate America,* and *Rachel and Her Children*

"An important contribution to American letters, both as theory and a documentation. I particularly appreciate the wide range of scholarship here as well as the lucidity. The case studies fascinate as do the commentaries, especially the last chapter. A MAJOR ACHIEVEMENT."
Louie Crew, PhD, Rutgers University; Founder of Integrity; Author of *The Gay Academic*

"Sears has not tried to impose one mold upon the youths he interviewed, but he has allowed them to speak for themselves: female and male, black and white, belle and redneck—all the wondrous diversity that perhaps someday the South will learn to appreciate and value. *Growing Up Gay in the South* should go a long way to overcome educators' silence. . . . PROVIDES MUCH INSIGHT into an understanding of the South in general, not limited to sexual issues."
Walter Williams, Professor of Anthropology, University of Southern California at Los Angeles; Author of *The Spirit and the Flesh: Sexual Diversity in American Indian Culture*

"SETS A NEW STANDARD for gay/lesbian sociology. The synthesis of cultural, regional, and institutional contexts with the narratives of young lesbian and gay South Carolinians creates a richer signification than the narratives alone would carry. Each narrative taps into the experience of countless others; and, while never losing its individual subjectivity, it reads simultaneously as a paradigm. As a result, a regional and generational cross-section of childhood and adolescence is brought palpitatingly alive—joys, confusions, lonelinesses, friendships, and the excitements of sexual awakenings and self-affirmations."
Donald N. Mager, Co-Chair, Gay and Lesbian Caucus for the Modern Languages (GLCML); Assistant Professor, Johnson C. Smith University, Charlotte, North Carolina

Growing Up Gay in the South

Race, Gender, and Journeys of the Spirit

James T. Sears, PhD

Harrington Park Press
New York • London

ISBN 0-918393-79-5

Published by

Harrington Park Press, 10 Alice Street, Binghamton, NY 13904-1580.
EUROSPAN/Harrington, 3 Henrietta Street, London WC2E 8LU England

Harrington Park Press is a subsidiary of The Haworth Press, Inc., 10 Alice Street, Binghamton,
NY 13904-1580.

© 1991 by Gay and Lesbian Advocacy Research Project. All rights reserved. No part of this work
may be reproduced or utilized in any form or by any means, electronic or mechanical, including
photocopying, microfilm and recording, or by any information storage and retrieval system,
without permission in writing from the publisher. Printed in the United States of America.

Cover design by John Paul Lona.

Library of Congress Cataloging-in-Publication Data

Sears, James T. (James Thomas), 1951-
    Growing up gay in the South : race, gender, and journeys of the spirit / James T. Sears.
      p. cm.
    Includes bibliographical references and index.
    ISBN 0-918393-79-5
    1. Gay teenagers — Southern States. 2. Homosexuality — Southern States — Case studies.
3. Homosexuality — Religious aspects — Christianity. I. Title.
HQ76.3.U5S43   1990b
305.9'0664 — dc20
                                              90-4993
                                            CIP

The 36 Sexual Rebels

Alston	Jackson
Audrey	Jacob
Brandon	Kevin
Brett	Kimberly
Carlton	Lenora
Cory	'Lizabeth
Darla	Malcolm
Drew	Marian
Elisa	Nathaniel
Everetta	Norma Jean
Fawn	Obie
Franklin	Olivia
Georgina	Phillip
Grant	Royce
Henry III	Steve
Heyward	Terry
Irwin	Vince
Isaiah	William

ALL HARRINGTON PARK PRESS BOOKS
ARE PRINTED ON CERTIFIED
ACID-FREE PAPER

CONTENTS

Foreword

For many lesbian and gay adolescents, high school is a lonely and often frightening place. Ridicule from teachers, violent harassment from fellow students, and other discriminatory school practices interfere with the ability of gay students to learn.

In 1984, while working on my doctoral dissertation in psychology, I surveyed ten of the largest school districts in the United States to determine the degree and nature of services provided for lesbian and gay youngsters, who make up a sizeable and well-defined minority of the adolescent population. Samples in the literature and testimonies from teenagers and advocacy groups indicated that services were, for the most part, non-existent. In order to confirm this, I sent a questionnaire to the head of guidance and counseling in each of the districts. This was followed by a telephone interview. Except for New York City's Harvey Milk School, an alternative school operated in connection with the Institute for the Protection of Gay and Lesbian Youth, services were entirely absent. Additionally the survey revealed a pattern of homophobia in the education system that systematically damages gay and lesbian teenagers, and takes the form of verbal and physical abuse, failure to discipline the abusers, and the perpetuation of a belief system which suggests that homosexuals are in every way morally inferior to heterosexuals. Generally, adolescent homosexuals were treated as invisible or as objects of hate and bigotry in the school.

It was against this background that Project 10, a counseling program for lesbian and gay youth, began at Fairfax High School in Los Angeles. Fairfax High is one of fifty senior high schools in the Los Angeles Unified School District, second only to New York City as the largest school district in the nation. Fairfax High School is located two blocks south of the city of West Hollywood along Melrose Avenue, a street of "New Wave" and "Punk" specialty shops. It has a student body of approximately 2500 students of mixed racial and ethnic backgrounds. Although West Hollywood with its large gay population is almost adjacent to the school, Fairfax students are neither more nor less sensitive to the issues of homosexuality than students from other schools in the Eastern part of Los Angeles.

Project 10 started because of an unpleasant incident involving an openly gay male student who had been transferred to Fairfax. From the day he entered he was physically abused by peers and verbally abused by teachers and peers alike. Finally, he dropped out of school entirely and turned to the streets, becoming one more casualty of a system that neither understands nor cares.

This offensive incident was brought to my attention and prompted me to investigate the background of Chris H., age 17, black, male, homosexual. Forcibly ejected from his home at age 14 for admitting that he was gay, Chris had been on the streets for about a year until he was placed in a juvenile detention home and finally a group home for lesbian and gay adolescents. All his teachers described him as "sweet," "nice," and of average intelligence with no particular learning disabilities. The only reason given as to why he encountered so much trouble in school was that he was gay. The story was always the same. He would enter a school and the students would harass him immediately. If he defended himself, either verbally or physically, he was taken to the Dean's office and reprimanded. The adults often added to his torment by their indifference or by making innuendoes or other subtle remarks about his homosexuality.

Chris' story is a metaphor for the dilemmas of gay, lesbian, and bisexual youth and the way these are played out in the school experience. Here was a young man — still a child in so many ways — who was separated from his family and black culture because he was gay, filled with shame, stigmatized by society, isolated from peers and positive role models, poorly socialized, and forced into dangerous sexual contacts. And in all of this, the educational system stood by blindfolded and mute.

Growing Up Gay in the South gives voice to the extraordinary struggle of lesbian and gay adolescents like Chris as they try to define themselves in a homophobic society. Through the lives of these "sexual rebels," Sears tells stories of courage and triumph in the face of defeat. *Growing Up Gay in the South* artfully blends the distinctive features of Southern life into the biographies of a young people who must make sense of their sexual identities and struggle in a hostile world. Sears gives visibility to a largely invisible population and in doing so he has made a wonderful contribution to the body of information on gay and lesbian youth. *Growing Up Gay in the South* takes the reader on a journey that few authors have been willing to make. It will make you laugh and cry—but most of all it will grip you with its candid blending of scientific research and matter-of-fact narratives. Although regional in its data, there is a universal quality that makes this book worthwhile for all readers.

Most of all, *Growing Up Gay in the South* is a symbol of the indomitable spirit of lesbian, gay, and bisexual youth. This book is a validation of them as good and healthy persons worthy of respect and deserving of attention by public educators and other professionals. With its extensive bibliography and data, *Growing Up Gay in the South* is an invaluable addition to the literature on adolescent homosexuality. It is essential reading for professionals working with young people and deserves a prominent place in college and public libraries. *Growing Up Gay in the South* is the quintessential blending of interdisciplinary scholarship, wonderful writing, and provocative thinking. It is a journey which we should all take.

Virginia Uribe, PhD
Founder, Project 10
Los Angeles Unified School District
Los Angeles, California

Preface

Growing Up Gay in the South is a wonderful book: mature, confident, elegantly written, and very moving. It is a stirring and, for me, disarming and revelatory look into the anguish that so many young gay people undergo in this society. This alone would make the book important. But, from another point of view, it is a wonderful portrayal of the way all kids grow up — the cliques that form, the sense of pecking order, the fear of being spurned, excluded, by the kids who form the "in-group" in junior high or high school; and this, I think, has relevance to almost anyone.

So, in this sense, this is a book about conformity and independence on a larger scale than sexuality. This will speak to everyone and I would hope, therefore, that *Growing Up Gay in the South* would be read by all who knew the longing to rebel against the often thankless norms that were held up to us. There is a rebel spirit in most children. Whether defined by sexuality, by religion, or by some less easily definable aesthetic impulse, it is part of the American grain, and in this respect, *Growing Up Gay in the South* is also very much in the American grain, though written "against" that grain, as most good literature is.

Growing Up Gay in the South is reminiscent of good fiction. It reminds me again and again of Eudora Welty and Carson McCullers. Its graphic details lend the book its gripping and idiosyncratic veracity — very vivid, sometimes bizarre, even Gothic items of pungent specificity.

I read *Growing Up Gay in the South* almost without interruption. It gripped me from the first page to the last. Although it is presented in the format of a work of sociology, I read it as enormously compelling narratives, filled with the pain and love of all good fiction and nonfiction. It is a critically essential novel about gay youth. But it is also an important portrait of the coming-of-age of all young people in this country. The secret anguish of adolescence has rarely been more meaningfully portrayed.

Jonathan Kozol
Byfield, MA

Acknowledgements

Many people contributed to this project. I particularly wish to thank Tony Deiulio, William Rose, Joel Taxel, Dennis Carlson, and Anne Trousdale for their comments on earlier drafts of this book. Support for this project was provided by the Gay and Lesbian Advocacy Research Project, Inc., the College of Education at the University of South Carolina, and the South Carolina Guidance Counselor's Association. In particular, I wish to thank Lorin Anderson, Norma Deery, Leonard Pellicer, and Sam Vause. This book also benefitted from the work of three talented and committed librarians, Tara Fulton, Cathy Eckman, and Gary Geer. I also wish to thank Louie Crew and Carter Wilson for their critical reading of the manuscript and Jack Huberman for his thoughtful editing. John DeCecco's insights and patience as I worked through earlier versions of this book are kindly acknowledged as are my extended conversations with J. Dan Marshall who was an important source for refining and testing many of these ideas. Central to the book, of course, are the 36 young Southerners who let me glimpse into their lives and share them with you. Finally Bob Williamson, to whom this book is dedicated.

Copyright Permissions

Grateful acknowledgement is made to the following for permission to reprint previously copyrighted material: Audre Lorde for "Sister Outsider," excerpted from *The Black Unicorn* (New York: Norton), © 1978 by Audre Lorde, all rights reserved; Ron Romanovsky for "Paint by Numbers," music and lyrics by Ron Romanovsky, © 1978, all rights reserved, available on *I Thought You'd Be Taller* by Romanovsky and Phillips, distributed by Fresh Fruit Records—FF 101; Ron Romanovsky for "Carnival People," music and lyrics by Ron Romanovsky, © 1986, all rights reserved, available on *Trouble in Paradise* by Romanovsky and Phillips, distributed by Fresh Fruit Records; Holly Near for "Put Away," words by Holly Near, music by Jeff Langley, © 1976 by Hereford Music, all rights reserved, used by permission, available on *Imagine my Surprise* by Holly Near, distributed by Redwood Records; Gloria T. Hull for "Poem," © 1979 by Gloria T. Hull, all rights reserved; and Geoff Morgan for "Homophobia," lyrics and music by Geoff Morgan, all rights reserved, available on *It Comes with the Plumbing* by Geoff Morgan, distributed by Pi-Gem Music and Nexus Records—KC 102449.

Introduction

In 1986 I returned to Georgia for the first time in many years. I came back home to attend the twentieth reunion of my high school graduation. My former classmates of Cross Keys High were clearly feeling confused by my presence. I had been a leader in my high school days (captain of the debate team, president of this and that, student council, etc., etc.). They might have remembered that I was the student speaker at the graduation ceremony, and a few might have recalled my editorial in the school newspaper attacking our DeKalb County School System's segregation.

Given my prominence, perhaps they were not surprised that—twenty years later—I also seemed to be the most prominent person among our number. From my biographical blurb in the *Class of 1966 Reunion Booklet*, they learned that I had received my PhD at age 24, and was now a professor at a major university. One ex-classmate, who did not recognize me, asked if I knew that one of our classmates had published four books. When I explained that I was that person, his mouth literally fell open.

Another classmate, hearing that I now live in Los Angeles, asked "How can you stand it out there, with all those weirdos and liberals?" "Easy," I replied, "I am one." With that, I opened the *Reunion Booklet* to my blurb and handed it to her. I had made sure to include in there the fact that I was president of the board of directors of the International Gay and Lesbian Archives, and had been a chairperson of the American Historical Association's Committee on Lesbian and Gay History, as well as an officer of a gay rights political organization. By the time that she read that I taught a Gay Studies course at my university, and was author of an award-winning book on the social acceptance of homosexuality in many American Indian cultures, her eyes were practically popping out. The only word that seeped through her pursed lips was a quiet

"Oh." She shortly afterward mumbled an excuse to get something, and I never saw her after that.

Others of the students (mostly the ones who were now living outside the South) reacted in the other extreme, practically throwing themselves at me, in order to let me know that my being gay was fine with them. That was quite nice of them, though I had to gently explain to a few that I was there to have a good time rather than to explain what it was like growing up as a homosexual. I think I was the first openly-gay person some of these people had ever met.

Yet, other students were decidedly cool toward me, and I figured out that it was not due to the bright Hawaiian flower-print shirt I was wearing. They were uncomfortable, it was clear, with me. Here I was, confounding all their stereotypes (well, maybe not all), in a decidedly confusing manner. Not only are gay people supposed to slink around in the shadows, but they are also (as countless fundamentalist preachers reiterate) supposed to be "anti-family." Yet, I arrived for this reunion with my mother and father, who had come down from their current home in North Carolina to meet me for this visit in our former hometown. I could see my classmates' questioning looks, as they pondered my parents happily interacting with their openly-gay son.

Sexual liberationist activism, homosexual Indian, Gay Studies, proud parents — I'm sure all this was more than some of these people could handle. It was precisely for this experience that I had made the return trip to Georgia.

I wanted to talk with those who had loudly told fag jokes in our school lunchroom, to the great delight of students and teachers. I wanted to see the reactions of those who in tenth grade had asked me why I "walked like a girl," and why my good friend Barbara (she preferred to be called Barb) acted "like a man." I wanted to see Mike Hitt (appropriately named), who had beaten me up on more than one occasion because I did not fit his notion of masculinity. Unfortunately, he was not there — I was told he had committed suicide a decade before.

One person I was lucky enough to meet was my favorite teacher. He let me know how proud he was of my accomplishments. Later, he telephoned me to tell me that he himself is gay. He said he recognized, even when I was his student, that I would be gay. A long silence passed after he said this. Then I told him, "Do you realize how many years of self-searching struggle I could have avoided, if you had told me this twenty years ago?" I explained to him how much I needed a gay role model, a person who could provide me with a sense of pride and a sense of how it might be possible to structure my life course as a gay man. No matter how loving and supportive my parents might be, this was a role that they would never be able to provide me.

I had known that this teacher was a bachelor, and I knew he always attended our high school football games with another unmarried male teacher. I was sexually attracted to both of them, but it had never — never — occurred to me that they were homosexual. I had absolutely no role model, no real person to connect me with reality. All I had were the statements of homophobic preachers and silly fag-bashing adolescents.

Though I had received a very good education at Cross Keys High, in this one respect that school had dismally failed me. It had failed to prepare me for the reality of my life. Those lessons had to come later, and at greater cost.

When I confronted this teacher with my regrets about all the missed opportunities, he responded, "I would have liked to have been honest with you, but if this had become known I would have lost my job." I knew that. Still, I resented his compliance with a system that forces us to hide our positive contributions to society, while only bringing up homosexuality when there is a scandal. I resented my similar compliances in my own past. I resented the way the gay and lesbian movement has been intimidated by the radical Right — from Anita Bryant's "Save Our Children" campaign to the ravings of North Carolina's Senator Jesse Helms. I resented the way we had been slow to provide assistance to lesbian and gay youth, by insisting upon and supporting openly-gay projects in the schools, through scholarship programs, media campaigns, radio shows, telephone counseling lines, and rescue missions for oppressed gay and lesbian youths who all too often spend their adolescence suffering in isolated silence.

With all this in mind, I wrote a letter to the principal of Cross Keys High, offering to fly out at my expense, to address the school's student body. I explained that I would forego my usual speaking fee because of my sense of commitment to students who might be in precisely the same spot as I was twenty years before. I never even received a reply.

That principal could not reply, because Southern polite society has not yet faced the fact that lesbian and gay youth exist. Because it is so necessary that this reality be accepted, this volume is extremely important. Jim Sears has not tried to impose one mold upon the youths he interviewed, but has allowed them to speak for themselves. He has included female and male, black and white, belle and redneck, in all the wondrous diversity that perhaps someday the South will learn to appreciate and value.

What this book shows is that, despite the gains of the gay rights movement, growing up gay in the South is still as terrifying as ever. The three institutions that most affect children — the family, the church, and the school — have been the major sources of oppression for lesbian and gay youth. Perhaps the most tragic failure has been the schools' unwillingness to address homosexuality as a subject for education. With educators' silence, youths are left with no beacon of light by which to question their prejudices. Homophobia flourishes, and many talented youngsters who might have contributed to the South's progress are either stifled or exiled.

Professor Sears' book should go a long way to help overcome this silence. His commentaries show a wide reading in the new scholarship on sexual variance and gender studies. His analysis provides much insight into an understanding of the South in general, not limited to sexual issues. The quotes from the gay and lesbian youths themselves provide moving portraits of those who, despite all the obstacles they have had to face, have survived. They are survivors, who have much to teach us all.

When I was growing up in the South, from the small town in North Carolina where I was born, past the time when I took my first job working at Georgia's Stone Mountain Confederate Memorial State Park, to the time when I studied Southern history and culture at the University of North Carolina, it was popular to blame the striving for black people's civil rights on "outside agitators." What this book proves is that this new generation of Southern lesbian and gay youth are not outsiders at all. They are no more outside their culture than are the previous generations of gay Southerners, from

Tennessee Williams to George Washington Carver, from Bessie Smith to Rita Mae Brown. Some of us have left the region, fleeing the intolerance that is as thick as the mosquitos. But whether we have left or not, we always carry our Southernness with us. We are not outside, but integrally inside. We are the sons and daughters of the South, descendents of the slaves who broke the red Georgia clay and brought forth a Cotton Kingdom, descendents of the Mississippi Confederate soldiers who brought the region to its knees in a futile struggle to retain that Kingdom. We are a reflection of the South's strengths and tragedies, we are the inheritors of the Southern inclination to rebel.

We are in fact the South's new rebels, and in some respects our rebellion is just as revolutionary as our Confederate and civil rights foreparents. It is revolutionary because almost every Southern family — if they will just be honest with themselves — has at least one lesbian or gay relative. Our rebel message is so revolutionary because it is so banal. That message is simply acceptance: acceptance of our human diversity, and recognition of the reality that some of us are just "that way." For aiding in this effort of understanding and acceptance, Professor Sears and each of the youths interviewed in this book deserve out heartfelt thanks and deep respect.

Walter L. Williams, PhD
University of Southern California
Los Angeles, California

Chapter 1

Peering Through Prisms
of Sexual Rebels

(T)he meaning of any beautiful thing is, at least, as much in the soul of him who looks at it as it was in his soul who wrought it.

Oscar Wilde, "The Critic as Artist"[1]

THE HISTORICAL SETTING

Growing Up Gay in the South is unique. It portrays the childhood and adolescent experiences of 36 Southern lesbians and gay men as they attend school, explore their sexuality, and make meaning of homosexuality.[2] These sexual rebels were not cut from a single mold. Each has journeyed along a different path. You will come to know intimately the thoughts, experiences, and feelings behind 13 of these voices. You will come to recognize Vince's easy going manner crowned with a broad smile, Norma Jean's childhood scars hidden behind her pugnacious determination, Cory's cynicism and biting sarcasm masking a desert heart thirsty for love, and Obie's deep-seated resentment of her father complicated by her commitment to family. Thirteen of the book's chapters are biographical portraits of these and other homosexual youth growing up in the countryside, the cities, and the suburbs of South Carolina. Some were tomboys or sissies; many were not. Some are from poor families, a few are from wealthy ones. Some were high school athletes or cheerleaders; others were "brains" or "freaks." Some come from two parent homes and some from single parent families. Most are from religious families, most usually Southern Baptist, others belong to rival denominations or religious sects, and a few have no religious home at all.

These are white and black children of the much ballyhooed "New South." They were born in the heady years of the New Frontier and the Great Society. They have come of age as voters during the Reagan Revolution. Their childhoods span from the late sixties to mid-seventies. By the time most had been enrolled in first grade, James Earl Ray, Sirhan Sirhan, and Charles Manson had performed their deeds of terror, Neil Armstrong had just walked on the moon, Jackie Kennedy had once again walked down the wedding aisle, and Rita Mae Brown had walked out of the New York NOW office helping to form the Radicalesbians. Woodstock, Czechoslovakia, and Chappaquiddick entered the news terrain of political geography as Fire Island, Provincetown, and Key West were claimed as free territories by their gay patrons. The race riots of Detroit and the blackened churches in Mississippi were still smoldering as slogans such as "black power" and "power to the people" burned in hearts, raising hopes or heightening fears. The "homophile movement" had given way to "gay liberation" as the neurotic homosexual figure portrayed in the successful off-Broadway production of *Boys in the Band* was eclipsed by the militant image of lesbians and gay men clashing with police in the Stonewall Rebellion. Homosexuals were beckoned to "come out of the closet" through the efforts of the newly founded Metropolitan Community Church and *The Advocate*.[3]

During their six years of elementary school, the 36 Southerners who were interviewed for this study would live through the break up of the Beatles, the Olympic tragedy in Munich, and the unrest at Kent, Jackson, and Orangeburg State campuses. They would witness battles: Ali versus Frazier; Taylor versus Burton; Vidal versus Buckley; Agnew versus the press; Spasky versus Fischer. Watergate would banish Nixon, the Jackson Five would supersede Jefferson Airplane, the American Psychological Association would remove homosexuality as a mental disorder, and Jimmy Connors would unseat Arthur Ashe. Disney World opened its doors to the public, China opened its door to the world, and the National Gay Task Force opened doors in Congress. Spurred by the formation of the gay ghetto and identification of a gay market, magazines like *Blueboy* and *Cruise* began production. As these public events unfolded, these sexual rebels endured private events: loneliness, family strife, childhood sex play, and the meaning of color, incest, and death.

As most of these participants entered adolescence, Jimmy Carter became the first Deep Southerner since the War Between the States to be elected to the presidency, Anita Bryant's *Save the Children* campaign had been launched, and the first Apple microcomputers were shuffling off the assembly line. As these young adults were awakening sexually, the country was startled by the incident at Three Mile Island and homosexual communities were incensed by the assassination of Harvey Milk. During adolescence, their first full decade passed before them. Another decade, the 1980s, would herald a series of firsts: the first woman in space; a major political party adopting the first gay rights plank in its national platform, the first reported case of Gay Related Immune Deficiency (GRID). As words such as "queer" and "dyke" were assuming more personal and critical meanings for these sexual rebels, theater productions of *La Cage aux Folles* and *Torch Song Trilogy* were receiving critical acclaim. For these homosexual Southerners, adolescence bridged the death of Mao with Reagan's 49 state re-election landslide, the mysterious and much publicized deaths of a handful of citizens from Legionnaire's Disease with the complexities of a less publicized virus felling thousands of young men. During this eight year period marking adolescence, these participants would travel from the Jamaican reggae music of Bob Marley to Michael Jackson's "Victory Tour," from the Olympic feats of Romania's Nadia Commaneci to that of West Virginia born Mary Lou Retton, from the journeys of an African taken slave in *Roots* to Harlem's roaring *Cotton Club*. For most of these adolescents, however, Christopher Street had not become Main Street, AIDS had yet to enter their personal vocabulary, and the contributions of Harvey Milk, Audre Lorde, Harvey Fierstein, Holly Near and many others had yet to be a source for pride.

The young adults portrayed in this book are members of a transitional generation bridging the turmoil and social consciousness of the sixties to the "New Age" and spiritual consciousness of the nineties. Their lives bind the epoch march on Washington of 1964 with the landmark march on Washington of 1987; their lives blend the dissident chords of "We shall overcome," to the jubilant cheers of "Run, Jessie, Run"; their lives connect the humiliating resignation of Walter Jenkins after his arrest in a men's D.C. washroom to the overwhelming re-election of openly gay Congressman Barney Frank. Their lives are living testimonials of the best and worst of preceding generations. They witnessed the struggle for lesbian and gay rights from the adoption of the model Illinois penal code to the high court ruling on the *Hardwick* case. They lived through the *de facto* segregation of schools and buses to the de jure desegregation of classrooms and neighborhoods. As they lived through these public events and struggled with their private feelings, these participants became sexual rebels.

THE REGIONAL SETTING

As a region of the country, the South is defined by its history and culture. The 11 states of the Confederacy comprise the Old South. South Carolina, the first center of Southern culture (Charles Town), the home of John C. Calhoun (the architect of the nullification crisis of 1832), the first state to secede from the Union, the site of the first Civil War engagement, and the birthplace of the "Dixiecrats," is the site of this study. Because of its prominent role in Southern history and its biracial population (as opposed to Louisiana Cajuns and Texas Hispanics), South Carolina, perhaps more than any other state in the region, epitomizes the Old South. It is not, however, the entire South. Readers living in the hills of Arkansas, the Louisiana bayous, the sprawling cities of Atlanta, Miami, and Houston, or the red-clay towns of Georgia must judge how similar their experiences are to the Carolina Southerners portrayed in this book.

Growing Up Gay in the South is important because the experiences of lesbian and gay-identified Southerners have long been neglected. Researchers, however, have not neglected the South. In their unapologetic devotion to church, community, and family, Southerners most visibly reflect those conservative values that for many define the heartland of America.[4] Social science research has repeatedly shown the South to be less tolerant than other regions of the country on political and social issues. Racial attitudes, in particular, have distinguished the South from other parts of the country in the public mind.[5] However, in the 1980s, as other regions of the country have become less liberal, the South has become less conservative. For example, Southern youth (under 30), while expressing less political tolerance than their Northern peers, were more tolerant than young Southern adults of the previous decade. On sexual and racial issues as well, young people in the South remained more conservative than their Northern counterparts — but this difference too was narrowing as Northern youth in increasing numbers expressed more conservative attitudes. These and other changes led one social scientist to conclude, "The regions do appear to be becoming more alike, but this trend is the result of Northern change and transformation."[6]

Focusing on the historic gap between North and South, we sometimes overlook the differences within the South: between rich and poor Southerners and among various Southern subcultures.[7] In South Carolina, for example, there has always been an up-country radical populist-agrarian tradition which for generations has been at odds with the mercantile and planter interests of the tidewater region. The South has a long history of electing populist politicians, and social scientists have demonstrated that working class Southerners are more liberal on economic issues than generally assumed.[8] Excluding racial issues, these subcultural differences explain much of the variation between northern and southern attitudes regarding social welfare policy, law and order issues, and minority rights. The most conservative views are held by Southerners from the top of the socio-economic pyramid. Southerners with low incomes or living in rural areas are no more conservative than their Northern counterparts and less conservative than their "high-brow" Southern neighbors.[9] As political scientist Earl Hawkey notes, "Laying a blanket indictment on the South as representative of a distinct conservative political culture generally is not justified. Conservatism is a many splendored thing and does not appear to be confined to one region or to one group of people."[10]

This convergence of Northern attitudes with Southern values and the tendency for people under 30 in both regions to harbor more conservative views, may mean that the phenomenon of acquiring a lesbian or gay identity in the South may be much more representative of the United States as a whole during the next decade than is the gay and lesbian experience in the nation's coastal and industrial cities.[11] Yet, most studies on lesbian and gay issues have been conducted in metropolitan areas of the industrial North or far West, particularly California. These studies fail to represent the conservative context within which these 36 South Carolinians grew up. And, they will mirror less and less the social reality for homosexual Americans growing up in the nineties.

I began this study with several questions. How do young people, living in the South, view homosexuality and themselves as sexual beings? Did these young men and women experience problems in elementary and secondary school? If so, to what degree were these difficulties associated with coming to terms with their sexual feelings? I began by assuming that growing up in the South differed qualitatively from other regions of the country. After four years of research, I conclude that the Southern experience differs in degrees but not in kind. Racism does not disappear when one travels north of the Mason-Dixon line and neither does heterosexism. Belief in God, the importance of family, and the value of honor are not exclusive virtues of Southerners. The standardization of the school curriculum, the homogenization of American culture through television, transportation, and communication, and the ascendency of the federal government in the everyday lives of its citizenry have *lessened* the differences between growing up in Bamberg, South Carolina and Rochester, New York. The differences, though, have not disappeared — a point made by Chris Mayfield in her wonderfully edited collection of Southern children's voices:

> "Growing up southern" . . . The words evoke a tide of images, both bitter and sweet: overalls and organdy, hot green fields, cool brown creeks, Grandma's front porch, lengthy and complicated family connections, Mama's fried chicken and biscuits and Granddaddy's cane syrup, "colored" water fountains and "white" ones, church, chores, Dixie, and hot dark dangerous summer nights. Today's southern children get their biscuits as often from Hardee's as from Mama. On Saturday

afternoons they're as likely to cool off in the local shopping mall as in a shady spring-fed swimming hole. But Grandma and Grandpa and Uncle Joe and Cudn Elaine loom large in the lives of today's southern kids, just as they did in those of earlier generations. . . . "colored" and "white" labels are less blatant, but they still constrict the futures of this generation's southern children.[12]

Southern children not only are enveloped in social conservatism but are more likely to confront social ills. South Carolina, like its neighboring states, has made remarkable strides in reducing infant mortality, poor housing, and illiteracy by improving health care, social services, and education. Even so, the gap between the South and other regions of the country has not narrowed and South Carolina is generally near the bottom of state by state quality of life comparisons. The state is second from the bottom in average life expectancy and third from the top in its infant mortality rate; South Carolina is one of the top ten states in the percentage of persons below the poverty level and one of the bottom five in per capita income. One quarter of the South Carolina population is unable to read; the state ranks third in the number of prisoners per 100,000 of the population; and the percentage of South Carolinians who exercise their voting franchise is the second lowest in the United States.[13]

In some respects, the drama of growing up and acquiring a lesbian or gay identity in the South, and particularly the Carolinas, may seem distinctive from that in the rest of the country. But as you will discover, the typical story is familiar in outline: the struggle for identity and self-understanding; the power of oppression and the pain of repression; the presence of fear, triumph, silence, and courage; the absence of forbearance, trust, support, and certainty.

THE ORGANIZATIONAL SETTING

A five-sided, crystal prism is a useful metaphor for understanding *Growing Up Gay in the South*.[14] Just as the observer's point of reference determines which light a crystal prism reflects, so too does our stance determine what we observe in a prism of a particular person. *Growing Up Gay in the South* uses five vantage points. These range from the impact of religious values and rituals to the attitudes and reactions of Southern peers and teachers. Each of these points of reference enriches our understanding of the experience of these sexual rebels as they construct a sexual identity.

From the first vantage point we peer into how Southern religious life influenced Vince's and Malcolm's understanding of their emerging homosexual feelings and affected their eventual adoption of homosexual identities. These chapters probe the pervasiveness of fundamental Christian values and beliefs which continue to set the South apart from other regions of the country. For both blacks and whites living in the South, the pulpit and the prayer book have been a critical, albeit taken-for-granted, force in everyday Southern life. The relative lack of cultural diversity has permitted the hegemony of "mainstream" Christian values to touch every segment of Southern life. The belief in the inerrancy of the Bible, the recitation of prayer in some public schools, the reliance on Scripture to justify social policies, and the expectation of regular church attendance defined Vince's and Malcolm's everyday world. Most lesbian and gay youth in this study first viewed their same-sex feelings and behaviors from this religious perspective. And, family and friends often judged these sexual rebels from that same vantage point. Religious experiences, also, spurred the journeys of some, as Vince's musical interest, developed under the tutelage of the *True Tones*, illustrates.

From the second vantage point we peer into the biographical "prisms" of Norma Jean, Royce, and Jacob to observe how race, gender, and social class define sexual perimeters in Southern communities and affect the construction of a sexual identity. These boundaries are, in part, vestiges of the antebellum South and of the changes wrought within the reconstructed South of the twentieth century. The restrictive public boundary between inter-racial dating or marriage is, in part, a manifestation of the long-held image of the sexually virile black male and the defenseless purity of the white woman. Though often these boundaries have been crossed in the steamy darkness of midnight passion, no Southerner thoughtlessly trespasses over them. However, these boundaries are more than historical; they are psychological. These boundaries, simplistically represented in mental images or social metaphors such as "White Trash," "The Gentleman," or the "Oreo," are reconstructed by each generation of Southerners. These social metaphors are the result of the changing intersections and conceptions of race, gender, and social class in the South. The archetype of the "Southern Belle," for example, with its expectation of female virginity and its origins in securing a suitable beau for the nineteenth century planter's daughter, is celebrated today in highly stylized rituals such as Charleston's exclusive and secretive St. Cecilia Society, whose annual ball introduces daughters of the Confederacy, escorted by Citadel cadets, into South Carolina society.

The portraits of Norma Jean, Royce, and Jacob underscore the degree of elasticity in sexual boundaries that young people of different backgrounds within southern communities experience. Poor and female, Norma Jean represents the antithesis of the "Southern Belle." Her biography illustrates how social class and gender delimit sexual choices and meanings. Royce's portrait illuminates how sufficiently high status in a small Southern community can be enough to silence sexual innuendo and restrain would-be bullies. Jacob's story depicts his conflicts between practicing homosexuality and choosing an African-American identity.

From the third vantage point, the Southern family, we peer into the prisms of two other sexual rebels, Terry and Obie. Within a culture ravaged by pestilence and war, bloodlines are more enduring than money. In the South, perhaps more than in other regions of the country, a primal relationship exists between the land and its people, and among family and kin. Through the family name, land is passed from one generation to the next. Respect is accorded to those town families whose names bear a quiet dignity. Participants in this study acknowledged the importance of family name and family honor. They also noted that concerns about such matters generally surfaced when their *public* reputation was questioned or ritual symbols and gestures were disregarded. The lives of some of these sexual rebels were dominated by such concerns. As a consequence, their inner selves mirrored the appearances which they portrayed.

This division between public and private spheres in the South, however, can liberate as it can imprison. The town hair stylist can rave and banter to *her* heart's content as long as she respects the sensibilities of the blue-rinse set and preserves family honor and family name. The appearance of wrong-doing rather is more central to Southern family life than the commission of wrongful acts. Obie challenges this accepted form of social hypocrisy within her family. In contrast, Terry celebrates this social ambivalence between the public and private selves seeking to balance his sexual freedom with his relatives' concern for family name and family honor.

The lives of Cory, Alston, and Everetta illustrate the fourth vantage point, childhood feelings and behaviors. These sexual rebels attend different types of schools, confront a variety of family dilemmas, and experience a variety of sexual feelings. They construct different meanings about their childhood experiences, same-sex feelings, and emerging identities.

Many elementary school boys and girls like Cory fit the norms for childhood behavior. Never experiencing sexual harassment, they may occasionally engage in such harassment themselves. These are the "kids." During adolescence, they eventually will come to terms with feeling different—with being queer. Until then, however, these children experience what most teachers, counselors, and parents perceive to be typical Southern childhoods. Beneath these surface appearances, however, lurk sexual feelings and untold experiences that will profoundly affect the manner in which they will cope with "feeling different or being queer" during adolescence. There are also a few "outcasts" found in every elementary school. These children, generally boys, evidence subjection to verbal and physical abuse. Sometimes the abuse continues throughout their schooling experience. Often their behaviors or appearances do not fit the gender-specific norms of their culture and community. Alston is an outcast. Though he did not clearly understand the words used to batter him during childhood, he felt different at a very early age. There are other students like Everetta who do not behave in a fashion suitable for a little girl, yet are *not* the butt of jokes or the target for torment with sexual innuendo. These are "the tomboys." As adolescents or adults, some of these children, like Everetta, will identify themselves as lesbians.

Our fifth vantage point will be the culture of junior and senior high school, as seen through the eyes of Olivia, Phillip, and Brett. These rebels handle their emerging sexual feelings and developing relationships with others differently. As their heterosexual-identified classmates enjoy the support of their friends, teachers, and parents, Olivia, Phillip, and Brett struggle with their same-sex feelings in an inhospitable and, at times, dangerous school environment. The attitudes and feelings of others make the pilgrimage from childhood to adulthood more difficult than it normally is: Olivia abandons her homosexual relationship with Kris as rumors and innuendoes spread among her friends; Phillip fails to enter into any relationship lest he confirm others' suspicions; associating with homosexual students, Brett finds himself torn between a supportive teacher and gay students pressing for him to proclaim his homosexual identity, on the one hand, and his own reluctance to assume such an identity, on the other.

Stymied by fear and shame, these teens' psychological growth and development languishes. In lunch rooms, adolescent gossip and crude comic stereotypes violate their human dignity. In classrooms, the exceptional teacher expresses concern about their hurt and hardship. With not-so-hidden expectations, the school institutionalizes heterosexism while homophobia exacts a heavy psychological price from Olivia, Phillip, and Brett.

The pervasiveness of fundamental religious beliefs, the acceptance of racial, gender, and class community boundaries, the importance of family name and family honor, the unbending view of appropriate childhood behaviors, and the intensity of adolescent culture constitute the Southern psychic landscape on which these participants sketch their biographies and color their sexual feelings and experiences. From these five vantage points, *Growing Up Gay in the South* unfolds chapter by chapter as lesbians and gay-identified men candidly share their attitudes and feelings about themselves, their families, and their schooling from childhood through adulthood. They speak of private tragedies and public accomplishments; they speak with words of bitterness, determination, and joy; they speak, in the present, of their past and their future.

The concluding chapter explores the paradoxes of homosexual communities, identities, and culture. The chapter places the struggles of these 13 sexual rebels within a broader context of journeys of the spirit in which sexual difference is viewed as a gift as much as a burden.

The 13 women and men highlighted in *Growing Up Gay in the South* were chosen on the basis of their experiences and diverse backgrounds. Consideration was given to their ability to communicate these experiences and to their willingness to invite the reader into their lived worlds. These biographies portray the diversity of people who identify themselves as gay or lesbian and delineate a spectrum of prejudice and problems encountered as sexual rebels. Sexual rebels are disparate youths who have wrestled with tragically disconnected and apparently distorted sexual lives but who no longer hide or ignore the truth of their "moral deformity." *Growing Up Gay in the South* is a cacophony of voices revealing conflicts between public and private worlds in the New South; a series of histories of innocence lost and journeys to selfhood begun; a human testament to the process of social questioning in the search for psychological wholeness.

THE THEORETICAL SETTING

I was born in a Midwestern farming community that had a checkerboard flatness. My world was clearly divided. Adams always followed Jefferson Street; First Avenue never crossed Second. In my town, as in the black-and-white television world of the Andersons, Cleavers, and Nelsons, there were no shades of grey. There were no long-kept secrets. As a white, middle-class male, I learned through my family, my school, and my church how to dress, what to think, and when to repent. I learned that only girls wore dresses and sported stylish, long hair. I learned to write within the broad-lines of my ruled paper as I sat beneath an American flag and a scantily clothed crucified Christ. I learned that God punished sinners but loved the repentant. I learned that homosexuality was sinful; that *I* was a sinner.

The sexual rebels portrayed in this volume are from a different generation and a different region of the country than myself. *Growing Up Gay in the South* is portraits of Southern youth which will be of interest to a variety of readers. For readers struggling with their same-sex feelings, these are journeys into the worlds of others sheathed in sexual mythology and social prejudice. For those in the helping professions these portraits of Southern youth coupled with scholarly commentaries provide a synoptic and interdisciplinary understanding of homosexuality grounded to personal contexts. Lesbians, bisexuals, and gay men may find *Growing Up Gay in the South* an opportunity to reflect upon, if not relive, their childhood pasts. The challenge to the canons of gay/lesbian liberation orthodoxy will provoke some activists while inspiring others to consider the long-range impact of their strategies. Scholars may use the data presented from these case studies, and accompanied by an extensive bibliography, as a platform for academic debate as well as further inquiry.

Growing Up Gay in the South is not a compilation of "coming out stories." This study explores the various intersections of sexual, gender, racial, and social class identities through the biographies of 13 South Carolinians; it examines the personal and social significance of acquiring a lesbian or gay identity within Southern culture, and describes the journeys of young adults in their search for Self. These 13 portraits, followed by scholarly commentaries, form a mosaic revealing a deceptively simple argument: **Sexual identities are socially constructed**. *Growing Up Gay in the South* develops this argument along five lines.

First, *being* "gay, lesbian or homosexual" is a modern-day phenomenon. Just as "homosexual" is a 19th century, enlightened, medical construction, "gay" and "lesbian" are social artifacts popularized in post-Stonewall America. However, the basic emotional and erotic attraction to members of one's own sex is not a social artifact. As scholars using such diverse methodologies as those of Freud, Dover, and Kinsey have demonstrated, *human beings are diverse sexual creatures*: Our ability to relate emotionally and physically to other human beings is not limited to the opposite gender. Kinsey shocked Americans more than 40 years ago when he reported that nearly half of the adult population engaged in both heterosexual and homosexual activities. Concluding that the world is not divided into sheep and goats, he stated that "patterns of heterosexuality and patterns of homosexuality represented learned behavior which depends, to a considerable degree, upon the mores of the particular culture in which the individual is raised."[15]

Second, *human beings interpret and reinterpret their lived experiences*. Reinterpretation is not a consequence of failed memory but an attempt to reconcile personal identity with one's past. It represents an ability to reflect upon our many selves and to reconstruct them into a more meaningful Self through the soft light of introspection. It also represents our need for psychological wholeness. It is a response to the cognitive anxiety of confronting conflicting self-images.

Third, the reconstruction of personal identities is not done within a social vacuum. On the contrary, *sexual biographies are integrally related to society*. Society provides the collective cultural history, social scripts, and language that form the foundation for these constructed identities. The personal meanings of our regional, social class, racial, gender, and sexual identities are inextricably woven into a culture in which being from the north or south, upper class or working class, black or white, male or female, homosexual or heterosexual have social significance. While the intersections of region, social class, race, gender, and sexuality vary for each person, their existence and importance within our culture are social facts.

Fourth, the gay and lesbian liberation movement is essentially a political effort to establish legal and social space for homosexual-identified persons. As such, *many gay and lesbian activists work within and build upon the history, scripts, and language of the culture within which the movement was born*. By using history, scripts, and language of the old, they create space within the existing social, political, economic, and spiritual paradigm. Only thus can the practice of sexual minority politics, the creation of lesbian and gay communities, the development of a homosexual-identified economy, art, and religion rest comfortably within the very culture whose history, scripts, and language have defined them as cultural outsiders.

Fifth, homosexual loving and love-making within this culture transforms Southern adolescents into cultural outsiders—sexual rebels. This is a gift as well as a burden since *sexual identities can be as oppressive as they are liberating*. These sexual rebels suffered and eventually rebelled against the straightjacket of compulsory heterosexuality. In the process, most found self-understanding and sexual meaning through adopting a lesbian or gay identity. Yet, such self-identification limits potential sexual experiences, segregates people, splits the spectrum of human sexual capacity into either/or categories, and lessens opportunities for growth of the spirit.

THE RESEARCH SETTING

Can a homosexual scholar study homosexuality? One lesbian researcher states the issue forthrightly:

> As an insider, the lesbian has an important sensitivity to offer, yet she is also more vulnerable than the nonlesbian researcher, both to pressure from the heterosexual world—that her studies conform to previous works and describe the lesbian reality in terms of its relationship with the outside—and to pressure from the inside, from the lesbian community itself—that her studies mirror not the reality of that community but its self-protective ideology.[16]

At the heart of this question is our understanding of social science research and our concept of "objectivity." A century ago, German sociologist Max Weber wrote, "the very recognition of a scientific problem coincides personally with the possession of specifically oriented motives and values."[17] Above all else, social inquiry focuses upon the personal and the person. Before being a researcher, a person is first a member of a particular culture.[18] It is within that culture that the person's view of the world is constructed. Though this world view generally remains unexamined, cultural anthropologists and interpretive sociologists resonate to the phrase, "an unexamined life is not worth living." As the most renowned scholars in these fields—Margaret Meade, Bronislaw Malinowski, Ruth Benedict, W. I. Thomas, Robert Redfield—gained a better understanding of other cultures they were better able to appreciate and bracket their own cultural preconceptions. Though I do not claim the expertise or experience of a Meade or a Cooley, I do bear witness to the power of reflexivity that peering into another culture affords. I have thought often about my Midwestern, rural boyhood as I listened, watched, and felt the everyday sounds and experiences of Southerners: black and white, affluent and poverty-strickened, male and female. Through this intra-personal process of observation and reflection, my understanding of these sexual rebels as well as knowledge about myself has deepened.

But, can a homosexual white male researcher understand and adequately tell the stories of women or persons of color? Those who answer "no" would logically have to demand that the late newscaster Max Robinson only report the news of Black America, that Tennessee Williams or Carson McCullers restrict their insights to people of their own gender, or that Marlee Matlin refrain from assuming roles of non-deaf persons. The test is not one's ability to remain objective but one's capacity to be empathetic. Proper questions for the anchor on the evening news, the playwright, the novelist, the actress, or the social science researcher are, "Have you immersed yourself into the world of the other?", "Have you portrayed its richness and complexity?", and "Have you treated your informants/characters fairly with respect and understanding?"

Social scientists cannot expect to discover The Truth; we can aspire to convey the various truths held by others. Despite this simple fact, our admiration of empiricism reigns unquestioned. Truth, we presume, can be algorithimized into coefficients, probability tables, and regression formulae. Knowledge, we believe, is a simple distillation and ordering of sensory data. Objectivity, we surmise, is the product of precise instrumentation and rigorous controls. These commonly held beliefs ignore the fact that the "instruments themselves (are) elements of this world,"[19] that "knowledge is always, in part, subjective,"[20] and that "if men define situations as real they are real in their consequences."[21] Social science research, at its worst, imposes an order to social phenomenon and labels that construction "reality." At its best, social science research provides an interpretive framework which, at that historical moment, seems to make the most sense.

In *Growing Up Gay in the South*, I have struggled to achieve the latter. This endeavor will be judged a success if the parent of a gay son or bisexual daughter, or the former friend of a gay student or classmate of someone who is simply rumored to be gay can say, "Now, I better understand and can empathize with your struggles." This endeavor will be judged a success if the white gay man closeted in Peoria, the lesbian-feminist active in San Diego, or the black student coping with bisexuality in a Mississippi high school examines the values, experiences, and behaviors of these 36 Carolinians and thereby gains insight into the richness, the multiple dimensions of human sexual experience.

To facilitate this judgement the book's appendix displays data on each of these sexual rebels in a variety of tables and figures. These data allow the reader-as-researcher the opportunity to test the adequacy of my interpretations, to explore hypotheses which I may not have considered, and to compare their life histories with those portrayed in this book. The appendix also includes a description of the study's methodology and a discussion of related methodological issues.

REFERENCE NOTES

1. Wilde, 1972:158.
2. Only a handful of studies have been reported that examine *any* aspect of education and homosexuality vis-à-vis gender, race, or region (e.g., Fischer, 1982; D. Smith, 1985). Given the lack of interest and support within and outside of the education community, this is not surprising. The few monographs which have focused on the childhood and adolescent experiences, attitudes, and concerns of homosexual adults are presented either in statistical form lacking insight into the human condition or in anecdotal extracts absent a theoretical framework (e.g., Alyson, 1980; Baetz, 1980; Bell, Weinberg and Hammersmith, 1981; Harry, 1982; Saghir and Robins, 1973; Glenbard East *Echo*, 1987; Gottlieb, 1977; Heron, 1983; Hite, 1981; Spada, 1979; Stanley and Wolfe, 1980; Trenchard, 1984; Trenchard and Warren, 1984). Further, the principal focus of these studies has been the urban, white homosexual.
3. For a social history of the modern gay rights movement and culture, see; Abbott and Love, 1972; Altman, 1971; Altman, 1982; Bronski, 1984; D'Emillio, 1983b; Humphreys, 1972; Licata, 1980-81; Marotta, 1981.
4. As a philosophy, conservatism views human beings as imperfect creatures who, left to their own selfish interests, would create an anarchic society. Limited government acknowledges the need to preserve public order while recognizing that any government drawn from the hand of humankind is beyond perfectability (Schuettinger, 1970).
5. Corbett, 1982; Hawkey, 1983; Key, 1949; Nunn, Crockett and Williams, 1978; Reed, 1972; Stouffer, 1955.
6. Hawkey, 1983:54.
7. Corbett, 1988; Wallerstein, 1988.
8. Davidson, 1972; Mathews and Prothro, 1966.
9. As the South becomes more industrialized and urbanized, this agrarian-populist tradition is eroded. "As the old South passes away, so do some of its

benefits as well as its drawbacks. The populist-agrarian tradition in the South has been a positive social force not only in the South, but for the entire nation. Its death may well herald an increase in the ideological distinctiveness of the South rather than its reduction'' (Hawkey, 1983:70).

10. Hawkey, 1983:67-68.

11. This, of course, is quite opposite to the thesis of the northernization of the South popularized by scholars such as Current, 1983 and Edgerton, 1974.

12. Mayfield, 1981:ix.

13. South Carolina Division of Research and Statistical Services, 1990.

14. I am indebted to Janet Miller (1990) for her suggestive use of the prism metaphor.

15. Kinsey, Pomeroy and Martin, 1948:660. In his later work (Kinsey, Pomeroy, Martin and Gebhard, 1953:450), he went on to state: ''Exclusive preference of behavior, heterosexual or homosexual, comes only with experience, or as a result of social pressures which tend to force an individual into an exclusive pattern of one or the other sort.''

16. Krieger, 1982:108.

17. Weber, 1946:60-61.

18. Gouldner, 1971.

19. Schultz, 1970:54.

20. Morris, 1966:121.

21. Thomas, 1927:576.

Homosexuality and the Religious South

Protestantism reigns supreme in the South to an extent un-matched in this hemisphere.

Kenneth Bailey,
Southern White Protestantism in the Twentieth Century[1]

The importance of the Protestant religion in everyday life is certainly not unique to Southerners.[2] Americans have a long history of seeing themselves as God's chosen people. While tolerating a diversity of religious beliefs ranging from Judaism to Mormonism, Americans, in general, remain no less committed to belief in God, the specialness of their new Zion, and the righteous certainty of their earthly role to evangelize the world for God and Democracy.[3]

Southerners share these core beliefs with citizens of other regions of the country. Unlike people in other regions, however, Southern Christians often are more orthodox, their reading of the Bible is more literal, and their religious rituals are more flamboyant.[4] Gracing the steeples of most southern churches are Baptist or Methodist crosses. For whites, the dominant denomination is the Southern Baptists and for African-Americans it is the African Methodist Episcopal Church. The power of Southern religion is evident in activities ranging from marches on state capitols protesting racial segregation to marches around health care clinics decrying abortion on demand. The pervasiveness of Southern religion is captured in literary works such as Erskine Caldwell's *God's Little Acre* and Sinclair Lewis' *Elmer Gantry*. The South has produced such preachers of national prominence as Charles Grandison Finney, Billy Graham, Martin Luther King, Jr., J. Frank Norris, Billy Sunday, and Jimmy Swaggart.

A majority of South Carolinians, black and white, are conservative Christians. They are Southern Baptists and African Methodists, Congregationalists and Jehovah's Witnesses, many subdued by the fear of an Old Testament God, lying prostrate to God's will. Crippled by grief, guilt, and despair, they are fervent believers in rebirth and redemption, the blood of Jesus Christ, the power of the Holy Ghost, salvation and eternal damnation.

South Carolina is a land set apart by suffering as much as by love. It is a land of tent revivals, cable television preachers, and evangelistic amusement parks. Belief in Scriptural exactitude is impressed upon children's minds, the template of the soul. In Sunday school, girls, clothed in modestly trimmed white cotton dresses, absorb metaphysical absolutes: temptation, original sin, hell, and Satan. Wearing their best J. B. White brown suits, boys learn of the great earthly morality play in which their role is to be a witness for Jesus. South Carolina is a state in which righteousness *is* enforceable as ministers overwhelmingly favor strong laws regulating liquor sales, gambling, pornography, and marijuana.[5] South Carolina is a state in which any discussion of homosexuality is barred by law in sex education for grades K-7, and any discussion of homosexuality beyond grade 7 must be placed in the "context of instruction concerning sexually transmitted diseases."[7] South Carolina churches have contributed to change as well as stability. The moral authority and political framework for the Civil Rights Movement has its origins in the southern black church. The relatively peaceful school desegregation movement of the early seventies owes much to the inter-denominational and inter-racial cooperation of ministers and their congregations.[7]

Not surprisingly, then, religion greatly influenced the formative experiences of many of these 36 lesbian and gay Carolinians. This influence is illustrated in the biographical portraits of Vince and Malcolm. In the words of the great southern writer Flannery O'Connor, they learned that "evil is not simply a problem to be solved, but a mystery to be endured.''[8] Whether on the grooves of an Elvis Presley album or through the effeminate mannerisms of a boy worshipping in a Kingdom Hall, evil is neither something to tolerate nor understand; it is a simple fact of everyday life.

REFERENCE NOTES

1. Bailey, 1964:ix.

2. The lineage of Protestantism is represented in the thinking of such diverse groups of men as: Roger Williams, Jonathan Edwards, and Cotton Mather; Benjamin Franklin and Thomas Jefferson; Woodrow Wilson and William Jennings Bryan; and Warren Chandler and Josiah Strong. Currency engravings, the rise of the land-grant colleges, the inception of Scouts and the Young Men's (and Women's) Christian Association, and the passage of the 18th Amendment reflect this Protestant vision of America.

3. I have found the work of Bellah, 1975; Lippy and Williams, 1988; Marty, 1970; and Marty, 1981 most useful in reflecting upon the influence of religion on the American consciousness.

4. Religious regionalism has characterized the United States since the 17th century. In order to understand the unique structure, style, ritual and theology of Southern religion, I have found the following works most useful: Baker, Steed and Moreland, 1983; Bolton, 1982; Eighmy, 1972; Harrell, 1981; Hill, 1967; S. Hill, 1972; Hill, 1980; Hill, 1983a; Hill, 1983b; Hill, 1987; Hill, 1988; Issac, 1982; Mathews, 1977; Reed, 1986b; Stark and Glock, 1968; White and Hopkins, 1976; Wilson, 1985; Yance, 1978.

5. Sauds & Guth, 1981.

6. South Carolina Comprehensive Education Health Act, 1988:7.

7. For an insightful analysis of the relationships between the white and black Southern Baptists and their ministers during the years preceding and immediately following the *Brown* decision, see Blackwelder, 1979; Manis, 1987.

8. O'Connor, 1969:209.

Chapter 2

White Churches:
The Southern Baptists
and the Fundamentalists

VINCE AND THE TRUE TONES

*This is not the age of the thinker; it is the age of the doer. If
you try to think crossing a highway or street, some fool will
run over you.*

Bob Jones, Sr., *Gothic Politics in the Deep South*[1]

Vince is an articulate gay man of twenty-three with a broad-rim
smile and a Southern twang. Born in the mountains of the Piedmont, his father, Vernon, operated a machine shop outside the
house and was the chairman of the deacons for the local Southern
Baptist church. Vince's earliest memories are enjoying baths with
Vernon at the age of two. "Sometimes through our bathing experience he would let me place my hand on his chest. I loved doing it. I
started judging older men: was he someone I wouldn't mind laying
my hand on his chest?" Vince's mom, Melba, worked at home and
served as the church's assistant music director and secretary. Vince
remembers:

I'd come in for Sunday school. Then we would have worship
at eleven o'clock. After church my mom's side of the family
would always have get-togethers with lots of food and music
to go around. There would always be lots of people. My
mother was the youngest of nine children and all of them were
horny little devils so they all spread out into a rather large clan.

Then we'd have training union an hour before the Sunday evening service.

Vince's fascination with music began at a very early age. "Mom was making an album while she was carrying me." At the age of five, he remembers listening to his mother's country and western albums:

> One night we had company over and my mom was playing records — that was real hip to play records for your company. Mom played all her albums saving Jailhouse Rock for last. She knew that I was scared to fuckin' death of that song. At last she put it on. I was in front of the stereo and I let out a yell. I took out the front door and went running for grandma's, stumbled onto her porch, and put my head onto her lap.

At this time, Vince began identifying more with his mother, as his father "started to be the master of the house":

> I was never hit. "Whuppings" is what they called it. I never got one of those although I always wish I had. Instead of hitting me a few times with a belt, which would have caused a few welts and hurt maybe ten minutes, I had to go without television, my stereo, and my drums. I was a very good boy.

When Vince started school he cried every morning as his mother prepared him to leave home. By the end of first grade "David, Sam, and me were the three most popular boys. Darlene, Debra and Margaret were the most popular girls. We were the boy and girl triplets." Throughout elementary school, Vince still remained a bright and likable student. He enjoyed playing little league football on Saturdays, drums for a Gospel group on church nights, and softball with the church team during the summers. He also did well in school. His parents developed an academic reward system: each "A" would earn him ten dollars, and five dollars was given for each "B." Vince recalls, "I was raking up fifty to sixty dollars every time report cards would come around." Vince also began enjoying childhood sex play with his cousin:

Whenever I would go see my grandparents, I would see Clift. Me and Clift would go fall in the bedroom which was just right off from the living room. We would just close the door, lock it, and go at it. It began as childhood curiosity: show me yours and I'll show you mine. It progressed from there. It felt wonderful. I remember that I always thought that I was going to get pregnant from Clift.

By the time Vince entered sixth grade, he knew he was a "homosexual":

It is so vivid. I was in the sixth grade. I had just heard the word *homosexual* and I knew what it meant. But, at the time, I didn't know the social stigma that went along with it. We were waiting in line to get on the bus and I told my second cousin, George, "I am a homosexual. I make love to men." Then I forgot about it.

A year later Vince began to understand the social meaning of homosexuality.

One morning George and I were riding the bus. We were the only ones in junior high on it. George looked across the aisle at me and yelled, "Hey, Vince. Do you 'member that time you said you were a homosexual?" If I could had made myself into melted butter I would have been running all through my seat. Everybody was going "Ahah!" George realized he shouldn't have said what he said because he tried to take it back right then. I learned when I made that one slip with George that I would never slip again.

During junior high school, Vince and his fellow classmates began exchanging "fag jokes":

That really became a code word for some of the boys on the team. Anybody who was a little different was labelled "fag." We didn't understand what it meant. We had been told a homosexual was some depraved, drooling, old man who went around the park feeling around young kids, seducing young boys, and had the personality of a frog. It was morally reprehensible. It was the ultimate scarlet letter: gay, fag, pansy, queer, sissy, dick-sucker.

Although he was president of his Sunday school class, by eighth grade Vince no longer attended his Southern Baptist church on a regular basis. His father discovered a sexual liaison between Vince's mother and the church's softball coach. "The affair was over when Dad found out. It was just the fact that he could never bring himself to trust her again and that Mom thought Dad should forgive." Vince suffered during this time of emotional upheaval:

> My parents had asked me jokingly, "If we were to divorce, who would you live with?" I would always think to myself, "That will never happen." Then suddenly here I was confronted with it. I was very torn emotionally. My mother got suicidal at the time. I went through a period of about a year where I was almost phobic of the thought of coming home because I didn't know what Mom had planned for the night. One night I sat in the living room with her hands held in mine because she had pills that she was going to take. It was her way of crying out for help because her 18-year marriage was falling apart.

During early adolescence, Vince continued to engage in homosexual activity with one or two close friends, his grades slipped, and he started to write "dark poetry." He also had a heart-to-heart talk with his Sunday school teacher about his homosexual feelings:

> I only told him because I was so damn attracted to him. I had these big fantasies about telling him, "I'm gay" and he'd say, "Me, too. Let's do it!" Of course, that didn't happen. I told him I wanted to talk to him about something that was really bothering me. But I didn't know what to say. So, he started a game of 21 questions. He said, "You haven't got some girl pregnant, have you?" I said, "Far from it." Finally, he asked, "You don't think you're a homosexual do you?" I said, "Yeah." I couldn't bring myself to say, "Yes, Baxter, I am a dick-sucker." He asked me if I had done it with anybody. I lied. We talked. He didn't say, "You damn sinner, get

on your knees." He said, "Any time you need me just call." I would call twice a week. I was like a fuckin' leach. I think he got tired of it. I finally gave up. He never said he didn't want me to talk about it anymore. I was just smart enough and picked up on the vibes.

Vince continued his sexual exploration, experiencing "my first piece of womanhood." During his parents' separation, Vince was alone in the early evenings. A friend of the family, Carolyn, would sometimes come to stay with him. He and Carolyn, who was a year older, "ended up making it or making an attempt to make it." Vince continues: "I don't know if I got it or not. All I know is that it was so dry, I didn't think I was going to have any skin left." Asked why he even bothered with Carolyn knowing his feelings toward men, he responded, "In the back of my mind I thought maybe if I did it with a girl I would never want to do it with a guy again. I was realizing no matter how you dress it up and try to make it look fancy, it's tough being a fag." Vince's sexual fantasy life was also active. Every day during industrial arts class he would sit, stare at his teacher, and imagine engaging him in sex. "Just the things he said were enough to provoke a sexual response," Vince remembered.

In the turmoil of his parents' breakup and coping with his sexual feelings, Vince changed congregations and became involved with a fundamentalist Gospel musical group, *The True Tones*. "I was saved and baptized when I was six years old. After that, I'd cuss and I didn't read my Bible. Then, in tenth grade, I joined *The True Tones*." The group toured the Southeast in a customized bus and cut records in a private recording studio. Vince considered himself lucky to join the group.

I said to myself, "I'll be a good ol' boy and straighten my act up now that I'm playing with a good group like this." For the first year I got back into my Bible. I started praying—"If this is so wrong, God, why don't You do something to change me?" But, I still practiced homosexuality. Then, one day we went to a town in North Carolina to sing at an Indian charismatic church. There were people banging their heads against windows and doors, dancing up in front of the podium and fainting, and other people coming up and covering them with sheets. I was trying to keep my mind straight and remember what I was playing on the drums. About that time, a little voice inside said "Give up Rock 'n Roll." The next thing I knew I was leaving my drum kit behind and I went up to Billy Rob [the group leader] and said, "I think God wants me to give up my Rock 'n Roll." He let out a yell and said, "Hallelujah!" The whole group got down and prayed with me. That was on Saturday night. The next Friday we had practice. I brought $800 worth of albums and poured paint thinner on them and struck a match. It didn't last but for about two weeks before I was missing my old *Kansas* album. I was depressed. I could have shot myself for doing something that stupid. Personally, I think I was a victim of mental illness that night. It must have been a spontaneous, psychosomatic, neurotic, induced response.

Vincent continued with *The True Tones* for the next two years while clandestinely listening to *Yes*, *Genesis*, *Kansas*, and *Rush* and surreptitiously engaging in homosexual activities.

I still had the wool pulled over their [the group members'] eyes. But inside I was deeply depressed. There was nowhere I could go when I was in high school to get information about what I was from people of my own. I didn't know anything about rest areas. I couldn't have even gotten to them if I'd wanted to 'cause I didn't have transportation. I couldn't go to a gay bar. Homosexual-oriented material just was not within my grasp.

I reminded Vince that he came across material supportive of being gay when he was about 15. He quickly responded:

Oh, yeah. There was one book in the school library, but I never had the courage to check it out 'cause it had "GAY" written on it. But, I did sneak a few peaks at it. It was a prize winning novel written by a man about how he felt about his homosexuality. I wanted to check that book out *so* bad. But, I didn't. I just knew that whoever the librarian was that stamped my card would look at that book, see that it was about being gay, and automatically say, "Why Vince, you're a faggot, aren't you?" So, I never got to read it—except for the cover.

Throughout high school Vince maintained a "straight image." He was a solid *B* student and a second stringer on the school's football team.

I played because I liked to. I wasn't playing to prove that I wasn't gay. I just enjoyed it. I also found it enjoyable being in the shower sometimes. It was a nice view. There were quite a few football players that trotted through every now and then.

During high school Vince also edited the high school newspaper, wrote for the school's literary magazine, and had a steady girlfriend, Terri.

I met Terri in tenth grade. She came to see me play one night. I wasn't ashamed of my classmates coming to see me play although the Vincent that played drums on the stage with this Gospel group was a much different Vince than played football. She started that night to like me. We never had sex, but she was a very beautiful girl. I was always comfortable with her. We talked intimately, not about sex, but I knew personal things that had gone on in her life and I told her personal things that had gone on in my life. We would talk a lot on the phone. She would call every night. Talking was the highlight of our relationship. I could discuss feelings with her that most "macho guys" wouldn't think of doing. You know, guys aren't supposed to be sensitive and wonder about things that aren't of a manly nature. Just recently I met her out at the bar with her female lover. It surprised the hell out of me. We hugged, we laughed, we cried.

Beneath his carefully manicured image "no one had any real idea of what the real Vincent was like."

Although I didn't do anything in high school, it wasn't because there wasn't time. The only reason I didn't do anything then was because I was so afraid of being found out. If someone in my high school would have gotten caught in an explicit homosexual act, they would have had to leave town. I may have passed up some great opportunities while I was in high school. But, I never wanted to wear the scarlet letter of being a fag.

There were a few students in the school who wore the scarlet letter "not because they were caught sucking anybody off but because people just saw forks in their personalities. They had some kind of feminine characteristic" about them which other students in the school quickly picked up on and ridiculed.

These people didn't fit the picture of the perfect male. Whenever the top jocks felt threatened they would strike out and call them "fags." Then there were the rednecks. We called them "The Ropers" because they were all alike. They had four-wheel drive trucks. They wore Levi's, plaid shirts, and cowboy boots. Their jeans always had a circular place in the back of their hip pocket where they had their can of Skull chewing tobacco. They thought the sun set on Hank Williams and Alabama. Friday and Saturday nights they were up on Main Street cruising chicks and drinking Budweiser. For them fags were worse than demons and useful only to kick around when their old ladies weren't available.

Though Vince was different he got along with most students. He could stand out in the school hall and talk about Kahlil Gibran or swap fag jokes with his football buddies. He could play an original piano piece at a school assembly or smoke dope with "The Ropers" before going to industrial arts. Though he would have liked school to be different, he played the cards dealt to him and he played them well.

As far as folks in high school were concerned I had it made. But, you know, your mind is constantly running and *the issue* was always confronting me. Sure, I would like to have gone through high school and tell people who I was and for them to tell me who they were — with no strings attached. But a man knows the difference between something that is realistic and what is not. It's like hoping to find a nickel in your pants' pocket and dreaming about winning the Irish Sweepstakes.

When Vince was a high school junior, he had the opportunity to tell his mother who he really was. As he was cleaning out his closet one Saturday afternoon, Vince came across a scrap of paper in an old pair of jeans. On the faded paper was a list of male classmates he found attractive and the kind of sexual activities he would like to perform with them. Stuffing it in his pocket, he quickly forgot about it. A few days later Melba, his mother, discovered the list while washing clothes.

I was in the living room playing the piano. She came in and asked, "What's this?" holding that piece of paper in front of me. I said, "Sit down, Mom. I think we have to talk." I went on to feed her the biggest piece of bullshit that you ever heard of in your life. I told her that ever since I had had Carolyn I thought I was a homosexual. But, I told my mom about my new girlfriend, Terri and said, "You know I'm not gay, mom." She wanted to believe it and so she did.

Vince was tempted, though, to tell Melba about an incident which occurred the year before. "Mom met this guy on Thursday night, dated him on Friday night, brought him home on Saturday morning, and I had him Saturday night. The next day he got baptized." But, Vince chose to be discreet.

After Vince completed high school, he felt increasingly uneasy about his participation with *The True Tones*. Criss-crossing the Southeast six days a week, life on the road was hard, the pay was low, and sexual frustration was high. By that time, Vincent had developed a "crush" on Tracks, the lead singer who was separated from his wife. "Again, I went through this mind set that I would tell him I was gay, and even though he was married and had a young kid, he would admit to me he was gay too." Vince vividly recollects when he finally confided in Tracks about his secret:

> It was the night of the final episode of *MASH*. Mom came in and muttered, "When are you going to start dating girls, Vince?" and stomped out. It was almost like a play. I got to thinking about it while I was watching the show. The 4077th was breaking up and it was pretty fuckin' sad. After it went off I went to my room and started crying. I couldn't stop crying. I left Mom a note on the table telling her that I had to go see Tracks. It was 11:30 but he wasn't home. I sat in the driveway and cried until he returned. I cried when he got out of the car, when we got into the house, and when I talked to him. I was crying until he said, "What's wrong?" I blurted out, "I'm gay!" I stayed with him that night. We prayed. Tracks knew that God would give me strength to overcome this problem. I finally fell asleep on the couch; he slept in his bed.

For the next two months, Tracks acted differently toward Vince. Paula, Tracks' wife, had returned home. She whispered to Vince one night while cooking hamburgers on the grill, "Something is eatin' at Tracks. He's laying awake all night long. He's not sleeping." A short time later, Tracks confronted Vince: "I haven't seen you make any progress in changing what you are." Feeling that Vince should leave *The True Tones* until his problem was resolved, the two agreed to talk to Billie Rob, the group's leader.

> We told Billie Rob and he cried. Oh, that was touching. He couldn't believe his little drummer boy was a fag. They really liked me at that time, since this was after I had given up Rock 'n Roll. I still had the wool pulled over their eyes, but I was really getting into the services. I told him that I drew my strength from being on stage, which was bullshit. I just didn't want to quit playing drums. Billie Rob suggested counseling with Stew Crawford, a fundamentalist minister who was their preacher at the time. I got Billie Rob to let me stay in the group while the preacher was trying to save me from Satan.

Vince also visited the Reverend Johnston, the preacher for one of the largest Southern Baptist congregations in the area.

> He was very honest. He told me that whatever he said in the room would be very different from what he preached in church. "I have to take a different stand when I am in the pulpit but in here I'm not like that," he told me. At this time I was on the border line of religion. I was already starting to form doubts. But, I really respected him. When I told him that I really didn't believe in all of that, he wasn't offended. He was just there for me. He said, "Get close to the Lord, find you a good lover, and be happy."

About six weeks later Vince wrote Billie Rob a letter thanking him for his help and concern, but bowing out of *The True Tones*. He concluded his letter saying, "The Vince I am now is not the one I started out to be nor the one you like, but it's the one I am. Thanks for everything." Vince does not regret for a moment his time with *The True Tones*:

> It gave me a lot of experience meeting different people. I saw a larger segment of the social strata than a lot of people I grew up with saw. I learned there's a big difference between Katie, Texas, Greenville, South Carolina, and Hartford, Indiana. It's almost like I assimilated all the data from the places I had been, the people I'd seen, and was able to make a decision about myself.

At 20, Vince sat down with his mom and told her he was gay. "I didn't know how she was going to take it. My mom had talked to me about masturbation and it didn't embarrass me or her. It seems like she was liberal to a point but when she was conservative, by God, she was conservative. She could have easily said, 'If he's gay that won't bother me in the least.' But, she didn't." Melba's first response was one of shock and admonishment, exclaiming "I'd rather rot in hell than to see one of my kids in a homosexual situation." Over the course of the next year and a half, however, Melba became more comfortable with Vince's homosexuality. She even warmed up to his lover of one year, Frank. On his last birthday she told Vince, "I love you and there's nothing you can do that can make me not love you. But, I'm still praying that God will get a hold of you and that He will convert you to the straight and narrow path."

At 22, Vince relayed a message to his father about his homosexuality. He followed this up with a telephone call inviting Vernon out to dinner. Vince slowly traveled the 90 miles into North Carolina. In a somber silence, his mind raced through possible scenarios of meeting with a father he had not seen for two years. During dinner, Vernon was supportive and sympathetic as Vince discussed his sexual orientation. Vernon politely asked questions and listened intently. Following dinner, they returned to his father's home for six more wrenching hours of discussion.

> My dad is very religious. He claims to have visions. At the same time he has a girlfriend that he sleeps with three times a week. He likes Jimmy Swaggart but he also takes a shine to Jim Beam. At the house, he told me that he really believed that I didn't have any choice in what I had become. "Your orientation," he said, "is the result of some form of demonic possession." My mouth hung open. He took me back to when I was three years old and I let out that yell to Jailhouse Rock. He asked, "Why were you so afraid of that song?" I shrugged my shoulders. He told me that was a real significant point in my life. He thought the demon entered my soul through the grooves of that Elvis Presley record. Then, he warned me never to bring my friends or lovers to his home. I asked if that was because he was unsure about his own orientation; he exploded. We haven't talked much since.

Today, Vince is enamored with the religions of the Far East which emphasize meditation and reincarnation. He bears no hard feelings toward his parents, his Gospel friends, or their religions. Sitting on a cushion, Vince reflects:

> I have become aware that people can't help the way they think. Some Baptists and Fundamentalists are the finest people in the world. But, I just can't accept everything verbatim. Some people can't help the way they feel. When I hear some redneck

calling somebody "faggot," it doesn't provoke feelings of anger inside me. I feel pity. This boy is only mimicking what he has been taught as the Gospel Truth.

COMMENTARY

As a child on the brink of adolescence, Vince coped with a church scandal, the divorce of his Christian parents, and the understanding of the sinfulness and stigma attached to his homosexual feelings. As an adolescent on the brink of adulthood, Vince grappled with his crushes on older men, learned from playing on the Gospel circuit, disclosed his homosexuality to his parents, and made peace with his God. Throughout this time no one suspected a muscular guy who played football, cracked fag jokes, kept a steady girlfriend, attended fundamentalist church, and sung in an evangelical Gospel group could be gay. These roles, coupled with his outgoing personality, hid his scarlet letter from others. The Southern Baptist beliefs of his mother and Reverend Johnston, as well as the fundamentalist convictions of his father, Billie Rob, and Reverend Crawford combine to form a useful vantage point from which to peer into the prism of Vince's story. In order to make sense of Vince's biography, an understanding of the history and beliefs of these two related but distinct religions is necessary.

Theology and History of Southern Baptists and Fundamentalists

As anthropologist Clifford Geertz has documented, religion and culture are inextricably tied together.[2] Just as Utah has been influenced greatly by the Church of Latter Day Saints, and the Southwest by Roman Catholicism, so the Deep South has been affected by the Southern Baptist Convention. Though Southern Baptists have church organizations in every state, more than 20,000 of their churches are located in the South, the vast majority serving small congregations located in rural areas. Together with the United Methodists, they account for a majority of the Southern church population — a demographic fact that has remained unchanged for two centuries.[3] South Carolina played a pivotal leadership role in the growth of the Baptist denomination and in the birth of the Southern Baptists. The first Baptist church in the South was formed in late seventeenth century Charleston under the pastoral guidance of a New Englander. South Carolina formed the first statewide association of Baptists in 1821, and, under the leadership of South Carolinian William Johnson, broke from the Northern Baptists (later to be called American Baptists) to form the Southern Baptist Convention in 1845.[4] Today, with more than 700,000 members, South Carolina boasts the third largest concentration of Southern Baptists in the United States.

These "regenerated believers" and their present disciples share a belief in the inerrancy of the Scripture, profess a faith in the Spirit of God gained through personal religious experience, proclaim a heartfelt dedication to Jesus Christ through immersion into baptismal waters, demand local and lay management of a congregation's affairs, and emphasize the importance of the evangelistic enterprise and religious education. However, as southern scholar Samuel Hill, Jr.[5] recently wrote, "literalism in Biblical interpretation, while characteristic of Fundamentalism, is not all that distinguishes it from other forms of conservative Protestantism. . . . On the whole, the South is an evangelical territory of more moderate forms—Fundamentalism being the most extreme variety within that diverse family." He concludes that while this particular brand of evangelical conservatism has become more common during the past three decades, particularly in the Southern highlands of the Carolinas, "that approach to religion does not dominate the region nor serve as the central resource or axis for national Fundamentalism."[6] Emphasizing the healing of hands and speaking in tongues, Holiness and Pentecostal worshippers reflect this more radical brand of fundamentalism which some mainstream Baptist congregations find embarrassing.

Like their more radical fundamentalist brethren, Southern Baptists are known for their conservative views on theological as well as political matters.[7] At its 1946 Convention, the Southern Baptists agreed that "the New Testament [is] the divinely inspired record and interpretation of the supreme revelation of God through Jesus Christ as Redeemer, Savior, and Lord."[8] While American Baptists have argued that "the Fundamentalist view of faith, which requires assent to and acceptance of Biblical evidence at every point, is not our historic Baptist position;"[9] it remains inviolable to Carolina Baptists. Consequently, the Scriptural admonition (e.g., Luke 1:15, I Cor. 6:10) against the sale and consumption of alcoholic beverages is translated into social policy through dry counties and Sunday "blue laws"; the Biblical role of the wife vis-à-vis her husband (e.g., Eph. 5:24, Mark 10:6b) is used to justify the rejection of the Equal Rights Amendment; the Old Testament God's blessing on Chanaan as slave (Gen. 9:27) and the command of servants to obey their masters (Eph. 6:5) were used to support segregation of the races; and apparent Biblical condemnation against homosexual behavior (e.g., Rom. 1:18-32, Lev. 18:22) is employed as justification for state sodomy statutes and the restriction of information provided in sex education.[10]

Religion and Homosexuality

South Carolina is the heartland of the Protestant evangelistic South. On its northwest corner, resting on 155 acres of prime real estate, is Bob Jones University, a fundamentalist high school and college campus. On its north central border lies Heritage USA, formerly the third largest theme park in the country operated by the now defunct and scandal-ridden PTL Club. Near its Atlantic coast is the Baptist College of Charleston, a private liberal arts school which strives for "academic excellence within a Christian environment." Within the state there are more than a dozen Protestant-supported colleges. Scattered throughout the state, alongside dirt roads or crowded together in small towns, are nearly five thousand Christian outposts where networks of family and kin worship and pray. These Christian fortresses guard South Carolina against the isms: evolutionism, ecumenicalism, secular humanism, communism, pluralism, globalism.

In this land of true believers, religion is an anchor in the maelstrom of everyday life.[11] The rituals of religion, such as baptism, worship, marriage, and burial, provide a heavenly strand through this earthly maze of temptation and suffering. They give sustenance to individuals in time of tragedy and provide an interpretive lens for them to make sense of an apparently capricious world in which God will ultimately triumph and the good will be saved through personal faith, repentance, and conversion. Through this lens, Melba and Vernon try to make sense of their son's homosexuality. Using this focus, Billie Rob and Reverend Crawford lecture Vince that the abomination of homosexuality can only be righted through ritualistic cleansing of the spirit. From this perspective, the price of sin and wickedness is terrible and costly. A century ago this price was paid through the shedding of Southern blood and the despoilment of young Southern manhood. Today it is exacted through the quick, though painful deaths of God's most recent plague upon those who violate His temples of the Holy Ghost.[12]

Reverend David Alben (fictitious name) is a native Southerner graduating from a Tennessee high school right after World War II and ordained as a Presbyterian minister in 1954. "Father Dave" has ministered to gay people since the early seventies north and south of the Mason-Dixon Line. "Being a clergyman and representing the church there is an immense barrier between them and me," he says. "I represent the very engine of oppression that they're lashing out against." As a pastor of southern Metropolitan Community Church,[13] he worries that his church is becoming a "dumping ground for the name brand churches' unwanted gay youngsters. I'm glad to deal with other people's discards. I've built a whole network of churches out of them. But, I think it's loathsome of them. It cuts the kids off from stuff that's precious to them." For Father Dave, this religious tradition connecting family and community is particularly important for adolescents like Vince who must cope with being gay and Christian. There is though, according to Father Dave, an "immense gulf" between growing up gay in the South of the forties and the New South of the eighties:

> Before Stonewall there was nothing except for Mattachine and Bilitis. I remember reading the *City and the Pillar* right after high school. I don't remember how I got a copy. How do you get a copy of this book? You can't go up and ask for it. If you do you've labelled yourself. You just got the book the best way you could. When I grew up and came out, if you possibly could you went to New York; Los Angeles was second choice — nobody spoke of San Francisco. You tried to go to a

major urban center to find anonymity and to lead a double life. If you couldn't do that you were apt to have a very hard time of it and eventually you would wind up as the town queer, a drunk, or killed somewhere. Today you can go to Atlanta, you can go to Nashville; there are lots of places to go. And, if you stay in a little town, because transportation is so easy and communications have totally changed, you can have support: news, media, books, music.

Despite the enormous changes outlined by Pastor Dave, Vince reports an isolation and loneliness not too dissimilar from the Tennessean's hometown of the 1940s. Vince, who graduated from high school in 1982, laments:

Back then, I didn't feel very knowledgeable about homosexuality. Inside I was deeply depressed because there was nowhere I could go. I wasn't old enough to go to a gay bar even if I would have known where one was.

Nevertheless, for Father Dave there is a pronounced distinction between growing up gay today compared to 40 years ago; indeed, today the distinction between southern and northern homophobia is insignificant:

These kids don't have a true Southern accent and they think their grandmother talks funny. They read the same magazines, they hear the same music, they see the same television and films [as northern kids]. Of course it's true there are a lot of very loud forceful rednecks in the South but they have their opposite number in the milltowns up and down the Ohio River Valley. Today, what is the difference between the rural southern fundamentalism and the kind of crap that goes on in a Catholic church on Boston's south side? I don't like to hear, partly because of my own regional pride, Southern fundamentalism having to take the lumps when Wisconsin Lutherans are guilty of exactly the same kind of homophobia. I despise it in all of them and I have nothing but contempt for it. It's easier in a Northern town of thirty to fifty thousand not to be involved in church than it is in a Southern town, but that's the only break you get today.

Again, this is a perspective that Vince does not share:

It is easier to be gay in Atlanta than in a small town in South Carolina, just as it is easier to be gay in Chicago than some jerk-water town in Iowa, so that's the same anywhere you go. But, South Carolina is one of the fuckin' notches in the Bible Belt. Mr. Bob Jones is right up the road here. You got to be discreet. Also you got to realize that Southerners are stubborn. The hardest thing for them to do is to change their minds because "that's the way it has always been." Like they're still flying the fuckin' Confederate flag in Columbia; nobody has the balls to take it down. They're just stone-headed; they won't look at the facts.

Though Vince's experiences have been more limited and idiosyncratic than Father Dave's, both draw upon personal experiences as the basis for their conclusions. There have been few empirical studies on Southerners' attitudes toward homosexuality or homosexual persons. A recent study that examined regional differences found that whereas a majority of non-Southerners profess tolerance toward such minority groups as atheists, communists, and homosexuals, a majority of Southerners do not. The study concludes that "the main source of regional differences is the large number of Protestant Fundamentalists inhabiting the South. . . . which is independent of the effects of economic variables."[14] This finding conforms to those of other studies reporting relationships between personal background and beliefs, and attitudes and feelings about homosexuality. People with negative attitudes report less personal contact with gays and lesbians, fewer (if any) homosexual experiences, a more conservative religious ideology, and more traditional attitudes about sex roles than those with less negative views. Those harboring negative attitudes toward homosexuality are also more likely to have resided in the Midwestern or Southern regions of this country, to have grown up in rural areas or in small towns, and to be male, older, and less well-educated than those expressing more positive attitudes.[15] While these studies support Vince's claim of the

South's more homophobic tilt, they do not challenge Father Dave's assertion that other religious denominations outside the South, though having less influence in regional politics and culture, are no less conservative than their Southern counterparts.

Vince's story also portrays the relationship between sexuality and fundamentalism. The explicit condemnation of the most lurid sexual acts from the pulpit and the rhythmic writhing of charismatic Christians to the tribal beat of *The True Tones* ignites sexual energy within the sanctity of the wooden church or revivalist tent. Poor whites like Vince's parents, the Lesters of *Tobacco Road* and the Waldens of *God's Little Acre*, can furtively indulge in their lust while condemning those who express their sexuality honestly.

Vince was the only participant in this study to receive private affirmation of his private life from a religious figure. During that brief conference with Reverend Johnston Vince's sinfulness and guilt were absolved. What might have happened to Vince had his church or Bible Study group celebrated the Old Testament love between Ruth and Naomi or the deep bond of affection between Jonathan and David? Had the silent reproof within Vince's Baptist congregation or the wrath of Yahweh promised by the true believers in his Gospel group been dispelled, would his journey of the spirit have changed? Though no one knows for certain the answers to these questions, certainly the promise of comfort to all who enter the church proved false when Vince entered through its doors.

REFERENCE NOTES

1. Sherrill, 1968:222.
2. Geertz, 1973.
3. Bailey, 1964; Fields, 1983; Quinn, Anderson, Bradley, Goetting and Shriver, 1982.
4. For understanding the development, growth, and influence of the Southern Baptists, particularly in South Carolina, I am indebted to: Baker, 1966; Baker, 1974; Gaustad, 1980; Hays and Steely, 1981; Hudson 1979; King, 1964; Owens, 1971; Owens, 1980; Townsend, 1935; Wallace, 1917; Wesberry, 1966.
5. Hill, 1988:1506.
6. Hill, 1988:1506. For a discussion of the relationship between Christian Evangelism, Fundamentalism, and Protestantism in the South, see: Bailey, 1964; Hill, 1988; Marsden, 1980.
7. Stark and Glock, 1968; Stark and Bainbridge, 1985. Though a more mod-

erate wing exists within the Southern Baptists, during the past ten consecutive years, the evangelical Christians have enjoyed a majority of representatives to its annual convention, placing persons who share their religious views in executive offices, committees, and college boards. For a discussion of the recent evolution and politics of American neo-conservative Protestantism see, Hedstrom, 1982.

8. Quoted from Wamble, 1976:206.

9. Wamble, 1976:208. This quote, however, is misleading as it reinforces the popular misconception of the South as the bedrock of fundamentalism.

10. Kelsey, 1973. For a critique of these Biblical interpretations and their translation into public policy with suggestions for a broader theological understanding, see: Bailey, 1964; Bartlett, 1977; Boswell, 1980; England, 1980; Furnish, 1979; Horner, 1978; Lance, 1989; McNeill, 1976; Nelson, 1980; Scroggs, 1983. Of course, since the words of the Bible are accepted as Creed and not subject to debate, the theological and hermeneutic arguments put forth by these authors will hold little sway with conservative Christians. Their social and political beliefs are rooted in religious faith and in the conviction that accepting Jesus Christ as their personal savior excludes tolerance for homosexuality or acceptance of homosexual persons. Nevertheless, appeals for religious compassion and understanding have been written by a number of ministers or members of religious denominations. These include: Batchelor, 1980; Brick, 1979; Cook, 1988; Feinberg, 1981; Halloran, 1979; McNeil, 1988; Pennington, 1981; Pittenger, 1967. Reflections of personal difficulties confronted by gay Christians and Jews include: Beck, 1982; Curb and Manahan, 1985; Fortunato, 1982; Krody, 1977; McNaught, 1981.

11. For arguments supporting this position, see: Gaustad, 1980 and Shortridge, 1977.

12. 899 AIDS cases have been reported in South Carolina as of February 1990. The actual number is estimated to be much higher.

13. Founded in 1968 by Rev. Troy Perry, MCC is the only gay-centered Christian denomination (Birchard, 1977; Perry, 1972).

14. Jelen, 1982:85.

15. Fyfe, 1983; Herek, 1984; Morin and Garfinkle, 1978; Stark and Bainbridge, 1985.

Chapter 3

Black Churches and Sects: The African Methodists and the Jehovah's Witnesses

MALCOLM AND THE YOUNG PIONEERS

The church really represented all that was left of African tribal life, and was the sole expression of the organized efforts of the slaves.

W. E. B. Dubois, "The Philadelphia Negro"[1]

Malcolm is the youngest child in a family of five brothers and five sisters. Seven, including Malcolm, come from one marriage; two are from his father's first marriage; and one from his father's "escapades." Because of his father's alcoholism and inability to pay rent, the family moved to "the projects" when Malcolm was four, remaining there until he was nine years old. "It was a total shock to me," Malcolm recalls. "I had never been around kids like that before. It was really bad. There was an intense amount of violence." There was also religious conflict and psychological violence within his family.

Both my parents were involved in cults. My father belonged to a church called "The House of Prayer." This church is not well known among whites. My mother, because of the fanaticism of my father's cult, joined the Jehovah's Witnesses. Both religions thought that everybody else was wrong: Catholics, the Jews, the Methodists, the Presbyterians. They were all wrong except for their own religion. It was very intense and confusing for me because my mother felt that my father was the type of person that he was because he didn't have his relationship with God straight. My father's religion was at constant odds with my mother's religion. I was really a pawn between my parents.

As Malcolm grew up, he began to share his mother's views:

Mom tried to help me to see, according to her way of thinking, that the reason he was extremely violent and derogatory was because he was still enslaved to Satan's manipulations, alcohol, and the religion that he was in. She felt that demonic forces were holding him in this state of being. So, when I looked at my father, I saw Satan. When I looked at my mother, I saw God.

Beginning at the age of four, Malcolm walked door to door with his mother and sisters proselytizing for the Jehovah's Witnesses. As a "vacation pioneer," he and other children were "pushed into field service" for 75 hours a month. "If you weren't eating, sleeping, or resting at home," Malcolm remembers, "you were out in the field. Every thought and every feeling was directed toward religion." Except for school activities and sexual adventures, religion consumed Malcolm's active childhood and adolescent life.

Also beginning at age four, Malcolm enjoyed childhood sex play with neighborhood friends:

The lady next door had lots of kids, like my mom. She had a son, Morris, another boy and a few daughters. When our parents weren't around, we would play with each other. We would touch each other. We would actually have orgies. I'm talking about three-, four- and five-year olds!

His older brother of 11, Ernie, also engaged him in sexual activity. "I didn't really want to," Malcolm recalls. "I could sense that it was more of a power thing with him than an expression of love or even passion." By the tender age of four, Malcolm asserts:

I knew I was going to be a homosexual because I saw what was considered natural and what was considered normal in a relationship between the men and women that I was around. I looked at it and it did not seem right to me. I didn't see any beauty in it at all because there was hardly ever any beauty there. It was sexual lust and passion, obsession and possession. There was very rarely any love there at all.

Malcolm recollects, "I remember being just basically a happy person. That is, until my mind would drift back to the times that I was involved in the sexual escapades. That was always in the back of my mind no matter what I was doing. I was constantly being harassed by my memories."

Malcolm, though, was harassed by more than his memories. Due to bussing, he began third grade in a middle class, predominantly black, suburban neighborhood school located on the other side of town.

They were calling me "fag" and "sissy," but I was so naive I didn't really know what those words meant. I remember being in class and the other boys and girls would walk away from me. I felt an intense amount of guilt and self-hatred. When the others called me names and stuff, I assumed they were right. I had very low self-esteem.

Malcolm's low self-esteem and self-hatred were exacerbated by the reactions of his parents:

I was embarrassing to them, especially to my father. If some of the neighbors came around, my folks didn't want me to say anything. They did not want me to be there with them. They felt like somehow there must be something wrong with me. When we were in the projects and I would play with other kids, there were times when my mom would tell me to come in. She would say, "Those kids don't want you to play with them." She always made me feel like there was something wrong with me.

This negative reaction to Malcolm's effeminate behavior was sanctified by the church elders:

> By the time I was nine or ten I started to get a lot a flack from the church. I would be going from door to door with an elder in our Congregation. I would be standing there getting ready to knock on somebody's door to tell them about my faith and love for Jesus. He would say, "Why are you walking like that? Why do you talk like that? Do you have any idea how these people are looking at you? You're degrading God's name." It was just devastating. They said that I had a "swish" and a certain whine in my voice. My minister would tell me, "I ought to get a tape recorder and tape your voice. You're a disgrace."

For a person committed to Jesus and to the Church, such criticism had a damning impact:

> If you were going to be like Jesus Christ and His sheep, you were supposed to be innocent. You were supposed to listen to the elders. They knew what they were talking about. They had been out there in that corrupt world. So, when they told you something, you did what they told you to do. Needless to say, it was very confusing and caused me to have an intense amount of self-hatred.

His family moved from "the projects" into a middle class African-American neighborhood in 1970 when Malcolm was in the fifth grade. Malcolm was bussed again, this time to an upper class, predominantly white school. This was his first exposure to being black in a white-dominated culture. He was particularly surprised by the behavior of some of his teachers.

> Being so innocent and naive, I thought I liked the school. But, there was a certain amount of racism there that was so obvious and flagrant. The white adult teachers showed favoritism toward some of the white kids there. My mom was very worried about me. But, there wasn't much she could do about it.

He also continued to experience harassment: "I was weak. I wouldn't fight back. I wouldn't say anything. I was always afraid. I was always scared. That gave other persons who were insecure about their sexuality or their own strength a chance to get one over on me. They did that constantly."

The following year Malcolm attended a large middle school as a sixth grader. He continued to experience problems because of his effeminacy and race:

> I was just a little bit out in left field. I still really didn't know what was going on. I was in my own little world. That's when the abuse and the harassment got absolutely vicious. I'd get on a bus full of students with a bus driver who doesn't care. He's a teenager himself. He's stoned. He's not paying any attention. The kids would just go haywire. Every day I was called "fag" and "nigger." People would pick fights with me. They would throw things at me like rocks and shoes. I would never go to the back of the bus. I would sit at the front in a seat by myself because nobody wanted to sit next to me.

In school Malcolm was a poor student and terrible in athletics. Few teachers were concerned about his welfare and most who expressed concern inevitably compared him to his brothers — all of whom had played football.

> The teachers didn't say anything to me to let me know they were concerned with me as a person. When they did it was always comparing me with my brothers. I remember the principal of the school coming to tell me that Ernie, my older brother, was a very good role model. He put him on a pedestal. One day I had just come out of the cafeteria and was sitting with the misfits. I was just sitting there scared because there was so much violence at the school. I'll never forget when the principal came and said, "Ernie was a football star. He was really well liked at this school. I think you should be that way too." The principal looked upon me as being a disgrace to Ernie and my other brothers because I was so feminine.

Malcolm became a "pioneer" in the Jehovah's Witnesses during the ninth grade. "Every thought, every feeling was directed toward religion," he recalled. After school Malcolm would go into his room, shut the door, and read from his Bible for hours. When he was not at home he was proselytizing in the field one hundred or more hours a month, attending conventions, and giving sermons. Malcolm's actions were motivated as much by denial of his homosexual feelings as by his affirmation of his mother's religion.

> Homosexuality was considered the most awful sin that anyone could commit aside from outright worship of Satan. It was the most terrible thing in the world that anyone could ever do. Very rarely would they mention it in church because it was considered something that was so base and so depraved. I felt that the reason why I was having these homosexual feelings was because I was an imperfect human being. I had sinful tendencies. That was why I should pray all the time and I should be so busy in church. If I prayed all the time and stayed active in the church, maybe somehow I could appease God in some kind of way and He wouldn't be so angry at me for those spurts of homosexuality.

In ninth grade, also, Malcolm adopted a different strategy to cope with his peers, who in middle school had harassed him because of his effeminate behavior. Part of his carefully crafted strategy was the pursuit of academics:

> I became an honors student. I became really popular because honors students were considered to be elitist. You weren't supposed to harass anybody if they were studying. You can pick on a fag or a sissy, but you don't bother a brain. I felt that if I became a brain, nobody would pick on me anymore. That's exactly what happened.

Malcolm carefully staged other aspects of his public self:

> I had to become more masculine. It was an effort, but something I did. I would make myself walk a certain way. I would make my voice sound a certain way. I would make myself sit a certain way. It was total insanity; I was not being me.

At the time, however, Malcolm was "elated" with the change. His teachers knew "it was really strange but they just thought that I was a good student and a good person for other students to pattern themselves after." His parents, the minister, and the Congregation at the local Kingdom Hall also treated Malcolm with more respect. He continued to project this new image until the end of his freshmen year.

During that summer, Malcolm developed a friendship with Wesley, a man seven years his senior and a member of the Congregation. Wesley was "very entertaining and just a funny person. He was such a girl," recalls Malcolm. The reaction of the Congregation and Malcolm's father to this newly forming friendship, though, was less positive:

> My mom invited him over to our house one evening for dinner and my dad came home. We had dinner and everything. My mom was getting ready to take Wesley home and my dad was sitting there talking to him. After we took him home and came back my dad just flew off the handle. He went berserk. He yelled, "That guy's gay! He's a faggot. He's a sissy. I don't want him around my son. Malcolm will become more feminine. Don't you see he's trying?" This made my mom angry. So, she had Wesley over as often as she could.

With his mom's approval, Malcolm and Wesley became best friends and Malcolm "just let go. I didn't care how I acted or what people thought of me any more because he didn't." Despite Malcolm's determination to "let go," the influence of religion and the power wielded by his Congregation greatly affected his thoughts and behaviors as the following year in school would prove.

In the tenth grade, Malcolm had the opportunity to attend a public alternative school in which students worked at their own pace and teachers focused on the affective needs of adolescents. "You didn't sit at desks, you sat at tables. You didn't call the teachers by their last name, you called them by their first names. You didn't raise your hand to be excused, you just got up and left." Malcolm remembers when he first confronted the issue of homosexuality in the school:

> It was a class on death and dying. There was this girl in class who was one of the most beautiful females I had ever seen in my life. Lydia had breasts out to here. Everything was in proportion. Long, thick, wavy black hair. She was a goddess. Everyone was shocked to find out that she was a lesbian. I

thought it was something terrible. I was taught to think that when you sin, you were sinning against God. You were actually offending God and you were sinning against yourself as well. I tried to get her to see this because I believed it. I carried my magazines and books around with me all the time. But, Lydia wouldn't accept it. She really tried to get close to me. She was very affectionate, very warm. But, I kept pushing her away because she was a lesbian. I knew that there were other gay people at the school. Deep inside I cheered for them. But, I couldn't do what they were doing because it was a sin. It was wrong. As a Christian, I was supposed to be a witness for God. I was supposed to live that lifestyle. I'd say, "Look at what it's doing to your mind, your body, your health, and the spiritual side of you. As a Christian, I am not doing those things. See how happy I am?" Lydia would tell me, "You're not happy. I know you're not happy, Malcolm. No matter what you show me in the Bible, I know you are not happy." Of course, I would deny it.

Despite his best efforts to deny his sexuality, Lydia saw through Malcolm. She expressed her understanding, love, and support. "Sometimes I think about her now," Malcolm pauses for a long drag off his cigarette. "I wish I could see her. She really tried to get close to me and help me."

Malcolm's teachers at the open school also tried to reach him. He remembers:

They would have described me as a good person with a lot of ability to achieve but a person who was really screwed up in the head because of his parents' religions. Sometimes they would look at me and shake their heads. One time a teacher tried to get me to read *Mr. and Mrs. Bo Jo Jones* — about this guy who had gotten this girl pregnant in school. The moral of the book was that you shouldn't have sex before marriage and that you should be responsible as a teenager. I was reading this book at home and my mom saw me reading it. She saw on the cover a girl and a boy facing each other who looked nude. She said, "Take that book back to school!" She didn't even open the book to see what it was about. That upset my teacher. She just looked at me, shook her head, and didn't say one word.

During that year "school was great but home was really bad." The only child still at home, Malcolm suffered from his father's physical and verbal abuse, the raging conflict between his father and mother, their religious fanaticism, and repression of his homosexual feelings. Malcolm seriously considered suicide several times during that year.

I was trying so hard not to kill myself and to protect my sanity. I might have been able to pick up a Bible and read it but I couldn't pick up a book and really get into it. While I was trying to keep my mind on the Bible I couldn't keep up with math, history, and those things. It was hard enough trying to keep up with the Bible. And then I had to put up with my father and with the constant screaming and yelling. It would just blow my mind. I really should have been put into a home and taken out of that environment. I was a very sick child and I knew my parents were sick. I'd talk to my mom and I'd say, "Mom take me out of this because its doing this to me." But, my mom was just so obsessed with proving my father wrong that she used me to try to make him look bad. I lived in constant fear. I used to sleep with knives under my bed. My father would try to barge into my room. Sometimes I'd have to push the chest of drawers in front of the door to keep him out. He felt that I was a bad person because of my being in a religion separate from his and because of my sexuality. Every time he saw me he was calling me a "fag."

Malcolm looks back at his adolescent years in disappointment.

I wish that teachers would have realized, especially after seeing me tote around all that religious literature and just talking to me, that I was spaced-out. If there had been only some way they could have gotten the authorities to come to my house and taken me out of that environment—I've known that to be done before. Teachers see a student come to school with bruises on his face and they take notice. I came to school with marks on the inside and they walked away. Maybe they were too afraid, maybe they just didn't have the power, maybe they didn't want to be bothered, maybe they just didn't care.

As a sophomore, Malcolm began dating Surlina, a tall, muscular woman seven years his senior. "We didn't actually have sex," says Malcolm. "We fondled, caressed, and did a lot of heavy petting. I did not like her." Why did Malcolm continue to date a person he did not like?

> I saw myself falling from grace. I knew that if I did not change my femininity and my feminine characteristics that I would eventually be looked upon with disgrace in the Congregation. I knew that was going to hurt me. I did not want to marry someone who I loved and then have my marriage fall apart. She didn't love me either. The only thing she was concerned about was getting a husband.

Following his graduation from high school, Malcolm married Surlina. They moved to another city and joined another Congregation of Jehovah's Witnesses. It wasn't too long before the elders there also expressed concern about Malcolm's mannerisms and demeanor.

> The elders said, "Hey! You can't act like that. Do you have any idea how people in this Congregation are looking at you?" They told me to change my voice and grow a mustache. I was 18 years old and married. There was a part of me that believed these men were actually anointed and appointed by God Himself through the power of the Holy Spirit to judge anyone. There was another part of me, though, that was horrified at the thought. I knew that they didn't care about me or love me at all. I knew they were rotten to the core.

Not long after arriving in town, Malcolm's sexual interest in men was tempted. While waiting for Surlina at the hair salon one afternoon, he strolled through the multi-level shopping mall. He stopped to use the third floor men's room. He remembers:

I was washing my hands and I looked up in the mirror and saw this guy. I didn't think about it but I spoke to him. He spoke back. I saw these other guys in the restroom. It didn't click what was going on. I left. As I was walking down by my wife's hair salon, he was standing there looking at me. I said to myself, "This is it." I went up the escalator. When I got up the escalator to turn around he was standing there watching me. I thought, "How did he get up there that quick?" I said to myself, "Well, this must be it." I walked over and asked him, "Are you gay?" He said, "Not particularly." He told me he wanted me to come with him. He took me to the very same restroom where he had cruised me and we did our little thing—the first time I had made it with a guy since I was 10 years old.

When Malcolm and Surlina returned home they had sex. "It was strange," Malcolm recalled. "My body went through all the motions but I felt no pleasure at all." Within two weeks Malcolm had entered a relationship with another man. He confided in his wife:

I told her that, since things were so bad, if she wanted to get a divorce to go ahead, because I had been with another man. In our religion you can't get a divorce unless a person has been unfaithful to you. We met with the Church committee and they talked to me. They asked, "Who all knows that this happened?" I said, "My mom and my wife." They said, "Well, you understand that because this is now a public matter we are going to have to publicly announce that you have been reproved." "Sure," I said. Now, I really wanted to be excommunicated and wanted Surlina to get the hell out of my life. But we stayed together.

Malcolm started going to the gay bars. He enrolled in a gym where he exercised daily and lost 30 pounds. His short hair grew and he got a perm. The sun bleached his silky fine hair. Malcolm was changing. He was in conflict with his wife, his church and, most of all, himself:

The elders started coming down on me heavy. They would come by my house and meet with me. I was frightened; I was drained. I was so weak emotionally and mentally. Deep down I didn't want to leave the church. I didn't want them to excommunicate me. I felt I wouldn't have anything to live for. See, I was told from day one that without the church you're nothing; you're as good as dead. So I ran from them. I moved back home. I really didn't want to go home but there was another part of me that felt like I had to in order to keep my sanity.

Within six months Malcolm experienced disfellowship for leaving his wife. He was alone. An outcast among family and friends, within a few months he petitioned to be reinstated. For another year Malcolm met weekly with a committee of three Witnesses who would ultimately determine if he was truly repentant. "Can you imagine meeting with people for a whole year and not having one even look at you?" Malcolm asks. After the weekly meetings he would leave the Kingdom Hall and go to the gay bars or baths. "I would say to myself, 'This is the last time.' But, it never was. I would leave that garbage and go to church where no one would even talk to me because they were waiting to reinstate me and see proof of my repentance. I was devastated mentally, physically, and spiritually."

Malcolm was finally reinstated. His reinstatement, though, brought no inner peace to himself or domestic tranquility at home. Soon, the cycle started again. At church Malcolm was told, "If you're truly repentant why don't you change the way you walk and talk?" At home Surlina demanded to know his whereabouts and expected him to stay with her at home on nights and on weekends. "I tried to do it. But, even though I had everybody's approval, I didn't have respect for myself. I decided I wasn't going to change. Some people can do it. They can put on a certain act and then go home and dress in drag. They are mentally capable of doing that; I couldn't." Malcolm left his wife for the second time:

I was staying with my brother, Ernie, because neither my parents or other family members wanted me to stay with them. I was someone who was unclean. I became an all-out slut. I got really heavy into drugs and alcohol and was whoring around. I couldn't hold a job because I was an alcoholic and drug addict. I was trying to deal with my sexuality, the church, and the way my family was reacting to me. I started to hang with other gay men in the neighborhood and they would come over to the house and party. Finally, my brother just blew up. We got into an argument at my sister's house. I was drunk and stoned and could barely reach up to scratch my chin. He was an ex-football player and three times my size. He beat me so bad that I had to be hospitalized. To this day I still feel some pain.

Malcolm drifted from place to place living off friends, tricks, or the local mission house. His tail-spin ended with a short-term relationship. During the six month affair, Malcolm found a job and quit drugs. "I had lost my self-esteem. I almost killed myself with drugs, alcohol, and promiscuity. I lost my self-respect. I'm getting it back now." Though they broke up at Christmas, he and his former lover continue to see one another every day. For Malcolm his most important task lies ahead:

My name is still on the church's record. I have written a letter to tell them that I want to be disassociated from them. I'm planning on mailing it this week. I've been putting it off for a month. But, I really have to do it. Once I get this letter in the mail — it's sitting right there on my nightstand next to my bed — then I'll be free of it. But, my mom told me that, if I do mail it, she won't be able to talk to me anymore. Even though I have decided to separate myself from the church, there is still a lot of religion ingrained in me.

COMMENTARY

Within Malcolm's secret whirlpool of sexual feelings, religion was the anchor to his African-American community and family who looked with horror on homosexuality and effeminacy. But, religion prevented exploration into a room hidden from himself and others. The black religious tradition blends African tribal customs and spirituality into the Euro-American religious experiences. The theme of religion as liberation for the oppressed, the religious belief in justice through redemptive suffering, and the conviction of the coming of

God's justice characterize black religious thought. Black religious thinking is a useful vantage point for peering into Malcolm's prism of experience.[2]

Theology and History of Southern Black Sects and Churches

The majority of Southern African-Americans who participated in this study were brought up in the traditional churches of the Southern black community: The African Methodist Episcopal Church, its sister denomination, the African Methodist Episcopal Zion Church, and the National Baptist Convention. There also were several religious sects represented including the Jehovah's Witnesses, the House of Prayer for All People, and the Church of God in Christ, whose membership rolls have a disproportionate number of southern blacks compared to whites. Whatever denomination or sect in which these participants claimed membership, they all acknowledged the pervasive role of black churches in their communities, confirming African-American scholar C. Eric Lincoln's statement: "There is no disjunction between the black church and the black community. The church is the spiritual face of the black community, and whether one is a 'church member' or not is beside the point . . ."[3]

The House of Prayer for All People and the Church of God in Christ sects emerged in slave society where traditional African religions were barred, colonial Christianity was not satisfying, doctrinal rivalries gave rise to revivalism, and segregationist practices were long-standing.[4] These sects have flourished for generations. In his recent study of black sects, Joseph Washington, Jr. describes these churches as "lower class, small, loosely organized, local, perfectionist, ascetic, unstable, antiecclesiastical, antistate, lay-oriented, isolationist, exclusive, future-oriented, short-lived, and rigidly moral."[5] Washington views the permanence of these black sects as "a testimony to distress and crisis as a way of life among blacks . . . [they] are rooted in substantial qualities of the authentic black experience."[6]

Another sect, the Jehovah's Witnesses, boasts many black members among its 46,000 congregations worldwide.[7] The church's missionary workers in African-American communities and its stated opposition to ethnic and racial prejudice have made it the most attractive sect for blacks in the South. This sect commands absolute obedience of its members to the Governing Body, recognized as the spokesman for Jehovah. Members' direct contact with the church is through the local Kingdom Hall and a variety of publications, including *The Watch Tower*, issued by the church, which members are expected to read and distribute. Believing that faith without works is dead, elders of the Jehovah's Witnesses impose a strict code of ethics upon their fellowship, ranging from traditional behaviors of males and females to sexual practices. For example, *Your Youth: Getting the Best Out of It*, one of the many publications of this sect, devotes an entire chapter to "masturbation and homosexuality." It concludes, "Even though you find yourself having a hard struggle to break a masturbation habit, never feel that Jehovah God and his Son Jesus Christ have given up on you. If you sincerely keep working to overcome it, they will kindly and patiently help you."[8] Violation of these strict moral and doctrinal beliefs result in "disfellowship" in which other Witnesses, including family, are barred from any interaction with these "eternally damned" persons.

The belief is that members will live forever on an earthly paradise following the Battle of Armageddon (which will spare the 144,000 predestined souls who constitute the heavenly class); accordingly, non-Witness contacts are expected to be minimal. Thus, the conflict between Malcolm's parents and his mother's determination to inculcate him with the church's beliefs at an early age is understandable. By adolescence Malcolm had restrained his homosexual and masturbatory activities, since the Church taught:

> Masturbation is self-abuse, and a masturbator needs to deaden his sexual appetite in order to please God. He needs to cultivate the self-control that is necessary to de-emphasize sex in his life and to leave his sexual organs to adjust to any pressures in the normal way. How? He must keep busy in theocratic pursuits, in meeting attendance, field service, making return visits, conducting Bible studies, helping others spiritually.[9]

Malcolm also adopted a more masculine demeanor and proclaimed his faith through daily public outreach activities. At 13, Malcolm accepted fellowship in the church. At that point, the power of the Congregation, its ministry, and his mother were united through love, respect, and fear. Like John Grimes in Baldwin's *Go Tell It on the Mountain*, Malcolm's self-hatred and homosexual urges were sealed within this Christian triangle. Surrendering his sexuality to God, the abrogation of this union of the Jehovah God, family, and community by Malcolm would cast him into the ranks of the "eternally damned." Listening without disgust to Lydia's proclamation of sexual liberation, the flaunting of effeminate behavior (especially in the public world), or failing to marry Surlina or another woman were all sins of varying gravity. From adolescence through adulthood Malcolm's rebellious acts (associating with Wesley, cruising in the mall) alternated with acts of contrition. Malcolm abused drugs, consumed alcohol, and engaged in other acts of degradation rather than spurn his mother, desert his black congregational community, and renounce his Jehovah God. Unwilling to be cast into the fires of eternal damnation, he chose to descend into a well of loneliness and despair.

The Jehovah's Witnesses and other black religious sects differ significantly from southern black mainstream denominations' liturgy and theology. Churches such as the African Methodist Episcopal reflect the distinctive ancestral heritage and experiences of African-Americans.[10] For example, the Euro-American Protestant concept of purity, sin, and salvation is quite different from the West African tradition rooted in three hundred years of American slavery and oppression. Rural anthropologist Bruce Grindal, who has expended considerable effort studying black religion, asserts:

> God and Devil — good and evil — are not always simple propositions, especially for black people whose historical experience has been twisted between the oppression and sham of white moral justice and the perceived sense of individual and collective inadequacy. Black religion places little emphasis upon moral purity or upon a hard-and-fast distinction between the saved and the damned . . . Salvation, or the union of people with God's spirit, is not so much a release from sin as a release from suffering in a world that is inherently sinful.[11]

For many black congregations, their church and its rituals of conversion and worship affirm the primacy of kinship and their solidarity with their black brethren. The Gospel message is more directed toward social renewal than personal salvation, pastoral care is more temporal than spiritual, and congregational concern is more with acts of racism within the surrounding community or in South Africa than with threats of communism within the local university or in Central America.

In the antebellum South, the plantation master had the responsibility to provide for the religious instruction of his slaves. For some this was done through plantation prayer meetings while others were taken to their master's white church. During such services Southern ministers:

> [U]sually restricted their occasional sermons on slavery to the reciprocal duties of masters and slaves — "servants," as they preferred to call them. They dutifully and dully preached obedience and submission to the slaves, who normally seized the opportunity to catch up on their sleep. They had something more useful to say to the masters, who normally stayed awake. Slave ownership, they insisted, entailed Christian obligations, to be scorned at the risk of a master's immortal soul.[12]

Beyond those slaves who attended worship services either on the plantation or at the master's church, there were a handful of blacks who were allowed to preach on the plantation and a few free blacks and slaves who attended independent black churches, such as the Savannah Baptist Church or Charleston's Bethel A.M.E. church.[13] Plantation slaves were sometimes assigned ministerial tasks and, occasionally when state law permitted, church associations bought them to work under the supervision of a white minister or, on rare occasions, set free to preach the Gospel.[14] It was not until the second decade of the 19th century that any systematic efforts to evangelize the slave occurred in the South through the efforts of South Carolina planter Charles Pickney.[15] Despite the increasing tensions between southern whites and the slave population during the 19th century and the restrictions placed upon African-Americans by state legislatures following events such as Denmark Vessey's failed insurrection in South Carolina, these efforts continued. As late as 1859, for example, a Charleston slave was allowed to preach to his own Baptist church when granted permission from his master.[16]

The spectrum of the Southern black religious experiences spans from sects such as the House of Prayer and the Jehovah's Witnesses to mainstream denominations such as the A.M.E. and Southern Baptist churches. Each of these denominations, like their white counterparts, connects black persons with their God and their community. In concert with one another, these denominations shape the everyday life of believers and non-believers alike.

Religion and Homosexuality

Despite differences in theologies and experiences, Southern black sects and denominations share a common commitment to family buttressed by the church. Black scholar J. Roberts writes:

> One of the most serious internal problems of blacks is family disintegration. It would be nigh impossible to find a group of people who have been able to survive great hardship without strong familial ties. The destruction of the black family has been deliberate during our sojourn in this country. Although the black man's mere survival is a miracle of grace, it appears that the black church, as "invisible" and as a visible institution, has nurtured this suffering race and kept it alive.[17]

The church and the family are the bulwark of African-American communities. The black church has always been the center of secular as well as spiritual fellowship.[18] One scholar of religious studies concludes that, as in the traditional African society, religion in the black community "is not a sometime affair. It is a daily, minute-to-minute involvement of the total person in a community and its concerns."[19] Under the watchful supervision of the church elders, the congregation provides assistance to members in times of crisis and chastises those whose sinfulness shame the community. Jacob, one of the participants in this study and a Southern Baptist, underscores the critical and unique role that religion plays in his black community.

The white community is a little more open-minded, even in the South, about homosexuality. With the black community it's more strictly religious as far as our faith and upbringing. The basic Baptist doctrine is the same, but I think the roots go deeper for blacks. Because of slavery, religion was the only thing we had to rely on. You get these stories passed down to you about your ancestors. Our ancestors had to work and they had to pray. That was the way of life: working and praying. It was their prayers and their work that got us to this point. Those roots are instilled in me. That's why the religious aspect goes so deep. "You got to do right. You got to live by the Bible." That's why we're here in the first place—because our ancestors did that.

The life stories of African-American males as different as Malcolm or Jacob (portrayed in Chapter 6) illustrate how their families' religious faith and its intersection with black community, culture, and history complicates their emerging homosexual identity. The experiences of Malcolm living under the watch tower supervision of his elders is an extreme example of the more common difficulty that lesbian and gay persons of color confront. The late journalist Joseph Beam, in his anthology of black gay writing, remarks:

Because of our homosexuality the Black community casts us as outsiders. We are the poor relations, the proverbial black sheep, without a history, a literature, a religion, or a community. Our already tenuous position as Black men in white America is exacerbated because we are gay. We are even more susceptible to the despair, alienation, and delusion that threatens to engulf the entire Black community.[20]

Grant's biography tempers Beam's words. Historically, ministry and teaching have been prestigious careers in the African-American community. In this respect, Grant, the only son of an African Methodist Episcopal minister and an elementary school teacher, is privileged. For the first ten years of his life Grant lived along the western edge of the Carolina low country in what used to be the heart of the cotton kingdom. In his soft-spoken voice, Grant recalls the life of a minister's son:

You're always in the public's eye. I had certain responsibilities; I had certain things I had to uphold. Like when all the kids used to go to the neighborhood store after Sunday School and before church, I couldn't go. I always had to pay my money in church. They could save their Sunday School money to go to the store. Later I had to perform certain duties besides going to Sunday School like working on this Board or singing in the choir. There were times that I didn't want to but I didn't have the freedom or choice to say, "no."

Grant is proud of his religious heritage: "The African Methodist Church is a story in itself because of its traditions. It's a good religion to be in." Grant recounts the history and contributions of his church. Prior to the War between the States only several dozen black-controlled churches existed in the South.[21] The first truly independent black church was the A.M.E. Church formed in New England after its free blacks experienced discrimination within the white church. Rooted in the Wesleyan tradition and methodist principles, its founders blended Yankee virtues with black identity to form the Union Church of African Members in the second decade of the 19th century.[22] Within several years, a convention in Philadelphia united the small congregations of five Union churches into the A.M.E. Church, under the tutelage of a respected black businessman and founder of the Free Africa Society, Richard Allen. Charleston was the first southern site of an A.M.E. church. It closed in 1822, with a membership of more than 1,400 persons, following Denmark Vessey's aborted slave uprising and the subsequent hanging of 34 blacks. Another A.M.E. church was not established in the southeast until 1865. During the interim, Grant's black Methodist ancestors, like their Baptist counterparts, either worshiped at the plantation missions or participated in segregated worship services in white Methodist churches.

As Grant underscores, the A.M.E. church achieved a number of "firsts" including being the first African-American interstate organization established in the country and electing the first black Protestant bishop in America. Despite his respect for the tradition and accomplishments of the A.M.E. church, at 18 he stopped attending the church his father pastored. "I was really under a lot of pressure." Interestingly, Grant's mother has had a more difficult time adjusting to his poor church attendance than has his father. Grant is quick to point out, "I like the A.M.E. church. In a different place, in a different setting, I could see myself going back to the church." Grant's dislike for attending his father's church had less to do with its position on homosexuality since "our A.M.E. church is not as strict as the Southern Baptists. Our church never really stressed so much that 'God condemns homosexuals.'" Grant, who has not disclosed his homosexuality, simply was fearful of "letting my parents down" in the eyes of the Congregation.

Freelance writer George Stambolian asserts that this less negative experience of homosexual blacks in the church, as reported by Grant, became more common in the decade of the eighties:

> [P]rejudice does exist in the Black community. A great number of progressive Blacks want to think that if Black people are gay, it's because Whites made us that way. . . . But today those ideas are changing, partly because the Black church is changing. Black ministers are beginning to say that homosexuality is part of what people are and that it need not be castigated for being a legitimate form of human sexuality.[23]

Though homosexuality was never embraced in Grant's church, its position was nonetheless more liberal than that of the churches of other black participants in this study, particularly Southern Baptists. Kimberly, noting that "the church is really the foundation of the black community," stresses that "in my church it's preached that homosexuality is wrong. They quote Scripture and the people believe it." Heyward reiterates this observation as he recalls attending his African Methodist church during college in the early eighties: "Every time I would go the preacher would be hammering away at that. He'd say it was a sin and they were going to hell for it."

Though African-Americans in this study, like their white counterparts, reported varying degrees of animosity expressed in their churches toward homosexuality, all emphasized the importance of religion in their family, community, and history. Most, too, noted a tendency to link homosexuality with effeminacy and the white community. Jacob recounts:

> I often hear my black friends say that so and so committed suicide. They say, "I know he wasn't a black person because black people don't kill themselves." Suicide sounds like something a white person would do, just like homosexuality. Even though there are a lot of black homosexuals, a lot of blacks do not want to accept that fact. A homosexual thing is a white thing.

Malcolm repeats these observations: "To be effeminate, black, and gay — blacks really can't take that. If you're white, gay, and effeminate — that's okay." African-American novelist Ann Shockley is more acidic in her assessment of the relationship between black religious beliefs and homophobic attitudes:

> The threat of being gay, queer, funny, or a bull-dagger in black linguistics is embedded deeply within the overall homophobic attitude of the black community, a phenomenon stemming from social, religious, and biological convictions. The enmity toward homosexuality has long been rampant in black life, and is flagrantly revealed in the words of Minister Addule-Baqui of the male-supremacist Black Muslim religious sect: "The dressing of man for another man's sexual companionship and the dressing of a woman for another woman's sexual companionship is an evil, lowly, foul thought."[24]

African-American religious leaders, such as Richard Allen, Henry Highland Garnet, Nat Turner, Malcolm X, Henry Turner, Adam Clayton Powell, Sr., and Martin Luther King, Jr., reflect the many strands of black religious thought. So, too, do the unique stories of Malcolm and Grant. These persons, like the denominations themselves, reflect different journeys in a struggle for human dignity and social justice. Like black religion itself, their personal experiences were forged in the African heritage, molded by antebellum culture, defined by Reconstruction, war, and depression, and etched in the struggle for civil rights. The personal tragedies experienced in Malcolm's life, like characters in *Black Boy* or *Say Jesus and Come to Me*, may symbolize to some the essential meaningless-ness of life. But, as Wright concluded, the "meaning of living came only when one was struggling to wring a meaning out of meaningless suffering."[25] In that case, Malcolm's decision to mail the letter to his Congregation will mark an important point in his journey of the spirit.

African-American lesbians and gay men report that this religious tradition is a mixed blessing. Religious rituals and spirituals ground blacks living in white America in a community of shared history and values. Religious theology also distances them from this com-munity and its history. Lesbians and gay men of color in this study often chose exile from either their homosexual feelings or their black communities.

Noting, "The black church is the single most important institu-tion in the black community," theologian James Cone laments the lack of attention it has paid to women's and gay rights. "It is al-ways much easier to tell the truth about others," writes Cone, "But the critical test of the gospel that we preach is whether we can tell the truth about ourselves. For I believe that the gospel of Jesus demands that we tell the truth about our churches that claim to be Christian but in fact have denied that faith with devilish deeds."[26] This new gospel of compassion and self-criticism was too late for Malcolm whose devilish deeds of homosexuality and effeminacy were the object of scorn and disfellowship.

REFERENCE NOTES

1. DuBois, 1967.

2. For a recent summary of scholarship on African-American religion, see Cone, 1988.

3. Lincoln, 1974:115.

4. Mitchell, 1975.

5. Washington, 1984:69.

6. Washington, 1984:79.

7. About 18 percent of all its U.S. church members are black. I am indebted to the following resources in the development of this section: Botting and Botting, 1984; Gerstner, 1978; B. Harrision, 1978; Penton, 1985; Raboteau, 1988; B. Stevenson, 1968; Whalen, 1962.

8. Botting and Botting, 1984:130.

9. Botting and Botting, 1984:130.

10. For further explanation of the distinctive history, theology, and structure of black religions in the South, the reader is referred to the following: Baer, 1984; Bennett, 1982; Cone, 1984; Grindal, 1982; Harrell, 1971; Lincoln, 1974; Lincoln, 1985; Raboteau, 1978; Sernett, 1985; Washington, 1964; Washington, 1984; Wilmore, 1972; Woodson, 1972.

11. Grindal, 1982:97-98.

12. Genovese and Fox-Genovese, 1988:21.

13. For a particularly interesting, though dated, analysis of the changing relationships between whites and blacks during the first one hundred years of the Southern Baptist Convention, see Valentine, 1980.

14. Baker, 1974.

15. Loveland, 1980.

16. Wesberry, 1966. At the time of the War Between the States, 68 black churches existed within this country; 30 of these were in the South (Lincoln, 1985). The formal separation of blacks from white Southern Baptist and Methodist churches did not occur until Reconstruction. In 1866, for example, South Carolina blacks formed their own independent associations of Baptist and Methodist churches. Within a year of Appomattox, the A.M.E. church boasted a membership of more than 20,000. Within twenty years about one hundred A.M.E. Zion churches crowded the North Carolina-South Carolina border and a new convention of South Carolina Baptists boasted more than 100,000 members. As the last Federal troops were withdrawn from South Carolina, black membership in white churches was nearly non-existent (Baker, 1974; Jones, 1984; Richardson, 1976; Valentine, 1980).

17. Roberts, 1971:60.

18. Cone, 1984; Frazier, 1949; Frazier, 1964; Raboteau, 1978.

19. Washington, 1984:30.

20. Beam, 1986:17.

21. The very first black church in the United States, a Southern Baptist congregation, was established in the third quarter of the 18th century at Silver Bluff, South Carolina.

22. I have found the following sources of particular use in preparing this section: Baldwin, 1983; George, 1973; Payne, 1969; Richardson, 1976; Walker, 1981.

23. Stambolian, 1984:135.

24. Shockley, 1984:268.

25. Wright, 1966:112.

26. Cone, 1984:98.

Homosexuality and Southern Communities

The things we see, hear, smell, and touch affect us long before
we believe anything at all, and the South impresses its image
on us from the moment we are able to distinguish one sound
from another.

Flannery O'Connor, *Mysteries and Manners*[1]

Regions within a country are sometimes thought of strictly in terms of geographic boundaries: the region of Northern Spain bounded by the Pyrnees, the Pampas region lying in central Argentina; the Upper Peninsula of Michigan, which has threatened to secede from its lower half; and, of course, the Southern United States, which did secede. But, these geographic and political boundaries reflect historical and psychological boundaries as well. They define a "community," whose members are bound by commonly held beliefs, values, and experiences.

The South's distinctiveness from the rest of the United States is evident in American literature, history, and the arts.[2] South Carolina is one of five states known collectively as the "Deep South." Its 46 counties range from the low-country on the east coast — the heart of the aristocratic rice plantations — to the Piedmont area in the northwestern part of the state — the industrial center dotted with half-empty towns bearing mill owners' names. South Carolina has become more industrialized, its people more schooled, its politicians less strident, and its culture less insular. More than anything else, though, *South Carolina is a state of mind*, born of history, bounded by war, defeat, reconstruction, and desegregation. Proud of its ideals and customs, many of the three million residents view themselves as confederate nationals first and Southerners second. Theirs is a collective memory of an idyllic past captured in its Gothic architecture and romance literature; a history of the firing at Fort Sumter, the defense of the Alamo by South Carolina natives Travis and Bonham, the oratorical skills of statesmen John Calhoun, James Hammond, and "Pitchfork" Ben Tillman, and the ministerial contributions of Richard Furman and James Thornwell. Theirs is also the less remembered collective history of the contributions of the poor, the black, and women such as Septima Clark, Sarah and Angelina Grimke, and Harriet Tubman. This land of plantations and palmettos was under a state of siege for most of its history: Cornwallis, yellow fever, abolitionists, hurricanes, Sherman's army, carpetbaggers, the boll weevil, freedom riders, pirates, daylight savings time. This is a culture in which the antebellum, patriarchal ethos is rooted in Southern honor, Christian faith, and an extended family.

Skin color, social class, and gender are the contemporary boundaries of many a Southern community. The social metaphors used by participants in this study imperfectly reflect this social topography: the good ol' boy; the nigger; the oreo; the redneck; the Southern Belle; the gentleman; and white trash. These metaphors suggest boundaries between blacks and whites, expectations for males and females, and responsibilities of rich and poor, and also reflect beliefs about romance, marriage, and sexual practices. Most importantly, these metaphors provide the psycho-historical basis for identities constructed within Southern communities. They are the mirrors with which these sexual rebels judge others and identify themselves.

A Thumbnail Sketch of Southern Social Metaphors

Bubba, the good ol' boy: An un-lettered working class Southerner with child-like simplicity and ox-like determination. He has more erections than problems, and his colorful stories outnumber the keys hanging from his 40-inch belt. Good-natured, unpretentious, and reliable, he respects the law, pays taxes, and attends Sunday church. Most often found at fishing holes, hunting grounds, and stock car tracks, the good ol' boy is a likeable, 100 percent American.

Nigger: An African-American who refuses to accept his caste-like assignment in a white controlled community. His utter disregard for danger, emphasis on sexual virility, extravagant spending on outlandish material goods, and hedonism reflect his seething, though often unacknowledged, anger about living in a racist society. "Rednecks" and "white trash," by using this term in a derogatory manner, unwittingly betray their fears about their marginal status in Southern society. Within poor black communities this term, or its variation — "one bad nigger" — is often used complimentarily, underscoring resistance to white domination.

Oreo: A contemporary version of a 19th century Uncle Tom who associates more with whites than with members of the black race. An assessment of the worth of this character mirrors one's political views. For some, this person is an icon of kindness, patience, humility, loyalty, dignity, and forgiveness in the face of barbarity and injustice. For others, he or she is a servile, de-sexualized, domesticated, assimilationist whose religious fatalism and blind trust in divine deliverance bankrupts the continuing struggle for equality and freedom in a white controlled society.

Redneck: A town bully whose speech is fouler than his breath. He loves to watch cock fights, encourages dog-fights, and drives a pickup truck with a loaded rifle hanging in the rear window. Beneath his sweat drenched hat are half-fermented thoughts of women in bondage and burning crosses. Having just enough schooling to be dangerous, his essential traits are meanness and selfishness.

Southern Belle: Before the sexual upheaval, this unmarried, white upper-middle class woman had a limited education confined to the Bible, history, and well-chosen literature. Today,

the Southern Belle simply pretends to have a limited educa-
tion. The larval form of the Southern Lady is the debutante at
Charleston's St. Cecilia Ball wearing a sleeveless, all-white
Oscar de la Renta ballgown.

Southern Gentleman: The inheritor of an aristocratic lineage
(sometimes the product of too frequent intermarriages between
first cousins) and the beneficiary of a Southern liberal education, he enjoys the prestige of his position without the accompanying power. This self-assured gentleman with natural dignity of manner is often trotted out for *Southern Living* photos
and honored at annual historical events. His affable and understanding demeanor disappears only when an outsider attempts
to destroy established customs or seeks membership in his social circle.

White Trash: The grassless yards of white trash are filled
with broken toys, dismantled cars, and half-fed barking dogs.
Their lack of "proper raisin'" is reflected in earthy conversation punctuated by impolite interruptions from a six-year old
clothed in a soiled dress with a runny nose. "More the victims
of strong germs than weak genes, poor white trash were
looked down upon by blacks and whites alike and considered
hopelessly deficient in character as well as resources."[3]

These taken-for-granted social metaphors were carried around in
the heads of many Southerners interviewed for this study.[4] Some
Southern white girls, like Molly Bolt in *Rubyfruit Jungle* or Norma
Jean in this study, prefer climbing trees to fussing with hair. Norma
Jean finds her lowly social status a barrier to her desire to break into
the "right school crowd." As a member of the Up Country elite,
Royce finds that few students or teachers are willing to cross the
border of class and social ranking to challenge his effeminacy and
alleged homosexual activities. Jacob must deal with pint-sized versions of redneck bullies like Stanley Kowalski of *A Street Car
Named Desire* as he struggles with his sexual and class identities
within a middle-class black community.

These metaphors may or may not correspond to any objective
social reality. The power of these metaphors, though, lies in their
ability to simplify a complex social system, to facilitate the con-

structions of personal identities, and to describe codes of sexual conduct considered appropriate within and between social groups. Norma Jean, hanging around the old oak tree, is expected to "suck face" with good ol' boys and country rednecks. The authorities wink at Royce's homosexual escapades masked in deception and discretion. Jacob learns early of the boundaries between black boys and white girls.

These metaphors shift participants' focus from forces which define, maintain, and reproduce a culture to those which merely reflect it. Most importantly, they shape the self-images of Norma Jean, Royce and Jacob while limiting possibilities of transcendence from these socially constructed identities. As John Reed observes in his classic study of social types, while every Southerner gets a menu from which to choose, not all choose from the same menu:

> Individuals . . . are offered a menu of social types. But culture writes the menu, defines the range of alternatives. We make our character, but we must make it out of the material at hand. . . . [T]here are strong pressures to internalize a role, to make it part of one's self.[5]

In this study, these metaphors enable us to ask critical questions about the formation of sexual identities: How do these Southerners make meaning of their sexuality within their limited social menu? How do these metaphors affect the way these young people define themselves sexually? How are sexual thoughts and deeds of these youthful Southerners interpreted within their particular southern communities? These social boundaries and metaphors, then, are a useful vantage point for exploring another dimension of *Growing Up Gay in the South* and peering into the prisms of experiences of three Southerners: Norma Jean, Royce, and Jacob.

REFERENCE NOTES

1. O'Connor, 1961:197.
2. Carole Hill (1977) provides an excellent overview and discussion of Southern culture and approaches social scientists have used to study it.
3. Boney, 1984:39.
4. I have found the following works most useful in developing these ideas, providing the appropriate examples, and suggesting many of the colorful meta-

phors: Abbott, 1983; Atkinson and Boles, 1985; Bartley, 1988; Boney, 1984; Cash, 1941; Davidson, 1972; Flynt, 1979; Fraser, Saunders and Wakelyn, 1985; Gutman, 1976; Hundley, 1979; King, 1975; McKern, 1979; Moses, 1982; Owsley, 1949; Parkhurst, 1938; Reed, 1986; Roebuck and Hickson, 1982; Scott, 1970; Stember, 1978; Strong, 1946; Tate, 1977; Taylor, 1961; Wiggins, 1973.

    5. Reed, 1986:7.

Chapter 4

"White Trash" and Female in a Southern Community

NORMA JEAN, ROTC, AND THE LIVE OAK TREE

"Now class, honey, is something you just ain't got," she
*would jive herself. "I mean, like cool, girl, you just weren't
there when they passed it out, You've done missed that boat
altogether!"*

Carol Seajay, "The Class and the Closet"[1]

Norma Jean was three years old when her mother, Eva, took a
waitress job at a Christian barbecue hut. Eva scuttled her three year
marriage to an army sergeant after suffering one too many drunken
batterings. For the next 13 years, Eva slipped in and out of male
relationships, often leaving Norma Jean and her younger brother,
Roy, to fend for themselves.

A short, pugnacious girl with an oval face and a scraggly frame,
Norma Jean unquestioningly followed adult orders. "I was very
rule oriented. What they told me to do, I did. I did what was expected of me — nothing more. I didn't have a lot of incentives to do
much more." Though she spent time talking with girls at school
most of her time was spent with males. "I guess you can say I was a
tomboy," recalls Norma Jean. "I played with a lot of little fellas.
Since I grew up in a predominantly male environment, we'd all play
football and that kind of thing."

Norma Jean does not clearly recall her childhood. A mediocre
student, she looked forward to school simply because it was a way
"to get out of the house. I associated being home with some of the

problems that I had with my family." After school she would go home to watch television and to read schoolgirl romances until her bedtime. Her most serious home problem was repeated sexual abuse by her father (who would visit home occasionally), as well as by uncles, cousins, and other men who dated Eva. "I've blocked out a lot of my past because of that," Norma Jean explains. "It's still hard for me to imagine sexual intercourse happening to me at that age." Asked why she never reported this to her mother or to another adult, she replies:

> I felt like I couldn't get out of it. I couldn't say anything. Who would believe me? I was doing it to myself. I thought I was seducing those men. I thought it was *their* right. I told my mother about the incidents with my father three nights before she died. We cried together. She told me that she had been sent to reform school for running away after being raped by her stepfather and accused by her mother of lying—to get out of reform school she ended up marrying my father.

Divorced and living in a small town, Eva and her children's economic status and social reputation were marginal. Norma Jean was not a member of the "right group" at school and a day seldom passed without her little brother getting into a fight protecting the family name. Norma Jean remembers an incident at the local Southern Baptist church in which their lowly status was publicly proclaimed. "My mother had a miscarriage; she was not married. After she got back from the hospital we went to our church. The minister gave a sermon and mentioned how having babies out of wedlock was a sin. He said, 'We have one amongst us,' and pointed my mother out."

At the beginning of Norma Jean's sixth grade, Eva remarried. Norma Jean remembers:

> We were buying this house—then Eddie stepped in. He wanted to buy a new house. So, we moved out to the country and bought this house. Then it burned down. So we got a trailer and we put it out there. But, Eddie couldn't hold his job. He took money from where he was working. From then

on it was downhill — I guess you could say we were poor white trash.

Norma Jean's relationship with her stepfather, Eddie, was not positive though he was one of the few adult males who never sexually abused her. "Before my mother remarried, there were different men living with her. Then Eddie stepped in. I didn't like him. I don't like him. I never will like him. I think I was also afraid of him because of the relationships with the male members in my family." Norma Jean also resented living in a rural community. "We were in the real sticks. I go down in the area even now. There's still a dirt road that washes out when it rains. We didn't know our neighbors like we did when we lived in town. All we had were trees." She spent most of her time alone playing make-believe.

Though her grades never rose above average, Norma Jean found school in the country more enjoyable than town. Since "people didn't have any predispositions of how they felt about me," she tried to associate with those outside the boundaries of her social class. "Inside my head people were in different classes, higher, lower, whatever. At school I wanted to be around the popular in-group. These were kids who were good looking, popular, had good grades, involved in a lot of activities. These were kids whose families seemed well-off and happy. Maybe I felt it would rub off." Seeking affection and affirmation, she hung around them without any hope of becoming part of their group.

> I didn't think of myself as a very friendly person. I saw myself as short, fat, and ugly. Nobody wanted to be around me so I felt being around them I could at least get some residual affection. Not that they gave it to me but being around them I could just feel it among themselves.

Norma Jean's presence was tolerated for a brief time. Then an incident occurred.

> There was this really small girl in our class. One day I was trying to prove to somebody that I was strong. I wrapped my arms around her waist, picked her up, and carried her around the classroom. You know, little girls just don't do that. It

chilled out a lot of people and my friendship circle sort of changed. I started hanging out with the next highest group. But, I was still alone in the crowd.

Norma Jean had no interest in boys during middle-school. Given her concern to be well-liked and, at least, on the periphery of a circle of friends, she participated in the daily banter among female classmates.

> When they talked about boys, I talked about boys. When they talked about doing interesting things with boys, I'd seem interested and give a lot of supportive conversation. But, I'd never commit to anything. I'd never outright lie unless it came right down to it. When they started talking about real feminine things like makeup and stuff, I'd leave because I'd feel uncomfortable.

The summer before Norma Jean entered ninth grade, Eddie abandoned the family. The family moved back to town to live in a rented trailer. Norma Jean attended a middle-class, predominantly white high school in Columbia. The next three years were more enjoyable in school because of a new found interest: junior ROTC. "I could take either PE or ROTC. I figured they're not going to make me run up and down like PE so I signed up. ROTC gave me direction. It gave me clear objectives. I could do them and excel at them — like drilling with weapons." With a sparkle in her eye, Norma Jean asked, "Would you like for me to demonstrate?" Standing up she spouted:

> The officer would step in front of you and ask, "What is the nomenclature of your rifle?" I would say, "Sir. The nomenclature is the M190383, a Springfield, lightweight, manually operated, magazine fed, brief shorter weapon, sir." I felt very good about ROTC. You can sort of tell.

During these ROTC activities Norma Jean had a place in school; there was meaning and direction for what she did. Outside of ROTC she was an "outcast." At lunch time, she associated with two other outcasts in the school cafeteria: Marty, "an obese fella who was a science fiction freak," and Hilda, "a real slight, quiet, pimply-faced girl who was into art."

Although she enjoyed ROTC, she was given a difficult time by other ROTC members.

> They were real mean toward people who were at all different. I was known as a "boy/girl" because people thought I wanted to be a boy. They said I did all the things that the boys did. I wanted to be an officer. God! Did I want to be an officer. I wanted to be on the drill team. They didn't like that. Girls didn't do stuff like that. Unlike the other girls in ROTC, I was more masculine and more rural. Nobody accepted me, my authority, or my ideas because I was a girl.

Norma Jean attempted to cross these boundaries seeking affection and identity through her association with the ROTC group which expressed little toleration or kindness to her. Trying to gain their favor, Norma Jean routinely made fun of her outcast friends, Marty and Hilda.

> It was a real paradox. How could I be friends with the people I'm making fun of? But, it's easy sometimes. I guess I made it easy. I wanted so much to be identified with the people in ROTC that I came up with jokes and lies about these people who were different. Then, I'd be friends with Marty and Hilda because they accepted me as I was and didn't make any real demands on me. But, I did my best to meet the demands of the ROTC people by making jokes so that they wouldn't look at me so much as a "boy/girl."

Norma Jean identified herself as a heterosexual person throughout adolescence. "If I had known a person who was gay, I just might have wanted to talk to her about it—without anybody seeing me. Not because I was gay but because I've never talked to anybody who was that way." Norma Jean did not begin to date, however, until the tenth grade when she would go out with Marty or Mickey, an "ROTC man." Her feelings of attraction for these boys were rather weak: "I was sexually attracted to them. I mean, it was expected that I would go out with fellas. Sometimes, I guess, I liked making out. I liked kissing. But, that was all I liked doing. So, I provided a real problem to some. I never had intercourse.''

Norma Jean, however, continued to be molested by her mother's adult boyfriends. "It was very sporadic," she recalls. "I didn't bother with it. When it happened, I forgot about it—I tried to anyway.'' During this time, Norma Jean became interested in her physical education teacher. "I thought she was real cute. I was sort of attracted to her but I didn't admit that to myself or to others. I'd say, 'Gosh! She's an ugly bitch.'" Within Norma Jean's world, neither homosexual behavior nor identity existed: "It wasn't an option. If I felt an attraction, I'd say, 'I just want to be friendly with her,' or, 'She's just a nice friend.' Sexuality would be taken away. I wouldn't attribute my friendship to that kind of thing.''

Eva died of complications associated with diabetes the summer before Norma Jean's senior year. With the death of her mother, Norma Jean and her brother, Roy, went to live with their Aunt Felicia in a rural South Carolina town. They attended a lower-class, predominantly black school:

> We were country rednecks. In that school, country rednecks would go to the big tree in the school lot to smoke cigarettes. Girls sucked face with the guys or the girls stuck together and the guys did their thing. I was very much alone. I didn't like being with those people.

Neither Roy nor she got along with their aunt. "He argued with my Aunt Felicia. Nobody argues with Aunt Felicia. Roy left for a foster family first.'' Two months after her mom had died, Norma Jean was living with an upper-class foster family in the same town. She remembers:

> It was a big difference. Though my aunt had money, she didn't have the attitudes. I wasn't identified with the rednecks anymore. I didn't have to go out to the tree. I got a real different image of myself. When I changed families, I could really spend time with other kinds of students. These were people of a different class. Before I wasn't friends with them but when I changed families I could really spend time with these people.

Roy's foster parents, on the other hand, were "middle class in their money but not in their attitudes." He continued to hang around the old tree occasionally harassing Norma Jean for crossing her class boundary and leaving his world behind.

As the year progressed, and with the support of her well-placed foster parents, Norma Jean concentrated on her studies and participated in a variety of school activities including the drama and math clubs. Norma Jean's move to a more academic-oriented program with better grades is partly attributable to her change in schools. As she realizes, "When a little fish in a big pond moves to a little pond the fish seems to get bigger. It really doesn't. But, being mediocre at this suburban school was excelling in this rural school." The expectations placed by her foster parents and their status within this small rural community also were important. Norma Jean remains grateful for their support:

> I just saw something in Katie as my foster mother and she must have seen something in me. She helped me a lot. At the city school, before my mother died, I was in ROTC and that was it. When I first came to this school, they didn't have an ROTC program. It broke my heart when I found out. That one year, with Katie's help, I did more than I ever did at the other school.

With her foster family's support, Norma Jean crossed over another boundary. Katie and her husband "assumed that I would go to college. It was sort of a dream when I was in high school although before my mother died it wasn't even possible." Norma Jean's dream became a reality the next year.

"When I came to college," Norma Jean recollects, "I was still doing things that were expected of me. I dated a fella and became very involved with him. I probably would have married this fella had he not been killed. I was very emotionally attached to David before he died. We were very sexually active except for penetration." Five days before his birthday, David was killed by a drunk driver as he was bicycling.

Shortly after this tragedy, Norma Jean quit college, moved in with her grandparents, and began work at a convenience store. "I was sort of wishy-washy then. It was like, 'Now I am an adult. I've got to act like an adult but I don't know what to do.' So I tried to talk to people at work. I found out about this one woman, Charmaine." Norma Jean began to think about homosexuality. While working at the store, she became more conscious of her sexual feelings toward women. She recalls:

> Some women runners kept coming by the store where I was. After they finished practicing, all of these gorgeous bodies would just pile into the store to get something to drink. I became very sexually excited about that. I made sure that I worked the nights they practiced.

Norma Jean also began thinking about Charmaine in a sexual way.

> I had this real strong image of her being gay. I couldn't ask her. You don't ask people outright, "Are you gay?" So, I had to think of a story: One of my best friends told me that her roommate used to think that she was gay. Her roommate would leave the room and never change clothes in front of her. I asked, "Well, Charmaine how should I act? My best friend just told me that her roommate used to think she was gay. Damn! I think she is gay. How am I suppose to act?" Charmaine said to me, "What's different?" I said, "Well, she is gay now." She asked me, "What's changed about her?" I just kept saying, "She's gay." Charmaine said, "Well, nothing has really changed. You just know one more thing about her." So, I spent a lot of time with Charmaine.

As their relationship grew closer, Charmaine introduced Norma Jean to her roommate, Eloise. One evening she accompanied the two to a gay bar. "I hyper-ventilated the whole time I was there," recollects Norma Jean. For the next two months, she continued to accompany the two though "I had a hard time adjusting to thinking about being gay." Finally, she ventured out alone:

I wanted to find out what sex was like. One night I got drunk and propositioned three women. I went to a motel with the third one. I had my first experience of sex. I was real turned on. It was like, "This is it!" I felt really good about it. With women I felt I could express myself better and more freely.

Three days later Norma Jean moved in with the third woman and her lover moved out. Two months later they had broken up. Within that year, Norma Jean had moved into six different places and had four lovers. Throughout this time, Norma Jean continued to visit with Charmaine and her roommate, Eloise. Norma Jean and Eloise grew closer as they explored their different social histories which so strangely intersected. Eloise, a fiery red-head with a quick wit, is a refined product of generations of social grooming. Eloise was everything Norma Jean was not: feminine in appearance, schooled in private all-girls academies, born to a family whose ancestors were among the founders of Charleston. Despite or perhaps because of their differences, they became lovers, a relationship that has blossomed for more than a year. Norma Jean reflects on their 16 months together:

Eloise is a good friend. We talk about a lot of different things. We usually do all the things we can together except during school hours. We go to the bar five or six times a month. We regularly attend the gay meetings on campus as well as a women's group which is not homosexual in its orientation.

Eloise is completing her graduate degree in journalism while Norma Jean plans to become a social worker after finishing college, because, as she puts it, "I have a real identification with lower socioeconomic people."

COMMENTARY

Born into a traditional Southern community and a family of lowly status, the boundaries of Norma Jean's world were rather narrow. As a female, she felt the consequences of her subordinate role in a male-dominated culture. From her continued sexual abuse by men, she adopted a low self-image by assuming the guilt associated with such physical transgressions. Lacking conventional feminine traits and interests, she cast her lot with other outsiders like Marty and Hilda while struggling for leadership roles in the junior ROTC. As a poor white, she felt the limited options within a community in which caste and class have been synonymous for generations. During high school there was no visible alternative except for Norma Jean to hang out around the live oak tree, "suck face" with the boys, or talk with the girls. Even after her adoption by a family with the "right money and attitudes," her brother Roy pressured her to stay with "our sort of people." Not surprisingly, Norma Jean refused, noting, "I finally got to be part of the crowd I was trying to fight to be with in all those other schools." This change in her social status also opened up a variety of educational options such as pursuing drama and applying for college. In short, by the time Norma Jean graduated from high school there were more options on her social menu.

Boundaries Uniting Women

Despite these newly perceived options, marriage and heterosexuality were still Norma Jean's unquestioned destiny. Her lack of sexual enjoyment with men was eclipsed by the belief that sex was more biological than emotional and that the female role was more passive than active. Lacking the language of feminism and in the absence of same-sex experiences, being a lesbian never entered into the realm of possibilities — until she dropped out of college following her torrid and tragic affair with David. Childhood socialization notably affected how Norma Jean made meaning of her gender and sexuality. As Anna Durrell underscores:

> In cultures where women are viewed as socially passive, economically dependent, and sexually only "receptive" rather than appetitive, a young woman who wishes to be physically or economically active and to choose or refuse her own sexual partners is per se "deviant." For many women, this issue totally overrides any simple choice about being celibate or lesbian. Women's sexuality is so generally suppressed that girls often feel no attraction they could classify as sexual.[2]

This passive view of women pervaded Norma Jean's poor, white Southern culture. Only by crossing those cultural boundaries was Norma Jean able to choose beyond the limited social menu of her class and gender. Since leaving Aunt Felicia's home, the distance between Norma Jean and Roy, her brother, has grown. Roy is married and an active member in a fundamentalist Baptist church. Norma Jean remembers attending his wedding, "I had to refrain from laughing because of the vows. The minister turned to Roy's bride and said, 'You will look into his face as you would look into the face of God.'" While Roy maintains a traditional family and works at a local auto parts dealership, Norma Jean's horizons have expanded as she has attended college, attracted a female lover, and become active in women's groups. From the rural, poor, male-dominated community of her childhood, Norma Jean has crossed into an urban, middle-class, female-centered community during adulthood. In the course of that journey, she has acquired a sense of self-worth and a new identity. Looking back upon her past world, Norma Jean comments:

> Back in high school I was floundering for some kind of identification. I kept telling myself that I was an individual but I was so strange from everybody else. I didn't have any label or something to give myself to say, "This is the way I feel."

Norma Jean's association with Charmaine and Eloise helped to expand her menu of social options. At 21, she engaged in her first homosexual experience and a year later identified herself as a lesbian. While the role of women's groups and feminist thought will be discussed in Chapter 12, the importance that the lesbian community has played in the development of Norma Jean's identity and the enhancement of her self-worth is noteworthy. Through the encouragement of Eloise, she joined an informal women's discussion group with a predominantly lesbian membership and routinely contributed to the writing and production of a lesbian community newspaper. Both of these experiences provided her with much needed support and self-confidence.

Norma Jean's lesbian community was not geographical (such as the "gay ghetto" inhabited by homosexual males in larger cities) but social and psychological.[3] The community provided Norma Jean and other white middle- and upper-middle class women the opportunity to form extended kinship-type networks within which personal pasts could be shared and shared futures could be projected. Such interaction fostered a set of commonly held values and beliefs ranging from the primacy of women and female-female relationships to the integral connection between sexism and heterosexism and the necessity to cross gender, sexual, and racial boundaries in confronting the sources of oppression. Had Norma Jean not crossed the boundary of her social class through the providence of her foster family, she certainly would not have entered college and probably not have migrated to the city with its woman's subculture. Her relationship with Eloise, in particular, expanded those class-based horizons and eased her access into the women's network from which she has benefitted as well as contributed.

Boundaries Dividing Women

Southern author Rosemary Daniel writes, "The female attitudes so often caricatured are real: the manipulative magnolia and the hysterical matron *do* exist."[4] The social metaphor of "white trash," like those of the "Southern belle," the "good ol' boy" and others, conveys the distinctive historical and psychological boundaries which those of Norma Jean's class and gender often confront. As an individual, though, Norma Jean's biography enriches our understanding of the difficulty of growing up as a poor white girl in the rural South while challenging the social stereotypes that such a metaphor sometimes suggests, and which writer Sharon McKern describes eloquently:

> In earlier years, nearly all the classic Southerners were: Margaret Mitchell's belles and gentlemen soldiers, William Faulkner's half-wits and nymphomaniacs, Erskine Caldwell's low-rent po' white trash; Richard Wright's maimed blacks. Toss in one faithful mammy, a rawboned moonshiner or two, a quick black cook gifted with rare-but-simple wisdom, and you've got it: the celebrated Old South was one long Tobacco Road save for the carefree aristocrats gambling on Tara's lush lawns.[5]

Behind the Hollywood messages of *The Birth of a Nation*, the characters in *Song of the South*, and the props in *Deliverance* are the racial, sexual, and social class boundaries which define the New South. These form the boundaries of the sexual rebels' Southern psychic landscape. The childhood boundaries experienced by Norma Jean by virtue of her family's lowly social and economic status contrast sharply with those of her lover Eloise's participation in elite Southern rituals such as the debutante society, illustrating the gap that still exists between women of the same color in the South.[6]

These rituals are a key to another Southern social metaphor: the Southern Belle. Rooted in tradition, wealth, and family name, the debutante society underscores the fact that bloodlines are considered more important than money. Or, as a former Southern debutante remarked, "I am my father's daughter."[7] Female identity is defined in terms of male needs; women are separated from one another in their competition for men in the bed of power. In the words of Southern journalist Shirley Abbott:

> What the belle is after is not love but power — using the prettiest possible weapons, she is fighting a guerrilla war. . . . Being a belle has its risks, the worst of which is that she may be permanently seduced by her own propaganda. She may end up believing that she really is helpless and dumb and dependent, in which case she will cease to be a belle and become a victim.[8]

New Orleans, Charleston, and Raleigh are Southern cities in which the debutante tradition continues unabated. The St. Cecilia Ball,[9] held in Charleston on the third Thursday of January, the Mardi Gras Balls, most notably the Rex and Comus Balls, and the North Carolina Debutante Ball, held the first weekend after Labor Day, are the oldest and most exclusive. These Balls formally present the belle to society. The St. Cecilia Society is so secretive that no membership list exists and members know of each other only through attendance at society functions. The Society is so exclusive that membership is reserved for the oldest male son of long-standing Charleston families; divorce or other social disgrace results in expulsion.

While the likelihood of becoming a debutante is greatly influenced by family wealth and bloodlines,[10] a young woman does not wait to become a debutante at the age of 18. She is carefully molded for her role through years of social sculpturing. Her training begins with the work of her mother and governess inculcating common courtesies and lady-like behavior (the art of the curtsey, quiet demeanor, implacable table manners). It continues with her enrollment at a private school, weekly attendance at a dance studio (waltz, fox-trot, and rumba are essential), and mastery of horseback riding and tennis. With adolescence begins the more formal entry into "a social network that begins in high school and seems to continue through life."[11]

The "girls' committee," composed of older ladies who devote their lives to performing charity work and reliving debutante memories, invites the most eligible young women to "come out" each year. To receive these coveted invitations, the debutante's family must have money and social standing. The debutante, herself, is presumed to be a virgin.[12] As one insider noted, "If it's well known that she's not a virgin, unless she has extreme social connections and money to back it up, she may not be asked to come out. . . . She [must be] in good standing and conform to the ideal of womanhood that the debutante club is trying to project: chaste, beautiful, intelligent, having social graces."

The highlight of the season, of course, is the Debutante Ball at which the young woman is formally presented to society. "Presenting an eighteen year old daughter to society as a candidate for marriage," writes ex-Deb Cornelia Guest, "is an elaborate fiction."[13] The debut of these Daughters of the Confederacy (and its middle-class variation, the American beauty pageant) symbolizes the fantasized role of women: an *object* of beauty, chastity, and perfection placed above the turmoil of everyday life.

Following her debut, the post-deb will complete college and then marry. As she prepares for her wedding, the Southern debutante may enter the tradition of the past by reading the magazine of the future, *Southern Bride*. Publisher Alex Gant says, "Southern women have been celebrating tradition all along." This magazine "caters to the Plantation Belle. Or the woman who wants to feel like one.''[14] Underscoring its emphasis on bridal fashions, outdoor southern weddings, and Virgin Island honeymoons, Gant concludes, "You won't find articles on homeless people or starvation in India. . . . [F]antasy is better than reality.''[15]

Distanced by social background and experiences, the lives of Norma Jean and Eloise were never meant to cross. The rented trailer and the live oak tree were a world apart from the fox-trots and pre-deb dances. However, both young women were sexual outsiders within their own communities. Their lack of "fit" into their social slot led them to question the community values and family expectations of patriarchy and heterosexism. Through events of fate, they now inhabit a common sphere, the women's community — a situation which, as Rosemary Daniel notes, is far from unique: "In the South, lesbianism is usually visceral rather than ideological; high school dropouts fall in love with debutantes and college graduates; gay bars and parties are for cruising rather than intellectualizing.''[16]

Boundaries Within Families

Within Norma Jean's childhood town, the business of one person was the business of all. Another participant in this study, 'Lizabeth, also grew up as a poor white girl in a "lovin' town where everybody protects everybody else — unless you fall outside the norm. They don't deal with things that aren't normal for them." Homosexuality, as 'Lizabeth notes, is such a thing:

> One [gay] man mysteriously died in an "accident" involving a grain elevator. Another gay couple owned land and their own house on the north corner of the county. It got to the point that they would be getting stares when they walked into stores. There were some people who wouldn't even allow them to come in their stores. They finally got run off. In a small community, people here have the ability to make life miserable for you. All you have to do is say something to one person and it'll be over the entire county in 10 minutes.

Yet, those who cross the boundaries of sexual propriety within the family are seldom subject to such community prying. These "ghost relationships" between father and daughter, brother and sister, aunt and niece are seldom even acknowledged within the family.[17] As in the Sartoris, Compson and Sutpen families in Faulkner's novels, incest is the seamy, hidden underside of many households. In this study, five of the 12 women reported incestuous relationships with a family member. 'Lizbeth, for example, was sexually abused at an early age. From that point on, "I came to a place where if I have sex when I get married, that would be fine. If I don't ever have it again, that would be fine too." At 19, 'Lizbeth has just disclosed her relationship with another woman to her mother:

> She's sending me to a psychiatrist under the guise that I need to learn to deal with what happened to me when I was seven — which is true. I told her I thought that would be a good idea because it might help me, to some extent, open up to people. But, her ulterior motive is "once you learn to deal with this magically you're going to be straight again." I just can't convince her that I was having these feelings a year before I was raped.

Her mother's belief that lesbians are women who have had a bad heterosexual experience may appear reasonable to a casual reader of Norma Jean's biographical portrait.[18] However, sexual abuse of children is common in the United States. The likelihood of a female being sexually abused before she reaches her eighteenth birthday is one in four, according to a recent study.[19] Other studies have reported rates of child abuse ranging from 15 to 38 percent.[20] Lesbians appear to be on the high end of this range — a figure that is matched in this study.[21] Although lesbians are more likely to have a childhood history of sexual abuse than their heterosexual counterparts, with the exception of Norma Jean, the other abused women in this study reported same-sex feelings or erotic homosexual urges prior to such abuse. Moreover, incestuous childhood relationships do not account for the majority of women who identify themselves as lesbian. As 'Lizbeth candidly remarked. "I can't say that the incestuous relationships haven't hindered my opinion of men, but I don't hate them. Men are alright if they keep their space away from me. I simply don't want to have a sexual relationship with men. That's just not in my makeup."

Based upon her clinical work with approximately 50 women,

most of whom are lesbians, psychoanalyst Eileen Starzecpyzel borrows the Greek myth of Demeter whose daughter, Persephone, is abducted and raped by her uncle, Hades. Exploring the post-incest consequences and proposed treatment for the incest survivor, she writes:

> Like Persephone, we experience ourselves as motherless, as irrevocably marked by the incest trauma, as curiously powerful and mysterious, older and wiser than our contemporaries, but also as women who feel different and emotionally alone because of the double wounds of maternal loss and paternal seduction. We have never felt young because of the early blows we suffered, and only through healing can we reclaim our right to the playfulness we never enjoyed. The memory of daddy, abuser and lover, is the Hades to which we must compulsively return in memory and unreasonable guilt until we claim our own power to let go and move on to the powerful image of the Persephone returned.[22]

According to Starzecpyzel, who is a member of the Boston Lesbian Psychologies Collective, the result is a severance of the mother-daughter bond and an interruption of the child's psychosexual development. Consequently, "the primary issue for any incest survivor is lack of trust. Her mental and physical boundaries were violated, not just from the sexual assault(s), but also from earlier childhood experiences that taught her that the world was not safe."[23] The incest experience, then, complicates the process of developing a healthy and trusting same-sex relationship within a heterosexual culture in which such relationships are already problematic.

In a scant 24 years, Norma Jean has traversed several boundaries which defined her status within a small Southern community. Through the help of Katie, Charmaine, and Eloise, Norma Jean is no longer confined by the values of her working poor background. Her emotional and erotic feelings toward women have also broken through the shell of a heart hardened by male abuse and female neglect. Norma Jean's biography authenticates the insights of lesbian-feminist Adrienne Rich: "A mother's victimization does not merely humiliate her, it mutilates the daughter who watches her for clues as to what it means to be a woman.''[24] Not surprisingly, the pain endured by Norma Jean from the repeated crossing of sexual boundaries has been neither easy for her to express nor to transcend. Through her loving relationship with Eloise and the resources of the women's community, the victimization she feels may disappear. But if, like Persephone, she is to return as a "goddess" — more enlightened, freer — to revive the once fallow fields of her inner self, then she must continue to cross boundaries. Only thus will her journey of the spirit continue.

REFERENCE NOTES

1. Seajay, 1980:120.

2. Durrell, 1984:4-5.

3. Barnhart, 1975; Ponse, 1978; Ponse, 1980; Wolf, 1979. For reviews of these and other studies on lesbian communities, see: Krieger, 1982; Lockard, 1986.

4. Daniel, 1980:18.

5. McKern, 1979:10.

6. Like religious fundamentalists, debutantes are found throughout the United States. The International Debutante Ball held at New York's Waldorf, the Passavant Cotillion held at the Conrad Hilton Hotel in Chicago, St. Louis' Veiled Prophet Ball, and the Las Madrinas Ball where debutantes are presented at the Beverly Hilton Hotel in Los Angeles are, perhaps, the most sought after affairs. These certainly reflect the importance of this ritual among American aristocracy. Smaller and less prestigious debutante clubs exist in many other communities. In Columbia, for example, there is the Cotillion Club formed in 1890, which might be viewed as an AA farm club to the 18th century St. Cecilia Society. For a brief discussion of the Cotillion Club, see Henning, 1936.

7. This section is based primarily upon interviews with former debutantes, escorts, and officers of debutante societies. I have also found the debutante guidebook authored by Cornelia Guest (1986), as well as various handbooks published by the Terpsichorean Club to be most helpful.

8. Abbott, 1983:106-107.

9. Although this is frequently referred to as a ball, strictly speaking, it is the presentation of the season's debutantes escorted by cadets from the Citadel.

10. These societies are segregated by race/ethnicity as well as by social class. Parallel societies, such as the Young Men of Illinois in New Orleans, or the Blue Revue Gala in Columbia, have been organized by African-Americans.

11. Ashley, 1978:2c.

12. Prior to the 1960s, debutantes were expected not to date before their coming out.

13. Guest, 1986:85.

14. Snead, 1988:4e.

15. Snead, 1988:4e.

16. Daniel, 1980:227.

17. Lilian Smith (1949) used this phrase in her discussion of miscegenation in the South — another great taboo in Southern society.

18. This, of course, is just one of several myths associated with the development of lesbian identities. For a review of other myths and the research related to them, see: Potter and Darty, 1981; Sang, 1978.

19. Seattle Institute for Child Advocacy, 1985.

20. Finkelhor, 1986; Finkelhor and Hotaling, 1984; Wyatt, 1985.

21. Gundlach, 1977; Meiselman, 1978; Simari and Baskin, 1982. Further, from 80 to 90 percent of these abuses are perpetrated by a person known and trusted by the child. In nearly one-half of these cases, the molester is the child's father or stepfather (Pierce and Pierce, 1987; Seattle Institute for Child Advocacy, 1985; Sgroi, 1982) and the act is initiated during prepubescence (Burgess and Holmstrom, 1979). For recent reviews of research into incest as child abuse, see: de Young, 1985; Vander Mey and Neff, 1986; for perspectives of incest victims, see: Thorton, 1983; Hill, 1985. Again, these findings parallel those of this study. All but one of the participants (Obie) who experienced sexual abuse reported the source to be family members or trusted adults.

22. Starzecpyzel, 1987:266.

23. Starzecpyzel, 1987:275.

24. Daniel, 1980:13.

Chapter 5

A Gentle-man
in a Southern Community

ROYCE AND THE ROCKVIEW COUNTRY CLUB

Homosexuals who stay in Southern small towns often have money, and Southerners of any class have enough ancien régime in their bones to permit the aristocracy forms of decadence that they would not permit to lesser folk.

Florence King, *Southern Ladies and Gentlemen*[1]

Royce comes from the back country of the Piedmont Carolinas dotted by small towns whose names evoke the isolation and ruggedness of the region: Tigerville, Caesars Head, Rocky Bottom, Nine Times, Woodville, Six Mile. The youngest of four children born to an upper-middle class family, the horizons of Royce's childhood were wider than those of Norma Jean's. "Our house was on the corner. A block away was my grandmother's house. There were no houses between us. I had aunts a block away in each direction." Royce's father, Pete, owns several businesses and served as the town's police chief for several years. Royce's mother is very artistic and works as a designer for a locally-owned company. She also was secretary of the Southern Baptist church for 25 years. Royce benefitted from the position of his family in town affairs and by being the youngest in a family with teenage sisters.

I was spoiled rotten. I had two older sisters. When I was born I was like a doll to them. They used to fight over who was going to feed me and change my diapers. My father and I also had a good relationship when I was growing up. I remember I had the measles and was put to bed. I was going crazy. I wanted chocolate ice cream. I made one of my sisters call my father at work. He left work, went to get chocolate ice cream, and brought it home to me.

Seventy-seven students graduated in Royce's senior class. Two-thirds of them had been with him since the first grade. "We all grew up together," Royce reminisces. "A new kid coming in got shunned." Learning his ABCs from his mother and sisters, he was eager to learn to read as he began the first grade. Royce's favorite childhood hobbies would soon be reading mystery books and collecting coins. He also had a flair for the theatric:

My mother has pictures of me when I was seven or eight doing "little plays" for her that I had made up in my own little mind. I always lived in a fantasy world. I had a make believe friend, Beau. I talked to him constantly. He did whatever I wanted him to do. If I wanted to play parade, he wanted to play parade, too. If I wanted to ride bikes, he wanted to ride.

Royce was a likeable classmate and talented student who displayed some less than manly traits during childhood. Although he was anxious to learn how to read, going to school was another matter altogether. "I was scared to death. I cried everyday until the end of the second grade. I guess you could say I was a mamma's boy." His second grade teacher served as his "second mother," and Royce finally made the emotional transition from home to school.

During recess at elementary school, Royce would often be found playing on the huge sliding board or jumping rope with four or five friends—boys and girls who would be his classmates through high school. Royce remembers a teacher fussing at him as he jumped rope during recess: "Don't do that. Go down there and play football with the boys." He and the other boy ignored the directive and continued to play with their girl classmates:

I understood what she was saying. I was starting to hear the term "sissy" a lot. I was pegged with that label. I was still likable. I was not the outcast. I was part of the group. It didn't really bother me. If they threw a rock at me or picked up a stick, I probably would have told someone. But it didn't bother me. I was probably screaming just as mean things back to them.

Royce occasionally got into fights on the playground and could be a "pest" in the classroom. "We would get the outcast — a person that would do anything to be liked or to be a part of the group — to do mean things to another little gang. 'You can be part of my group if you'll go over there and trip Lisa or throw mud at Bobby.'" During third grade he recalls forcing Rebecca, the only Jewish girl in class, to kiss him. Later "we were boyfriend and girlfriend. Our desks were always side by side. If somebody tried to move in on my girl, it was like fights. We became arch rivals in high school."

During third grade, integration occurred in the town. Two African-American students entered Royce's classroom. Racial strife, though, touched Royce more profoundly than it did his other white classmates. Right before Thanksgiving his father, as chief of police, shot a black man to death:

> Civil rights had just sort of come to the forefront. We were getting threats — a lot of which were directed at me. I didn't understand it at the time. I was being left at my aunt's house or my grandmother's house. The worst part of it was the huge trial. There was not a courtroom big enough, so they did it on the high school stage.

Though his father was found innocent of all charges, he resigned his position. The event alienated him from the rest of the family. He started to drink heavily. Royce's childhood memories include "incidents where he was screaming at my mother and I was screaming for everybody to shut up. He never went to my younger sister's wedding because of the trouble in the family. I haven't gotten along with him to this day." Though Royce generally remembers a happy childhood, this incident placed great strain on his family. Royce recalls that "He couldn't handle a lot of things. I cannot remember my father going to any school function after that happened until I graduated from high school."

By the time Royce was ready to enter the sixth grade the school had become over-crowded. His class was moved into what had been the town's black school. Isolated from the other elementary school children, Royce and his classmates were bused for lunch everyday. He also began noticing things: a copy of *Playboy*, a deck of his father's playing cards with nude women, his best friend's physique.

It was like hero worship with this guy that I had been friends with all along. I don't know why it suddenly clicked to think that way. I would do anything to be Laddie's friend. If he was playing softball at recess, I'd play softball. Me and my friend used to sneak my father's deck of playing cards out of his cabinet and look at it or steal a copy of *Playboy*. I was doing it by myself, too.

In the summer before his seventh grade, Royce and Laddie first explored sexuality:

We were constantly together and spending the night at each other's house or camping out. We put a tent up in the back yard playing strip poker to see each other's bodies. That progressed into masturbating in front of each other. Then, I instigated oral sex. Laddie was purely passive. He let me on two occasions because I was curious about it. I wanted more to happen.

Royce, Laddie and their fellow classmates left the solitude of their sixth grade classroom to attend high school. At first, attending a school that ranged from grades 7 through 12 was overwhelming. "It was frightening," Royce recalls. "It was almost like starting over. You're going from being the top to the bottom." Royce quickly adjusted to this new world through the help of several older students and his family's status in the small community:

Luckily, I was adopted by three high school girls as their little brother. A lot of it was family connections and the family name. They took me under their wing. In seventh grade, I would pass them in the hall and they made it a point to speak to me in front of my friends. If you've got a tenth, eleventh, or twelfth grader speaking to you that makes you a little better than anybody else. Soon being a seventh grader wasn't frightening; it was a challenge.

Royce associated with the same group of friends he had had since first grade. "The top students," Royce remembers, "were always together and placed in the same classes." Continuing to do well academically, he participated in extra-curricular activities. His effeminate behavior also disappeared. He was no longer pegged with the label "sissy" by his classmates. He began "talking dirty," telling "fag" jokes, and cussing:

> That's the age when you first learn to cuss out loud. The worse words you could find the better. Because of my older brother and a neighbor, I had access to *Playboy* and *Penthouse*. I thought it was great to be able to read one of those jokes and then go to school and repeat it to my friends. Talking dirty was the big thing.

Royce also started to drink alcohol:

> By the eighth grade, those of us who were part of the "right families" in town—those who controlled the city, had the money and the businesses, and had been there forever—were slowly included in group things like the Country Club. We'd go out after the football games or go out for pizza and would have a drink or liquor in the car. It took me years to like beer. I would drink half a beer and think I was going to die because it was so terrible.

Though Royce continued to "feel different, I didn't think of myself as gay or queer," his mind and interests began to wander beyond the town's boundaries: theater, performing arts, art decoration; Charleston, Atlanta, New York. "I desperately wanted out of town," Royce confesses. While his friends were reading *Hot Rod* and *Guns*, Royce's interest turned to *GQ* and *The New Yorker*. "I started discovering fashion," he recollects:

> I was very big on new styles. Mom had no qualms about spending money on clothes for me. I can remember the other guys wearing blue jeans and plaid shirts. They knew I was different. I was the first guy to wear a jump suit to school. The first guy to wear his jeans tucked into his boots. The first person to carry a back pack.

Though his classmates no longer labelled him "sissy," they knew Royce was different. As he entered adolescence, his new found sexual feelings had emerged. From the summer of his sixth grade he had begun experimenting with sex. Throughout seventh grade, he and Laddie had enjoyed boyhood exploits in the silence of the night. As they neared the completion of seventh grade, however, their sexual relationship ended. "Laddie started getting uncomfortable with it. He started clicking with other friends. I think I alienated him a little." During the next four years, Royce was not involved in another relationship. He often thought about his feelings for other guys; there was no one, though, with whom to share these feelings.

As a tall and lanky freshman, Royce was a natural on the hardwood floor. He made the junior varsity basketball team. He also was elected mascot for the varsity team. "I enjoyed both," he remembers. "I would play JV basketball, take a shower, put on my mascot costume, and cheer at the varsity basketball game." Since the "Red Devils" had never had a male mascot for their team, Royce's mother made a boy's costume with "red pants and suspenders with black sequins and white turtle neck with sequins spelling out the team letters." Though Royce occasionally got "little snide remarks" from his teammates, "I'd learned just to let them go over my head. Nothing phased me." As a high school student, Royce continued to hang with the town's right families in and out of school.

The majority of our jocks at our school were also the brains and sort of the preppies. They were also the ones promoting alcohol and drug use. These were the rich kids. They had access to liquor and drugs. A couple of them were from divorced parents so they threw wild parties at their houses. I used alcohol and drugs to be part of the crowd. I would drink a lot of wine because I could handle the taste of that. Liquor I hated. Everybody was smoking pot. I tried it but I'm allergic to smoke. I got very addicted to uppers. I don't know why I did it. It just made me feel good. It gave me as much energy as I wanted to have.

Royce expended this energy on school activities ranging from sports and student government to the yearbook and school theater. He was well-liked and did well academically. Never dating girls, he continued to have unemotional sexual encounters with other boys. Unlike Malcolm, he had no remorse for his sexual behavior. Like Vince, he enjoyed sex and took it at its face value. Then, at 16, Royce fell in love with Jason—a handsome boy with light brown hair and a captivating smile, and the son of the president of the Rockview Country Club.

I was editor of the yearbook. He was the photographer and a year younger than me. My parents owned a mobile home park and had several trailers that they rented. I was living in one. I had become the school porno king. I had every magazine and stag film at my disposal. At the yearbook meeting, Jason and I were talking and I said something about him coming over. We had been friends, but never close friends. He came over and we started looking at magazines. At some point, he said something about going to bed and fucking. I remember my reply was that there wasn't enough time. He said, "There's time enough to suck some cock." That was the first time I really heard somebody just come out and say it. I knew I wanted to but I'd never known how to approach it. I said, "Let's go." Next thing, we're in bed. The next morning, I'm in love.

That next morning Royce felt on top of the world. Within a short time, Royce started making more demands on the relationship. Jason was stunned. For Jason, the relationship was simply sexual; for Royce, it was essentially emotional. "To him I think it was, 'I haven't gotten a girl yet, so you're the next best thing.' You know, 'This is our outlet.' It was like every two days. The more that it happened, the more emotionally involved I got."

Unknown to one another, each had disclosed their secret to another close friend. "At times, there would be four people sitting in the yearbook staff room that knew what was going on. They would know if there was a fight going on or something." Two of the staff at the high school were also aware of the sexual liaison existing between Royce and Jason. The boundary between the public and private worlds worked to Royce's advantage.

> The guidance counselor knew I was sleeping with Jason because we were constantly signing each other out of school. We'd go to my trailer and fool around in the middle of the day. She must have followed us one day. But, she was very nonchalant, saying "I know that when you've been signing out to 'go take photographs for the yearbook' you've been going to your trailer. I think you should be more discreet." Another time, the assistant principal took some of us to Myrtle Beach. Everybody was assigned four to a room except for Jason and I. We had a room to ourselves. Now, both of them knew without knowing. They weren't being hypocritical. Sex is just not a topic that's open for discussion in the South. You're brought up not to discuss it.

Royce's schoolwork was unaffected by his newly acquired homosexual identity and his emerging relationship with Jason. "If anything," Royce remarked, "I think I tried harder to impress him." Royce, however, felt alone. "I thought I was the only one having a relationship in school. I actually, at times, thought I was the only gay person in school. It wasn't until years later that people were coming up to me at the bar saying, 'I was in high school with you.' For Royce, *being gay*, unlike most of the participants in this study, was not a problem. This was not true, however, for Jason:

He was in a situation with a guy that was in his class. The guy told him that he knew about what Jason and I were doing. He wanted to go to bed with Jason. Jason was appalled that somebody knew. It really bothered him. He was really scared to be labelled gay. I reckoned myself to what I was. I just wanted to kill the guy.

Emotionally, though, *being involved* in a gay relationship was a problem for Royce.

By my senior year I was having many emotional problems dealing with Jason. He was truly my first love — my first broken heart. I was being rejected on the one hand but was also being physically attracted and encouraged by him on the other. It hurt having him come over and having a physical thing and telling him, "I love you," and then him leaving to go out with a girl or to make it with other guys. I got to the point of figuring ways to commit suicide. I thought it would end that hurt that was going on inside and hurt him, too. There was no adult that I would even dare approach to talk to about it. I kept it all bottled up inside.

Asked why he did not speak with the counselor who was aware of his sexual relationship with Jason, Royce said:

In my school, guidance counselors were there to offer career advice, hand out college catalogues, and do tests. I never considered going in and saying, "Look, I'm sleeping with Jason. What should I be doing about it? Why is it driving me crazy?" That was never an option. Sex is not something that one discusses in public. I'm not even sure if I had said something that she would have known what to say or do about it.

In Royce's town, people chose to ignore what they did not care to see — particularly among the well-to-do families:

In my town, the Rockview Country Club group was your typical Southern, old family group. It has always been accepted that their sons and their grandsons would all be members of the Country Club. It was like when the quarterback of the football team (who I later found out was gay and was having an affair throughout high school) was doing drugs, they looked the other way because of his family and what he achieved at school. I guess, if I had been a very poor student and openly gay, I might have gotten more flack. But, I was a student body leader. I was president of several clubs. People looked up to me and listened to my ideas because of my being part of that right family group and being a good student. It's like if a student happened to ride the bus to school and didn't dress very nicely they could have been the most intelligent person in the world, but they would have been put in a lower standing academically. One guy, who later dropped out of school, was part of the upper class families and had the right family name. He was stupid. He was burnt out on drugs all the time. But, he was still allowed to pass along.

I was taught very Southern manners: "Yes, Ma'am." "No, Ma'am." Always offer a guest a seat and refreshments when they come to your house. In the South, you keep your nose out of other people's business. It's not polite to ask how much a person makes. It's not polite to ask who they're sleeping with or ask who other people are sleeping with. Sex is not a topic that's open to discussion in the South. There are certain things you don't discuss. If you have an uncle that's been put away for being mentally insane or incompetent, that's just not discussed. "Uncle has gone away to recuperate." Same with a drinking or drug problem. There's great family pride and you don't air your dirty linen in public. That's how you're brought up. You have family secrets, and that's what they remain.

Even within the family, there are secrets shared by all but acknowledged by none. Few parents or their children choose to cross the boundary between the public and private worlds on such an intimate matter as sex. Royce's sexuality is one such example. Though Royce has yet to "come out" to his parents, he suspects that both know.

She's seen me in bed with guys. Not having sex, of course. But one time I thought I had locked the door and me and this other guy were in bed, both of us naked, under the covers, hugging. She walked in and it was like, "If you can tear yourselves apart from each other, breakfast is ready." At the time, I sort of wrote it off as her thinking we were cold and were trying to stay warm. Lately, though she's been making statements of support and concern. Like a guy in our town came home to die with AIDS and his parents didn't even know about him. She's mentioned that to me a couple of times. I think that is her way of saying to be safe and careful. Same with my father. I know he suspects and feels uncomfortable about the issue. Like when I was in my first two years of college I was a theater major. He told everyone I was majoring in math.

Though Royce enjoyed membership in the town's elite social circle of friends and families, and was relatively free to do as he pleased, he was not satisfied. By tenth grade, he knew he had to leave the town if he ever wanted to pursue a career of interest to him.

Knowing what I wanted and what I wanted to be, I had to get out. There were those that had no further aspirations but to follow in their father or mother's footsteps. It did not bother them to stay. But me and Rebecca [the Jewish classmate with whom he enjoyed a childhood courtship] knew we had to get out. Everybody was going to Clemson. She wanted to go to Yale to be a doctor. I was looking for a good theater school.

Royce never found that "good theater school," and chose instead to attend a small, private college in the Piedmont area. Later, he decided to go into retailing where he could apply his skill and interests in fashion and set design in the everyday world of commerce. After completing college, he worked his way up to a managership of a large department store in a large city in the Piedmont. Lacking the social and political connections which he enjoyed in his home town, Royce was fired last summer. His employer refused to give him specifics simply noting that "my work did not reflect their store image. I got very frustrated because I knew my work was good." Pausing, Royce says, "I'm tired of playing politics. I want to have my own business doing free lance-home decorating, consulting, and weddings." Royce is planning to return home and open his business.

COMMENTARY

As an academically gifted and athletically talented white male from an affluent family, Royce had a relatively tranquil experience growing up gay in the South. Compared to Norma Jean, the zone of toleration was broad and expansive for him. Those who noticed Royce's clothes chalked it up to Southern dandyism. Those who suspected a liaison between him and Jason "knew without knowing." Royce's path through school was eased considerably by his membership in the town's "right families." Harassment due to his sissy-like behaviors in elementary school was minimal, his entry into high school was facilitated by placement in classes with students of similar social and economic backgrounds, and his treatment by school authorities was influenced by his family's standing in the community and his position as a student body leader. Like Vince, Royce was blessed with an outgoing personality and popularity which allowed him to serve as the team's first male mascot and wear fashionable clothing or jewelry with little intimidation. This "sissy" side of Royce, however, was counterbalanced by the conscious telling of "fag" jokes and by his role as the school's "porno king." Just as Vince used religion to escape from wearing his scarlet letter, so Royce used his social standing as shelter from the more negative consequences that normally befall boys brandishing outlandish clothes and effeminate behaviors.

Boundaries Within Classes

To an outsider the boundaries of Royce's world appeared open and expansive. From Royce's perspective, they were psychologically and geographically confining. Like his Jewish classmate, Rebecca, he sought to escape the small town environment which offered respectful protection but limited opportunities. Unlike Eugene Gant in *Look Homeward, Angel*, Royce has yet to make his romantic pilgrimage. His abbreviated journey to a nearby urban area ended with a pink slip—perhaps thought by his employer to be colored appropriately. Royce is returning home in muted shame.

Psychologically, Royce also felt the borders of his position enveloping him. Just as religious fundamentalism magnified Vince's existential crisis, so did the respect and discretion exercised by Royce's classmates and teachers make coping with his homosexuality difficult. Royce accepted these same-sex feelings with little difficulty. However, being involved in a closeted relationship with another high school student presented an array of problems. The most vexing of these was his inability to talk about this relationship with adults who were aware of but refused to acknowledge his homosexual feelings or his relationship with Jason. Sex, as Royce noted, is a private matter. Given his status in the school community, students and educators refrained from publicly challenging Royce about suspicions they may have privately held. Thus, while Royce's social position and personal qualities protected him from the most overt homophobic viciousness, it also isolated him from persons and resources of which he was in desperate need.

The effect of social class on growing up gay has been examined extensively by sociologist Joseph Harry. In his analysis of 1556 questionnaires from gay men in the Chicago area, he found that those coming from middle- and upper-income families expressed less guilt than those with working class backgrounds. Further, Harry reported that blue-collar respondents who were more troubled as adolescents by their emerging homosexual feelings were more likely to attend college than their non-guilt-ridden counterparts.[2] In his search for trends and central tendencies, however, this quantitative study may have overlooked the significance of idiosyncratic responses that fell outside the statistical norm.

Contrary to Harry's work, this present study found an inverse relationship between these 24 Southern males' social class backgrounds and guilt associated with their same-sex feelings and behaviors. Male participants from working poor backgrounds started to feel good about the assumptions of their homosexual identity more than a year (18.6 years) before their upper-class counterparts and eight months earlier than those from middle-class families. For example, Irwin comes from a working poor background and felt positive about his sexuality at the earliest age (14 years) of participants in this study. Boasting a family whose wealth and name extend back for generations, Kevin was the oldest (24 years) before his sense of homosexual guilt and shame began to dissipate.

Examining the relationship between homosexual guilt and college attendance within socio-economic groups, Harry's generalizations may require modification. Three white and three black men from working class families participated in this study. The three white men matched the pattern Harry found. Brandon, who attended college, started to feel good about his homosexuality at the age of 22; Steve and Alston, neither of whom attended college, reported such feeling three to five years earlier. The opposite occurred for the three persons of color from low-income families. Irwin and Franklin reported feeling good about their homosexuality at ages 14 and 18, respectively. Both attended college. Malcolm, who did not attend college, was 21 before his sense of guilt lessened. As the biographical portraits of Malcolm and Brandon in this study reveal, factors other than family economic background influenced feelings of homosexual guilt and self-loathing.

The small number of cases examined in this study, of course, do not obviate Harry's findings which are based upon a much larger sample. They do, however, provide an opportunity for a case by case analysis to illuminate these patterns. Though social class is an important vantage point from which to examine Royce's experiences, it neither defines Royce as a total human being nor does its role in his life automatically generalize to other gay males who are the products of privileged families. In fact, Royce was the *only* male from the upper-income group in this study to attend college without a sense of guilt accompanying him. The others, Henry III, Carlton, Drew and Kevin, did not begin to feel good about their homosexuality until their early to mid twenties. Hence, family social standing in the community alone does not guarantee that a gay son will escape childhood harassment or readily adopt a homosexual identity. Other factors contributed to the unease which these participants suffered in coping with their homosexual feelings and behaviors. Henry's biography illustrates this point.

Like most of the inhabitants of this southeastern corner of South Carolina, Henry III shares more in common with his fellow Tidewater aristocrats than with Royce and his Southern Appalachian culture heritage. Historically, there has always been a cleavage between these regions of South Carolina. Two centuries ago the mountain folk in the Carolina back country had to deal with Cherokee Indians, while the rice planters on the coast were more concerned with the "negro problem." Today those along the coast are interested in attracting the tourist trade while those in the Highlands are more concerned about enforcing "blue laws." In post-Revolutionary America, voters in the Piedmont tended to support the more agrarian-oriented and democratic policies of Jeffersonian Republicans like Charles Pickney, while the more commercial-minded Coastal residents opted for the Hamiltonian Federalist such as Thomas Pickney and John Rutledge.³ In post-Reagan America, state politicians must balance the textile interests and conservative social philosophy of the up-country with the tobacco interests and free-market philosophy of the low-country.

Blessed with attractiveness and wealth, Henry III grew up along The Battery of Charleston in a house built by his pre-Revolutionary War ancestors. When he was five, Henry remembers complimenting another boy on his good looks. As he grew up, these romantic feelings deepened but adopting a gay identity "was never a possibility. It was impossible for a nice downtown boy like me to be gay." Until sixth grade, the word "gay" had no significance to him:

We were talking about a short story. In one scene there was a door and light coming out from it. The teacher asked, "Why is this important?" I raised my hand. "Well, to anybody in the street, light coming out of the door would make them think that there is music and gaiety inside." Now, I meant gaiety as in joviality. But Harden, the boy sitting next to me, laughed and mocked, "GAYiety." I wasn't exactly sure what he meant. I knew it wasn't good. Later another classmate wrote, "I am queer" on my notebook. I thought that was sort of neat because it meant that she thought that I was individualistic. When I got home my mom saw the notebook. She was real quiet and very thoughtful. Then she explained to me about queers. She told me that was not a good thing to be identified with. I had no idea that there was anything sexual about these men. I just thought that they were somehow strange and weird. They liked to dress up in women's clothes and they hung out in the park. I thought that they cruised in anonymous cars. I thought they were old. I thought they tried to pick up little guys. As far as I knew, homosexuality was unnatural, wrong, horrible, and barbaric. I assumed that the natural way was for men to be with women. That was the way of my par-

ents; that was the way of people on television; that was the
way of all my friends' parents; that would be my way.

Henry never engaged in childhood or adolescent homosexual activity. Though he lived a privileged life, neither his family's social
standing within an aristocratic city nor his costly education within
an elite school environment allowed the bitter cup of harassment
and self-loathing to escape from his lips. "I had problems of self-
esteem when I was in high school. But, I remember thinking that,
even if I had no personality, that at least I had a pretty face." De-
testing sports, preferring the company of girls, boasting a bland
personality, speaking with a lisp, and acting feminine, Henry
quickly became known as the school fag. "I hated to walk away
from groups because you wonder what they say to themselves when
their heads go together. It was the worst feeling in the world when
you meet someone for the first time and to be greeted with 'I've
heard about you.'" He silently shouldered the burdens of such labelling. Henry's emotional suffering surfaced in behaviors which
only compounded his adolescent problems:

I felt isolated throughout high school. I didn't talk to anybody.
I was just weird—just flat out warped. I went through a shop-
lifting period. I didn't have anybody to hang around so I'd go
downtown and shoplift. Also, I had about five or six good
friends but somehow I thought that they weren't really my
friends and I had to work at winning their friendship. I would
just get really temperamental. Something would happen and I
would just get pissed-off out of all proportion. I would just feel
like they were all rejecting me. I would get really depressed.
I'd go to school and I'd go to the library to read until it was
time to go for class. . . . I'd draw all the way through class. I'd
go to my next class and I'd draw all the way through that.
Then break would come and I'd go somewhere to be alone
unless I decided, "Okay. I'm going to have friends now." So,
I'd go to find my friends and try to join in their conversation.
Then I'd go to class and I'd draw some more. . . . I was
always scraping by. . . . I just floated through high school—in
a daze.

During high school, Henry did not connect his feelings for other men with the possibility of "being gay." It was not until the age of 19 that he had his first homosexual experience. At the time, "I just told myself, 'I had strayed.'" A year later he first entertained the idea of adopting a homosexual identity:

> Before I had gone to France, I was in my dorm room thinking, "Is it so awful to be gay?" If you've never thought or considered the possibility that you might be gay you can't understand what a thunderbolt that question is. It is just one sentence, but it slams in your face. Twenty years of upbringing — everything you've ever absorbed or been taught or heard. All that time you're taught that it's awful to be gay. But, I thought that some people are gay and seem to be happy and quite normal. Then I thought maybe it is possible to be gay and happy and normal. That was a revelation. About a week later I had enough nerve in my mind to ask, "Am I gay?"
>
> Then I went to France on a six week study tour. There I had a very long conversation with the professor. He told me about himself and his experiences. For the first time in my life I started to think about my feelings toward men. There was another guy in our group that I wanted to get to know better. But, then I started thinking that maybe I really wanted more from him — maybe I would like to get to know him better in bed. That was the first time I had said it out loud and made the connection in my mind. What I wanted ever since I was five or six watching Marlo Thomas' boyfriend on television was to have a man in my bed!

Despite similarities in affluence and sexuality, there were marked differences between Royce and Henry. Royce attended the town's only public high school in a small town; Henry was schooled in a private academy of distinction in South Carolina's most elegant city. Royce was outgoing and athletic; Henry preferred the solitude of an artist. Royce worked more diligently in school to impress his teenage lover while Henry languished in academics as he struggled with submerged homosexual feelings. Royce engaged in homosexual activity in junior high school; Henry was in college before enjoying such an experience. Both had opportunities denied to Norma Jean and avoided pitfalls that befell her by virtue of her family's social stature and her gender. However, the social standing of Royce's and Henry's families within their communities was less important than the communities within which they were raised and the idiosyncratic behaviors and attitudes which they brought into them.

Boundaries Between Classes

Royce's anecdotes — the quarterback using drugs and demonstrating little academic achievement, the poorly clad student placed in a lower high school track, and the upper class student burnt out on drugs yet passed along from grade to grade — underscore how community boundaries between social classes permeate the school and translate into educational opportunity and achievement. Recent sociological studies have documented such differential treatment accorded students.[4]

In a classic study by Aaron Cicourel and John Kitsuse, high school counselors were found to play a pivotal role in allocating educational options to students. These opportunities were often provided on the basis of social class and related characteristics, such as appearance and character, rather than upon academic ability or vocational interests.[5] The reproductive role of schools in sorting students on the basis of social class (as well as race and gender) have been documented repeatedly by more recent studies using a variety of methodologies.[6]

Ray Rist's masterful study of kindergarten students attending an all-black school, for example, revealed that the groups to which students were assigned within a few days of their school careers correlated strongly with their socio-economic backgrounds. Those kindergarten students whose families were on welfare or had a single-parent were more likely to be assigned to the poorest group — independent of testing or evaluation. Moreover, little mobility between these assigned groups was evidenced as these students entered second grade.[7] As sociologist William Sewell notes, the effect of social class continues throughout the schooling process, translating finally into the probability a child will attend college:

We estimate that a higher SES [socio-economic status] student has about a 2.5 times as much chance as a low SES student of continuing in some kind of post-high school education. He has almost a four to one advantage in access to college, a six to one advantage in college graduation, and a nine to one advantage in graduate or professional school.[8]

The student culture also has been vividly documented in educational ethnographies ranging from Phillip Cusick's, *Inside High School* to Fred Wiseman's cinema verite film, *High School*.[9] The social boundaries among Southern students are reflected in high school cliques ranging from "The Ropers" and the "air-head blondes" described by Vince to the kids hanging around the live oak tree sketched in Norma Jean's biographical portrait. Participants in this study readily recalled identifiable groups of students within their high school. Those with upper-class family backgrounds, like Cory, Olivia and Royce, were more likely to identify themselves with the "band people," "the jocks," and the "preppies," whereas those with working poor and blue collar backgrounds, like Irwin and Alston, were more likely to associate with the "Bible-belters" and least likely to associate with the "freaks." In general, this group associated with fewer cliques than their upper income counterparts.

These boundaries among social classes (as well as between races) also are evidenced in gay community life in the adult world. Reflecting Southerners' penchant for individualism and their heart-felt belief in discretion, no clearly recognizable gay or lesbian communities exist in South Carolina. This clannishness among Southerners, as well as their tolerance for eccentricity, desire for privacy, and reverence of social class, translates into sparse attendance at assemblies of the Metropolitan Community Church or at gay and lesbian organizational meetings in South Carolina. Few persons in this study participated in such activities within the 12 months preceding their interview.

"Even in the modern South," Edmund White wrote in his travels in gay America, "gays still form a masked cadre."[10] Not until the mid-eighties, with the emergence of AIDS and the promise of Draconian state legislation, has any viable statewide organization of gay men and lesbians formed and endured. Most of the conservatively estimated 100,000 gay-identified South Carolinians live in palmetto closets socializing with a small group of friends of similar social rank, occasionally visiting a gay bar, or criss-crossing the traditional cruising areas in cities or along interstate highways. A myriad of honeycombed cells of lesbians and gay men flourish. Seldom do these tight-knit groups cross gender, class, or racial boundaries, and entry into these mini-gay communities is difficult. One participant notes how "It's very cliquish here in South Carolina. Gay people are very clannish and it's hard to break into a clique."

Gentlemen such as Royce enjoy and maintain their public respect by practicing their homosexual lifestyle in private. The "flaunting" of one's sexuality as either a flaming queen or a gay activist disturbs the sensibility of the Southern gentleman. Subtleties — the occasional double-entendre, wandering eye, or inflected voice — are his preferred codes of communication. Exclusivity is his trademark. The gentleman prefers to socialize privately with a small circle of friends who share common interests and backgrounds. In Columbia, South Carolina, those gentlemen active in the bar scene frequent the exclusive President's Club which routinely screens and rejects applicants. On occasion they also may appear at the Oasis, a discotheque catering to a young, fashion-conscious crowd. Southern gentlemen like Royce or Henry would never think of visiting the Back Alley, a hangout for hustlers, pool sharks, and dusk-to-dawn drinkers; the Last Roundup, a bar for down-home, country folks; or the Sugar Babe, a black night club on the "other side" of town. As a passing glance at any *Bob Damron's Address Book* will attest, gay men's bars throughout the country cater to particular clientele. The difference in the South is the degree to which boundaries between these bars' social milieux are drawn and the difficulty of breaking into a clique once inside the bar door.

The same characteristics which make Southern communities difficult for strangers to join and for community activists to organize are the ones which make life so comfortable for those who have the right family name, skin color, or genitalia. Royce's personal qualities and his small Southern hometown's idea of acceptable behavior extended the boundaries for his hushed world of homosexual desire.

The up-country's respect for privacy and social rank and Royce's willingness to assume roles harmonious with heterosexist assumptions (enjoying pornography, engaging in athletics, swapping fag jokes with cans of beers) gave him a rather broad social latitude. In communities such as his, freaks wearing sequined jump suits and reading *GQ* can be accepted as "eccentrics" while poorly dressed effeminate boys can be trashed as fags. This closeted comfort, unfortunately, has its costs; it can make one forget about the "other" world outside of cozy hometown limits. "Tired of playing politics," Royce retreated back behind familiar boundaries — trading one game for another. Returning to the safe harbor of his hometown, he will sit again in a game that makes life more comfortable for those able and willing to play by the house rules.

REFERENCE NOTES

1. King, 1975:171.
2. Harry, 1982:173-180.
3. Further information about the Appalachian South may be found in Coles, 1967; Coles, 1971; Higgs and Manning, 1975; Wilkins, 1970; Williams, 1961.
4. For a review of these studies, see: Eggleston, 1977; Hurn, 1978; Persell, 1977. Also, for a further elaboration of the ideological dynamics at work within schools, see: Apple, 1982a; Apple, 1982b; Apple and Weiss, 1983; Carnoy and Levin, 1985; Giroux, 1983; Giroux, 1988 as well as the seminal works of Bernstein (1977) and Bourdieu and Passeron (1977).
5. Cicourel and Kitsuse, 1963. See, also the classic study, *Pygmalion in the Classroom* by Rosenthal and Jacobson, 1968.
6. Ball, 1981; Bowles and Gintis, 1976; Carlson, 1980/81; Cicourel, Jennings, Jennings, Leiter, MacKay, Mehan and Roth, 1974; Cusick, 1983; Erickson, 1975; Everhart, 1983; Jencks, 1972; Mehan, 1978; Oakes, 1985; Ogbu, 1978; Rist, 1973; Rosenbaum, 1976; Walker and Barton, 1983; Willis, 1977.
7. Rist, 1970. For an ethnographic study examining the values expected by kindergarten teachers, see King, 1976.
8. Sewell, 1971:795. See, also: Sewell and Hauser, 1976.
9. Cusick, 1983; Powell, Farrar and Cohen, 1985.
10. White, 1983:249.

Chapter 6

Black or Gay
in a Southern Community

JACOB AND THE BUS BOYCOTT

There is a need in any group to card anyone crossing its boundaries. Any black man who admits to a prowhite preference will be carded. And if he [does so] frequently, his commitment to the black group will be doubted.

Julius Johnson, "From a Black Perspective"[1]

Jacob lived on the western edge of the Carolina Low Country where Cotton was once king and bottom lands wrap around small towns. "You would have to go elsewhere to enjoy any kind of recreation," he remembers. "Whether it's going to a decent movie or doing some nice shopping. It's a very quiet town. It's pretty much set in its ways." About one-half of the town's population was black, including Jacob. Though racial integration was instituted when he was in elementary school, the county continued to maintain two elementary schools, two middle schools, and two high schools—one predominantly white and the other predominantly black.

Jacob's earliest and fondest childhood memories were those occasions when his mother would leave him with three crippled children of a neighboring family. "They sort of adopted me as their little brother. All three of them were bedridden and it was a joy for them to have me around to play. They used to dress me up in little girls clothes." The youngest in a middle class family of six, Jacob was encouraged by his parents to explore his intellectual, social, and artistic talents. Since his brothers and sisters were of high school age at the time Jacob entered kindergarten, he found himself worried about being with other children his own age. Jacob remembers his first day in school:

> I was always a mamma's child during that stage. I cried the first day. Then, I discovered that I was a people-person. I liked to be around people. Since I didn't have a lot of playmates prior to kindergarten, that was a whole new experience. After that first day, I had no problems.

During childhood, his parents supported him in his artistic interests: he took private piano as well as art lessons. Jacob was encouraged to develop his social and leadership skills: he organized neighborhood street carnivals, conducted parades on his street, and formed social clubs. "They always expected me to be in the middle of planning something. They expected a lot of kids to hang around the house because I was in charge of something."

Jacob also excelled in school: "I was the teacher's pet. I thought it was great. I had no problems with it because, in first grade I looked at the situation and thought, 'I've got 12 years of this. I'm going to have to get along with these people.' I saw it as politics, even at the first grade." Jacob did not suffer at the hands of his classmates as the "teacher's pet." During the first and second grade, Jacob was a class leader and had his "own little group" on the playground. He enjoyed school, respected his teachers, got along well with his classmates, and performed well above average academically.

In second grade Jacob remembers an incident which was his first introduction to the concept of homosexuality. Jacob's family was attending a May Day celebration at the town's park. There were music, clowns, and food. In the center of the park was a May Pole with children dancing around.

> A woman got out of her car. She had on a house robe. She took it off and started running through the crowd to the May Pole. She didn't have any clothes on. People started fainting and crying. I was a very inquisitive child. I didn't understand

what was going on. My father explained to me that it was a scandal. The [woman's] family was having problems because their son was homosexual. He left it at that. My head boggled. I really didn't understand it at the time.

At the beginning of Jacob's third grade year, racial integration began. Though he remained in what was the school district's all black elementary school, some of his friends were transferred to the other school. A small proportion of whites, mostly working class kids, were bused to his school. "I basically didn't look at them as being white kids," Jacob recalls. "It was just getting to know new students." Integration allowed Jacob the opportunity to make new friends. Celeste became a particularly good friend:

I liked her because she was smart. I *was* the smartest kid on the block, then she comes. It was just fun to be around her. We were more mature than the other kids in the class. We used to play during recess. It didn't really dawn on me that she was white and I was black. Integration, though, was a big thing in my hometown. You would hear the adults talk about how much trouble there would be. I used to ask my mom if I could go over to visit Celeste. She would make excuses. Celeste would ask if she could come over to visit me and her parents would make up excuses. We remained friends, though, through junior high school.

By the time Jacob had entered fifth grade, he was actively involved in sports as well as schoolwork. He also began to assume more responsibility at home:

I would come in from school and my mom would have everything done. The only thing I would have to do is eat supper and do my homework. Then I'd go visit friends. They were slaves compared to me. I was like, "What's going on, Bro? Why are you doing all of this? Why can't your mamma do this?" Then, I realized that maybe I could take on a little bit more responsibility.

In fifth grade, Jacob also had a new "girlfriend":

> I went through these little love letter stages: 'Do you like me?'
> It was the thing to do, so I wrote Raphael a letter and we dated
> for a while. We took two classes together. I walked her to
> school and carried her books—then I found out we were dis-
> tant cousins. I told Raphael, "I don't care how distant you are,
> you're my cousin. That's how I was reared. It's wrong, so we
> can't do this."

As Jacob entered his last year in elementary school, he came to
realize the meaning of being an African-American in a rural Southern town. On weekend nights, Jacob and some of his friends, along
with many of the kids in the county, would go to their "hang out":
The Star Crystal, the town's skating rink. One Saturday night in late
spring a black classmate got into a fight with a white girl. During
the argument, the white girl's brother yelled out "Niggers!" Fighting broke out among blacks and whites. For several weeks it was
the talk of the county. About that same time, Jacob's sixth grade
teacher asked him to come by her classroom after school.

> Mrs. Green said, "Until last year, Jacob, Celeste had been
> doing much better than you. But you've made a big improve-
> ment. Big enough to be class valedictorian." She told me how
> important that was and how proud she was because I was
> black. I asked, "Why should that make a difference?" In a
> nutshell, she summed it up. "As far as being black, you have
> to do better. You have to give 120 percent over the white per-
> son." That stuck with me. When I got to junior high school, I
> *had* to make the top ten. In my hometown, there had never
> been a black person to make the top ten. From the day Mrs.
> Green talked to me, that was the goal I set for myself.

Not only was the meaning of being black impressed on Jacob's
young mind, sixth grade was also the time of his sexual awakening.
He recognized his strong attraction for guys at the age of ten. "I just
felt more comfortable around guys. My best friend at the time, Rodney, we had a lot more to talk about, laugh about, joke about than I

did with girls." He and Rodney never explored sex. The summer following his sixth grade year, however, Jacob was coaxed into engaging in sex with Lester, a high school-age neighbor.

> He used to come over to my house a lot during that summer. One particular day my mom and dad weren't around. I showed Lester some magazines my brother had. He suggested that we have sex. I really hadn't been exposed to sex. I hadn't even started masturbating. I said, "No. I don't think I want to do that." Lester prodded and coaxed me. So, I just sort of let it happen.

This began a non-emotional sexual relationship that continued through Jacob's thirteenth birthday. At first he was bothered by these sexual activities:

> I had always been very religious and I knew enough as far as my Baptist faith that it was wrong. I remember at a revival the year before a preacher talking about homosexuality. So it kind of stuck out in my mind. But, homosexuality was never mentioned at my house. If it was, my parents would pretend they didn't hear it, except for that one time with my father. I knew it was wrong, but I could not go to my mom and tell her about the incident. So, I was angry at Lester. But, I knew I did enjoy it and that I wasn't really interested in girls.

That fall, Jacob left his black dominated elementary school for a predominantly white junior high school. "There was a lot more competition as far as grades in classes," Jacob noted. He was placed in the most advanced group. In most of these classes, he was the only African-American. He continued to earn good grades as well as engage in after school activities. He also continued to see Lester. "I would never call him and say, 'Let's have sex.' I would maybe go over and visit him knowing that there was nobody home. I knew that it would happen." Jacob also became more aware of his homosexual feelings while attending mandatory gym class in the seventh grade. "You had to use the showers. I looked at other guys' bodies and became aware of my physical attraction toward them."

As Jacob tried to cope with these emerging homosexual feelings and his occasional homosexual activities, his religious upbringing tugged at his insides:

> I went to church every week and I studied my Sunday School lesson. I used to tell myself that I knew that God would forgive me for my sins. Even though I knew I was doing them over and over. I would pray every night, "God, forgive me for my sins." It was like, you do whatever you want to do during the day, but at night don't worry about it, because you're going to pray and the Lord is going to forgive you.

Jacob didn't label himself gay until 16; the central core of his identity, however, has always been color. "I'm proud of my black heritage," Jacob proclaims. "I wouldn't trade it for anything." During junior high school Jacob continued to excel in academics. He became involved in student government and the drama club. At the end of his seventh grade year, he was named to the "Superlatives" for being the most studious. "That's when people started looking at me as being a scholar. Throughout junior high and high school I never made anything lower than an 'A'." Beginning in junior high school, Jacob felt under increased pressure:

> I knew at this point that my whole family thought I was the smartest person in the world. My parents got to the point where they didn't seem to even look at my report cards. They would just sign them because they knew I had made good grades. One time I switched report cards on them just to see if they would notice. My mom said, "Jacob! These aren't your grades. These can't be yours." So, I guess they paid some attention to them.

Three years later, Jacob completed the ninth grade having achieved his goal of making the academic top ten and graduating as class valedictorian. He had also become adept at hiding his sexual feelings from friends and family. As a high school student, Jacob continued to demonstrate superior academic and leadership skills. Being a black male was central to his identity.

It was still very much a racial situation in my high school. As far as being on top in academics or student government, I always had a strong sense of being black. I had to let it be known that I was not a "token." It meant a lot to be able to win as president in a class that was 70 percent white.

Being an adolescent black male in the rural South in the late '70s, the boundaries for Jacob's behavior were clearly circumscribed by his race. Despite civil rights progress, being an African-American still exacted psychic and, at times, physical costs. Though he was elected class president, he felt his election was at least partly due to a sense of tokenism among students and faculty. Jacob's actions often were viewed by himself and others through a racial lens—a perspective, as the following school bus incident illustrates, which sometimes placed Jacob in physical peril:

I drove a school bus during high school. We had a busing problem with the whites on a bus that went to a black school and vice versa. I tried to be a very strict bus driver but there were still fights on my bus. There was one particular incident in which a big white child got into a fight. I got him suspended off my bus. He had been in so much trouble that when he got suspended off my bus he also got suspended from school for three days. His parents came to my bus and started to hassle and threaten me. I had to have police escorts for a week. Later the director of busing started coming down on the black bus drivers and being real unfair. I got elected to be spokesperson for the black drivers. I led a protest and we walked off our jobs. They didn't have buses for a whole day. There was chaos because nobody was there to drive all the black kids' buses. The administration was all over me saying, "You're class president. You can't do this." And, I was like, "No, but you see, I'm black . . ."

By virtue of Jacob's school-related activities and achievements, Jacob's effeminate mannerisms and lack of interest in girls were rarely questioned by friends or family. "It was like, 'He don't have time for girls. He's smart. He's doing his books.'" Jacob often

played off this theme: "I knew there were a couple of girls interested in me. We would talk and I would play the intellectual role. It
was like, 'I guess he really doesn't have time for me.' That's how I
would psych them out." When his younger sister would ask about
girlfriends during family dinner, he arrogantly replied, "I don't
think there's a girl out there good enough for me. Besides, I don't
have time. Look at my grades." Jacob's parents would back him
up, saying "He doesn't have time for that, child. He's working on a
scholarship for college."

During high school, Jacob did "hang together" with a peer
group composed of a roughly equal mixture of boys and girls. This
group included some "Platonic girlfriends." Jacob remembers one
with particular fondness: "We were real tight. We had our classes
together and we were in a lot of other things like honor society and
going to parties and meetings. We just used to do things automatically together. I think that's what really kept all the people from
asking." Nevertheless, a few adult neighbors suspected that Jacob
might be gay because "I wasn't out getting dirty and playing football." Had he been pressed by his sister or an adult, he would have
denied it saying, "Are you crazy? I'm not gay!" Asked why his
parents, who likely heard the neighbors' gossip, did not confront
him on the matter, Jacob popped, "Maybe they were afraid of me
saying, 'Yes.' I think that may have been why my parents never
mentioned it to me."

As he progressed in high school, Jacob's physical attraction for
males strengthened. At tenth grade, his first year in high school,
Jacob began initiating sexual encounters with other boys his age.

> The guy next door to me claimed to have had sex with my first
> cousin, Larry. I didn't believe him. I just couldn't believe
> Larry would do something like that—he was just too good
> looking. So my next door neighbor had me hide in the closet
> and he called Larry over. The idea was that when they got to
> the point when they were really going to do it, I was to come
> out of the closet and surprise him. Well, it didn't work out that
> way. I stayed in the closet the whole time. My friend yelled,
> "Wait a minute, Larry! Jacob is in the closet." My cousin
> thought he was just trying to make up something. When Larry

came to the closet and looked around, he didn't see me; I hid behind some coats. My friend just went on ahead and went through with it. When Larry was on his way out, my friend asked, "What are you going to do? Go over to Jacob's house?" That's when I jumped out of the closet and said, "Why should you go over there when I'm here?" Larry was really surprised. About two weeks later Larry was visiting our house and we just started talking. He asked if I'd consider doing it with him. Now, I had always found Larry very attractive so I said, "Sure."

Jacob had been very reticent in establishing any public relationship with his distant cousin, Raphael, during the fifth grade. However, he had no reluctance crossing family boundaries for private sexual encounters with his first cousin, Larry. The sexual significance of these routine encounters, though, had a more profound impact on Larry than it did on Jacob.

My cousin, Larry, and I did it. I can't count the times that we had sex. Larry felt even guiltier than I did. It was like, "We're not supposed to do this." I was like, "Why don't you chill out? What's wrong with you." He would never label himself as being homosexual. He would get real depressed sometimes. He'd say, "Why does this have to happen? Why can't I be normal." I'd say, "You're not normal?" Larry said I knew what he meant. I said, "No, I don't. I always consider myself to be normal."

Jacob, though, occasionally struggled with deep-seated religious guilt. As late as his senior year he was making promises to his God that he would stop this homosexual activity. Jacob remembers: "I still had that religious side to me. I would do it and I would make promises to myself that I would stop. I ordered the little porno novels. I would get into my moods where I would say 'No. This is wrong,' and burn them. I'd get back into the mood and buy some more."

Jacob privately proclaimed his sexual identity during his sophomore year, confessing to himself, "Well, you know you like to have sex with guys so that makes you a homosexual." He refused to place himself in the same category as those labelled "faggots" at his high school. There were about 10 "hard-core faggots" in his school of 1500 students. "In that little group, most of the guys were open about it. They were very effeminate acting. They openly said, 'Yeah I'm interested in guys. What are you going to say about it?'" Jacob would "pass for straight and I really didn't associate with them. They were pretty much social outcasts." However, he was tuned into the news about gaylife, and often thought about the problems confronting those who openly acknowledged their homosexuality. "I'd sit back and analyze situations that gay people were in," Jacob recollects, "like the people that struggled for gay rights or that got thrown in jail." Although he didn't associate with the "faggot group" in high school, he empathized with the problems they were confronting. He felt their harassment was unjust. "I was reared that you don't judge a book by its cover and you can't just say things about people." With his reputation for his willingness to stick up for others, few were surprised when Jacob finally called a friend down for such harassment. "One of my best friends used to make jokes about them and used to pick at them. I finally said, 'Have you ever been to bed with that person?' He couldn't say 'yes' and he wouldn't say 'no.' He just didn't say anything. So, I said, 'Then you can't talk.'"

Throughout adolescence, Jacob's primary concerns were issues associated with the color of his skin, not the gender of his sexual partner: "We did not get black history in my high school. I yearned for that. I went out and got it on my own. Most of the gay materials I read were pornographic materials or those little pamphlets you pick up at a club." Unlike Larry, Jacob "never got into depressed states. It would be a struggle but I never wanted to change my life." Six years out of high school, Jacob declares, "I'm proud of my black heritage but I wouldn't want to be straight." During adolescence, however, Jacob was not ready to disclose his homosexuality to his family or peers. In his role as class president, Jacob would talk with some of his classmates who were suspected of being gay, but he didn't associate with them. When attending school proms he chose "the prettiest girls" to escort and made sexual passes at them, fearing that if he didn't "they would go back and tell." Jacob participated in many of these types of activities "because it was a social thing. As president of the junior class, I had to be there. It was more like President Reagan entertaining heads of state. It's expected of you when you're in a certain position."

As a junior, an incident occurred that "probably changed my whole life." Jacob fell in love. He met Warren, a young black man who also sang in the community choir. Warren was a senior when "we started to have sex. It started to be an emotional thing. He got to the point of telling me he loved me. That was the first time anybody ever said anything like that. It was kind of hard to believe that *even after sex* there are really feelings. We became good friends." Then an incident occurred:

Warren was interested in this guy who he was not sure was gay. He made advances toward him and it was a very ugly scene. But, he didn't tell me about the scene. The next night he came to my house and said, "Let's go riding. I want you to stop by this guy's house. I just want to see if he's home." We went to this guy's house. His mother was at home. The guy evidently had told his mother what had happened. When my friend got to the door, his mother came outside. Warren just turned back around, got in the car, and drove off. Later, the guy told his mom that it was my car. She called my parents and told them, "I don't know what Jacob is into but his friend has made advances toward my son. You should talk to Jacob."

That is the first and only time my mother ever mentioned anything to me. When I got home that night she called me into the bedroom and asked, "Does your friend like other guys?" I said, "Why would you say that?" She replied, "Because I got this phone call" and so on. I said, "I really don't know what he does." She paused and then asked, "You don't like other guys, do you?" I quickly said, "No." She told me that she didn't want me to associate with Warren. I knew right then, "I can't tell her this because it will really hurt her." That is the only time I really felt intimidated or really scared about anyone finding out about me liking other guys. I can remember that night just as clear. It hurt me because I had to lie to her.

This relationship, lasting until Warren graduated from high school, "reaffirmed my homosexuality. Before, I had never come into contact with someone I truly loved. But with Warren I had become emotionally involved."

As a senior, Jacob was finishing his college preparatory courses, preparing for the college entrance examinations, and having occasional, unemotional sex with his next door neighbor, Lester, and his cousin, Larry. The weekend before Jacob graduated valedictorian, things changed. Jacob met Gordon.

> I was at church and my choir was singing. Gordon came up afterward. He was an older man. He was telling me how much he enjoyed my directing, singing, and playing. He spoke French. He asked me for my name and telephone number so I could do a program at his church. I told him I had taken French in school. My sister was standing there while Gordon said "Parlez vous Francais." I said, "Oui." He then said, "I would like to get to know you better." It's a good thing my sister didn't know French. She would have eaten it up.

> Gordon came to my graduation and gave me a gift. One night we were just riding around. We had never really talked about being gay. Suddenly he said, "Do you want to make love." I really did want to have that kind of relationship but I was also sort of disappointed. Although he was a very attractive man, I had sort of wanted this to be a "big brother" kind of thing. We had sex that night. We spent the whole summer together. I really got emotionally involved with him.

Though his relationship with Gordon lasted only a summer, Jacob's identity as a black man and commitment to academic excellence continued throughout his college years. His skin color not his homosexual behavior continued to shape his life's work and goals. In less than four years, Jacob completed college with honors and found a job in state government. Declaring himself gay is less important to him than expanding the opportunities and influence of African-Americans. For example, Jacob recently founded an organization, "Black Together," whose two dozen black-gay members regularly meet to share friendship and to work on social projects within the African-American community.

At 26, he enjoys a network of friends, regularly attends parties and seeks same-sex dates. But, he has yet to disclose his homosexuality to his mother. Thinking back upon the incident with Warren, Jacob comments: "If she asked me that question today," he pauses, "I really don't know. I don't think she would ever ask me — I think she knows. But, I don't think she wants to hear the answer. It's like if you hear it then you know it for certain. My parents are like 99.9 percent sure. But if they hear it they're going to be 100 percent sure. They don't want that degree of certainty."

COMMENTARY

Jacob inherited a Southern world turned upside down by the *Brown* decision of 1954, the Montgomery Bus Boycott of 1955, and the registration of nine black students at Little Rock's Central High School in 1957. Born during President Kennedy's first year in office, scenes such as Bull Connor commanding fire hoses and police dogs in Birmingham and George Wallace straddling the university door remain only as fragmentary memories of late night, kitchen table conversations among relatives. Jacob progressed through elementary school during a time of moderation, as middle-of-the-road South Carolina politicians like Governor John West and Senator Ernest Hollings defeated strident segregationists. The decade of the seventies marked the first time since the importation of slaves ended in the first decade of the nineteenth century that more blacks entered the state than departed from it. It was a decade of comparative racial quiet as South Carolina students peacefully integrated while their parents viewed the racial turmoil in the Boston schools from their living room sofa. The seventies were a decade in which Jacob found an identity.

The Old and New Black Middle Class

The boundaries within African-American communities have been drawn for generations.[2] E. Franklin Frazier noted in his pioneering Depression era work:

In most cases the social differentiation of the Negro community is not built upon occupational differentiation of the population, but represents the efforts of those who have achieved some culture and education to enforce standards and recognize distinction in behavior. . . . In a Southern city, for example, the small elite will be composed of a few school teachers, a couple of physicians, a dentist, postal employees, and one or two other families who have acquired a superior status because of family, property or sometimes because of some unique position in the white community.[3]

The ancestors of this old black middle class described by Frazier were antebellum free black artisans and gentry living in Southern port cities and Northern commercial municipalities. From the ashes and hopes of Reconstruction, Jim Crow laws undermined their economic autonomy while elevating their status within newly formed black communities.[4] The restrictive immigration laws and the industrialization of a Post-World War I workforce spurred the growth of this middle class which enjoyed its greatest pre-Civil Rights prosperity during the Harlem Renaissance of the twenties. The "new black middle class" emerged in the decades following the *Brown* decision. Writing in the mid-fifties, Frazier first recognized the emergence of this distinctive group:

Those members of the new middle class who have been able as the result of education and larger employment opportunities to rise to middle class status have intermarried into the old middle class. Since the new middle class are not the true heirs of the old middle class with its solid virtues which had some real meaning among a privileged caste behind the walls of segregation, they seek to confirm their new status by conspicuous consumption.[5]

During the intervening three decades, educational and occupational opportunities have expanded and political and social barriers have lessened. Within the span of two generations, the black middle class in America has increased four fold and now represents four of every ten African-American workers.[6] Writing near the end of three decades of expansion, two social researchers underscore the dilemmas confronting many new middle class blacks in the late eighties:

> One major problem of the black middle class is that as more and more blacks seek and gain entrance into the middle class, they become engaged in a continuous effort to stabilize their class position for themselves and their children, within the institutional structure of their community, which is partially but not totally regulated by the standards of the larger society. Thus, members of the black middle class are in a quest for "community" — that is . . . buying a home . . . family stability, white-collar occupations, political participation and a high level of education . . . behavior patterns and life-styles appropriate to the middle class and . . . increasing their sociocultural identity and unity . . . As such, the black middle class must contend with both internal and external community forces, demands, standards, norms, values, and reactions.[7]

Jacob and his family are not members of the new black middle class. With his weekly piano lessons, exemplary academic performance, and passion for social leadership, Jacob reflects the values of the old Southern black gentry. His biography, juxtaposed with that of Nathaniel's story, illustrates the contemporary boundary between the old black bourgeoisie and the new black middle class. Nathaniel's story illuminates how forces within the new black middle class can affect the identity of a black man with homosexual feelings.

Nathaniel's father is a commercial truck driver and his mother is the head of nursing at a metropolitan hospital. Nathaniel has lived his 18 years in upper-middle class neighborhoods. He attended two of the nation's finest co-educational military academies from the first through the ninth grades. "I wanted to get out [of the academies] but my father wanted me [to stay] there. My father was basically scared of my mother who was the big bread winner of the house. He couldn't take it so he took all of his anger out on us kids."

Nathaniel did reasonably well academically though his first love was sports. "I was basically a quiet student that always worked and who did his best in doing what I had to do. But, I really love to run, just getting away, you know.'' By the time Nathaniel was in fifth grade, ''I was noticing guys. Not knowing that I was gay—just curious about guys. I thought it was wrong and I kept wondering, 'Why am I attracted to men?''' At 13, he engaged in sex with another boy; a few months later Nathaniel had a steady girlfriend, Delta, with whom he also shared sexual intimacy. For the past five years he and Delta have gone steady; for the past year and a half he also has been dating Hodding. Delta is black; Hodding is white. Noting ''it's rougher being black and gay,'' Nathaniel claims that if homosexuality was more acceptable, ''I probably would be strictly homosexual. When I got Delta, it was like a cover. I was having sex with a man but for security I got a girlfriend and we've stuck together.''

Finally, in tenth grade Nathaniel attended a public school. He was elated, ''because I didn't have to wear a uniform and didn't have to carry myself as a military student anymore. I could let loose. I started wearing tight clothes. I really wanted to get an earring in the wrong ear but I didn't want no one to know I was gay.'' As a high school senior in this predominantly white, upper class school, Nathaniel seldom associates with other blacks. ''I wanted to be like one of the preppies. I hang out with the jocks and the preps at school. My black friends sometimes give me a hard time because of the way I dress and the neighborhood I live in.'' Nathaniel also has confrontations with the ''redneck-druggies. They called us 'little pukes.' They are the hicks who hang out on the back porch, wear these rebel shirts, and run a four wheel drive.'' Though occasionally harassed by them for his effeminate behavior, the jocks and preps stand behind him. ''I guess they said, 'Gay guys don't wrestle. Gay guys don't have a girlfriend. Gay guys don't drive a '69 Chevelle.' So I must be okay.''

In Nathaniel's suburban world, social class and family status are important considerations. His association with the preppies, disinterest in rap music and black history, and fondness for white men clearly distinguish Nathaniel from Jacob. In Jacob's rural county town, race was the important social marker. Both his inability to

bring Celeste home after school and the fracas that spring night at
the Star Crystal illustrate the rural Southern boundary between his
county's black and white citizens in the seventies.

Like Jacob's, Grant's family is from the old black bourgeoisie.
Grant's light skin is a historical reminder of the elasticity in sexual
relations during the antebellum era, the special role of light-skinned
servants in the operation of the Big House, and the premium placed
on mulatto women and children by the old middle class. Shy, withdrawn, and bright, Grant changed schools in sixth grade when the
family moved to a mid-size city. Unlike Nathaniel, he had difficulty
adjusting to suburban white culture:

> Most of the kids I went to school with were really wealthy.
> There was always a sense of inadequacy. I just didn't fit in. I
> didn't have the money. It was like the kids had bicycles and I
> didn't. I wanted one. When I finally got a bicycle, everyone
> was into mopeds. I was always late.

Grant lacked status at this school because of his parents' financial
situation and his skin color. Grant's academic ability also proved to
be a liability in this situation. One of three African-Americans in an
accelerated class of 29 students, Grant underscores the problems he
faced in this new environment:

> It is really hard on black kids, especially if they are in acceler-
> ated classes. You get all of this negative feedback. It's done in
> a subtle way. I don't even think it's intentional. Whenever
> references are made to blacks, you can tell in the intonation of
> the teachers' voices — they tense up. Or, when you would go to
> the gymnasium for awards night and everybody is mostly
> white and a black comes up to the stage and gets an award —
> people start moving around in their chairs and you hear things.
> This is *still* the South. It's like being black is abnormal. Unless
> you're white, you're not normal. You would also get it from
> other blacks who were in the regular classes. They would al-
> ways say that you were being "uppity" because you were in
> that class. They'd say you were trying to act like an "oreo."

They'd shy away from you and then the only people you have
to associate with are whites. It was a vicious cycle.

Speaking of the "black community," or for that matter general-
izing about any minority group, diminishes differences among sub-
groups and undervalues the power of individuals to transcend those
boundaries. Grant, a son of old middle class parents, one a school
teacher and the other a minister, was labelled an "oreo" by his
more rowdy and less respectful black classmates. Jacob, also the
product of an old middle class background and the recipient of academic honors, was not. Jacob's primary identity is black. He eagerly represented his fellow black co-workers in the bus walkout
and his fellow students as the first black student body president.
Nathaniel, a son of new upper-middle class parents, is concerned
with joining the right groups and wearing the most fashionable
clothes. Projecting a bisexual image, he has little interest in African-American culture or his black heritage.

The Black Middle Class, Homosexuality, and Social Opportunity

Race separated Jacob's personal and social worlds in the school
community; homosexuality separated Jacob's private and public
worlds in the African-American community. Though Jacob was
successful in crossing the racial boundary in school, as evidenced
by student elections and academic awards, he has been less successful in transcending the sexual boundary within his black community. As a high school student, he refused to associate with the
"hard-core faggots" and used books and girlfriends as a heterosexual "front." As an adult, he is active in black community affairs
and has formed his own organization, but is reticent in identifying
himself or his organization as gay-related. "Its purpose is to pro-
mote cultural education and social achievement. It is *not* a gay organization."

Some observers of African-American communities have noted
differences between poor and middle class blacks' reactions toward
homosexuality. For example, Cheryl Clarke writes:

The poor and working class black community, historically more radical and realistic than the reformist and conservative black middle class and the atavistic, "blacker-than-thou" (bourgeois) nationalist, has often tolerated an individual's lifestyle prerogatives, even when that lifestyle was disparaged by the prevailing culture. Though lesbians and gay men were exotic subjects of curiosity, they were accepted as part of the community (neighborhood) — or at least, there were no manifestos calling for their exclusion from the community.[8]

This is underscored by John Soares who notes that the middle class black families "are so persistently monitoring their social standing that any family member departing from their peer group norm would experience a certain degree of ostracism. But, for what appears to be the majority of working class black people, gay lovers and steadies are accepted by or even into the family . . ."[9] These observations may explain why none of the middle class participants in this study — Jacob, Grant, Nathaniel, and Heyward — have "come out" to their families, while all of the working class males have done so. It is important to note, however, that none of these African-Americans reported significant differences in their black communities' feelings toward homosexuals or attitudes about homosexuality. Irwin, a working class African-American, echoes the sentiment of these black males:

> First, the South is conservative. When you're black in a black society and you're gay it's even harder. Blacks don't want it to be known because they don't want to mimic or imitate white people. They see it as a crutch and they don't want to have to deal with it. That's what they have been taught. They would do all sorts of things to deny that someone in their family is gay or that they're gay.

The observations of Clarke and Soares also have been challenged by a recent analysis of National Opinion Research Center Data. Examining dimensions of liberalism and conservatism among white and black Americans, Richard Selzer and Robert Smith found that poor and working class black Southerners held the most conservative views on social issues ranging from abortion on demand to homosexual rights.[10] This same study reported that blacks were more liberal than their white counterparts on economic issues but that whites were more likely to support homosexual rights. African-Americans were also much more likely than whites to perceive the need for further efforts in economic and social equality for minority Americans.

Though participants like Jacob have enjoyed benefits and opportunities unimagined by the previous generation, the social menu for blacks is still different than that offered to whites. Understandably, Jacob's concern for social opportunities among blacks in housing, education, and politics is more visible than his interest in furthering homosexual rights. Many African-Americans in South Carolina share Jacob's assessment that economic and social barriers have yet to be eliminated.[11] Overt racist comments and actions are not generally heard or seen in the state. Racist attitudes and behaviors, however, lie just beneath the surface. As one Southern, white attorney, commented "it's more under the table. . . . We are still a segregated society."[12] These attitudes and behaviors are reflected in the "symbols, expletives, ritual speeches, gestures, [and] half-understood impulses"[13] relating to housing patterns and schooling opportunities as well as participating in social clubs and local politics.

Though few, if any, blacks live in certain residential areas, headlines in South Carolina's major newspaper read, "Realtors Say Housing Law Won't Stop Discrimination,"[14] and a prominent Columbia realtor is reported saying "There is no discrimination in the Columbia real estate market . . . blacks are afraid of moving into white neighborhoods where they will not be accepted."[15] Though black and white students attend the same public schools, African-Americans may find restrictions on extracurricular activities. A high school golf coach sent a letter to his fellow South Carolina coaches informing them that blacks would not be allowed to take part in an upcoming tournament because of the local country club's long-standing practice of barring African-Americans. This letter, stated the coach, "was not intended to offend, but to inform participants in order to avoid an awkward situation on the course."[16]

Though persons of color have now entered into middle- and upper-level management in South Carolina, a black IBM executive recently was transferred from Columbia to New York after being refused membership in an exclusive club, though he was nominated by one of the state's most powerful financial executives. Labelling the discrimination practices of the state's private social clubs "an American form of apartheid,"[17] the social analysis by the executive secretary of the South Carolina NAACP was in sharp contrast to the response of the president of the private club who, when asked why there were no black members, simply stated, "I have no idea."[18]

Though African-American voter participation and representation has increased since the 1965 Civil Rights Act,[19] less than one-sixth of South Carolina counties have near equal representation among blacks and whites.[20] In counties that use at-large elections and where the black voting population ranges between 16 and 38 percent, there are no black council members. Counties, like Barnwell, maintain racial discrimination through the at-large system. The council chairperson of Barnwell County (composed of a 38 percent black voting bloc) can benefit from discrimination and preserve democratic appearances by insisting that this "makes council members responsible to all the county."[21] The blame is placed elsewhere — generally at the doorstep of African-American communities. Barnwell's state representative simply concludes the absence of a black council member is because "There's been no effort on the county level by the black community."[22]

Since Jacob graduated from high school in 1980, the boundaries between his private and public worlds have loosened more than those between the white and black communities. This is true not only in the heterosexual world of housing patterns, schooling opportunities, social clubs, and local politics but in the homosexual bar and dating scene as well. Within gay communities, the division between black and white still exists. Jacob elaborates:

I have a cousin who lives in New Jersey. One of his friends who is black and gay came down to visit me during last Fourth of July. This was his first time down South. We went out to the clubs. I didn't really tell him anything. When we got to the disco he started to ask me questions. Like, "Why are all the blacks on this side and the whites over here?'' I told him, ''That's just the way it is. You're down South. We do it subconsciously whether we're gay, heterosexual, or whatever. We do it in restaurants, on the job, in churches, and at the bars.''

This lack of social integration reflects the racism and homophobia within both the white and black communities. Speaking about attitudes within his black community, Malcolm declares:

> If they are going to see you with a man at all, they would rather see you with another black man. I think it goes back to racism and slavery. There was a time when whites owned blacks. If they think you're gay and you're with a white man, they think that he's your sugar daddy or you're a snow queen. If you happen to be a masculine type, then they think that the white is just using you to get that black stuff from a stud.

Choosing Between Black and Gay Identities

The late black historian and theologian James Tinney observed that homosexual blacks like Jacob are often caught in the cross-fire between allegiance to their racial heritage and emerging gay communities:

> Since the sixties, there has been a growing emphasis on the wholeness and self-determination of the Black community wherever it is located. This has meant a visibly increased sense of loyalty to Black institutions and Black social cohesiveness. Similarly, since the seventies, there has been a growing emphasis on the existence of the gay community in whatever city it is found. This has meant growing support for lesbian and gay institutions. Yet Black lesbians and gays have often found themselves ''caught in the middle'' (so to speak) since the ''two-ness'' of identity (to use a term of W. E. B. DuBois) reflected in being both Black and gay was not wholly approved in either the Black or gay communities. To maintain comfortability in the Black community, particularly in those places that cultivate Black culture and Black solidarity, many

have felt a need to downplay their homosexuality. . . . And in order to maintain comfortability in the gay community, others have felt a need to downplay their Blackness.[23]

This need to downplay one's race or sexuality was reflected in the differing biographies among the black males who participated in this study. As Jacob's biography portrays, despite accusations from some that he was "too white," blackness was the core of his identity. As a black adolescent, Jacob assumed a responsibility to his race: president of the junior class, leader of the bus boycott, class valedictorian. The allure to gay pornography was secondary to his interest in black studies. From that afternoon in Mrs. Green's classroom to the bus boycott to his first meeting of Black Together, Jacob's commitment and identification with his fellow blacks has been unswerving. Asked to choose between "being black and being gay," Jacob unhesitantly answered, "I'd choose to be black. I'm proud of my black heritage. I wouldn't trade it for anything." Three other male participants also primarily identified themselves as black: Irwin, Franklin, and Malcolm. Irwin, for example, commenting on the difficulty of being gay in the black community, remarked:

> I'm black. I am going to remain black. I prefer being black although you have a disadvantage because of the color of your skin. You have to work harder, sleep less, and eat less to achieve and to be recognized. In my society, it's all right to see a white gay person. You would accept that as opposed to seeing a black gay person in a black society. The majority of black men are bullies. They don't want to be confronted with being gay. They call them "faggots" or "hunks." They won't say "sissy" because sissy sounds too pretty.

Unlike Jacob or Irwin, Nathaniel downplays what he (and popular culture) has constructed as his black identity. "I just don't get into break dancing. I never did get into Fat Boys strings. I don't get into sprayed t-shirts. I don't like rap. I'm not a part of them." Similarly, Grant identifies himself less with skin color and more with homosexuality. "The ideal situation would be for me to be white and gay in the South," he discloses.

The differences in primary identity between Jacob and Grant or Nathaniel and Irwin are imperfectly captured in the distinction made by some black scholars and observers between "gay-blacks" and "black-gays":

> Gay blacks are people who identify first as being gay and who usually live outside the closet in predominantly white gay communities. . . . Black gays, on the other hand, view our racial heritage as primary and frequently live "bisexual front lives" within Black neighborhoods. . . . It would be wonderful if the two groups could meet, communicate, and share one another's strengths. Unfortunately, gay Blacks are usually so mesmerized by and so assimilated into the white gay culture that Black gays tend to write them off as hopelessly lost and confused. Black gays are often so strongly into our African-American identity that we would rather die than be honest enough with our homosexuality to deal with it openly.[24]

These observations are documented in a dissertation written by black clinical psychologist Julius Johnson. During the late seventies, Johnson studied 60 black men whose primary identification rested with their skin color or sexuality. While both groups viewed the larger African-American community as unsupportive, he found black-gay men, like Jacob, more likely to date other blacks and to be less open about their homosexuality. Conversely gay-black men, like Grant, generally dated white men and became assimilated into the white-gay culture. Of the seven black males who shared their experiences as sexual rebels, four of those — Franklin, Irwin, Malcolm, and Jacob — could be classified as black-gay men. Interestingly, with the exception of Jacob, all of these men were from poor and working class families. The three men whose primary identity was closer to the gay lifestyle and community — Nathaniel, Grant, and Heyward — had middle class backgrounds. The reasons for adopting one identity over another, however, is more complex than simply family socio-economic status. Grant is a useful example.

Regularly frequenting gay white bars, dating white men, and preferring a white-gay identity, Grant is a gay-black man. The basis for his identity is situational. According to Grant, there are limited options available to homosexual black males in the South. Unlike Johnson's San Francisco-based sample, South Carolina has no identifiable black, homosexual organizations. "If you're black and want to exclusively date blacks you may find yourself alone a great deal of the time," Grant warns. Noting the difference of cultural climate between Columbia and Washington, DC (a metropolitan but still very Southern community), Grant observes:

> I didn't hear about a gay rights movement in South Carolina the whole time I lived here. When I moved to Washington they were having a street festival at DuPont Circle. It would not be unusual to see two men walking down the street holding hands. If gays did something like that here they'd be lynched, mobbed, or have rocks thrown at them. The gay scene in South Carolina is secretive and private.

Thus, Grant attributes his primarily gay identity to the isolation experienced in the rural South. This point is echoed by free-lance writer John Soares: "Chances of finding an active and productive social life in the black gay community are far better in key cities with large black populations than in cities and areas sparsely populated by black people."[25]

Though Grant is reasonably well integrated into the predominantly white Southern gay community, he remains closeted in his African-American community. He leaves the door open for his entry into a black heterosexual lifestyle:

> I'm a realist. If I'm going into politics I think I would have to get married. For the sake of companionship and emotional stability, I could easily see myself rejecting everything that I've gone through and trying to lead a straight life. I can see myself married to a lesbian — "a marriage of convenience."

Grant's ambivalence toward his constructed gay identity and Jacob's hesitancy to openly identify himself as a gay man are different than Royce's decision to remain closeted in his small up-state hometown. The politics played by Royce and the rules of the game experienced by Jacob or Grant are different. This difference is rooted in the varying intersections of racial and class boundaries. As Julius Johnson comments, "To be vested in that [Third World] community is by definition to be political. Blacks who move very heavily into the gay bar scene tend to move out of the black community."[26] Thus, homosexual blacks who work within African-American communities to expand the social menu for blacks often remain covert. But, as Johnson further notes, "Black gay men do not see their covertness as being closeted."[27] The construction of their sexual identities is integrally connected with their understanding of being a black male in the South.

Frantz Fanon, the author of *Black Skin, White Masks*, wrote: "Without a Negro past, without a Negro future, it was impossible for me to live my Negrohood. Not yet white, no longer wholly black, I was damned."[28] From his childhood memories of Mrs. Green's classroom and the Star Crystal to the bus boycott and the formation of Black Together, Jacob has maintained his African-American identity while gaining entry into the white world of politics and commerce. Jacob has not lost his sense of black history, black community, or black identity. For other black males interviewed in this study, however, the principal boundary line over which daily battles of oppression and prejudice are fought is sexuality, not race. The allure of Dupont Circle for Grant or the desirability of inter-racial dating for Nathaniel is more potent than establishing a primary identity as a black man. The black men highlighted in this chapter have re-drawn their boundaries of identity differently. These boundaries reflect the differing influences and emphases on race, class, and sexuality. These identities constructed from their understanding of race, class, and sexuality pose problems as well as present possibilities.

Some, like the expatriate Fishbelly in Wright's *The Long Dream*, seek escape from their African-American identity while others, like Ralph Kabnis in Toomer's *Cane*, struggle with the ambiguity of black identity in the South. As Jean Toomer realized, these identities separate people from one another and, however re-drawn, reflect a fragmentation of self out of harmony with being. Thus, "Mr. Costyve Duditch," travelling the world at whim, is free from the responsibilities of life but remains bounded by his spiritual rootlessness. Such journeys afford no opportunity for self-knowledge, for the boundaries of mechanical thinking remain.

REFERENCE NOTES

1. Beame, 1982c:55.

2. The black middle class in America has been the subject of careful study by a number of scholars during this century. See, for example: Blackwell, 1975; Durant and Louden, 1986; Frazier, 1925; 1939; 1949; 1957a; Kronus, 1971; Landry, 1987.

3. Frazier, 1939:79. See also: Frazier, 1968b.

4. Berry and Blassingame, 1982; Billingsley, 1976; Frazier, 1939.

5. Frazier, 1957b:297.

6. Durant and Louden, 1986; Landry, 1987. Nevertheless, as reports from the National Urban League document, this expansion has not equaled the expansion of the white middle class nor has it eliminated the vast numbers of black Americans who comprise the underclass of the black community.

7. Durant and Louden, 1986:261.

8. Clarke, 1983:206.

9. Soares, 1979:265.

10. Selzer and Smith, 1985.

11. Huguley, 1987.

12. Monk, 1987:5A.

13. Wyatt-Brown, 1982:22.

14. Page, 1987.

15. Huguley, 1987:16A.

16. LeBlanc, 1987:14A.

17. Associated Press, 1987a:15A.

18. Associated Press, 1987a:15A.

19. Though black voter turnout in the 17 southern states has risen to 42.5 percent, in South Carolina election day turnout by black voters is near the bottom at 29.1 percent (Associated Press, 1987b).

20. Tuten, 1987.

21. Stuart, 1987:8B.

22. Stuart, 1987:8B.

23. Tinney, 1986:72-73.

24. Smith, 1986:226-227.

25. Soares, 1979:264.

26. Beame, 1982c:26. For a detailed analysis see J. Johnson (1981).

27. Beame, 1982c:26.

28. Fanon, 1967:138.

VANTAGE POINT THREE

Homosexuality and Southern Families

We all grow up with the weight of history on us. Our ancestors dwell in the attics of our brains as they do in the spiraling chains of knowledge hidden in every cell of our bodies.

Shirley Abbott, *Womenfolks*[1]

The War of Secession destroyed the Old South. Its culture, though, is preserved within Southern families — black and white. Thus, challenge to the integrity of Southern families undermines the very foundation of Southern society. Homosexuality is such a challenge.

As a black lesbian, Obie's life story is one of strained and lost relationships as she challenges the authority of her father, questions the submissiveness of her mother, and hides her homosexual feelings. The structure and covenants in a black family, the "threat" of women-loving women to its stability, and the relationship between a mother and her daughter are discussed in Chapter 7. The integrity of the family is no less important in Terry's biography. However, he explores his homosexuality and constructs his sexual identity within the framework of family interests and traditions. Chapter 8 examines the multiple meanings that honor has for three gay sons of the Confederacy and their varying relationships with their parents.

From the vantage point of the family we view Obie's and Terry's biographies. A theme in both stories is reconciling the individual interests with the tradition of the family. Beneath the veneer of ethnic restaurants, high-tech industry, and interstate cloverleafs of the New South, there rest the underlying social codes of the Old South.[2] Family rituals foster codes such as honor, respectful politeness, and tolerance of eccentricity as its members negotiate ties of intimacy among one another.[3]

For those who are unable or unwilling to adopt these social codes, being a sexual rebel is difficult, perhaps needlessly so. Thus, like Caddy in *The Sound and The Fury* who rebels against family codes, disregards social taboos, and acts on her feelings, Obie lives with the possibility of being cast out by family and friends. She may become, in Mary Daly's phrase, "A Terrible Woman" whose objective is "not zeal for martyrdom, but zest for life."[4] There are others, however, like Terry, who appreciate the distinction between the domestic and public worlds and who carefully walk the tightrope between the merely idiosyncratic and the abnormal, between the flamboyant and the brazen, and between satire and contempt. Of course, respectful compliance with family and social codes does not guarantee a pleasant childhood. These portraits illustrate the complexity of Southern experience and challenge the image of the South as "a simple land of catfish and honeysuckle."[5]

REFERENCE NOTES

1. Abbott, 1983:1.
2. In a recent update of his 1960 study of the South, sociologist John Shelton Reed (1986b:91-92) concludes, "Cultural differences that were largely due to Southerners' lower incomes and educational levels, to their predominantly rural and small-town residence, to their concentration in agricultural and low-level industrial occupations—those differences were smaller in the 1960s than they had been in the past, and they are smaller still in the 1980s. . . . On the other hand, most of those differences that were persisting in the 1960s are still with us, as predicted. That persistence, I believe, supports the argument that these are cultural differences of a quasi-ethnic sort, differences with their origins in the different histories of American regional groups, not merely epi-phenomena of different levels of current economic and demographic 'modernization.'"
3. Bossard and Boll, 1950; Cheal, 1988.
4. Daly, 1984:245.
5. Fields, 1983:74.

Chapter 7

Questioning Authority
in a Southern Black Family

OBIE AND THE BREAKING OF TIES

Went out last night, had a great big fight,
Everything seemed to go on wrong;
I looked up, to my surprise,
The gal I was with was gone

Where she went, I don't know
I mean to follow everywhere she goes;
Folks said "I'm crooked." I didn't know where she took it,
I want the whole world to know:

They say I do it, Ain't nobody caught me
Sure got to prove it on me;
Went out last night with a crowd of my friends,
must've been women, 'cause I don't like no men.

Ma Rainey, "Prove it on Me Blues"[1]

Obie's family traces its ancestry back to 18th century Savannah where their forebears arrived on ships from Africa's west coast. During the past two centuries her ancestors have experienced the pain of being separated from kin during slavery, the joy and dashed hopes of Reconstruction, the tyranny of Jim Crow, and the promises of the Great Society in a still segregated South. Throughout those two centuries, Obie's family survived. During the past two generations her family has modestly prospered. At her parents' middle class home, resting on their fireplace mantle, are family portraits. There is a picture of her great-grandfather, Virgil, who scraped together enough money to purchase the family land. To its right is a portrait of Obie's paternal grandmother, Louise, whose prudent saving and iron determination allowed her two sons to attend college. The youngest of these two sons, Vernon, is Obie's father.

Vernon has a white collar job in the Federal government. His income is sufficient to allow Adele, his wife of 27 years and mother of his three children, to work at home. Obie proclaims:

> I've always considered myself to be raised by one parent, my mother. Whenever I make a major decision I think about her and how she is going to perceive me. And, how she is going to perceive me is largely affected by how others are going to perceive me. Appearances, I've learned from my folks, are everything.

Obie's relationship with her father has been strained for as long as she could remember. "I didn't feel like I could talk to him about anything. The way he is, if you say anything to him then you're questioning his authority. Sometimes I do question his authority because he's so obnoxious." No one else in the household dares to challenge Vernon's authority. The relationship between Obie's parents is troubled: "Mom never talks to Dad about her feelings or concerns," Obie reveals. "My mother has friends, but they're gossip friends. But she doesn't have true friends that she can rely on. Dad has no friends at all. He can't even talk to my mother."

Adele's submissive behavior to Vernon has frustrated Obie's unconditional love for her mother and cemented a distrust for her father.

> My dad dismisses family life. He's on the road and when he comes home he doesn't speak to us too much. But, in our religion [Jehovah's Witnesses] the father is supposed to take the lead in instructing, raising, and disciplining his children. My mom has always gotten a lot of flack whenever she tries to take over his role. But, the church elders don't understand that if anything is to get done Mom has to do it. My mom is always submissive to my dad who is a church elder. She would never

go to the other elders and say, "I don't think my husband should be an elder since we are not doing family things in the right way." You don't air your dirty linen in public and you sure as hell don't go up against your husband.

As a child, Obie was the picture of a happy, little girl with her braided hair and silky black skin, her sweet tooth and her giggles. She was popular among her classmates, and enjoyed playing jack fish, jungle gym, and jump rope with them during recess. The occasional ridicule she received was for the people with whom she associated.

A friend of mine, she and I would go and play in the kindergarten yard. After a while these guys — I've always had trouble with boys — they were teasing us. They were saying things like, "Aren't they cute? Look at the two little girls. Aren't they cute? Don't they look sweet? Don't they make a nice couple? Don't let your parents see you playing together. No wonder the little boys don't play with you." I didn't know why they were teasing us but she seemed to get her feelings hurt. It didn't bother me.

The first time Obie heard the word "queer" was in third grade:

I had a friend who lived near me. Max was real nice looking. But, he looked more like a girl than a guy. He had real nice hair. He was Lebanese. He had pale skin, dark, curly hair, blue-green eyes, and nice eye lashes. He used to wear pastel shirts. We used to play together. This other boy, Lance, kept calling him "queer." I thought "queer" meant "funny" because we used to say things were queer or odd all the time at my house. But Lance said, "Isn't he queer?" and then he asked me, "Why don't you run off with your girlfriend?" Max got really upset, pouted, and ran away. Some of the other kids said they were going to tell the teacher because Lance was saying bad words. I asked them, "What do you mean by queer?" They said, "Sissy, fag." But that didn't mean anything to me at the time.

Obie did not make the connection between "queer" and feelings toward the same sex until the fifth grade. For part of that year, Patrick, a college student, assisted her teacher. "He would come to school two or three days a week," Obie remembers. "Most of the things he did were games and art." One day,

> Patrick asked Lance to volunteer to help him teach this game. The boy said, "I'm not going to come up there with you." Patrick said, "Stand up or I'm going to send you to the principal's office." So, Lance stood up. Patrick tried to show him what he was to do. Then, the boy said, "Take your hand off me, you sissy." Patrick got really mad and turned red. "What are you talking about?" he asked. He told the boy if he wasn't going to cooperate to leave and go to the principal's office. The boy said, "Okay, Miss Priss. I'll do what you want," and he left. Patrick looked like he was about to cry. Then the teacher came back and said, "I saw him going down to the office. What happened?" She and Patrick started talking quietly and the kids started talking. One boy whispered, "Yeah. He's a fag." His sister replied, "My mom knows him and he really is gay. He has a boyfriend and they live together."

After school, Obie and Ginny, Patrick's sister, were walking home together, hugging one another, and singing. Suddenly, Lance sneaked up from behind and yelled, "I see it's contagious. You have the same disease as Patrick. Why don't you get some straight people in your family?" Obie recalls:

> That is the first time I heard the word "straight" used in that way. I didn't like anything Lance ever did. He used to call me "nigger" and things like that. He would just hit me because it was funny. I went all the way through high school with him. He was really ignorant.

Since her parents were Jehovah's Witnesses, Obie was not permitted to play with many of her friends after school. The family would attend church three times a week: Sunday for two hours; Tuesday for one hour; and, Thursday for two hours. "They were real strict," she notes. "You're not supposed to curse, so we couldn't associate with the bad kids who used that language. My friends were either those who Mom knew or who were Jehovah's Witnesses.''

In junior high school, Obie was considered a bright but stubborn student by her teachers. Her marginal grades reflected an unwillingness "to work up to my capacity. I could have done better but I just played around a lot.'' Unlike most of the other junior high school girls, Obie didn't date boys.

> There always have been guys who I have been friends with, who I was half interested in, and who liked me a lot. But, whenever I would spend even 15 minutes with them I wouldn't feel right. Not that they weren't fun to be around but I couldn't kid myself into thinking that I was attracted to them.

Her lack of interest in boys was not questioned because of her membership in the Jehovah's Witnesses: "Most of my friends, other than the ones I had at school, were Witnesses. What they teach or believe is that kids don't date unless they're really contemplating marriage. I didn't think of dating as a social sort of thing.''

Obie first engaged in homosexual activity with her friends, Lorraine and Shelly, at the age of 13. "I didn't think anything was wrong with it,'' she recalls. I didn't feel bad or guilty. I liked it. And, usually when it happened the other person initiated it.'' The following year, Shelly had a talk with Obie. "She told me what we were doing was bad. Soon, she started saying things about me like I was square because she was liking boys.'' With the exception of Lorraine, the other girls broke ties with Obie. A short time later, she and Lorraine also underwent a painful separation. She recalls:

> Her father had gotten cast out of the Congregation because he was bisexual. If you are baptized and you do something against doctrine then you get "disfellowship'' which means you get cut off from family and church. Ninth grade was when she and I were being separated by my parents. I was feeling bad about that because she was really the only friend that I had. Lorraine moved right after ninth grade. For a long time after she moved I didn't have any friends. It wasn't that I

couldn't, but I was just kind of in a depression. I was sad because she had gone.

Though Obie was not ashamed of her emerging feelings for other women, she did not handle the stress of isolation well. Obie was depressed, contemplated suicide on more than one occasion, and attempted it once. Though she spoke to other students in school and at the Kingdom Hall, she didn't have any close ties with anyone, including her family.

After a year in isolation, Obie made friends with two white classmates: Jimmy-Robert and Beau:

> They were different from everyone else. Everyone called them "punks"; they shaved their heads. People talked about them, too. They called them "queer" and stuff. But, it wasn't like we really discussed it. I didn't know that for a fact. In fact, they didn't know it for a fact.

Unlike Obie, they were often subjected to intimidation and harassment by their fellow students. Beau, in particular, was having a difficult time in high school. He decided to write a paper in English about homosexuality. Obie offered her help. She advised him to write about those who refused to allow children with AIDS to attend school — not homosexuality. But, "he was stubborn and he was very angry. A lot of people were picking on him. He had not even admitted to himself that he was gay. The paper was very emotional." A few days later in the corridor Ms. Bowman, Beau's English teacher, invited Obie into her classroom for a private conversation.

> "Sometimes I really wonder about you and your friends." Ms. Bowman began to laugh. She told me that Beau had just written this paper about homosexuality. "Now, Obie, I'm not advocating homosexuality and I'm not against it. But, reading that paper really made me want to hit him on the head. Beau's paper is so negative. He sounds like a raving queen."

Through her friendship with Beau and Jimmy-Robert, Obie was introduced to Connie, a white girl whose dress and reputation

placed her among the school's outcasts. Obie had already acknowledged her sexual feelings for females before meeting Connie in her
junior year of high school. Connie was also interested in a romantic
relationship. Soon she and Connie began dating and within two
months were "going steady." Though no one, except for Jimmy-
Robert and Beau, knew for certain of their relationship, some students within the school began labelling them "dykes." Obie remembers: "We all used to hang together. Other students always
used to say, 'Look at the dykes.' So we were always the 'dykes and
queers.' But, we didn't care. It didn't matter if we were or we
weren't."

These incidents sparked many private discussions between Obie
and Connie. Obie remembers one of these: "We were wondering if
we were deciding too fast. If we really should just not label ourselves and just experiment. Connie was always one to say, 'I don't
think we should knock it [heterosexuality] until we've tried it.'"
This air of caution on Connie's part was exacerbated by Obie's
parents. The two were not allowed to visit one another because
Connie's father also had experienced disfellowship by the Jehovah's Witnesses. Obie's parents constantly badgered Connie to become a Witness for the sake of her family and discouraged Obie's
friendship with her. By the spring of Obie's junior year she and
Connie decided to stop seeing each other "not only for our parents'
sake" but because of different expectations about their relationship:

> We saw each other and had sex but it wasn't exclusive. I was
> free to see someone else and she was, too. And, that was what
> happened. I didn't choose to see someone else because I really
> wanted it to be exclusive. She wanted to see someone else — a
> guy. She was feeling guilty and bothered by her sexuality.

Though they continued to be friends, their special relationship
ended. Obie plummeted into another depression. "It was like any
time I would ever meet someone," she remembers, "the personal
tie was broken."

At home Obie was also tiring of family life. She felt, "My dad
didn't seem to be particularly concerned about me and my mom

didn't want the same things for me that I wanted." Obie's depression intensified. Her psychology teacher, Mr. Martin, asked Obie to stay after class one day. Mr. Martin was "the type that seemed to me I could trust." She continues:

> He was saying something to me about, "Obie you seem depressed all the time. Is there anything I can do to help you? What I really think you need is a boyfriend." I said, "You mean a girlfriend." He goes "You're really serious aren't you?" I said, "Yeah." He asked me "Do you just not think about guys or do you just not like guys?" I said, "I like them. I like to talk to them. But, I just don't think of them that much sexually or emotionally." Then he sighed, "I guess that's your choice."

Asked why she did not seek Mr. Martin's help or that of one of the school's guidance counselors, Obie exclaimed, "You're kidding! They were dumb and very narrow-minded." Despite the rumor around school that one of the counselors was a lesbian, Obie did not want to have anything to do with these adults.

> Mrs. Watkins was supposedly a lesbian and a witch. You know how kids are; they say things. I really didn't have any idea if she was a lesbian but I knew for a fact that she was married and had kids. She wasn't the type that I trusted. It's like if you're on a street corner and you don't have a watch. You're not going to ask the first person you see wearing a watch. You're going to think about who you will ask.

Obie missed a lot of school that year as a result of her bouts with depression and conflicts within her family. In order to enter school as a senior the following year, Obie attended summer school. "I remember sitting in summer school and Connie was all that I would think about." As summer neared its end, Obie completed her coursework only to find that Connie was moving to another state.

> I got really down and depressed. I wanted, of course, for her
> to stay. Before they left I wasn't able to see her. I hadn't seen
> her for almost a month. I knew tentatively they were going but
> I really didn't get to see her and say goodbye. She didn't leave
> an address. It wasn't good.

Obie traveled to Florida to escape from her problems. During her
two week visit, she stayed with her relatives and spent some time
with Denise, whose brother was Obie's uncle by marriage. Denise
had been "wild" ever since Obie had known her. "We were just
friends, but not just friends," Obie wryly smiles. Denise's mother
was a strict Jehovah's Witness. "She's a real snoopy type. She
always tells me that I'm not living right and that God is not going to
have a place for me." On Obie's first visit at Denise's house she
learned that Denise was about to be baptized. "Her parents gave her
an ultimatum: become baptized or get out of the house. Her parents
had taken her bedroom door off its hinges. She had no privacy.
They scanned her mail and they tapped her phone. I'm like, 'You
can't want to be baptized.' But, she goes 'I really want to.'" A
week later, Obie spent another evening with Denise. They had a
long talk:

> She was crying. She gave me this Jehovah's Witness book that
> had a chapter on "Homosexuality and Masturbation." I was
> dying. I thought this was the funniest thing I had ever seen.
> She told me, "I've had to change myself. I have to make my
> life right. There's more to life than having a good time. This is
> not what God wanted." I said, "What God wanted never
> seemed to be a major concern of yours before." Then she
> cried some more.

Returning home for the beginning of school, Obie still felt bad
about herself and her broken ties.

> It seemed like I couldn't be where I wanted to be. I wasn't
> happy in school. I didn't feel like I was going to go anywhere.
> My parents were hassling me then about what I was going to
> do. I said I wanted to go to art school. They didn't want to pay

for it and they didn't want me to go. They said, "Obie, you can do something better with your life like be a missionary."

Obie quit school on her eighteenth birthday and enrolled in adult education to "escape all the bull shit" at school. Her mother was bitterly disappointed. "I always took it for granted that all my kids would finish high school, would wear the mortar board, and would walk down the aisle," Obie recalls her mother saying. "Thanks for lightening my load," Obie responded. "That's not something one takes for granted. Not everyone is into the pomp and circumstance of graduation, Mom." Though Obie regrets making her mother unhappy, she is glad she dropped out of school.

Quitting school made it more difficult for Obie to live at home. Her parents continued to express their concern about the people with whom she associated and her apparent lack of concern with the family image. She began to see Paul, a foreign-exchange student, regularly. The two shared much in common including their homosexuality. In March, Obie learned Paul had been diagnosed with AIDS. She spent a great amount of time during the next few months "being supportive." Despite Paul's repeated requests for Obie to move into his apartment and Obie's interest in doing so, she didn't want to cause more problems within her family:

> I thought, "If I separate myself from them now then that means I can't ever go back." Moving in with a gay guy would have separated me from my family permanently. For my parents to know that I was living with someone who had AIDS, that would have killed them. They would have gotten the police to bodily remove me from his place.

Before Paul's departure for Europe at the end of the summer, he invited Obie to come with him. Again, she was torn between her allegiance to her family and her affection for Paul. After prodding, cajoling, and begging, Paul finally convinced Obie to go with him. In order to prevent her family from interfering, they devised a plan. Tickets for a Saturday IceCapade show were given to her family. Obie recollects: "Paul came by to get me when they were gone to IceCapades. I panicked. I was ready but then I chickened out. I just knew that would be it with my family, that that would be the last time I would see my mom, and that things would never be the same between us." Paul left without Obie.

During the next three months pressure mounted on Obie. Paul telephoned Obie twice a week. An underlying sadness accompanied each conversation. Though he had not shown any AIDS-related complications, Paul was anxious for Obie to visit him. Obie was completing her GED and searching for work. She was also helping Beau cope with his homosexual feelings while her mother was accusing them of being lovers: "If you move out with Beau and it becomes common knowledge that you are living with a man. . . ." Vernon was working out of state and was gone for weeks at a time leaving Adele to attend to family matters. Two weeks before Thanksgiving Vernon returned; Paul was waiting to hear of Obie's decision for her to visit him; Beau's father had just thrown him out of the house; and Obie's GED coursework had ground to a halt. She remembers:

> Paul was supposed to call me Tuesday to hear of my decision of whether I wanted to go. He called me on Monday instead and asked if I had made up my mind. He sounded like he had given up and just couldn't take it anymore. I was still talking with Paul when my dad came home. He put his things in his room. He didn't say hello or anything. He had been gone a month. He was about to walk out when Mom goes, "Where are you going?" He didn't say anything. So I said, "Mom asked you a question." He yelled, "I'm going out." I said, "Gee, Daddy. You just came home. You've been gone a month. You haven't even spoken to us. We only want to know where you're going." He walked out. Mom went to bed crying. I was like, "I can't take this anymore." That just pushed me over and I took a bottle of depressants. I woke up in the hospital three days later in intensive care.

Following Obie's attempted suicide, Adele cautiously watched her every move. She pleaded with Obie for the sake of the family never to attempt such a terrible stunt again. "I tried to help her understand why I tried to commit suicide. But it was so alien to her. Mom buries her emotions. She suppresses her feelings about her and Dad." Adele relentlessly pressed Obie to attend Congregational meetings and to become baptized. Obie describes her thoughts when deciding whether to accompany her mother to such meetings:

> I don't want to go, but in the end I will go, because I know if I don't go what's going to happen. I know what's going to happen to her at the meeting and what's she going to say to me when she comes back from the meeting. If I don't go she will come back and say, "Well, BB asked about you and so did Eloise and Rudy." Now these are three people who don't care or give a shit about me. These are three people who, if I am there will not smile in my direction, but will sneak up to me and say, "Oh! It's so nice to see that you dropped in for a meeting. What brought you here? Where have you been?" I tell my mom, "The only reason that they ask you about me is that they want you to tell them where I am so that they can have some gossip to spread." She'll just go on saying something like, "Brother Leroy's talk dealt with such and such. I thought it was really beneficial. You should have heard it." Then I'll say something like, "I'm glad you liked it Mommy and that you found it beneficial to you. But, it's really not beneficial to me. If I wanted to hear it I would have gone." And, then she goes, "I'm trying to share with you, Obie." I reply, "Why don't you share with your husband?" "Well, he don't like to talk about it," she says. I interrupt, "You come in here trying to force these views on me but you can't even get your husband, who supposedly is religious and an elder, to talk to you about this shared belief." She says, "Obie, you're being divisive. Think of the family."

Now, 19, Obie has a better opinion of herself. She has already disclosed her sexual identity to her close friends. Reflecting upon her self-disclosure, Obie remarks, "It was pretty easy to come out to my friends. But, if I was able to come out to my parents I feel like I would be a lot more comfortable with myself. Right now I feel like there is this cloud hanging over me." Obie's difficulty in "coming out" to her parents is complicated by the contradictory sets of relationships among family members. "I want to tell them but it seems so impossible. If I told my mother that Beau and I were living together and sleeping together she would be able to handle that. That, to her, is normal. That's what sinners do. But, being gay is going against nature; it's going against God; it's going against the family."

Caught in the cross-fire of adolescence, growing up gay in the South is complicated by Obie's contradictory relationship with her parents: she has little respect for her father but she yearns for his attention; she fears losing her mother's love but will not mold herself into her mother's image. In candor, Obie says:

> Every morning I get up and say, "Obie, today's the day that you're going to tell Mom you're gay and then pack your shit and leave." I just can't do it. I love my mom even though she makes me sick. And everything that I have ever done seems to have been what she didn't want me to do — like not completing high school and marching in that graduation ceremony. A lot of times when I get really down it has nothing to do with me but it has a lot to do with her. Things that I have not done or have done have been because of her. I don't want to become what she wants me to be but I still want her to accept me. I want so much for her to be proud of me. I know there are certain things that won't make her proud of me. Being gay is one of them.

If the importance of family ties and Obie's fear of losing her mother's love were not so pronounced then coming out would be less difficult. As she works through this difficulty, Obie secretly reads lesbian and gay books. In each book she finds a new insight, a memorable passage, or an admired character. Recently, her mother found one of these books in Obie's closet. A cat and mouse conversation followed:

> She asked me, "Do you want to tell me something?" I go, "About what?" "I found a book that I don't think that I would advise you to read laying in your closet. Do you want me to show it to your father?" I say, "No. He never discusses books

he reads with me." Upset, Mom says, "Well, I'll let you discuss it with him if you want to."

Despite such incidents, Obie's parents appear unaware of her homosexuality and the problems associated with it.

> You know parents blind themselves. They see what they want to see and they observe what they want to observe. My mom can blind herself to my dad's drinking. The church elders can blind themselves to the dissent in our home. As long as it is not confronted everything is okay. As long as it is not in the public eye. As long as people don't know about it, it won't hurt us.

COMMENTARY

Conflicts between adolescents and parents often explode into family crises when they expose wounds hidden from the everyday, healing sun of trust and honesty. Obie's repeated confrontations with her father and mother, added to her unwillingness to share an important part of herself, strained family relationships and placed mounting pressure on Obie. As a lesbian struggling within her minority culture, itself marginalized by the dominant white culture, Obie's story is a series of battles fought out on the front lines of a Southern black family. It is a battle over the integrity of the African-American family. It reflects the struggles of black women and of women who love women. It is a test of wills between mother and daughter and of their capacity to love.

The Integrity of the Black Family

As discussed in Chapter 3, the church and the family have been the bulwark of the African-American community as generation following generation have confronted challenges to the black spirit.[2] From the economic hardships during Reconstruction to the collapse of the Southern Depression economy and the social turmoil of the Civil Rights movement, African-American family structures have evolved. Obie's is the latest generation of a Southern black family that survived and modestly prospered during the past nine generations.

Obie's family is not a haven from a heartless world; it is a social arrangement propped up by private truces. Some of these were forged years ago when the roles of husband and wife in a middle class black family were less ambiguous. Other unspoken covenants have been made in the course of their 27 year marriage, as two struggling parents coped with a daughter who seldom refrained from challenging the apparent hypocrisy of these covenants. Though Obie is a child of a two-parent family, Vernon leaves the day-to-day operations of his family in the hands of Adele. When he is not on the road, Vernon prefers to spend his time with the men or reading in the solitude of his room. Contemptuously, Obie declares that her father "dismisses family life" as her mother quietly assumes family responsibilities.

This husband/wife pattern parallels the study of 38 Southern black families in the mid-sixties, and challenges the stereotype of the matriarchal household. Virginia Young states, "men are usually accorded or assume authority in the home. Women act as though their husbands had authority . . ."[3] Thus, while Obie's family biography does not correspond to the popularized version of the unstable black family headed by a single, strong-willed mother,[4] Obie's family structure more truly represents the Southern norm.[5] Unlike many black Southerners who participated in the Great Northern Migration, Obie's parents have steadfastly maintained their Southern roots and values.[6]

During the past two generations, this two-parent family model has changed markedly as the proportion of households headed by females has increased dramatically. Sociologist Robert Staples concludes that the decline of the nuclear black family is a reflection of the "greater sexual permissiveness, alternate family lifestyles, increased divorce rates, and reductions in the fertility rate.'"[7] Lamenting this decline, he states:

> The basis of a stable family rests on the willingness and ability of men and women to marry, bear and rear children, and fulfill socially prescribed familial roles. In the case of women, those roles have traditionally been defined as the carrying out of domestic functions such as cooking and cleaning, giving birth to children and socializing them, and providing sexual gratifi-

cation, companionship, and emotional support to their husbands. There is abundant evidence that Black women are willing and able to fulfill those roles. Conversely, the roles of men in the family are more narrowly confined to that of economic provider and family leader. There are indications that a majority of Black American males cannot implement those roles.[8]

Staples cites homosexuality as one of the reasons for the black male's inability to fulfill his role. This "shortage of desirability of Black males in the marriage pool," is augmented by '800,000 Black men [who] are not available to heterosexual Black women.'"[9] The existence of black lesbians is not mentioned in Staple's assessment of the state of the black family. The fact that many lesbians and gay men marry and have children is another subtlety often lost upon crusaders for the African-American family.[10] Further, this analysis fails to place the decline of the black family within a larger structural framework in which racism, sexism, classism, and heterosexism intersect.

These perspectives, however, have been challenged by a number of black women. Psychologist June Butts reminds readers of *Ebony* magazine: "Individual homosexuals have been a part of the Black race during our entire history on this continent. We have worked together, worshipped together, and together faced loneliness — all within the context of Black family life — and we have survived as the Black Family to this very day."[11] Furthermore, Carrie McCray argues that these rigid family roles have seldom been found in the African-American family:

Harsh social realities have made flexibility of role a necessity for Black families. We could not live with the unrealistic societally determined rigid role prescriptions, which were not always applicable to us. For family survival in crises, the Black woman has often had to take on the role that carries out the instrumental function of the family. . . . In some groups in our society, male-female roles traditionally have been more distinct. The father has been the provider, protector, and disciplinarian; the mother's role has been that of a homemaker, taking care of the children and providing the emotional-expressive functions. However, historically, for most Black families this clear-cut distinction never existed.[12]

Arguing that blacks are ignorant about the sexual politics of their experiences and haunted by the mythology associated with each gender, Michelle Wallace in *Black Macho and the Myth of the Superwoman* challenged the myth of the satisfied black woman more than a decade ago:

> Though originally it was the white man who was responsible for the black woman's grief, a multiplicity of forces act upon her life now and the black man is one of the most important. The white man is downtown. The black man lives with her. He's the head of her church and may be the principal of her local school or even the mayor of the city in which she lives. She is the workhorse that keeps his house functioning, she is the foundation of his community, she raises his children, and she faithfully votes for him in elections, goes to his movies, reads his books, watches him on television, buys in his stores, solicits his services as doctor, lawyer, accountant. She has made it quite clear that she has no intention of starting a black woman's liberation movement. One would think she was satisfied, yet she is not.[13]

For crusaders of the family, blurring of sex roles or accepting homosexuality threatens family stability. This linkage between the integrity of the black family and African-American culture and the belief that transgressions of gender or sexual norms erode that integrity are at the heart of heterosexist and misogynist writings, ranging from *Soul on Ice* to "Black Woman." Such beliefs fuel negative attitudes about homosexuality within black churches, communities, and families.[14]

The conservative social attitude of African-Americans is not the only factor affecting Obie's struggle to selfhood.[15] Malcolm and Obie, who were expected to conform to rigid sex roles and to marry, shared a common religious background. The conservative attitudes expressed by both sets of parents were certainly aggravated by the Watchtower theology. Obie, too, was fearful of losing ties to her family, particularly her mother, whose rejection through disfellowship would have been devastating to both. Lacking any personal ties to other black lesbians, Obie would have been banished by her family and set adrift outside her African-American community. She states, "There are fewer reasons why a person who is black would want to acknowledge her homosexuality."

Obie's fear of losing her mother's love and disgracing her family shaped her most critical decisions, ranging from departing with Paul for Europe to the disclosing of her homosexuality to her parents. Obie perceives as inevitable a choice between cutting family ties or loving and living with another woman. Her dilemma is the silent tragedy within this Southern black family. She struggles to break the covenant of silence into which she and her parents have entered.

Women-Loving Women and the Black Family

Women have traditionally played an important role in the black family as well as the black culture and American society.[16] Seldom have their contributions been acknowledged. Even the most famous African-American women such as Sojourner Truth, the first black woman to publicly support women's rights, Ida Wells-Barnett, a journalist battling lynching atrocities, Zora Neale Hurston, the grandmother of modern black literature, Mary McLeod Bethune, the great Southern educator, Mary Church Terrrell, the founder of the National Association of Colored Women, and the talented playwright Lorraine Hansberry are often treated as nothing more than footnotes in the panorama of male-scripted history.[17] It should come as little surprise that the lesbianism or bisexuality of black women such as Ma Rainey, Bessie Smith, and Alice Dunbar-Nelson is all but forgotten.[18]

Though willing to acknowledge their dual oppression, black women have been less able and willing to go beyond their brothers', husbands', and fathers' struggle against racism. In the ground breaking book, *A Voice from the South*, Anna Cooper, a noted educator and civil rights activist, wrote in 1892, "The colored woman of today occupies, one may say, a unique position in this country. . . . She is confronted by both a woman question and a race problem, and is as yet an unknown or an unacknowledged factor in both.'"[19] These concerns of black women have since been acknowledged in plays such as *For Colored Girls*, novels such as *The Women of Brewster Place*, anthologies like *This Bridge Called My Back*, and popular works such as *Black Macho and the Myth of the Superwoman*.[20] Unlike Anna Cooper, who had argued that the profound differences of experiences and conditions between white and black women necessitated black women to fight within the overall black struggle, these works publicly challenged the black man's status in the community, in the family, and in the bedroom. As Jacquelyn Grant writes:

> [A]s long as the Black struggle refuses to acknowledge and deal with its sexism, the idea that women will receive justice from that struggle alone will never work. It will not work because Black women will no longer allow Black men to ignore their unique problems and needs in the name of some distorted view of the "liberation of the total community."[21]

The day-to-day struggles of distinctive black women occasionally have been portrayed by sensitive and gifted male writers.[22] There is, for example, the distant and unyielding welfare mother, Mrs. Thomas, in *Native Son*, the warm and affectionate Elizabeth Grimes dominated by her hypocritical minister-husband in *Go Tell It On the Mountain*, and the proud, religious, and strong-willed Mamma Hawkins in *The Soul Brothers and Sister Lou*.[23] These fictional characters mirror the real life worlds of African-American women as portrayed by Charles Willie in his descriptive case studies of 18 families.[24] There is, for example: the profoundly religious Gladys Fisher who with her husband of 28 years has raised eight children in a relationship characterized by love and equality; Coreen Jones who maintains a five-room apartment for her four children on her cleaning lady's wages and her grandmother's social security; and the middle-aged, fussy but understanding Mrs. Hines who teaches high school in the city but lives in the suburbs with her husband, the undisputed head of the household, and their three children.

These characters underscore the diversity of African-American families and the women who are their foundation. Obie's biography represents one of many unique stories that could be told. Sadly, the experience of women-loving-women in a black family has not been told in these novels or case studies. Perhaps this is due to the gender of the authors. Lesbianism, after all, is the most blatant challenge to the black male. Lesbian feminist writer Ann Schockley declares, "the independent woman-identified woman, the black lesbian, was a threat. Not only was she a threat to the projection of black male macho, but a *sexual* threat too — the utmost danger to the black male's institutionally designated roles as 'king of the lovers.'"[25] In contemporary novels written by African-American women, such as Alice Walker's *The Color Purple* and Toni Morrison's *Tar Baby*, the complexities and contradictions of being black, female, and lesbian are portrayed.[26] Celie in *The Color Purple* was psychologically and physically abused by her father and husband. Through her relationship with singer Sugar Avery she began to feel good again. These childhood feelings of low self-esteem were also evident in Obie's story. Supportive and loving female relationships, however, were absent. A female bond, evidenced between Nel and Sula in *Tar Baby*, was something Obie has sought in vain.

> [I]t was in dreams that the two girls had first met . . . so . . . they felt the ease and comfort of old friends. Because each had discovered years before that they were neither white nor male, and that all freedom and triumph was forbidden to them, they had set about creating something else to be. Their meeting was fortunate, for it let them use each other to grow on . . . they found in each other's eyes the intimacy they were looking for.[27]

Though Obie identified herself as a lesbian at the age of 16, the eyes of Lorraine and Connie never connected with her in intimacy. Obie's uncertain and abruptly ended relationships plummeted her into depressions. She was unwilling to pay the cost of family loss which would likely have enhanced her self-esteem and enabled her to enter into a supportive, loving relationship with another woman. Obie's deep depressions and suicidal behaviors reflect the inner suffering of a woman singing the blues in solitude and despair.

Another black participant in this study, Kimberly, recognized the costs of such isolation:

> You begin to doubt yourself. You begin to doubt your feelings. Are they really authentic? I think it's very unfair for young people to have to go through it. If there's no outlet, if there is no one there for them to talk to, what are they to do? A lot of people withdraw altogether. A person that could be a really beautiful person becomes a real sour person. They don't experience the joys of life.

Christine Carrington notes that those who fail to experience the joys of life, plummeting into depression and harboring low self-esteem, suffer the powerlessness unique to black women—"straight" or "gay"—in American society:

> [W]omen are more depression-prone than men because of their peculiar status in society. Women are powerless and oppressed as a group, a result of both sexism and traditional role socialization. . . . Critical to an examination of depression in Black women is the element of loss of self-esteem. . . . For some Black women, there is the task of generating all of the forces within them to repair their damaged self-esteem—the task of "healing their own wounds." Self-hate has to be replaced with self-love, indignity with dignity, depriving love objects with nurturing love objects, feelings of victimization with feelings of power and self-mastery.[28]

Obie's family lacks the trust and honesty for the healing of these wounds. Obie, though, clings to the *possibility* of love in an embattled family, rather than the *uncertainty* of lesbian love outside of it. She has yet to echo Ma Rainey's dare, "prove it on me," or to join the *For Colored Girls* chorus in singing "I found God in myself and I love her fiercely."[29] Paradoxically, such confidence can only be asserted by a woman who views herself no longer as a victim, and has realized that love of self cannot be conditioned upon love from others.

Mother-Daughter Relationships

Like Mamma Hawkins in *The Soul Brothers and Sister Lou*, Adele mixed her strong religious faith with her reluctance to see Obie assert her independence outside of the family. Obie hid her homosexual feelings as well as her feelings of love from her mother, while seldom refraining to chastise Adele's submissiveness to her husband, whom Obie despised. Obie's unresolved anger with her mother, her undercurrent of love for her, and the rejection of her father form the groundwork for a psychoanalytic interpretation of her lesbianism.

Popularized through psychoanalytic literature is the theoretical contention that a child's relationship and contact with parents significantly affects psychosexual development.[30] Lesbianism is said to result from the child's failure to turn away from the "mother-object," the inability to resolve her "Oedipus complex," strained parental relationships, or poor heterosexual experiences during childhood.[31] Thus, discovering at the age of three or four that she is physically inferior to the male ("penis envy"), Obie, according to traditional psychoanalytic theory, turns away in anger at her mother but fails to embrace her father. This latent mother-daughter attachment and overt rejection of the father is thought to lie at the heart of lesbianism.

While there is no empirical evidence to validate this psychoanalytic claim, there are studies that substantiate a difference in the quality of mother-daughter relationships for heterosexual and homosexual-identified women.[32] One study, for example, found that nearly one-quarter of the lesbian sample, compared to less than one percent of the heterosexual female sample, reported a poor mother-daughter relationship.[33] Similarly, there is some evidence to suggest that girls who recall their fathers as being detached or hostile are more likely to identify themselves as lesbian,[34] though these findings are far from universal.[25] Moreover, these studies report parent-daughter relationships in white families. A rare study comparing 75 black and 125 white lesbians reported black mothers more likely to be away from home than mothers of white lesbians (a likely effect of race and class), but failed to note the strength of the mother-daughter relationship.[36] Such research has led one scholar, in an exhaustive review, to assert: "There is no obvious conclusion to be drawn from the data available about the parental factors that may contribute to lesbian development. . . ."[37] This conclusion has been echoed by other researchers.[38]

Nevertheless, the mother-daughter theme weaves through many of the biographical portraits presented in this study. The stories of the three black lesbians—Obie, Kimberly, and Lenora—all are characterized by their love-hate relationships with their mothers and their hatred for their fathers. Like Obie's, Kimberly's biography reflects a loving disgust for a mother whose submissive behavior to her husband greatly strains the family.

In many ways, Kimberly is the mirror opposite of Obie. Kimberly is an attractive and poised woman with sugar brown skin and long wavy hair. Though she is the same age as Obie, Kimberly refuses to label herself a lesbian, makes every effort to put forth "a straight image," and desires a bisexual identity. Born in rural poverty, her parents, Virgil and Thelma, married early, worked hard, and entered the new black bourgeoisie. "My father didn't like taking orders from other people so he stayed in there until he could secure enough money to venture out on his own. And, he's been quite successful. He is an entrepreneur. He owns real estate and several small businesses." Thelma works as an office assistant. "She has gone back to night school for her high school diploma. She's a bright person, but she just underestimates herself. She has no faith in her ability to do anything." Kimberly confesses, "I've always been her confidant. Mom would tell me things that a kid should not be told about her marriage. But I always listened since she didn't have anybody else to talk to."

The middle of three children and the family's only girl child, the relationship between Kimberly's parents, like that of Obie's, has not been particularly good.

> They've had a real rocky marriage. Mom married my dad simply because she had my brother out of wedlock. Mom didn't have a good family life so she figured that was a way out. But she didn't know what she had married into. Dad was a rowdy, hell-raising womanizer. He abused my mom the first few years of their marriage, he hasn't been faithful, and he really

doesn't care if my mom knows about it. I began to build up this hate for my dad when I was just a little kid.

Like Obie, Kimberly's relationship with her parents remains strained. Her feelings for her father, who was rarely around when she was growing up, are, as her remarks make evident, unfavorable. Her feelings for her mother are a mixture of love and disappointment.

This past summer my dad hit my mom after she accused him of being unfaithful. This was the first time in a long time he has abused her. She told him, "I'm just really tired of you keeping these girlfriends of yours. The children are grown and I've stuck with the marriage this long only so that we would be insured of having a good life materially." I've lost a lot of respect for my mom. There are women who would get out of a situation like that. But, Mom doesn't have confidence in herself.

Though Kimberly was never exposed to the topic of homosexuality during childhood, "I remember having this huge crush on my third grade teacher. From that point on I became aware of my feelings for women but I pushed them out of my mind. I didn't know how to explain it and I didn't understand it." Kimberly's sexual feelings did not emerge until this past year when she first engaged in a homosexual relationship.

A sociological interpretation of the ambivalent maternal feelings harbored by Obie and Kimberly differs substantially from the psychoanalytic one. Here, social theory and the concepts of resistance and reproduction are especially salient.[39] For the mothers of both Obie and Kimberly, their historic role as preserver of the Southern black family and the dutiful follower of their husbands' authority, sanctioned through the church and the community, was paramount. Relying on religious faith and the security of the family, Adele and Thelma trusted in the Lord and invested themselves in their children.

From data gathered in a nationwide survey of black women conducted in 1980, Gloria Joseph found black daughters, as adults, commonly "expressed respect for their mothers in terms of strength, honesty, ability to overcome difficulties, and ability to survive."[40] Though most daughters expressed misgivings about and dislike for particular aspects of their mothers, Southern African-Americans were the least critical of their mothers, viewing them by and large as warm and loving. Joseph claims that familiarity with the family circumstances allows the daughter to assume an empathic understanding:

> Black daughters learn at an early age that their mothers are not personally responsible for not being able, through their individual efforts, to make basic changes in their lives or the lives of their children. This recognition enables daughters *in later life* to be more appreciative, understanding, and forgiving of their mothers. . . ." (emphasis added)[41]

In the case of Obie and Lenora it is this very familiarity that engenders feelings of ambiguity toward their mothers. Both daughters feel that their mothers are not mere victims of family circumstance but, in fact, contributors to the strife within the family; rather than preserving the family, Obie and Kimberly feel, their mothers contribute to its destruction. This difference may be explained as unrealistically harsh adolescent criticism which, within a few years of adulthood, will soften as they become more appreciative of their mothers' circumstances and behaviors.[42]

At 19, Obie's anger is directed at a mother she perceives as submissive to her husband and oppressive to her. Adele does not question the authority of the Southern black family as Obie has often done and as Celie ultimately chose to do in *The Color Purple*. Obie's anger blinds her to Adele's strength of heart and courage of conviction. Ironically, Obie's reluctance to break her homosexual silence, coupled with her fear of breaking family ties, mirrors the very image she holds of her mother. Obie realizes that the affirmation of homosexual desire is a rejection of the authority of the Southern family. She has yet to understand, however, that the love between mother and daughter need not cease and that the marginality and oppression felt by both have a common root. The tragedy of Obie's relationship with her mother is best expressed in the poetry of Audre Lorde:

We were born in a poor time
never touching
each other's hunger
never
sharing our crusts
in fear
the bread became the enemy.[43]

REFERENCE NOTES

1. Lieb, 1981:124.

2. The following resources are particularly helpful in understanding the history of the African-American family: Engram, 1982; Frazier, 1932; Frazier, 1939; McAdoo, 1981. I am indebted to the following authors for their insights into the black family of the Deep South: Abbott, 1967; Bethel, 1981; Gutman, 1976; Johnson, 1967; Simkins and Woody, 1932; Taylor, 1976; Tindall, 1967; Woodson, 1918.

3. Young, 1970:271. Several other Southern studies found a similar pattern among many African-American families (Hyman and Reed, 1969; Maxwell, 1968; TenHouten, 1970).

4. Elkins, 1968; Frazier, 1932; Frazier, 1939; Moynihan, 1965. These scholars were careful to emphasize that the black family's instability was due to external factors (slavery, northern emigration, ghettoization, unemployment). Recently, scholars have either revised or refuted this view. Though they differ on the influence of the African ancestry and slave masters on the black family, they assert that the integrity of the African-American family generally was not violated in the antebellum South, that a strong sense of family continued from slavery into freedom, that nuclear families were the norm through the early decades of the twentieth century, and that most African-American households were not matrifocal in structure or characterized by an absent father (Babchuk and Ballweg, 1972; Billingsley, 1968; Blassingame, 1971; Fogel and Engerman, 1974; Genovese, 1974; Gutman, 1975; Gutman, 1976; Harris, 1976; R. Hill, 1972; Johnson, 1969; Jones, 1982; Lewis, 1975; Owens, 1976; Rawick, 1972; Willie, 1981a; Willie, 1981b). For a review of the field of black family research see: L. Johnson, 1981; Taylor, 1976; Zollar, 1985.

5. Historian Arnold Taylor (1976:166) in his synthesis of Southern black culture since the War of Secession wrote, "despite economic and social strains, the two-parent family has continued to exist down to the present as the representative family in the South. In 1900, when the bulk of the black population throughout the nation resided in the rural South, there was little structural difference between black and white families. . . . By 1975, however, for reasons that are not yet clear, the proportion of two-parent families among blacks had declined to 61 percent. Until recently, however, blacks in the rural South diverged less from the

two-parent pattern than those in other regions of the country. . . . [T]he great majority of black Southerners have subscribed to the ideal of the nuclear family since the end of the Reconstrution era. . . ."

6. This migration from the South between the two world wars occurred for several inter-related reasons: the blatant racism in the rural South, the industrial opportunities in the North, the institution of European immigration quotas, and the depressed Southern farm economy. As Billingsley (1968) notes, this migration generally favored younger men who left their families behind to be sent for at a later date.

7. Staples, 1987:275.

8. Staples, 1987:278.

9. Staples, 1987:281. For a further discussion of the decimation of black males, see: Franklin II, 1984.

10. Ebert, 1980.

11. Butts, 1981:144. Audre Lorde (1978:33) makes a similar point, writing "Instead of keeping our attentions focused upon the real enemies, enormous energy is being wasted in the black community today by both black men and heterosexual black women in anti-lesbian hysteria. . . . [T]he unmarried aunt, childless or otherwise, whose home and resources were often a welcome haven for different members of the family, was a familiar figure in many of our childhoods."

12. McCray, 1980:73-74. Support for this position is found in the historical work of Genovese (1974) and Gutman (1976).

13. Wallace, 1978:14. Similar sentiments have been expressed by activist Kathleen Cleaver: "Women are always relegated to assistance, and this is where I became interested in the liberation of women" (Grant, 1982:147).

14. Cleaver, 1968; Baraka, 1971.

15. Recent empirical studies detailing inter- and intra-racial differences on social issues ranging from abortion to homosexuality include: Colsanto, 1988; Seltzer and Smith, 1985; Welch and Combs, 1985.

16. Hooks, 1981; Giddings, 1984. Useful resources documenting the contributions of black women are: Aptheker, 1982; Davis, 1982; Green, 1983; Harley and Terborg-Penn, 1978; Hull, Scott, and Smith, 1982; Lerner, 1972; Noble, 1978; Oshana, 1985; Sterling, 1979; Sterling, 1984.

17. It is not that there is an absence of writings by women of color but that their writings have been ignored or downplayed. In a recent review of black literature, Calvin Hernton (1985:2), a professor of black studies at Oberlin College, wrote "The fathers and purveyors of black writing have been men, and the male authors have portrayed male heroes, male protagonists. The complexity and vitality of the black female experience have been fundamentally ignored."

18. Several important sources for the works and contributions of black lesbians include the recent anthologies of black lesbian scholarship and literature (Moraga and Anzaldua, 1981; Smith, 1983) and the bibliography of lesbian writings (Roberts, 1981).

19. Cooper, 1969:134.

20. Shange, 1977; Naylor, 1983; Moraga and Anzaldua, 1981; Wallace,

1978. These are a few of the chorus of diverse voices representing the spectrum of the African-American women's community.

21. Grant, 1982:147-148.

22. The development of this thesis is found in Gloria Wade-Gayles' insightful analysis of several classic sociological studies on the black family such as *Negro Family in the United States* and *The Strengths of Black Families* juxtaposed to five major novels including *Native Son* to *Daddy Was a Number Runner* (Wade-Gayles, 1980).

23. Wright, 1940; Baldwin, 1953; Hunter, 1968.

24. Willie, 1981b.

25. Shockley, 1984:269.

26. Walker, 1982; Morrison, 1974.

27. Morrision, 1974:51-52.

28. Carrington, 1980:265-267.

29. For an interesting discussion of the sexual politics underlying the black women's blues tradition, see: Carby, 1986; D. Harrison, 1978.

30. Freud, 1964; Bieber et al., 1962; Hampson and Hampson, 1961; Mowrer, 1953; Tyson, 1982; Wrate and Gulens, 1986.

31. Bene, 1965; Deutsch, 1945; Poole, 1972; Freud, 1922; Freud, 1963a; Freud, 1963b; Freud, 1963c. More recently some feminists and gay scholars (e.g., Chodorow, 1978; Hencken, 1982) have argued that this model, properly used, can offer insight into the lives of lesbians and gay men. Most feminists and gay scholars, however, assert that the psychoanalytic model is inherently misogynistic and homophobic (see, for example: Donovan, 1985; Greer, 1970; Millett, 1970).

32. Bell, Weinberg, and Hammersmith, 1981; Kenyon, 1968b; Saghir and Robins, 1973.

33. Kenyon, 1968b.

34. Bell, Weinberg and Hammersmith, 1981; Kenyon, 1968b; Miller, Mucklow, Jacobsen and Bigner, 1980; Symonds, 1969; Thompson, Schwartz, McCandless and Edwards, 1973.

35. Shavelson, Biaggio, Cross and Lehman, 1980.

36. Bass-Hass, 1968. Just as there has been a tendency to view the African-American family through the lens of the white experience, so, too has there been little appreciation of the distinctions between white and black mother/daughter relationships. In her discussion of black mothers and their daughters, Gloria Joseph (1981:76) asserts, "To discuss Black mother/daughter relationships in terms of patterns of White mother/daughter relationships would be to ignore the explanations and interpretations of Black women regarding their own historical and cultural experiences as Black women."

37. Richardson, 1981b:35.

38. See, for example, Bell, Weinberg, and Hammersmith, 1981.

39. Bernstein, 1977; Bourdieu and Passeron, 1977; Horkheimer, 1972; McCarthy, 1978.

40. Joseph, 1981:94.

41. Joseph, 1981:96.

42. In other areas, Joseph's data conform to the pattern of the three black women interviewed in this study. For example, both studies reveal negative messages conveyed by mothers to their daughters about men. In Joseph's study, the content of these messages varied by region. The image provided to Southern black daughters by their mothers is that men are abusive, whereas mothers from the urban North were more likely to stress the unreliability of black men. In this study the themes of physical abusiveness and marital infidelity were common among the three case studies.

43. Lorde, 1978b:106.

Chapter 8

Honoring and Carrying on the Family Name

TERRY AND THE TWO TUX PROM

The South was not founded to create slavery; slavery was recruited to perpetuate the South. Honor came first. The determination of men to have power, prestige, and self-esteem and to immortalize these acquisitions through their progeny was the key to the South's development. . . . [I]n the South today devotion to family and country, restrictive views of women's place and role, attitudes about racial hierarchy, and the subordination of all to community values remain in the popular mind to an extent not altogether duplicated in the rest of the land.

Bertram Wyatt-Brown, *Southern Honor*[1]

Terry was named after Terrence Cardinal Cook of the archdiocese of New York. Terry's father, Vito, was raised as an Italian-Catholic in Queens. During World War II, Vito was stationed at Fort Jackson, an army post located on the outskirts of Columbia, South Carolina. There he met Vivian-Lee, a young woman from an old Southern family whose fortunes had fallen on hard times during the past century. Terry, talking in a melodic twang, recollects: "My mom was reared in the country. She wasn't a big city girl. She's a Southern Belle raised by my grandmother who spoiled her rotten. When she got married she didn't even know how to make coffee."

Vivian-Lee converted to Catholicism and had ten children, the youngest of whom was Terry. When Vito died last winter of emphysema, they had been married 41 years.

Terry grew up in a lower middle class neighborhood in Columbia. At 22, he is chubby with curly brown hair receding rapidly from his forehead. He and his lover of three years, Todd, work together at a supply company in the city. On weekends Terry plays instruments and sings in a band. Weeknights, the couple enjoy home life, often listening to Terry's enviable collection of polka albums. Though Terry would like to work full time in the entertainment business, his chief goal is simply to be happy. "I don't want to be a tycoon. Material things aren't that important to me. Living life and enjoying it, that's important."

As a child, Terry escorted his mother to church every Sunday. They enjoyed a special relationship. "I was the son that she could talk to. If she ever had a problem with Dad, she would talk to me. I was her 'little listening box.'" Terry would spend Sunday afternoons with his mother playing cards and sipping tea while his father and older brothers watched sporting events on television or played tackle football in their oversized back yard.

The gentleness and refinement of his mother sharply contrasted with the male-dominated household in which Terry was raised. A round-faced young boy, Terry remembers hearing his older brothers calling one another "faggots" as they played. At four years of age, Terry was watching television with the older children one June evening. His father sat comfortably in his imitation leather recliner, gazing down at the local newspaper. On an inside page was a story of a three-night disturbance between homosexual men and police at a gay bar in Greenwich Village. Throwing down his newspaper, his father shouted, "I don't know what I'd do if any of my kids grew up to be a faggot." Terry looked up to see the towering figure of his father, his angular face reddened with anger, stomp out of the living room.

Terry's father seldom displayed tenderness or understanding. "He didn't rule with his mind; he ruled with an iron fist." Terry recalls lying in bed with the flu at eight years of age:

> This is one of the big events in my life that I will never be able
> to get out of my mind. My older brothers were picking on me
> saying, "You're not sick." I got upset and started to cry. My
> father came into the bedroom. He slapped me in the face and
> said, "Be a man." He walked out. I thought to myself,
> "What is a man?"

During elementary school, Terry constantly heard from his public school teachers that he "could do better." Though he seldom
applied himself to his homework, he never caused trouble and genuinely enjoyed learning. "I just liked to learn. I always had questions. Sometimes I would wonder why some teachers, if I came up
with an answer that was different than theirs but was right, made me
look bad in front of the other students."

By second grade, Terry had a felt sense of difference. This difference centered on a vague feeling of attraction toward other males.
"I noticed myself looking at the male underwear ads that came in
the newspaper when I was a little kid. I would get close to see if I
could see an outline." He did not experience any type of harassment or intimidation, however, by his classmates.

It was not until late middle-school that his classmates began to
look at Terry as being different. His behavior changed. His church
attendance faded and he adopted the role of a prankster. Always a
"happy-go-lucky" person, Terry began to get into a bit of trouble.

> I acted like a boy scout until the last two weeks of my eighth
> grade. I threw them all in a whirl when I got caught for
> "smoking pot." A friend of mine had bought this bag for two
> dollars. It was just leaves in which a guy had put some seeds in
> it. But, we didn't know. We had never smoked the stuff be-
> fore. We smoked a joint that was about as big around as a
> quarter. We didn't get high although we thought we did. I
> stuck it in my cigarette pack and put it in my sock. That's
> when I got suspended for the last two weeks of school.

Sent home, Terry confided in his mother, who advised him not to
tell his father right away. When Terry owned-up to his deed he
explained to his father that it really was not marijuana and that it

was all a misunderstanding. Vito had little interest in engaging in such a murky discussion. For him, the facts were straightforward: Terry had been suspended from school and he had a pack of cigarettes on him. For a man dying of emphysema this deed deserved punishment.

During early adolescence Terry also was first exposed to sex with a group of his fellow classmates. He smiles broadly as he reminisces: "Back then they called it 'horn holding.' Five of us would meet at Jake's house because his parents didn't come home until late. I thought it was great! We got to experiment with different kinds of stuff. I was always willing."

Terry pursued a general education curriculum in high school. He did well in mathematics and science but performed poorly in English. Never forced to do his homework at home, Terry was described by some teachers as "lazy." His grades, ranging from B's to D's, reflected the lack of attention he placed on school work. During his freshmen year, Terry's brother was a senior. He was captain of the football team and one of the stars of the school's championship basketball team. "I wasn't into sports all that much. But, I played because Denny did and my mom signed me up. I was on the football team and the basketball team, too. But, it was embarrassing."

After Denny graduated, Terry felt free of his family while he was attending school. There was no one for Terry to be compared to on a daily basis nor anyone to report back about Terry's daily school adventures.

> I started finding more people like me that I could relate to. I became a "weirdo." We would just do stuff to be different in the music that we listened to and in the way we would dress. We would dress more flamboyantly. This was the preppie era and everybody was wearing alligators. We'd take the alligator off and turn it upside down and draw a little arrow sticking through it. We'd wear rap shades before anybody knew what they were. We'd come to school with our hair dyed pink.

In tenth grade, Terry began to notice that the afternoon boyhood sex circle was thinning out. "Eventually it was just me and this one other guy. Then he had to get married when he got his girlfriend pregnant. That's when I started to realize that I was different." Terry's difference, though, was felt from the inside. He did not behave in a stereotypical effeminate manner like a fellow classmate.

> I didn't hang around Chris because I didn't want to be associated with him. But I wouldn't pick on him like everybody else either. They would ask me, "Why don't you pick on him. Are you a fag, too?" I told them it was none of my business what he wanted to do. So some guys started calling me a faggot.

About this time two seniors, Dalton and Laura, told Terry that they were gay.

> We were all good friends—*Rocky Horror Picture Show* freaks. I was attracted to them because they were different. I felt like I could relate to them. They also told me that there were other people my age in school who were gay. Dalton asked me if I was gay. I said, "Yes, I am." Then he said, "Do you know that Jimmy is gay?" It was like, "No!" He was my best friend. We worked together. We were in band together. We worked on projects together. I had no idea that he was gay too. I found out that Jimmy was Dalton's lover. Jimmy and I became even closer friends.

Terry entered his junior year with a network of about nine gay students. "We ate lunch everyday together. We would borrow people's I.D.'s and go to gay bars. I would pick up a little slang like, 'get it girl,' and 'Miss thang.' I'd say those around school. Soon we were talking in a complete code. No one else understood." As Terry experienced greater harassment from other students, this small group of friends became his lifeline.

> It was a support group. We all made jokes about those who made jokes at us. Plus I would learn how to throw things back at them like saying to some redneck, "I'm more man than you'll ever be and more woman than you'll ever get." It took

their little bullets away from them. They were sort of like, "Well if it doesn't bother him why pick on him?"

Terry did not tell anyone outside his network that he was gay until the end of his senior year. This was not because he was uncertain about his sexual identity but "I felt like that would give them the edge on me. I figured if they didn't know for certain then they had nothing to base their accusations on."

In his senior year, Terry was called in to see Mrs. Setzler, the school's guidance counselor. Jimmy and Dalton had been having problems with their relationship and Jimmy had gone down to talk with her. She asked Terry if he had any problems with "your lifestyle." Terry answered, "No. Not as long as nobody beats me up." Terry felt comfortable talking with Mrs. Setzler. "She was always a super nice person. I felt like I could be open to her."

Around this time, Dalton gave him a worn copy of *Reflections of a Rock Lobster*, the autobiography of a gay student, Aaron Fricke, who insisted on taking a male date to his high school prom. "That was the first book I ever read that was pertaining to coming out. I related to it. It made me feel proud of him because he stood his ground. I could say, 'I'm proud to be gay.'" As spring neared, Terry began thinking about his senior class prom. He talked with his friends about the upcoming event. One woman in the group, Shirley, expressed an interest in attending but snapped, "I ain't wearing no dress to no prom. I don't like wearing dresses. I don't even own a dress." Terry thought for a moment and then proposed that they both wear tuxes:

> She goes, "We can't do that." I said, "Why not? Be daring. What are they going to do? It's our senior year." She said, "Okay." She wore a tux with the little frills, a big red corsage, and butched up hair. I wore the one with pleats, a white corsage, and greased back hair. We wanted to make her look a little more feminine. When we got to the prom there were lots of people who were saying, "You're ruining our prom." Whenever we danced if you were at a distance you'd think that two guys were dancing together. The preppie girls were especially concerned about what people thought. But, I said,

"You're not just supposed to have it your way. The prom is for everyone. If you don't want to see us, don't look at us."

Asked if he had considered taking a male date, like Aaron Fricke had done, Terry offered, "that would have been too radical. We joked about doing that, of course, but I never seriously thought about it. Everybody in the whole neighborhood, including my parents, would find out. My father would have been ridiculed at work. The family name would have been up for ridicule."

Despite Terry's association with the school's fringe population, his flamboyant dressing, and his fascination with "being different," he was always careful to steer these activities away from his family life. Terry's boldness ended at the school parking lot. "I would do things that I knew wouldn't come back to my family from their friends." At home, he was careful not to disclose his well-concealed sexual feelings and behaviors.

Throughout high school, he continued to date Pauline, his "regular girlfriend. I liked her personality, that's what first attracted me to her. We were in the band together and we got to know each other. We dated. She was extremely religious so we never had sex. It was more of a friendship." When Terry was 16, his mom found several *Playgirl* magazines stuffed between the mattress and springs of his bed. "I lied to cover it up saying, 'They're Pauline's. Don't let her know that you found them. She'll be embarrassed. She won't want to come over again.' I think she wanted to believe me. If she knew for sure that I was gay then she would feel like she had failed." As far as his family was concerned, Terry thought, everything was concealed.

When Terry was 18, his older sister asked him one day if he was gay. "I couldn't believe she actually asked me," Terry said. "'Yes.' I wasn't going to lie about it." She put her arm around Terry and said, "Well, I have a friend who is that way. She's my best friend. I just want to let you know that if you need any help or need to talk, just come to me." Terry breathed a sigh of relief. He decided to tell Pauline, with whom he had just broken up the month before.

She already knew that Jimmy was gay so I figured it would be okay to tell her. But, she just went to tears. She said our relationship "was all a lie." I tried to explain to her that it wasn't. I told her that I really loved her and that I still had a place for her in my heart. But, she wouldn't listen.

At 22, Terry has long stopped dating women. The importance of the family and the necessity to carry on the family name, however, continues to haunt him:

There are no male grandchildren on my father's side of the family. There has to be to carry on the family name. Somebody has to carry it on. My mother feels strongly, especially with the death of my father, that we must continue the family line. She would hate to think that our generation is the one that ended it.

Though Terry is the youngest of five boys, he is willing to accept this responsibility if it falls to him. "I wouldn't mind giving somebody the family's name. But, I wouldn't get married. I would have to find a way to do it other than that. Maybe a surrogate mother. I also would like to have a child that I could raise with the point of view that he wouldn't have the problem of satisfying his parents."

Terry graduated from high school in 1982. During the intervening five years, no one else in the family has asked about his sexuality. "I figure my sister didn't go up to my father and say, 'I'm heterosexual.' So why should I go up to him or my mother and say, 'I'm homosexual.' If they find out, they find out; if they don't, they don't." Terry is not reluctant to assert his gay identity as an alumni, however. At the time of the interview, Terry was organizing the five year reunion of his high school class. "I'm really looking forward to seeing everyone. I can look through my twelfth grade class and see a lot of these people at the gay bars now who weren't out when we were in high school. I guess my class just bred a lot of homosexuals."

The five years, however, have taken a toll. Terry spends some of his time with high school kids who are dealing with their sexuality. Being gay or being suspected of being gay in high school, according to Terry, is more difficult today:

I know this one guy who has just turned 18. I feel sorry for Kerry. He knows he's gay. He loves guys but he's afraid of AIDS. Kerry is so worried about it he doesn't know what to do. I keep trying to explain to him that you can still have a sexual relationship as long as it is safe. I also tell him you can have an emotional relationship. But, AIDS has made growing up gay more difficult. There are so many people out there who are still ignorant about AIDS and that believe homosexuals cause it. It makes people like Kerry more scared to let somebody know that they're gay. Being gay in the South was never easy; with AIDS, it just that much more difficult.

COMMENTARY

Terry's experiences, as well as those of Brandon and Carlton, can be explored from the vantage point of the Southern family and the themes of family honor and the bonding of fathers and sons. The code of honor sometimes places family interests and tradition ahead of individual needs. At other times it allows the individual to engage in discreet but unseemly behaviors. Family relationships, particularly those between fathers and sons are important. Through the father, the past becomes the future as family name, inheritance, and heredity are bestowed on the son. Some gay-identified Southern men, like Terry, accept these responsibilities and try to compromise individual needs with family interests. For others, like the young Bayard in Faulkner's novel *Satoris* or Brandon and Carlton in this study, the certainties of a father's past have vanished, yet they feel trapped by family tradition and honor to uphold them.

Honor and the Southern Family

Enduring great economic misfortunes and rooted in the chivalric ideals of their antebellum past, Southerners have placed more importance on family and family honor than on outward manifestations of wealth.[2] Honor is sometimes equated with inner virtue and personal courage, as when Scout's father in *To Kill a Mockingbird* defends a black man accused of raping a white woman. At other times honor is tied to public repute and conformity to community values breeding destructiveness and contempt, as evidenced in the life of would-be aristocrat Thomas Sutpen in *Absalom, Absalom!*.[3] Family honor and loyalty to family sometimes overshadow feelings of personal desire and self-worth. Such was the fate of Major Lacy Buchan, the antebellum gentleman in Tate's *The Fathers*, so consumed by the outward trappings of society that he loses his individuality. Discarding family tradition, though, also is costly. As the romantic hero George Posey finds, family and tradition may simply be exchanged for loneliness and rootlessness. Terry, Brandon, and Carlton feared personal loneliness and rootlessness as they grew up in South Carolina and constructed their sexual identities.

Family honor remains as an antebellum vestige. Historian Martin Duberman has unearthed letters which document homosexual behavior between two South Carolina gentlemen. These illustrate the importance of family honor coupled with a toleration of dishonorable but discrete activities. In two letters, written in the spring and autumn of 1826, 22-year-old Thomas Jefferson "Jeff" Whithers wrote to his friend, James H. Hammond, of their playful bedtime exploits.[4] Writing from his college residence in Columbia, Jeff asks Jim:

> I feel some inclination to learn whether you yet sleep in your Shirt-tail, and whether you yet have the extravagant delight of poking and punching a writhing Bedfellow with your long fleshen pole — the exquisite touches of which I have often had the honor of feeling. Let me say that unto thee that unless thou changest former habits in this particular, thou wilt be represented by every future Chum as a nuisance. And, I pronounce it, with good reason too. Sir, you roughen the downy Slumbers of your Bedfellow — by such hostile — furious lunges as you are in the habit of making at him — when he is least prepared for defense against the crushing force of a Battering Ram.[5]

As Duberman notes, the letters suggest no emotional involvement but a rather "free-wheeling attitude" toward sex. Carefully preserved in the hidden recesses of the Caroliniana Library, a considerable part of his essay details the problems he confronted in pursuing and publishing these letters. For example, Duberman faced numerous obstacles from the curator who painstakingly sought to avoid a conflict between the interests of the historian and the honor of the family. When Professor Duberman insisted on a formal decision, the curator declined his request, citing a concern that publication might "result in embarrassment to descendants."[6]

The curator's respect for family honor and the reluctance to publicize behaviors of this type (about 150 years after the event) is a legacy of the Old South. So, too, is Southerners' fondness for polite conversations and their unwillingness to confront (or tolerate) private behavior in public. Had these letters been made public during their lifetimes, the careers of both men would have been ruined and the family names would have been shamed. These deeds, though perhaps rumored, did not become public knowledge and both men went on to enjoy the paradox of public restraints coupled with private liberties that characterized Southern society.

Behind public symbols, ritual gestures, and physical appearances there exist private worlds where Southerners like Jim Hammond or Terry may express their individuality in forms of their own pleasing. Within these worlds sexual relations between members of the same sex may occur. Unlike the Calvinistic North where discrepancy between public sexual image and private sexual behavior is viewed as hypocritical, such behaviors escape public vigilance and regulation as long as they do not violate the code of family honor by becoming public knowledge.[7] As Terry and Royce come to understand, this code celebrates the individual and tolerates the idiosyncratic.

There is a seamy side, however, to Southern honor. In a study of Southern ethics and behavior, Bertram Wyatt-Brown claims that Southern honor "itself was defective. Its reliance on shame distorted human personality and individualism, forcing even the good man . . . to lose himself in the cacophony of the crowd."[8] Brandon's story differs from Terry's and illustrates how one can become a victim of Southern honor.

Brandon is a thin young man of 23 with a frail build, freckled face, high-strung voice, and effeminate mannerisms. A loner, with few friends and "never a best friend," he grew up in "a traditional Baptist family: man, woman, children, and dog" within a working class neighborhood. The only brother of two older sisters, Brandon's loyalty to his family, respect for his parents, and belief in God have dominated his life. "I still believe in the traditional family and traditional values," he says with a quixotic sigh.

Born to a mild-mannered father and over-protective mother, Brandon's devotion to his family is coupled with feelings of shame and disappointment. "My parents slaved for us," he declares. "They've used up their lives on us." These unselfish efforts, he believes, have been dishonored through his constant humiliation in public and sporadic, sinful activities in private.

Preferring to play the clarinet rather than football, Brandon's childhood memories are full of taunts and torments. He remembers his parents taking their "hide-away" money to buy him a Cub Scout uniform. He enjoyed spending time with his den mother and learning about arts and crafts, but his experiences in activities such as camping were traumatic. "Back in Cub Scouts we went on a camping trip. The other scouts would say, 'Are you a fag?' I didn't really know what it was. I'd answer, 'Yes.' They'd all laugh. Everyone was yelling, 'Fag!' That will always stick in my mind: 'Fag! Fag! Fag!'"

These taunts and torments carried over into the school yard and occasionally invaded the sanctity of the classroom. Brandon was ashamed to confide in his parents about such harassment. At the age of eight, he felt trapped and lonely. In elementary school, "I had so many things cluttered up inside. I couldn't deal with them." When Brandon was in fifth grade, his eldest sister got her first high school yearbook. The whole family was excited. They slowly paged through the glossy black and white pictures while the younger sister played Christian hymns on the piano. "I found myself looking at the boys more than the girls. I was looking at the basketball players, the swimmers, and the football stars. I wanted to be like them. I didn't just want to have a body like that; I wanted their bodies." A short time later Brandon attended a sex education class provided by the school:

> A family doctor came and talked to the boys and the girls separately. I was given a booklet with a whole bunch of questions in the back. He described to the boys the changes that

were going on with our bodies. He told us it was perfectly normal and not to worry. Well, in the back of the book a lot of terms were defined.

Brandon pauses and appears squeamish. "You know the terms. I don't want to say them." After a moment, he relents: "Terms like birth control, sex, wet dreams, and—homosexual. It stated that homosexuals preferred to have sex with someone of their own sex."

Unlike the other male respondents interviewed during this study, Brandon is visibly bothered when speaking about explicit sexual matters. Words such as *masturbation*, *oral sex*, and *wet dreams* are punctuated with embarrassed looks and long pauses. At 23, these terms, like his homosexual urges, are things that he would prefer neither to discuss nor encounter. Asked to describe a homosexual person, Brandon says, "A person who desires and fulfills unnatural desires with someone of the same sex. I satisfy my urges at particular times." These cravings separate him from his family and his God.

Brandon's story contrasts sharply with Terry's biography. Though Brandon suspected a couple of his fellow students might be gay, he never approached them. "At that age nobody is going to admit it 'cause it is too much of a risk." Both acknowledged their homosexual feelings at the age of 16; Brandon, however, did not adopt a gay identity. "I never could stand it when anybody would say the word 'gay.' I would be terribly embarrassed." Brandon spent Sunday evenings away from home. After services his church group would go find a bite to eat and then waste some time by riding around. Occasionally, they would drive up and down State Street. A wide boulevard divided by palmettos and protected on either side by monuments, museums, and government buildings, this has been a Columbia cruising street since antebellum times. "They would kind of ride around and laugh at (pause) you know. They'd go by and ask, 'Are you queer?' I wasn't into the name calling but I did enjoy looking at the crop of nice men."

Unlike Terry, Brandon endured physical and verbal harassment while attending high school. He dealt with these problems in solitude. "I would come home and feel horrible not wanting to talk to anyone. My parents would ask, 'How was your day?' I would say,

'None of your business, just get off my back.' They aged tremendously during that time." Though his parents suspected something was bothering Brandon, sexuality was mentioned only once in the family home:

> We were having dinner, the whole family, including my grandparents, were at the table. We were talking about my dog who had been sick. He was just laying around in the sun doing nothing, just moping. My sister pipes up, "He's a fag dog just like Brandon!" I just waited for a response. There was a few moments of prolonged silence. It was horrible. Then someone asked about the weather.

Brandon was determined never to have this topic broached again within the family. Asked if he had thought about confiding in his grandmother, the most supportive member of his family, Brandon barks, "NO! NO! NO! Never! It would tear her and the family apart." Brandon struggled to preserve appearances at home while sacrificing his own desires for those of his family. He stopped cruising with his friends on State Street, began to date a girl for whom he felt no attraction, and when *Boys in the Band* was aired on television, allowed his parents to switch the channel without murmuring a word. "I never told them what was wrong. They always knew something was wrong. I couldn't put them through it. They would be too hurt. It would be embarrassing for them and bring shame upon the family. I just couldn't put them through that."

Brandon's commitment to his church is as strong as his ties to family; yet his homosexual feelings and behaviors dampened his commitment to Jesus Christ.

> I'm glad I grew up in the Baptist church. I couldn't live without it. I've had two sermons in church where they say there is a way out: hear Jesus Christ. I know that's true but I can't commit myself to Him. I'm doomed. I know He is forgiving, but when you just downright do it when you know you aren't supposed to, even though you know you are forgiven, how can something like that be forgiven? It's all one big struggle. I wouldn't like to repeat any part of my life. I just figure, Bran-

don, you are going to die anyway. Look ahead toward that time.

Brandon is caught in the crossfire between public posturing and private posing, between ritualized beliefs and sexual feelings, between family expectations and personal desires. Like most children born in the religious South, Brandon felt badly about shaming his God. These feelings were the result of many a Baptist Sunday service, during which "they bring up sex, drugs, drinking, and money," and many a family Sunday dinner at which "the importance of behaving in public and preserving the good name of the family" was heard. "You hear it so often it gets into your skull." As an adult, Brandon vigorously clings to the belief that his "impure" thoughts, "unmanly" behavior, and unspeakable deeds are "Biblically wrong and evidence of our turning into another Sodom and Gomorrah." The fear of hurting his family or his family abandoning him affects Brandon greatly.

> All my friends have had family problems of some sort. There is one guy who just got thrown out of his house. I know one girl and three other guys who have gotten disowned by their families. Three of them chose to tell their parents. I don't dare tell mine.

Unlike Terry, however, the pains that Brandon has experienced and hidden from his family have affected him greatly. To avoid bringing dishonor to his family and embarrassment to himself, Brandon continues to live a compartmentalized life:

> My church is one life. I abide by certain things there. Family life is another. At home I blow up more. I keep my bar friends away from my family. The people who I go to the bar with is another life. There, I'm more of a flame. And, then there is the street life where I do things that I shouldn't. That's something you don't talk about even to your bar friends.

Though Brandon wishes that he did not lead these separate lives and pursue these social lies, he laments, "it's just one of the things I have to live with." Living with these conflicting roles and often contradictory values explains Brandon's seemingly inexplicable beliefs and paradoxical actions:

> There is this heavy set guy dressed up as a girl that comes out to host the show on Sunday nights at the bar. She turns the spotlight on the crowd and says, "Are there any queers out there tonight?" Well everyone cheers. It causes me to laugh and not take it so seriously. But, I still just can't stand those words. Also, I don't like how guys at the bar come on to people, the smoking and the drinking, and the language. It's just so anti-God, so anti-family. It's another Sodom and Gomorrah. You know, the more bars they have the more they want to legalize relationships and then they want to adopt children. It's getting further and further to erode the family. I think we are being punished with AIDS to let us know you just can't do stuff like that and get away with it.

Brandon still dreams of a "house, wife, child, and dog. I would like for it to happen, but I don't think it can. I see myself as being a homosexual. I know I am. I ask, 'Why was I made like this?' " As a born-again Christian, Brandon views himself as a deceitful son and a purveyor of "unnatural desires." As the family's only son, he hears his duties of marriage and fatherhood beckoning. At 23, Brandon finds himself checkmated on God's earthly proving ground. "I ought to be put away. I'm not safe on the streets." Then, Brandon smiles: "Well, maybe I'll never have a home, wife, and kids, but I can always get a fag dog."

Brandon's story affirms the difficulty that family honor sometimes poses for Southerners. In his case, Wyatt-Brown's generalization is accurate: "The interior contradictions of honor [hold] men in shackles of prejudice, pride, and superficiality."[9] Masterful dancers around truth, Southerners are the great preservers of appearances. There is a respect for an individual's privacy or, less gingerly, an unwillingness to confront private idiosyncrasies in public. The whole town might know about Cousin Randolph's fondness for men; but as long as these behaviors are kept to himself, no one will publicly acknowledge them. This storehouse of collective private knowledge, in part, is what identifies a Southern community. Southerners evidence a "determined ignorance of the seamier facts of life. Even the most innocent Dear Old Thing knows what Town Fairy is and what he does, but the blue-rinse set simply refuses to think about it. Their blind spots are so calcified that eventually they actually forget that Town Fairy is Town Fairy."[10] In those rare instances when a person's shadowy actions are exposed, this willful ignorance is transformed into shock and repudiation. Meg Segrest writes:

> So here you have a situation where an entire town expects a man to be — or pretend to be — abnormally perfect . . . [and] when he cannot live up to it, the whole situation is potentially tragic. He and his family can be destroyed by people who might sorrow to do it, but who cannot conceive of challenging the community's world view.[11]

Public exposure shames the family. This betrayal of family honor is a profound act in a region where honor has been inseparable from hierarchy and entitlement for generations. Not surprisingly, many homosexual sons of the New South, adhering to codes of family honor in the Old South, willingly choose bare toleration over ostracism. Not surprisingly, the parents practice determined ignorance as their sons sexually rebel: Terry's mother meekly accepts an explanation for *Playgirl* magazines or Brandon's parents quickly turn the dinner conversation to the weather. As Brick asks Big Daddy in *Cat on a Hot Tin Roof*, "Who can face the truth? You?"[12]

Parent-Son Relationships

According to psychoanalytic thought, male homosexuality results when the normal developmental relationships between a son and his parents do not progress, or, more specifically, from the failure to resolve "Oedipal desire" or "castration anxiety."[13] Perceiving the father as a rival for his mother's affection, the "normal" child of four of five years old fears his father's anger for such feelings and fantasizes castration as punishment. In order to resolve this castration anxiety, the boy child's desire for the mother is replaced by wanting to be like the father. Identifying with the father, the child vicariously enjoys the mother's love. The boy child then will develop appropriate gender role behaviors and will seek out another woman in adulthood. According to this traditional interpretation, poor father-son relationships or close mother-son relationships arrest a child's psycho-sexual development.[14]

In this study, only three of the 24 male participants (Royce, Cory, and William) reported a close relationship with their father as they were growing up. There are, however, other explanations for a distant father and his estranged son. For example, Kurt Freund and Ray Blanchard, discussing three studies of the relationships among father-son distance, homosexual orientation, and cross gender behavior, posit that "not homosexuality *per se* but much more likely feminine gender identity is the true correlate of indifferent or antagonistic father-son relations. . . . Those individuals who reported the greater degree of cross gender behavior in childhood also tended to report the worst relationships with their father."[15]

Of the males in this study, the effeminate did indeed have worse relations with their fathers. Fourteen males displayed cross gender behavior in childhood or adolescence; only two (Isaiah and Henry) reported a relatively good relationship with his father. The reasons for the distancing between fathers and their effeminate-acting sons varied with the other 12 individuals. For example, Malcolm's distancing probably was the result of his father's rejection of the effeminate behavior. However Alston, portrayed in Chapter 10, distanced himself from a father he perceived as domineering and hostile. Ten of the 24 males conformed to social-sex role expectations during childhood and adolescence. The other two males (Cory and William) who reported a close relationship with their fathers were in this group. The other eight, however, reported antagonistic or indifferent relationships with their fathers. The supposed linkage between a distant father-son relationship and homosexuality is, therefore, far from universal.

Terry, for example, did not display effeminate behaviors yet reported a hostile father. Terry's relationship with his mother (becoming her "little listening box"), however, was close. With the exception of Carlton, Cory, Heyward, and Kevin, males in this study reported a positive relationship with their mothers as they were growing up. Even those like Isaiah, Henry, and William, who enjoyed a good relationship with their fathers, reported feeling closer to their mothers.

These findings parallel some research studies but conflict with others.[16] In a recent review of research on gender identity and mother-son relationships, C. Anne Mallen concludes:

> "It is unclear whether relationships of homosexual males with their mothers follow any particular pattern."[17] Further, data supporting a strong mother-son relationship among homosexual men may be no different than the bonding between heterosexual sons and their mothers. And, given the design of such studies, it is not possible to determine whether there is a *causal* relationship between close mother-son relationships and the development of homosexuality. The only large scale study designed to examine such causal relationships, *Sexual Preference*, found no empirical support for this thesis. Based upon a statistical technique known as path analysis, researchers affiliated with the Kinsey Institute examined the interrelationships among a variety of variables to explain homosexuality. They reported, "neither unusually close nor unusually negative mother-son relationships can be considered important in the development of homosexuality among our male respondents."[18]

By focusing on individuals and their sexual struggles, *Growing Up Gay in the South* reveals unique as well as common factors regarding the relationships between family patterns and homosexuality. This study's conclusion, however, does not differ from those of these Kinsey researchers. Terry's biographical portrait represents the archetypical image of a homosexual male with a distant and antagonistic father coupled with a close and loving mother. In contrast, the following brief biography of Carlton describes a distant mother and a demanding father whom he constantly seeks to please.

Carlton's parents come from poor, rural families. In two decades they built a good business in a metropolitan area. As Carlton entered elementary school, they bought a home in an exclusive suburb. They had arrived. Unlike most of the participants in this study, Carlton still enjoys an active sexual life with his college girlfriend—the first woman with whom he has been intimate. He has, however, had strong sexual feelings for other males since the age of nine and has engaged in homosexual behavior since the fifth grade. "I like both sexes," proclaims Carlton. "I go on binges in cruising. I may go as long as a week without even caring at all to really cruise, then I may go cruising different times during the day and several days at a time."

As a child, Carlton enjoyed music and drama. "I was a sensitive person. I didn't engage in rough and tumble games or brainless and brutish activities. I had no violent feelings and it was hard to get me angry enough to feel like fighting." Carlton got labelled early as a "fag." "Being thin and comparatively graceful, I didn't get into just walking around with my knuckles dragging on the ground. A lot of guys put on this very stiff walk so they would look macho. I was not into that game." Carlton's slim and coordinated physique contributed to his talent in gymnastics, track, and swimming. In middle school he joined the swim team. "I won a lot but I didn't enjoy the feeling and the pressure of competition. I would dream constantly about swimming. 'On your mark, get set, go!' I'd jerk and wake up. I got involved with swimming to please my father. At least, I thought it would please him."

Throughout school Carlton was a good student who earned B's but seldom pushed himself academically. By the time he was a high school freshman, though, Carlton acknowledged his homosexual feelings. Struggling with them, he was fearful that others would find out about his secret. "I desperately needed to find out what it was with me, 'Am I normal?' 'Is this bad?' 'Will it change eventually?' But, I didn't know and I didn't dare ask. I felt like everything I did was under scrutiny." His fears of disclosure, lack of information, and need to please his father produced pressures that were most acute in sports:

I felt like I had to be ultra-careful in the dressing room. I couldn't let my eyes wander. I couldn't let anyone suspect the slightest thing. I found myself putting up more of a front in sports than anywhere else. I felt like it was such a proving ground—proving my manhood to my father, to the other guys, to myself. But, no matter how much I proved myself, it didn't seem to change anything. No matter how much I competed and bested others it didn't seem to matter how my father felt.

Just as Obie felt a strong need to please her mother, so Carlton felt toward his father. Fear of displeasing parents was integrally connected with a fear of losing the mother-daughter or father-son relationship. Obie and Carlton also struggled with severe bouts of depression lasting day after day. Sometimes Carlton's depressive state would be triggered by a "sad feeling and other things would just start pouring in: things that did happen, things that I fantasized could happen. They would just pile up more and more as my depression became deeper and deeper." Other times his depressions would begin with feelings of unreleased anger.

At the age of 20, Carlton entered private therapy. "We talked about my family and relationships with people. When I faced these things that the therapist thought I couldn't see, it just took care of itself. Sexual orientation wasn't the real problem; there were other things in my life like my relationship with my parents. I wasn't communicating with my mother and I was very worried about disapproval from my father." With the help of his therapist, Carlton "came out" to his father. He remembers:

> We were sitting out on the porch on an early summer evening. I got tired of hearing remarks about how I was hanging around with gays and how Jeremy was a bad influence. Finally, I just came out and said, "Well, Dad here's how it is with me." I told him how I had felt ever since I was young. I was hoping he would take it really well. I was very nervous. He was pretty understanding, though he was not pleased. He didn't condemn me or kick me out of the family. But he did tell me that he would be very disappointed if I chose that way of life completely. He talked about owing something to the family and not only thinking about myself. I was pretty amazed at his honesty. That hurt. He seemed so open and accepting and then he went and said that. Who knows if I can ever actually please him?

Within the Southern family, honor and tradition played an important role in the lives of these three gay men. Terry, like Brandon and Carlton, felt a sense of duty to honor and carry on the family name which, at times, made being a sexual rebel difficult. Considering marriage or staying in the closet became attractive options in such southern families in which the antebellum concept of honor is passed down from one generation to the next. As Bertram Wyatt-Brown notes, "one did what others thought right and honorable, not what the heart or other parts of the anatomy prompted."[19]

The differences among these three men far exceed their similarities. The classic pattern of distant father and close mother portrayed in Terry's biography contrasts with that of Carlton's distant mother and demanding father. Each man may fulfill his family obligations, but in a different manner. The importance of parental affection and its impact on growing up varied considerably. Brandon is a victim of Southern honor trapped by tradition, family, and religion. Like a maimed character in a Flannery O'Connor short story, he believes that "traditional manners, however unbalanced, are better than no manners at all."[20] Terry, on the other hand, has learned to work within Southern culture while adapting a private homosexual lifestyle and identity. He, like Meg Segrest, understands that "Southerners have a high tolerance of and appreciation for eccentricity, a knowledge in our heart of hearts that everyone is a little strange. It is from this playful, private sense of strangeness that people maintain sanity and protect one another from the life-destroying institutions and norms to which they give lip service."[21]

REFERENCE NOTES

1. Wyatt-Brown, 1982:16-17.

2. Wyatt-Brown, 1982; Wyatt-Brown, 1988; Kim, 1977.

3. The evolution of honor in the literary tradition of the South is aptly discussed by Wyatt-Brown (1988).

4. Withers completed his studies in law from South Carolina College and eventually assumed the judgeship of the state's Court of Appeals. In 1861, he was sent to Montgomery, Alabama as one of South Carolina's delegates to the Confederate convention. Hammond, a commoner, married into a wealthy Charleston family and entered politics. As Congressman, Senator, and Governor representing the people of South Carolina, Hammond was a pro-slavery advocate, a religious moralist, and heir-apparent to John C. Calhoun.

5. Thomas J. Withers to James H. Hammond, 15 May 1826. Hammond

Papers, South Caroliniana Library, Columbia, SC. Quoted from Duberman, 1980/81:87.

6. Duberman, 1980/81:96.

7. Interestingly, in Hammond's case, one "critical flaw" — the seduction of young women — was made public by kingmaker Wade Hampton II, who learned of his daughters' violations at the hands of Hammond. In 1843, following Hammond's refusal to withdraw his name from nomination to the U.S. Senate, Hampton made public the scandal. Threatened with being horse-whipped, Hammond retired in shame to his plantation at Silver Bluff. Dishonored by his sexual violations, none of Hampton's four daughters ever married (Faust, 1982). For a discussion of this case vis-à-vis the place of sexuality and women in the antebellum South, see D'Emilio and Freedman, 1988 esp. pp. 85-108. Another interesting case is that of William Percy, a great Mississippi poet-bachelor and member of a prominent Southern family (Baker, 1983). His fondness for young men has been asserted by Mader (1978) in his introduction to an anthology, *Men and Boys* in which Percy's poem, "A Page's Song," appears as well as by a relative of Percy, William Armstrong Percy III (1990). According to Percy, William Armstrong Percy, known affectionately as "Uncle Will," spent considerable money on young men (including his scandalous purchase of a new car for a young black man during the depths of the Depression) and took several of them under his wing. One of these men, Walker Percy, who lived with Uncle Will from the age of 14 to 26, fondly remembers these years in his introduction to *Lanterns on the Levee* (Percy, 1973). Percy's alleged homosexuality, however, has been staunchly denied by Walker Percy. William Perry, who is seeking to "bring Uncle Will out of the closet," claims that Walker Percy's homophobia and concern for "family honor" lies at the root of his denials.

8. Wyatt-Brown, 1982:22.

9. Wyatt-Brown, 1982:22.

10. Segrest, 1985:158.

11. Segrest, 1985:63.

12. Williams, 1955:92.

13. Freud, 1963c; Legman, 1950. For a critique of psychoanalysis see, Eysenck, 1986, and for a reasoned and supportive argument outlining the modification of the psychoanalytic interpretation in recent years with respect to homosexuality, see Hencken, 1982.

14. Bene, 1965; Bieber, Dain, Dince, Drellich, Grand, Gundlach, Kremer, Rifkin, Wilbur, and Bieber, 1962; Buhrich and McConaghy, 1978; Buhrich and McConaghy, 1979; Evans, 1969; Freund et al., 1974; Hatterer, 1971; Mallen, 1983; Stephan, 1973; Symonds, 1969; Thompson, Schwartz, McCandless, and Edwards, 1973; Thompson and McCandless, 1976. Some support for these findings has been provided from empirical studies (Bell, Weinberg and Hammersmith, 1981; Millic and Crowne, 1986; Siegelman, 1974; Siegelman, 1981; Sipova and Brzek, 1983) though these findings have not been universal (Schofield, 1965), and no differences were found between homosexual and heterosexual-identified men with low neuroticism scores (Siegelman, 1974). The interpreta-

tions, however, vary widely and the authors of one of the largest studies of homosexual and heterosexual men (Bell, Weinberg and Hammersmith, 1981:56) conclude, "the quality of the father-son relationship (like that of the mother) is not a very good predictor of a boy's eventual sexual preference." Marvin Siegelman (1981:511), after years of empirical work with non-clinical samples of heterosexual and homosexual men, concluded that "The evidence to date, however, does not indicate that any particular parental background is typical or generally present in the development of most or all homosexuals or heterosexuals. This writer is becoming more and more impressed with the likelihood that sexual predisposition is an incredibly complex, multi-faceted, and individualistic personality trait. . . ."

15. Freund and Blanchard, 1983:21. This hypothesis is also suggested by Millic and Crowne (1986:245) who state, "rather than being antecedent to the development of homosexuality these were parental reactions to the discovery of their son's sexual orientation." At least one research study has confirmed this relationship (Sipova and Brzek, 1983). As Millic and Crowne (1986) noted, these differences between homosexual and heterosexual men's parental relationships also may be due to distortion in recollections.

16. For example, Saghir and Robins (1973) and Stephan (1973) report mother-son relationships to be related to the son's identification as homosexual. These findings are contradicted by others (Bell, Weinberg and Hammersmith, 1981; Mallen, 1983; Siegelman, 1974).

17. Mallen, 1983:57.

18. Bell, Weinberg, & Hammersmith, 1981:45.

19. Wyatt-Brown, 1988:114.

20. O'Connor, 1969:200.

21. Segrest, 1985:76.

A few "outcasts" are found in every elementary school. As adolescents or adults, many of these children will identify themselves as lesbians or gay men. There are other students for whom such words will come to have a special meaning only in adolescence. These students, like Everetta in Chapter 11, are viewed by their elementary classmates as distinctively different. They do not, however, become the butt of jokes or the target for torments with sexual innuendo. These are "the tomboys."

Other elementary children, like Cory portrayed in Chapter 9, fit the norms for childhood behavior. Never experiencing sexual harassment, they may occasionally engage in such harassment themselves. During adolescence, they will eventually come to terms with feeling different—with being "queer." Until then, however, they experience what most teachers, counselors, and parents perceive to be typical Southern childhoods. Beneath these surface appearances, however, lurk sexual feelings and untold experiences that will profoundly affect the manner in which they will cope with their sexuality during adolescence. These are the "kids."

There are similarities between and among the outcasts, tomboys, and kids. Everetta and Alston come from poor, rural homes. Everetta and Cory both engaged in heterosexual relationships, one marrying and the other fathering a child. Alston and Cory had lovers and performed "drag" while in high school. None of them excelled in school; all of them brandished psychological shields.

There were also differences. Alston often was harassed for his effeminate mannerisms; Everetta's tomboyish behaviors were simply ignored. Unlike Alston, Cory was fond of his father and had little emotional attachment to his mother. Though they sensed a "difference" about themselves, the meaning of this difference was interpreted differently by them and by those around them. Each experienced ambivalence as they struggled in their journeys of the spirit and constructed their sexual identities. Cory, an arrogant, insensitive punk, for years assumed a passive role in sexual encounters refusing to adopt a gay identity. Alston, a naive, sensitive, and unassertive boy, engaged in sex with other boys well before he understood the term homosexuality and assumed a gay identity. Everetta, a strong-willed girl, fawned over girlfriends as early as the third grade but refused to declare a gay identity for fear that "if you say you're a homosexual, then you are and you can't change it."

The biographies of Cory, Alston, and Everetta are examined from the vantage point of gender and sexuality. The constructed meanings of behaving like a male or female and being "straight or gay" is important to our understanding of the psychosocial context of these sexual rebels.

REFERENCE NOTE

1. Cather, 1936:50.

Chapter 9

The Kids

CORY AND THE LITTLE REDNECK HELL-RAISERS

> *Paint by numbers*
> *Color in the lines*
> *March in rhythm*
> *Never out of time*
> *Walk in single file*
> *Learn the system*
> *Conform to the style*
>
> *But that's not how Picasso painted*
> *That's not how Beethoven played*
> *They rearranged tradition*
> *And history was made*
> *That's not how Picasso painted*
> *That's not how Beethoven played*
> *They dared to be different*
> *And did it their own way*

Ron Romanovsky, "Paint by Numbers"[1]

Cory was the only child born to a mild mannered father and a "hell-raising" mother. Lucy worked nights "tendin' bar" in the Carolina low-country; Cecil had a desk job with the Federal Government. "My mother is by far the more dominant," Cory asserts as he takes a drag from a Salem Light 100. "My father, though, was the one who took care of me. He was always here." Cory always had a special relationship with his father. In kindergarten Cory refused to sing the national anthem because of its line,

"Where our fathers died." His relationship with his mother was cool. "My idea of being around my mother for an extended period of time is that she would pick me up at school and we would go to the Tastee Freeze for hamburgers. She'd drop me off at day-care where Daddy would pick me up."

Cory has a half-brother and a half-sister from Lucy's first two marriages. Both of them are well into their late thirties. For most of his childhood, Cory was treated as an only child. Being "surrounded by adults" and having little contact with his mother, Cory assumed responsibility earlier than most children from middle class homes. "I was cooking my own breakfast before I was 10," he remembered. "At seven o'clock, Daddy was already gone and Mamma was still in bed. An explosion wouldn't wake her up."

At 21, Cory has a muscular frame, ruddy complexion, and short blond hair. Never at a loss for a sarcastic comment, Cory chain smokes and drinks Chevas Regal—when he has the money. Cory's earliest memory is wrecking the family station wagon at the age of four. "I threw it in reverse and ran into the garage across the street. I found that pretty exciting." During childhood, Cory had a passion for collecting: comic books, coins, stamps. He also spent hours watching cartoons on television or playing in big piles of sand at a nearby construction site. "I was very stand-offish. I had a couple of close friends but don't ask me their names." Outside school with his neighborhood pals, he would spend hours "wandering around 200 acres of undeveloped woodland along the Ashley River, going up under the bridge and chasing wild dogs." Inside school, Cory spent most recesses on the swings; "I'd swing until I puked."

Cory was born the day after Thanksgiving and started school a year later than most children. An "average student," Cory enjoyed school—until the third grade:

I had a teacher, a royal biddy, who literally turned me against school. By the time she was finished, I was completely anti-social. Mrs. Mabley was in the process of dying with lung cancer. She would cough up blood in the trash can. She singled me out. One day, in front of the whole school when my mamma came to pick me up, she said, "You need to take that child to see a doctor. He's sick." She didn't mean that I was physically sick. Mamma took me to the doctor and slapped the doctor's report down on her desk at noon the next day. Mamma and Mrs. Mabley almost came to blows several times. I hated her. I started cutting school.

Through the sixth grade, Cory was a quiet, moderately popular, precocious student who teachers felt needed to put more effort into his schoolwork. Outside of school, unknown to his teachers or parents, Cory was a "little redneck hell-raiser": callous, spiteful, manipulative. "I didn't get in trouble at school. It was outside of school where I was a little hellion. School was too structured; there was always someone watching."

Throughout elementary school, Cory was just "one of the kids." One of his pals, Reggie, was a wiry, black skinned, unassuming boy. Reggie's father was a trawler captain. When his parents were not around, he and Cory occasionally engaged in sex play. "It was really pathetic and tame," Cory recalls. "But, I didn't have any trouble dealing with it." Well before he had entered middle school Cory had progressed beyond these childhood exploits. He established a relationship with his baby-sitter's husband:

> He would get stoned out of his gord on codeine and valium and walk around the house with no clothing on. When she was some place else, he would read to me from a somewhat filthy magazine with my asking. I coaxed him into showing me what oral sex was. I was completely passive. When it was over, it was like, "Okay, that was fun. Show me something more."

Always on a search for the unexplored and forbidden, Cory dismisses these childhood sexual encounters as "just lust." He adds, "Never was there true love — until 17."

The year Cory began middle-school, Lucy and Cecil petitioned for a divorce.

> It was a mess. I was despondent. I had basically figured out that it was all my fault even though for the past five years they had been having violent fights. Daddy started drinking more. I was having a hard time dealing with why they weren't together. I didn't want to go to school. I'd say, "I don't feel

well." I was placed on drugs to counteract hyperactivity. I slept through the last three months of fifth grade.

Cory also developed a school-age crush on a male classmate. At 12, Jessie "was extremely cute, a little sports fanatic, and ultra popular. He was one of the main reasons I made it through school that year." Cory's attachment to Jessie grew as he entered puberty.

> I started going crazy. He looked better everyday. I did not do anything during that time, I just looked a lot. It bothered me that I wasn't in a position to do anything. But, I just couldn't go up to him and say, "Hey, Jessie I'm horny for you."

During sixth and seventh grades, Cory was still pretty much of a loner habitually hanging around the counselor's office. "I was like the counselor's sidekick. I was not into talking with him 'cause I had no real problems." Cory claimed an old desk that was idle and set up shop. "Nobody ever bothered to tell me 'no,'" Cory remembers. "It was some place to go in the morning when everybody else was just bumming around. It was a place of importance. I was already craving power."

When his parents separated, Cory and his father moved into his "Granny's house." Not coming from particularly religious parents, living with his grandmother was a rude awakening. "Mamma had no use for God; when things got tight, Daddy looked to God. Daddy always left the choice of religion up to me. He didn't want to put me into any particular type of religious setting until I was old enough to make up my own mind. I've been to everything from a synagogue to an A.M.E. church." Cory's grandmother, though, was different. "At Granny's house, I went to Sunday School. Granny was a bit of a preacher. She'd tell me what I should or should not do even when I wasn't doing anything wrong."

Within six months Cory and Cecil moved into their own house a block away from grandmother's house. Lacking the scornful supervision of his grandmother, Cory formed friendships with a new group of kids:

We were little redneck hell-raisers. Probably one of the happiest times of my life. I was constantly sneaking out of the house in the middle of the night. Daddy comes home and falls asleep in the recliner after cooking dinner, completely exhausted. I go out and do my thing. Just go out and wander around. Chase the big kids and find out what they were doing. I started smoking. I was also becoming very anti-social: egg and rock throwing, fire crackers, and other such things. Like I got involved with the police explorers. I learned all their codes and frequencies and for the next seven months fucked up every single bust they had.

By seventh grade, Cory's outside behavior occasionally lapped over to the classroom.

I remember English class. There was a pair of twins: Billie and Bobby. They were two total basket cases. One day Bobby decided that he had to go to the bathroom. But, he didn't want to get up to go. So, he just went right there. I picked him up and threw him out the window. It was only a one story building, but I still got into trouble.

Cory usually attended the school sponsored dances. He and his little group would line the gym wall during after-game dances telling dirty jokes and leaving occasionally to torment one of the "sissies" or to set off firecrackers in the girl's bathroom. Girls, as an object of sexual attraction, held little fascination for Cory. The opposite, however, was not true:

By this time the girls that found me attractive decided to tell me. But, I was attracted to extremely masculine, somewhat vicious females. There was a blond-headed, big girl, Wendy. She had tiddies you wouldn't believe. Well, Wendy decided she was going to chase me down at recess one day. She pinched me until I bled and then sent me a Valentine's card. I didn't care much for females.

In the summer of his fourteenth year, Cory threw some clothes in a bag and hitchhiked to Key West, Florida. When he arrived, he telephoned his father. "I told him to expect me back at the beginning of school. Daddy was under the impression that I had a friend whose family had moved down there. But, Daddy had no control — none." Cory had an eventful summer:

> I met a guy named Mario who dealt cocaine for the Florida mafia. He wanted someone on his arm who was pretty. I was well taken care of. I did a lot of drugs, drank a lot, and spent exorbitant amounts of money. I was sitting around one day and put on this pair of shoes. It was like, why not? I started doing drag. I had a very, very good State of Florida I.D. I would go to the bars, do drag shows, wear a full length mink coat and hand-beaded dresses. With the amount of backing that I had and the attitude I had developed, I was in demand. I remember coming back from Miami one night throwing my wig and pumps onto the interstate and waking up on a float in a swimming pool the next morning with nothing on but a camisole.

Cory returned home at the end of August. "When I left for Florida," he remembers, "I was still calling my father 'Father'; when I came back I was calling him Cecil." In his freshman year, Cory was smoking lots of pot, dropping acid, hanging around his group of "hell-raisers," and dealing drugs. His school behavior deteriorated:

> I gave every teacher problems. We were at each other's throats constantly. I used to cuss teachers out in the classroom for their lack of teaching ability. I was reading on the college level. I had no tolerance for school. I had no tolerance for homework. I spent too many hours at school as it was. I thought, "Why do I have to go home and do this shit too? Why do I have to do this work because in my class they can't add two numbers?" I did absolutely no homework but I had an "A" average. They were giving a substandard education in those classes. I knew it. It was not a situation of trying to get the best out of the best students. It was trying to bring the students in the back of the class up to par.

The only harassment Cory experienced was from teachers. By Cory's account he became "a vicious, mean, totally self-confident, rude asshole. If somebody stood in my way, I had no problem about stepping on them." He was in constant battles with his teachers; three-day suspensions had little effect on Cory's behavior. One of the school counselors tried to work with Cory. "In a few words, I told her to 'kiss my ass.'" None of his friends were aware of his summertime adventure. During high school he dealt drugs, completed courses with minimal effort, and served as the *de facto* leader of two school cliques: the "freaks" and the "rednecks."

> The rednecks were lower class, drove pickup trucks, smoked a lot of pot, drank beer and listened to AC/DC. The freaks were listening to Nina Hagen. I was the only link to buy decent marijuana. If you wanted it, you had to go to me. Everybody wanted it. I never sold more than any one person could handle. I never sold anything that was dangerous. I never catered anything that could be used for mainlining. I catered straight pills in small milligrams, marijuana, and small amounts of cocaine.

From school officials to the town's detective, Cory often found himself the target of suspicion. "I was suspected of everything from housebreaking to stealing cars," Cory says wryly. "Dealing drugs was something they never knew about." Selling drugs allowed him to be free of "my Daddy's money" and to occupy a place of importance among his schoolmates. In his search for power and influence within the school, Cory associated with every clique in school with the exception of the "Bible Belters":

> I had no tolerance for them. One of them, Ronnie, was also on the football team and his father was pastor of a church. He used to hassle the outcasts making faggot comments and faggot jokes. I remember friends of mine who were not gay being reduced to tears because of these jibes. So, I had a friend of mine a bar in Florida come up and seduce him. He never opened his fuckin' mouth again. He knew if he did his father would be disgraced.

Cory's association with the other cliques, such as the "snobs, the basket cases, the outcasts, and the brains," were at his choosing and on his terms. With relish, he remembers:

The brains wanted nothing to do with me. But, I was president of the computer club. On occasion they would need research that could only be done on the computer. I could understand anything they'd say. I could come up with things they couldn't even understand. So, they had to come to me. The jocks showed me respect after I had one of them hauled away in handcuffs after he punched me and broke my glasses. I pressed charges against him for the value of the glasses and won. I tore up the little bill the Court gave me and told him, "I just wanted to prove a point." After that, I had no problems.

Cory continued to engage in sex with other guys; he also continued to deny his homosexuality. He always assumed the passive role:

Daddy and a friend of his were out running the streets some place and Gary [a college-age friend of his father] and I were left alone together. I was asleep but I was close enough to being awake that I could actually hear noises. Gary began showing attention to me and I continued to feign sleep. For the first three times I played like I was asleep. He knew that I was awake, that was painfully obvious. He never attempted to do anything that I had any problem with him doing. It was not forceful.

At 16, Cory also found himself assuming a passive role with a female student:

Daddy was in the Bahamas and I threw an incredible party. I got extremely messed up. That night Bessie picked me up — she was a BIG girl — and put me on my daddy's waterbed. All I remember is her sitting on me. I don't know how she managed to accomplish it but nine months later she has a child. It looks like me, too. She has never asked me for anything except, when I feel I'm ready, to give the child my name.

Cory did not identify himself as "homosexual" until the age of 18. "I was attracted to guys but these erotic feelings I wrote off as lust. Never have there been true emotions." Never, that is, until the summer between Cory's junior and senior year.

> I found out that Winston [who Cory had known two years earlier from biology class when he had developed a "crush" on Winston] was coming back to stay with his sister for the summer. I got into a frenzy trying to get in touch with him. The night he came back, I called him. I walked up to the store and got myself a pack of Salem Light 100s. I walked back to his sister's house and we went into the woods. We sat there and talked from midnight until seven in the morning.

Three days later they slept together. At that moment Cory's emotional and physical feelings were married. For the first time in his life, he began to explore the possibility of being gay:

> I was sitting on the front porch for the longest time. I called Daddy out. I said, "I think I might be gay." He looked at me; "That's okay, I figured it out. The only thing that upsets me is that you are probably going to have a hard life in front of you." Later I was furious. I thought it was insulting. How dare he know this and not tell me? He knew something that I myself didn't know yet. He had caught on to the fact that as we would drive down the road, two out of three times my eyes would follow a scantily clad male. But, I never thought about it.

Cory's relationship with Winston lasted only a few months. On a blustery autumn day Cory hitchhiked to Winston's home town to visit him for the weekend.

> He looked at me and said, "I love you. It's been marvelous. But, it has been too much for me. It would kill my mother." I went back home and died. That is the day I lost all use whatsoever I had for that person. It ended right there. Yet to this day, I still love him. That person has been haunting my life for years.

Cory remains bitter about his relationship with Winston. He confided in a high school classmate, Trudy. "That's when I came out of the closet and she introduced me to Hank." Hank had strawberry blond hair, green eyes, and was Cory's age. As his anger and love for Winston slowly burnt out, Cory's love for Hank deepened. A year after he and Hank had been lovers Cory told him, "I love you."

At 21, Cory has gained insight into himself. Pouring another glass of Chevas Regal, he confesses:

> I built up walls in high school because I did not want to deal with other human beings. That's why I didn't fall in love until I was 17. That's why it was such a painful experience for me to fall in love. I let someone in. If homosexuality would have been acceptable I wouldn't have built so many walls and been so angry. But, this is one region of the country where you can get killed walking down the street differently. Everything is hush hush. Everyone is afraid. The word "gay" scares people.

As with Vincent and Royce, it was not until after Cory had graduated from high school that he discovered the existence of other classmates who, like himself, had remain closeted and in fear.

> Almost a full eighth of my graduating class has come out of the closet. A good number of them are lesbians. There were a lot of people who were having to repress things about themselves and having to put up with a lot of unnecessary guilt.

Three years later, repressing homosexual feelings and staying in the closet is still the norm at Cory's old high school. Growing up gay in the South is still difficult for today's high school student:

> I have a friend who is 17. He didn't find out he was gay until three months ago. Of course, he was gay all along but he never really looked at the facts. He was always afraid to look at them. It's hard living in the South and being gay. Here you have no place where you can go. In Florida, if you're 16, gay, and want to meet someone else you can go to a juice bar and get around people your own age. Here, you can't get into the bars. You're stuck cruising along The Battery or at the rest areas. It's not psychologically healthy. "Gay" is just a dirty word down here. It used to be the thing to ride down the road and yell "nigger." You don't do that anymore because they'll tear your car apart. So they go down to The Battery and yell

"faggot," or go to the rest area with a baseball bat. It's hard growing up gay in the South.

COMMENTARY

An arrogant and insensitive boy, Cory played on the swings until he "puked," tormented sissies, and led a group of redneck hell-raisers. In a world in which the images of homosexual men are sensitive boys with high pitched voices and a fondness for dolls who grow into effeminate queens dripping with sarcasm or dirty old men lurking around dimly lit parks, Cory could not have been a "homosexual." His biography shatters such stereotypical images. Beneath his heterosexual veneer, however, was a boy trapped within a culture of heterosexual words and images. As a silent prisoner of the flesh, Cory was confused and lost in a cell invisible to friends, family, and teachers.

Through Cory's prism of experience, we begin to explore the development of childhood homosexuality and examine the crucial distinctions among homosexual feelings, behaviors, and identities. Cory's boyhood traits and masculinities allow us to begin this three chapter exploration of gender and sexuality by examining the varied psychosocial patterns of homosexual feelings, behaviors, and identities among children and adolescents. In this commentary, particular attention is paid to genetic explanations for gender identity and homosexuality.

Gender Identity and Homosexuality in Childhood

Based upon extensive interviews, Professor Alfred Kinsey, who devoted his professional life to the understanding of human sexual behavior, concluded that "many of the adults who are actively and more or less exclusively homosexual date their activities from pre-adolescence."[2] Kinsey's conclusion is borne out by Cory's biography and other research studies.[3] For example, one study reports nearly two-thirds of homosexual-identified men masturbated with another boy before adolescence — more than double the frequency of self-reports from heterosexual-identified men.[4]

In this study, however, neither a majority of males or females reported such childhood sexual behaviors — though males were much more likely to report such incidents than females. Cory, like 10 of the 24 males in this study, engaged in homosexual behavior prior to adolescence, whereas only one female did (Everetta, whose biography appears as the third chapter in this section).

This difference between men who identify themselves as gay and women who identify themselves as lesbian reflects a fundamental difference in early childhood socialization patterns. As discussed in Chapter 11, in Southern culture, gender identity and gender role, like racial identity, take precedence over a child's sexual identity. Just as Jacob's (and many other African-Americans) primary childhood identity is racial, so too does the importance (or lack of importance) of being female or male color a child's behavior and the expectations that others have regarding such behavior.

Cory's biography illustrates the gender role socialization tolerated, if not encouraged, among boys. Cory was characteristically rebellious, independent, adventurous, sharp-witted, and quarrelsome. Intellect was prized over emotion and street smarts over school knowledge. Cory's boyhood was different from some of the other males in this study. Unlike Malcolm, Cory's voice was low and his gait sure. He lacked Royce's social sensitivity as well as Jacob's personal convictions. Like Vince, he swapped "fag" jokes but he never had close friends. But unlike Brandon's, Cory's lack of friends was a deliberate choice: he associated with others when it suited his interests. Cory never let his guard down and he never winced about "stepping over" others. He distrusted closeness, and hid himself behind a mask of smugness, toughness, and vindictiveness. His search for mastery over others left little time for a reflective journey into his feelings toward boys or his passive role in sexual encounters. For Cory, sex was power, and those who expressed feeling were held in contempt. Though he repeatedly engaged in homosexual behavior, he refused to acknowledge his same-sex feelings until he was 18.

Assuming a typical boyhood, Cory was spared the verbal and physical abuse inflicted upon effeminate children such as Alston, whose biography appears in the next chapter. Ten of the 24 males participating in this study conformed to social sex role expectations during childhood. Again, this is fewer than the three-fourths of gay men, reported in two separate studies, who did not recall displaying inappropriate sex role behavior as children.[5] Regardless of the proportion, males in this study like Cory and William, who assumed boyhood traits and expressed masculine interests, were not spared inner pain and torment as they coped with their sexuality.

William is a strapping man of 27. Soft hazel eyes highlight his rugged face. As a boy, he remembers tramping through the woods of the Piedmont on fishing and hunting jaunts. At school, sometimes he would "get my butt whipped" for not getting an 'A' in conduct due to "cutting up" in class. "I used to get a paddling almost every fricking day for yapping in class. I'd have to take notes home. I can remember never bringing home an 'A' in conduct during second grade. I hid my report cards." Despite his difficulty in controlling his tongue, William was a good student, popular among classmates and teachers.

He first remembers hearing "the word" riding the school bus in third grade. An older boy asked William if he knew "what 'a queer' was. I think they called someone 'queer' on the bus. I was the young kid on the bus and I think they thought it was kind of funny." At home, he asked his stepmother what "queer" meant. She replied, "It would be the same way as a black person being called 'nigger.' It's not something you want to be called and it's not accepted behavior."

By 11 years of age, William remembers feeling attracted to males. During recess, he particularly liked playing touch football with the older boys. As he approached adolescence, he also engaged in the ritualistic torment of girls that often signals a boy's first bout with "puppy love." "There was this one girl named Karen," William remembers. "She was probably the prettiest little girl in the school. She made a rise in my Levi's. I'd send notes with my name or another guy's name attached to it." In sixth grade, William experienced the same arousal when watching the school's principal. William recalls:

> I even fantasized about him. Then I'd try to chase it off with something else. That confused me a lot. I think I chose not to

think about it. You know how you can sometimes? You have these little fantasies but you learn how to release things. I think once I dealt with that I would just sort of not think about it. I put it in another little compartment and shut the door.

Unlike Cory, William did not engage in any childhood sexual activities. As he approached adolescence, he remembers "being confused finding some of these guys that I saw attractive and knowing that it was not what I wanted to be and not what I wanted to be called. I would not connect the two things. I would justify it in my own mind by telling myself they were really nice looking and wishing that I looked like that." William was particularly reluctant to connect his own feelings with being "queer" after the incident with Donnie:

> Donnie was a very unusual guy. His parents didn't have a lot of money so he wore clothes that were way out of style. He acted weird. Like when his father would bring him to school he'd always peck his dad on the cheek right before he got out of the car. He also walked sort of funny. He wasn't in any group. Donnie was one of those little loners. I'd always see him out in the morning before everyone went into school. Donnie would always stand by himself. I didn't see anyone around him unless someone was there to pick at him.

Mid-way through the seventh grade, William remembers an incident after school on the gridiron involving Donnie and several football players:

> I was playing football. Donnie asked some of the guys that were on the football team if he could give them a blow job in the bathroom. These guys said, "Sure let's go." They got him in the bathroom and beat him up. That got around school real quick. It was the big event of the week. So, Donnie and these three guys were taken to the principal's office. The principal asked, "Did you say this?" He said he did. So, he suspended Donnie for three days and let the other guys go. That was what

confused me at that early age. That's what I thought gay people were about and I wanted no part of it.

William did not have his first sexual experience until he was 18.
At 22, he labelled himself "gay," and told his brother about it two
years later. He remembers:

> I had really come to the point of saying to myself, "Well, if
> Mom and Dad just come out and ask, I'm not going to lie
> about it anymore. I'm so fed up with lying." Finally, some
> fart tells my brother, "You know, William is queer." So, he
> comes and tells me, "I heard that you're gay." Well, I had
> lied so much. It was just eating the shit out of me. So, when he
> finally asked I just said, "Well, now that you've mentioned it,
> yeah." He dealt with it pretty well. He was silent for a few
> minutes. I knew how much it disgusted him. At first, he was
> seeing sort of what I'd seen in the beginning. He mentioned
> Donnie that night. I said, "Well, Gene, it's weird because
> I've seen a lot of them. They range from being like Donnie to
> totally different from him. Some act just like you!" He started
> seeing something that he had not seen before. Now he sees
> things a little bit different.

The biographies of William and Cory portray a different image of
the "homosexual" than is stereotypically caricatured in an Eddie
Murphy movie or a John Rechy novel. These two biographies also
represent extremes of age of first homosexual experience: Cory's at
seven years of age and William's at 18.

According to research, the exact proportion of gay men who report childhood homosexual encounters is undetermined. That such
a relationship exists, however, is undeniable. A variety of studies,
including those conducted by Frederick Whitam, underscore this
"very close connection between one's first—usually childhood—
sexual contact and one's adult sexual orientation."[6] There are two
important caveats to be mindful of as one interprets this statement.

Though studies document the same-sex childhood explorations of
many homosexual adults, *most children who engage in such childhood behavior do not continue such behavior into adulthood*. Many
more children have same-sex erotic feelings or engage in homosex-

ual behavior than later assume a homosexual identity in adulthood. In Kinsey's seminal studies, case histories of sexual behavior of thousands of children, adolescents, and adults were analyzed. By second or third grade, Kinsey found that most children become involved in exploratory sex play with *both* sexes.[7] Sixty percent of the preadolescent boys admitted to homosexual activity. The mean age for the initial homosexual contact for boys, reported in several studies, is about nine years.[8] The incidence of homosexual behavior among girls is estimated to be from one-third to one-half less than among boys;[9] but the mean age for a girl's first homosexual experience is younger than that for boys.[10]

Though the number of adults who engage in primarily homosexual behavior is difficult to determine, it certainly is nowhere near this 60 percent figure. A recently released study, using more dated survey data, reported that fully 20 percent of adult men have engaged in some form of homosexual behavior.[11] In Kinsey's classic studies of the human male and female, he found that 37 percent of the total male population and 13 percent of the female population had at least some overt homosexual experience from adolescence through adulthood. The number of women and men who exclusively engage in homosexual behavior, however, is considerably less: According to Kinsey, eight percent of adult males, and one to three percent of females (sampled in the late forties).[12] Thus, most boys who engage in same-sex behavior during childhood do not continue it into adulthood. The ever dwindling circle in Terry's "horn holding" group illustrates this point.

Secondly, though patterns of homosexual childhood behavior are found in many adult homosexuals, *childhood same-sex behavior is not causally linked to adult homosexuality*. The psychiatric-based study, *The Sissy Boy Syndrome*, illustrates the interrelationship between biology and environment. The metaphor for the study were identical twins, Frank, Jr. and Paul. Richard Green, the study's author, states:

> Divergent socialization experiences during boyhood shaped gender-role behavior as "feminine" in one twin [Paul] and as "masculine" in the other. However, the twins' later sexual orientations do not differ as much as with most of our other

previously "feminine" and "masculine" boys. This is explainable by the constraining influence of their common genetics. Their similar genetic contributions to sexual orientation define the limits within which their childhood experiences can modify later erotic behavior.[13]

The constraining influence of a common genetic code, as several other identical twin studies posit, does not dictate the "sexual orientation" of such children. In some cases, one twin may adopt a heterosexual identity as an adult and the other a homosexual one.[14]

Nevertheless, there have been persistent efforts on the part of some researchers, most notably John Money and Gunter Dörner, to provide a biological explanation for homosexuality.[15] For more than 30 years, John Money of the Johns Hopkins University and Hospital has been conducting research on the relationship between human hormonal balance and gender and sexual identities. Based upon his extensive research and review of other research studies, Money concludes that prenatal hormonalization of the brain influences even if it does not absolutely determine "sexual orientation." Unequivocally rejecting the concept of "sexual preference," he writes:

> In the human species, a person does not prefer to be homosexual instead of heterosexual, nor to be bisexual instead of monosexual. *Sexual preference* is a moral and political term. Conceptually it implies voluntary choice, that is, that one chooses, or prefers, to be homosexual instead of heterosexual or bisexual, and vice versa. Politically, sexual preference is a dangerous term, for it implies that if homosexuals choose their preference, then they can be legally forced, under threat of punishment, to choose to be heterosexual. The concept of voluntary choice is as much in error here as in its application to handedness or to native language.[16]

In recent years, Money has been careful to steer away from the biological determinism of other researchers such as Dörner. Money notes that "sexual orientation in adulthood cannot be attributed to any variable that is either exclusively nature or exclusively nurture. . . . [T]here is no human evidence that prenatal hormonalization alone, independently of postnatal history, inexorably preordains either orientation.''[17]

Perhaps the most intriguing biological research has been conducted by the East German, Gunter Dörner. Based upon his research with laboratory rats and upon study of human sexuality, Dörner argues that homosexuality is determined by the differentiation of the hypothalamus in the fourth and fifth months of pregnancy resulting from androgen levels in the fetus. In his review of Dörner's work, philosopher Michael Ruse summarizes these findings:

> [A] male fetus exposed at the age of four or five months to normal (that is, average) high levels of androgen will, as an adult, have a male sexual orientation — he will be a heterosexual attracted towards females; while a male fetus exposed at the same age to low levels of androgen will, as an adult, have a female sexual orientation — he will be a homosexual attracted toward males. A female fetus exposed at age four or five months to normal (that is, average) low levels of androgen will, as an adult, have a female sexual orientation — she will be a heterosexual attracted towards males; while a female fetus exposed at the same age to high levels of androgen will, as an adult, have a male sexual orientation — she will be a homosexual attracted towards females.[18]

Ruse further cites evidence from human studies regarding similar (though not identical) response patterns of homosexual males and heterosexual females when injected with estrogen, compared to the responses of heterosexual males.[19] The hormonal feedback response of the homosexual males was characteristic of what one would expect of persons with a female differentiated hypothalamus.

Such studies are evidence of a biological link to the development of homosexuality. However, these studies have been conducted on limited samples of human subjects; the results are therefore open to interpretation. Further, these studies, like those of Alfred Kinsey, have focused exclusively on sexual behavior. But, as the biographies of Cory and William underscore, exclusive focus on sexual behavior is inadequate for an understanding of the psychosexual development of children and the adoption of a sexual identity in adulthood. Ruse concurs: "There is a lot more to gender identity and sexual orientation than the effects of bodily fluids, however vital. . . . [W]hat has to be conceded (and what has certainly been conceded by me) is that human homosexuality centres primarily on feelings, desires, and fantasies, with behaviour somewhat secondary."[20] It is to these areas which we now turn.

Homosexual Feelings, Behaviors, and Identities

"There is a general problem of how you get from the genes to the biochemical product, to the desire, and then to the behavior," states sociobiologist James Weinrich. Acknowledging the importance of non-biological factors, he adds, "There has to be the very important question of how orientation, a feeling, a desire, translates into actual behavior. And that's something that obviously is very dependent on the culture."[21]

What are the relationships among homosexual feelings, behaviors, and identities? How does culture affect the development and understanding of each of these? There are important distinctions among these, as the biographical portraits of these sexual rebels as well as studies in the social and natural sciences illustrate. In addressing these questions, I believe that homosexual (as well as heterosexual) identity is socially constructed more than it is biologically determined.

Feeling same-sex emotional or erotic attractions, engaging in homosexual behavior, and acquiring a homosexual identity are four qualitatively different components of the childhood/adolescent homosexual experience. In this study, on average, participants were first aware of their emotional attraction to members of the same sex at the age of 9 1/2. Approximately three years later, these sexual rebels reported homoerotic feelings. On average, their first homosexual experience occurred at the age of 14 1/2 and they designated themselves "homosexual" three years later. These findings coincide with other studies employing larger male and female samples,[22] and supports the contention of Kinsey Institute researchers who consider "homosexual arousal and activity as *part of*, rather than a contribution to, a homosexual preference. . . ."[23]

Data reported in such studies are valuable in that they underscore the distinctions among these different components of the homosexual experience. However, they often hide the diversity and complexity of the human sexual experience behind frequency counts and median scores. Further, they suggest to the casual reader an invariable linearity in homosexual development that belies the distinctiveness of human beings. Biographical histories provide an opportunity to explore the degree of diversity.

These four components can be configured in a variety of ways — 24 possible permutations. Only four were found in this study; the most dominant pattern was for participants first to report feelings of attraction to the same sex followed by erotic same-sex feelings, then to engage in homosexual behavior, and finally to label oneself "homosexual" [Attraction - Eroticism - Behavior - Identity (A-E-B-I)].[24]

A young person may feel a same-sex attraction but, like William in this study, not act upon it until early adulthood. Though he was first aware of being attracted to other males at the age of 11, William did not engage in any homosexual activity until the age of 18 when he first acknowledged his erotic feelings for men. During adolescence his sexual fantasies were nearly exclusively homosexual; however, he never engaged in such activity during high school, nor did he identify himself as "homosexual" until he was 22.

This pattern (A-E-B-I) was found in 21 of the 36 case studies including those of Royce, Georgina, Vince, Norma Jean, Jacob, Malcolm, and Obie. These data, however, hide the significant variation in the ages at which these events occurred. For example, Malcolm was first aware of his same-sex feelings and eroticism at the age of three, engaged in homosexual behavior at four, and at five labelled himself "homosexual." Georgina, on the other hand, was aware of these feelings at the age of six, felt erotic urges at 12, engaged in homosexual activity at 14, and labelled herself "homosexual" at 17.

The second most common pattern among participants in this study was for homosexual identity to form prior to homosexual behavior (A-E-I-B). Six of the participants, including Brandon, Lenora, and Elisa, fell into this pattern. Like William, Elisa did not engage in homosexual activity until her mid-twenties. However, she was first aware of her attraction toward females at the age of five and by the age of 13 had labelled herself "homosexual" as she became aware of her erotic feelings for women. As a self-identified "homosexual," Elisa more or less exclusively fantasized about other women during adolescence without engaging in any sexual activity:

> I remember when I was a little kid saying that I was going to marry women. I remember in science class the teacher would talk about people who had chromosome problems and who weren't really women. That always terrified me 'cause I figured I was one of them. In high school there were three of us girls who worked at this hamburger joint. The other two would kiss each other just out of affection and hold hands. They thought people should express themselves. I wouldn't do that because they didn't have the same feelings as me. For me, it wouldn't have been just signs of affection. I thought that I could suppress it the rest of my life. I knew I might be a homosexual and that really scared me. I thought what they did to people like that was to lock them up.

For both William and Elisa, emotional and erotic feelings were distinct from homosexual behaviors and identities. There were three persons in this study, however, whose homosexual behavior preceded same-sex feelings and identities. One of these participants, Cory, reported having homoerotic feelings well before feelings of emotional attraction (B-E-A-I); the other two, Grant and Heyward, indicated that the attraction to the same sex followed their first homosexual encounters but preceded their erotic feelings (B-A-E-I). This evidence bears out Thomas Weinberg's observation that "Actual sexual experiences are neither a necessary nor a sufficient factor in labelling oneself as homosexual."[25]

Cory engaged in homosexual behavior and fantasized about members of the same sex but did not identify himself as "homosexual" or attach any emotions to these sexual encounters. He was aware of erotic feelings for members of the same sex as early as age seven, but first acknowledged his emotional feelings for other men only at age 17 when he fell in love with Winston. Though no one, except Malcolm, engaged in homosexual activity earlier than Cory, he was one of the latest to identify himself as "homosexual." Eleven years separated these two points in Cory's biography — longer than any other participant, with the exception of Grant.

Cory's passive role in earlier homosexual situations and his lack of emotional feeling for males and of a homosexual identity are analogous to situational homosexuality — i.e., the homosexuality of, for instance, prisoners and boarding-school students who are permitted limited physical contact with members of the other gender; youthful male hustlers turning "tricks" for a place to sleep or to earn money to take their girlfriends to a movie; and married men who occasionally engage in the "tearoom trade."[26] In such situations, assuming an "active" role in same sex activity does not imply homosexuality;[27] the sex is connected with power, dominance, or control, but not emotion.

With Cory, then, we can distinguish between erotic and emotional attachment, as well as between homosexual behavior and homosexual identity. There are, of course, other possible configurations. As noted above, there were two other people in this study who engaged in homosexual behavior prior to developing either emotional feelings or erotic attractions for members of the same sex. However, in both cases, feelings for the same sex were *followed* by erotic feelings at about the age of 12 or 13. Both of these cases, Grant and Heyward, are African-American males who, like Cory, reported sexual initiatives coming from other persons.

Grant started having sex with his teenage cousin at the age of seven though he did not first have emotional or erotic feelings toward males until he was 12. Grant first labelled himself "homosexual" at the age of 19. He remembers his first homosexual experience:

We engaged in sex from the time I was seven until I was 14. He forced me to do it. He told me that if I told, bad things would happen. As time went on, I became more and more comfortable with it. It really didn't bother me. Looking back at it now, I don't think I wanted to have sex with him. But, the feelings that were soon to be there were being expressed by him at the time.

Heyward first engaged in homosexual activity at the age of 12, though he did not develop emotional or erotic feelings toward other boys until a year later and did not identify himself as a "homosexual" until he was 20. Heyward recalls:

> In small Southern towns you always have your different characters. Everyone has their "Bubba" and, I found out, everyone has their town fag. Dexter was a year behind me in school. He was very feminine acting. First they called him "sissy," and then they called him "faggot." Well, I used to go riding my bike in the afternoons. One day I just happened to see Dexter coming in the opposite direction. Something told me to turn around because I didn't want to be seen in public with him. But, I kept on going. He stopped. Being the person that I am, I stopped to talk to him. We stopped in front of an old, abandoned house. He asked me to come back there with him. After that, I was scared. I was scared that somebody saw us or that Dexter would go back and tell. Knowing that I had been with this person would have been highly embarrassing. I don't know what my parents would have done. Believe it or not, I met him again. We did it a couple of more times. But, up until my junior year in college, I didn't think about what it meant. I just wanted to do it.

Thus, three cases in this study followed the B-E-A-I and B-A-E-I patterns; three others, Terry, Alston, and Henry, experienced homosexual behavior as the second event in their biographies, which followed an A-B-E-I pattern. Note that *all six cases were males*; no female in this study engaged in homosexual behavior without first experiencing emotional and erotic attraction for other women.

Terry, Alston, and Henry reported first feeling attracted to members of the same sex, then having a homosexual encounter, followed by erotic arousal and concluding with the adoption of a homosexual identity. As described in Chapter 8, Terry already felt an attraction to males by the second grade which was followed by a long series of sexual encounters with a "horn-holding" ring of neighborhood boys beginning at the age of nine. It was not until age

12, however, that Terry first had erotic feelings for males; four years later he labelled himself as "homosexual."

Henry's pattern was the same though the ages at which he arrived at each step were quite different. Like Terry, he felt emotional attraction to other boys in primary school. For Henry there were no erotic feelings for men until a year after his first homosexual experience which occurred at the age of 19. During high school, he recalls his lack of sexual interest:

> When I was in high school, I liked to walk around The Battery in Charleston. While I was just out walking, guys would start to follow me in their cars. After a while I figured out that these guys were gay and they were following me because they wanted to take me home. Somehow, I thought that was really neat. I liked guys to follow me in their cars because it just reinforced the idea that I was pretty. That was neat! Sometimes I'd see how many cars I could get to follow me at one time.

The Battery was where, at 19, Henry had his first homosexual experience. Telling himself that he had "strayed," as noted in Chapter 5, he didn't even consider the possibility of "being gay" until his junior year in college. "I really didn't understand being 'straight' but I felt all the time I had to make people think that 'I'm straight.' In my own mind, I thought, 'Yes. I am straight.' If I had actually sat down and honestly thought about it, I would have realized that I was gay much earlier. But, there were a lot of things that I just didn't think about."

Before embarking on his trip to France, at 20 years of age, Henry first began to seriously think about it. It was while attending his Episcopalian church one summer night:

> We were all standing in line to say goodbye to the minister. I was bored so I started to play this game with myself. If I could take anyone in this room that I wanted to into another room and have sex within the next five minutes, who would I take? The important thing was that it had to be within the next five minutes. I had always told myself that I was "straight" because I had affections for girls. But, I was never initially at-

tracted to them until I got to know them. Even when I got to
know them I was never sexually attracted to them. So this five
minutes was important because I couldn't get to know them to
like them; I had to like them first. Well, I came up with three
guys. I went home and thought about that. I started masturbating while thinking about these guys.

When Henry returned from France, following conversations with
his professor and sexual fantasies about a fellow classmate, he continued to reflect:

When I got back I just wanted to think quietly to myself. Then
one night I was over at a girl's house who I had gone to high
school with. She asked me to go outside with her. We sat on
the sidewalk. She told me about another girl who was from our
high school who was living with another woman. At first that
really surprised me. Then, I remembered that I always felt a
sense of closeness with that girl. I was never exactly sure why.
I said, "Good, that's the way it should be for her." Then my
friend touched me and said, "I know. That's something that
I've been wanting to tell you for a while. There's just no other
way to say it except that I know and it's okay." My first reaction was to deny it. Then, I thought for a moment. I said,
"Yes, I am." There was just this tremendous release. But, it
was such a struggle not to say, "No, I am not." I just stopped
fighting something that I shouldn't have been fighting at all. It
was such a relief and it was so nice to know that someone else
knew and it didn't make any difference.

This feeling of relief contrasts with Cory's resentment toward his
father for withholding information. In both cases, however, it was
through the process of reflecting and making sense of prior homoerotic feelings and behavior that each proclaimed his homosexual
identity. *Making these sexual feelings and experiences personally
meaningful is done within a cultural context.*
    Two of the participants in this study, Kimberly and Nathaniel,
have engaged in homosexual behavior but have not identified themselves as "homosexual." One final participant, 'Lizabeth, has
identified herself as "homosexual" but has yet to consummate her

feelings through a physical relationship with another woman. In all three instances, participants reported feelings of attraction first, then the onset of erotic feelings. These three persons are simply in the process of assuming the two most common patterns found in this study (A-E-B-I and A-E-I-B) — assuming that Kimberly and Nathaniel eventually assume homosexual identities and 'Lizabeth consummates her homosexual feelings. 'Lizabeth and Nathaniel, however, evidence bisexual identities as measured through the Klein Sexual Orientation Grid, and Kimberly falls almost within the bisexual range,[28] and so such an assumption may not be valid.

Kimberly was first aware of feeling attracted to other girls at the age of eight. "I felt like I could relate to them more so than males. I had a huge crush on my third grade teacher. From that point on I became aware of my feelings. . . ." Throughout school Kimberly "fit in." An outstanding student, she was class president for three years as well as a star athlete. She casually dated during high school, although she never engaged in any type of sexual activity with males or females. Her feelings for the same sex were "just something I pushed to the back of my mind." For Kimberly, a homosexual person is someone "who has chosen an alternative life-style and expresses her feelings for the same sex." Based upon this definition, Kimberly does not define herself as a lesbian. She remembers talking with others about sex in high school: "I used to sit around and listen to the girls talk about it. A lot of the girls became sexually active in ninth grade. I abstained; I am still abstaining." Kimberly recalls one incident in which she was challenged to perform sexually with a male. "I was dating this guy. We had been dating from about a year. It felt so unnatural. Once he brought up the question of a sexual encounter. I just stuck to my guns and told him, 'I don't believe in premarital sex.' But, there were some heated moments."

At 18, Kimberly first had sex with a woman. Three years later she is "seeing a girl," but continues to date guys. But, she also remains uncertain about her sexual identity:

> I can see an attractive guy and say, "I wouldn't mind going out with him." I'm still finding out about my sexuality. I'm

still learning about myself. It might be that this is a phase I'm going through. I don't know. I feel very comfortable around females. I feel comfortable around males when it's on a friendly basis. But when it starts to get deeper that's when I get uncomfortable.

Kimberly's ambivalent thoughts about her sexuality were echoed later during the interview as she changed her mind regarding the origins of homosexuality. "I think homosexuality is inborn. I don't think you have any control over it. It's just something that's there for me. It's just a matter of time before I realize it and begin to deal with it."

Unlike Kimberly, 'Lizabeth has yet to have a sexual relationship with another woman. Like Kimberly, she was first aware of feeling attracted to other girls at an early age. For 'Lizabeth, a homosexual person is someone "who is sexually attracted to members of her own sex. I have friends who are attracted to other women. But, they're not feeling the same thing that I am inside." A year ago, at the age of 18, 'Lizabeth labeled herself a "homosexual. I have a sense of peace about me that I've never had. I don't have to play any games. I don't have to pretend that I'm straight when I'm not. It's like a weight has been lifted off my shoulders." During the past two months, 'Lizabeth has been "going steady" with Laureen who is two years her junior. "I want to live at the beach with my fiance. She or I would like to have children and just grow old together at the beach." A month before her interview, however, 'Lizabeth's mother discovered love letters Laureen had written her. A heated conversation followed:

> She tells me it's a phase. She says, "How can you possibly know that you're gay? You've never been to bed with anyone yet!" "Fine," I say. "You want me to go out and sleep with somebody to find out if I'm gay?" Then she says, "You messed around with a girl. Why can't you mess around with a guy?" I just looked at her. "Exactly what do you mean? Laureen and I have never had sex together. We talked about it and decided we weren't ready for that. What do you want me to

do? Go out and marry a guy or sleep with him so I can figure out that I'm stuck in a marriage that I don't want?''

Though 'Lizabeth may have come to terms with her own sexuality, she has not resolved this matter with her mother. "My mother keeps telling me that the heterosexual norm would be so much easier to live under. But, I had to live that way for 18 years and it wasn't easier. It was screwing me up in my head."

The distinction between behavior, sexual attraction, emotion, and identity are clearly important, yet are constantly overlooked, by both laypersons such as 'Lizabeth's mother, and by researchers such as Gunter Dörner. In terms of the sequence of these four components, most (30) of the participants in this study evidenced one of two patterns: Following awareness of same-sex feelings and the acknowledgement of homoerotic feelings, they either labelled themselves "homosexual" or engaged in homosexual behavior.

The search for sexual identity is important politically as well as personally. There is no incontrovertible evidence to assert that homosexuality is an outcome of genetics nor are there conclusive studies documenting its acquisition following birth. Nevertheless, as discussed in Chapter 15, one of the most frequent claims by lesbian and gay activists is that homosexuality represents an "orientation," and one of their greatest fears is the use of biotechnology to prevent homosexual-linked hormones from developing in fetal tissues. Paradoxically, activists are equally afraid of the concept of homosexuality as "sexual preference" — i.e., that people *choose* to be gay or lesbian. This would mean that presumably, through secular or Christian counseling, one could choose to stop being a homosexual.

"Being gay," however, can often only be understood through its opposite, "being straight." This sexual dichotomy, rejected long ago by Alfred Kinsey and Sigmund Freud, is difficult for some of the participants in this study, such as Nathaniel and Kimberly, to straddle. Others, like William and Elisa, simply reconstruct their heterosexual feelings and experiences as fraudulent as they proclaim their new found homosexual identity. Reducing sexual response to an either/or category, however, simplifies the complexity of the human sexual experience and transforms unique journeys of the human spirit into simple equations for "Christian living" or into jingoistic canons of "gay liberation." Interestingly, many fundamentalists and gay rights advocates share a common assumption: an untested belief of the *essentiality* of sexuality. The next two chapters challenge this belief by examining how human beings construct the very meanings of maleness/femaleness, masculine/feminine, and heterosexual/homosexual.

REFERENCE NOTES

1. Romanovsky, 1984.

2. Kinsey, Pomeroy and Martin, 1948:171.

3. Bell, Weinberg and Hammersmith, 1981; Jay and Young, 1979; Whitam, 1977a.

4. Saghir and Robins, 1973.

5. Bieber, Dain, Dince, Drellich, Grand, Gundlach, Kremer, Rifkin, Wilbur, and Bieber, 1962; Whitam, 1977b.

6. Whitam, 1977a:9-10.

7. Kinsey, Pomeroy and Martin, 1948; Kinsey, Pomeroy, Martin and Gebhard, 1953.

8. Kinsey, Pomeroy and Martin, 1948; Sorensen, 1973; Finger, 1975.

9. Kinsey, Pomeroy, Martin and Gebhard, 1953; Pillard, 1974; Wyatt, Peters and Guthrie, 1988.

10. Kinsey, Pomeroy and Martin, 1948; Kinsey, Pomeroy, Martin and Gebhard, 1953; Sorensen, 1973; Finger, 1975.

11. Fay, Turner, Klassen and Gagnon, 1989.

12. Kinsey, Pomeroy and Martin, 1948:650-651; Kinsey, Pomeroy, Martin and Gebhard, 1953:474. The narrow, clinical criteria used to define sexual orientation and the use of prison populations in the sample may well have resulted in misclassification of persons and an inflated proportion of homosexual persons (Harry, 1984). Some of these concerns are addressed in Kinsey's biography penned by Wardell Pomeroy (1972).

13. Green, 1987:351-352.

14. Davison, Brierly and Smith, 1971; Green, 1974; Klintworth, 1961; Mesnikoff, Rainer, Kolb and Carr, 1963; Parker, 1964; Zuger, 1976. Though, as in much of the research on homosexuality, these findings and conclusions have not gone uncontested (e.g., Puterbaugh, 1984).

15. Dörner, 1976; Dörner, Rohde, Stahl, Krell, and Wolf-Günther, 1975; Money, 1980; Money and Ehrhardt, 1972. For a critique of such work, see S. Baker, 1980; Birke, 1981; Birke, 1982; Fausto-Sterling, 1985; Gartrell, 1982; Hoult, 1983-84; Van Dyck, 1984; Weinberg, 1984. A review of both Dörner's and Money's work is to be found in Ruse, 1988:84-129.

16. Money, 1987:385.

17. Money, 1987:397-398.

18. Ruse, 1988:110.

19. Ruse, 1988:122-23. The specific studies Ruse cites are: Dörner et al., 1975; Dörner, Rohde, Stahl, Krell, and Wolf-Güther, 1976; Gladue, Green, and Hellman, 1984.

20. Ruse, 1988:116, 118.

21. Quoted in Thompson, 1983:47-48.

22. Studies of males include: Dank, 1971; Harry and DeVall, 1978; Roesler and Doesler, 1972; Troiden and Goode, 1980; McDonald, 1982; Van Wyck and Geist, 1984. Studies of females, like this one, follow similar age patterns with the exception of a later age for first homosexual experiences. See: Gramick, 1984; Califia, 1979; Kooden et al., 1979. An elaboration of gender as well as racial differences in this study is found in Chapter 12.

23. Bell, Weinberg and Hammersmith, 1981:104.

24. See Appendix, Table 2.

25. Weinberg, 1983:300.

26. David, 1970; Fishman, 1934; Gathorne-Hardy, 1978; Giallombardo, 1966; Halleck and Hersko, 1962; Humphreys, 1970; Lockwood, 1980; Proper, 1978; Reiss, 1961; Sykes, 1958; Wooden and Parker, 1982.

27. These meanings assigned to passive homosexual relations are also found in Mediterranean-based cultures (Brandes, 1981; Carrier, 1980).

28. See Appendix, Figures 1 and 2. Interestingly, while 'Lizabeth is a self-defined lesbian, the ratings on the KSOG place her in the bisexual range whereas Kimberly, who is ambivalent about her sexuality, falls within the homosexual range.

Chapter 10

The Outcasts

ALSTON AND THE ROCKY HORROR PICTURE SHOW

Let's hear it for the people of the stage
And the silver screen and the printed page
Give us a place where it's okay
To laugh and cry and to feel our pain
jesters and clowns and carnival people
Trying to make it a little bit easier
Singing and playing so fine
All in a day's work, all in a lifetime

Ron Romanovsky, "Carnival People"[1]

Alston has come further than the mere 50 mile distance between his home town and the capitol. He sports short blond hair with a rag tail, wears a suit and tie, and speaks in a distinctive Southern accent. He vividly remembers growing up in a town of 1,200 people: "There was one main street. Everyone knew what everyone did. There were few churches but lots of church activity and only a few blacks lived on the outskirts of town." More than a few of the town's inhabitants were related, in one way or another, to Alston. As far as his eyes could see, there were aunts, grandmothers, uncles, and grandfathers. "I lived right among my father's relatives. One of his brothers lived on one side, the other brother lived behind us. His sister lived over to the side and his mother lived practically in our backyard."

Members of Alston's extended family did not get along with one another just as he seldom got along with his brothers and sisters. "We all loved each other. But, I guess it was a kind of had-to-love." Alston and his brother, Luther, were the only two children from their parents' marriage. "Luther was very Civil War. He liked armies and guns." Within the family there was also a brother and two sisters from the parents' prior marriages. "My grandmother adored my father's first wife but couldn't stand my mother. Other Southern families are very close but not my family. We were pitted against each other. Luther picked on me a lot. He was a lot like my father."

Bart, Alston's father, was an independent trucker spending most of his time on the road. Alston has few kind things to say about him:

> He was bald on top and had a pot-bellied stomach. If you did something wrong, he was usually there. He would let out a yell and stomp toward you in his bare feet and a tank top T-shirt. It was like a buffalo running up on you. With me, his favorite thing to do was to kick. He kicked me a lot. He beat my older brother, too — beat him so hard once with a stick, he got welts on him and bled. He beat my younger brother with a folding ruler. He hit my sister once but he never hit my mother. He tried once. She told him she'd kill him if he did it again.

In contrast, Alston's father treated the oldest sister with kid gloves: "Tammy was my father's pet. He worshiped the ground she walked on. If she needed a new pair of shoes, he would take the money for food and spend it on her. Nothing she ever did was wrong."

Alston was born at home, delivered by two neighbors in 1962. One of them was "the church lady who would come and pick us up on Sundays. She was hard-core Southern Baptist: no dancing, no drinking, no smoking." Alston fondly reflects upon his early childhood:

> That was a fun time. I didn't really have a worry in the world. We weren't rich. My family was very poor. My father sent home money but we didn't have a lot to provide ourselves with material goods. We had to make our own fun and use our own imagination to escape from not having.

Alston's favorite forms of escape were bicycling and watching television. When his dad was at home, Alston was often seen riding around the six blocks on either side of Main Street:

I was a loner. I only had a few times when friends came home
and spent the night. The rest of the time, I stayed by myself
and was left to my own imagination. I'd go places and put
myself in different situations. I was also a TV-holic. I especially liked disaster movies and scary stuff. I'd sit down and
write plays and skits.

In school, Alston spent little time on homework and had a lackluster
academic performance. "There was no big emphasis placed on
grades at home. Mom would just say, 'If you don't pass, they'll put
you back a year.' So, all I had ever worried about was just passing
at the end of the year." What he disliked most about school, however, was being around other kids — especially in the close and un-
supervised setting of the school bus:

It was a little scary. There were just lots of kids. The way the
bus traveled we were the next to last people to be picked up.
When we got on, the bus would be practically full. I was effeminate and there were people on the bus who did not like my
older brothers and sisters. We didn't wear the better clothes;
we wore hand-me-downs with holes in them. People didn't
think us anywhere near their equals. I was picked on a lot.
People didn't want me to sit down. They'd make a face or say
something.

During recess Alston would play by himself or jump rope with the
girls. Alston reminisces, "All the other boys were out chumming
around and playing football or tag. The girls treated me a little nicer
than the boys did." Alston was routinely harassed by his classmates. "Sissy' kind of stuck with me until about seventh grade,"
he recalls. "Then it turned to 'fag'. I was a loner, an outcast."
Alston's relations with his teachers also were poor:

I really didn't listen a lot to the teacher. She would tell the
class to stop talking and I would still be talking. She would tell
the class to stop drawing and I would continue to draw. She
singled me out and made me stand in the corner and ridiculed
me before the class. They all picked up on it and started ridi-
culing me.

Imagination was more important to Alston than homework. By third grade he was earning D's and F's. He simply refused to apply himself. "The third grade teacher came up with a new torture that I had not been exposed to before," Alston pauses; "She'd draw a circle on the board and make you stand in front of the board for 10 minutes with your nose in the circle without moving while the rest of the class laughed at you."

Despite Alston's lackluster performance in the classroom, he was always placed in the "B group" in the class—"The kids who weren't the super smart ones but those that applied themselves in different areas." Not coincidentally, this was the same group to which his brother and sister had been assigned. Alston continues:

> My first grade teacher, Mrs. White, had had my sister, Tammy, and my brother. She knew from the moment I walked in there: "You're Tammy's and Luther's brother, aren't you?" She had me pegged from the start. "Well, I know you're going to be just like them." Others kids would come in and she'd say, "Oh! You're Linda's sister. We're going to get along just fine." There was one black girl in the "B group." The rest of the black children were in the "D group."

Bertie was one of the other students in the "B group." One day Alston asked his parents if she could come over. "That's very nice,' they said. Then they met Bertie. It kind of freaked them out. This little girl that I wanted to bring home was black. My mother was kind of speechless."

Alston's sorry school performance and his classmates' persistent badgering continued through fourth grade. Fifth grade was an important year for Alston, for he was assigned to the "A group." His teacher, Miss Langston, made a lasting impression on him:

> I liked her because she shaved her eyebrows off and drew them on with a big crayon. She had a big bouffant hairdo. I sat up front in the class. One day the principal's son, Derek, who was just a little hellion, took my books and threw them in the garbage can. I just broke down in tears and cried my eyes out. Miss Langston ridiculed Derek in front of the entire class for having mistreated me and made him apologize to me. With tears in his eyes, he apologized. Before when I was mis-

treated, it was overlooked. She was the first teacher I remember calling someone down.

Alston began to bring his school work home and even started reading a bit. "Miss Langston," he asserted, "she made me see something."

One winter day Alston returned from Miss Langston's class and found his uncles and aunts sitting around the kitchen table talking quietly. The church lady, Mrs. Mosely, was comforting his mother. His older sister, Tammy, was crying, and Luther had tears streaming down his face. Alston asked, "What's going on?" "Your father passed away," he was told. Alston reflects:

> I just stood there and thought, "Oh." Then I went outside and walked around a bit. I thought, "He's gone." I was almost relieved. He was out of the way now. He wasn't going to bother me. I wasn't going to be beat anymore. Everyone cried except me.

After Bart's death things changed for Alston in school. A potted plant arrived from Miss Langston's class. "That was kind of a point where there was a little recognition made, a little acceptance. But, people still made jokes about me and called me names." His appreciation for Miss Langston, though, was genuine: "Miss L. did a lot of changing in me. She sat me down and said, 'I'm going to pass you even though your grades are horrible. I think you can do better and you should.' I respect her because she had taken up for me."

Alston began his last year in elementary school as a sixth grader with high expectations.

> When I got off the bus and got in I walked around and looked for my name on the sheet. People who had been in the "A group" the year before were there. They all greeted me, "Hey, how are you doing? Welcome back." I came in and sat down. About an hour later the principal came and said, "You're not supposed to be here. We've made a mistake. You're supposed to be back in the 'B group.'" He took me out and put me back with the people I had been with in the fourth grade — kind of like being knocked back down and put into an old situation and surroundings. People in the "A

group,'' like Derek, just laughed at me. They became the jocks and the cheerleaders in high school.

Despite this setback, Alston's grades continued to improve with the support of Miss Langston. He visited with her frequently. "When I would do good on tests and things, I would bring them down to her. I'd say, 'Look what I've done.' She always offered encouragement." Alston also felt differently about his classmates' harassment. "It was getting to the point," he recalls, "that 'sissy' didn't hurt as much. I just kind of accepted that as a pet name." There were limits, however, to Alston's tolerance as his most memorable childhood tale reveals:

> Wilbur moved in new at sixth grade. He happened to be in the "B group." He went along with the crowd. He'd call me names and stuff. "Sissy" was his favorite. My teacher got up and left the room one day. Wilbur started in on me, "Sissy! Sissy! Sissy!" I was sitting two seats over from him. I got up from my desk and walked around to him and squeaked, "What did you call me?" He sat there for a second and got a sheepish grin on his face and said, "Sissy." "That's what I thought you called me." Whack! I slapped him as hard as I could — backhanded. The class just roared. I walked back and sat down. The teacher came in. They all got real quiet. Wilbur is sitting there kind of stunned. Then the class starts tattling on me. "Alston got up and slapped Wilbur." The teacher just looked at Wilbur and looked at me. "Well," she said, "he probably deserved it." From that point on we became good friends. He was like one of my best male friends in high school. I think it also got me some respect. That was the first time I ever stood up for myself.

Alston entered junior high school the following year.

> We were moved into an area of the school we weren't allowed to go into when we were in the sixth grade. There was kind of an unspoken dividing line — a long hallway that connected down to the other part of the school. Past the doors of the cafeteria led into another world, another part of the school. There were lots of breezeways and classrooms. If we were

caught out in that area going up to the sixth grade we were paddled. That was a taboo area. Suddenly, we were allowed inside. There were all these new teachers, classrooms, and hallways. It was real disorienting and, at the same time, it made me feel older. Instead of being the big kid on the playground, suddenly I'm small again. There were all these seniors and big black men that liked to pick on me.

Though he continued to experience harassment at school, his grades steadily improved. In the seventh grade, Alston started being more of a "teacher's pet," doing extra credit work in his classes and talking with the teachers in the library during recess. Soon he became a solid "B" student. He also became less introverted. During lunch, he associated with two older female students, one of whom went to his church. Eating at a big round table off to the side of the cafeteria, Alston listened more than he talked. It is here that he remembers hearing his first "fag joke":

There was a joke about a little boy who finds two flies on top of one another. He asks his mother if there are boy flies. His mother says, "Yes." Then he asks her if there are girl flies. His mother thinks, "Oh, no. He's learning about the birds and the bees and he is much too young." So, she says, "No, son. There are no such thing as girl flies." The boy goes back into the other room and swats the two flies. As they fall to the floor he mutters, "Faggots."

Alston laughed along with everyone else. But, "it didn't dawn on me that they were talking about a guy and a guy together. I was still pretty naive. When someone would say the word 'sex,' I would blush."

Throughout his childhood, Alston rarely thought about sexuality or engaged in sexual activity. "I really hadn't come to grips that I really liked guys. It was still a big brother sort of thing." There were several occasions, though, where older men would show affection to him:

When I was young, Father would bring in trucking buddies with him. They'd come in and they would stay for a week or so in the spare bedroom. They seem to have singled me out. I started calling them "uncles." Anything I wanted they gave to me. They liked having me on their laps. This one man, Ben, used to get us in his car. My mother turned us over to him because he was like a friend of the family. She would always send him pictures of us kids. He would take us out and buy us drinks and kiss us a lot. Finally, it got to the point that I didn't want to be kissed anymore. I told my mother about it, "Ben likes to kiss." My mother told me to put vanilla flavoring on my lips and that if he kissed that he'd get a bad taste. For the longest time I would put vanilla flavoring on my lips. But, there was a lot of holding and fondling. I liked him, though. Those are fond memories.

Alston's first real sexual encounter occurred when he was a high school freshman. His mother was a wrestling fan. "She used to watch it on television, go to the matches, and get involved in it so much that she'd be screaming and be beating on the person next to her," recollects Alston. Soon the entire family became involved with a group of semi-professional wrestlers. They would routinely stop by the house on the way to or from a local wrestling match. "They were nice looking," remembers Alston. "I liked being with them. I felt an attraction." Occasionally, some of the wrestlers would sleep over. One night was particularly memorable for Alston:

He was sharing my bed. I was kind of waiting for it and it happened. I had my first orgasm, but it was hand-wise. I was so naive that when I was fixing to experience the orgasm I thought I was fixing to pee. He explained it to me. No one ever took me aside and explained the birds and the bees to me. I felt older. I felt a little more knowledgeable. But, I didn't look at it as being homosexual.

Alston and his family criss-crossed South Carolina and Georgia with these wrestlers on and off for more than a year. "We would see them get into the ring and be the worst of enemies, then they would get back in the van with us and have their arms around each other. I guess they were bisexual. They did it with themselves; they did it with my sisters; they did it with me.''

There were other instances in which Alston's attraction for men surfaced. One day he borrowed a book from another freshman. ''Tight Pants Ricky would bring bondage books to school. He gave me one about some girls' school where they would torture the girls and have sex. The cover had two good looking guys on it.'' Alston fantasized steamy sex scenes with the two guys. During this time, however, he had yet to associate his same-sex experiences with homosexuality, identify these fantasies as homosexual, or label himself a homosexual. But, he continued to endure the verbal and physical harassment from his fellow students. His experiences of humiliation were petty but constant. He recalls one typical incident at the school:

> I had to go from the bottom floor to the top floor. If you were going up the stairs, you were against the wall; going down, you were against the rail. When I was changing classes I had all the books in my hands looking down and walking up. I'd hear someone mutter ''Faggot'' and have my books knocked down. People are walking over me as I am trying to gather my books. I don't have time to turn around and see who said it.

Alston had been spending nights at Wilbur's farm house where they would ride horses, jump on the trampoline, and play in the barn. Occasionally, Hollis, a fellow classmate, would join the two-some. In their sophomore year, Hollis invited Wilbur and Alston to join his family for a spring weekend at a Charleston beach.

> We were walking down to the far end of the beach which I later found out was where a lot of cruising went on. That's when Hollis told me that he was ''gay.'' That surprised me a little since we had become such close friends. Then, I found out that he and Wilbur had been playing around on and off in the barn. That really surprised me.

Though Alston had not made the connection between ''being gay'' and ''homosexuality,'' he told them that he, too, was ''gay.''

In Alston's high school of 300 students, no subterranean gay group existed. At times, even Hollis and Wilbur avoided associating with Alston at school.

> It seemed like every class had their *one* homosexual, their *one* scapegoat, their *one* outcast. I was the one in our class. I was picked on and harassed for it. Hollis had a different reputation. He didn't give a shit. He didn't do good school work and he was proud of it. He was caught in the ball park with this girl one time so his reputation was okay. At times, I was comfortable "being gay" in high school. I just wish that I wouldn't have been harassed. What made me feel uncomfortable was hearing the word "faggot" and being hassled in the halls. That's what hurt.

Before the end of that school year, Alston finally made the connection between "homosexuality" and "being gay":

> It was near the end of the tenth grade. I was on the bus with a girl named Trisha. I don't know how the subject of men-loving-men came up but she said, "That's homosexuality!" I'd heard the term but then it finally dawned on me what it meant. I said, "I didn't know it was a sin." Trish said, "Oh, yeah. It's in the Bible. Sodom and Gomorrah, you know." That really made me think.

Before that time, Alston had sporadically attended the local Baptist church accompanied by the church lady, Mrs. Mosely. It was not until his conversation with Trisha that Alston made the connection between having sex with another man and homosexuality. With Trisha's help, Alston confessed his sins and entered his "church phase":

> Trisha went to the pastor for me and told him. When I got there he already knew what I was there for. He helped me along with it. He told me the standard things: God loves you; He doesn't want you to be a homosexual; you'll burn in hell if you don't change; come down for your call to altar tonight and repent, kneel, and pray — just the general stuff. At the end of service, they had the call to altar. Everyone was standing there

singing. I walked down the aisle. I went to the front, got down, prayed, and asked to be forgiven. A couple of weeks later I was baptized. I became born again!

Alston accompanied his mother to church every Sunday. "Mom wasn't as hard-core as I was. But, I think the proudest she ever was of me was whenever I was involved with the church."

During the next six months, Alston's public life changed. "I was trying so hard to be something else. I burned movie sound tracks that they said were 'devil music.' I spouted gibberish and Bible verses." Alston also began dating. He went steady with Willa, another church member. "She threw the shot put. She was into track. She had a short butch haircut. She was a very tough, masculine girl." Giving Willa his class ring, he escorted her to their junior prom. Prom night was an important event in Alston's life:

> It was a disco prom. As I stepped through the shimmering streamers hanging down, there was a table over to the side where all the jocks and cheerleaders were sitting. Derek saw me and whispered. I put my hand out. Willa took my hand and stepped through. The entire table turned and looked like, "There's Alston with a girl!" We stayed long enough to get our pictures taken, went out to eat at the Hungry Fisherman, and then went to see *Rocky Horror Picture Show* for the first time.

Rocky Horror was the "turning point" of Alston's young life:

> Tim Curry changed my life. I went, "Wow!" The costumes, the grandness, the singing, the dancing, the decadence. I was just overpowered. My senses were blown completely apart. I left the theater going, "What a movie." Willa was like, "Yeah." I dropped her off at her house and went home. I thought about it and thought about it. I went a few more times by myself. Then I got the nerve up and bought a corset and got a costume together. I started going to the theater in costume. It started becoming a ritual. One day I ran into some people who I knew from my home town. They were like freaked that I was there dressed. They didn't recognize me because I had a big

wig on. That's when I started developing these friends away from school. The movie just caught us and changed us all. It made life so much easier. It didn't matter anymore. I had something. I had meaning in my life.

Soon his night time activities became the object of jokes and sarcasm among his classmates. "Some of them, I heard, were in the audience on nights when I would strut down the aisle and do my little show. It got back to school and there were remarks made about it. But, they didn't hurt anymore. It all kind of stopped hurting. I had a shield, something to protect me." His mother also was aware of his dressing up, wearing makeup, and going to the theater. "I'd tell her, 'I'm getting acting experience, Mamma.' She just kind of ignored it. She didn't want to face up to it."

Attending born again church services three nights a week and playing to the *Rocky Horror* show audience on Saturday nights, Alston led a "double life." After several months it began to take its toll:

One day I looked in the mirror and I didn't see me. All I saw was Mrs. Mosley. All I saw was the pastor. All I saw was the Congregation looking back at me. I couldn't see myself! I said, "This has got to end."

Within a short time, Alston had eased himself out of the church and became a weekend regular at *Rocky Horror*. A short time later, one of his *Rocky Horror* friends, Buddy, telephoned Alston to ask, "Do you want to go to a bar tomorrow night where there are shows and gay people meet?" Although Alston was only 17, he agreed. The next evening, Alston entered The Twilight dressed to go on stage:

We walked into this bar and there were men kissing men, men dancing together, everyone was smoking cigarettes and drinking. It was like everything your mother told you about hell. Here it is. There were so many people that made me feel so much better and stronger. We walked in and I stood over in the darkness for a few minutes. Then they said, "Now welcome

to the stage . . . What's your name?'' I came out and did a
show. I got a dollar tip.

For the next seven years, Alston assumed the name ''Velvetta
Spike.'' As his senior year progressed, he was increasingly unwilling to ''take shit'' from anyone. The little boy who had once stood
up for himself in sixth grade once again adopted an offensive posture:

> I knew that people were going to pick on me regardless, even
> when I got out of high school, so I decided to give them some-
> thing to pick on—something that was my shield. I had no
> qualms about stomping right up to someone and cussing them
> out if they looked at me the wrong way. I became a vicious,
> nasty, little queen. I didn't take shit from anyone.

Four weeks before Alston graduated from high school, he experienced his first ''big romance.'' Buddy's friend, Mike, who had
since moved to Chicago, was in town for a short time and wanted to
meet someone. Buddy introduced him to Alston.

> Mike played cat and mouse with me. He shocked me and
> freaked me out. He was cute, he talked a lot. We hit it off real
> good. We ended up at Buddy's place. That was the first time I
> experienced anything all the way. I got up the next morning at
> eleven o'clock. I was supposed to have been at school at eight.

When Alston returned home at midday, his mother was out looking
for him. When she finally returned, Alston simply told her he had
spent that night at Buddy's and apologized for not calling her.
Though his mom was suspicious, she said nothing else about the
matter. A few days later, she asked Alston where he was going
every night.

> I said, ''I'm going to The Twilight.'' She said, ''What's The
> Twilight?'' ''It's a bar where they do shows.'' Then she
> asked, ''What shows?'' ''Well, you know. Just shows. People
> acting and doing pantomime. It helps out with my acting,
> Mamma.'' She's like ''Okay.'' She didn't put two and two
> together.

About a week later Buddy and Alston had a quarrel. On his way home, Buddy dropped Alston's bar costume at his mother's house.

Buddy wakes my mom up at one in the morning. He says, "Alston forgot these. Would you please give them to him?" He gives her my fish net stockings. Now, Mom has seen me wear these for the *Rocky Horror* thing but she still hasn't put two and two together. She asks Buddy, "Where's Alston?" Buddy says, "Oh, he's at a queer bar hanging out with a guy he likes." "Beg your pardon," Mom says. "He's at The Twilight, you know."

Well, I get home in the morning. Mom is sitting there at the table with her coffee. "Did you have a nice time?" "Yeah," I say. "Did you enjoy the bar?" "Yeah," I go. "Did you enjoy all the men?" "What?" I'm speechless. "Buddy told me." I just say, "Gotta go to school, Mom. See you later." I leave.

I come in from school that afternoon and there is my sister, Tammy. Mom pulls all the standard lines. "Where did I go wrong?" "How can you be this way?" "What did we do?" She starts to cry. I go in my bedroom and get one of those *Cruise* magazines. I show her pictures of guys dressed like girls. I say, "Look, Mamma. A lot of people do it. It's nothing out of the ordinary." Then she hits me with a low one. "You just ruined my world, Alston." I turn around and storm out of the house.

I get down the street a ways and my car runs out of gas. I get out and start stomping down the road when who should pull up beside me but Buddy. This stretch of road has three houses where people from our church live. They're all sitting out on their porches. They see little Alston, the church boy, stomping down the road cussing and screaming at this guy in a car. I call Buddy every name in the book at the top of my lungs. He peels out. A few moments later Mom's car pulls up. "Where's your car? Do you want to come home?" I yell, "Not until you accept me for what I am." "Please, " she begged, "we can talk about this at home." I get into her car. On the way home she says, "I won't talk about this if you don't." I said, "Fine."

The next day, Alston moved out of the house. Living with friends from a neighboring town, Alston heavily indulged in drugs and alcohol.

> The whole thing with high school just crumbled. It didn't matter any more. I missed days from school. I'd come in the middle of the day hung over from the night before. I had always been teachers' pets and they were freaked out. The guidance counselor took me into her office and sat me down: "Alston, are you all right? I'm going to ask you a question and I want you to tell the truth. Have you been doing drugs?" I said, "Yeah, I've been doing a few." She asked me what was happening. I wouldn't tell her. I didn't trust her. I didn't want to share it with anyone in school because they had treated me like an outcast. I didn't feel they deserved to know that part of my life. I turned in my last term paper, my last book report, my final exam and I left them behind.

Alston had no contact with his family for over six months. "I found my own group of people. There was no need to be a loner anymore." He moved into a boarding house, continued to abuse drugs and alcohol, did "drag" at The Twilight, regularly wrote to Mike in Chicago, and began attending college. His living expenses and college tuition were paid through his father's social security.

Finally, Alston started to see his mother for brief visits. Each time he purposely shocked her: "I did acid last night, Mamma. I'm doing a Quaalude right now.' Each time I would tell her something just a little bit worse. Finally, she was immune to it all. Her standard comment was, 'If that makes you happy, Alston.' I freaked her out until nothing I did bothered her."

Alston continued to entertain Twilight audiences as "Velvetta Spike," for several years. He became Mistress of Ceremonies and head female impersonator ("Don't call us 'drag queens.' We'll scratch your eyes out."); besides choreographing the shows, he appeared doing Liza Minelli favorites such as *New York, New York*, *Cabaret*, and *City Lights*, and has also performed as Little Orphan Annie who, nearing the end of her song, is beat up by a band of hoodlums, as well as Sister Mary Magnum who quickly strips to reveal leather underwear and a T-shirt reading "Guns for Nuns."

Alston enjoyed scouting for new talent and teaching the "new girls" the fine art of female impersonation. One of his favorites was Timmy, known professionally as Foxie Ritz. Alston first spotted Timmy when he had entered the 1983 contest for Miss Collard Festival in a neighboring South Carolina town.

> It wasn't supposed to be a contest for men. But Timmy just went there, did her talent, and won. She rode in this little redneck town's parade and her picture appeared in the state's newspaper. Another guy won it the following year. That's when the town fathers stopped having it. They said it wasn't right to have men get up in dresses to be judged by other men and looking better than the women.

Alston recognizes a freedom peculiar to the South. "People who grow up gay in the North are jaded. Even though it's hard down here, we're in the country. You can roam with your imagination here. It's a little bit more relaxed." The conservative views on gender and sexuality take on an air of ambivalence in the Southerner's imagination. Alston remembers even his father engaging in this type of playful charade:

> We were raised hard-core Baptists. They hate fags. But, they still have this nutty tradition in my church called 'the womanless wedding.' There is a bride, a groom, flower girls—everything except women. Dad's favorite part of play was the soprano soloist. He had this giant blonde wig and a purple sequined gown. It wasn't 'till years later that I realized that my dad did drag.

Alston quit working at The Twilight about two years ago. No longer a female impersonator, he wears a pin-striped suit, a fashionable tie, and short hair. It is difficult to envision him as Velvetta Spike.

What you see before you is a different Alston. If you had known me two years ago, you'd be flabbergasted. That's why my mother is finally proud of me again. I've been through a 180 degree change on the outside. I used to have purple hair that stood out to here and shaved all around the back with a rat tail that hung down. I *was* Velvetta Spike.

Now a computer specialist, Alston has changed his name back and assumed a new image. He no longer belongs to the *Rocky Horror-Twilight* group:

I've lost their respect. They feel I've sold out. But, I had to do something. I didn't want to end up a bag lady on the streets at the age of 60. I didn't want to be living off my friends for the rest of my life. I had to have a future and something to look forward to even if it doesn't fit with *their* image of who I am.

Alston does not regret any of his experiences. He has profited from them. From his relationship with Mike, Alston has now formed a mental image of a homosexual person:

This is someone who loves a member of his own sex intimately. It goes beyond the sexual. If it's indiscriminate sex here and there, a blow job in the park when the lights are dim, or some big truck driver or jock wanting to get into his own little fantasy world, that's just sex. You're really homosexual when you can fall in love with someone of your own sex and freely admit to yourself that you are in love with that person. Forget what the rest of the world thinks. You're in love. You may not want to tell the rest of the world, you may still be in your closet. But, if you can admit it to yourself that you truly love this person, then you've become a homosexual.

Alston still harbors painful memories of his harassment in high school:

If there had not been such a taboo on being gay or being feminine; if people had not ridiculed me for it as much, it would have been a lot easier. In dealing with myself there was no problem. Those were my feelings. They didn't embarrass me.

The thing that was so hard and painful to deal with was all the name calling, the snickers and the laughs, the elbows in the side, knocking my books down or snatching them and throwing them in a garbage can. That's what hurt.

Reflecting on the importance of being oneself, Alston momentarily assumes the demeanor of Velvetta Spike. He snaps his fingers and crosses his legs. His raspy voice carries a reflective message:

If you don't really have to worry about risking your life or being stabbed to death, then be whatever you want to be. If you're young, you have the chance to do what you want, to be what you want, and to feel good about it. I've seen some wild things and been to some wild places, honey. But, I've met a group of people who genuinely loved me for who I was. And, babe, that's what is important.

COMMENTARY

In the South, where sexual and racial divisions are so pronounced, it would be unusual to find an elementary school that did not have its share of "outcasts": boys like Alston, who fail to conform to social-sex roles, face a particularly difficult time growing up in the South. In a state that ranks fifth in the nation for Department of Defense payroll on a per capita basis, boasts eight major military installations, and seats half of its Congressional delegation on the armed services committees,[2] Rambo-like strength and macho appearance are held up as an ideal. Like the effeminate Biff Brannon in McCullers' New York Cafe,[3] Alston, a thin young man with a soft face and a shrill voice, is the antithesis of this Southern icon of manhood.

The importance of *acting* like a male is a common theme in the childhood biographies of Southern males. Bedridden with a high fever, Terry's father slaps him and admonishes Terry to "be a man"; Vince masks his poetry writing and piano playing behind football and a girlfriend. The embarrassment felt by parents whose sons display effeminate behavior or interests was also common. Royce's father informs friends his son is studying mathematics instead of theater; Malcolm's father forbids his son to talk in front of neighbors.

Traveling with some professional wrestlers, Alston soon found out that the rigidity of these gender behaviors and roles is an artifact of the mind, not a reflection of the world. Yet most parents, teachers, and classmates believed that "being a man" was biologically prescribed, not culturally constructed. Three misconceptions were commonly held: First, effeminate boyhood behavior continues into adulthood. Second, male roles and traits are the same everywhere. Third, assuming female traits or roles dishonors male status and family prestige. Each of these assumptions are challenged in the following, first section of this commentary. Additionally, the peculiarities of Southern culture which sometimes allow for greater toleration of cross-gender behavior are discussed. The second section examines the relationship between cross-gender behavior in boys and homosexuality. Here, the distinctions between gender and sexuality are explored. Additionally, the relationship between race and childhood harassment is examined.

The Cultural Construction of Boyhood Effeminacy

From a very early age, children in the United States are exposed to gender appropriate behaviors ranging from assignment of household tasks to expectations for dress and demeanor.[4] Fourteen of the 24 males participating in this study failed to conform to gender norms during childhood. With the exception of Royce, these boys reported harassment. This harassment is, in part, attributable to three misperceptions about boyhood effeminacy. Following corrective statements and discussion about boyhood effeminacy, the degree of tolerance for such behavior within the context of Southern culture will be explored.

Not all children who engage in these cross-gender behaviors become effeminate adults. Alston's and Brandon's childhood effeminacy carried over into adulthood. For several other participants in this study, however, "defeminization" occurred in adolescence.[5] For example, Malcolm consciously chose to adopt masculine mannerisms during his first year in high school and Isiah permanently changed his behavior at the onset of puberty.

Isaiah is an only child. His parents were very open about discussing sexuality; he remembers holding a book before he could read with pictures and drawings explaining reproduction. At the age of four, he had "vague attractions" to other boys and "I had the impression as a young child that I would not fit into the patterns that I was supposed to." Isaiah did not want to play football. He preferred to play with girls and was labelled "sissy" in elementary school. "That was something that they could recognize. I was a whole lot less guarded about how I acted back then." By the time Isaiah entered middle-school, however, he "was acting the way other people expected me to act. I just had to learn how to act other people's way."

Both Malcolm and Isaiah changed their offending behaviors and acknowledged that their more conventional masculine behavior resulted in less harassment. Not surprisingly, some psychologists and parents seek to facilitate "defeminization." Clinical practitioners such as Richard Green claim that counseling enhances these effeminate boys' social and psychological adjustment and their comfort with being male.

Such an approach, of course, is not without its ethical and political dilemmas. As one critical reviewer of Green's work noted, "It's a little like trying to teach highly ghettoized blacks how to behave more 'properly' (don't jive too much, straighten your hair, whatever) so they won't get traumatized by the racists—without going after the racists."[6] Thus, other practitioners assert that parents and professionals should create an environment of respect and acceptance, and assist the child in coping in a healthy manner with adverse reactions from less sensitive persons and in understanding the reasons for such harassment.[7]

Changing outward mannerisms, however, does not divert children's sexual interests or assure that they will be any more comfortable with themselves. Alan Bell, Martin Weinberg and Sue Hammersmith, sex researchers at Indiana University, simply state, "You may supply your sons with footballs and your daughters with dolls, but no one can guarantee that they will enjoy them."[8] Further, "defeminization" innocuously suggests that a boy's adoption of "female" traits is the problem, whereas, in fact, the problem is adult misogyny. Outwardly repudiating male dress and demeanor is a visible rejection of male power and prestige: an effeminate boy-child who becomes an adult "drag queen" is as unwelcomed in a gay rights lobbying group as he is in a Chamber of Commerce luncheon.

A second point to consider when admonishing a young child for displaying inappropriate gender behavior is that *"appropriate" and "inappropriate" gender behaviors are culturally based*. Anthropologists report a wide variety of human gender arrangements.[9] Their findings portray a rich tapestry of male behavior and suggest that this great elasticity in gender roles and traits is culturally ordered, not divinely ordained. In New Guinea, for example, the interests of men in the Tchambuli tribe include art, gossip, and shopping while women adopt what we might consider masculine roles. On the Trobriand Islands, both husband and wife nurture and care for their children. In northern Madagasgar, Yegale men assume their wive's surnames, perform domestic duties, and obediently comply with female demands. These and other studies are discussed in Ann Oakley's influential work. She concludes:

> Quite often one finds these examples of masculinity and femininity in other societies dismissed as eccentric, deviant, peculiar, and irrelevant to the mainstream of human development. This is an absurdly ethnocentric view. . . . [T]he chief importance of biological sex in determining social roles is in providing a universal and obvious division around which other distinctions can be organized. In deciding which activities are to fall on each side of the boundary, the important factor is culture.[10]

Even within cultures known for relatively rigid codes of male and female behavior, there are acceptable forms of cross-gender behavior for males.[11] Womanless weddings are routinely held in churches within rural communities of the South as fundraising events. In Japan there is the centuries-honored Kabuki tradition in which men assume theatrical roles as women. In Africa, Masai boys wear women's clothing for several months following circumcision. In Holland, on the island of Marken, boys are dressed as girls until they reach the age of seven. In the United States, even the society pages consider Halloween and Mardi Gras appropriate occasions for such cross dressing.

While the concept of maleness varies from culture to culture, no society has ignored the temptation to extend physical differences between "males" and "females" into its language, social structure, or ideology. This "sexing of the world," notes British anthropologist Allen Abramson, occurs when "objects and roles tend to become imaginatively annexed to either the male or the female in a way that, conjunctually, may appear to be 'natural' and eternal."[12] As these objects and roles become thus reified, those who deviate from them are often ostracized. But to claim that such behavior is "unnatural" is to ignore the spectrum of human diversity and to simplisitically and artificially divide the world into gendered halves. "We perceive," notes William DuBay, "vaginas and penises not just as anatomical facts but as meaningful signs representing basic beliefs about human nature. In short, our beliefs in the differences between male and female go far beyond visible cues offered by human physiology."[13]

A third point to consider is that even in those societies in which gender role divisions are similar to our own, the *cultural responses to cross-gender behavior differ markedly*. For example, Kenneth Clark, in his classic study, *The Nude*, noted that mockery of male queens at gymnasia can be found depicted on Greek vases; and Kent Gerard and Gert Hekma's *Pursuit of Sodomy: Male Homosexuality in Renaissance and Enlightenment Europe* is filled with accounts of effeminacy used as evidence in sexual prosecutions of the period.[14] In contrast, within 19th century American Indian cultures, males who did not conform to masculine behavior or dress often assumed special ceremonial roles as healers, shamans, and seers.[15]

Parents of a PaPago Indian son, for example, who suspected that he might be different would "build a small bush enclosure. Inside the enclosure they place a man's bow and arrows, and also a woman's basket. At the appointed time, the boy is brought to the enclosure as the adults watch from the outside."[16] After the boy enters the enclosure it is set afire. If the boy takes the basket in hand as he flees, he is recognized by the tribe as a *berdache* — a position of respect and economic status within his community. This social script, detailed by ethno-historian Walter Williams, illustrates the power of the cultural context in making meaning of "being different":

> Native American religions, above all else, encourage a basic respect for nature. If nature makes a person different, many Indians conclude, a mere human should not undertake to counter this spiritual dictate. Someone who is "unusual" can be accommodated without being stigmatized as "abnormal."[17]

Interestingly, the status of berdachism changed radically as the Native American culture was colonized and Anglo values were imposed on the reservation. Two scholars comment on the impact of cultural colonialism on the *berdache* in Native American communities:

> On many reservations today the status of the *berdache* has declined, and younger individuals who would formerly have taken a respected position in their tribe are currently stigmatized and lost in a society that is no longer independent of colonial control.[18]

> The tribes have forgotten. Instead, this [*berdache*] role appears only as a ghost. At least that is all that remains in Case 1, who is considered nothing more than a harmless amusement, allowed to sit around in women's clothes, to weave, and to sleep with men. No one thinks he is under the influence of the gods; he brings no magic, nor is he its recipient. He is fully secularized, thought of without drama as a gay man who wants to act like a woman.[19]

For today's Native American children the cultural meaning of "being different" and the cultural rules for gender appropriate behavior insure that their effeminate peers will be met by ridicule rather than respect.

The phenomenon of the *berdache* illustrates the difference in importance assigned to cross-gender behavior and its linkage to sexual behavior by 19th century Native American culture and Anglo culture. According to anthropologist Harriet Whitehead:

What differs is the center of gravity in the two gender systems. For the American Indians, occupational pursuits clearly occupy the spotlight, with dress/demeanor coming in a close second. Sexual object choice is part of the gender configuration, but its salience is low; so low that by itself it does not provoke the reclassification of the individual to special status. In the Western system, the order of salience is virtually the reverse.[20]

A similar point is made by Will Roscoe on his case study of the Zuni *berdache* We'wha:

> In their [Zuni] world view, the social roles of men and women were not biologically determined but acquired through life experience and shaped through a series of initiations. . . . The rites observed at We'wha's death . . . best reveal the Zuni view of the *lhamana*. To prepare the body for burial, We'wha was dressed in new female clothes. But beneath the dress, a pair of pants was slipped on—symbolizing the fact that, while *born* male, We'wha had *learned* the traits and skills of women. The Zunis did not entertain the social fiction that We'wha had crossed sexes to become female.[21]

Unlike the *berdache*, within more recent American cultures boys who display effeminate behavior are labelled "sissies" early in life and often are castigated as "faggots" by the time they enter junior high school.[22] In the South, though, Royce's biography illustrated family name and social class can rescue a lucky young man from such overt hostility during adolescence. For those effeminate males who lack Royce's social position, however, there is another window of opportunity: Southerners' toleration for eccentric behavior and their fondness for politeness. These provide gay men as different as Terry and Alston an eddy of freedom they would not likely enjoy in another region of the country. "People down South are more showy and everybody is worried about how everyone looks. But," Terry adds, "you can be more flamboyant here—that's expected." This expectation of flamboyance and politeness enables the South to honor Tennessee Williams and attend "womanless weddings" even while censuring school libraries with homosexual literature and enforcing sodomy statutes. Not surprisingly, female impersonation has blossomed in the South. "In today's drag world there is a seemingly endless number of contests and pageants. Indeed, there are as many titles as in female beauty pageants, even in the South, where every girl seeks to be 'Poultry Queen,' or 'Cotton Queen,' or 'Queen of the Forests.' "[23]

For some female impersonators, like Alston, a central feature of their act is "camp."[24] Noting that the "essence of camp is the unspoken amusement derived from knowing something is camp without having to explain why," cultural writer Vito Russo declares it "is something of a secret code, it has become one of the mainstays of an almost ethnic humor which has been formed for defense purposes over the years. . . . [and in] aiding people in forming images with which they feel comfortable in a hostile culture."[25] Camp is Alston's shield against the world where sissies become outcasts and faggots are bashed. He taunts this world by parodying feminine mannerisms and parading in female dress. He mocks through humor, bitchiness, and sarcasm.

There are two types of female impersonators working the bars, discos, and clubs in this country: stage impersonators and street impersonators. Like Virginia Hamm in *Torch Song Trilogy*, the stage impersonator performs live and earns a respectable living. Like Velvetta Spike in this study, the street impersonator pantomimes his music and seldom makes enough to support himself in a comfortable style. Since the early nineteenth century, the stage impersonator represents the crown jewel of this profession in the United States. In recent decades, however, he has been far outnumbered by street impersonators.[26] In her two-year study of female impersonators in the late sixties, anthropologist Esther Newton describes the "street fairies" as "jobless young homosexual men who publicly epitomize the homosexual stereotype and are the underclass of the gay world. . . . Street impersonators are never off stage."[27]

Unlike many street impersonators, Alston didn't merely mouth the music. He choreographed the Sunday shows, hired the performers, and interacted with the audience in a game of verbal roulette. He was, in the words of Esther Newton, a "camp queen":

The camp queen makes no bones about it; to him the gay world is the "sisterhood." By accepting his homosexuality and flaunting it, the camp undercuts all homosexuals who won't accept the stigmatized identity. Only by fully embracing the stigma itself can one neutralize the sting and make it laughable.[28]

Brandon is one of these homosexual men targeted by the camp queen's humor. Attending an occasional Sunday night "drag show," he is fraught with ambivalence as he finds the show both comforting and disgusting: "It causes me to laugh and not take it so seriously. But, I still just can't stand those words." But, of course, listening to the words in a *different context* is precisely the Camp Queen's strategy:

> The camp ethos or style plays a role analogous to "soul" in the Negro subculture. Like soul, camp is a "strategy for a situation." . . . Like the Negro problem, the homosexual problem centers on self-hatred and the lack of self-esteem. But, if "the soul ideology ministers to the needs for identity," the camp ideology ministers to the needs for dealing with an identity that is well defined and loaded with contempt.[29]

Alston and Brandon exemplify two very different paths taken by small town, "sissy" boys. Alston's public assertiveness and acceptance of his sexuality contrast sharply with Brandon's timid and closeted existence. Perhaps nowhere is this difference more clearly stated than in their definitions of homosexual:

> **Brandon**: "A person who desires and fulfills unnatural desires with someone of the same sex."
> **Alston**: "If you can love someone, you can become a homosexual."

Boyhood Effeminacy, Adult Homosexuality and Effeminate Behavior

Undergirding parental concern and peer harassment over cross-gender behavior among boys is its association with homosexuality.[30]

On both logical as well as empirical grounds the linkage of homo-sexuality to social sex roles is questionable.[31] Michael Ross, a se-nior faculty member at the South Australia Medical School, suc-cinctly writes:

> The view that homosexuality is associated with deviant social
> sex role implies that all homosexuals will contain attributes of
> the opposite sex. It is clear from past research, however, that
> there is little agreement on this. . . . [G]iven the lack of empir-
> ical evidence of a consistent relationship between social sex
> role and homosexuality, it is important to understand the more
> subtle aspects of the relationship that may stem from social or
> cultural assumptions.[32]

One of these subtleties is the distinction among sex, gender, and sexuality.[33] Like most effeminate boys, Alston has a male identity. Although he has no desire to become female, his effeminate charac-teristics were noticeable before he entered elementary school.[34] His attraction to other boys began late in elementary school and he first labelled himself as "homosexual" at the age of 15. Being born male or female, exhibiting masculinity or femininity, and desiring men or women are three human components which can be arranged in several distinct combinations reflected in terms such as hermaph-rodite, transvestite, bisexual, sissy boy, transsexual, and homosex-ual. While biological sex is established at conception,[35] gender iden-tity (personal conviction about being male or female) is thought to develop between 18 months and four years; the internalization of cultural expectations for gender roles is believed to be established between the ages of three and seven years of age; and the claiming of a homosexual identity is found to occur in one's early twenties.[36]

Though there is no established *causal* relationship between boy-hood effeminacy and the development of a homosexual identity, these two components overlap in some individuals, such as Alston. One method to examine the link between boyhood effeminacy and adult homosexuality has been through clinical study. One of the most elaborate studies is *The Sissy Boy Syndrome*.[37] This 15-year study of extreme cases of boyhood effeminacy, conducted by psy-chiatrist Richard Green, followed 66 effeminate boys into early adulthood and compared them with a matched sample of volunteers. Green found that two-thirds of the effeminate boys experienced homoerotic fantasies compared with none of the remaining 34 volunteers. In a long term follow-up of 55 boys referred for treatment of their early effeminate behaviors, Bernard Zuger also found two-thirds of them to have an adult homosexual orientation.[38] Other clinical studies report similar patterns providing support for the contention that gender non-conformity in childhood parallels adult homosexuality.[39]

Survey sampling of homosexual adults also supports a relationship between boyhood effeminacy and adult homosexuality.[40] "Prehomosexual boys," according to Frederick Whitam, are most likely those who play with "gender-inappropriate" toys, practice cross-dressing, engage with girls in play activities, and shoulder the label "sissy" assigned by other boys.[41] A more extensive empirical study of the childhood play activities reported by approximately 800 heterosexual and homosexual-identified adults concluded that masculine sports activities and feminine behavior most clearly distinguished these two groups of males.[42] Further, homosexual males scored lower than heterosexual females in the frequency of childhood sports activities, and nearly one-quarter reported enjoyment in playing with dolls as a child. In a related study, the absence of masculine behaviors and traits was more powerfully related to adult homosexual identity than the presence of feminine traits and behaviors.[43]

In *Homosexuality*, philosopher Michael Ruse, noting the abundance of "evidence suggesting that homosexual men have tended to have had atypical childhoods when compared to heterosexual men," cautions that "Not every homosexual has differed from the (heterosexual) norm. . . ."[44] In this present study, 14 of the male participants (58 percent), including Alston, spoke of effeminate traits and interests during childhood. At the time of their interviews, however, one-half had assumed more masculine behaviors and engaged in gender-appropriate activities. Alston is the most dramatic example of this gender role conversion.

The findings of this study fall within the rather wide range reported by other researchers.[45] They report between 27 percent and

67 percent of their gay male samples lived an effeminate childhood. For example, in a study of 1,500 heterosexual and homosexual men, nearly one-half of the gay males were labelled "sissy" during their school years compared to five percent of their heterosexual classmates. These researchers report a lower range (16-41 percent) for children engaged in cross-dressing, and Joseph Harry, among others, has also commented on the large number of homosexual males, estimated between two-thirds and four-fifths, who "defeminize" during adolescence.[46]

Much more commonly, gay men report having had a general feeling or sense of *difference* during childhood. All of the males who were "outcasts" in this study volunteered that they "felt different" from their fellow classmates. Consistent with other studies, the most frequently recalled manifestations of this preadolescent sense of difference were a general sense of alienation, feelings of gender inadequacy, excitement in the presence of other males, lack of any common specifically "male" interests, and effeminacy. Nearly three-fourths of the men in the recent Kinsey study, for example, reported feeling a sense of difference during elementary school—double the percentage of heterosexual males who felt different.[47] Other studies report similar findings.[48]

It is worthwhile to underscore that some children who come to identify themselves as heterosexual adults share these feelings of difference with their homosexual counterparts. But these heterosexual men are likely to interpret such feelings—a sense of alienation from or being different than, say a rugged All-American boy classmate—differently. Richard Troiden speculates, "The same childhood feelings which the adolescent heterosexual may come to redefine as the initial signs of, for instance, artistic sensitivity may be reinterpreted by the teen-age male who later becomes homosexual as the first stirrings of homosexual interest."[49] *This reinterpretation of childhood events to fit into constructed sexual identity is the most provocative but least researched aspect of sexual development.*

Of course, the interpretations that we draw from these studies, like those linking a weak father or a strong mother with homosexual behavior, must be critically examined. First, none of these studies establishes a *causal* relationship between boyhood effeminacy and adult homosexual behavior. Second, most homosexual-identified adults do not report effeminacy in childhood or display effeminate characteristics in adulthood. As one of the most prominent group of researchers notes:

> [W]hile gender nonconformity appears to have been an aspect of the development of homosexuality in many of our respondents, it was by no means universal, and conversely, gender nonconformity does not inevitably signal future homosexuality. . . . No particular phenomenon of family life can be singled out, on the basis of our findings, as especially consequential for either homosexual or heterosexual development.[50]

Nevertheless, other researchers have made rather dramatic assertions. For example, Fred Whitam and Michael Zent write, "Early cross-gender behavior appears to be an intrinsic feature of male homosexuality. . . . "[51] Such a generalization has been properly challenged by J. M. Carrier, a member of the Gender Identity Research Group at UCLA. Labelling such statements "unwarranted and misleading," he points out the use of skewed research samples and the liberal interpretation of data.[52] Though such figures dwarf the effeminate childhood behaviors reported by heterosexual men (e.g., gay men are three to six times more likely to report cross-gender characteristics during childhood compared to heterosexual men),[53] in most studies they have represented a *minority* of gay men sampled.

The full complexity of gender behavior cannot be understood without consideration of certain other factors; for instance, class. Effeminate males in this study who adopted conventional gender behavior in adulthood tended to come from middle and upper income families. This coincides with Joseph Harry's data gathered from a sample of 686 Chicago homosexual men. In that study, Harry found "a greater persistence of childhood cross-gendering among gay youths from blue-collar households."[54] His study, however, did not report the effect of race on adult effeminacy and homosexuality. It is noteworthy that in this study all of the African-American males who reported effeminate behavior during childhood or adolescence (Grant, Heyward, Irwin, and Malcolm) continued such behavior beyond adolescence.

Race also complicates the equation of childhood harassment. The experiences of Grant illustrate the impact that race has upon the quality of life for young black males who deviate from accepted sex roles. Black effeminate male children like Grant experienced greater problems in elementary school than Alston, his sissy-white counterpart. Attending all-black elementary schools, Grant was harassed because of his effeminacy. Attending school within an integrated setting, he was harassed because of his race.

Historically, ministry and teaching have been prestigious careers within the African-American community. From this vantage point, Grant, the only son of an African Methodist minister and an elementary school teacher, is privileged. For the first 10 years of his life Grant lived in a rural area between Columbia and Florence. As discussed in Chapter 3, being a minister's son was difficult for Grant.

During his first five grades, Grant attended the all-black school at which his mother taught. "The kids were very, very vicious," he recollects. Being of small stature and having little interest in sports, "Most of the time I felt alienated and was picked on: 'faggot,' 'sissy,' 'queer bait.'" His mother, aware of the harassment, advised him, "Don't let it get to you." Academically, Grant did not suffer; socially, he did: "I just had the feeling that I wasn't like everybody else. Everybody was picking on me. They would all play together, I just would stay by myself."

Although he was often the object of fag and sissy jokes, "I never made a connection. When you're young you just don't have all the pieces to the puzzle. There were always jokes about sissies and queers, but that never connected in my mind with watching men on television and feeling good about seeing them when they took off their shirts." Grant did not make the "connection" between "faggots" and "homosexuality." He interpreted these jokes as a statement of physical weakness, not sexual predisposition.

Shy, light-skinned, and bright, Grant changed schools in sixth grade when the family moved to a mid-size city. As noted in Chapter 6, Grant had a difficult time adjusting to the upper-income, white school. Despite his superior academic performance, he continued to face harassment — generally on the basis of his race. Harassment came from both whites and blacks. Grant endured the subtle harassment among his white teachers who would "tense up" or accord unintentional favoritism to his white classmates. "The only blatant harassment I got, I got from black students. Very seldom did I get called 'faggot'; it was mostly 'oreo.' They would always say that I was trying to act like an oreo — trying to be uppity."

Asked which label, "oreo" or "faggot" hurt most at that time, Grant quickly replied:

> Being called an "oreo" was worse than being called a "faggot," since I never really made the connection with the word "faggot" and being a "sissy." It was never really defined in my mind. Even when I went to Venice Beach — the attitudes and atmosphere in California were completely different than anything I'd ever seen in South Carolina — and saw guys holding hands, I didn't think of them as "sissies." I never made any connection between what they were doing and myself.

June Butts, professor of psychiatry at Howard University College of Medicine, writing in *Ebony*, counsels a worried mother whose son, like Grant, was effeminate:

> Her daily fear is that the other boys in the projects will molest her young son because he has certain sensitivities, certain mannerisms, that the other boys consider "effeminate." I have counseled this mother and have told her that it is not her son who carried within him the seeds of our destruction; those seeds, the threats to our cohesiveness as a race and to our continued survival as a loving family, are carried by the others who have confused manliness and Black Manhood with brute force.[55]

This mother, like Malcolm's parents, might also fear the public role he may adopt in adulthood. Malcolm declares, "To be effeminate, black, and to be gay — they really can't stand it. If you're white gay, and effeminate, that's okay." Unable to adopt a role compatible with the "bad nigger" social metaphor, effeminate black boys turned gay black men sometimes adopt the most visible homosexual role in the African-American community: the street sissy. According to John Soares, "The street sissy typically excels in flamboyance and confrontation — ass kicking. Hardly ever admired, he is always respected." This role, like other roles in homosexual communities, exacts a cost upon those who assume it. Soares continues:

> But like all people who step into roles institutionalized by whatever culture, they most commonly find themselves trapped. One cannot be a street sissy part-time any more than one can be the baddest motherfucker on the block part-time. Neither does this institutionalized role allow for creative personal growth and development. It is a cultural prison that obscures endless possibilities for a homosexual life-style for adolescents who would love members of their own sex.[56]

Soares, however, ignores the fact that financial status dramatically affects the range of possibilities for a homosexual lifestyle — in black or white communities. Middle class blacks, for example, can assume the identity of a "street sissy" late Saturday night yet be transformed Sunday morning into a prayerful, upright church elder, and retransformed Monday into the macho Manhattan office manager. The "street sissy" is, in part, imprisoned by circumstances of poverty as much as by his culture and himself.

Black or white, being a "sissy" is equated with becoming a "faggot." As an outcast, Alston coped with his emerging sexuality by wearing a badge of the gay community: the camp queen. In the process, Alston found the strength to continue without the support of family, church, or school. As Velvetta Spike, Alston challenged the icon of Southern manhood and bolstered his weakened self-image. The identity of Velvetta Spike, like the earlier one of Alston the sissy, was eventually discarded much to the disappointment of many of the Twilight girls. The adoption and discarding of gender and sexual identities is evidence of their social construction; this fact, that we can exchange as well as create social masks (albeit some more readily than others), opens up endless paths of possibilities in one's spiritual journey; mistaking one's outer mask for the many selves we call "oneself" obscures such possibilities. It is from this vantage point that we now examine Everetta's biography.

REFERENCE NOTES

1. Romanovsky, 1986.
2. Fladung, 1987.
3. McCullers, 1940.
4. Broverman, Vogel, Broverman, Clarkson, and Rosenkratz, 1972; Duncan and Duncan, 1978; Goldstein and Oldham, 1979; Lipman-Blumen, 1972; White and Brinkerhoff, 1981.
5. Harry, 1983; 1985; Whitam, 1977b.
6. Mass, 1986:56. Moreover, as Money and Russo (1979) found in their longitudinal study of nine effeminate boys, "nonjudgmentalism" was a critical factor that contributed to these boys' healthy adjustment in adolescence and adulthood despite their continued "non-traditional" social sex role behavior.
7. For a discussion of a humanistic approach to working with gender non-conformists, see: Coleman, 1986; Rebecca, Hefner and Oleshansky, 1976.
8. Bell, Weinberg and Hammersmith, 1981:189, 191.
9. Davenport, 1965; Denis, 1967; Frazier, 1913; Hodges, 1973; Mead, 1935; Munroe, Whiting and Holly, 1969; Murdock, 1937.
10. Oakley, 1972:58, 156.
11. Talamini, 1982.
12. Abramson, 1984:196.
13. DuBay, 1987:44.
14. Clark, 1956; Gerard and Hekma, 1989.
15. There have been several recent essays on the Native American culture and the status of the *berdache*. See, for example: Forgey, 1975; Miller, 1982; Roscoe, 1988; Thayer 1980; Whitehead, 1981. The most authoritative work is that of Walter Williams (1986). Some ethnographic work (e.g., Blackwood, 1984a) has been devoted to the female equivalent which is discussed in Chapter 11.
16. Williams, 1986:24.
17. Williams, 1986:14.
18. Williams, 1986:14.
19. Stoller, 1976:536.
20. Whitehead, 1981:97.
21. Roscoe, 1988:129.
22. Green, 1973.
23. Real, 1983:47.
24. There is a distinction between "doing camp" and "doing drag." Doing drag transforms our thinking through a change in physical appearances; doing camp transforms our common-sensical thinking through language (E. Newton, 1979). Terry, in this study, mixed gay argot with a quick wit, an eye for incongru-

ity, and fondness for the dramatic in his two tux prom. Alston's friend, Timmy, assumed the dress and demeanor of a woman, Foxie Ritz. Alston combined both elements. In Susan Sontag's (1978:277) classic essay on camp, she speaks of it as a "sensibility . . . a mode of aestheticism . . . disengaged, depoliticized" and provides examples ranging from fondness for Tiffany lamps and old Flash Gordon comics to Wilde's epigrams and the dandyism "in the age of mass culture."

25. Russo, 1979:206.

26. For an interesting history of female impersonation in the United States and Great Britain, see: Baker, 1968.

27. Newton, 1979:8.

28. Newton, 1979:111.

29. Newton, 1979:105.

30. For example, Green and Money (1966) noted the interrelationships between effeminacy, role-taking, and stage-acting among a small sample of effeminate males during childhood, and another group of researchers (Hellman, Green, Gray and Williams, 1981) have reported interrelationships between cross-gender behaviors, homophobia, and religiosity among transsexual and homosexual men. This association of effeminacy with homosexuality is not an assumption made only by researchers. Effeminate males are more likely, based on limited information, to be characterized as "homosexual" by laypersons than those who appear to fit the sex role norm (Dunbar, Brown and Vourinen, 1973).

31. Coleman, 1986; Freund et al., 1974; Mannion, 1976; Richardson, 1981; Ross, 1983; Taylor, 1983; Zuger, 1984.

32. Ross, 1983:3-4.

33. Shively and DeCecco, 1977.

34. This parallels findings by other researchers (e.g., Green, 1969; Zuger, 1984) that effeminacy and cross-gender behavior in their clinical studies is most common among boys six years of age and under. Lebovitz (1972:1288), however, reports on two groups of effeminate boys, one that displayed such behaviors prior to the age of six and another that displayed them only after 10 years of age, noting that the first group was the most likely to evidence the most severe "malignancy of the symptom."

35. There are case studies of individuals whose genetic and anatomic characteristics do not match at birth. These children, raised male or female according to their physical characteristics, fail to develop gender-appropriate secondary sex characteristics during puberty and thus face a conflict between their gender and biological identities (Imperator-McGinley, Peterson, Gautier, and Sturla, 1979; Money, 1970; Money, 1987; Money and Dalery, 1976; Money, Devore and Norman, 1986; Money and Ehrhardt, 1972; Money, Hampson and Hampson, 1955).

36. Dank, 1971; Gramick, 1984; McDonald, 1982; Troiden, 1979; Van Wyck and Geist, 1984; Vance and Green, 1984.

37. Green, 1987.

38. Zuger, 1966; Zuger, 1970; Zuger, 1978; Zuger, 1984.

39. Bates, Bentler and Thompson, 1979; Bieber, Dain, Dince, Drellich,

Grand, Gundlach, Kremer, Rifkin, Wilbur, and Bieber, 1962; Green, 1976; Green, 1987; Lebovits, 1972; Money and Russo, 1979; Stephan, 1973.

40. Billingham and Hockenberry, 1987; Grellert, Newcomb and Bentler, 1982; Saghir and Robins, 1973; Whitam, 1977b; 1980.

41. Whitam, 1980.

42. Grellert, Newcomb and Bentler, 1982. Though such studies have been criticized for retrospective bias (Ross, 1980), this study sought to establish validity through comparison of the heterosexual adult sample with an earlier study of children's play preferences.

43. Hockenberry and Billingham, 1987.

44. Ruse, 1988:39.

45. Bell, Weinberg and Hammersmith, 1981; Harry, 1983; Harry, 1985; Saghir and Robins, 1973; Whitam, 1977b.

46. Green and Money, 1966; Harry, 1983; Whitam, 1977b.

47. Bell, Weinberg and Hammersmith, 1981.

48. Bell, Weinberg and Hammersmith, 1981; Bernard and Epstein, 1978; Blanchard, McCankey, Roper, and Skiner, 1983; Green, 1974; Grellert, 1982; Grellert, Newcomb and Bentler, 1982; Harry, 1983; Heilbrun and Thompson, 1977; Hockenberry and Billingham, 1987; Kenyon, 1968b; LaTorre and Wendenburg, 1983; Money and Russo, 1979; Poole, 1972; Saghir and Robins, 1973; Thompson, Schwartz, McCandless and Edwards, 1973; Troiden, 1979; Whitam, 1977b; Zuger, 1978. These findings, however, have not gone uncontested (e.g., Lebovitz, 1972).

49. Troiden, 1979:364.

50. Bell, Weinberg and Hammersmith, 1981:189, 191.

51. Whitam and Zent, 1984:435.

52. Carrier, 1986:89.

53. Harry, 1983.

54. Harry, 1985:11.

55. Butts, 1981:144.

56. Soares, 1979:266.

Chapter 11

The Tomboys

EVERETTA AND THE "CINDERELLA COMPLEX"

You dressed in gym socks and tennis shoes
So you could ride your bike to school.
Your starched white shirt tucked in a skirt revealed defiance.
While matching sweaters were the rule
And while the other girls dressed and went to dances
You played mazurkas at home

Holly Near, "Put Away"[1]

Everetta, the youngest of three sisters, was reared during the mid-sixties in a sparsely populated county at the end of a dead-end dirt road. Her parents, Thurmond and Mandy, brought to their new family several additional children from previous marriages. One of these was Jake. "I never figured out if he was my real brother," acknowledges Everetta. "But, as far as I was concerned he was." Her last faded memory of Jake was his leaving for Vietnam. She has not seen him since. Everetta has vivid memories, though, of her Cinderella-like family relationship with her two natural sisters:

> Penny failed the seventh, eighth, and ninth grades, and the first grade, too. But Daddy never abused her. He never hit her or kicked her or anything like that. He bought her a car even though she had failed all those grades! The other, Julia Mae, was the prettiest and the wittiest one. She had health problems, though. She had sclerosis. She had to have surgery and a pin put in her back. She was untouchable, too.

In contrast to her two older sisters, Everetta enjoyed a less than charmed childhood. Short and husky with a determined smile and weather-beaten skin, she recalls her responsibilities at 12 years of age:

> First thing in the morning, when it was still not daylight, I had to get up. We had a farm and I had to do as much work as I could before I went to school. I rode my bike to the peach shed. I worked on a conveyer belt grading, working my way up to loading the trucks. Then I went to school. I came home and worked until it was dark. When I failed there was constant beatings from Daddy.

When Everetta was not doing her chores, working in the peach shed, or going to school she would wander in the woods, walking along the nearby river journeying into "my own little space." She remembers going to bed as soon as possible to escape from the often heated arguments between her parents. Everetta also would escape through reading Mark Twain books, and *Boy's Life* or *Hot Rod* magazines — a skill she learned through the efforts of her father:

> I remember learning to read before I went to school. Daddy brought home a big book and told me to learn to read it. So, I tried to read it. Then he would come back and say, "Could you read any of it?" Some words I could. He would make me sit down and he'd read it. Then I'd read it after him until I got it. When I got to first grade, I was reading at the third grade level.

In first grade, Everetta experienced her first crush: It was on Louise, a third grader she came to know in her reading group. Everetta began writing little notes to her. "I wanted to be around her as much as possible. But, she thought it was sort of strange. She didn't really want to be around me that much. It went on for a while. I didn't give up real easy."

During elementary school, Everetta's teachers found her to be smart but disruptive. Though she earned A's and B's and was reading two levels above her grade, she was often punished by her teachers for engaging in playful mischief, such as throwing airplanes, that was considered unlady-like in school. She recalls: "The boys liked to pick on me for some reason. I wouldn't let them. I would fight back. Most of the other girls, you know, they were just too femme." During recess, Everetta generally would be found rough-housing with the boys while her female classmates jumped rope, played on the swings, or talked quietly on the school steps. Seldom would a school day go by in which Everetta, wearing heavy-rimmed black glasses bandaged together with tape, did not return home without soiled or torn clothes. Her parents, though, did not seem too concerned with Everetta's tomboyish behavior. "It was like, 'You'll outgrow it,' so I wasn't really given a hard time about being a tomboy at that age."

As Everetta advanced in elementary school, her attraction to girls became stronger. Though she had no close friends, she had repeated crushes on other girls a year or two older than herself. Her second childhood sweetheart was Lynette. Everetta constantly followed her about school and sent her notes. "I nicknamed her 'Tally' because she was so tall," Everetta remembers. "She'd wear skirts. I would roll down the hill so I could see up under her skirt. It felt natural. She didn't like me either. It wasn't until later that I kind of understood a little bit about why she didn't like that."

When Everetta was in fifth grade, her mother left home for a while. Mandy was an alcoholic.

> Everyday she would be drunk. When I got home from school and Daddy would come in from his maintenance job, they'd fight. She'd kind of go crazy and throw things. Daddy was also physically abusive. If you spilled something, you were slapped. If you didn't want to eat a certain thing, you were slapped. If you didn't do all the work you were supposed to do, you were slapped.

Though she never felt particularly close to her mother, Everetta was saddened by Mandy's departure. When she returned several months later, Everetta was very happy. "I cleaned the bathtub and did other chores for her. I was thinking if I did more of something that she'd stay. But, then she left again. I didn't see her for a long time." Before leaving, though, her mother found cards that Everetta had written to different girls and notes about her feelings toward them.

"She took them out of the drawer and burned them. I can't remember her saying any words. I just remember her anger and my anger that she had burned them. It wasn't brought up anymore."

Everetta had her first sexual experience during this time. Sleeping in the same bed with one of her female cousins, she found herself caressing and kissing Linda. Afterward, she "felt fine." About that same time, Everetta and a male cousin, Hook, spent the night at her grandmother's house. He asked Everetta to come to his room "after granny is asleep and we'll play." Everetta continues:

> I said, "Okay." I thought we were going to play on the lawn or something. He was the instigator. I had no idea what was going on. I don't believe it was his first time. I didn't feel good about having done it. I liked the other, with my girl cousin, better. I thought what happened between me and her wasn't sex since you hear sex is marriage. They don't tell you not to be naughty with the girls.

As Everetta entered middle-school, she continued to get into fights, play sports with the boys, and write notes to girls. Tracy became the target for Everetta's attentions:

> I had a baseball glove. I had her name and mine written all over it. I tried to explain to her how I felt. I remember being in school and telling her the only way I knew how: "There are three kinds of fruits. There is one where you are crazy. There is one that you eat. And, there is one where you are a girl and like other girls." That's how I explained it to her. I told her that I was the third one and that I liked her. She kind of went along with it for a while though we never touched or anything. Then, she got tired of it and asked the teacher to make me get her name off my glove. I told the teacher, "This is my glove and Tracy can't make me take her name off it." Well, teachers don't like that kind of attitude so, of course, I got into trouble.

Everetta's sense of difference became more apparent during middle-school. And it was then that this sense of difference was first given a name.

There was this kid named Billy. He decided he also liked Tracy. I thought that it was just too bad. Now, for some reason or another, Tracy and I ended up having to ride the same school bus home. He wanted to sit by her but I was sitting next to her. He told me, "Get up, 'four eyes'"—that was my nickname back then—"you shouldn't be sitting by Tracy unless you're queer." We fought over her on the school bus. I got in trouble and ended up getting licks from the principal.

Still, Everetta really "didn't understand exactly what 'queer' meant. I just knew I was different. I went through a stage that I thought that somehow God had made a mistake and that I really would have rather been a boy." Everetta recalls an incident with her father:

> *Real People* came up with a segment about this real tall guy who was very ugly and this short, ugly woman. She wanted to be the man and he wanted to be the woman. They had kids, too. They were going to reverse their sexes and still be together. I remember Daddy saying, "I think them people ought to be taken out and be shot." At this time, I was feeling I don't want to be a woman. I like to play sports. I like to play rough. I like girls. I don't like dresses. I don't like makeup. I don't cross my legs. So, I'm sitting there thinking, "Yeah, maybe something like that. . ." Then Daddy says, "What do you think?" I said, "Yes, sir."

Everetta and her father seldom had conversations, however. After her mother had gone, Everetta found herself more and more alone. She was often left to fend for herself:

> Daddy had girlfriends in and out. My older sisters were at my mother's a lot. He was gone most of the time and I got a lot more freedom. He'd ship me off to different places, which was fine with me. I could go over to friends' houses and stay a night or two. Most of the time we'd have frozen pizzas and weenies at home.

Particularly after the school bus and glove incidents, Everetta had a difficult time fitting in with any of the groups at school.

The kids just didn't accept me as much. The boys were getting old enough that they didn't like a little girl hanging around with them. The girls were all into their own thing. You know, being real pushy acting and talking like, "Ain't that boy cute?" and other things that I had no comprehension of. I was kind of an in-between. I didn't fit with the boys and I really didn't fit with the girls. I stayed mostly by myself.

Her continued fighting with boys (and often winning) earned her the nickname, "Rock." Though Everetta continued to be the object of scorn and ridicule, her classmates' motivations were still uncertain. "I wasn't sure why they didn't like me. I didn't really think it had anything to do with my liking girls. I thought they were harassing me because I was little, wore patches, and wasn't good looking."

A welcomed relief during seventh grade was her teacher, Mrs. Munn. Everetta found her very friendly and supportive. "I always had a feeling that she knew something inside of me was gay," Everetta confesses. "She was the first teacher I actually ever connected with. I acted up and was late to her class a lot. I guess I was looking for attention. She'd reprimand me but she also understood why I did those things." Mrs. Munn, though, was an exception. Her other teachers, like Ms. Peagler, were less understanding.

I always wore this blue jean jacket with fuzz inside. That jacket was everything to me; it was my identity. No matter what the weather was like, I would wear that jacket to school. Ms. Peagler would say, "That's not right, Everetta. You don't need to be wearing that kind of jacket, walking like a boy, talking like a boy, and acting like one." One day I left my jacket behind in her classroom. I went back later and asked her, "Did I leave my jacket here?" She teased me. She wouldn't tell me whether I left it there or not. Then she sat me down and told me how a young woman should and should not act and what a young lady should and should not wear.

But Thurmond, Everetta's father, was unconcerned about his daughter's boyish mannerisms. Everetta declares, "He didn't really care. I think he really wanted a son. At home, I was out with him chopping wood, clearing land, mowing grass, and fixin' the house."

In addition to persisting with her boy-like behavior, Everetta continued to pursue her interest in girls. During seventh grade Everetta would walk Veronica to school every day, carry her books for her, and accompany her to her classes. "Veronica liked boys. She ended up getting pregnant and leaving school. But, she let me do this anyway. We were close enough that I didn't have to write her notes. We could just talk. But we never really talked about how I felt."

Although Everetta did not date in middle-school, she did write notes to one or two boys, let them accompany her to a class, and occasionally allowed them to kiss her. "I kept trying to like boys," recalls Everetta. "But it was never comfortable. But, I thought I just needed to keep trying even if I didn't like it or it wasn't comfortable." Her feelings for girls, however, persisted.

As her feelings deepened, Everetta started "taking pills, smoking a little pot, drinking vodka here and there." In eighth grade Everetta found herself in the same class as her former fifth grade sweetheart, Tracy. She tried to get close to Tracy by moving their seats together during science class. As in the baseball glove incident years earlier, Everetta was rebuffed. "Tracy didn't want me being around her," recalls Everetta. "I honestly loved her. I wanted to hold her and kiss her. But, I knew I couldn't." Doing poorly in her schoolwork, Everetta was harassed by other students and abused at home. At 13, Everetta could see no exit:

> I took everything I could get my hands on: cold medicines, Nyquil, Tylenol, a whole bottle of aspirin. I couldn't sleep at all that night. I'd break out in a cold sweat and then I'd get real, real hot. My ears were ringing constantly. The next morning, I told my father I was too sick to go to school. He said, "You're going anyway." I couldn't make it through the school day. I couldn't hold my head up and my ears were still ringing.

Everetta confided to her cousin, Linda, who told their teacher. Everetta was placed in the nurse's office and met with the school district's psychologist for the first of many sessions. During the next three years, Everetta and Dr. Dorothea Chapman developed a supportive relationship to the point where she would go and stay with Dr. Chapman:

> We kind of got close talking about different things at home: my mother, my father and him being abusive. That was when the first ideas of homosexuality came up. During that time is when it kind of fell into place. You know, I liked girls therefore I was gay, or homosexual, or lesbian. The terms came together at that time. I denied it when it fell into place. I wouldn't admit to myself that I was gay but I knew that I still had feelings. I didn't want any labels. At that time, I was still trying to be what I was supposed to be. And, if you say you're a homosexual then you are and you can't change it.

Everetta failed school that year. In order to continue into the ninth grade, she attended summer school, paying for it from her summer work. During the summer, her father re-married. "He came home one night." Everetta recalls him announcing, "'This is your mamma.' I said, 'I ain't calling her mamma.' He yelled, 'You will and you won't do a thing until you do.' I was very stubborn. I didn't do anything." Like Thurmond, her stepmother "was more attuned to my two sisters." For Everetta, it seemed like "there was just another person in the family who was against me." There was no Prince Charming for Everetta.

"From then on," Everetta remembers, "things were never as good." Ninth grade was more or less a rebellious time, when she became involved with a gang of four or five other girls:

> I fell in with this group led by Moose. She was a real large girl. She looked like me, acted like me, and talked like me. It was never discussed, either. She kind of got me into her crowd—the drug crowd. By this time, I was into drinking anytime I could get away with it. I was taking any kind of pills, smoking pot, Quaaludes, uppers, downers, prescription.

"Rock" also continued her sexual activities with her two cousins, Linda and Hook. Asked why she continued to have sex with Hook, she replied:

Probably for closeness. He liked me when I did. I wanted to be liked. It was hard to say no to Hook for some reason. I would go through a period of saying no and he would break me down again. I just kept feeling worse and worse about it. With Linda, it got more enjoyable. It didn't feel wrong.

Despite her problems at home, her relationship with Hook, and her poor schoolwork, Everetta did enjoy some success during her freshman year. She was named "best actress" in the drama club and she found an interest in the vocational arts:

I was a real brain for things like small engine repair and basic electricity. I took half a semester of home economics. I couldn't stand it. But, you had to have some time in it. You had to sew this little stuffed animal. I paid someone to do that just so I'd pass. As soon as I could, I got out of it. I took welding. I was usually the only girl in there.

There were girls in some of the classes. Tracy was in her woodworking class. With the help of Dr. Chapman, Everetta had her "last talk" with Tracy. "I explained some of the things in my childhood and why I thought I was the way I was. We had a real good talk and decided to be friends. But, we never were actually close. But, it seemed like I resolved something with her." This talk was probably more important to Everetta than to Tracy. "I really did care about her and I wanted her to understand that I didn't mean any harm."

In addition to her shop classes and the basic English, math and science courses, Everetta also was expected to take physical education. Though athletically talented, she tried to get doctors' excuses from PE in order to avoid the showers. "I was very bashful and shy about my body and how it compared with others. I was uncomfortable, too, because I really wanted to look at the other girls." Fortunately, Ms. Hightower, the PE instructor, often kept Everetta after class to further develop her athletic skills. One day, Everetta made a connection:

I thought, "She looks sort of like me. Maybe she feels the things that I feel." I kept waiting for her to say "It's okay. You're all right." But, it never happened. I thought that if she had those same feelings then she knew more about what I was going through than Dr. Chapman. It would have been nice to know someone older, like Ms. Hightower, who had struggled with this, too.

Everetta's love and admiration for Dr. Chapman, however, has not diminished over the years. "If she hadn't been there I probably would have killed myself. She really was a good influence and real supportive even though she couldn't give me the things I needed as far as being gay."

During the tenth grade, Everetta met Kerri and they soon became good friends. With Hook and Linda watching on the bus rides home, Everetta would "just sort of pick at her" sitting together, holding hands, and whispering that she liked her. It was not long before Everetta's stepmother "had gotten a whiff of this." Her stepmother's suspicions about Everetta's sexuality were lessened only by her concern about Everetta's choice of a black girlfriend.

Troubled by the rumors of her classmates and the suspicions of her stepmother, Everetta decided that she "wanted to try to be straight again and to do what all the other girls were doing." Everetta decided to go on her first date:

> This guy at the peach shed asked me out. Unfortunately, Gareth only wanted one thing. Hook had told him what I had done. But, I didn't know all this. I thought Gareth actually liked me. So, I come in and ask my stepmother. She says, "You know you're too young." I guess I was 15. I said, "Yeah. That's possible." She says, "No." "Okay," I said. I took out my little piece of paper that I had phone numbers written on. "I'll just give Kerri a call and see if I can maybe go over there." She says, "I will talk your Daddy into letting you go." That's all that was said.

Gareth escorted his date to the cinema. *The Rose* was the feature film. "Have you ever seen that movie?" Everetta asks. "The bathroom scene hit me real good. I identified with that scene a lot.

When you identify with something, that makes you understand a little bit." Gareth, though, was not interested in the cinematic virtues of the film. Everetta continues:

> It was half way through the movie and Gareth says, "Let's take off and go do something else." We wound up at the peach shed and it ended up being the same old thing. Again, I couldn't say "no." I felt like I had been used.

Her first and only high school date a fiasco, Everetta struggled with her sexuality. Her drug use became more prevalent and her studies continued to slide. She remembers "it was a constant struggle inside of what I should do and what I wanted to do. Drugs quieted the struggle. It quieted everything." One morning, Moose gave her a half of a Quaalude but "it was pure angel dust. I didn't know that at the time." It did not take long for the drug to have its effect:

> I was sitting in junior English class and I asked the teacher if I could go to the bathroom. He bitched a little bit and said, "Yes." Some time went by and he said, "Why didn't you go?" I'm sitting there saying, "I'm a good desk." I finally was able to get up and I ran out of the class. I'm running into lockers and things. The school nurse found me. She knew that I had been taking drugs and the psychologist did too but they were trying to keep it quiet at this point. They didn't want me to get into any more trouble. But, they couldn't. I was totally out of it. The principal was pumping me for information. "Where did you get the drugs?" He kept asking and I kept lying. Finally, I ended up telling him, "Moose!" I went in the hospital and got expelled.

Everetta was released from the hospital three days later and Dr. Chapman had already arranged for her to be reinstated at school. Thurmond, however, had other plans. Unknown to her, he had arranged for her commitment to the state mental hospital in Columbia. "I was a total mess," recalls Everetta. "I was nothing like I was the day before I took the drug. I thought I was going back to the doctor. My family tricked me. They had my suitcases hidden in the trunk and Daddy had already signed me into the [mental] hospital.''

Everetta's experience at the hospital set the stage for her ill-fated marriage.

> While I was in that hospital I had a guy walk up to me from out of the blue. I didn't know him and he didn't know me. He said, "Don't ever admit to yourself you're gay. I've lost my family, lost my home, lost everything because I admitted I was gay.'' I was 15 at the time. I told myself [then that], when I decide to admit it, I will look in the mirror and I will say, "You are gay."

The hospital released Everetta several months later. Taken away from her father by social services, she was sent to live with her natural mother. Everetta had not seen Mandy for years. This arrangement lasted only a brief time as her mother's alcoholism and their poor relationship forced social services to place her in a juvenile home. The "home" was no place for Everetta. No suitable alternative, however, could be found; Everetta returned to Mandy. Months passed. Everetta wrote long letters to a boy she met during her hospital stay. Lonnie-Wayne, just barely 18, had a baby face, a farm-hand's body, and a mind of a mule.

Everetta realized that her only hope for leaving her mother and moving beyond the grasp of social agencies was marriage. Her Prince Charming had the power to release her from the bondage of state and family. Everetta recalls her short-lived marital arrangement with Lonnie-Wayne:

> He liked me more than I liked him. He honestly loved me. He wanted to marry me. I was willing to try. My mom signed for us to get married which got me out of her place anyway. I lived with him and his parents. He slept with his brother and I slept on the couch. He knew I was struggling. I had talked with him about it before we got married. That was okay for a week or so. Then, he got real impatient. I knew it would hurt him even more if I couldn't be what he wanted me to be, so I wasn't going to let him be with me until I decided. I told him, "Give me two weeks. If I decide to stay with you, then I will

> be with you in every way that we are supposed to be." So, I
> decided. I looked in the mirror, I said, "You are gay," and I
> left him.

Lonnie-Wayne refused to accept Everetta's decision. She was
unable to get the marriage annulled and he refused consent to a
divorce. Everetta waited. Three years passed. After coming into
some money from an automobile accident, he consented. At 18,
Everetta became a free woman.

After leaving Lonnie-Wayne, Everetta participated in a voca-
tional-rehabilitation program. "I never thought that I was crazy in
the first place. But," she admits, "that drug did affect me pretty
bad." During this time she met an older woman, Lucinda, who
worked in the program's office. As their friendship grew, Lucinda
invited Everetta to live with her.

> That didn't work out either because Lucinda was an alcoholic.
> She'd let me drink and then I would try to make advances
> toward her. She kept telling me, "No way, kid." Then, one
> day she got tired of it. "Okay, you go jump in the bed and get
> undressed," she said. I tucked my tail between my legs and
> ran off like a little puppy. There ain't no way I was goin' to
> fool with an older woman.

Moving out of Lucinda's house, Everetta admitted herself to a drug-
abuse treatment center. As important as her therapy was the relationship she established with another young lesbian, Debbie.
Everetta's first genuine relationship blossomed, until one fateful
day:

> I kept a diary. Debbie was in it. This girl that I shared a room
> with read it and told everyone. A big meeting was called to
> discuss it. One of the counselors pulled me over and asked,
> "Are you gay?" I said, "As far as I can believe in my heart
> and soul, I am gay." She asked me what I wanted to do about
> it. There was a lot of whispering and talking going on. I said,
> "I guess I'll just tell them the way it is." So, I got up in front
> of all those people and told them I was gay. It wasn't easy.
> After the meeting, I found out that five or six other people

were gay, too. We formed our own little group and nobody really bothered us.

Finding a part-time job at an automobile supply company, Everetta left the center and began attending Alcoholics Anonymous meetings. One evening, Cinderella met her princess. "I can remember the day and the time," reminisces Everetta:

> Azelea walked into the room with her 17-year-old daughter. She was 35 at the time; I was still 18. She had broken up with her lover of four years. I was a little rooster flying around the place. Azelea first thought I was interested in her daughter. The next day we went to the gay outreach church. At first, she didn't like the age difference. I had to chase her a little bit. But we both knew there was something there. I kept her alive because she was heart-broken. She kept me alive because I was just a street kid. She is very intelligent; I have all the common sense. We've grown together.

COMMENTARY

This commentary focuses on two fundamental questions: What does Everetta's story tell us about our social understanding of the female experience? What does her story tell us about the relationship between being a tomboy and becoming a lesbian? In addressing these questions, we will examine the limitations of gender and sexual identities, examples of lesbianism in other species, times, and cultures, and patterns of tomboyish behaviors.

The Cultural Construction of the Female Experience

At a very early age, children learn what it means to be male and female in American society.[2] Despite this early, prolonged, and extensive socialization process, some children fail to comply with gender role norms. Greater tolerance for such deviation, however, is extended to girls.[3] Whether reading *Hot Rod* magazine, disrupting class, or standing up against boys, Everetta's childhood behavior was not of great concern to her father or teachers — in contrast with Alston's experience.

The proportion of males and females in this study who failed to conform to sex-typed personality traits and interests were the same; roughly 60 percent of these participants displayed cross-gender behaviors during childhood. The consequences suffered by these nonconformists depended on the child's gender:[4] Unlike Alston and other male "outcasts," women participating in this study seldom reported extensive *childhood* harassment. All but one (Royce) of the 14 males in this study who displayed gender inappropriate behaviors experienced sustained harassment; only one woman, Darla, discussed in Chapter 13, reported these problems.

Since tomboyishness is "more common, more tolerated, and more likely to represent a passing phase than sissiness,"[5] not surprisingly, Everetta was told "You'll grow out of it." Generally, tomboys experience reprobation from adults only when their actions fall well outside the accepted behavior or if it continues beyond childhood. In the case of Everetta, her father, who wanted a son to do the chores, did nothing to discourage such behavior. It was not until the seventh grade that she was taken aside by a teacher, Ms. Peagler. Lectured on the appropriate demeanor and dress for "young ladies," Everetta's classmates distanced themselves from her.

A similar pattern of harassment was found among others who insisted upon carrying their tomboyish behavior beyond middle-school. Six of the seven women describing a tomboy childhood reported harassment in *adolescence* for "being different." Five of these women, including Everetta, continued to display tomboyish traits or dress as adolescents. The other, Olivia, portrayed in Chapter 12, though effeminate in dress and traits, faced harassment because of a rumored relationship with another female student. Again, this contrasts with the effeminate boys, one-half of whom assumed appropriate gender roles by adulthood.[6]

Conventional studies of gender socialization fail to explain the issue of sexuality and its relationship, if any, to sexual identity. Michele Barrett observes:

[F]ew of these studies systematically engage with the question of sexual practice, or erotic behaviour, and how this does or does not relate to socially acquired gender identity. This absence . . . reflects the marginality of sexuality in the conventional socialization approach. One possible reason for this situation might be that by and large studies of gender socialization tend to argue a strong case on the social and familial pressures towards conformity and the acceptance of heterosexual gender identity.[7]

Barrett goes on to point out the importance of the distinction between gender and sexuality and the relationship of these concepts to the social structure. The impact of socially constructed categories and attributes associated with gender and sexuality extends beyond the individual. Thus, while gender expectations of adults like Ms. Peagler and the sexual demands of boys like Hook exacted a psychological toll on Everetta, it is the oppression of *all* women within a larger structure of social, political, and economic relations that is of utmost concern for some scholars and activists. Scholars from a variety of academic disciplines have argued that categorizing human beings according to their role in the biological process is central in the reproduction of their culture. Sociologists Kenneth Plummer, David Greenberg, and Ann Oakley, feminists Simone de Beauvoir and Mary Daly, cultural anthropologist Claude Levi-Strauss, social theorist Michael Foucault, and linguist Guy Hocquenghem have all explored the ideological aspect of the construction of gender and sexuality.[8]

This position is clearly articulated in Gayle Rubin's classic essay, "The Traffic in Women." In part, she asserts:

The division of labor by sex can therefore be seen as a "taboo": a taboo against the sameness of men and women, a taboo dividing the sexes into two mutually exclusive categories, a taboo which exacerbates the biological difference between the sexes and thereby *creates* gender. . . . [T]he social organization of sex rests upon gender, obligatory heterosexuality, and the constraints of female sexuality.[9]

In a more recent scholarly work, Sondra Farganis, examining motherhood as a social institution and femininity as a social construction, argues:

> [W]hat it means to be a woman, or gendered, is neither fixed nor indeterminably variable, but that interaction between how one defines oneself and the historical circumstances which encase the act of selfhood. The rooting of a "feminine character" in time and place allows us to see it as political, as subject to the social arrangement of the particular society. . . . What the feminine has come to mean is a result of a socially arrived at definition, made legitimate as a consequence of the power and influence of those in a position to define it.[10]

Thus, the social construction of gender and sexuality (i.e., the transference of biological divisions of maleness and femaleness into social categories), the delegation of human roles and traits according to conceptions of femininity and masculinity, and the proscription of same-sex activities rationalizes a particular way of organizing society—patriarchy.

Patriarchy is a system of social arrangements in which the female is economically, politically, and psychologically dependent upon the male.[11] This dependency extends from her roles in the private sphere (housewife, mother) to her status in the public arena (worker, consumer), and is reflected in her comparatively weak control over her economic and reproductive destiny.[12] Through patriarchy the body politic is ideologically reproduced by distinguishing "male" and "female"; the subsequent division of opportunities and rewards, traits and interests, privileges and responsibilities are accorded by gender.[13]

This social arrangement, while reflected in the products conceived and marketed in big city boardrooms, is rooted in small town bedrooms. Everetta's dependence on Lonnie-Wayne to carry her away from her family and his refusal (sanctioned by state statute) to consent to a divorce illustrate these patriarchal relations. These relations also are evident in her being used for sex by Hook and Gareth, and Thurmond's control over "his" family.

Legislators may prop up forms of patriarchy (e.g., divorce law, marital rape) but it is legitimized by hundreds of thousands of cultural cops who define the significance of gender and delimit meanings of sexuality. Everetta's peers and Ms. Peagler played an important, though unreflective, role in this process. Through humiliation and reward these cultural cops enforced gendered norms; through jokes and harassment they discouraged same-sex behavior.

From this perspective, children like Everetta and Alston who continue to flaunt their deviant gender behaviors challenge more than social sensibilities; they challenge the foundation of our social system. The ability to define and delimit appropriate gender behaviors and expressions of sexuality is nothing less than the power to shape society; conversely, those who threaten to defy these roles challenge the hegemony of patriarchy. As "in-betweens," lesbians like Everetta are the cultural bandits of the New Age. The emergence of gender studies, the success of feminist and gay collectives, bookstores, and publishers, the emergence of festivals ranging from Wiminfest to the Gay Games, and the blossoming of lesbian/gay music and humor are visible examples of this New Age. These are, in Christine Riddiough's words, "part of a culture of resistance that has helped gay people survive and fight back. . . ."[14]

The emergence of this New Age of public and private relationships signals the crumbling of a world view spanning two millennia of everyday social discourse. The fear of a social Armageddon lies at the root of misogynist attitudes, sodomy statutes, heterosexist curricula. A 13-year-old tomboy or a 17-year-old drag queen does more than threaten persons with insecure gender identities; they threaten the social order. But, as Mary Daly rightly points out, this is an idle threat if lesbians and gay men merely reverse sex roles and bifurcate relationships into roles such as "butch/femme" or "dominant/submissive":

> Such standardization of persons into roles is antithetical to radical feminism, which is concerned with overturning the sex role system. Lesbians may also be radical feminists, but the fact of choosing women rather than men as sexual partners does not of itself necessarily challenge sexist society in an effective way, any more than choosing men as sex partners necessarily supports sexist society.[15]

Choosing same-sex partners does little to end heterosexist society. For radical lesbian feminists like Carol Kitzinger, the greatest dangers are privatizing homosexual relationships, characterizing lesbians as basically the same as heterosexual women, reducing lesbianism to only a small part of what constitutes a human being, and asserting that lesbianism poses no threat to either heterosexuality or the larger social and political structures. She declares:

> [O]ur 'inner selves' — the way we think and feel about and how we define ourselves — are connected in an active and reciprocal way with the larger social and political structures and processes in the context of which they are constructed. It is for this reason that, as many radical and revolutionary movements of oppressed peoples have argued, 'the personal is the political.'[16]

According to radical feminists, the activists who dominate lesbian/gay organizations have not yet clearly declared all-out war on the patriarchal system itself. Radical feminists argue that these leaders are too timid and abuse the insight "the personal is political" by interpreting it as a license for personal freedom within the system, not as a mandate to change the system itself. Feminists such as Kitzinger, Farganis, and Rubin, conclude that the lack of such a declaration evidences the bankruptcy of liberal thought and progressive politics.

However, lesbians and gay-identified men who posit *either* the liberal or radical feminist position or those who adopt homosexual identities based upon these ideologies may, in the end, find themselves no more liberated than before. Exchanging compulsory heterosexuality with the canons of liberal gay or radical feminist orthodoxies provides little nourishment for a journey of the spirit. As discussed in Chapter 15, the insights these positions offer may come at the expense of personal wonderment and, ultimately, the very liberation they so ardently advocate.

Everetta's biography clearly depicts her reticence in adopting a homosexual identity. Recalling her time in counseling with Dr. Chapman, Everetta remarked: "I didn't want any labels. At that time, I was trying to be what I was supposed to be. And, if you say you're a homosexual then you are and you can't change it." The power of naming is, indeed, profound. It was important for Everetta to name her oppressors and personal demons. The power of naming, though, may become debilitating. Confusing the simplicity of names (e.g., "four-eyes," "tomboy," "lesbian") with the complexity of the thing named ("Everetta") may lead her into a maze of mirrors in which her identity becomes a mere reflection of others.

Eventually, Everetta and Alston gazed into the mirrors of their souls. Alston, to his horror, only saw members of his Congregation staring back at him; Everetta realized that she could not be the woman of Lonnie-Wayne's fantasies. Each chose a homosexual identity. Other life-choices followed: Everetta left her husband and sought a divorce; Alston divorced himself from the Congregation and participated in the weekend rituals of *Rocky Horror*. Where do they go from here? Alston has departed the security of The Twilight and discarded his identity as Velvetta Spike; Everetta has entered into a relationship with her Cinderella princess and forsaken her identity as an unattractive, drug-dependent kid.

Lesbianism and Tomboyism

Homosexual relations among females are found across times, cultures, indeed, even throughout nature.[17] Dolphins display a wide variety of sexual behavior, including homosexual, and female homosexual behavior has been observed in wild langurs and other primates.[18] In human societies, pre-colonial western North America, for example, female *berdache* were valued warriors among the Kutenai people and respected shamans in the Mohave tribe.[19] Susan Cavin describes lesbianism ranging from pre-Christian Athens to the 17th century Amazonian societies. Of this earliest period, she writes:

> [T]he earliest recorded history, art, and literature of western society documents the existence of lesbians: Ruth and Naomi among the Hebrews (pre-800 B.C.) in the Bible; Sappho's poetry on Lesbos (c. 600 B.C.); Aristotle and Plutarch describe female homosexuality in Sparta (c. 400 B.C.); Aristotle also describes homosexuality sanctioned by the Cretan constitution and among the Celts; lesbianism has been reported in Athens (450 B.C.) and in Rome (A.D. 100).[20]

Women who dared love other women also include: Queen Christina of Sweden, Gertrude Stein, Bessie Smith, Catherine the Great, and Susan B. Anthony.[21]

Finally, lesbianism occurs in a variety of contemporary societies.[22] In southern Africa, !Kung girls first engage in sexual play with other girls before participating in sexual activity with boys.[23] In western Africa, one of the twelve marriages practiced by the Fon of Dahomey is that of "giving the goat to the buck" in which one woman marries another.[24] In eastern Africa, the Swahili Muslims of Mombasa, while observing sharply defined gender roles, accept lesbianism.[25]

Despite routine occurrences of same-sex behavior in other species, across time, or among other contemporary cultures, female homosexuality is less documented and, possibly, less prevalent than male homosexuality.[26] For example, the female *berdache* was a relatively rare phenomenon in Native American culture compared to the male *berdache* described in Chapter 10. Anthropologist Harriet Whitehead posits an explanation:

> [T]he phenomena of adult reproductive processes added to and underscored an image of femininity that could weaken and be counterbalanced by masculine occupations only if the physiological processes themselves were held to be eliminable. Throughout most of North America, they were not so held, at least not for that period of a woman's life when she was realistically capable of taking up the hunter-warrior way of life. Becoming a member of the opposite sex was, therefore, predominantly a male game.[27]

In this study, assuming the traits and demeanor of the opposite sex is an acceptable *female* game in childhood. Seven of the 12 lesbians described a "tomboy" childhood and, with the exception of Darla, reported little harassment for such behavior. This is consistent with other studies which have found a substantial proportion (up to three-fourths) of homosexual women recalling greater childhood preference for competitive games or male dress and less interest in dolls or female demeanor.[28] Everetta's repeated desire to "become a boy" is also a common phenomenon. For example, two-thirds of Saghir and Robins' sample of 54 lesbians expressed similar sentiments.

These data should be interpreted with caution. First, as Marcel Saghir and Eli Robins note, "They were not, however, actual wishes of sex change but rather ideas of regret for not being born as a male and a wishful desire to become a boy or a man, mostly through fantasy and imagination."[29] Another important caution, as detailed in Chapter 10, is that there is no evidence that cross-gender behaviors are causally related to homosexuality. In heterosexual women, for example, tomboyish behavior is common. Studies have reported between 16 and 48 percent of heterosexual women engaged in such behavior during childhood.[30]

Finally, there were discrepancies found between data provided by lesbians participating in this study and findings reported elsewhere. One widely quoted research study includes the statement, "All those that were tomboys in childhood gave a persistent history of avoidance of girl playmates. . . ."[31] However, Everetta eagerly sought girl playmates who generally rebuffed her advances at companionship. Despite Everetta's attraction to a string of slightly older girls during childhood (Tally, Tracy, Veronica), she was never able to woo them. They found her behavior as threatening and unattractive as that portrayed in the *Real People* segment she remembers watching with her father.

The life stories of the seven tomboys in this study revealed a variety of behavioral patterns as they acted upon meanings of gender and sexuality from early childhood through late adolescence. Four sought girl playmates during childhood; five maintained their tomboyish traits and demeanor during adolescence; and one adolescent was not subjected to harassment. These patterns are evidenced in the stories of Elisa, 'Lizabeth, and Kimberly.

Like Everetta, Elisa displayed boy-like mannerisms and interests but preferred the company of other girls. Elisa's family moved from the North to the South when she was 10. The family's fortunes also moved downward. Elisa's father worked in restaurants and later, when his business folded, in the cotton mills of the Piedmont area. Elisa recalls her childhood play behavior:

> I was real attracted to pretty women but I identified more with men. When me and my friends played, I was Joe, the guy. When we had dancing lessons, I was the guy. I always identified with the man. I remember when I was a little kid about four or five saying to my mom that I was going to marry a woman. She just said, "Girls don't marry other girls."

By the time Elisa approached adolescence, her feelings for girls strengthened, though she began to date boys:

> I was infatuated with a female friend when I was 12 or 13. It wasn't just like a buddy type thing. It was a crush you get on somebody of the opposite sex — only this was my friend. I had fantasies about her. After I would have them for a while, I would feel guilty and fantasized about something else. But, no one labelled me as gay until late in high school when I developed a close friendship with this girl. Her brother started a rumor about us. But, there was no attraction between us. We were just friends. At the same time, I didn't feel comfortable around boys. I didn't feel it was natural. It was kind of forced. Although I did have a boyfriend, it was a puppy love kind of forcing. I'd go out on dates and it was always awful. I had a terrible time. I never had sex with any of them!

At the end of high school, Elisa was still uncertain about her gender and sexuality:

> I was really scrawny and people were always asking me if I was a boy or a girl. My boyfriend's friends would say my shoulder blades stuck out more than my chest. I had the nickname "aircraft carrier." I think they thought of me as asexual.

Like Elisa, 'Lizabeth displayed boy-like interests and dress as she was growing up. Unlike Everetta and Elisa, she seldom associated with other girls.

> I never felt like I fit in to begin with. But, a lot of my "looking gay" had to do with my attitude not with my dress. I can look now at other females and they can dress exactly the way I did and still look like the most feminine thing in the world. My

mother can wear jeans with paint all over her and look like she stepped out of *Vogue*. I can wear nice jeans and a shirt and still look like a dyke. It has a lot to do with the fact that I tend to be very aggressive, very competitive. I also never had the desire to allow myself to be vulnerable or show my feelings to anybody. I don't cry in front of people. I also have a "If you try to hurt me, I'll get you for it" attitude. People say that's not being very feminine. You know, women are supposed to be meek and let men take care of them.

'Lizabeth's "masculine" behaviors and "unfeminine" attitudes continued through high school at which time she found herself the target of harassment. "I was tormented about everything. I was tormented for not looking feminine enough. I was tormented about being skinny. People kept saying, 'You're not very feminine. You must be gay.'" 'Lizabeth "compensated by calling attention to anything male that walked down the street. It didn't much matter whether they were good looking or not. But, it made people think I was strongly boy-crazy when, in fact, I wasn't at all."

The harassment experienced by tomboys turned adolescents was found for all the women in this study who continued to exhibit masculine traits or behavior beyond childhood. Kimberly, who "demasculinized" during adolescence, was not harassed during high school. During childhood, she excelled in sports, did well in school, and had little problem "fitting in" with the other kids in school. On the playground she would champion the little guy. She recalls:

I was a little tomboy. I always hung around with the guys because I was really athletic. I could beat most of the guys in anything. I would protect kids when bigger kids wanted to pick on them. I'd protect them, especially girls. Guys would always pick on girls. I remember in third grade there was this black guy and white girl. It was like "blacky and whitey." I thought she was really a nice person. The guy started picking on her about being white. He was saying, "Black is better." He was going to jump on her but I intervened. I stuck up for her.

By adolescence, gender roles changed and Kimberly with them:

> Around the eighth grade, I realized that I was different than
> the guys. Competitions that I used to win I started coming in
> second and third. I started hanging out with the girls. We'd
> always get together and say, "I like so and so." I fit right in. I
> didn't stand out. I just fell into the pattern of "You're sup-
> posed to have a boyfriend." So, I got a boyfriend. I never
> really felt comfortable. But, it was like something that I had to
> do.

Everetta also persisted in dating boys even though she suspected
she was different—"the third kind of fruit." Unlike 'Lizabeth,
however, Everetta was genuinely struggling to fit into her prescribed heterosexual norm by "dating" Hook and Gareth. But,
there was no one to rescue Everetta from her fondness for girls, the
peach shed, or the hospital. Lonnie-Wayne was not her Prince
Charming. The problem was not his lack of love for her but her lack
of insight into herself. Finally, one morning she looked at herself in
the mirror and acknowledged her search was for a princess not a
prince. Living at one rehabilitation center and then another,
Everetta searched for her princess. She found Azelea.

Aside from her mannish characteristics, Everetta's portrait contrasts with that of the lesbian icon, Stephen Gordon, popularized in
Radclyffe Hall's *The Well of Loneliness*. Everetta lacked the emotional security of a father's love and the financial security of a family estate. Most importantly, while Stephen was forced to give up
the woman of her love for a man, Everetta chose to leave her man
for her Princess Charming. Through her relationship with Azelea
Everetta's journey continues:

> There is a strong emphasis on being a woman and being femi-
> nine in the South. But, I work at a parts place. I get dirty from
> the top of my head to the bottom of my toes. These redneck
> men accept me. They're country boys and they're into hunting
> and drinking with the wife staying at home. "You're an ex-
> ception," they say. "But, you're not my wife." Of course,
> they don't know about Azelea. I tell them I have a boyfriend.
> But, I wouldn't change being gay. I love Azelea more than

anything. She has taught me a lot. Azelea says, "Don't ask me to stand up for gay rights if you're not going to respect yourself enough to act respectable." I'm beginning to respect myself.

REFERENCE NOTES

1. Near, 1978.

2. Broverman, Vogel, Broverman, Clarkson, and Rosenkratz, 1972; Duncan and Duncan, 1978; Goldstein and Oldham, 1979; Lipman-Blumen, 1972; McRobbie, 1978; White and Brinkerhoff, 1981.

3. Kagan, 1964; Lynn, 1961; Saghir and Robins, 1973. None of the tomboyish girls in this study, however, were from wealthy families where more conventional behavior might be in keeping with the grooming of southern debutantes.

4. Sears, 1989b.

5. Saghir and Robins, 1973:201.

6. Though substantial scholarship has been devoted to sissiness, "defeminization," and homosexuality, little research has been done on tomboyism, "demasculinization," and lesbianism. This reflects both the relatively little stigmatization associated with childhood tomboy behavior and the centrality of male-oriented research.

7. Barrett, 1980:63.

8. de Beauvoir, 1952; Daly, 1973; Foucault, 1978; Greenberg, 1988; Hocquenghem, 1978; Levi-Strauss, 1969; Oakley, 1972; Plummer, 1975; Plummer, 1981.

9. Rubin, 1975:178-179.

10. Farganis, 1986:80, 196.

11. Eisenstein, 1979; Foreman, 1977; Lerner, 1986. Patriarchy, of course, is found in socialist as well as capitalist countries as Eisenstein (1979:24) makes clear. "The overthrow [of an economic system] does not necessitate the destruction of patriarchal institutions either. Although practiced differently in each place, the sexual division of labor exists in the Soviet Union, in Cuba, in China." This is evident in a recent essay by Joanne Passaro (1987), who examined the revolutionary as well as reactionary conceptualizations of gender in revolutionary Nicaragua.

12. Barrett, 1980; Bentson, 1969; Hartmann, 1981; Zaretsky, 1976.

13. Chodorow, 1978; Hartmann, 1981.

14. Riddiough, 1981:86. For further elaboration of the role of lesbian and gay communities in redefining taken for granted identities, roles, and experiences, see: Bronski, 1984; Ponse, 1978; Wolf, 1979. But, as I will argue in Chapter 15, these very communities also pose the danger of reifying sexual identities, gendered roles, and homosexual experiences.

15. Daly, 1973:125.

16. Kitzinger, 1987:62.

17. Denniston, 1980; Geist, 1971; Goldstein, 1982; Hunt and Hunt, 1977; Trivers, 1976; Weinrich, 1980.

18. Akers and Conaway, 1979; Goldfoot, Loon, Groenevald, and Slob, 1980; Hrdy, 1975.

19. Roscoe, 1987. From the time of creation, the Mohave believed that there have been homosexual persons who have served according to plan (Neithammer, 1977).

20. Cavin, 1985:43.

21. For other examples of lesbianisn across the annals of time, see: Abbott and Love, 1972 (esp. 107-134); Cavin, 1985; Fisher, 1965; Foster, 1975; Goldstein, 1982; Grier and Reid, 1976; Katz, 1976; Myron and Bunch, 1974; Rule, 1975.

22. Adam, 1986; Blackwood, 1984a; Blackwood, 1984b; Blackwood, 1986; Cavin, 1985; Ford and Beach, 1951.

23. Shostak, 1981.

24. Herskovits, 1967.

25. Shepherd, 1987.

26. It has also been of less concern in most societies for a variety of different reasons (Goldstein, 1982).

27. Whitehead, 1981:93.

28. Grellert, Newcomb and Bentler, 1982; Heilbrun and Thompson, 1977; Saghir and Robins, 1973; Whitam, 1977b.

29. Saghir and Robins, 1973:195.

30. Gundlach and Reiss, 1968; Saghir and Robins, 1973.

31. Saghir and Robins, 1973:194-195.

Sexuality and Adolescence:
Peers, Queers, and Tears

Dear God, I am fourteen years old . . . I have always been a
good girl. Maybe you can give me a sign letting me know what
is happening to me.

Alice Walker, *The Color Purple*[1]

Adolescence is a modern day cultural construction bridging
childhood with adulthood.[2] Adolescents struggle between identity
and role confusion as they contend with a variety of developmental
tasks: establishing an identity independent of parental authority,
feeling comfortable with body image, developing social skills and
abstract reasoning skills, forming memberships within peer groups,
internalizing a moral and ideological code, and making vocational
decisions.[3] Coping with homosexual feelings is an unacknowledged
task since those who exercise greatest control of the adolescent's
environment — parents, teachers, and peers — operate under the heterosexual presumption. This premise is articulated through the daily
scripts of classroom conversations, manifested in the ritualized behaviors promoted in school-sponsored activities, and represented in
school icons such as the jock and cheerleader.

Olivia, Phillip, and Brett passed through adolescence with a heavier burden than their heterosexual-identified counterparts. These Southern youths felt an absence of peer and adult support. They found few opportunities to discuss their concerns with their friends; seldom did an adult extend a helpful hand. They had no openly gay, lesbian, or bisexual role models and, unlike their heterosexual peers, they lacked opportunity to develop social skills or to experience trust and intimacy in fledgling same-sex relationships.

In order to explore one's sexuality, there is a need for a "dual dialectic"[4] within oneself: the willingness to reflect upon the consequences of one's actions and to delve into one's inner self. The childhood biography of Olivia is a human testament to the difficulty of engaging in this dialectic. Olivia was out of touch with herself during adolescence. Unwilling to express feelings or attitudes which were at odds with what was thought acceptable, her social and emotional development languished. For example, she split her public and private self: Beneath the veneer of good grades and extracurricular activities, she engaged in a long-term closeted homosexual relationship. This fragmentation of the public and private self further delayed her psychosocial development.

As Phillip entered adolescence, tensions and conflicts arose between his emerging sexual interests and his presumed heterosexual identity. Taunted and tormented by homophobic thugs, Phillip seldom felt at ease. Drifting through the labyrinth of courses, classrooms, and high school clubs, he also failed to embark on the inward journey to "another country." In the process, he adopted a variety of self-destructive coping strategies.

For each participant, acquiring a homosexual identity gradually culminated in early adulthood, with each "coming out" to parents, siblings, or friends. Brett's biography portrays not only the negative attitudes and feelings held by peers and educators but also pressure from other gay students to declare a gay identity. His period of struggle with same-sex feelings and development of a sexual identity was one of anxiety, wariness, and tumult, culminating in a whirlwind of family anger and disgust when his homosexual feelings were disclosed.

These biographies include high school environments in which few people would want to find themselves even briefly, let alone be able to learn. Beneath the surface of films such as *Sixteen Candles*, or television sit-coms like *Head of the Class* lies the everyday torment of innuendo, fear, and intimidation. Olivia, Phillip, and Brett knew few students like Molly Ringwald or teachers like Charlie Moore. In reality, high school is a world dominated by peer pressure, structured by heterosexuality, and overseen by well-meaning but insensitive educators; a harsh world in which to nourish personal and sexual identities.

REFERENCE NOTES

1. Walker: 1982:1.
2. The concept of adolescence, like the earlier construct of childhood, is a phenomenon of the industrial age. During this century, adolescence itself has been expanded and now bridges a 10-year span between the onset of puberty to graduation from college, or the graduation from high school for those who marry or enter the workforce. See, Aries, 1962; Teeter, 1988.
3. Archer and Waterman, 1983; Erikson, 1968.
4. Macdonald, 1975.

Chapter 12

Relationships

OLIVIA AND THE SILENCED RELATIONSHIPS

> *"Your silence*
> *will not*
> *protect you"*
>
> *"Our speaking is stopped*
> *because we fear the visibility*
> *without which*
> *we can not really live"*
>
> *You quietly stand there,*
> *annealed by death,*
> *mortality shining:*
>
> *"Whether we speak or not,*
> *the machine will crush us to bits—*
> *and we will also*
> *be afraid"*
>
> *"Your silence*
> *will not protect you."*

Gloria T. Hull, "Poem"[1]

Olivia, a Southern feminist who has lived throughout the Old Confederacy, seldom minces words. "In the Deep South," she bluntly states, "they are blatant racists, they don't like uppity women, and they don't like gays. They are very verbal about their prejudices. In the Southwest, they were more subtle." Raised in an upper-middle class Southern family by her football coach father and her Southern Baptist mother, Olivia has not always spoken out. Throughout her childhood and adolescence she chose to remain silent about things dearest to her.

Olivia is a 23-year-old lab technician with wind-blown auburn hair and golden skin. Her favorite childhood activities were playing the piano, singing in the choir, and competing in sports — especially basketball. She also enjoyed school. A diligent, conscientious, and able student, Olivia rarely earned a grade below an A. At recess, though, she seldom associated with females. During elementary school, "I didn't spend time playing tiddlywinks with the girls on the sidewalk. I'd go over to jump rope just to see what the appeal was. But jumping rope and hopscotch bored me." Olivia preferred more rugged games like basketball and "smear the queer":

> Somebody takes the football and runs around. Everybody, maybe 30 kids, tries to tackle him. You didn't want to be queer; you didn't want the football. But if you get it, you better run like hell. You have to pass the ball off before you get tackled. I had two other female friends who would go do that.

One of those girls, Cynthia, was a close friend. "I had a habit of picking females out of the class that I wanted to teach how to make a basket or something. These females had absolutely no athletic ability. I would teach them how to run or make a goal. Cynthia caught right on. I thought, 'That's great. I finally found a female friend who can do this stuff.'"

There were limits to Olivia's tomboyish behaviors. When she was in the second grade several of her male classmates promised to show her their notebook if she would pull down her panties. She agreed. Spotting this indecent act on the playground, a teacher paraded Olivia to the principal's office where she was immediately sent home. The boys were not punished. Olivia remembers the reaction of her father:

> My dad sat me down. He just sat there. It seemed like eternity. Then he went into this very degrading talk about right and wrong. He said, "Don't you understand right and wrong? Haven't I taught you that this is something little girls don't do?" He couldn't understand me; I couldn't understand him.

Olivia, however, learned her lesson. During the third grade, she attended an integrated school. Half of the students were from the neighborhood in which the school was located and the other half, like Olivia, were bused in from an outlying suburb. She recollects:

> All those things that were never talked about out in the white middle class schools, these young black kids knew. I was hearing "fuck" for the first time and seeing a lot of very lewd graffiti. My parents were like, "What are we going to do with this girl being exposed to all of this?" I was scared all the time. I was scared I was going to get knifed, pushed, or cursed because they were very mean black children. I remember this one guy, James. He pulled his pants down for those of us who were sitting around. All the other girls at the table took a peak, but not me.

Before the next school year her family moved Olivia to a suburban school. Olivia found herself working comfortably within a familiar school environment. "I loved it. I was back in middle class America. Everybody was white. I could relate. Everybody was the same social class. Nobody talked about sex anymore. Everybody was just like me."

Although she continued to play rough and tumble games with the boys, she also assumed the role of "matchmaker" for her class. "My time evened out. I spent time talking with my close girl friends, trying to get couples together or worrying about my own little things. I would find somebody that I thought was cute, get somebody to go tell him that I liked him, and he would tell them that he liked me and so on."

At nine years of age, Olivia was familiar with boy-girl relations. Three years earlier, she had already began to experiment sexually with little boys in the neighborhood. "I didn't have a term for being sexually excited at that age, but it was erotic. I knew it wasn't something I wanted to tell my mother because it had something to do with your 'private parts' which were naughty and nasty. So, I knew I was doing bad, but that didn't stop me." From second through seventh grades Olivia had a childhood crush on Oliver, a boy her age whose parents were friendly with Olivia's mother and father. By seventh grade, they began experimenting in more advanced sexual play. "One night our parents let us all sleep in the same bedroom. My mother did not realize that 12-year-olds had sexual feelings. That was the first time I got to see an erection. It was just extraordinary!"

Though Olivia recognized the evil of such heterosexual deeds, her strong feeling for other girls "just wasn't talked about at church or at school." Olivia first became aware of these feelings at six years of age. Her first female crush was the family's 14-year-old baby-sitter, Mary Louise. Olivia remembers: "I just loved being around her. I had never felt that way before. I thought she was pretty. She had long blond hair, blue eyes, and a great body. She'd wear her little cut off Levi shorts. I just adored her. When she had dates, I remember thinking, 'That guy is so lucky.'" Unlike the sex play in which she engaged with the neighborhood boys and Oliver, acting upon these same-sex feelings was "a gray area that I didn't want to tread into." By the end of the second grade, however, Olivia had recognized that her feeling for Oliver and the baby-sitter "wasn't the same. I felt attracted to my little sweetheart, but it wasn't this 'wow' feeling." The next time Olivia would experience that "wow" feeling was when she was 10.

At that age, Olivia came across the word "lesbian" while reading *The Chaplain of Bourbon Street* which her mother thought had a poignant religious message. "I came across this word. I didn't even know how to say it. I asked my mom. As she passed through the room, she said, 'That's when two women feel for each other like I feel for your father.' This was a completely new concept to me. I remember trying to filter it through my own experience but I really couldn't get a handle on it. But, I kept it in my brain." That same year, Mary Louise, a neighbor four years Olivia's senior, would come over to baby-sit Olivia and her younger brother. "I remember getting this — it wasn't a sexual urge — I just wanted to be next to Mary Louise. I didn't know what it was that I was feeling. I didn't label myself a 'lesbian' or call myself a 'homosexual.' I just started wondering about myself."

During sixth grade, Olivia was friends with another girl who "I could tell she liked me the way that I liked Mary Louise." On one occasion they touched one another. Olivia harbored both good and bad feelings about that experience:

> We poked around on each other's breasts. I thought, "This makes me feel embarrassed and sort of icky." So, I said to myself, "This is good. Maybe I'm not physically attracted to women after all. Maybe I am normal." I definitely used that word even though I didn't know what was abnormal. I knew that being normal for a female was not having any emotional feelings for a woman. I also knew that I had very strong emotional feelings for Mary Louise. But, I couldn't talk to anybody about it.

At the beginning of her seventh grade year, Olivia learned that her family was moving to east Texas. It was several months, however, before the move actually occurred. Olivia struggled with the fact that soon she and Mary Louise would be separated. Olivia recollects, "I started a five-year diary. Every day you would have to turn a page. It just hurt like hell to turn a page because I knew that was a page closer to the day when I was going to have to leave Mary Louise. It was killing me. It was so hard because I couldn't express it to anyone. They would have said, 'You're this upset because you don't want to leave your baby-sitter?'" As the weeks passed, Olivia decided to share her feelings with Mary Louise:

> I hadn't told her from the time I was 10 years old until that March. All this time I had all this feeling welling up inside of me. I kept saying to her all fall and winter, "I've got something I've got to tell you." She kept saying, "I don't want to hear it." At this point, I was not a child anymore. I was a young lady. We were both adult women in my mind. I remember begging her, "No! Don't go home. I have to tell you tonight." She said, "No. I don't want to hear it tonight. I think I know what you are going to say and I don't want to hear it." Lo and behold she left me a Valentine card. She told me in this card that she loved me. I thought, "Wow! This is great." This is the way I feel, but I still couldn't tell her. So finally I got up enough guts to go out and to write on a big rock, "I love Mary

Louise." Then I told her, "I can't tell you but you can just go out to this place and you'll see how I feel." She did. When she came back, I told her I loved her. She said, "That's very sweet. I love you too." I'm like, "No. You don't understand." I thought, "No. That's not the way it is supposed to be." That's when I knew I just didn't love her like a friend loves another friend.

Though she would correspond with Mary Louise throughout adolescence, Olivia's grades and behaviors during the seventh and eighth grades suffered. Once again she found herself in a "tough school. It was not middle class and the education was not as good. I just didn't try. I was snooty, rebellious, and angry. I'd tell the teacher, 'You can't give me a B. I've never had a B.' 'Yes, I can. Go sit down.' But, I would not stay in my seat. I'd go talk to people over here and over there. This was so unlike me, but the teacher had no feelings for me. I felt nobody knew me, nobody cared a thing about me, nobody understood me." Olivia added: "I think a big part of that was leaving and feeling powerless to stop it. My dad didn't give a damn why I didn't want to go. I was being a nuisance; I wasn't being supportive."

Like many other adolescents, however, Olivia's identity rested in large part on the opinions others held of her. She remembers entering the boy/girl "game" during junior high school:

My friend would tell me, "I have a crush on such and such." We would talk about this at length. If she could just get these guys to pay attention to her the world was hers. I just didn't ever have what Janice had for these guys. Because she was very overweight they would end up liking me. For the game, I'd say "Okay, he is kind of cute. If he asks me to go with him, I'm going to go with him." And I would. Janice would get really upset. She said I always stole her boyfriend.

As these coupling rituals continued, Olivia "started to realize that they really were into it. It wasn't a game to them. The girls really felt like that toward these boys. I realized that it really wasn't the same for me." Looking back at her childhood experiences and feelings, Olivia reflected: "I didn't know why I was different. I don't want to say that I was different because I was gay. I was also different because I was very studious. I was also different because I was very religious. I had a lot of dimensions. It made me a very different kid."

Olivia's eighth grade graduating class went on to two high schools. "Most of the lower class people and the Mexicans went to Eastside High. All of us went to Northside. I was happy again. I could relate to these people." Olivia entered womanhood with a vengeance her freshman year:

> I decided that ninth grade was going to be the time that I was going to start wearing makeup, that I was going to dress fashionably, that I was going to carry a purse. I was excited about doing those things. I still am. When you do them you get all this attention. Presto! It pissed me off. I made myself look just a little bit different and I get all this attention. I thought, "You are really shallow."

Olivia's feelings about Mary Louise drifted into memory as she participated in a variety of school activities including sports, band, and academic clubs. She also began to pay more attention to "fag jokes" and to the "queer" label. "I thought it was terrible. But, I didn't say anything. I had realized that my feelings about Mary Louise, even though they were gone, were 'gay' feelings. I had finally put a handle on them. So, I could relate to whoever was being pointed at." During her freshman year Olivia met Kris:

> We talked a lot. She had just gone through her parents' divorce. I had just gone through this terrible move. We were in a lot of classes together. I started doing things with her family. She became my true best friend. In February, I told Kris that I loved her; she told me she loved me. She reacted in a very emotional manner but still nothing physical. That summer her mom, her brother, Kris, and I went to family camp. We got our own tent. Right before we went I had this dream. It was the first time I'd even dreamt of being with a woman. I was kissing Kris. I told her about that. I said, "That was a weird

dream. I don't know what it means. I think I could be queer."
She goes, "No, you're not." I said, "Yes, I am." I told her
that I was attracted to her. Even though she couldn't understand it, she was real sweet. She just sat down and said, "I
don't know what to say. I don't know anything about this."

Midway through Olivia's sophomore year, at 15, her relationship
with Kris became sexual. It was then that Olivia first labelled herself "homosexual." "We were both enjoying it very much. I had
never felt anything like that before. It was so special." As their
relationship blossomed, they kept it to themselves. Olivia was frustrated with the need for secretiveness: "It was hard as hell to have a
relationship because I wanted so bad to tell people how happy we
were. She loved me and I loved her. It was so great but I couldn't
tell anybody. It really hurt."

Despite Kris and Olivia's closeted relationship other students in
high school began to talk about them. Finally, Harvey, a friend of
Olivia's, confronted her:

I was asked as a junior, "Are you and Kris gay?" I said,
"No." Then Harvey said, "If you are or you aren't, you act
like you are. If you don't want people to talk about you, don't
act around her like you do." I said, "What do you mean?" He
said, "Well, you stand about this close together to talk.
You're constantly talking to her across the band room. You're
looking at her all the time. You're always fiddling with something on you." I was shocked because I didn't realize I was
doing any of this. I thought, "Shit! People know. What's going to happen to me? My reputation will go right down the
tubes." It was just devastating.

Evidence of Harvey's concern already was surfacing in the band
group. Olivia spotted phrases like "Olivia and Kris are lezzies,"
and "Kris and Olivia like to fuck with dildos" scribbled on the
band room chairs. Kris and Olivia decided to be more aloof in public. Olivia quit band. Determined to squelch these rumors, Olivia
began dating boys in the school. "I was terrified of people not

liking me," she admits. "I had to have people like me. I was obsessed with that." She remembers:

> Peter really liked me. He was a jock and he looked the part. I was plotting by this time. There were no feelings there. I had him purely for show. He was there for two years. I did some things for him sexually. We had a pretty good time. But I wasn't getting the same thing out of it as he was. I yearned for Kris. It really made me mad that I couldn't have her.

In a high school of 2,000 students and dozens of cliques Olivia was able to confine these ugly rumors to a group of 40 people. "The people in the band did not associate with the jocks, the freaks or the other groups so all these rumors were going in this one clique and no one else noticed." Olivia also arranged for Kris to accompany her and Peter on "double dates" including junior and senior proms. "We were all dating and playing the game. It wasn't until later that I found out that some of my other friends were also gay. But, back then everybody kept it to themselves."

Outside the range of public view, however, Olivia and Kris continued their relationship. Both, however, harbored reservations about its morality:

> Kris and I prayed a lot. We asked forgiveness for doing anything that wasn't right and to be showed if what we were doing was really wrong. I felt like God knew that I loved Kris and that if He allowed us to go without getting caught that He was supportive. "Maybe," I thought, "He doesn't like homosexuality in general but that Kris and I are special. Maybe He realizes that our relationship isn't based on sex but on love."

Despite her ambivalence about the relationship and the necessity to disguise her homosexuality under a cloak of heterosexual activity, Olivia graduated valedictorian. "It got real hairy in high school with sexuality," Olivia confesses, "but I kept my grades together. The stress has always shown in my face."

Her relationship with Kris provided the support and nurturance Olivia desperately needed. For their senior year, Olivia arranged with Mrs. Christenson, the guidance counselor, for their identical class schedules. "I was afraid we wouldn't have classes together. It was a terrifying thought. I knew that as long as I had Kris to talk to and she had me, we didn't need anyone. I was a 'goody-goody' and Mrs. Christenson was really nice. She said 'okay.' But, I'm not sure she knew what was going on."

Olivia remains feeling dumbfounded by the apparent lack of awareness or willingness of her teachers and counselors to confront this topic:

> They didn't really understand. Like, if I was teaching high school I would pick up on these things right away. But, Mrs. Christenson didn't. She tried to show support for my very close friendship with Kris. I remember her telling me once, "You and Kris are really special friends. You will be able to get together 50 years from now with your families and sit down and talk. It will be like you've always been together." If she and the other teachers wouldn't have completely ignored the fact that this actually goes on and tried, at least, not to have been scared of even saying the word "homosexual," then I would have felt like they could have been talked to.

Despite the perceived lack of understanding about her "special relationship" with Kris, Olivia is glad that she did not have a circle of gay friends within high school. "I couldn't have handled it. If we would have had a circle of gay people, we would have been the social outcasts. I wouldn't have been able to have been nearly as superficially happy as I thought I was."

At the end of her senior year, the family moved to South Carolina. At the time, Olivia said to herself, "It's just rough being gay. I'm off to somewhere else wherever Dad is moving. Who knows, I may never meet another gay person in my whole life."

Nearing the end of her adolescence, attending a large university as a freshman, and living with her parents, Olivia was depressed. "Life was dismal. I was really thinking about not living anymore. It was so traumatic. I didn't have anybody to talk to. I didn't know any gay people here. I didn't have Kris anymore. It was a lonely, terrible time." Olivia spent her first two years in college as a social isolate. Majoring in psychology, she was finally exposed to sup-

portive material about homosexuality and a knowledge of the contributions of lesbians and gay men to society. "In psychology I was
told over and over again that it was okay to be gay. Plus in my
English and history classes I found out all these details about people
who were gay. Those are things I didn't hear in high school."

In the summer following her sophomore year, Olivia went to live
with her grandmother. There, to her astonishment, she found out
her cousin, Jennifer, was gay. Jennifer introduced her to the lesbian
bar scene. "I felt I was finally around a bunch of people I could
relate to even though they drank too much and stayed out real late."
When Olivia returned from summer vacation, she was feeling better
about herself. She began to frequent Lambda House, the town's
lesbian bar. Then, her father was told that Olivia had been seen
entering a "queer bar."

> Once again, my father dealt with me. Dad and I never talk
> except when there's a crisis. Then he talks to me. It's not
> Mom, who is my really good friend and who knows me; it's
> Dad who is a total stranger. My father sits down and asks me if
> it was true. I said, "Yep, and so is. . . ." I rattled off about 10
> of my friends. That was a mistake. He declared, "We're not
> allowing you to talk to any of those people any more. You're
> not going to write to them or speak to them again." I go,
> "What do you mean? I'm 20 years old. You can't do that."
> He said, "Yes, we can. If you decide to continue living like
> that we will no longer support you. You will find yourself very
> alone, young lady." They changed our phone number. I was
> not allowed to go out of town. They told me that I couldn't be
> trusted. Basically, the message was that I was a louse, a big
> shit, and a total failure in life.

Olivia was angry, hurt, and depressed. She cried a lot. She ignored her parents; they ignored her. Olivia withdrew into herself,
associating occasionally with two women from her family's church,
Beverly and Monica. While her father was heavily involved with
the fall sports season, Olivia's mother began to reach out. "If you'd
like to get some Christian counseling, your father and I will pay for
it," Olivia recalls her mother saying. "I had enough psychology to

know that that was no good." As fall faded into winter, Olivia began to spend more time with Beverly and Monica. "I was so depressed that I finally told Beverly. Then, lo and behold, a week later she told me about her. I was dumbfounded. She had no idea about me; I had no idea about her. Meanwhile, my parents thought they were just nice church girls."

During that year in college, Olivia's interests broadened to women's studies. She began to take interdisciplinary courses ranging from the psychology of women and the sociology of sex roles to women's literature and history. "I came across *The Color Purple* in one of my classes before it came out as a movie. It was really great in how it portrayed the relationship between the two women; the movie wasn't. In another class I did research on women's music and found out that Janis Joplin was gay." These studies had a profound impact on Olivia:

> Before I could define myself or define my sexual orientation for myself and get on with my life, I had to feel good about myself as a person. Those classes really helped. Before I was thinking I'm just a female. I am lousy. Like my parents forced me to talk with a minister. He and they were probing and poking about my sexuality. They all tried to make me feel real guilty. I broke down in a puddle of tears. But, then those courses showed me that it's a good thing to be female and to love a woman.

In the spring of that year, Olivia moved in with Beverly. At the time of the interview, Olivia and Beverly had been lovers for three years. While distancing themselves from Olivia's family has eased tension, it has not resolved the family impasse. "Now it's like, 'If you'll at least pretend that you're not gay, then we'll accept you.' My parents will not overtly recognize my relationship with Beverly. If they want to be like an ostrich with its head in the sand, then I'll let them deal with it that way."

In retrospect, the only decision that Olivia regrets was not "coming out sooner. Had I come out earlier I would not have gone to South Carolina. I would have stayed with Kris. I probably would have gone to college with her. We might still be together; we might not. But, I wouldn't have let my parents run my life.''

COMMENTARY

Relationships for any human being are as important as they are complicated. Among other tasks confronting adolescents is learning how to develop healthy social and emotional relationships with peers. For young people like Olivia this task is complicated by a hidden sexuality that is at odds with school, community, and family expectations. In fact, the very activities that allow the adolescent to develop and refine skills in heterosexual relationships, such as school dances or private talks with parents and peers, frustrate such development among adolescents struggling with homosexual feelings.

Olivia's relationship with Kris quivered silently in the heterosexual thunder of school and community cultures. Ms. Christenson and Mary Louise did not really hear Olivia's expressions of fondness for women. The not so silent intimidation of peer pressure and harassment stilled the relationship between Olivia and Kris. The emotional sustenance in women-loving-women and the shared solitude of a relationship with another woman were purged of eroticism. Harvey's devastating advice, the slurs etched on school chairs, and Olivia's need for social approval quieted an already whispered relationship. Olivia and Kris knelt in prayer to a heterosexual God for blessing upon their relationship ''not based on sex but on love.'' Unknown to Olivia and Kris, continuing their relationship rested on their willingness to name and proclaim their relationship, not upon the willingness of others to sanction it.

As Olivia's story illustrates, sexual identities and behavior are integrally related to the quality of relationships which develop between persons of the same gender. Thus, the first part of this commentary examines patterns of sexual behaviors and sexual identity among participants in this study. The second part discusses different types of homosexual adolescent relationships. Differences between males and females as well as between African- and Anglo-Americans will be discussed throughout the commentary.

Adolescent Sexual Activities and Identities

Researchers have demonstrated what perceptive educators have long known and evangelical Christians have long feared: adolescents engage in sexual activities. For example, in a recent national survey, 87 percent of the teenagers reported having had a "boyfriend" or "girlfriend," and two-thirds of these "daters" report heterosexual intercourse.[2] By the age of 18, most males and a near majority of females have had sex; by the end of adolescence seven in 10 young women and eight in 10 young men have had sexual intercourse.[3] The average age for women to experience sexual intercourse in the United States is 16.2 years; for men, it is 15.7.[4]

The AIDS crisis, however, has transformed this social fact into a political issue. Rejecting the concept of "safe sex," would-be guardians of morality have insisted that there is no "safe sex" outside of heterosexual marriage. Consequently, they oppose the distribution or sale of condoms, the explicit teaching about the transmission of AIDS, and the discussion of "alternate sexual lifestyles" to high school students on grounds that these will encourage adolescent sexual activity, undermine the family, and legitimize immoral behavior. For example, in South Carolina, the politics of AIDS has produced legislation banning any formal discussion of homosexuality in the public school curriculum and emphasizing sexual abstinence.

Eighty percent of the participants in this study engaged in sexual activity during high school; two-thirds of those participated in homosexual activities while the rest engaged in heterosexual behaviors. The women were as likely as the men to engage in same-sex experiences prior to identifying themselves as lesbian or gay, although the time gap between these two events was much more pronounced in the males (2.7 years) than the females (4 months).[5]

The pressure to perform sexually with a member of the opposite sex was less evident for these Southern men. Olivia, like two-thirds of the females of this study, engaged in heterosexual activity compared with approximately one-third of the males. Additionally, females experienced heterosexual activity at an average age of 11.5; males, on average, experienced their first heterosexual activity three and one-half years later — the exact opposite to what has been found in general studies of adolescent sexuality.[6] These Southern women also reported a significantly greater length of time between their first heterosexual and homosexual experiences (5.5 years vs. 1.5 years) than the men.

These findings differ from studies of homosexual populations from other regions of the country; for example, Thomas Roesler and Robert Deisher reported that two-thirds of the homosexual-identified males in their study had engaged in heterosexual activity.[7] A recent study of 29 young homosexual men, ages 15 through 19, reported that all but three of these white, middle-class men engaged in homosexual activity during the past year and that about one-half had heterosexual experiences.[8] A more dated study of 25 lesbians between the ages of 13 and 17 found that 13 had engaged in hetero-sexual activity and slightly more than one-half of these had reported a lack of enjoyment in such activities.[9] The small samples of these studies and the different time periods in which they were conducted render problematic any conclusions about regional differences in sexual behavior.

Gender differences, however, have been found consistently in large-scale studies of human sexual experience.[10] In this study, there were also differences in how lesbians and gay men experi-enced and interpreted their sexual feelings during high school. For example, while high school students, lesbians were more likely to have had bisexual fantasies and were more inclined to have been sexually attracted to both genders. Further, as indicated in Olivia's biography, they were more likely to report an emotional closeness with girls and to have spent more time in same-sex socializing. These Southern men, on the other hand, were more likely to have engaged in homosexual behavior and to have been sexually at-tracted to members of the same sex during their high school years.

Females were also more likely than males in this study to label themselves homosexual prior to finding supportive materials on the topic. For Olivia, like most of the participants, self-designation pre-ceded entry into the homosexual culture. Though this contrasts with several other research studies on lesbians, the findings of this study parallel those of Jeannine Gramick, who reported that three-fifths of her sample of 97 lesbians identified themselves as such prior to their entry into the lesbian culture.[11]

By the time these sexual rebels were interviewed, the gender differences evidenced during their high school years generally had disappeared. Gay men, however, were still more likely to report having more homosexual fantasies than females and, in general, were more willing to adopt a homosexual identity than females; however, when asked to think of their "ideal" world, the women in this study were less likely to hold an ideal sexual identity that was different from their present homosexual identity. In fact, they tended to report a slightly more homosexual identity in their ideal worlds. Gay men, on the other hand, were much more likely to posit an ideal world that was bisexual. Homosexual males viewed the bisexual or heterosexual norm as a more ideal personal identity than did their female counterparts. These findings may be due, in part, to the primacy of the male and the value of manliness still upheld in our culture, and to the growth of the women's movement and feminist thought during the past three decades. For gay men, there is no visible exit from patriarchal beliefs; for lesbians, feminist institutions and ideology provide an important counterweight to the hegemony of these beliefs. For all participants in this study, the impact of culture on the construction of their sexual identities is evident. The polymorphous nature of human sexuality, documented by Professors Freud and Kinsey, is submerged by culture and recast into molds of individually constructed sexual identities.

In this study there were other differences between Southern homosexual men and women regarding sexual experience and behavior differences, similar to those reported elsewhere. For example, females in this study were more likely to have been married, to have had more stable, same-sex relationships, and to have had fewer sex partners; males were more likely to have engaged in "cruising activities," to have engaged in sex prior to identification as "homosexual," and to desire a heterosexual identity.[12] Important differences among males and females in the meanings constructed around these sexual feelings and experiences were also evident. Lesbian participants, more often than gay men, attached emotional-romantic meaning to same-sex relationships prior to engaging in homosexual behavior, defined the term "homosexual" in an emotional-romantic context, and denied the legitimacy of their homosexual feelings.[13]

Not surprisingly, the meanings constructed by these homosexual young adults correspond to those images and values most visible in the lesbian and gay communities: the image of a woman-identified woman as a nurturing and loving person who enjoys enduring, feminine friendships and long-term, monogamous relationships with her lover; the image of an affluent, white male who enjoys mainstream gay magazines such as the *Advocate*, whose eyes shop over the clothes and bodies of models in *Gentlemen's Quarterly*, and who endures erotic, lustful, and transitory relationships in the shadow of AIDS. Participants' comments about their definitions of homosexuality and their relationships with same-sex partners illustrate this difference. Women participants in this study were more likely to stress the emotional and spiritual component of their relationships (e.g., "A homosexual person has intimate love for a person of the same sex." "Sex is fine, but the emotional part is more important.") whereas men tended to place much greater emphasis on the sexual aspect (e.g., "A homosexual is someone who has sex with the same sex.").

Given the differences in experiences and the meanings constructed from these experiences, some scholars have concluded that lesbians have more in common with heterosexual women than they do with gay men.[14] This study supports this assertion. Women who love women are not the counterpart to men loving men. The thoughtlessness and, at times, callousness of researchers, writers, and activists — particularly males — to the female experience has led one feminist to chide, "We have been told more about the lesbian woman than we have about women who are lesbian,"[15] and another to comment scathingly that women have more in common with trees than men.[16]

Not all lesbians are feminists, not all feminists are lesbians (indeed, not all feminists are women).[17] The majority of women in this study did not identify themselves as feminists, though most were aware of feminism's basic tenets and spokespersons. Feminism is an important component in the lives of a few of these sexual rebels, such as Olivia and Marian.

Marian is 24. Her biography illustrates how her emerging homosexual feelings were coupled with the adoption of a lesbian identity through the power of feminist thought and women's culture. During her adolescent years, sexuality was simply not a concern.

> I dated Dale in high school for about three years. He was one of my best friends. We got along real well on an intellectual basis. We did a lot of things together. We were both involved in the same types of things: athletics, honor society, student council, dances. But as far as a sexual attraction, I did not feel that at all. I never really had to deal with it with my boyfriend because our scenes were basically kissing and hugging.

Marian recollects her best friend going on about boyfriends. "I remember being totally bored. I could never share. She was sharing her feelings with me and I was never able to share my feelings about being different." Asked what she would have liked to have said to her friend, Marian said: "I am different and I don't know why. I am going out with this guy and I don't have the same feelings: They're just not there." Marian did not tell anyone this sense of difference or her lack of feelings for her boyfriend. To those who knew her, she appeared the perfect student. Marian reminisces:

> I was the little role model for teenagers. I did not smoke or drink. I played athletics, worked hard, and wore a dress to Church every Sunday. But, I didn't know myself. I didn't have any individual identity. I was somebody that someone else created. I did well in high school, but I don't feel like I questioned. I knew the rules and I followed them.

For Marian, a product of a Catholic education and a model of Southern womanhood, sexuality was simply not an issue. "I did not hang around the cliques in high school that talked about sex. Mostly, I would be with the jocks who talked about the next ball game." She interpreted her lack of feeling for her male suitor through a Victorian perspective, considering women's proper place to be gracing the virginal pedestals of unflowering womanhood. Marian never considered lesbianism seriously: "I didn't think I was homosexual because I had the stereotype about it: I did not hate men and I was not butch. I saw myself as different, but I didn't know what it was. I felt the convent calling out to me." Knowing oneself was not only unnecessary, but potentially dangerous: It opened up a world of possibilities within a personal and social system of limited options.

> You can't learn until you start to question things. Had I not gone to college, I probably would have gotten married and had kids. I could have gone through life and identified myself as heterosexual and still have been homosexual. You may have more of an emotional attachment with the female sex, yet still get married, have kids, and still not quite fit in — still not know yourself.

Marian started questioning the traditional view of sexuality when she was enrolled in a sociology course as a college junior. As she studied the taken-for-grantedness of gender roles, she explored women's music and feminist scholarship. She recalls:

> [The professor] didn't do a lot of lecturing; we mainly sat around and talked and questioned ourselves: whether or not I had to wear a dress, how much make up I had to put on, who was to pay when dating. Then I started questioning other things I had been taught. I had felt like the female is supposed to be a bit more passive. I had played that role for a long time. I realized that I didn't have to fit into that role. I could actually venture out on my own. Then I went to a woman's music festival where Rosemary Kirk talked. She is a lesbian and wrote a book about coming out. I could really identify with that since she was a Catholic.

Marian wanted to do something with her life but "felt if you identify yourself as being gay then your whole world closes in on you." Then, she experienced her first homosexual relationship. "This feeling of not fitting in anywhere was just totally flipped over. It was like, 'Wow!' I was aroused. I was emotionally involved. I felt like the world fit together a little bit more."

To paraphrase the poet Audre Lorde, Marian had failed to recognize the shape of her name.[18] Through feminist social, political, and intellectual networks she renamed her feelings and desires. College and women's studies, in particular, had a profound influence on her self-image and the affirmation of her sexual identity. Olivia echoes the impact that such courses had upon her, while acknowledging feminism's lowly status within the student culture:

> I didn't feel good about myself as a person. Those feminist classes really help women feel a lot better about themselves. The guys that take them say they're real biased and they're full of crap. But for a girl it is really uplifting. You realize that you have been made to feel real yucky all your life.

The women's movement helped Olivia and Marian choose a lesbian identity. The movement also provided opportunities for them to network with other feminists and feminist groups, and the new literature, conferences, and festivals provided a vibrant framework for personal support and information exchange. As Olivia and Marian came to realize, lesbian feminism is viewed as an alternative lifestyle, a political act, and a critical focus for both theoretical analysis and social reform. Their same-sex feelings were integrally connected to women's communities with sexually diverse membership.

From Barbara Ponse's 75 in-depth interviews within an urban lesbian community, she identified women like Marian and Olivia as "elective lesbians." Unlike most women in this study, Marian and Olivia have a

> discontinuous or "mixed" history of sexual-emotional relationships (often heterosexual experiences followed by homosexual experiences), and second, an imposition of continuity of meaning through retrospective reinterpretation. The elective lesbian reviews her heterosexual past and finds it fraudulent . . .[19]

For many white women living in the South, the script of heterosexuality[20] is a cultural fact, not a conscious decision. Within Southern culture, female identity is defined through male needs: sexual stimulation, social domination, and personal exploitation. Sex is divorced from sexuality; sexuality is separated from emotionality; emotionality is detached from companionship.

Wedded to feminism, the act of women-loving-women is as

much a political act as it is a personal choice. As Christine Browning and others have defined it, homosexual expression "poses a threat to the phallocentric power structure which clearly defines women in terms of their relationship to men";[21] thus, growing up lesbian has numerous liabilities. First and foremost, a lesbian is a woman. Secondly, she is a woman who spurns men. As a woman-identified-woman, she suffers from economic, social, and sexual inequalities, particularly in the South.[22] She lacks economic parity with men — "gay and straight." This inequality deprives her of self-sufficiency. As Marian observes: "Even gay men, as males, earn more money. Therefore, they potentially have more power. With lesbians, as long as we don't have any money, we can be treated like witches." Third, a lesbian is defined in terms of her presumed heterosexuality. Georgina was first aware of her attraction to other girls at the age of six; by 12 she was fantasizing about them while engaging in heterosexual activities. She remembers:

> I was not feeling society's normal way so I tried to be overly straight . . . I cut my hair, wore makeup, and French-kissed. I would go out with guys just to prove to me and everybody that I was normal.

A similar pattern is observed in Elisa's biography. Though Elisa had strong sexual fantasies about other women, she did not engage in any homosexual behavior during childhood or adolescence. Elisa married her boyfriend, Wade, right after high school since, after all, through marriage a woman gains legitimacy. In this matrimonial bond, though, Elisa often assumed the role of a supportive actress to her husband in both public and private surroundings. "When my husband went off to boot camp, my mom would discourage me from going out with my friends. I was married. I was not supposed to have any friends. The world centered around my husband." Elisa's marriage to her marine husband lasted less than five years. Since her divorce, she has been involved with a woman: "Before meeting Ginny, I didn't think that relationships would last no matter what they were. Now I think that they will. When I think of the future, I think of Ginny and I together. When I was married to Wade, I thought I had a loving relationship; I didn't. You don't miss not having it until you have one."

In a traditional culture, women are expected to serve the sexual needs of their male partner. Though recent research suggests that these gender-based expectations have relaxed somewhat, most of the women participating in this study underscored a lack of sexual satisfaction with their male partners.[23] In the phallocentric wonderland of adolescence, the sexual gratification of these Southern women was outside their cultural boundaries. The expectation of enjoyment was absent. Not surprisingly, women like Olivia and Elisa placed little sexual significance on their displeasure with such activities. As one researcher of lesbian identity formation concluded:

> Since she is socialized into heterosexual social roles and behavior by a strong emphasis on heterosexual dating during this [adolescent] period, homosexual identification is obscured or delayed. Repression or even denial of same-sex feelings and attractions may result from societal expectations, particularly from family and peers, of heterosexual patterns. Because she operates primarily in the heterosexual and heterosocial world, which insists that female sexual satisfaction is dependent upon a male, she does not recognize her own homosexual sources.[24]

Other adolescent women like Olivia played "the game," using suitors such as Peter as heterosexual fronts or going on "double dates" as an excuse to be with one's same-sex lover.

As noted in previous chapters, being a Southern lesbian is sometimes easier than being a gay man. Not only is greater tolerance extended for cross-gender behavior during childhood, but there is a greater tolerance for emotional intimacy and public gestures of affection. As Olivia commented:

> If I have to be gay, at least I'm female. People don't notice as much. It's okay to tell your close friends, "I love you." If you're seen in public kissing a woman that's okay. You can be physical, warming, sensitive, and caring. If you're together all the time with another woman, you're just a "giddy little female who likes to do things with her woman friends." Being a

gay man seems like it would be the hardest thing. If you fall short as a man, you fall a hell of a lot farther than if you fail to measure up to the image of Southern womanhood. In this culture, it's simply not as important being female as it is being male.

Olivia has reinterpreted her adolescent sexual experiences and feelings through the prism of lesbian feminism. Now she recognizes her early desires as lesbian, and can also more powerfully explain her womanly status within Southern society. But *is* her newly acquired homosexual identity more genuine than her identity of adolescence-past? Is the script of homosexuality not also a culturally influenced personal decision? If so, have these sexual rebels found their true sexual identities or have they merely reconstructed past sexual experiences and feelings to correspond with their present and perhaps ephemeral understanding of themselves? In an interview a decade from now, would Olivia have come to feel her 20s were as fraudulent as her adolescence? Would it disclose a self-assured lesbian whose sexuality is no longer the core of her identity, or might it reveal a bisexual who continues her inward journey?

Society is divided not only along sexual and gender lines but along racial lines as well. In examining the development of sexual identities, it is useful to explore the construction of racial identities and the interrelationships between the two.

"Being Gay is no rebellion," wrote a black gay activist, "gaining a Gay identity is. . . ."[25] But, prior to acquiring a gay identity, African-Americans have a racial identity. Race simply compounds the problem confronting homosexual-identified blacks, as James Baldwin's artful portrayal of Rufus Scott and Montana Arthur suggests. Scott, a black who cannot escape from the racism and provincialism of his country, is lost in the misery and shame of New York homosexual life. Arthur, a famous black Gospel and soul singer struggling with his sexual identity and his family, seeks refuge in the black churches and revival tents of the civil-rights torn South. Rufus and Montana both come to the same end—untimely deaths. But while alive, they cope with their suffering as victims of racism and heterosexism differently: Rufus dives into the black water of despair; Montana sings his blues away.[26]

Black gay men suffer a double oppression and identity conflict; black lesbian women, triple. Experiencing multiple identities can be overwhelming and can result in a fragmentation of identity, loss of Self, and despair. Given the multiple oppression felt by homosexual blacks, it would be surprising if the development of their sexual identities paralleled that of whites in this study. Little research, however, exists in this area. African-American participants differed from their white counterparts on several dimensions of sexual identity during adolescence. White lesbian and gay youth in this study were more attracted to members of their own sex and more likely to have experienced same-sex fantasies. During high school, black participants' sexual fantasies and feelings were less homosexually-oriented than their white peers; African-Americans were more likely to adopt a bisexual lifestyle during high school and whites were more likely to adopt a heterosexual lifestyle. Several of the black participants asserted that these findings were due to a tolerance for bisexuality within their African-American communities.

By the time participants in this study had entered adulthood, these differences in homosexual fantasies, attraction, and lifestyle had disappeared, and other differences emerged. During the time of their interviews, white participants were more likely to socialize with the same sex than the African-American lesbians and gay men. And, white lesbians and gay men tended to identify themselves as more homosexually-oriented than their black peers.

The co-relationship of gender and race to the emerging sexual identities of these sexual rebels was also examined by tabulating scores on sexual identity using the Klein Sexual Orientation Grid.[27] While differences in both the individual dimensions and summative scores were found between blacks and whites, and between males and females at the time of this study, no differences between black and white males or black and white females were found. The lack of significant differences between participants of the same gender but different race may be an artifact of this small sample; however, it may suggest that for each person, a racial *or* gender identity is the more salient biographical fact in one's life.

A co-relationship, however, was found between race and gender and participants' desired sexual identities. Summative scores differed significantly between black and white females as well as between black and white males. White females were more likely to hold a homosexual identity in their ideal world than black females; black males were more likely to maintain their current bisexual identity whereas white males sought movement in a heterosexual direction. Taken together, these data support the hypothesis that a tolerance for bisexual behavior may exist within the African-American community.[28] Furthermore, these data suggest that gender may be a more powerful discriminator between white homosexual males and females than between black homosexual males and females.

All African-Americans participating in this study believed that their communities held more negative attitudes toward homosexuality than they have observed within white communities. As Heyward states:

> In my black community it's looked down upon more. You're shunned more and you're talked about a lot more than in the white community. There are a lot more whites that I know whose parents know about them than black. The whites accept it a little better than the blacks do.

This lack of toleration for overt gay or lesbian identification within the African-American community juxtaposed with its greater acceptance of bisexuality may also explain, in part, the willingness of black participants during adolescence to adopt a less heterosexual lifestyle than whites yet to identify themselves less strongly as gay or lesbian as adults. Interestingly, only two of the 36 participants have yet to label themselves "homosexual." Both are African-Americans.

Racial, gender, and sexual prejudice, of course, exists on both sides of the Southern color line. Recognizing these different prejudices, Malcolm, for one, senses prejudice against gay men in both the black and white communities as more pervasive than racial prejudice. Asked if given the opportunity to alter *either* his skin color or homosexuality which he would choose, Malcolm unhesitantly says, "If I could choose only one, I'd just prefer being straight and black." His response, though, is less a reflection of the homonegative attitudes within his African-American community than those within the white community. He continues: "Gay white men are not considered as good as straight black men. They're looked down on. Most Southern whites prefer to be in the company of straight black men than to be around gay white men."

Another interesting finding is that, when given the option to change gender, none of the males—black or white—would choose to become female, while several of the females opted for a male identity. These responses reflected a political understanding of the role of women in society much more than a physiological prefer- ence for the other gender. Particularly for women of color, growing up lesbian in the South poses existential dilemmas. Lenora clearly expresses the powerlessness and vulnerability of being female in a patriarchal society and the alienation and anger of being black in a white-dominated culture, feelings which are magnified through the stigma of homosexuality. She recalls her experiences speaking be- fore a group on the college campus:

> At one dorm a guy kept using blacks as an example. He was like, "Our oppression is different from your oppression." For me, oppression is oppression. I'm always on the bottom. Color really has no bearing on me. I try to stay away from racial issues which black people really hate. You're supposed to stand behind them and back them all the way. Of course, they won't stand behind me and back me even though I'm black.

In writing about the black lesbian in white America, feminist activist Anita Cornwell reiterates this sentiment and warns: "[T]he moment I or any other Black forget we are black, it may be our last moment. For when the shooting starts, *any* Black is fair game. The bullets don't give a damn whether I sleep with a woman or man, their only aim is to put me to sleep forever."[29] An interview with a black gay activist by George Stambolian also echoes these themes of differing identities and mixed allegiances:

> It's important for gays to call themselves gay, and for Blacks to call each other Black. It's a choice we make to name our- selves instead of being named by others. . . . The legacy of Stonewall is that we all joined together, not to say to a system of oppression, "You must accept me," but to say, "I am

here, I am human, I have dignity, and therefore I will not allow you to destroy me or change me. You must deal with me as I am, not as you prefer me to be." Well, how can we say that to society, and not say that to each other?[30]

However, the terms "homosexual," "black," or "female," are in contradistinction to "heterosexual," "white," or "male." But a gay person, an African-American, or a woman is more than her or his linguistic opposite. To define oneself in relationship to one's opposites is not truly defining oneself as it tacitly accepts either/or distinctions (e.g., a homosexual person is someone who is not sexually active with the opposite sex). Further, such naming reaffirms the validity of the names themselves. Believing there *are* such entities as blacks and whites, males and females, homosexuals and heterosexuals, people respond accordingly. There is a failure to see beyond these names and to recognize their element of cultural construction. The difficulty for those who are oppressed is to define themselves without reference to their oppressors. Liberation groups (e.g., activists in the gay/lesbian, black, feminists movements) are of little help in the creation of these *individual* identities since they are born from the belly of the beast itself.

Not surprisingly, persons like Lenora and Obie who struggle with sexism, racism, and heterosexism during adolescence and into adulthood are often placed in the absurd situation of choosing among several identities — none of which may fully represent their Self or facilitate the journey of the spirit. Although the feminist community has made overtures to black women, black lesbians in this study were not involved in the women's community nor did they experience the support reported by Olivia and Marian. This failure to incorporate black lesbians into the women's community and the difficulties confronting participants like Obie and Lenora in the black community have been addressed by others.[31] As the authors of one book focusing on contemporary lesbian and gay issues note:

Women of color are given a very difficult choice if they think of coming out as lesbians: to be true to their racial identity or to their sexuality. . . . If a woman [of color] makes the difficult choice to live openly as a lesbian, she had, until recently, been forced to rely on a white lesbian community . . . the most visible lesbian culture today was developed by white women for white women, and the lesbian of color is faced at every turn with ignorance, racism, and her own invisibility.[32]

Women of color in this study grappled with their sexual identity in greater isolation. Black, female, and lesbian, Obie struggles mightily:

In the South, being black and lesbian is looked at harsher than being gay. I don't think that there are no black lesbians. I just think that they are more afraid of being ostracized. It's a social caste type of thing, it's not really accepted. In the South, there really aren't that many upper middle class blacks. Of those that are, it's expected that you marry and procreate.

Ignorance and racism are present within the African-American community as well, according to Lenora:

Black women always think a gay woman automatically wants them to sleep with them or will rape them. If I told a white woman, she'd go, "Oh." That would be it. I think black people view it very negatively. Just this past week we hired this new black girl who found out that I was gay. My boss told me she was really afraid to work with me. She asked him if I would bother her. It just really bugged me because the white girls that know never talk about it or say anything.

Some also feel that the black lesbian threatens the black man. For example, in referring to the renaissance of the new black man, author Ann Shockley writes:

The independent woman-identified woman, the black lesbian, was a threat. Not only was she a threat to the project of black male macho, but a *sexual* threat too — the utmost danger to the black male's institutionally designated role as "king of the lovers."[33]

Clearly then, the development of homosexual identity during adolescence is shaped by each person's racial and gendered context. Gender exerted an enormous influence on the manner in which male and female participants made meaning of their same-sex feelings and experiences; for example, though participants did not differ on their public sexual lifestyle during adolescence, females were more likely to have had opposite sex experiences, to attach greater emotional meaning to same-sex relationships, and, as adults, to be more comfortable with their emerging homosexual feelings. Race also complicated growing up gay in the South among homosexual blacks in this study. They experienced isolation within their black communities, had fewer opportunities to meet others who shared their gender and racial inheritance, and confronted oppression from a variety of sources as they struggled with sorting out their multiple identities.

Adolescent Sexual Relationships

Sex, as many high school students will freely admit, is an integral part of school life. Though educators, parents, and legislators — particularly in the South — are reluctant to formally integrate this topic into the school curriculum, covert sexual instruction comprises a large part of the hidden curriculum at any high school: the exchange of lustful looks in the hallway or romantic notes in the classroom; half-glances in the shower or erotic day dreams in study hall; the homoerotic comradery of sports teams and the sexual energy pulsating in even the most boring of classes. At any given day in any particular high school these feelings span the sexual continuum, yet only those at the heterosexual end are publicly acknowledged and sanctioned. When sex education is formally discussed in health or biology class it is most often heterosexual mechanics which are presented (leave it to schools to make even the most interesting subject emotionally dry, moralistically rigid, and intellectually sterile).[34] School dances, especially prom night, socialize boys and girls into their presumed heterosexual destiny. For the homosexual-identified student, high school is often a lonely place where, from every vantage point, there are couples: couples holding hands as they enter school; couples dissolving into an endless wet kiss between school bells; couples exchanging rings with ephemeral vows of devotion and love.

Add to this environment a mirror-opposite set of attitudes and feelings about homosexuality and it should come as little surprise that the vast majority of the sexual rebels participating in this study engaged in heterosexual relationships: most dated while in high school and only a slightly smaller percentage (two-thirds) went steady with a person of the opposite gender.

Some, like Norma Jean and Kimberly, dated simply because it was expected. Kimberly remembers when she first started to date: "It's not like I wasn't attracted to guys — I was — but it was when it started getting down to the intimate part when everything just kind of turned off." Though she never engaged in heterosexual behavior during high school, Kimberly maintained a steady boyfriend: "It was like I was just going through the motions. It was expected of me, so I did it. I'd kiss him or embrace him but it was like I was just there. He was probably enjoying it, but I wasn't."

Others like Olivia and Georgina dated as a cover for homosexual feelings and liaisons. Georgina entered adolescence with a vengeance. Here she first realized "I was not feeling society's normal way so I began to try to be overly straight." She continues:

> In sixth and seventh grades you start wearing make-up, you start getting your hair cut, you start liking boys — you start thinking about letting them "French kiss" you. I did all those major things. But, I still didn't feel very satisfied with myself. I remember I never really wanted to be intimate with any guy. I always wanted to be their best friend.

Like Kimberly, Georgina dated in high school but never felt comfortable. Dating was her heterosexual proving ground:

> I would go with guys to prove to me and everybody that I was normal and like everybody else. Our little group, Priscella, Carolyn, Kris and me, we all had a guy to go with all the time. I'd go with the guy just for the sake of going with him. I would find one guy, get real close to him, break up with him, and go with someone else.

There were some, however, for whom such an elaborate one-on-one charade was impossible to perform. For those high school students like Grant, "group dates" were used to maintain their heterosexual images. Grant remembers going "on a lot of group dates. Just a gang of us going out to the movies. You would pair off with somebody but there were always six or eight of us there." For others like Fawn "fake dates" were another alternative. She remembers:

> We took fried chicken into a movie theater pretending we were on a real date. We'd go cruising down Abbey Drive all the way up to the highway—that's what you did on Friday and Saturday nights in high school. If I was seen in the car with a boy, we were on a "date." But, we were just out cutting up and having fun. That way neither of us had the pressure of going on a "date."

Erving Goffman has observed that every person engages in "scripts" during daily life, and "[A]lmost anyone can learn a script well enough to give a charitable audience some sense of realness in what is being contrived before them."[35] "Reading" from heterosexual "scripts" dispensed in great abandon during high school was a simple way to prevent embarrassing questions or dangerous innuendos from arising and manifesting into rumors.

One-sided dates, group dates, and fake dates provided these sexual rebels heterosexual cover. In Kimberly's case, a rumor about her lesbianism never got off the ground. "The guy I was dating told me about what Suzanna had said. He didn't believe it and neither did anyone else because I had always kept the image up." In a similar fashion, by the time Nathaniel was a sophomore "I knew I liked having sex with other men but I didn't label myself gay. I started meeting homosexual students in the school but my other jock friends stood up for me: 'He's not a fag. He has a girlfriend.'"

There were other scripts as well that allowed some of these Southerners to hide their same-sex feelings behind a mask of heterosexuality. Though he first became aware of erotic homosexual feelings at the age of 13, Jackson didn't identify himself as homosexual until six years later. It was three more years before he began to feel good about his sexual identity. Throughout high school, he dutifully read from his heterosexual script, going steady with several girls. Occasionally, however, he would engage in homosexual behavior.

> These sexual experiences I had in high school weren't real pleasant to me. They weren't things that I felt much control over or savored. Typically it happened when I was drunk or there was an older person who I sort of looked up to who initiated the things.

Grant echoes this theme:

> My first attachment to another man was in the twelfth grade. We would go out and ride around. One night we were out and we were smoking and getting high. We were sitting in an apartment parking lot and he put his arm around me. At that point, I asked him "Are you gay?" He said, "No." We were both so high. I just thought we were just totally bombed. I just dismissed it as that.

Heterosexual scripts, such as the "I got drunk" scene, permitted some Southerners to engage in homosexual behavior without acknowledging their homosexual feelings. Joel Hencken provides a laundry list of other types of sexual scripts sometimes adopted by men engaged in homosexual activity. There is the "I just get done" script in which someone like Cory assumes a purely passive role; the "it's just physical" construction in which Royce's boyfriend, Jason, attaches no emotion to his same-sex attraction; the "I was just horny" story by which same-sex activity, such as between Jacob and Lester, is justified in a moment of opportunity and deprivation; and the "I was just experimenting" version in which Terry's "horn holding" gang engaged in homosexual activities viewed as a developmental process leading ineluctably to heterosexual adulthood.[36]

A recent text in adolescent psychology estimates that between 7 and 10 million adolescents engage in same-sex behavior and retrospective studies of homosexual adults report that about one-third did not engage in same-sex behavior during high school.[37] In this study, two-thirds of the participants, including Olivia, engaged in homosexual activities while in high school. However, less than one in four actually "dated" or "went steady" with a person of the same gender. As Olivia's long term affair with Kris attests, homosexual relationships and liaisons do occur in high school. These range from the most casual "cruising" activities to "going steady." For some participants like Vince and Everetta, sexual behavior was restricted to an infrequent sexual partner. Others, like Grant, had repeated sexual relations with the same person but did not consider themselves to be "dating" that person, "going steady," or acquiring a "lover." And, there were participants like Olivia, Royce, Obie, Jacob, and Alston who dated a special person during high school.

Grant was sitting one day in the principal's office with another boy. He recalls:

> We had just gotten into trouble. Suddenly, he said "Why don't you meet me in the bathroom after school?" I looked at him like he was crazy. I said, "Yeah," but passed it off as him not being serious. In retrospect, though, if he had meant it as picking on me he would have said it in front of a gang of people. He didn't. It was one-on-one—which is what he wanted.

Grant also remembers having occasional sex with the school's star football player but "our relationship at school was very limited. We would see each other and barely speak but after school we'd see each other a lot. He had his image that he had to keep up and, since it was rumored that I was gay, he didn't want to get a close identity with me."

Of the 11 participants who reported having a same-sex "lover," most involved little emotional commitment on the part of the other party or were of a very short duration. For example, Royce's feelings toward Jason and Obie's toward Connie were not reciprocal. Further, Cory's relationship with Winston and Alston's with Mike lasted a couple of months. There also were occasions, however, when the participant was the one who chose to remain detached from the relationship, as the case of Irwin depicts.

Irwin was involved sexually with another black high school student when he was 14 years of age. Attending a small 7-12 school, Irwin was a good student and active in student government. He first met Benji in the eighth grade. Though they attended different high schools, Irwin knew from the moment they met of his deep attraction for Benji. "We just started talking. He was musically and academically inclined and, like me, he wasn't into sports." On Saturday's they enjoyed long conversations while riding around the countryside or playing music. Irwin remembers:

> I suspected he was gay and so I said certain things. I knew how to talk to guys. I don't know where I learned it but it was like how a girl would talk to a boy. "You've got some good eyes." "I'm looking forward to seeing you tomorrow." Each time I said these certain things I would gauge his reaction. Finally, he told me he had very strong feelings for me. Around that time, he asked me if I had ever been to bed with a guy. I said, "No." So, he told me about his experiences. I was a very curious person. That June, I had sex for the first time.

Their relationship continued on Irwin's terms. "I had to be in control. If I wanted to talk to him or see him it was up to me. If he wanted to see me, I would not let him if I didn't want to." Irwin continued with the relationship for nearly two years before he labelled himself gay at the age of 18. "I just told myself that 'I'm in love with this guy but there's other things that take priority over that. This will have to be secondary and take the back seat because of my family and friends.' They were more important to me than being in love with Benji. They had first priority."

Olivia's ghostly relationship with Kris stretched over a four-year period. As their relationship silently crumbled amidst rumor and innuendo, Olivia resorted to "double dating" and talking with the school counselor to maintain their school and social contacts. Despite the many adversities, their relationship was the longest reported by any participant during high school. However, there were no other persons to share with them their joy of being together, to resolve petty personal conflicts, or to judge the maturity of their relationship.

Psychologist Christine Browning described the pros and cons of late adolescent homosexual relationships, noting that such affairs

> may enhance the development of the individual's adult identity
> by validating her personhood, reinforcing that she deserves to
> receive and give love. A relationship can also be a source of
> tremendous emotional support as the woman explores her
> goals, values, and relationship to the world. . . . [But], when
> the relationship reflects a premature commitment motivated by
> fear of loneliness or isolation, it can potentially inhibit the in-
> dividual's growth.[38]

Olivia and Kris were able to get along quite well despite the lack of
counseling and in spite of the intense pressure among peers at
school. Georgina's two-year relationship with Kay is a not-so-
happy love story complicated by these very factors.

Georgina graduated from pot to speed as she entered the ninth
grade. "Speed keeps you going, keeps you from getting tired."
High school represented Georgina's "facade years. I was always
wanting to be entertaining and for people to like me. Speed seemed
to make that easier." During high school, Georgina adopted the
dress and demeanor of a Southern woman. A gregarious, musically-
oriented woman with chestnut hair, she continues to enjoy the image of Southern womanhood. "When people think lesbian, they
think dyke and butch. Gosh! That just makes me sick. I love being a
Southern woman. I love being feminine."

Georgina's first serious relationship began at the age of 14.

> I was in the band room dancing and making a fool out of
> myself when I spotted a real cute student. He looked, he
> walked, he talked, he acted like a guy. But, there was some-
> thing different about this guy. I asked someone, "Who is that
> cute guy?" "That's my sister." I went, "Sister, ugh?"

A few days later, Georgina was talking with Patton, the only openly
gay student in the school, when Kay, the "cute guy," sat down to
join them. During the conversation, Georgina hinted around that
she had never done anything with a woman. Patton left for class
leaving the two to talk. "I said, 'So, I don't ever see you around
here.' She nodded, 'Yeah, I'm around,' and wrote her address on a
piece of paper." The next afternoon, Georgina walked three miles
to her house.

As I was walking up to her she was talking to somebody in the car. She looked up and shouted, "There she is!" She looked at me again, "What the hell are you doing here?" We went for a walk arm-in-arm. Suddenly, she stopped. "Georgina, are you cold?" I wasn't. "Well, calm down." I started shaking and she kissed me. She pulled back and said, "I'm glad we got that over with." We continued to walk. All the time I'm thinking, "What am I doing here? This is not right." I was so confused.

Kay also harbored ambivalent feelings about their emerging relationship. One night when Kay slept over at Georgina's house, she woke up to hear Kay's soft voice. In the far corner of the bedroom, Kay was kneeling. "Dear Lord, forgive me for the way I am." Georgina's parents were also uncomfortable with the budding relationship between the two girls: "She was so butch that after she went home my parents said, 'We don't want you to ever talk to her again.' I knew why. I wanted them to tell me why. They wouldn't."

Telling her classmates that she and Kay were "just good friends," Georgina was fearful that they also might pick up on her relationship with Kay. Georgina latched onto Robert, a lanky but handsome freshman. "For three years, we were the cutest little couple. I really had no feelings of love for him. I was just using him. I thought of him as a good buddy; he was a terrible lover."

As time passed, friends began to ask Georgina about her special relationship with Kay. She would insist that the two were "just close friends." But others began to treat her differently. "I couldn't understand why nobody would hang around me. I didn't understand why nobody liked me anymore. I couldn't understand why people looked funny at me." In desperation, Georgina talked with Robert:

I asked him, "Why doesn't anybody like me? Why doesn't anyone talk to me?" He just said, "Maybe because you hang around that dyke, Kay." I was stunned. I thought, "They do know. They can tell even though I'm not telling them anything." I just felt like I was going to lose all my friends. So, we suddenly broke up. They asked, "Why aren't you and Kay friends anymore?'' I just said, ''Because we were tired of people talking about us.''

Georgina continued to date Robert throughout high school and attended the junior and senior proms with him. She ignored Kay. For Georgina, ''High school was a drag. There are so many cliques. And I had to be a certain way, otherwise 'We just don't like you.''' Georgina wishes things could have been different. ''If everybody would have accepted everybody, I would have stayed with Kay.'' Daydreaming, Georgina visualizes ''walking down the school hall holding Kay's hand or kissing her off to class. I'd feel like I could be myself and not try to kick those walls back up.''

No person in this study had an overt homosexual relationship while attending high school. That homosexual relationships do develop (and occasionally prevail) in high school despite the school's heterosexist curriculum is noteworthy in itself. For most participants in this study, however, establishing such relationships became easier after they left the everyday life of high school with its incessant rumor mills, cliques, and peer pressure.[39] Engaging in adolescent relationships, even after high school, however, was generally more difficult for blacks participating in this study than for their white counterparts.

There are a variety of reasons for this. First, despite the similarities among the sources of oppression confronting African-Americans, women, and lesbians as well as their common agenda of ending discrimination and fostering positive identities, sexual politics have not found a common ground.[40] Unlike their white counterparts, there was little literature about black women that directly touched the lives of Kimberly, Obie, and Lenora. As Kimberly puts it: ''I've read some feminist literature but there isn't much out there as far as being black. I have come across two books and they're not even in the library or sold in the bookstores. You have to order them from California.'' Jacob, who has recently separated from his lover, faces a similar dilemma in his futile search for literature on black male relationships.

The problems confronting persons of color who identify themselves as lesbian or gay are difficult to ignore. The struggle against oppression, however, will meet with success only through the coupling of shared agendas. For example, the second class status of African-American women within the black community has been attacked by lesbian-feminist Barbara Smith, who writes, "A blueprint was made for being Black and Lord help you if you deviated in the slightest way."[41] Similar criticisms can be made of the gay rights movement which, in the past, has been associated with white men of affluence.

According to Cherrie Moraga Lawrence, "Without an emotional, heartfelt grappling with the source of our own oppression, without naming the enemy within our self and outside of us, no authentic, nonhierarchical connection among oppressed groups can take place."[42] However, "naming" can, itself, be a form of oppression. The enemies are not Anglos, men, or heterosexuals: Racism, misogyny, and homophobia are part of our cultural heritage; they are embedded in categorical and artificial concepts and terms (black/white, female/male, homosexual/heterosexual) which, paradoxically, are part of the everyday language used in the process of naming.

Naming oneself "homosexual," "black," or "female" constructs an identity in relationship to what one is not: Selecting oppositional words to those in the oppressor's lexicon validates spurious categories that become the very engines of oppression. For example, to affirm one's homosexual feelings, "come out," and declare a lesbian or gay identity there is a concomitant reaffirmation of heterosexuality; to proclaim that "one person in ten is gay" is to concede or at least imply that the other nine are "straight." To declare that *every* person has the capacity to form emotional, physical, and spiritual relationships with both males and females and that those at one of the two extremes on the sexual continuum are, at best, a minority and, at worst, sexually fixated, rocks the ideological warships of lesbian/gay activists, fundamental Christians, and social researchers alike.

The coupling of agendas among dispossessed "minorities" can occur through a shared exploration of the oppressive elements of everyday discourse and life scripts. Language, not politics, is the basis for a shared agenda because language, not politics, is at the root of oppression. Failing to bridge these chasms among oppressed groups through the coupling of racial, gender, and sexual agendas exacts personal as well as political costs; a fact not lost on African-American gay men like Grant and Heyward.

Grant went to live north of the Mason-Dixon line for a couple of years. Upon his return he observed, "If you are a person who has no problem with being involved with someone of a different race, then it may be a problem for you here. " He outlines the problems faced by those engaged in interracial relationships within Southern gay communities:

> It's rather difficult being black and gay in the South and to date the kinds of people that I like. Number one, I don't get the opportunity to meet them. Number two, if I do meet them they have some hang up about it. Most of them do. I ask people to dance and they turn me down because I'm black. They say they can't dance with me in public because they don't know how their friends would react to it.

Underscoring the more overt racial boundaries in the South, Obie notes her difficulty in seeking relationships:

> Being gay in the South is just like the racial thing here. If you're used to it not being a really big deal then you might have to get used to being ridden a little bit more down here. Also, there are more black males that are gay than there are lesbians. If you want a black lover then you would have a better chance if you're male.

Despite the cultural difficulties of interracial dating there appears to be more of it within the homosexual community than in the heterosexual (a fact that few activists appear to capitalize upon). These interracial relationships face other obstacles as well. Jacob, whose good friend, Heyward, has a white lover, comments:

> I have a black lover. There are a lot of things that my lover and I do together that they don't do. I think it's because his lover is white. My lover and I can go to church together; they go to separate churches. My lover and I belong to Black Together [an informal black community group]; he belongs, but his lover doesn't.

At 25, Heyward has enjoyed a three-year relationship with his white lover, Jerry. They have lived together for the past two years. Heyward has not disclosed his homosexual identity to his parents and he remembers when his mom first met Jerry last summer. "She liked him. She asks about him but she doesn't say very much to me about him. I think she knows we are and there's nothing she can do about it." Heyward and Jerry deal with conflicts arising from the crossing of racial boundaries. For example,

> When we first started seeing each other, we used to have these arguments about dressing. He's been all around: Ft. Lauderdale, New York. He was really into the gay scene and had this T-shirt and jeans with everything showing. So, before he came into my community I tried to have a discussion with him about how he should dress. I told him that in the black community it's looked down upon more. You're shunned and you're talked about a lot. They just seem to take things like being masculine and being feminine a little bit more seriously than whites do. So I tell him to come a little more conservatively dressed. He got real mad.

The difficulties of black/white relationships within the gay community were outlined several years ago by the founder of Black and White Men Together. According to Mike Smith:

> There aren't only cultural disparities but, more importantly, economic ones. The white partner in a relationship will often have a greater income than the black one, and, like it or not, that's going to affect them. And sometimes that will lead to a consciousness gap. I've heard black men lament that their white lovers don't seem to give a damn about racial issues.[43]

Some white male Southerners interviewed for this study were sensitive to racial issues. Vincent, for example, commented:

> It's easier being a white gay male in the South. If you're good at hiding, it's a lot easier. If you're a straight black male the incriminating adjective there is not straight; it's black. Black is

always seen. The incriminating adjective for me is gay and that's not always seen.

Black or white, male or female — coping with same-sex feelings complicates the already complex adolescent task of developing meaningful relationships. Some women, like Olivia, enter into heterosexual relationships to divert attention from their homosexual ones; other women, like Kimberly, played the heterosexual game, feeling unease but unable to identify its source. While women in this study were much more likely to engage in heterosexual relationships and activity, many of the males adopted a variety of sexual scripts to rationalize their homosexual behavior while refraining from heterosexual contact. Race, particularly in the Old South, further complicates relationship building. A black gay male, for example, must deal with different sexual myths embraced by each race. As Daniel Garrett writes, "The white community has made blacks into strangers: creative, exotic, passionate, violent; and the black community has made black gay men into strangers: emasculated, sensitive, weak."[44]

What the lesbian and gay communities have made the "homosexual" into, the benefits and costs of that personal as well as social transformation, and the myths embraced by many living in those communities will be discussed in Chapter 15. First, the attitudes and feelings of students and high school educators to these sexual rebels will be explored.

REFERENCE NOTES

1. Hull, 1983:lvii.
2. Coles and Stokes, 1985.
3. Hass, 1979; Guttmacher Institute, 1986.
4. Zelnick and Shah, 1983.
5. The Appendix presents these and other data outlined in this section.
6. Coles and Stokes, 1985; Hass, 1979; Sorensen, 1973.
7. Roesler and Deishler, 1972.
8. Remafedi, 1987a.
9. Kremer and Rifkin, 1969.
10. Coles and Stokes, 1985; Hass, 1979; Kinsey, Pomeroy and Martin, 1948; Sorensen, 1973.
11. Gramick, 1984. Research studies which reported different findings are:

Abbott and Love, 1971; Faderman, 1984; Ponse, 1980; Vance and Green, 1984. There also has been some disagreement regarding whether homosexual males engage in homosexual behavior prior to suspecting that they might be gay. See, for example, the conclusions of Weinberg (1987:149) in comparison to those of Troiden and Goode (1980:387) regarding the order of these two milestones.

12. Parallel findings have been reported elsewhere. See, for example: Bell and Weinberg, 1978; Cotton, 1975; Freedman, 1971; Goode and Troiden, 1979; Kinsey, Pomeroy, Martin and Gebhard, 1953; Saghir and Robins, 1973; Thompson, Schwartz, McCandless, and Edwards, 1973.

13. Similar patterns found by other researchers underscore the profound influence of culturally constructed and personally internalized images and values. (Cotton, 1975; Beck-Fein and Nuehring, 1975; Gramick, 1984; Hedblom, 1973; Ponse, 1980; Riddle and Morin, 1977; Simon and Gagnon, 1967; Van Wyk and Geist, 1984.)

14. Gagnon and Simon, 1973; Groves, 1985; Hedblom, 1973; Kinsey, Pomeroy, Martin and Gebhard, 1953; LaTorre and Wendenburg, 1983.

15. Krieger, 1982:106.

16. Griffin, 1980.

17. Hess, 1983.

18. Lorde, 1978b:87.

19. Ponse, 1980:194.

20. The script of heterosexuality manifested in both sexual behavior and sexual identity precludes alternate scripts from becoming viable options (Laws and Schwartz, 1977).

21. Browning, 1984:24.

22. The quality of life for women in South Carolina is rated fifty-first in the nation (Cherow-O'Leary, 1987).

23. Wyatt, Peters and Guthrie, 1988.

24. Gramick, 1984:34.

25. Lockwood, 1974:16.

26. Baldwin, 1979.

27. Klein, Sepekoff and Wolf, 1985. Participants completed this grid, which includes seven dimensions: sexual attraction and fantasy, social and emotional preference, and sexual self-identification, lifestyle, and behavior. Each dimension is an interval scale with continuous graduations between exclusively heterosexual and exclusively homosexual. See the Appendix for specific data on participants' scores and more information about the grid.

28. Recently, activist Max Smith (1986:226) estimated that 10 percent of homosexual blacks are "out" and live in the gay white community. Most "view our racial heritage as primary and frequently live 'bisexual front lives' within Black neighborhoods."

29. Cornwell, 1983:25.

30. Stambolian, 1984:132, 135.

31. Bennett and Gibbs, 1980; Cauthern, 1979; Combahee River Collective,

1982; Cornwell, 1978; Hemmons, 1980; Hood, 1980; Joseph and Lewis, 1981; Neverdon-Mortin, 1978; Smith, 1982; Terborg-Penn, 1978.

32. Klein, 1986.

33. Shockley, 1984:269.

34. Sears, in press.

35. Goffman, 1986:72. For a recent discussion of sexual scripts, see Simon and Gagnon, 1986.

36. Hencken, 1984.

37. Nielsen, 1987; Schofield, 1965; Troiden, 1979.

38. Browning, 1987:51.

39. For a discussion of the problems confronting lesbian and gay adult relationships, see: DeCecco, 1988; Harry and DeVall, 1978; Larson, 1982; McWhirter and Mattison, 1984; Moses and Hawkins, 1982; Silverstein, 1981.

40. For insights into the similarities and differences confronting minority groups, see: Beame, 1982a; *Black Scholar*, 1979; Yearwood and Weinberg, 1979.

41. Smith, 1983:xl.

42. Stanley and Wolfe, 1980:189.

43. Quoted in Beame, 1982b:22.

44. Garrett, 1986:102.

Chapter 13

Peers

PHILLIP, EDITH,
AND THE THREE MUSKETEERS

First I learned it was evil,
Then I got liberated and learned it was sick.
And now I see things differently,
But that early training won't quit.
Sometimes it feels just like a wall,
or a river in me that froze.
But though I can't really touch it,
It keeps me from getting too close.

Now it's homophobia
in the locker room when I took gym.
Homophobia,
It keeps me from touchin' my friends.

Geoff Morgan, "Homophobia"[1]

Phillip has blue eyes, thinning blond hair, and a small build. At 20 years old, he is timid and aloof. Until Phillip enrolled at the University, he had spent his entire life in a mid-size town on the Carolina coast. He and his younger brother lived in a middle-class neighborhood. Raised in a God-fearing home, Phillip attended church three times a week until his senior year in high school. His father, Kenneth, is a deacon in the family's Southern Baptist church while his mother, Delores, teaches Sunday School.

Phillip's parents married as teenagers. His grandfather had died a month before the wedding. "For the first couple of years my grandmother raised me. Those nights when I wouldn't stay with her, I'd sit in front of the window crying for her to come pick me up." Phillip's special relationship with his grandmother continued throughout childhood:

> She devoted her life to me. She would get off work and pick me up from nursery. She would leave Steve, my younger brother, for Mom or Dad to pick up. Everything I needed, she did for me; everything I wanted, she got for me.

Phillip's favorite childhood pastime was watching television, particularly the "soaps and movies with real plots and emotion. I hated superficial movies, like *Rambo*." He remembers watching television with his father, who made pejorative comments about some of the men who appeared effeminate. "My dad would always make this joke about them 'ready to bend over at the drop of a hat.' He was very anti-gay. My mom really didn't want to know anything about it." Living in an all-white, middle-class neighborhood, Phillip also endured his father's racist comments.

When Phillip entered elementary school, his teachers were pleased with his academic ability but somewhat concerned about his shyness. "I remember being given my own book and a list of assignments to complete for the next couple of weeks while the teacher would teach the rest of the class. Most students didn't pay me any attention. I was very shy and distant." Phillip usually was found on the playground alone or "on a rare occasion with another outcast guy like myself." After school, Phillip would spend late afternoons at his grandmother's house. He rarely played with the neighborhood children, though he remembers being harassed by one particular girl:

> Edith was very moody. She'd hate one person. The whole neighborhood would get behind her. That one person would be stoned. They would be the total outcast. No one would have anything to do with them. Usually that one person was me.

Phillip experienced racial integration in the fourth grade. The town's all-black elementary school was emptied and its students bussed to the surrounding white schools. About one-third of Phillip's fourth grade classmates were African-American. "Many of my friends that year were black or female. I began to take personal objection when my dad cracked nigger or fag jokes."

The next year, however, Phillip was placed with the advanced group. In this class, Phillip was given more responsibility. He also had greater expectations placed upon him, which included being less introverted. Phillip enjoyed the advanced class:

> I pretty much got away from the redneck kids but lost my black friends. The redneck kids gave me 10 or 15 times more hassles than the others. They would be picked up after school and climb into pickup trucks with shotguns in them. They had a very backwoods attitude.

During fifth and sixth grades, Phillip matured. He became more open and assumed greater responsibility. He also crossed the threshold into adolescent sexuality:

> In fifth grade the boys around me were waking up sexually. There would always be these little conversations. I was just a fly on the wall. Intellectually, I understood what they were talking about but biologically I didn't have any understanding. Then one day in the summer after sixth grade I woke up. A friend of mine, Timmy, stayed over and something happened. That experience opened up the door to a lot of questions. I knew what it meant for two guys to be together.

The following day, Timmy told other kids in the neighborhood of his exploits with Phillip. "Timmy was a year younger than me. He didn't know there was any stigma attached to it. It was just like, 'Hey, guess what Phillip and I did last night? We sucked each other off!'"

Phillip began to experience more harassment from those in the neighborhood. For the first time words like "faggot" and "queer" were targeted against him. Then, one night his parents' house was egged.

My dad got the neighborhood kids together to ask them why they did it. He made me and my brother go into the house. I was standing inside listening. One of the older ones said, "You think we're such little devils and your kids are always angels? Let me tell you what Phillip did." I thought, "Shit! Here it comes." Then, he told my dad. My father is very violent and often would just blow his stack. I got real panicky and went to my room. My dad came into the house and sat alone in the living room for three hours. He just sat there. No television or anything. Finally, he called me in. "Billy said that Timmy said that y'all sucked each other off. I just want to know if it is true." Given his penchant for heavy spankings, I lied. He said, "Well, I just wanted to know because I thought maybe it would hurt you in later life." I could feel his hurt. I could feel how he felt like he had no control over the situation.

Back from summer vacation, Phillip ambled up the red brick steps of Strom Thurmond Junior High School. At the top of the steps was Edith. A group of "redneck brats" were behind her. Phillip feared something like this would happen:

The night before I started seventh grade, Edith called me up. She said, "I hope you know I have a lot of friends. I told them all about you. We're going to make your junior high days pure hell." I was very nervous about it. Sure enough, she had told all her friends. They'd just throw shit at me, make jokes about me, and say stupid things like, "I hear you suck dicks."

Phillip experienced some of his worst harassment in his seventh period gym class.

All of Edith's ninth grade friends were in there with me. They'd make jokes, push me around, and pick on me. I was always used to being protected by the teacher. But Coach Burris was different. He loved it when they picked on me. He was one of the good ol' boys. He wouldn't do anything about it and sometimes he'd just laugh.

This harassment and fear took an immediate toll on Phillip. He began "not feeling good" at the end of fifth period each day. Finally, after several weeks his father blew up. "What does 'feel good' mean? Are you sick or just don't want to get schooled?" Phillip was afraid to tell his parents of the problem:

> At first, I told my mom about being hassled in gym. Her answer was to call the principal. So, Mr. Cokley gets the guy in there and gives him a paddling. The next day he and his friends were even more intent on torturing me. Parents just don't understand retaliation.

The next semester, Phillip was assigned to study hall during sixth period. Here he met two other boys, Ernie and Scott, with whom he became good friends. Ernie occasionally had been harassed in gym class and, though "not my educational equal," was talkative and friendly. Scott's parents were atheists and "they didn't give a shit about anything." Spending time with them made the remainder of Phillip's school year pass more easily.

When he entered eighth grade, Edith and most of her gang were gone. Phillip was exuberant:

> I flourished in eighth and ninth grades. I was more at ease and did better in school. I had more friends. Like Ernie, Scott and myself were the three musketeers. We were always together. They had a lot of other friends and my relationship with everybody else depended on them. But, I still had this shadow of "faggot." But, I was very comfortable — if you can be comfortable with being called "faggot."

During Phillip's eighth grade year, Timmy entered seventh grade. Though he and Phillip continued having sex throughout junior high school, Timmy never associated with Phillip during school. "When Timmy came to junior high he saw what was going on. He woke up to what that stigma could do. So, we weren't friends in school. We just waved and said 'Hi' in the halls."

Phillip dated girls in junior high school, including Jackie. "I actually liked her. It's hard to believe a girl could be so wanton. We never made out that much so she found an older guy who really wanted to stick it to her. She broke up with me. That really hurt. That was the last time I ever went with a girl who I really liked.''

By ninth grade the three musketeers spent most of their time together as Ernie began to experience more harassment:

> Ernie was weird. He really was a total faggot. Even now, he's a flame. I did about as much as I could do about being swishy and stuff. But, as far as acting straight, there was only so much Ernie could do. So, we just turned it into a game and played like we were faggots. I never slept with Ernie or Scott, but at school people would look at us funny. We'd do shit like all sit together at one little drafting table. In our English class there were these bitchy girls so we'd always call Ernie ''our gynecologist''; it would embarrass the hell out of them. You know, if someone calls you ''faggot'' and you just sit there stone-faced, they don't know what is going on in your head. But, if you let them know that you don't give a shit and laugh at them, then they have the problem. People just concluded that if ''he can laugh about it then he really isn't a faggot.''

In tenth grade, Phillip entered a high school with 1,200 students. Earning his driving license, getting a part-time job, and enjoying his friends from junior high school days, Phillip began to party and skip school. Tenth grade was Phillip's favorite year; his parents had mixed feelings:

> They saw me doing a lot of bad things but they also remembered the years when I didn't have any friends as pretty dismal. So, in a way, they were glad to see me getting out, doing something, and having some fun — even if it included drinking. After all, my dad was young when he got married and was really heavy into drinking but he grew out of it. So, he couldn't bitch.

Though Phillip's grades slipped to B's, he enjoyed school. He was involved in the honor society, the church group, and academic clubs. ''My teachers were friends. We would go to their houses as club leaders. They looked out for the few in my group." Interestingly, it was precisely because of Phillip's close relationship with some of his teachers that he chose never to discuss his feelings toward other boys or the harassment he suffered:

> In my hometown there was no one I could talk to and there were no role models. My hometown is still in the dark ages. Homosexuality is just something that's not talked about. It simply doesn't exist. There wasn't anything in the library except medical definitions. There was never anything pro gay. I couldn't talk to my teachers about it because they were just too close and to ask them would be like risking them not liking me.

As a junior, Phillip no longer hung around Ernie and Scott because of different class schedules and Phillip's new job as a supermarket bagger. One day when Phillip went into work a neighborhood boy was spreading the word about Phillip and Timmy. "This kid was talking to someone leaning in. The other guy said, 'Yeah, but that doesn't mean he still does it.'" The head bagger, Terry, put a stop to the hurtful gossip. Phillip remembers:

> He immediately jumped on them and they didn't say anything more. I began to have the most fantastic crush on him. Terry was the perfect male: very handsome, very tall, very mature. He was always asking me to help him close up. He even got other guys to go home early so it would just be me and him to sweep up. I think he had a crush on me, too, although we never did anything. But, that didn't matter. I realized that being with another guy was more than just playing around in a tent. I actually had emotions for Terry. With the girls I dated, we never made out because the emotion just wasn't there. But, then I met Terry and I had an awakening. Things finally came together. I understood my attraction toward men. That's when I first put the label that I was gay on.

Phillip disclosed his homosexual identity to his parents when he was 18 years old. The summer between high school and college Delores made the off-handed comment, "If either of my two boys were gay, I wouldn't want to know about it." Phillip remembers deciding "I was never going to be happy in my hometown. I decided I was going to the university. It was far enough from home to sort out some feelings and a better place to meet up with gay people and gay organizations." But, Phillip returned home from college one fall weekend:

> I had some dirty magazines rolled up placed in a paper bag and stuck in a box that was taped up and placed in the my closet. "No one will ever find them," I thought. I came home and there's the box in my room with the magazines scattered on the bed. I thought, "Oh, shit!" I asked my brother if he had been going through my closet. He said he hadn't. I figured it was Mom. She is very nosy. So, I wrote this little letter saying that "I'm sorry you found out this way, but you shouldn't be so nosy. I'm not ashamed of being gay. If you want to talk about it or have any questions you come to me. I don't want to lose you as my parents. I love you." I put the note with the magazines in the box back in the closet. The next time I come home the magazines are out again. The note had been read. That Friday night something came on television about gays. Mom and I started talking about it. I told her about some of my lesbian friends. The next night we were talking about it again. I came out to her as I smiled. She returned the smile. I didn't know what she was feeling at the time. But, she wasn't mad like I thought she would be and she didn't burst into tears. So, I asked her, "Why were you in my closet?" She said, "I never was. It was your dad. He found them three months ago. He just told me three weeks ago. He has been upset. I came in one day and he was crying at the table. He told me about it. He was crying not because you are gay but because of the note you had written." Later, through my mom, Dad sent the message that he was having trouble with it but that he didn't want to lose me as his son. This was a 180 degree turn-around from the man who told the fag jokes.

Over the winter holidays, Phillip was living at home. One morning he had just finished showering when his father called for him to come downstairs. "Dad was reading a newspaper article. He read to me the AIDS statistics for the county where we were living. 'You know, Phil, we are going to have to be careful.' That was all he ever said."

When Phillip adopted a homosexual identity at the age of 17, AIDS had already received a great deal of national publicity. Consequently, "When I came out, I came out smart." He and his lover of one year have always practiced "safe sex," and, when they last visited Phillip's parents, they stayed in his room. It was "just accepted but not discussed." Two years later, Phillip's grandmother learned of his homosexuality:

> My grandmother called my dad one evening and was bitching at him because he and I were having some problems. My dad said, "There are just some things going on in Phil's life right now that you need to stay out of. Don't ask any questions." Well, she got incensed. She calls my Aunt Caroline who I had talked to about things. My grandmother says to her, "If I ask you something about Phillip will you tell me?" My aunt goes, "Well, yeah." Grandma asks, "Is he a homosexual?" Aunt Caroline laughs and replies, "Yeah." Grandma got really upset. "Is there anything we can do for him?" My Aunt Caroline laughs some more and just says, "No, he's happy. There's nothing you can do for him. He doesn't want anything done for him." Grandma has never said anything to me but she hugs me a lot, constantly calls to check on me, and talks about AIDS.

COMMENTARY

Politeness and discretion always have been prized in the South. Florence King once wrote, "It's all right to segregate people as long as you don't hurt their feelings."[2] In the wake of school desegregation, however, ritualistic harassment, crude jokes, and vicious pranks among students have fallen onto a more despicable group: queers, dykes, and fairies. In the era of AIDS, "faggots" have become the new "niggers" of the American South.

In schools where the ostensible purpose is education, harassment and intimidation are overlooked as ignorance and prejudice flourish. Discussion of homosexuality, particularly in Southern schools, is relegated to hallway gutter gossip, classroom sexual slurs, and locker room queer-baiting. As Phillip's biography shows, the callous disregard of such malicious behavior among many educators is second only to the cruelty of the behavior itself. The first part of this commentary explores the nature of such prejudicial attitudes and feelings harbored by high school students.

In a society where sex is sold in toothpaste ads, portrayed in television "soaps," and highlighted in evangelistic sermons or behind the pulpit, it may be difficult to imagine an adolescent repressing his or her sexuality, but this seeming paradox is explainable through a cultural sleight-of-hand by which we glorify sex yet repress sexuality. Sex, as a commodity, is titillating; sexuality, as an integral part of our human identity, is foreboding. Sexuality is seldom discussed in the school's formal curriculum and, when such discussions do occur, healthy sexuality is defined as heterosexual. Within such a school environment, it should come as little surprise that lesbian and gay-identified students like Phillip must silently cope with their emerging sexuality as they struggle with internalized myths, worry about public exposure, and fear for their safety. The second part of this commentary explores a variety of coping strategies that these Southern youth employed during high school and the consequences of adopting them.

High School Students' Attitudes and Feelings

Nearly 20 years ago, three-fourths of the American population believed that homosexual activity was always wrong and that gay men should be barred as ministers, teachers, or judges.[3] During the intervening years, these attitudes have remained virtually constant although AIDS has had a moderately negative impact on public opinion.[4] The most negative attitudes are held by those who are poorly educated, strongly religious, and conservative; Southerners tend to have the most negative attitudes.[5]

The public school is a microcosm of this society. Educators have long argued that schools ought to be an embryonic environment for engaging young people in the art of democratic living and, in the process, move society further along its democratic path.[6] In fact, however, the hidden curriculum of the high school fosters conformity and passivity while seldom encouraging critical thinking, ethical behavior, and civic courage.[7] Within this environment, controversial ideas and individual differences are seldom welcomed by students. Homosexuality may be the most glaring case in point.

High school students' attitudes toward homosexuals and homosexuality reflect insensitivity, hostility, and ignorance cultivated through peer pressure and countenanced by adults designated as educators.[8] In a stratified sample of more than one thousand teenagers and 50,000 pages of transcribed interviews, Robert Coles and Geoffrey Stokes reported that three-fourths of the females and 84 percent of the males think that homosexual behavior is "disgusting." Further, if a friend of their same sex turned out to be gay, only one-third of the boys and one-half of the girls would remain their friends. Less than one in ten reported having a gay friend. In general, boys were more likely to express an irrational hatred of male homosexuals and were more concerned about being identified as gay than were females. The most tolerant group of adolescents were upper-income, white females who planned to attend college. Based upon analyses of these and other data, the authors conclude that "Despite the evidence of changing values, and despite the efforts of various gay activist groups to provide support for high-school kids in some parts of the country, homosexual teens remain likely to face at least strong disapproval and sometime brutality from their peers."[9]

These negative attitudes extend throughout the seven-year range that marks adolescence. In contrast to the public at large, late adolescents' attitudes toward homosexuality have become more negative during the past 10 years. In a comparative study of college freshman attitudes in 1987 with those held in 1977, today's 19-year old is more likely to be in favor of prohibiting homosexual relations. Overall, 53 percent (an increase of six points) held this position, males much more so than females.[10]

Given such negative attitudes, it is not surprising that, while the fantasies and feelings of the sexual rebels in this study were primarily directed toward members of the same sex, few associated those feelings with their *being* homosexual and most assumed a heterosexual lifestyle during adolescence. Among the difficulties cited by Southern guidance counselors who have known or counseled homosexual students, problems related to the school culture were thought to be the most pervasive. For example, eight out of ten observed that most homosexual-identified students in *their* schools are fearful of and indeed experience harassment, and feel isolated from their peers. Most counselors reported that homosexual students with whom they have worked experience greater personal difficulties than their heterosexual peers, and one in three agreed that most students have internalized negative attitudes about being lesbian or gay.[11]

Virtually every participant in this study told tales illustrating their classmates' disapproval of homosexuality. Most, too, were fearful of being harassed if they "came out" in school. Phillip was terrorized by Edith and her gang of hooligans, and Olivia dropped out of band to avoid the unseen torment of sexual innuendo etched graffiti on wooden band chairs. In order to avoid peer censorship, Alston remembers laughing at jokes about "faggot flies" and Vince volleyed barbs back and forth among his classmates. Two out of three of these Southern gay youth reported trying to pass for "straight" as high school students; less than one in five openly protested when friends exchanged "fag jokes." Audrey and 'Lizabeth breathe life into these statistics.

Audrey is the youngest of seven children born into a once wealthy family whose only Southern legacies are fading family portraits and the family name. "Folks," his parents were fond of saying, "respect you for who you are, not the kind of clothes you wear." From middle-school through his freshmen year in high school, he was an "outcast." Wearing big rimmed glasses and walking clumsily around the school yard, Audrey was usually the last chosen for sports teams and generally the first labelled different, sissy, or fag. Though Audrey was first aware of feeling attracted to other boys at the age of seven, he did not engage in any homosexual activity until 10 years later. Throughout adolescence, however, Audrey experienced homosexual fantasies and feelings. He recalls:

> I had homosexual fantasies constantly. If I had a heterosexual fantasy it was because I forced it upon myself. I figured it was a stage I would outgrow. Though I doubted my heterosexuality, I didn't suspect that I was homosexual. There is a fine line

between the two. I felt, since I could act like I was straight and was living a straight life, I would let it all reside in my mind.

Peer pressure dominated Audrey's day-to-day activities. "My social objective was to fit in," he says, "and homosexuality definitely was not fitting in." In order to "fit in," Audrey frequently swapped fag jokes and pulled pranks during high school. He remembers: "Me and a friend of mine, who later also turned out to be gay, would tell homosexual jokes constantly. Once we tried to play a joke on another friend by acting like we were faggots coming on to him."

Exposure to positive images of gay people was minimal; when it occurred, Audrey had mixed feelings:

One time some friends from school were going to a movie. There were two movies playing. One of those was *Private Lessons* and another was *Making Love*. I went to see *Making Love* with a girl. I chose it because half she was going and half because I wanted to see it. After the movie, I told the guys "I should have gone to see *Private Lessons*." They teased me for being the only guy going to see that movie. I told them, "It was a dumb movie anyway." I remember seeing parts in the movie that I enjoyed. The man in the gay bar or two guys hugging. It added a little bit to my fantasies. But, I was a teenager. I tried to act big and macho. Because of that, I kind of ignored the movie. When the guys did kiss I said, "Oh! Gross." I wanted to deny it in front of other people because I denied it in myself.

Peer pressure is at its zenith within the high school environment as broad social norms are reinforced and youthful sub-norms are developed.[12] Phillip was one of the few people in this study to understand the psycho-dynamics of peer pressure. As he noted, "If someone calls you 'faggot' and you sit there stonefaced, they don't know what's going on in your head. . . ." Lizabeth also found this an effective strategy:

We had a group of people at our school that we called the "snob squad." Basically, they were the most popular people in the school. They were the ones that all the little freshman would look up to and say, "God, if only they would speak to me my life would be made." They were the ones who were spreading it around that because my mom had a female roommate she was probably gay and that people shouldn't hang around with me. Now, the snob squad was very jealous of one of my friends in our group because she was very intelligent and attractive. One day she walked by and they made a comment like, "Fido gets all the guys." So we had our "First Annual Dog Convention." We had a big banner outside the house and roasted hot dogs. We even came up with dog nicknames for ourselves. We drove them up the wall because they couldn't get under our skins.

Three-fourths of these participants reported being harassed in high school because they were "different," and more than one-half reported being "picked on" very often. Norma Jean, Everetta, and Phillip endured the routine psychological torments and occasional physical intimidation inflicted by their fellow adolescents. Acknowledging that it was pretty tough being themselves in school, they felt isolated and mixed-up. Like Franklin, most felt their family did not understand them. They often dealt with torment and abuse in silent isolation. For African-Americans who were struggling with their sexuality, the burden of being black in a culture where white is preferred and gay in a family where straight is demanded intensified this sense of isolation.

Franklin's family returned to the South following the death of his uncle in New York City. He began adolescence living outside a small, predominantly black town in the Piedmont area of South Carolina.

Most of the town people are prejudiced — adding on to the fact that they already dislike you for the color, being gay is just a heavier burden. People were so open-minded in New York it didn't bother me that much. But when I came down here and I heard racial slurs I was surprised. Even though I had seen that stuff on television, I never thought it would happen to me. I just had to learn from it: I'm black in a Southern town where bigots live. In high school, I was ready to fight when someone called me "nigger." I learned from my parents not to pay any attention to them. But, I couldn't go home and tell my parents about being called "faggot." I just dealt with it. I felt real tied up inside.

Many adolescents feel "real tied up inside" as evidenced by the high rate of teenage suicide, drug and alcohol abuse, and delinquent behaviors. *High school students struggling with their sexual identities — particularly those from minority cultures — face greater difficulties.* For white students, educators, and parents who adopt a heterosexual identity within a white-controlled culture, this statement may have a hollow ring, due to their inexperience of being a minority. Within an alternatively constructed culture where, for example, matriarchal social institutions were controlled by lesbians of color, the difficulties of being a white, heterosexual high school male might be more apparent to them. If such a culture was penned by the talented science fiction writer Ursula LeGuin, readers of her story would marvel at the insensitivity and arrogance of leaders for allowing such human pain and injustice to continue unabated. But, as every white man knows, there is a line between fiction and fact; this line, as every minority knows, is as thin as the rationalizations used to justify our patriarchal version of "reality" reified by language.

Coping with Heterosexism

The average gap between participants' first homosexual feelings and first positive feelings about their newly acquired sexual identity was 10 years. During that decade of doubt, deception, and distrust, these sexual rebels coped differently with their same-sex feelings. Unlike their heterosexual counterparts, there was little awareness, understanding, or support provided by others. During the formative years of adolescence, these lesbians and gay men silently coped with feeling different or being queer, with verbal or physical abuse, and with their emerging homosexual feelings. The manifestations of their silent coping, however, were far from hidden.

Some hid themselves in a fog of drugs, others behind a stack of books. Some sought escape from the heterosexual world itself through suicide attempts and others sought to escape their homosexual feelings through heterosexual promiscuity. These desperate calls for help went unheeded by peers, family members, and educators. Heterosexism narrowed these adults' scope of human understanding, and stigmatization prevented these Carolina youth from asking their help.

Erving Goffman described at length two of the stages in the "learning process of the stigmatized person . . . his [sic] learning the normal point of view and learning that he is disqualified according to it. Presumably," Goffman adds, "a next phase consists of his learning to cope with the way others treat the kind of person he can be shown to be."[13] Adolescents' struggle with the stigma of homosexuality, or in Vince's words, the "scarlet letter of being a fag," is the root of a variety of coping strategies rooted in various forms of denial.[14] Some, like Kevin and Marian, denied their sexuality during high school. Others, like Everetta and Jackson, disavowed their homosexual feelings to themselves, while persons like Obie and Franklin denied their homosexuality to others. All danced around their sexuality. In this Alice in Wonderland ballroom of mirrors, sexual and social masks allowed these soon-to-be sexual rebels to hide their homosexual feelings, thoughts, and experiences. However, none of these sexual rebels escaped the burden of dealing with their sexuality—the burden was simply borne alone. As Jackson remarks, "Not dealing with your sexuality is dealing with it. That doesn't sound right, but choosing not to do anything is a conscious or a subconscious choice you make."

Acknowledging one's homosexuality at an early age, according to Gary Remafedi, an instructor of pediatrics at the University of Minnesota Hospital, also exacts a toll on gay youth. Based upon a study of a small population of gay adolescents, he concludes:

> The very experience of acquiring a homosexual or bisexual identity at an early age places the individual at risk for dysfunction. . . . Given the stigmata attached to homosexuality in contemporary American society, adolescents acquiring a gay or bisexual identity may have difficulty coping with the stressors. Younger gay adolescents may be the highest risk for dysfunction. . . .[15]

As these portraits depict, lesbian and gay-identified students indeed experience difficulties associated with these "stressors." The problem, though, is not with "coming out" early but with the "stigmata" of homosexuality creating a hostile or, at best, a nonsupportive school environment for gay students. Their subsequent denials of their sexuality are manifested in a variety of coping strategies ranging from academic achievement to substance abuse.

This position is documented in an empirical study of 200 adult gay men. As Illinois researchers Joseph Harry and William DeVall conclude, "teenage guilt seems to delay both coming out and self-definition and such delayed events are associated with attitudes that could readily impede successful later integration into the gay world. . . . Efforts by young gay males to conform to the heterosexual model in terms of sexual behavior create psychological problems for themselves both during their teenage years and later."[16] Others have reached similar conclusions.[17] It is precisely this lack of social support and interaction with bisexual men and women, lesbians, and gay men which impedes development of a healthy set of strategies to cope with others' reactions to one's homosexuality.[18]

Thus, the problem facing homosexual-identified adolescents at the most fundamental level is sociological, not psychological. In a comprehensive yet easy-to-read text on the counseling of gay youth, the authors write that these kids are particularly vulnerable because of their status as minors since

> They have no mobility, poor access to information, no rights in the matter of sexual preference; and they are legally and economically dependent on their parents. They are also surrounded by peers who are struggling with their own sexuality and enmeshed in the superconformist and highly antigay world of adolescence.[19]

Virtually every participant in this study said they wished they had had more supportive parents, teachers, and peers. Presumably, within a more sensitively structured environment, youngsters as diverse as Marian, Kimberly, and Jackson would have been able to cope with their sexuality in a healthier manner. Asked how adolescence might have been different had such an environment been provided, however, they responded differently. Marian replied:

> It would have helped to have known myself a little bit sooner. I would be a lot better right now because in your teenage years you're just experimenting. I would have said, "Wow! I'm a sexual being." It would have been better to have gone through it with my high school friends who were realizing that they were sexual beings. I was thinking I wasn't. If I had gone through that in high school, if the guidance counselors knew about it and they accepted it, if the students accepted it and if we talked about it in classes, then it would have been a wonderful experience for me. I wouldn't have had to deal with these damages and I could have gone on to learning more about content rather than to sit in class and think about all these other things.

Kimberly stated:

> I probably would have dealt with my feelings instead of pushing them aside and saying, "This isn't right." I would have felt comfortable not dating — serious dating. If I had chosen to have had a relationship with another female then it would have felt comfortable. I wouldn't have been so paranoid.

Jackson was less able to envision such a school environment:

> Gee, it's hard to talk about a world like that because it's so different from what is or ever will be. High school is not one teacher to each student, it's a lot of kids with a lot of peer pressure. Peer pressure controls everything at school: peer pressure among teachers not to teach what's unacceptable; peer pressure among students not to do what's unacceptable. I don't think its realistic to think that you could ever be openly gay in a public high school. It's unfortunate, but that's the way it is. You have to learn to deal with it the best way you can.

For many of these sexual rebels, however, dealing with it "the best way they can" was not good enough.[20] Lacking such an environment, there was a further delay in the development of their ego identity as well as the creation of a host of secondary physical, psychological, and social problems: Darla and Fawn engaged in heterosexual promiscuity; Henry escaped from school through drawing and daydreams; Jackson buried himself in academics; Obie attempted suicide; Kevin engaged in over-eating; Everetta and Darla abused drugs and alcohol.

Darla entered adolescence acknowledging her strong attraction for girls and fearing lesbianism. " 'I was not gay!' I told myself. I was like, 'I've got to stop this.' So, I started seeing guys constantly. I mean, I became a little whore." Darla remembers her first sexual encounter with a boy:

> Blythe was 16; I was 12. He was a guy in the neighborhood. He was nice looking. He was just trying to get it and I let him have it. He made the advance and I was like, "Sure. Why not?" This was one way for me to find out. I didn't like it then; don't like it now. I thought, "I may be able to stop myself from being gay." But it didn't work. I didn't like it, but I kept on. I just kept on with the guys just trying to prove myself not being gay.

Consistent with other studies, female participants in this study were much more likely to engage in heterosexual behavior than their male counterparts.[21] Nearly one-half of these female participants engaged in heterosexual activity during high school; less than one-third of the males had similar opposite-sex experiences. This and other related sexual strategies are cited by directors of a New York agency for lesbian and gay youth:

> We have had several cases of teenage lesbians who, as a means to hide, have become pregnant. They recognize that the family will accept an unwanted pregnancy more easily than a lesbian daughter. Other adolescent clients have married as a means to "prove" to themselves and others that they are not gay.[22]

Males may also engage in promiscuous same-sex behavior. For example, the earlier a male identifies himself as gay the more likely he is to frequent cruising areas.[23] Lacking "sex-free" and supportive environments to meet and interact with other gay youth, such as those provided by the Triangle Project in Los Angeles, or forced out of their homes by disappointed and angry parents, this finding is not surprising. "Turning tricks" for cash also provides a marginal means of financial support and justifies homosexual behavior and its accompanying identity.[24]

The difficulties experienced by adolescents in dealing with their sexuality may also be manifested in their school work. For example, one-quarter of a sample of 75 lesbians, ranging in age from 18 to 55, reported that their homosexuality affected the quality of their schooling experience.[25] This finding is based upon respondents' yes or no answer to a deceptively simple question, "Did being a homosexual affect your high school experience?" In a study of 29 gay and bisexual male teenagers, another researcher reported that two-thirds of these boys reported school-related problems specific to their sexual identity, problems ranging from poor test scores to verbal or physical harassment.[26]

It is to these students that the attention of some educators (and the media) has been directed through efforts such as New York City's public alternative high school for homosexual adolescents. The Harvey Milk School, established in 1985 under the sponsorship of the Hetrick-Martin Institute, serves about 40 students who are unable to function in the conventional school setting. While several students have graduated from the school, many re-enter a conventional setting as their studies and self-image improve.

In this study, 40 percent of the participants reported that their academic work in high school was *negatively* affected in their struggle for sexual identity. One such participant was Henry III. During high school, Henry denied his homosexual feelings and fantasies. As he silently coped with them, his school work suffered:

> I felt isolated throughout high school. I didn't talk to anybody. I was just weird for a while. Just flat out warped. I'd go to class and I'd draw all the way through class. I'd go to my next class and I'd draw all the way through that. Then break would come and I'd go somewhere to be alone unless I decided, "Okay. I'm going to have friends now." So, I'd go find my friends and try to join in their conversation. Then I'd go to

class and I'd draw some more. Then it was time to go home. I was always scraping by. The day the reports cards would come out, I'd always try to hide from my advisors because I didn't want to get mine. My parents were always disappointed in me. My teachers were always frustrated because they didn't know how to make me perform to my capacity. I just floated through high school—in a daze.

What about the other 60 percent whose school work was not negatively affected by their emerging sexual feelings? Though most participants in this study were estranged from their heterosexual environment, many coped in ways not viewed as problematic by teachers, counselors, peers, or parents.[27] The mediocre academic performances of Norma Jean and Vince, for example, would suggest no psychosocial problems to the casual observer. Students like Olivia and Jacob performed well academically and were involved in a variety of extracurricular activities. Such school performance, as their biographies revealed, did not reflect an equanimity within themselves.

These students are most ignored by researchers, social workers, writers, and parents. They may represent the silent majority of those in the student population who are struggling with their same-sex feelings; they do represent the majority of Carolina youth interviewed in this study.[28] Fearing disclosure of their homosexuality, these adolescents hide themselves behind their school work. Jacob was named valedictorian; Drew was honored with "the most studious" title as a senior; Jackson was labelled a brain throughout high school. This approach, of course, was restricted to those students who had academic ability and schooling interest. Participants such as Cory and Everetta lacked the interest, temperament, or ability to adopt this coping strategy. Jackson underscores this point:

I got good grades for a number of reasons. One, I am intelligent and have an aptitude for learning things quickly. I have the kind of thinking that it takes to get good grades in school. I don't try to be real creative; I just do the work and get it done. Second, if you get good grades you're accepted and everyone's happy, so there's no mess. [Third], the whole drive through high school and college was to get out of where I came from. I wasn't comfortable there; I didn't belong there. I would deny myself in order to meet that ultimate goal.

In his analysis of questionnaires from 225 gay men, sociologist Joseph Harry found that being a youthful loner and feeling guilty about one's homosexual feelings were positively associated with being a better student in high school and entering college. He concluded, "Given that the major cultural alternatives available in most high schools are the hedonistic culture of adolescents and the more serious intellectual, artistic, and vocationally-oriented ones of teachers and other adults, many gay youths appear to opt for the latter due to an aversion for the former."[29]

For students like Phillip, Jackson, Jacob, and Drew this was certainly the case. The relationship between the age of experiencing milestones of sexual identity and attending college, suggested by Harry, is also documented in this study.[30] For example, participants who had not attended college were more likely to confront psycho-sexual events, with the exception of first experiencing non-erotic feelings for members of the same sex, at an earlier age than their college-bound peers. For example, non-college participants, on average, had heterosexual relationships nearly four years earlier and homosexual relationships nearly two years before their college-educated cohorts. Non-college bound gay youth also labelled themselves at an earlier age (15.6) than other participants (17.7), and disclosed their sexual identity to their parents and friends a year or so earlier (19.2).

Each coping strategy exacts a psychological price; coping through academics is no exception. Drew recognizes this:

> In junior and senior high school you're kind of learning to be comfortable with yourself as a sexual person. You're learning about sexuality, and how to interact with people. I wasn't taught to be comfortable with myself. I was taught to hide that part of me rather than to develop it. As a gay person, I didn't learn to interact. I learned to hide and not let myself show at all. I'm having to go back and pick up a lot of remedial things.

For persons such as Drew, emotional disengagement meant a painful delay of some of the skills normally developed during adolescence. In the Aristotelian tradition, mind was detached from body and intellect was separated from emotion. The result was a compartmentalization of identity and a delay in the process of integrating sexuality with life's other aspects.

Phillip, for one, believes that he would have had a less difficult time with his first gay relationship (which occurred after high school) had he "come out" earlier and had the school environment been more supportive of sexual minority students:

> My lover, Johnny, had actual boyfriends who he went with from ninth grade on. Johnny is my first boyfriend. I'm not very good in the context of the relationship. I don't share very well. In adolescence when you have little relationships as a kid, each one is a test; each one helps you work toward that final relationship that you will make for life. I didn't have those experiences. Sure, I had some "girlfriends" but I really didn't care about the relationship. I didn't have any training as far as maintaining a relationship. I missed out on all of that.

Others interviewed in this study employed different strategies to cope with their emerging sexual feelings. One of the few scholars to explore the relationship between eating disorders and homosexuality is Laura Brown who concludes, "a lesbian who has a high degree of internalized homophobia is likely to be at very high risk for engaging in behaviors that will be emotionally or physically damaging. . . ."[31]

For Kevin, obesity not only reflected an internalized hatred of his sexuality but was a seemingly effective strategy for avoiding unpleasant questions: Why don't you date? Why don't you come to dances? Why are you uncomfortable talking about sex? After all, in our culture "fat" people aren't supposed to be sexual and seldom are they portrayed as sexually attractive. In Kevin's words, "If I was overweight I wouldn't have to face anything in my personal life. The opportunity to meet someone socially, engage in sex, or fall in love would not present itself." Kevin denied his sexuality and latent homosexual feelings by eating ("Food is friendly," Kevin noted), and becoming obese. This coping strategy, though, failed to resolve his primary problem.

My way of dealing with sexuality was not dealing with it. I got fat because that precluded me from personally dealing with relationships. I was a loner because that again kept me from having to deal with anything on a sexual level. I pushed myself away from everybody. But, if I would have gone on the way I was going I'm absolutely certain I would have killed myself. Nobody should have to be that miserable.

All through school, Kevin repressed thoughts and feelings about sexuality. "I basically didn't think about sex—period. It just wasn't something that crossed my mind." Kevin did think about food. By the time he had reached middle-school, Kevin was "twice what I should have weighed. I ate continuously. I would get on my bike, go up to the 7-Eleven, buy ten candy bars, and eat all of them. I would go to Bonanza and eat a half-dozen hamburgers. I would go to Dairy Queen and eat a quart of ice cream. I bought M & M's in the one-pound bag and would eat them in one or two days." Kevin's parents viewed their son's obesity as a problem rather than a symptom: "My father used to offer me money if I'd lose weight. It didn't work."

Kevin's weight continued to increase during his first two years of high school. He contemplated suicide: "I had the paraphernalia laid out and ready to go on more than one occasion." By the spring of his sophomore year, lost in dark and secretive thoughts, he stopped doing his homework. "I realized that there was something really different about me. I also realized just what it was. I couldn't handle it." Kevin pauses; "Two days later somebody just said something to me in the hall and I started crying. I dropped my books and started screaming. I don't remember anything else of that day. They took me to Columbia. I had a breakdown."

When Kevin returned home not many school days remained. "I just tried to block out that terrible day in my mind," Kevin remembers. He routinely visited a local psychologist. "We used to play *Monopoly* and things just to loosen me up. We talked about the possibility of being gay. It wasn't something we talked about very often—only once or twice over the course of about a year." The issue of sexuality was bitterly repressed:

I just absolutely refused to accept it. "It's not going to happen to me. This is not the way I am. It's not going to be that way. I'm going to get married. I'm going to have children. Those children are going to run down the steps on Christmas Day."

Kevin steadfastly denied his sexual feelings, seldom dealing with them on a conscious level. He recalls sitting in biology class during a presentation on sexually transmitted diseases. A slide of several effeminate looking men was displayed on the screen with text beneath it stating "'Homosexuals are not exempt.' Kids started yelling out Donald's name. My name wasn't yelled. But it made an impact on me." On another occasion Kevin accompanied Donald, also a student in his musical theater class, on an errand:

"Disco Donald" had to stop for something. I didn't really know that it [the place he stopped] was a gay bar. I knew it was a very different kind of bar. I was only in there for about five or ten minutes. I remember every second of it. There were two guys dancing together up on a platform. I remember lights and parrots in the windows. The bartender had a white shirt and thinning hair. I was galvanized.

That was the closest Kevin came during high school to confronting his homosexuality. "I know if I had accepted it," Kevin noted, "college would have been extremely different. Instead of driving through a parking lot of a gay bar yelling things, I should have gotten out of my car and gone in." As it was, many of Kevin's college activities were motivated by his denial of his homosexuality. "I would go to things where people weren't supposed to be gay. I went to the Mormon Church because Mormons weren't gay. I almost joined a fraternity because fraternity people weren't gay. I went to every football game. . . ."
Kevin graduated from college with a forty-two inch waist but without losing his contempt for homosexuals or his fear of homosexuality. He remembers:

Just prior to graduating from college, I still didn't accept anything. I didn't feel I had to. But, then my best friend in college told me he was gay. He not only told me, he told everyone. He had betrayed me. He was supposed to be "straight" because I only associated with "straights." I couldn't handle that. I couldn't talk to him. I had to get him away from me immediately. I sealed him away from me. I ignored him. I called him a fag behind his back and to his face.

But, that really forced me to confront it. I began to gain weight once again. I got very upset. I couldn't deal with it. I went up a few more inches in the waist. I went to New York. The first night I was there, though, I saw two guys kiss each other on the street. That had a great impact on me. That incident stayed in the back of my mind the whole time I was there.

On Thursday, August 15, I went down to the Village and sat in Washington Square Park for six hours. I walked down to the dock and sat at the end. It was warm and there were people all over. There was a guy standing out in front of a bar across the street. I watched him for a while. He looked damn good. I was confused. He was turning me on like I couldn't stand it. Some other guy came over and sat down next to me. He asked how I was doing. We talked for three hours. He told me that it wasn't really all that bad and that I would be okay once I accepted it. I still didn't believe him. But, he told me that my story was not that different from other people's stories although some people dealt with it better when they were younger. When we finished talking, he put his arm around me and gave me a hug. We said "goodbye."

I began to feel that maybe I was not that different after all. I was not alone. There *were* others. Other people have had the same problem and they have dealt with it. Now, I can. I knew there were certain things that had to change. The time had come to get on with my life. I got myself going. I lost weight [171 pounds], got rid of my glasses, had my teeth fixed, cleaned and bonded, and changed the way I dressed. I feel better.

Kevin's biography reflects self-hatred and a sexual loathing turned against himself. Like the other participants in this study, the coping strategy he employed was not only destructive but failed to resolve his sexual dilemma. In discussing these and other coping strategies, some may interpret these sexual rebels as somehow "maladaptive," "genetically-flawed," or "psychologically unfit.'' This tendency to ''blame the victim,'' of course, ignores the very system of heterosexual oppression under which these young men and women must struggle. As the co-founders of the Hetrick-Martin Institute for lesbian and gay youth noted:

> [I]n focusing on problems and coping strategies [there] is the possibility of giving the impression that homosexuality invariably leads to unhappiness . . . Nothing in our discussion should be construed as suggesting that the homosexually oriented, as a group, are less well-adjusted than their heterosexual counterparts . . . The fact of stigmatization *creates* situations and problems that must be resolved (italics added).[32]

As the biography of Kevin underscores, suicide is another coping strategy seriously considered by some gay and lesbian-identified youth. In the United States, suicide is the second leading cause of death, more than 5,000 deaths each year, and many more are not categorized as suicide. Twenty percent of all attempted suicides are made by individuals under 20 years of age. In a recent study of 313 midwestern high school students, about one in ten reported making at least one suicide attempt. Between 1960 and 1980, the rate of suicides for 15 to 24 year olds rose 237 percent, and attempted suicide rates are *at least* 10 times higher.[33]

As in the adult world, adolescents who actually commit suicide differ from those whose attempts fail. Whites have a greater proportion of attempted youthful suicides than non-whites. African-Americans are at the highest risk during childhood and adolescence. Females are more likely to attempt suicide and males are more likely to successfully complete it. Adolescent completers tend to be male, use a firearm, express suicidal ideas, engage in substance abuse, and be committed to dying. Those who attempt suicide are more likely to be female, demonstrate symptoms of depression, and employ less lethal methods.

Some young persons coping with their same-sex feelings ''cope'' by attempting suicide, although the actual rate of suicidal behavior among lesbian and gay-identified youth has been difficult to determine, given the heterosexual assumption operating in such research and the double stigma attached to suicidal and homosexual behaviors. Accurate information, therefore, about the suicidal behavior of lesbians and gay persons are, at best, speculative. More data are available on homosexual adults.

In two separate studies, nearly one-third of each small sample of gay males had attempted suicide.[35] A larger study of gay white males reported one-fifth had made such attempts.[35] With respect to those who seriously contemplated suicide, nearly 50 percent of 500 homosexual men reported doing so. White homosexual men are the most likely group to seriously consider or to attempt suicide: three times more likely than white heterosexual men, and one and one-half times more likely than African-American males. Though differences exist between the heterosexual and homosexual communities and between blacks and whites, when controlling for race, no differences between males and females are evident. About 40 percent of white homosexual men and women have contemplated or attempted suicide; about one in four black homosexual men and women have done the same.[36]

Noting that reliable data about suicidal behavior among gay and lesbian youth is scarce, a recent paper commissioned by the National Institute of Health concluded that young people struggling with their sexual identity are two to three times more likely than other youth to attempt suicide and that they may comprise 30 percent of all completed youth suicides.[37] In two other studies, one-third of male homosexuals, ages 16 to 19, reported suicidal attempts and roughly this same proportion of lesbians and gay men who had attempted suicide reported these acts occurring during adolescence.[38]

Though these findings suggest that suicidal behavior may be more common among adolescents struggling with their homosexuality, this conclusion is not unequivocal.[39] The relationship between youth suicide and homosexuality is far less settled than many gay activists choose to admit. Regardless of the numbers involved, it is certainly true that for some adolescents coping with their same-sex feelings there appears, in Sartre's phrase, "no exit" from the heterosexual world of privilege and prejudice except through the final "exit" of self-sacrifice.

The needless tragedy and human trauma of lesbian and gay-identified youth suicide is portrayed best in case studies. An outstanding compendium of such case studies is provided in Eric Rofes' book, *I*

Thought People Like That Killed Themselves. One of the most compelling stories is that of Kenneth Myers, a high school sophomore in a small Pennsylvania town who committed suicide in 1977. Rofes writes:

> In a suicide note, Myers explained that he was viciously taunted by his classmates and that his parents couldn't understand his anguished situation. His school teachers also provided him no support. As summer vacation came to an end and the next year in a hostile high school loomed before him, Kenneth Myers put a gun to his head and killed himself. Local gay activists responded to the suicide and presented the school administration with copies of *Lesbian/Women* and *The Gay Mystique*. Continuing to refuse to offer even token support or resources to lesbian and gay youth, the school's administration refused to put the books in the school library.[40]

In this study of Southern youth, two-thirds repeatedly contemplated suicide during high school; females, particularly African-Americans, were much more likely to have had such thoughts than their male counterparts.[41] Four of the participants—Everetta, Darla, Brandon, and Obie—attempted suicide. In these four cases the struggle of coping with their homosexual feelings was of varying importance. For example, Obie was attempting to cope with mounting pressure from a variety of sources, only one of which was "the cloud hanging over me" of coming out to her parents; Everetta's rejected love for Tracy and harassment from her fellow students were significant contributors to her failed suicide attempt.

Nevertheless, for a host of reasons, most of these sexual rebels chose not to act upon their morose thoughts. Certainly the difficulties experienced by Phillip, Norma Jean, Olivia, and Vince were no less serious than those of Obie, Darla, Brandon and Everetta. Four attempted suicide; two contemplated suicide; two never considered the option. A variety of individual and situational factors exists that make the lives of some young persons particularly vulnerable to serious thoughts of suicide. These include social isolation, anger, depression, exposure to repeated stress, feelings of personal inadequacy, and a less defined psycho-sexual identity.[42] The lack of social and institutional support is also a major contributor to suicidal behavior. Gay and lesbian-identified youth, in addition to normal conflict and ambiguity associated with adolescence, may experience strained and broken family ties, a lack of personal support networks, internalized homophobia, the absence of institutional recognition for relationships, and poor self-esteem.

As high school students struggle through the emotional highs and lows of adolescence, alcohol and drugs are commonly abused.[43] Eighty-five percent of high school seniors report they have used alcohol within the past 12 months; one in three have used marijuana during that same period.[44] Most studies of those factors which affect adolescent substance abuse cite gender, grade in school, socio-economic status, involvement in extracurricular activities, and community size.[45] In such studies, homosexuality is not considered. Coping silently with one's same-sex feelings certainly compounds the problems high school students confront during adolescence. While there is evidence of a greater abuse of alcohol among homosexual adults, few studies have examined this linkage among lesbian and gay-identified youth.[46]

One such study in the Midwest reports more than three-fourths of young gay men had used illicit drugs, with more than one-half meeting the medical criteria for substance abuse.[47] One explanation for substance abuse among lesbian and gay youth is psychological. James Gumaer notes that, "Those who do not express themselves to trusted others are alone and tend to become morose and suffer depression, which can lead to self abuse through alcohol and drugs."[48] A related explanation is non-acceptance of homosexuality. In a recent study of 20 gay men, Robert Kuhs concluded, "it is the internalized homophobia prior to having reached the stage of acceptance in the coming out process which is the root of alcoholism in gay men."[49] Another explanation is sociological. Lacking institutional and social support, young people often enter the lesbian and gay worlds through the front door or, if under age, the back door of a nearby gay bar or discotheque.[50] In the process, "they become exposed primarily to that segment of the homosexual world that is caught up, often compulsively, in the bar scene. . . ."[51] The centrality of the "bar scene" is summed up well by Grant:

> In the state of South Carolina the drinking age was 18 [it is
> now 21]. I don't think you can really identity yourself as being
> gay or start feeling good about yourself unless you go out to
> the bar in this state. There's just no other place to be around
> other gay people.

These sexual rebels relied less on the use of alcohol and drugs
than did subjects in the previously cited studies. About one-half of
the participants used alcohol or drugs during high school and one in
six acknowledged their use was coupled to coping with their sexual
feelings. These data are consistent with other studies which show a
lower level of substance abuse for rural adolescents.[52] The link between depression, homosexuality, and coping through substance
abuse is well illustrated in several of these biographies. In Chapter
11, for example, Everetta's problems with her father and her never-
realized relationship with Tracy, coupled with her inability to cope
with her homosexuality, result in drug abuse which "quieted the
struggle." In Chapter 7, Obie's separation from her one-time lover
and her conflict with her parents' religion, joined with her strong
family ties, result in extended bouts of depression.

Darla's excessive drinking and repeated explosions were symptomatic of her determination for her homosexual feelings to "stay
bottled up in me the rest of my life." When Darla entered high
school, her fellow students thought she was "real strange" and her
teachers considered her a "troublemaker." "I never did a lick of
homework," she remembers. "We'd always go to the third floor
bathroom, climb out of the window, smoke a cigarette, or a joint, or
drink a six pack of beer, and then go to class. I hung out with the
heads — the troublemakers in school. Everybody assumed I was a
troublemaker, so I lived up to the part." Though she went steady
with one boy for the next year and a half, she wasn't happy with the
relationship. But, "usually the only time we were together was
when we were trashed and then you're like, 'who cares.'"

During high school, Darla's grandparents built a cabin in North
Carolina and her parents would visit the cabin on weekends. Darla
would stay at home and have parties. At the beginning of her junior
year, Darla got a used car in which she and her friends rode around.

One day she picked Sylvia up at school. Racing down the road listening to Joan Jett, Sylvia asked Darla if she'd like to get Patsy, Sylvia's friend. When Darla was introduced to Patsy, she fell in love. "The first time she stepped foot in my Mustang it was like, 'I want her.'" Soon she and Patsy became good friends. "I gave her an extra set of keys to my Mustang. When I picked her up for school, I honked the horn and got on the passenger side. That was her car. Anything Patsy wanted Patsy got, come hell or high water." What Darla wanted most from Patsy, though, she never got nor did she ask. One weekend night a party was held at Darla's house:

> Patsy was going out with guys and I was going out with guys. Any time she was with a guy, I would get extremely jealous, and Patsy knew it, but she wouldn't say anything to me. We'd have a party and sit around and play quarters until everybody was trashed. Just one little thing would set me off and my whole temper would blow. This one night I was extremely drunk and Patsy was in my bedroom with Sean. I was so drunk I told them, "Go ahead in there and have fun." Later, I went to open my door and it was locked. I got pissed. I busted down the door. Right then I lost it. Sean ran bare-ass across my room. I grabbed a set of sheets and threw them at Patsy, "Get your slutty ass out the door." Then I came for Sean. I picked him up and threw him out the door bare-ass. He was in the middle of the yard screaming at me. I was screaming at him. Finally, I went out and kicked his ass from here to kingdom come.

In a tearful fury Darla returned inside and rammed her hand through a glass table. She calmed down and began to sob. Sylvia stooped down and said, "Come on Darla. Let's go wipe the blood off your hand." While the two girls were in the bathroom, Sylvia broached the taboo subject of Darla's sexuality:

> Sylvia goes, "Darla, talk to me. Tell me what's bothering you." I said, "No. I'm not going to tell you." Finally I said, "It's something that I can't tell nobody. Nobody will ever know. It will stay bottled up in me the rest of my life." She

goes, "Darla, by any chance are you gay?" I just looked at her and started bawling. I said, "I think so."

As we have seen, high school plays a significant role as these sexual rebels coped with their emerging sexuality and the accompanying split between the private and public self. The school, with its focus on school knowledge, psychological management, and bureaucratized social relations, represses personal meaning. Seldom viewed as a legitimate area of school concern, the expression of personal sexual meaning by a student is a risky endeavor. Not surprisingly, persons as different as Phillip and Darla engage in a "forgetfulness concerning their own meanings. They repress or submerge the unique meaning structure growing out of their own activity and take on the attitude and posture of the control agent."[53] In the process of adapting to an oppressive and alienating environment, these students may respond with withdrawal or aggression, suicidal or delinquent behaviors, eating or mental disorders, underachievement or over-achievement, drug or alcohol abuse.

The solution advocated by some educators, parents, and policymakers is to "just say no": Just say no to sex; just say no to drugs; just say no to alcohol. More liberally minded persons may modify this injunction to read: just say no to homosexual sex or sex without condoms, or just say no to drug abuse or addictive drugs. Parroting these simple-minded phrases, however, will do little to resolve the underlying problems of which these behaviors are symptomatic. In order to curb youth suicide or substance abuse among adolescents, we must be willing to affirm the healthy and important role of human sexuality in the school curriculum, affirm our children's opposite and same-sex feelings, affirm the importance of relationships between two persons—regardless of their gender, and affirm our willingness to face our own sexuality honestly.

REFERENCE NOTES

1. Morgan, 1980.
2. King, 1975:2.
3. Levitt and Klassen, 1974.
4. Schneider and Lewis, 1984; Schneider, 1987.
5. Schneider and Lewis, 1984. See also: Irwin and Thompson, 1977.

6. Dewey, 1916; Giroux, 1988; Newman and Oliver, 1967; Rugg, 1939.

7. Langton and Jennings, 1968; Litt, 1963; Newman and Newman, 1987.

8. Price, 1982.

9. Coles and Stokes, 1985:139.

10. Braungart and Braungart, 1988.

11. Sears, 1988a.

12. Coleman, 1961; Langton, 1967; Newcomb, 1966.

13. Goffman, 1986:80.

14. An excellent discussion of the dynamics of stigma and homophobia is found in Hammersmith (1987). Of related interest is: Martin, 1982; Martin and Hetrick, 1988.

15. Remafedi, 1987b:336.

16. Harry and DeVall, 1978:73, 75.

17. Malyon, 1982; Weinberg and Williams, 1974.

18. Martin and Hetrick, 1988; Plummer, 1975.

19. Moses and Hawkins, 1982:82.

20. The majority of these participants also grew up in a rural environment which further complicated this task. For an illuminating discussion of the special problems faced by rural lesbians and gay men, see: Moses and Buckner, 1982.

21. Manosevitz, 1970; Savin-Williams, 1987a; Schafer, 1976. In these studies, about one-half of the males compared to three-fourths of the females reported heterosexual activity. Another sample (Goode and Troiden, 1979) of 150 gay-identified men, however, found that more than 80 percent of the males engaged in opposite-sex behavior. Different sample populations, time periods, and operating definitions make comparisons of data on this dimension difficult.

22. Martin and Hetrick, 1988:169.

23. Roesler and Deishler, 1972.

24. Harlan et al., 1981; Hoffman, 1972; Reiss, 1961; Weisberg, 1985.

25. Hedblom, 1973.

26. Remafedi, 1987b.

27. Gagnon and Simon's (1973) findings that very few lesbians were "isolates" during their high school years parallel the data gathered in this study.

28. At present, adolescents portrayed in both the scholarly and popular press have been those who have consciously identified themselves as "homosexual" and who have manifested psychosocial problems. However, students who attend the Harvey Milk School or young people who visit the Larkin Street Youth Shelter in San Francisco probably represent a minority of the gay high school population. Participants like Royce, Olivia, and Jacob would never have been referred to such facilities nor would they have felt a need to visit them.

29. Harry, 1982:117, 122.

30. Harry, 1983.

31. Brown, 1987:299.

32. Hetrick and Martin, 1987:40.

33. Data described in this and the subsequent paragraph are reported in Aldridge, 1980; Allen, 1987; Harvard Medical School, 1986; Hendin, 1969; Hen-

din, 1978; Maris, 1985; Rickgarn, 1987; Smith and Crawford, 1986; Strother, 1986; Wellman, 1984; Young, 1985.

34. Remafedi, 1987b; Roesler and Deishler, 1972.

35. Bell and Weinberg, 1978.

36. Bell and Weinberg, 1978.

37. Gibson, 1983.

38. Bell and Weinberg, 1978; Roesler and Deishler, 1972.

39. Rich, Fowler, Young and Blenkush, 1986.

40. Rofes, 1983:44.

41. Noting the rising percentage of African-American women who attempt suicide, coupled with the virtual nonexistence of empirical data addressing this concern, Delores Aldridge (1980:278) noted, "The costs of having several negatively evaluated statuses are particularly high and lead to social bankruptcy when people simply cannot muster the resources to pay them."

42. Maris, 1985; Saunders and Valente, 1987.

43. The association of alcohol and drug use has been well documented. See, for example: Kandel, Treiman, Faust and Single, 1976; Wechsler, 1976.

44. Kerr, 1988:E5. See also, Johnston, Bachman and O'Malley, 1981.

45. For a summary of these studies, see Gibbons, Wylie, Echterling and French, 1986.

46. Although, the number of adult alcoholics in this country is estimated at 10 percent of the drinking population, alcoholism affects the lives of 20 to 30 percent of the lesbian and gay population. Compared to matched populations of heterosexual males, gay men have a higher incidence of alcohol abuse. Lesbians have more serious problems resulting from alcohol use than heterosexual women; one-third report alcohol abuse compared to five percent of heterosexual women. Discussing the relationship between homosexuality and alcoholism, a recent article concluded: "although lesbianism does not cause alcoholism, the relationship between the two may be important. . . . [A]lcohol may be used to cope with negative feelings about being lesbian" (Anderson and Henderson, 1985:521). For further reference, see: Diamond and Wilsnack, 1978; Hawkins, 1976; Kus, 1988; Lewis, Saghir and Robins, 1982; Lohrenz, Connelly, Coyne and Spare, 1978; Nardi, 1982; Nicoloff and Stiglitz, 1987; Noble, 1978; Saghir and Robins, 1973; Ziebold and Mongeon, 1982.

47. Remafedi, 1987b.

48. Gumaer, 1987:145.

49. Kus, 1988:27.

50. Kus (1988:32) discounts this theory, stating that all 20 of the gay male alcoholics he interviewed "drank abusively from their very first drink," which occurred prior to visiting gay bars.

51. Ziebold and Mongeon, 1982. For an elaboration of this argument, see: Warren, 1974; Weathers, 1980.

52. Gibbons, Wylie, Echterling and French, 1986; Napier, Carter and Pratt, 1981.

53. Macdonald, 1975:87.

Chapter 14

Educators

BRETT AND THE BASEBALL BAT

"I'm surprised Mommy let her sweet little boy play any nasty sports at all when the Big Dad was overseas," Bull taunted. "Your mouth has improved since I left, but you're still a mama's boy. You still haven't developed the Killer Instinct."

Pat Conroy, *The Great Santini*[1]

Brett is a tall, muscular young man of 19 with cold black hair and broad shoulders. He was born in South Carolina; his father, Clark, was an army officer. "Dad always likes things planned out. He makes a schedule of things and does them in the order they fall." Brett continues:

> He raised us by the hand and we learned quickly. I was always polite and very well mannered. I never caused any problems. Dad was always very persistent. If he wanted us to do something he'd keep telling us about it or he'd use sarcasm. It made me feel like, "I'll do it just to please you and get it out of the way."

Clark is now retired but his wife, Mildred, continues to work as a nurse at a Columbia hospital. "Mom was always there when you needed her. She was loving, caring, and understanding. Dad was the ruler of the house, but I'd always go to Mom first if I did something wrong."

Brett recalls playing pre-school games such as hide-and-seek and tag with the neighborhood kids. He and his older brother of two

376

years, Brook, also played with dolls. "Brook played with them differently than I did. I'd bend them out of shape; he was more gentle with them." Brett enjoyed kindergarten, "I was really creative. I'd be the first one with a new idea in art instead of doing the same old finger painting. I kind of lead the pack." As a first grader, Brett was average academically but continued to excel in artistic activities. He particularly enjoyed his weekly music class. During recess he and his best buddy would play rough and tumble activities, returning to class dirty and with scrapes and scratches. As a child, Brett enjoyed building model airplanes, solving picture puzzles, and reading Nancy Drew mysteries. He also used to go riding bikes and hiking in the woods with his best buddy.

Prior to Brett's entering second grade, his father was transferred to Europe. There Brett attended school on a military base. He continued to engage in typical boyhood activities like playing pranks on girls and playing kickball or using the monkey bars during recess. Sometimes, if his friends needed another person on the team to play football, he would agree. But, generally, Brett "did my own thing." Brett's grades also improved. Working at his own pace, Brett began to earn B's and an occasional A.

At 10, Brett and his family moved back state-side. Again, he did well in school, now earning more A's than B's. On the playground, though, Brett still demonstrated his independence. For example, he started playing Chinese jump rope. "At first they said I was a 'sissy.' But, I broke the ice and then friends of mine would come up, 'Can we join?' So, I just did my own thing." By sixth grade, Brett started to develop "real strong feelings for my best buddy. We'd stick up for each other like a man for his wife or a boyfriend for his girlfriend. It was another kind of love — friendship." In seventh grade, Brett started going on dates. "Having a girlfriend was a prerequisite for middle-school. So, I got two girlfriends." Brett would accompany them on alternate weekend nights to the neighborhood teen club. "We just kissed on the lips. But," Brett hastened to add, "we never messed around." During middle-school, Brett also dressed out for physical education class. "That's when I first heard the terms 'homosexual' and 'faggot.' I didn't understand it but I'd joke about it. Like this one guy would linger around from the previous gym class to see what we had so we began calling him 'faggot.'" Brett began to have wet dreams and to masturbate. He never had sexual feelings for other guys nor did he engage with them in same-sex activities. What he learned about sex he learned from his mother. She gave him a book on sex in seventh grade. "It wasn't graphic. It just told the simple truth with little diagrams."

At 13, Brett returned from Massachusetts to his home state of South Carolina. "We moved back and everything had changed: new roads, new buildings, the old neighborhood. My old buddies had moved just a couple of streets away to a new neighborhood. Their families were just a little bit higher than mine. I had just come back from six years on army bases where I met kids from all walks of life and different nationalities. I came back here and there was just one thing that mattered: prestige. The first thing I realized that I had to have was an Izod shirt." Though Brett bought one, he soon realized that he did not want to fit into the norm.

Before, when he agreed to play football with the guys or date girls, it did not bother him. But things had changed. Putting on that Izod shirt bothered him. "When I moved down here I went through a time warp. I didn't fit the definite stereotype of a Southerner. Most of my classmates had never left the South, except maybe for a trip to Atlanta. I had moved around a lot and experienced different cultures and ideas. I had changed. I realized that I didn't have to do what everyone else wanted me to do."

In eighth grade, Brett stopped dating. "In Massachusetts, dating was a prerequisite; in the South, it was a tradition. You were expected to find a soul mate to go through high school with. The ultimate girl was the Southern Belle. She had all the right clothes, the right makeup, the right hairdo, the pretty face. She just had a way about her." Brett did not follow tradition. He refused to date. He also was "shocked that they would sneak stuff out from their parents' bar, go out and drink, and have a hell-raising good time." Brett spent most of his school time hanging around his best friend, Theodore, "a small, skinny, wiry black boy. Everyone shut me out because I was the new kid, I didn't have a girlfriend, I didn't drink, and my best friend was black. I was different." Brett got nicknamed "faggie" since he didn't have a girlfriend. By that time, he had begun experiencing sexual feelings for other boys but "I knew it was morally and socially wrong so I didn't even acknowledge these feelings." With very little social activity, Brett spent most of his time studying at home. "I was kind of sad because I didn't have more friends and a clique," he confesses.

When Brett entered high school he was overwhelmed. "I first just saw it from the road. I was like, 'Wow!' It was massive. It had three different levels. There were so many different rooms and doors, hallways and stairwells. It took me two or three weeks to learn my way around — even then I was unsure." When Brett finally learned his way around school, he appreciated the diversity that such a large school provided. "There were more kids so you had more of a chance to meet different people." As a freshman, though, Brett continued to spend most of his time at home studying. "I had all this pressure on me from my family, teachers, and guidance counselors to do well and go to college and become somebody. I was scared. I just did what I had to do. I made A's and B's. It made me happy; it made everyone else happy." But he endured the occasional harassing comments like "faggot." "Sometimes they'd say it and I'd just shrug it off and then other times it would really get to me: 'They don't even know who I am, if I am or not. I don't even know.'" Other times Brett would experience physical harassment such as walking down the hallway between classes with a bigger student bouncing books on Brett's head. "I had tears in my eyes because of the pain. But, I just walked away. When I got to class and sat at my desk I was about to burst into tears. But, I didn't say anything."

As a sophomore, Brett was more eager to enter into the social aspects of high school — but on his terms. "I was myself but I always had my own little role to play." He hopped from clique to clique: "It was like the preps, jocks, and freaks against the blacks. With the preps I would go out somewhere to drink and dance. Some of the jocks were friends of mine. I understood they hassled me just to joke around so I didn't take it as hard as the other guys they hassled. With the band people, I'd go out to movies or miniature golf and pizza afterward."

Brett faced harassment of a different kind in the solitude of his bedroom. At nights, he experienced a recurring dream. A nude woman entered his room. Suddenly a muscular guy appeared. The guy disrobed; the girl disappeared. As he moved to embrace the

young man, Brett would awake in a sweat. "I just kept telling myself, 'it's just a dream. It's not going to happen.'"

Brett started to seriously question his sexual identity:

> In eighth grade I was like, "They're just stupid and they don't
> like me." In the ninth grade I was like, "It's just my imagina-
> tion." In my sophomore year I was thinking, "They might be
> right. But, I don't know because I've never done anything."
> So, I continued to act straight. I didn't want them to discover I
> was gay before I knew for myself. If they found out something
> about me that I didn't know about myself I would have been
> labelled. If it turned out I wasn't gay, then that was their mis-
> take, but I'd still have this label. If the label was going on, I
> was going to put it there!

As a junior, Brett began to speak to some of his friends about his
feelings and their sexual identities:

> I wouldn't come out and ask, "Are you gay?" I'd say, "This
> is how I feel about someone. Have you ever felt like this be-
> fore about the same sex?" If it was someone who had had
> these feelings, we talked. If not, I wouldn't bring it up again. I
> found out some of my friends considered themselves bisexual
> and one said he was gay. They asked me. I was like, "I don't
> know. I've never done anything." Then they asked me what
> my feelings were. I'd say, "Well, I lean more toward guys
> than girls." "So you're gay," they'd shout. But, I'd say,
> "You can't say that just because I have those feelings. I've
> never done anything physical so that means I'm not." I never
> denied it; I never accepted it.

Brett and his friends hung around with Mr. McLeod, the English
and theater teacher at the school. "He would kind of ease over and
talk with us and I got to know and trust him." Ever since Brett
could remember, there had been rumors about Mr. McLeod—but
they were just rumors. One time, in the midst of one of these group
conversations, Mr. McLeod leaned over to Brett and whispered,
"If you ever need to talk about anything you can come to me."

During his last year in high school, Brett became a "Big Cheese.

No one else had the courage to say 'none of your cliques are good enough. I don't need you.' But, I did.'' Surrounded by his friends, Brett rebelled against his father. He pierced his ear and began to buy his own "wild" clothes. "Dad hated this, of course. Mr. Army Man: men aren't supposed to do that. What are people going to think? Then Mom would say, 'In some countries an earring is a symbol that you're married.' I just laughed.''

Brett's group formed as remnants of the band and theater groups, some freaks and punkers as well as one or two jocks and preppies began to hang out at The Mix — an alternative, non-alcoholic dance club. Brett's grades dropped to C's with a couple of D's thrown in. But, he didn't care. "I was trying to be a class clown instead of a faggot. I was trying to lead them away from that idea. People kept trying to label me when I didn't know myself. So, I just kind of goofed off.'' Brett went to his senior prom, accompanying one of the females from his group, and had a great time. "Neither my brother nor sister went so I wanted to go. My brother was like a hermit and my sister spent all her time with the 'frocks' — freaks and jocks — who had their own little parties.''

A week after the senior prom, Brett met Ric at a drive-thru fast food restaurant. After they talked for a bit, Ric departed. A few days later Brett spotted Ric walking downtown. The two chatted and got a bite to eat. Finally, Ric invited Brett over to his apartment where they enjoyed sex. "I didn't have all these feelings for him. He wanted more. He wanted to make me love him. I couldn't. I didn't really know about love like that. I wanted to find more out about it and try it more.''

Brett confided in Mr. McLeod. "I told him things I didn't tell anyone else. He told me that he was gay. We compared notes on how it was for him when he was growing up, coming out of the closet, his first experience, and all of that. It put me at ease because here was a person who was older and more experienced in life.'' Asked if that wasn't the role of guidance counselors, Brett scoffed. "They never had any posters saying 'You can talk to us about this.' They just dealt with classes, grades, extracurricular activities and bullshit like that. I didn't trust them. Mr. McCleod put his trust in me and I put my trust in him.''

Two weeks before graduation, Angie and Lane, Brett's brother and sister, rifled through his bedroom one afternoon. They found a card written by Ric which Brett had forgotten to destroy. Brett recalls:

> Angie confronted me. She was like my dad in a woman's body. Angie is really powerful in her words and she can get physical if necessary. She said, "I need to talk with you." We sat down and she started talking normal but her voice built up. Soon she was clinching her teeth and making fists with her hands. In tears and anger she yelled, "I don't want a gay brother. If you're gay I'm going to disown you!" I was shocked that she was talking to me like this. I'm thinking, "How can she disown me?" She kept saying that I was becoming a different person. "I'm not different. The whole South is changing. Why pin it on me?"

Angie told their mother of the episode. "My mom goes, 'Well, I think you need to talk with your dad.' She didn't ask me if I considered myself to be gay or not." Brett remembers trudging up to the den and knocking on the panelled door. "It was the hardest thing I ever had to do. I said, 'I had an experience with another person.' He's like, 'Yeah. I already heard.'" Later that evening Brett overheard his parents talking. "It was like 20 questions: 'Where did we go wrong? What didn't we do?'"

Lane remained in his bedroom during Angie's confrontation with Brett. "He dwelled in the basement. He only came up for food and water." After the heated argument neither spoke to one another. "It was sort of like those comedy shows where the butler relays messages back and forth. I didn't want this to happen but I didn't want to stop being me. I was really confused." Lane's reactions were equally negative. "He became really campy and flamboyant in his actions toward me. He wouldn't talk to me or touch me. He'd also be really picky. If I was listening to music, he'd bitch to my mom that it was too loud." One summer evening Brett was alone with Lane:

I was going around the house getting my clothes ready to go out with a friend of mine. Lane started following me. He followed me into the kitchen when I went to get something to eat. He muttered something under his breath. "What did you say?" "Oh, nothing." I'd go to the living room; he'd follow me. Each time he got a little louder. I said, "Did you say something to me?" I was getting bothered by it, which is what he wanted to happen. He was provoking me to anger so I would do something that I would be truly sorry for. Finally, I turned around and started getting real campy toward him and became the stereotypical faggot, "Girl, that shirt looks so good on you. And the pants, it just does wonders." Lane hated this. He grunted and walked down to his room. The next thing I know he's wielding a solid wood baseball bat. He hit me on my foot and chipped a bone in one of my toes. Then he got scared and ran to the bathroom, locked the door, and braced it. I grabbed a lamp and ripped off the shade and started yelling, "I'm going to kill you, you bastard." I kicked the bathroom door with my foot and by that time I was screaming and crying in pain. I crawled over to the neighbor's house. They found me on the doorstep, sobbing "Lane's gone crazy!"

For the next week, Brett stayed at his grandparents' home. While he was recuperating, Brett had plenty of time to think and reflect. Finally, he called his father up: "I don't think I'm going to come back home." His father simply replied, "I think that's a good plan, Brett."

During the intervening two years, Brett hasn't seen much of his family. But recently things have been changing. Brett has moved into his sister's apartment for convenience. "In the beginning it was fine, but since I'm gay she automatically assumes I am promiscuous and have AIDS. I have to take an AIDS test this week and if I test positive she's going to throw me out." Unlike his relationship with his sister, Brett's relationship with his brother has not improved. "Lane is still kissing my father's ass to keep on his good side. He's 21 and still living at home." Brett's relationship with his father is cool: "Dad doesn't accept it. Lane was the black sheep of the family, now I am.'' A month ago, when Brett moved in with his sister, he and his mother had their first talk about his homosexuality since the incident.

> She was over at the apartment and she asked how my evening was. "It was great. I was out with my friends." Somehow she got on the subject of homosexuality. She goes, "What makes you think you're a homosexual?" I said, "What makes you think I'm not?" She went on, "Ever since you had that experience with Ric you have never said you were. Are you?" I pause, "Yes, I am gay." I was expecting tears and screaming. Nothing. "Well, I don't think you are. It's a phase." That made me frustrated. "Mom, I think two years is a pretty long phase, don't you?" But, she has been persistent in telling me to see someone who doesn't know the family. I haven't. I don't have anything to prove to her: I'm gay. I never really had any interest in women, sexually. I like them as friends, even best friends, but I've never really wanted to have sex with them or a relationship that I would like to have with a male. In high school, though, I was too busy proving that I wasn't gay to realize that I was. But, my body knew.

At 19, Brett doesn't go cruising. "You can never trust anyone because of AIDS. Besides, I don't need to cruise. People cruise me." Though he has dated several guys who have had lovers, Brett has yet to be involved in any long-term relationship. Instead, he writes poetry:

> Everyday:
> We wake up and get ready for work.
> We drive our cars on the same roads,
> the same highways.
> We park right next to your cars.
> We use the same bathrooms.
> We listen to the same music.
> We breathe the same air.
> We live in the same society.

So, why do you abhor us when we share so many of the same things?

Okay, so we love differently!
Why does that matter?
There is really nothing to fear from us
except the pain that comes from your ignorance!

COMMENTARY

Brett was more fortunate than many others interviewed in this study. He knew high school students who were gay or bisexual, he received the support of a closeted gay teacher, he was untroubled by drug abuse or poor grades, and he enjoyed the privileges of a white, middle class male in Southern society. Despite these advantages, Brett still confronted harassment that a heterosexual student of his ability and social standing seldom faced. Though he was physically and verbally abused in school, his greatest difficulties were at home: a hostile brother and sister, a stern father, and a well-meaning but parochial mother.

On the surface it would appear that school had little to do with Brett's plight and educators shared little responsibility for the actions of his family. This simply is untrue. Educators' unwillingness to address homosexuality in an open and educationally responsible manner certainly contributed to the homophobic responses of Angie and Lane. Educators' (and their local professional organizations') unwillingness to support lesbian and gay teachers made Mr. McLeod's frank discussion with Brett risky and exceptional. The indifference, insensitivity, and ignorance of those ostensibly responsible for providing guidance to students precluded counseling for Brett, Angie, and Lane, or referral to a specialist in family counseling. The invisibility of lesbian and gay-identified students meant that any support provided persons like Brett was serendipitous and accidental. The forming of gay support groups in Brett's and Terry's circles were by word of mouth — closed to all but a few insiders. Further, these groups, without any adult assistance and knowledge about homosexuality, sometimes pressured students like Brett into a declaration of their sexual identity before they were certain themselves.

This commentary focuses on the attitudes and feelings of educators toward the issue of homosexuality and homosexual men and women. The importance (and limitations) of lesbian and gay role models and the special difficulties faced by homosexual teachers are also discussed as the stories of other participants' are told. As one student told the Gay Teachers' Group of London:

> [M]ost of us hide our sexuality: if we are open about it or it is discovered, we risk verbal, physical and psychological violence at home, at school and elsewhere. We face the possibility of being thrown out of home by our parents . . . being verbally and physically abused by other students, and being sent to hostile doctors and psychiatrists to be "cured". . . . We are not even allowed access to knowledge about ourselves and our gay and lesbian brothers and sisters all around us: our lesbian and gay teachers are terrorised into hiding their sexuality from us, when they are the people with the most potential for helping us and supporting us — things we very rarely get from our parents or guardians. Our collective history is hidden or denied, having been excluded or purged from all teaching about history, music, art, and literature; sex education is confined to biological reproduction and childbirth, and our libraries are kept clean of any positive references to our existence — even negative references to us are often kept behind locked doors.[2]

High School Educators' Attitudes and Feelings

One of the more extensive areas of research in lesbian and gay studies is on adult attitudes toward homosexuality or toward homosexuals. With only a few exceptions, these studies have been conducted in metropolitan areas in the industrial North and far West.[3] Most assess peoples' attitudes toward homosexuality in the abstract rather than their reactions to individual homosexuals.[4]

Popularized by sociologist Weinberg, "homophobia" originally meant an irrational fear of homosexual persons.[5] Over the years, however, homophobia has been expanded to include disgust, anxiety, and anger.[6] Further, it has come to be used not only to the reactions of heterosexuals but the internalization of negative feelings by homosexual men and women.[7]

These studies often report the relationships between attitudes and personality traits or demographic variables.[8] Though such studies are not without conflicting data, Gregory Herek has summarized some consistent patterns.[9] People with negative attitudes report less personal contact with gays and lesbians, less (if any) homosexual behavior, a more conservative religious ideology, and more traditional attitudes about sex roles than do those with less negative views. Those harboring negative attitudes about homosexuality are also more likely to have resided in the Midwest or the South, to have grown up in rural areas or in small towns, and to be male, older, and less well-educated than those expressing more positive attitudes.

Quasi-experimental research studies have demonstrated that adult males harbor more homophobic attitudes or feelings than females and are more concerned about male homosexuality than lesbianism.[10] Further, those with less negative feelings or attitudes are more likely to have had associations or friendships with lesbians or gay men.[11]

Studies have also assessed the attitudes and feelings of people in the helping professionals toward homosexuality and homosexual persons.[12] These studies have found a heterosexual bias in these persons' professional attitudes and homophobia in their personal feelings. Only a handful of studies, however, have examined issues relating to homosexuality in the context of the public elementary or high school. These studies have focused on guidance counselors, teachers, high school students, principals, and gay/lesbian teachers.[13] While several studies have explored this topic with counselor trainees,[14] only two have examined the attitudes and feelings of persons preparing to be teachers.[15] With few exceptions, most education-related essays have been directed to school counselors regarding the special needs and problems of homosexual students.[16]

These limited studies on public school educators suggest that teachers, administrators, and guidance counselors, in general, lack the sensitivity, knowledge, and skills to address effectively the needs of students with same-sex feelings. For example, most school administrators would dismiss a teacher for disclosing her homosexuality to students; one-fourth of all college students preparing to teach at one institution acknowledged their inability to treat fairly a homosexual student or discuss homosexuality in the classroom; and less than one in five school counselors would willingly discuss the special concerns of lesbian and gay-identified students at a school faculty meeting.[17]

Three-fourths of the participants in this study reported that their high school teachers had negative attitudes about homosexuality and only six of these Southern youth talked to a teacher about their sexuality. In a study of a cohort group of 258 Southern college students preparing to become teachers, less than five percent reported that at least some of their high school teachers were supportive of homosexual students.[18] Not surprisingly, nearly one-half of this predominantly heterosexual sample had no idea of whether such support was extended by their teachers. Most, though, had first-hand knowledge of their teachers' attitudes about homosexuality and their willingness to discuss the topic in the classroom. Of those who had some basis for first-hand knowledge, more than 80 percent reported few or none of their high school teachers considered homosexuality an alternative lifestyle or that classroom discussion included this topic.

These findings parallel the assessments of 142 South Carolina school guidance counselors surveyed during the same time period.[19] The vast majority observed that few, if any, of their school's teachers were supportive of gay and lesbian students, discussed homosexuality in the classroom, or considered it an alternative lifestyle. Further, slightly less than one-third of these professionals indicated that their building-level administrators viewed homosexual concerns as legitimate topics for counselors to discuss with their school-age clients. Nevertheless, most guidance counselors reported knowing at least one homosexual student during their professional tenure, and four out of ten counselors have discussed homosexuality and homosexual-related issues among their counseling staff or have counseled students about their homosexual orientation. Despite their interest and contacts, few felt prepared to work with this special population, and less than one-fifth of the sample indicated that they had participated in programs to expand their knowledge about homosexuality.

As the social distance lessened, a greater degree of discomfort was expressed by counselors.[20] These counselors were much more likely than prospective teachers to adopt liberal positions on civil rights issues (e.g., decriminalization of consenting adult homosexual relationships) but to hold conservative moral views (e.g., homosexuality is a sin) and to fear personal contact (i.e., unwillingness to be around lesbians or gay men).[21]

Despite their personal misgivings about homosexuality, most school counselors assumed a non-judgmental and sometimes supportive role when dealing with homosexual students. For example, the vast majority believed that sexual concerns of students were legitimate topics for discussion and few expected homosexual students to overcome their same-sex feelings. Nevertheless, while nearly two-thirds of the counselors had known a student who had a homosexual orientation, less than one-fourth have chosen to counsel such students about it.

Those counselors working with older students and having more professional experience and formal education were most likely to express a willingness to work with sexual minority youth. Those spending a greater proportion of their time in administrative tasks such as testing and evaluating students expressed more negative attitudes and were less interested in the concerns of this special population. Consistent with studies of other segments of the population, counselors belonging to racial minorities and those with less education expressed more negative attitudes or feelings about homosexuality and toward homosexual persons.[22] However, in contrast to the respondents in these other studies, male counselors were more tolerant than their female counterparts.

Given these findings it is not surprising that most Carolina youth interviewed for this study reported high school educators adopting a neutral to negative position with respect to homosexuality. While they do not go out of their way to let students know of their availability to discuss personal issues, unlike Mr. McLeod in Brett's biography, neither do educators allow their prejudices against lesbians and gay men to enter into the classroom or affect intervention with students experiencing harassment. Nevertheless, school counselors were particularly singled out as insensitive, unknowledgeable, and distant.

Several sexual rebels, such as Franklin, spoke at length about the difficulty they faced in school as the result of the negative attitudes of educators. Most, like Nathaniel and Carlton, noted that this topic was simply avoided by teachers, counselors, and administrators in their school. Guidance counselors, in particular, were viewed as academic not personal advisors. A few of the participants like Georgina, however, relayed stories of supportive educators who made a difference in their adolescent lives. Examples of each kind are provided by these and other participants.

Franklin lives in a predominantly black South Carolina rural town. He remembers harassment from educators inside and outside the classroom:

> In high school, like the town, it was very hush-hush about homosexuality. You never talked to the students, teachers, principal, or counselors about it. They never talked to you about it. Even though I had two friends who were open and admitted it at the time, the teachers just ignored it and kept their feelings to themselves. But, the principal would always try to look out for the bad things these two were doing. He was always trying to get them for something. One day I was with my friends — when you are with them you are labelled — and this real flaming and feminine guy was telling someone off so the principal wrote him up and sent him to the "box" [in-school suspension].

Franklin also recalled an incident with his high school physics teacher:

> Mr. Jenson would usually drift away from the subject. He'd often bring up homosexuality. He mainly talked about the wrongs of it and how it was such a sin and that they should be condemned. I felt really bad.

Other participants reported similar incidents. For example, Fawn remembers one teacher who "hated me because she knew I was gay. She would fill out these forms that got me into trouble and then make comments like, "People like you. . . .""

Only a handful of participants, including Brett, reported speaking to a guidance counselor or teacher about their homosexuality. In general, they perceived these adults to be ill-informed and unconcerned and they simply felt uncomfortable talking to them. The image of counselors communicated to the participants in this study was summed up by Kimberly: "Our counselors had never been presented to us as someone there to talk about problems other than education. They were just there for grades, signing up for classes, tests like the PSAT, and finding colleges to attend."

Similar sentiments were echoed about teachers and their unwillingness to show concern for lesbian and gay-identified students or to express their feelings about homosexuality. A senior in high school, Nathaniel, recalls a recent classroom discussion dealing with homosexuality:

> In my sociology class we were talking about AIDS. One guy said, "I think gay guys are just sick. How could they do that? It's wrong!" One of my friends who is gay asks, "Why do you think it's wrong?" Well, everyone looks over to Miss L., our teacher, for what she thinks. She says, "I have no comment. I'm not even going to get into this discussion. I'm going to keep my opinion to myself." So we lingered on this topic for awhile. I kept my mouth closed. Another guy said, "If a fag makes a move on me, I'd whip his ass." I thought to myself, "Yeah, right. We had gotten in a fight earlier and I dogged him out." Then two of the football players joined in. One was on each side. So, I piped up. (I had just gone into wrestling, so I was safe. The people who had been calling me gay had been coming up to me saying, "Hey man, I'm sorry for calling you queer.") So, I say "If you don't try it, you never will know what's going on. You're just going on hearsay. How can you judge these people? They're people too, just because their sexuality is different."

This detachment of teachers from personal concerns and social issues was underscored repeatedly in conversations with these sexual rebels. Carlton stated:

Teachers seem to keep themselves so removed. In high school, teachers weren't people. They just lived in the school, went into the closet, stayed there over night, and then came out during the day, right? It was hard to think of them as real people. It was hard to interact with them. You know, a lot of the child's life is spent in school. If all that time is dealt with them through the book and not attending to any kind of personal needs, it just seems so ridiculous to me — stilted. It puts such a damper on what could be done.

Georgina's comments illustrate how quickly young people can pick up on teachers' personal detachment from their students — and how students can hide behind the role teachers expect them to assume:

Teachers don't see much of your inner self. They don't ask. It's easy to put on a face with teachers. For example, Miss Morrison wanted someone very Christian-like, a little angel. For her, I wrote in my English journal about Jesus and love all the time. Mr. Boozer was the band director. He wanted somebody with good leadership skills who could play well. He got that. Mrs. Laman, she liked slaves. So, if you volunteered for everything, like I did, she liked you. As long as you keep them happy, they think that you're well-adjusted.

Carlton is studying to become a teacher. Arguing that "a teacher is involved in growth and guidance and not simply to teach math, science or English," he asserts:

I would think that a student would be quicker to want to talk to teachers if they had been kind to them. If they had just started talking to me on a personal basis. Just to talk about interests, "Well, how's the rest of school? What do you like to do? I hear you're in chorus?" I might have more easily been able to bring it up. I remember this one woman, she was so hard. It would not have taken much for her to have asked me more personal questions. Like, "Carlton, how are you doing in school and I don't mean academically?" She possibly could have made me think about things that I hadn't even gotten up to the conscious level yet and then just leave it open for me to talk about them with her. If she'd only have said, "If you want to talk about anything, you can" — but she didn't.

Of course, as Darla's biography illustrates, being open to a student does not guarantee a response from that student. Darla was not ready to respond to teacher initiatives the way Brett and Georgina were. In ninth grade, Darla had Mrs. Taxel for sex education. "At first I hated her. All I heard throughout the whole year was that she talked about her little grandson. Sure enough, the first day of class that was the first thing she talked about, her stupid grandson." After several weeks of engaging in subtle but defiant acts in the classroom, Darla found herself confronted by Mrs. Taxel:

> I got ready to walk out after class. She stopped me and slammed the door. "Sit down. We're talking," she said. "I can't understand why you dislike me so much." I said, "Frankly, because you're a bitch." Mrs. Taxel saw my cigarettes hanging out of my pocket. "Are those yours?" I told her they were. "Can I have one?" I said, "Sure." I handed her one and I got one. We just sat there smoking and talking. After that, we became good friends. I could talk to her about anything — except being gay.

Most teachers, of course, are not as open or willing to engage adolescents on their own terms — let alone to broach the subject of homosexuality. Carlton appreciates the teachers' dilemma. "Looking back, they probably were aware but afraid to talk about my homosexuality. Besides, they probably didn't know what kind of reaction they would get from me if they had tried or if they were wrong." Nevertheless, Carlton is resentful about the inability or unwillingness of educators to try to communicate with him.

> I've felt cheated by school. I felt there was so much potential, so much I could have done and we didn't nearly approach it. I've lost time, and a lot of that can't be gotten back. It was as if I was there for a prison term or they were my babysitters without permission to do anything with me. Teachers act like they have total authority *and* that they can do nothing all at the same time!

This latter point is well illustrated by Franklin's observation of how teachers in his high school dealt with slurs. "The teachers weren't very tolerant as far as racial slurs. If a teacher heard it, she might write him up. If there was a sexual slur, like 'fag,' they would pay no attention to it. That told me they didn't feel homophobia was as important as racism." Carlton concurs:

> If a teacher got tired of hearing these derogatory remarks they would only say "stop" — never questioning as to why they were feeling that way or trying to make them think about what they were doing. Only that, "I just don't want to hear that." They would be a lot quicker to jump on other minority groups than homosexuals.

Despite the bleakness of these tales, there are educators who genuinely care about lesbian and gay-identified students and try to work with them; Mr. McLeod, Mrs. Munn, and Mrs. Seltzer, for example. Another was Laura Huggins, a counselor intern at the school Georgina attended.

In tenth grade, Georgina's lover, Kay, began to see Miss Huggins who after a while asked to see Georgina. Georgina stopped by Miss Huggins' office for a quick chat, and found her to be pleasant and mild-mannered. "She told me to see her if I had any problems." Six weeks later, Georgina discovered that Kay was seeing another girl; a violent quarrel erupted. Thinking that she had no one to turn to, Georgina suddenly remembered Miss Huggins' words:

> I wrote Miss Huggins a note and slipped it under her door. The next time she saw me, she said, "I know. Do you want to talk about it?" I told her all about my relationship with Kay. She acted as kind of an umpire in our fight. I remember her telling me, "You have different walls around you, Georgina. Every once in a while a wall will collapse and you'll kick it back up. Someday they will all come down and you will get hurt. You'll be tempted to put them back up again. But, don't." I really didn't quite understand what she was saying but it was a relief not to have to put on an act around somebody.

Miss Huggins helped to mend the quarrel between the twosome. Georgina continued to see Kay through her sophomore year. Georgina reminisces, "When you first fall in love, you're always caught up. Love is blind. You can't see what is really going on around you. I knew that Kay liked other people and wanted to date them along with me. She just wasn't ready to settle down." A short time later Miss Huggins completed her internship at the school. Georgina regretted her departure:

> If Miss Huggins would have stayed, I feel that I would have accepted myself a lot better. But, they didn't send anybody else. I remember after she left feeling so sad and needing to talk to somebody. All the time I kept thinking, "I can do what Patton did; I could try to kill myself. I was going to take some sleeping pills and eat them right before my mom came home. I thought, "If she catches me in time, I'll get to talk to someone." I didn't want to kill myself; I just wanted to talk to someone who knew what they were talking about.

Though Nathaniel never found an educator like Miss Huggins with whom he could speak frankly, he did receive advice early in high school from an adult working at his school. At 14, Nathaniel had not identified himself as gay though he knew that he enjoyed males physically as well as socially. He developed a crush on Reuben, a neighborhood boy three years his senior. The first time the two met, the older boy told Nathaniel, " 'Look, I'm gay. I want you to know this if you have any problems.' I had no problems with that and we soon became real close." Nathaniel continues: "One night we got some beer and got wasted, or at least acted like we were drunk. We started feeling on each other, grabbing one another. One thing lead to another and we just kept going."

Nathaniel also had sexual fantasies about girls and enjoyed their emotional company. About this time he started to date Delta. "I was scared, I really was. I was wondering if I was going to lose my feelings for Delta, who I loved, while I still really loved Reuben. Confused about these feelings, Nathaniel "thought about talking to the counselor, but I just didn't build up enough nerve." He finally sat down in the corridor after school one day and just cried. Sud-

denly he felt a gentle tap on his shoulder. Looking up he saw Ol'
Jessie, the school's janitor. His short grey hair stood out against his
black skin. Jessie invited Nathaniel down to his "office." Once in
the boiler room, the two pulled up a couple of crates and had a long
talk. "He told me that I was too young to even worry about being a
homosexual. 'Every man,' he said, 'has them feelings. You're going to look over at another guy in the bathroom and say, 'I'm big
enough. Can I satisfy this person?' Then I sat down and thought.
'Well, if it's normal for someone to have homosexual feelings, why
isn't it normal for a guy to try homosexual sex?''"

Having supportive adults such as Mr. McLeod, Miss Huggins,
and Ol' Jessie was certainly helpful to Brett, Georgina, and Nathaniel. Though most participants in this study said they would have
liked to have had such educators while attending high school, some,
like Audrey, Kimberly, Phillip, and Franklin, were much more reticent about such prospects. There were a variety of reasons for such
caution, including unwillingness of the student to assume the initiative, lack of trust in confidentiality, the worry of losing teacher
friendship, and personality differences. Audrey states, "I did not
have direct counseling. I'm glad because I don't know how I would
have acted. In high school, if it were to get out, I would have been
so embarrassed. I could not have stood the peer pressure." Kimberly remembers:

> I didn't talk to counselors because they're human, too. Homo-
> sexuality is taboo. People just kind of go bonkers when they
> hear that word or find out that somebody is homosexual. Even
> the adults act like kids. They don't know how to handle it. I
> thought, "I can't trust anybody with this information." You
> know, teachers talk.

This was echoed by Franklin: "I didn't want them to know my
feelings. I wasn't that trusting of them. I felt that they might tell my
parents." Phillip, who enjoyed close friendship with several teachers, feared sharing his sexual feelings because it would be "like
risking them not liking me."

In addition to knowledgeable and sensitive heterosexual adults,
the importance of gay and lesbian role models has been stressed by

professionals in a variety of fields.[23] Such persons are important for students like Everetta, who felt isolation and confusion, and for those such as Vince, who harbored stereotypically negative images of homosexuals.

Of course, there were no openly lesbian or gay teachers working at the high schools in South Carolina attended by these participants. Almost all of the participants in this study, however, suspected one or more teachers, and about one-fourth reported that they had a class with a teacher who they "knew" was lesbian or gay. For most, of course, "knowing" amounted to little more than hearsay and personal suspicions. There were, however, exceptions. The experience of Fawn illustrates the important personal relationships that can develop between student and teacher.

Fawn didn't label herself "lesbian" until she had graduated from high school. During her last two years in school, however, she hung around several teachers, two of whom were lovers, who helped her to feel good about herself:

> I didn't want to face what I was feeling at all about anything or anybody. But, I knew I cared about this woman a lot. She went out and bought some books and said, "Why don't you read this and tell me what you think?" She would get me into these conversations. However, the most embarrassing experience was when we were walking down the mall. She put her arm around me and kissed me saying, "I just want to let you know that I love you." I was so aware of being gay at that time even though she was straight. I just died. There were also two lesbian teachers in this group. I liked them a lot. They were good role models for me in the sense that it's okay to have feelings toward other people if you really do love them.

Lesbian and gay adult role models are critical for the *entire* student population. In reviewing the evidence regarding the adequacy of lesbians and gay men as role models, psychologist Dorothy Riddle concluded:

Rather than posing a menace to children, gays may actually facilitate important developmental learning. To offset the pressures of a heterosexual society toward adopting traditional sex-role behavior, gays often demonstrate a variety of alternative adaptations. Thus children have the possibility of learning that it is possible and may be rewarding to resist traditional sex-role socialization. In addition, children become exposed to the concept of cultural and individual diversity as positive rather than threatening.[24]

Or, as teacher-educator Pat Griffin notes, "pretending that there are no gay and lesbian teachers allows most students to go through school with their stereotypes and fears about gay people unchallenged."[25]

Ironically, as Griffin and others have detailed, while lesbian and gay teachers are well aware of the hostility and isolation that homosexual students confront, they are fearful of the personal and professional consequences that such public disclosure of their own sexual identity might have.[26] She writes, "Being a gay or lesbian educator requires a strict separation between personal and professional life. Moreover, teachers are united in the belief that to be publicly 'out' at school would cost them their jobs."[27]

Lorin Richards has taught English and coached sports at a large suburban South Carolina school for the past 10 years. He has never discussed homosexuality in public or private with his high school students. Asked if he had thought about mentioning Whitman's sexuality when discussing his poetry or focusing on modern day "scarlet letters" when reading Hawthorne's classic novel, Richards froze:

There is a kind of terror that runs through my mind when I think about that. There's a Pandora's Box that's opened with that. If I tried to deal with it in that fashion how would it be accepted? It's bringing that thing out into the open and making them think about it. I remember this one very blatant student went to the administration years ago and asked to have something like a gay meeting group. I wouldn't have the courage or stupidity to do that, but he did. The administration still jokes about that. So, I just don't know if students are mature enough or whether that's a subject that in this environment we can deal with. We teach things that are safe.

The great ambivalence felt by teachers such as Richards is reflected in his referral to homosexuality as "it," or "the issue." This ambivalence also is reflected in his teaching and being "out" in the classroom:

Most people who teach who are gay are not so much openly gay, although it's not a secret. But, it's not something that we go around and talk about with any of our peers on the faculty. It's basically a public thing that isn't public. I think maybe it's cowardice on my part. But, it's made me think a lot about how close to get around some students in some situations. I used to be a little more personal on the kind of things I talked about. You know how kids are always asking about your dating and stuff. Now, I try to keep myself from getting into the kind of relationship with a student or a class that allows those questions to come up. I don't want to have to lie.

Further, according to Richards, an openly gay teacher does not necessarily satisfy the needs of gay or lesbian students. He remembers, "There was one teacher who was very openly gay but in all the very negative, stereotypical ways. He was not the kind of a person that anyone would confide anything in." Richards also fears the consequences that public exposure might bring:

I know that among certain groups of students the thought about me being gay is there. They don't have any facts. But, it's one of those things that kids sense. It's scary. They know things that are true but they don't know for sure they know. These people really do get real close to that issue sometimes.

His fears of exposure are far from illusory. While less than 10 percent of a nationwide sample of junior high and high school principals would summarily dismiss a teacher for simply "being gay" more than one-half of the respondents would favor the revocation of

the teaching license should a competent and veteran teacher, like
Mr. Richards, disclose his homosexuality to students.[28] This despite
the fact that three-fourths of these principals reported that, in cases
where disclosure occurred, no negative effects in the school were
evident, and where problems did exist they subsided in a "relatively short time."

Nevertheless, even educational moderates question the conduct
of teachers who profess their homosexuality to students. In one
popular magazine, the authors bluntly assert:

> Parents and school authorities have a right to demand that ho-
> mosexual teachers refrain from using the classroom as a fo-
> rum. This is not to single them out for special limitations.
> Heterosexual teachers are expected not to parade their political
> or sexual preference before their students. If teachers are enti-
> tled to the full protection of their privacy, it ought to follow
> that they themselves are not going to void that privilege.[29]

Such an argument, of course, is comfortably blind to the daily parading of a heterosexual curriculum before its students, the isolation
and hostility experienced by homosexual students, and the simple
yet oppressive presumption of heterosexuality in everyday interac-
tions. The authors, too, are unmindful of the social fact, eloquently
elaborated upon by Guy Hocquenghem, that homosexuality ceases
to be a private matter when heterosexuality is woven throughout our
institutions, policies, and culture.

Fear and ignorance often dictate how people react to homosexual
educators. Lesbian and gay educators, however, often are woefully
unaware of the routine legal assistance provided by organizations
such as the National Education Association and the legal and bu-
reaucratic morass created when an educator's homosexual identity
is made public. Based upon legal research into this area, Karen
Harbeck concluded:

> Because of the complexities of the legal and social issues, and
> because of the seemingly limitless legal and financial re-
> sources on both sides, the courts appear to have tried to avoid a
> direct declaration concerning whether or not homosexuals
> have a constitutional right to teach school. As long as the judi-

ciary chooses to avoid taking the initiative on this controversial issue, tremendous room is left for negotiation and education. School boards seem more than willing to look the other way with respect to a teacher's homosexual orientation unless some indiscretion has occurred, and they certainly seem to be more willing to negotiate than to face the costly expense of litigation. . . . [C]redential revocation on the basis of homosexuality is a thing of the past.[30]

In a more general review of the legal implications of the sexual identity and classroom activities of homosexual teachers, Fernand Dutile, Professor of Law at the University of Notre Dame, recommends to school administrators:

[E]ven if school officials should learn of a teacher's homosexuality or of homosexual activity, no action should be taken against that teacher on the basis of undifferentiated fear, speculation as to what could happen, vague concerns about modelling roles or even the possible inference of school board approval to which retention of the teacher might give rise. Any action taken against the teacher should be based on actual and significant harm to the school system or the real likelihood of such harm. Surely, the objections of a few teachers, students or parents, especially in light of the likelihood that the real problem is theirs, not the teacher's, should not suffice.[31]

There is, though, a fundamental distinction between private or even public knowledge of a educator's homosexuality, and that person becoming an advocate for the needs and rights of sexual minority students or for the inclusion of knowledge about homosexuals and homosexuality in relevant topics of the high school curriculum. Here, the direct involvement of heterosexual and bisexual educators is essential. This direct involvement can, however, be solicited by homosexual teachers like Mr. Richards who privately or publicly disclose their sexual identity to faculty or students. Such acts not only raise the awareness level of other persons in the school, but can move well-meaning educators toward a variety of reflective and specific actions. As one heterosexual educator wrote:

When Geoff came out in the classroom his initial need for
support called on my beliefs in professional solidarity and led
to changes in my own attitudes to gays. I was forced to become far more positive when talking about gays, and became
sensitized to homosexuality and its problems for the first
time.[32]

The 36 sexual rebels portrayed in *Growing Up Gay in the South*
are survivors. They survived taunts and torments of childhood or
vaguely uncomfortable feelings about being different. They survived the combination of racial, gender, or class oppression with
homosexuality. They survived religious zealots and the importance
of honor in the Southern family. They survived fleeting homosexual
liaisons and long-term silent relationships. They survived incest and
rape, rumor and scandal, threats and beatings. In the silence of their
souls, they hid and they lied—but they survived.

Brett, Olivia, Phillip—these are the fortunate ones. Nameless
others have not survived. Some departed the heterosexual-oriented
world through suicide, drug overdose, or alcohol-related accidents.
Others entered the netherworld of closeted homosexuality through
marriages of convenience or baptismal waters. Others escaped into
worlds within worlds: the convent, the asylum, the prison. Some
have fallen into the black hole of lesbian and gay communities in
which the security of a ready-made homosexual identity often sup-
plants the search for a unique, authentic Self. They have not survived the heterosexual agenda to retell their lives; each of us share
responsibility for their untold stories.

There is, though, the next generation, one in which super-con-
ductivity will be as common as super-computers and in which the
Reagan-Bush years and the decades of dominance by Helms and
Thurmond will be but another era in the dustbin of history. Will the
generation see America become more like the Old South, or the
New South become more like the American ideal? Will it be a generation in which violence against lesbians, bisexuals, and gay men
is as socially unacceptable as violence against African-Americans
today, or will bands of skin-heads roam the land preying on the
weak and despised as freely as fundamentalist preachers now roam
the radio band preying on our fears? How we address the needs of

sexual rebels and the topic of sexuality in the schools is the bell-wether for the next generation. Our choices can make schools more educative and humane for *all* students. Our choices can make communities more just and more supportive for all people. On a common ground (economic justice, human rights), we must struggle against common evils (sexism, racism, heterosexism) and address common concerns (drug abuse, educational equity, community violence).

Nearly 40 years ago members of the Mattachine Society stood in a circle, joined hands, and took a pledge: "We are resolved that our people shall find equality of security and production in tomorrow's world. We are sworn that no boy or girl, approaching the maelstrom of deviation, need make that crossing alone, afraid, and in the dark ever again."[33] My generation passed childhood two decades ago. During the past quarter of a century, great battles have been fought (and many won) by lesbians and gay men on medical, legal, and moral fronts. These battles were fought to make the crossing from the heterosexual world to the homosexual community less lonely and the search for Self less painful. These victories, however, have not been so unequivocal. Although "being a homosexual" in the South is less difficult than it was four decades ago, although there are now established lesbian and gay communities throughout the country, and despite the flourishing of homosexual culture, a price has been exacted from this new generation. That price is to simplify the complexity of human sexuality. While struggling with one's sexuality is integrally related to the search for Self, adopting a gay or lesbian identity is not. As discussed in the next chapter, such identity may jeopardize that very search.

REFERENCE NOTES

1. Conroy, 1976:139.
2. Gay Teachers' Group, 1987:8.
3. Fischer, 1982; Gentry, 1986a, Gentry, 1986b; Haynes and Oziel, 1976; Lance, 1987; Young and Whertvine, 1982.
4. Hudson and Ricketts, 1980.
5. Weinberg, 1972.
6. MacDonald, 1976.

7. Lehne, 1976; Malyon, 1982; Margolies, Becker, and Jackson-Brewer, 1987.

8. For a summary of many of these studies, see: Fyfe, 1983; Herek, 1984; Larsen, Reed and Hoffman, 1980; Morin and Garfinkle, 1978; Taylor, 1983.

9. Herek, 1984.

10. Aguero, Block and Byrne, 1984; Braungart and Braungart, 1988; Coles and Stokes, 1985; Glassner and Owen, 1979; Hong, 1983; Larsen, Reed and Hoffman, 1980; MacDonald and Games, 1974; Minnigerode, 1976; Nyberg and Alston, 1977; West, 1977; Young and Whertvine, 1982. Conflicting data, however, have been reported using different samples or research instruments. For example, Sears (1988a) notes that male guidance counselors were less homophobic than their female counterparts and data from opinion polls (Irwin and Thompson, 1977; Schneider and Lewis, 1984) report no sex differences. Attributing these differences to population samples and attitudinal items, Herek (1986:565) in his review of this phenomenon, concludes "Males and females probably hold roughly similar positions on general questions of morality and civil liberties, but males are more homophobic in emotional reactions to homosexuality."

11. Aguero, Block and Byrne, 1984; Anderson, 1981; Gentry, 1986a, Gentry, 1986b; Millham, San Miguel and Kellogg, 1976; Schneider and Lewis, 1984.

12. Davison and Wilson, 1973; Fort, Steiner and Conrad, 1971; Garfinkle and Morin, 1978; Gartrell, Kraemer and Brodie, 1974; May, 1974; Pauly and Goldstein, 1970.

13. Dressler, 1985; Fischer, 1982; Price, 1982; Sears, 1988a; Sears, 1989a; Sears, in press; Smith, 1985.

14. Glenn and Russell, 1986; Schneider and Tremble, 1986a; Thompson and Fishburn, 1977.

15. Baker, 1980; Sears, 1989a.

16. Gumaer, 1987; Krysiak, 1987; Schneider and Tremble, 1986b; Sears, 1988a.

17. Baker, 1980; Dressler, 1985; Fischer, 1982; Sears, 1988a; Sears, 1989d.

18. Sears, 1989a.

19. Sears, 1988a.

20. Similar patterns have been found in other studies, leading one set of researchers to conclude, "[M]any people separate their moral censure of homosexuality per se and attitudes about the civil rights of homosexuals" (Irwin and Thompson, 1977:118). See also Gentry, 1986a.

21. Sears, 1988a.

22. Baker, 1980; Irwin and Thompson, 1977; Nyberg and Alston, 1977.

23. Griffin, 1989; Hetrick and Martin, 1987; Martin and Hetrick, 1988; Morin, 1974; Riddle, 1978; Ross-Reynolds and Hardy, 1985; Slater, 1988; Wein, 1982.

24. Riddle, 1978:53.

25. Griffin, 1989:4.

26. Fischer, 1982; Fogarty, 1980; Gay Teachers' Group, 1978; Griffin, 1989; Nickeson, 1980; Olson, 1987; Rofes, 1985; Smith, 1985; Woods, 1989.

27. Griffin, 1989:6.

28. Dressler, 1985.

29. Hechinger and Hechinger, 1978:164.

30. Harbeck, 1989:23-24,26. For a more detailed discussion of particular legal cases involving educators, see: Dressler, 1978; Hansen, 1977; Harbeck 1987; Lowe, 1978; Rausch, 1974.

31. Dutile, 1986:127-128.

32. Gay Teachers' Group, 1987:80.

33. D'Emilio, 1983b:68-69. D'Emilio chronicles the formation of the Mattachine Society—named after masked medieval figures whom some believed engaged in homosexual activity—which would be the first nationwide effort at homosexual emancipation.

Chapter 15

On Homosexual Communities, Identities, and Culture: Journeys of the Spirit

Detectives from the vice squad
with weary sadistic eyes
spotting fairies.
Degenerates,
some folks say.

But, God, Nature,
or somebody
made them that way.

Police lady or Lesbian
over there?
Where?

Langston Hughes, *Cafe: 3 A.M.*[1]

Langston Hughes wrote about a time lost to many of today's youth who have "come out" following the emergence of gay pride parades, Stonewall, and lesbian-feminism. This was the era of the Mattachine Society and Daughters of Bilitis, the Knights of the Clock and Bachelors for Wallace, of *One* and *The Ladder*, of *The City and the Pillar* and *Sexual Behavior in the Human Male*. There were no homosexual communities during those times; at best, there were loose secretive groups of men or women united in their oppression, exploitation, and fear. This era, described by Reverend

David Alben in Chapter 2, is contrasted with today's by author Donald Vining:

> It is no great problem today for one gay to identify another, at least in the urban centers. One simply goes to a gay bar, baths or film house and assumes that all those one encounters there are gay. Elsewhere one may find today's bold and liberated gays proclaiming their sexual and affectional orientation and their gay lifestyle by any of several means — from T-shirts that advertise their wearers as "Gay and Proud" to lambda signs, pink triangles, or an earring in the left ear. . . . It was not, however, always so easy for gays to single out from the mass of humanity those who would sympathize and empathize with their approach to life and sex. Certainly it was not so in my youth, when the social climate dictated discretion in announcing one's homosexuality and perhaps even more caution in approaching potential "sisters" or lovers. Mistakes in judgement could be costly in terms of both financial and physical well-being. Many a gay who erred in assuming that a Southerner's gentle manner indicated probable receptivity to advances found himself thrown out of school, discharged from a job, beaten up, jailed, disgraced, or several of the above.[2]

The clandestine and dangerous lives led by homosexual identified men and women continued into the 1960s. Prior to Stonewall, gay meccas such as San Francisco and Key West were little different than cities and towns throughout the country in their repression of lesbians and gay men.[3] Afterwards, in the midst of social turmoil — Civil Rights, the Women's Movements, Vietnam — homosexual communities emerged.[4]

It would be conventional wisdom to end these stories of sexual rebels with an essay placing their coming out experiences within the pageant of gay liberation: a celebration of the resilience of the human spirit and the power to name that which was without a name; of the shedding of false heterosexual identities; of the entry into gay communities. But a gay or lesbian identity can be as oppressive as it is liberating, as reactionary as it is revolutionary. It promises possibilities; it poses problems. Identifying oneself as a lesbian or gay man enhances self-understanding and raises social consciousness; it also limits potential sexual experiences, reinforces the norm of heterosexuality, reifies the "homosexual," and lessens opportunities for growth of the spirit. Becoming a homosexual invites further sexual categorization (e.g., butch/femme, top/bottom) and social segregation (e.g., leather, disco, male/female) within a society that too readily sorts, categorizes, and segregates people.

Through the biographies of these sexual rebels, this chapter explores questions posed by British sociologist Jeffrey Weeks:

> So what do we mean when we use the term "sexual identity"? Does it offer us the "truth of our beings," or is it an illusion? Is it a political trap that imprisons us into the rigid and exclusive categorizations of those arbiters of desire, the sexologists? or is it a necessary myth, the precondition of personal stability? Is it a snare . . . or a delusion, a cage . . . or an opportunity?[5]

ON HOMOSEXUAL COMMUNITIES, IDENTITIES AND CULTURE

To speak of *the* homosexual or *the* homosexual community is simplistic. The differences among homosexual persons have been noted throughout this study and are further evidenced in Edmund White's and Neil Miller's travels among the myriad of lesbian and gay communities.[6]

The emergence of gay liberation and the liberalization of civil codes spurred the establishment of urban communities. West Hollywood, The Castro in San Francisco, Greenwich Village's Christopher Street, Chicago's New Town, the Yonge/Wellesley area of Toronto, and Boston's Back Bay are territories marked by a more or less rigid social segregation of gay men from the outlying heterosexual and lesbian communities.[7] Lesbian areas such as Los Angeles' Echo Park-Silverlake, generally integrated within the larger feminist communities, find women who define themselves as "a community first of women and second of persons whose sexual practices are condemned by the dominant society."[8]

Though homosexual-identified women and men lived in these

metropolitan areas well before the Stonewall rebellion during the summer of '69, the contemporary terrain is contoured by the politics of sexuality and gender as expressed through a "gay culture," broadly represented through the arts, history, language, and lifestyle. Gay culture is a community of writers and poets of the past (e.g., Woolf, Isherwood, Sappho, Dickinson) as well as the present (e.g., Fierstein, Lorde, Albee, Brown). It is marked by an emerging body of "gay history" chronicling civilizations, personalities, and events of the past.[9] Gay culture is replete with formal and nonformal language represented by gay argot and icons. There also are several thousand gay-identified organizations spanning the religious, political, and social spectrums. These range from Gay Mormons and the World Congress of Gay and Lesbian Jewish Organizations to the Metropolitan Community Church and Gay/Lesbian Atheists, from the Alice B. Toklas Memorial Democratic Club to the Gay Republicans, from Dykes on Bikes to the Gay Games, from the *Advocate* to *Off Our Backs*, from the Lesbian and Gay Men's Chorus to Gay Mensa. Gay student and academic associations, bookstores and coffee-houses, courses in gay studies, radio programs and publishing houses, gay archives, and metropolitan directories listing professionals and businesses catering to the homosexual population — all attest to a burgeoning gay culture.

Gay and lesbian communities, however, are separated by psychosocial boundaries as well as geographical ones. In gay male communities, sexuality — "tamed" by AIDS and the politics of safer sex — remains the cornerstone.[10] Since Stonewall, sexuality not only has stimulated growth of these communities but has served to separate gay-identified males from other oppressed individuals. Prior to AIDS, John Lee wrote, "It is sexual pluralism and the emergence of public territories for the facilitation of numerous casual sexual encounters which ultimately energizes the development of a gay community."[11] In the midst of the AIDS crisis, Seymour Kleinberg bluntly states the gay dilemma:

> Before Stonewall, promiscuous sex was illegal, but it was no particular threat to health. If the heart and heat of gay politics has been to ensure the right to fuck who, when, and where one pleases, then the consequences now for the movement have a

rough poetic justice. The more that sex dominated the style of life, from discos to parades, with rights secured or not, the less need most men felt they had for politics — and the less others, such as lesbians, feminists, and minorities, felt the gay movement offered them.[12]

One challenge during the AIDS crisis is maintaining and strengthening gay communities on some basis other than sexuality. This may prove difficult if William Simon and John Gagnon's assertions that the homosexual community is an "impoverished cultural unit" and that homosexuals "often have only their sexual commitment in common" remain accurate.[13] It may also prove difficult if, as Dennis Altman contends, "because the new homosexual identity is promoted so assiduously through the gay media and gay marketing, many people who accept a homosexual identity feel pressure to adopt outward signs and mannerisms with which they feel uncomfortable."[14] Nevertheless, formations of grass-roots or national AIDS organizations, organized and operated by gay men with assistance from lesbians, bisexuals, and heterosexual individuals, attest to the ability of small groups within the gay community to organize themselves on a basis other than sexuality.

In contrast, within lesbian communities *gender* is the foundation for expanding social networks of women who share feminist values expressed through a variety of organizations.[15] Of course, there have been divisions and debates within women's groups; for example, Rita Mae Brown storming out of the New York office of NOW, or Del Martin proclaiming "I didn't join the women's movement to be told how to be a good girl." The intellectual, social, and political apparatus of the women's movement generally have bridged heterosexual, homosexual, and bisexual interests through common concerns of gender. Nevertheless, women in lesbian communities also face dilemmas. Reviewing nine studies that explore the relationship between lesbian identity and community, Susan Krieger summarizes

a few basic ideas: that in important ways lesbian communities define identity for their members; that they are experienced as extremely vulnerable in the larger society; that they are experienced as demanding conformity and commitment; that they require intimacy; and that they may threaten as well as support the development of individual identity.[16]

Thus, despite the different foundations of the gay and lesbian communities, both have been criticized for sacrificing personal identities on the altar of communal orthodoxy. This has had a profound impact on individuals, those communities in which they share membership, and the gay culture. For example, noted author John Rechy cautions that the very gay sensibility that allowed the arts to flourish is now vanishing. "Our art is in danger of extinction through a growing process of 'ghettoization' created by heterosexual institutions and nurtured by our own. The result is a metaphorical 'Castro Street' in which we see, and are seen by, only each other."[17]

Another example is the use of gay male argot: get it girl, trick, Mercy!, trade, Miss Thang, the sisterhood, fish, nelly, coming out, fag hag, and closet queen.[18] Some of these words, such as "trick" and "trade," are themselves borrowed from other outside groups and many serve to distance persons from one another by categorizing, separating, and sorting individuals.[19] One scholar writes:

> A group's specialized language or slang reflects much about its culture. The homosexual sub-culture, like all others, has its own slang which reflects that manner in which homosexuals perceive and structure the world in which they live. Much of the slang of the male homosexual directly reproduces traditional male attitudes toward women. For example, women are often referred to by their sexual organs; "fish" is a common term for a woman. . . . The derogatory term "fag hag" is used to describe a woman who enjoys the company of gay men. . . . There is also slang that refers pejoratively to effeminate homosexuals because they are "like women" and therefore are not worthy of considerate treatment.[20]

The process of stigmatization and ghettoization further exasperates the development of individual identity through the phenomenon of the "gay clone." Heterosexual institutions, particularly the media, have contributed to this by projecting a variety of homosexual social metaphors or icons.[21] Like Southern icons, they categorize, segregate, and sort people who lack an identity of their own. The power of these metaphors, though, lies in their ability to simplify a complex social system and to suggest codes of sexual conduct. For example, there is the image of the nelly man hidden in the gay sensibilities of *Charley's Aunt*, *Love, Sydney*, or *Boys in the Band*. There are the tragic, tortured, and self-hating characters like Martha Dobie in *The Children's Hour* and the mannish lesbian portrayed in *The Killing of Sister George*. Then there is the flamboyance depicted by Michel Serrault in *La Cage aux Folles*.

In recent years, there have been films, often by independent producers, that shatter these social metaphors (*Parting Glances*, *Torch Song Trilogy* and *Desert Hearts*). But these icons continue to dominate the gay landscape; clones, variously typecast as A-gays, dykes, and queen mothers, are found throughout homosexual communities.[22] Discussing "gay clones," a San Francisco-based writer noted, "Community and culture are a complex circulation of ideas and energy. Some folks out there, like Social Draculas, only drain that circulation. They add no new blood. Without some minimal contribution . . . we do not create, and we are candidates for clonedom."[23]

The use of divisive language and the assumption of false identities by lesbians and gay men do little for growth of the spirit. In her study of one lesbian community, social scientist Carol Warren warns, "a person who affiliates with the community and accepts a gay identity possesses a rarity in contemporary life: a total and all-encompassing core of existence by which to answer the question Who am I?"[24] And Joseph Hayes states, "Gay men might have to ask if the silent language of dress—most manifested in the clone look—might actually be a language trait preventing, rather than assisting, the liberation of the physical and the spiritual body."[25]

Homosexual communities certainly provide a much needed harbor for persons like Alston, tossed in the stormy seas of homophobia and heterosexism, to find companionship and security. But they also exact a price when individual identities are submerged. Alston's personal metamorphosis, entering the gay community as Velvetta Spike, was literal. Those years were not lost, fraudulent, or shallow—as Alston was quick to point out. He experienced love and camaraderie and his image of the homosexual world and himself expanded. But, Alston resisted the pressure to maintain the role of Velvetta Spike as he felt himself transcending it. Looking into the mirror of his soul once again, his community of sisters was all that was visible. Once again, he departed a community. Had he relented, the journey of his spirit would have ended. This pressure also was felt by Brett, as gay friends pressured him to declare his homosexuality. In Brett's words, "People were trying to label me when I didn't know myself."

The impact of communal orthodoxy also is evident in contemporary canons repeated by many persons representing the "gay community" or marketing "gay culture." Two examples are: "One out of ten persons is gay"; and "Coming out is a recognition of who you really are." Since Stonewall, these statements have become emblazoned in the homosexual creed. Few challenge or dispute these assertions. Exploring them allows us to examine the seamy side of those who advance "politically correct" ideas.

In her compelling essay about feminism, sexuality, and politically correct behavior, Muriel Dimen writes, "Politically correct is an idea that emerges from the well-meaning attempt in social movements to bring the unsatisfactory present into line with the utopian future."[26] As Dimen points out, the demands for political correctness presents feminists (and, as I argue, members of the lesbian and gay communities) with a double-edged sword:

> [Political correctness] creates visions of what is good, it seems sensible and self-respectful to try to live them out. . . . It is empowering; by psychological and ideological means, it creates the space for people to organize politically. . . . [But] when the radical becomes correct, it becomes conservative. The politically correct comes to resemble what it tries to change. For it plays on the seductiveness of accustomed ways of living, the attractiveness of orthodoxy. Its social armoring can lead the person away from self-knowing authenticity and the group towards totalitarian control.[27]

Within the lesbian and gay communities there are many examples of political correctness. Exploring two of them allows us to examine the interrelationships among homosexual communities, identities, and culture.

"How many homosexual persons are in the United States?" The orthodox response to this deceptively simple question is "Ten percent." *One in Ten* is a title of a popular anthology of writings by gay youth, *Project 10* is a school counseling project for lesbian and gay-identified adolescents in Los Angeles, and 10 percent is routinely cited in the gay media and by homosexual organizations. This claim, though, lacks the support of scholarship.

Given the diversity of the homosexual populations and the social taboo associated with homosexuality, "counting homosexuals" is not a simple matter of examining the latest census data (although the 1990 census may provide some evidence for the number of same-sex couples living together) or tallying those women who sport butch hairstyles and men who purchase pastel shirts. Further, attempts to develop a nationally representative sample of adult sexual behavior have been short-circuited by the now too familiar triumvirate of conservative politicians, fundamentalist ministers, and an apathetic public.

When questioned about the source of the often cited 10 percent figure, some cite the Kinsey data of the late forties. However, Kinsey and his colleagues focused on sexual contact and frequency, *not* sexual identity. Kinsey's famous scale is based on his subjects' sexual experience and "psychic" responses to individuals of the same sex. According to Kinsey, 10 percent of white males rated five or six on this scale for at least three years; eight percent scored six, and four percent exhibited exclusively homosexual behavior and reactions throughout their adolescent and adult lives. The figures for women were lower. Of course, if the claim was simply that the figures represented overt behavior and psychosexual responses (e.g., "About ten percent of the population currently engages in same-sex behavior.") then we would be on more solid ground — although, the disturbing distributions of Kinsey's samples as well as the age of the data merit concern.[28] But, to represent these figures in terms of a gay identity confuses behavior with identity.

In a system of pluralist politics with members of the legislature, judiciary, executive branch, and the media accustomed to thinking in terms of voter blocs and minority rights, 10 percent sloganizing becomes tempting. Political exigency overrides scholarly integrity. Nevertheless, scholars like John DeCecco, director of the Center for Research in Education and Sexuality at San Francisco State University, have vehemently opposed winning "acceptance of homosexuality through projection of a sanitized 'minority' image." He continues:

> The minority view is anchored to an idea of homosexuality, over 125 years old, as a core, personal identity, a concept for which, in all that time, there has never been any valid reliable genetic, hormonal, cortical, physiological, or psychological data. Moreover, *minority* is basically a quantitative concept, implying the existence of a smaller group embedded in a far larger group, the majority. Yet, it is difficult for many of us to believe that the majority of individuals over their life spans do not count among their most emotionally intimate and physically sensual relationships those with men and those with women. The real minority may be the few individuals whose relationships, heterosexual or homosexual, have been flawlessly and resolutely monosexual.[29]

The politics of minority rights makes the figure of 25 million lesbian and gay Americans compelling to any gay activist lobbying politicians. But, should any less concern be given to an oppressed minority because it represents five percent of the population, or, for that matter, only five persons? Clearly, the moral legitimacy of a minority's claim for fair treatment is not contingent upon its size. The use of the 10 percent figure, even if accurate, undermines the justifiable claims of those minorities who, through political alchemy, cannot transform their minority status into such an impressive, though illusory, constituency. It creates a community on the basis of questionable arithmetic and, as we shall see, through the reproduction of a homosexual identity.

The forging of homosexual persons into the lesbian and gay communities is the essence of "coming out." Coming out into these communities by Henry and 'Lizabeth was a sigh of relief: "There was just this tremendous release," Henry said. Similarly, 'Lizabeth stated "It's like a weight has been lifted off my shoulders." When coming out into lesbian and gay communities, many participants experienced what Carol Warren has described as the "phenomenological shock of encountering a stigmatized group and finding that they appear 'normal' and are not distinguished by bizarre physical markings of extraordinary appearance and behavior."[30] For example, William learned that not all gay men were like Donnie, and Terry's entrance into an informal "support group" of gay students resulted in his learning that his best friend was gay. They also learned the norms and roles within their homosexual communities and the canons of their culture. Using gay male argot, Terry and his friends communicated in a "code" among themselves while "putting down" their detractors. And, Henry states that "if I would have had actually sat down and honestly thought about it, I would have realized that I was gay much earlier."

Henry's statement, repeated by most of these sexual rebels, is the "I am because I am" canon of gay culture — the belief, articulated by Langston Hughes, that "God, nature or somebody made them that way." Based on this orthodoxy, coming out is a critical state in identity formation that "should help a person identify in a positive way with what she or he *is*."[31] A variety of scholars have elaborated on stages of the development and maintenance of homosexual identity beginning with the awareness of homoerotic feelings to the maintenance of a positive gay identity.[32] One of them, Diane Richardson, writes "in order for her [the lesbian] to be accepted within this subculture she must continue to maintain such an identity. In other words the social norms of the homosexual world serve to both affirm and confirm an individual's identification as lesbian."[33]

This confirmation process poses dangers recently explicated by scholars and therapists who have adopted a more constructionist orientation in understanding homosexuality. For example, one therapist writes:

> In my clinical experience I have met 14-year-olds who assert that the reason for their homosexuality is "I just am," and older men who object to my using terms such as "coming out" because "it implies someone wasn't *that way* all along."
> . . . Despite these essentialist beliefs of patients, I believe that

clinicians should take constructionist theories seriously. To do so provides people with a personal and political history of their lives that emphasizes the "choices" they have made — consciously or not.[34]

The canon of essentialism — "I just am" — permeates gay and lesbian communities. For example, Malcolm professes to have known he was going to be homosexual at the age of four and most Southerners expressed relief after acknowledging their "sexual orientation." Under the heading "Choosing to be Gay," the *Advocate* discussed John DeCecco's remarks in *USA Today*: "He reportedly asserted that people are born with a capacity of all kinds of sexuality but that most people limit behavior because of socialization. The trend toward 'biologizing' homosexuality, he said, is the result of a political desire to label people 'gay' or 'straight.'"[35] Dave Walter goes on to write:

> But what I find attractive about DeCecco's line of reasoning is its implied contention that sexual orientation is not only irrelevant but contrived. If we simply did away with the concepts of "gay" and "straight" and made sexuality a nonissue, then self-acceptance and societal acceptance and gay rights would also become nonissues. That is utopian thinking, however, and pushing a "we can choose to be gay" argument would, at least for the foreseeable future, provide us with more setback than advances.[36]

Dismissed as utopian, this statement illustrates the political basis for the "I am because I am" canon. Such pragmatism, however, allows for little tolerance of ideas or persons who adopt different sexual identities.

Bisexuality is a case in point. Several persons in this study — Nathaniel, Olivia, Carlton, and 'Lizabeth — consistently identified themselves (using the Klein Sexual Orientation Grid described in the Appendix) as bisexual. For Nathaniel it may have been more a bisexual front ("When I got Delta, it was like a cover. I was having sex with a man but for security I got a girlfriend"). But, Carlton simply declares, "I like both sexes." Kimberly, on the sexual borderline between bisexuality and homosexuality, describes a homosexual person as someone "who has chosen an alternative life-style." She adds, "I see an attractive guy and say, 'I wouldn't mind going out with him.' I'm still finding out about my sexuality. I'm still learning about myself."

Some lesbians and gay-identified men may interpret such biographies as fraudulent and bisexuality as damaging to the homosexual rights movement. Historian Martin Duberman wrote, "Most of my homosexual friends regard my admiration for bisexuals as suspect. They view self-designated bisexuals as people suffering from a failure of nerve, an unwillingness to take on the still onerous, still stigmatized image associated with being homosexual."[37] Nevertheless, after reviewing biological, anthropological, and historical research, Duberman concludes, "human beings will behave sexually as their culture tells them they should behave — and both the social cues and the behavior have varied through time."[38]

Scholars who make such assertions find little support from lesbian and gay rights leaders. The costs of such orthodoxy, though, should be apparent to all. "Having to think in terms of immediate political exigencies may limit us," states popular gay historian Jonathan Katz in an interview following the publication of the *Gay/Lesbian Almanac*; it "prevents us from raising issues that question current gay-movement orthodoxies."[39]

The identities of the new Advocate Man or Amazonian Woman born out of the struggles of Stonewall, nourished through homosexual culture, protected in homosexual communities, and maturing during the AIDS crisis are dependent upon these orthodoxies. Challenging these orthodoxies questions the legitimacy of these identities and threatens the existence of homosexual communities. These sexual identities and the communities which give them meaning have served us well, but as social artifacts, they also pose problems. One is confusing social artifacts with sexual destinies. Jeffrey Weeks explains this error well:

> Identity is not a destiny but a choice. But in a culture where homosexual desires, female or male, are still execrated and denied, the adoption of lesbian or gay identities inevitably constitutes a *political* choice. These identities are not expressions of secret essences. They are self-creations, but they are

creations on ground not freely chosen but laid out by history. So homosexual identities illustrate the play of constraint and opportunity, necessity and freedom, power and pleasure. Sexual identities seem necessary in the contemporary world as starting-points for a politics around sexuality. But the form they take is not predetermined. In the end, therefore, they are not so much about who we really are, what our sex dictates. They are about what we want to be and could be.[40]

Sexual identity as a "starting point" is a useful metaphor for understanding both the liberatory nature and oppressive potential of these identities. Laud Humphreys, tracing the emergence of the homosexual communities from a subculture prior to 1969 to a satellite culture a decade later, noted that the "Creation and maintenance of valid identity is the most important task with which we occupy ourselves."[41] For participants like Terry, Norma Jean, Olivia, and Malcolm, the Southern culture's emphasis on family, community, and religion were at odds with their sexual feelings and behaviors. In adolescence each of these sexual rebels "tries on identities that emerge from the cultural material available to [them] and tests them by making appropriate announcements."[42] During adolescence, Norma Jean tries on the identity of a junior ROTC brat and later finds herself bound by the live oak tree before being liberated by foster parents and a new social identity. Malcolm assumes the identity of an honors student in the ninth grade while undergoing defeminization. Sexual identities were also tried on. As Alston stood in front of his bathroom mirror, when Terry walked onto the prom dance floor, and as Everetta stood up in front of her therapy group, each announced her or his identity.

Humphreys continues, "To the extent that the cultural womb in which identity is formed is impoverished or limited, personal construction of valid identity will be thwarted and circumscribed."[43] While Southern culture thwarted their same-sex feelings and behaviors, it provided gender, regional, and racial identities for many of these participants as the unique biographies of Jacob, Norma Jean, and Vince revealed. The homosexual subculture though has provided values, models, heritage, and language which named and honored their same-sex feelings and behaviors.

But, as Humphreys concludes, "The emergence of a rich and varied satellite culture profoundly affects the quality and range of identities formed by its members."[44] However, it is the existence of this very rich and varied satellite culture coupled to the canons of orthodoxy driven by the exigency of "identity politics"[45] that jeopardizes the evolution of individuals and gay communities. The creation of the homosexual, despite the best intentions of pioneers such as Magnus Hirschfield, Havelock Ellis, and Karl Benkert, was a nineteenth century version of social control.[46] Political activists have long rejected using "homosexual" and advocated the term "gay," as witnessed in their long battle with the *New York Times*. One activist writes:

> [I]n speaking of ourselves adjectivally as *gay*, we in effect nullify the power of priests and psychiatrists to control our lives by stigmatizing us as *sodomites* and *homosexuals*. We become free spirits who cultivate an ancient art form long considered subversive by church and state. . . . Above all we acquire a history.[47]

Moving from classification to identification, gay replaced homosexual as the preferred human signifier for same-sex experiences in everyday social discourse. Nevertheless, sexual interest remains the basis for identification. Like the "working class," "gays and lesbians" *exist*. The task for activists is to transform their sexual interest into identities of community interest—in Marxist phraseology, from a class-in-itself to a class-for-itself.

Homosexual communities are less a celebration of cultural uniqueness than they are visible examples of the power of "compulsory heterosexuality"[48] to shape social realities of even the most critically-minded gay activist. They have become our twentieth century communities of social control.

"Homosexual/heterosexual" or "gay/straight" are dichotomous categories that reject the human capacity for choice, that simplify the complex connections among body, mind, and culture, and deny the essence of the spirit common to us all. These categories give the straight and gay person a sense of place, security, and identity. These categories allow each modern profession to apply its trade:

psychiatrists can treat, ministers can save, social workers can counsel, activists can organize, and advertisers can sell.

For example, the commodification of sexuality coupled with the recognition of the largely untapped market of affluent gay males has seen a burgeoning corporate-gay alliance in the construction of the new gay male. "What began as a street fight in 1969," notes freelance writers Nathan Fain and Brandon Jedell, "has become a calm conversation in phrases corporate America understands." Though these writers and probably the majority of gay men welcome this special attention and economic leverage, they ignore or downplay the ultimate costs and true beneficiaries. Kenneth Plummer makes this latter point succinctly:

> [T]he liberationists themselves have started to become their own source of regulation. "Homosexuals" were once regulated and defined by "experts"; now these experts need no longer do it, for the homosexual has assumed that role for himself or herself. Ghettoized and reified, "the homosexual" remains firmly under control in "liberated" capitalism.[49]

From the subtle appeal to gay men in Soloflex advertisements to the aggressive marketing strategies of Absolut vodka, homosexuals have been transformed from a 19th century medical image to an acknowledged demographic in the offices of Madison Avenue advertising agencies.[50] In the 20-year struggle to make Main Street cross Castro Street, Castro Street is *becoming* Main Street.

Thus, it should come as little surprise that the immediate task of maintaining and expanding homosexual communities does not always parallel the long-term interest of the individual. Homosexual architects and practitioners of the politics of pluralism reject a dialectical conception of human and cultural development. Change — either at the personal or social level — is viewed in its most pragmatic form: the forging of shifting alliances using tactics that maximize the likelihood of success. And the success — admittedly never an all-or-nothing proposition — usually comes in half-loaf compromises. Through persistence, however, progressive gains do result; in order to record these gains, however, one must play by the rules of the game. In the politics of sexuality, the game provides space to legalize a category of behavior but not to challenge the category itself. However, the transformation of an individual or a society comes when those playing by the rules realize that it is the game itself that must be changed. Thus, the most important contribution of two decades of community building and coming out since Stonewall will be the realization that the journey of the spirit requires deconstruction of the very categories which provide us sexual identities and the destruction of the very communities which have given us our collective identities.

The process of engaging in the struggle, not the results of the struggle, is the key for social and spiritual growth. The importance of the gay rights movement of the past generation has been the creation of communities, identities, and a culture; its success, however, must be judged on the ability of lesbians and gay men to let go and to journey beyond these social artifacts. Like Everetta and her blue jean jacket, the task of letting go will not be easy — no step in the journey of the spirit ever is.

JOURNEYS OF THE SPIRIT

Erotic attraction to members of the same sex within a Southern culture that lacks toleration for such feelings makes one a sexual rebel. This is a gift, as well as a burden. The sense of difference mentioned by many sexual rebels forced them to peer from the outside into a world that their classmates took for granted. Feeling sexually different in a society which stressed sexual sameness placed them in assorted conflicts which each struggled to resolve in his or her unique way. These struggles mark the journeys of the spirit.

At the beginning of this century an Armenian mystic, G. I. Gurdjieff, spoke of the importance of acquiring a "knowledge-of-being" — transcending the dream-like state of existence normally referred to as consciousness. Gurdjieff argued that ordinary people must work on themselves through the "reflecting of reality in one's attention upside down."[51] That is, as human beings we must become aware of our emotions, conscious of our bodies, and mindful of our thoughts through systematic self-observations and rigorous self-discipline.

The journey of the spirit is an exploration of, so to speak, a house of many selves, of which sexuality is but one, albeit important, room. The importance of feeling sexually different is not that we are, in fact, sexually different, but that in a particular historical moment within a specific culture those feelings have particular personal and social meanings. These meanings place us outside the world of respectability. This gift of difference prevents us from becoming too comfortable in an ephemeral world. This difference is our gift to seeing the world upside down.

This gift of difference, of course, is not reserved for the homosexual-identified being. Recent work by black female novelists have depicted the opportunities for self-understanding that accompany racial difference. Avery Johnson, a middle-aged widow in *Praisesong for the Widow*, goes on an inward journey, discarding the "shameful stone of false values" as she explores African wisdom preserved in the collective memories and rituals of the black Southern woman's collective culture. The abuse experienced by Celie at the hands of black men and rooted in racism and sexism is transcended through her sensual and spiritual relationship with Shug in *The Color Purple*.

These characters recognized that what is commonly referred to as "self" or the "ego" is really an amalgamation of many different selves whose voices reflect different states of being. The voices we tend to hear most are the most uninteresting (and familiar) parts of ourselves. These are the voices that allow us to get caught up in the most mundane aspects of everyday life. John Fortunato, in his book *Embracing the Exile: Healing Journeys of Gay Christians*, speaks of the importance of letting go of these voices of the ego: the "desire for worldy goods, power, status, relationships; the need for affirmation by other people; the need to keep our egos reassured that we exist by constantly defining ourselves apart from the other; the need to define ourselves at all; the need for the dualistic thinking that gives rise to the I-Thou dichotomy; the need for the security that leads to such a dualistic world view."[52]

The challenge is to become dead to what we have become in order to be resurrected into what we have the potential of being. For those wedded to gay, black, female, or Southern identities, the transcendence of these social selves may seem absurd, apolitical, or utopian. These identities, like the communities upon which they are built, are, to borrow a title from Christopher Lasch, comfortable havens in a heartless world. But, as James Baldwin noted in his introduction to *Nobody Knows My Name*, these havens exact a price:

> [N]othing is more frightening than to be divested of a crutch. The question of who I was was not solved because I had removed myself from the social forces which menaced me. . . . The question of who I was had at last become a personal question, and the answer was found in me. I think there is always something frightening about this realization. . . . And yet, I could not escape the knowledge, though God knows I tried, that if I was still in need of havens, my journey had been for nothing. Havens are high-priced. The price exacted of the haven-dweller is that he contrives to delude himself into believing that he has found a haven. It would seem, unless one looks more deeply at the phenomenon, that most people are able to delude themselves and get through their lives quite happily. But I still believe that the unexamined life is not worth living . . .[53]

Being different nudges us outside the perceived normalcy of everyday life to reflect upon our unexamined lives; it affords us the opportunity to see things not as they appear to be and the courage to peer into selves that we wish we might not see. Being different, though, is only an opportunity; one must still decide whether to take it. One of Gurdjieff's translators, Maurice Nicol, provides a useful metaphor:

> It is always a question of inner decision, of inner choice . . . Better states belong to higher levels of yourself. They are in you, as different levels. You can live in the basement or higher up. . . . But you have to see all this for yourself and get to know where you are in yourself. One has to learn not only whom to live within oneself but where to live in oneself.[54]

The absence of an identifiable self, like that of Joe Christmas in Faulkner's *Light in August*, prevents one from entering the house;

clinging to the crutch of our external identities prevents us from exploring the many rooms of the Self. This is why *exploring* one's sexuality is so important and *being* a homosexual is so fruitless. Each movement in life is an opportunity to journey into the spirit; each presents a crisis. Struggling with sexual identity is one example. Each crisis affords opportunities for knowledge-of-being. Each crisis gives rise to other opportunities (crises) from which further knowledge-of-being may result. Some lives may be composed of many movements; others just one or two. But, like a symphonic composition, it is the arrangement of the notes and the quality of the music, not the number of movements, that distinguishes a truly fine performance. And, as the late philosopher Alan Watts so eloquently pointed out, it is at life's end that our fellow travelers applaud our completed performances.

At each point, though, we may hide in our haven of identity and journey no further. Gendered, sexual, regional, or racial identities, as recent feminist and post-structuralist scholars have detailed,[55] are neither biological nor universal. They are constructs necessary to begin social-self understanding through the peeling away of the veneer of culture and ideology.

Too often, being homosexual is not integrating one's same-sex feelings into oneself but defining oneself by those same-sex feelings. Losing one's identity within the homosexual community is no more healthy than losing it within the heterosexual community from which we have departed. This is also true for those who cling to racial, gender, and regional identities. For example, Nathaniel and Jacob struggled with the "twoness" of their identities. From Mrs. Green's classroom to Black Together, Jacob embraced his black self while Nathaniel "never did get into Fat Boys strings," identifying himself more with upper-middle class whites. The question is not whether one accepted or rejected his "racial identity" but the degree to which these identities were used as a prism to peer into the Self. This search for Self is the crisis of identity depicted throughout American literature. It is found in African-American novels ranging from *Invisible Man* and *A Visitation of Spirits* to *Their Eyes Were Watching God* and *Zamie, A New Spelling of My Name*, portrayed in Southern characters like McCuller's Dr. Copeland, Wolfe's Eugene Gant, and Capote's Joel Knox, and described by feminist writers such as Kate Chopin and Lillian Smith. The searcher for Self, though, risks the trap of dwelling forever in an identity which in truth is no more than a temporary shelter. Both elements — change and stasis, movement and the momentary sense of certainty — are well expressed by Vince: "The Vince I am now is not the one I started out to be nor the one you will like, but it's the one I am."

To paraphrase Carl Jung, only personal integrity can guarantee that any journey does not turn out to be an absurd adventure.[56] That personal integrity rests on the willingness to explore each one of the many rooms or selves that we mistakenly label "our self." Each room which we explore marks an important part of our spiritual journey; to languish in any one after it has been explored is to stop journeying. Or in the words of Oscar Wilde:

> [H]e never fell into the error of arresting his intellectual development by any formal acceptance of creed or system, or of mistaking, for a house in which to live, an inn that is but suitable for the sojourn of a night, or for a few hours of a night in which there are no stars and the moon in travail.[57]

Others, though, looking around the room "through all the nooks and crannies of the cosmic map — if [they] dare to look and experience — can't help but be overwhelmed,"[58] so they elect to remain in a dusty corner. Some explore the entire room; others, like David escaping *Giovanni's Room*, leave with the room unexplored. In William's words, "Once I dealt with my homosexuality I would just sort of not think about it. I put it in another little compartment and shut the door." This compartmentalization, too, stymies spiritual development and prevents holistic integration.

The New Age spirituality of the "radical fairy movement" recognizes the importance of this journey of the spirit. Arguing that the movement for homosexual equality is dead and that the roots of the spirit-world have been cut, Mitch Walker talks about gay identities:

Humans don't come into the world with an identity; this identity must be made. Adult humans have to have such an identity because this is the source of *ontological security*. . . . These identity myths originate outside the individual and come in standardized forms like plastic molds. Because each individual is unique, such myths deny the true nature and potentials of that person. . . . The process of coming out is a quest for ontological security through the resolution of conflicting self-identities. At this point the Myth of the Homosexual comes into play. The Myth is a way of interpreting the aberrant feelings from the point of view of the falseself system. Since it's the only available myth providing a way of understanding the gay-defended situation, the confused person (and everybody else) comes to see themself as a "homosexual."[59]

Walker goes on to write, "I see gayness as a door, a source, a spirit, a lover, a teacher, or rather as sourcing, enspiriting, loving, teaching. It spirits me away somewhere magickal [sic], strange, profound."[60] However, identifying one's gayness as a door through which to commence a journey of the spirit is vastly different than placing gayness in the center of that journey (which Walker calls ROIKA: "the spirit-vision which has always been part of homosexual-identified people"[61]).

There is no such thing as the gay spirit; there is only the spirit. Much like the fabled superiority of "gay sensibility," advocates of the gay spirit, such as Mitch Walker, John Burnside, Mark Thompson, and Harry Hay, and movements like the radical faeries and the quarterly magazine *RFD*, posit an essential difference between themselves and heterosexual humanity. Harry Hay states the position well:

When we begin to truly love and respect Great Mother Nature's gift to us of gayness, we'll discover that the bondage of our childhood and adolescence in the trials and tribulations (dark forests to traverse with no one to guide us) of *neitherness* was actually an apprenticeship she had designed for teaching her children new cutting edges of consciousness and social change. . . . *It is from this spiritual* neitherness *that we draw our capacities as* mediators between the seen and the unseen, *as berdache priests and shaman seers, as artists and architects; as scientists, teachers, and as designers of the possibles . . .*[62]

Gay identity, like Southern identity, is an elaborate social fiction. The mind of the South, like the homosexualization of America, transforms contempt into distinction and refashions exiles into champions.[63] This dusting of reality by the wings of a fairy deludes us into believing that our differentness is our specialness. But, to paraphrase Buckminster Fuller, differentness is a verb — it energizes the journey of our spirit but it is not our spirit. As human beings we are all bestowed with the gift of differentness: sexual, racial, genderal, regional, and so forth. These differences are the portals toward knowledge-of-being; they allow us to see the world upside down; they are the moon and the stars that allow us to chart our journey.

REFERENCE NOTES

1. Hughes, 1958:105.
2. Vining, 1982:24.
3. For popular histories of such cities during this era, see: Hansen, Forrester and Bird, 1967; Sprague, 1983.
4. A variety of scholars have explored a variety of gay/lesbian communities including: Barnhart, 1975; Fitzgerald, 1986; Humphreys, 1970; Krieger, 1982; McCoy and Hicks, 1979; Ponse, 1978; Ponse, 1980; Russo, 1982; Tanner, 1978; Warren, 1974; Wolf, 1979. Gay historical studies during the past two decades examining the post World War II movement have chronicled the different strands of the homosexual rights movement ranging from the assimilationist tactics of the 1950s to the militancy of the 1970s and the AIDS challenge of the 1980s. (Adam, 1987; Bate, 1982; Cole, 1970; Darsey, 1981a; D'Emilio, 1983b; Escoffier, 1985; Licata, 1978; Licata, 1980/81; Levin, 1983; Marotta, 1981; Teal, 1971; Weiss and Schiller, 1988.) For more personal histories of these periods, see: Bell, 1971; Gooch, 1984; Karlinsky, 1983; Murphy, 1971; Norse, 1984.
5. Weeks, 1987:32.
6. Miller, 1989; White, 1983.
7. For explorations into these communities, see: Castells and Murphy, 1982; Kopkind, 1985; Lee, 1979; Levine, 1979.
8. McCoy and Hicks, 1979:66.
9. See, for example: Adam, 1987; Cavin, 1985; Grahn, 1985; Grier and

Reid, 1976; Katz, 1976; Lauritsen and Thorstad, 1974; Licata, 1978; Murphy, 1988.

10. The rapid emergence of grass roots organizations like the Gay Men's Health Crisis in New York City or the Names Project Quilt in response to the AIDS crisis, is a result of this gay infrastructure and has further served to develop it.

11. Lee, 1979:192. See also Padgug, 1987.

12. Kleinberg, 1987:136.

13. Simon and Gagnon, 1973:153.

14. Altman, 1982:103.

15. Lockard, 1986.

16. Krieger, 1982:105.

17. Rechy, 1984:26.

18. Many of these words have been used for decades by homosexual persons. See, for example: Chesbro, 1981; Cory and LeRoy, 1963; Legman, 1941; Rodgers, 1972. Lesbian and gay scholarship has also focused on language. See, for example: Hayes, 1981; Goodwin, 1984; Grahn, 1984; Taub and Leger, 1984; Tucker, 1982.

19. Crew, 1978; Hayes, 1976; Hayes, 1981; Stanley, 1970.

20. Blachford, 1981:188-189. A similar point is made by Kleinberg, 1987.

21. Bronski, 1984; Laermer, 1985; Russo, 1979; Wood, 1987.

22. See, for example: S. Berry, 1982; McDonald, 1982; Taub and Leger, 1984; Warren, 1974.

23. Alfred, 1982:22.

24. Warren, 1974:162.

25. Hayes, 1981:38.

26. Dimen, 1984:138-139.

27. Dimen, 1984:140-141.

28. Harry, 1984.

29. DeCecco, 1981:22-23.

30. Warren, 1974:156.

31. Jandt and Darsey, 1981:25 (my italics).

32. See, for example: Cass, 1979; Coleman, 1981/82; Dank, 1971; Plummer, 1975; Troiden, 1979. These and other studies are reviewed in Minton and McDonald (1983/84).

33. Richardson, 1981:119.

34. Hart, 1984:41-42.

35. Walter, 1989:23.

36. Walter, 1989:23.

37. Duberman, 1986:249.

38. Duberman, 1986:259.

39. Hall, 1983:39.

40. Weeks, 1987:47.

41. Humphreys, 1979:143.

42. Humphreys, 1979:144.
43. Humphreys, 1979:145.
44. Humphreys, 1979:145.
45. Alcoff, 1988.
46. Brown, 1970; Foucault, 1978; Hocquenghem, 1978; Kinsman, 1987; Lesselier, 1987; Plummer, 1981; Weeks, 1981.
47. Stone, 1981:21.
48. Rich, 1980.
49. Plummer, 1981:55.
50. *The Economist*, 1982; Russo, 1981; Stabiner, 1982.
51. Gurdjieff, 1950:1233.
52. Fortunato, 1982:73.
53. Baldwin, 1961:11-12.
54. Nicol, 1957:162.
55. Bulkin, Pratt and Smith, 1984; Caplan, 1987; Foucault, 1978; Greenberg, 1988; Irigaray, 1985; Kristeva, 1980; 1981; Laurentis, 1984. For useful reviews of this scholarship, see: Alcoff, 1988; Culler, 1982; Dreyfus and Rabinow, 1983; B. Martin, 1982; Mitchell and Rose, 1982.
56. Jung, 1955:93.
57. Wilde, 1926:147.
58. Fortunato, 1982:102.
59. M. Walker, 1980:16, 32.
60. M. Walker, 1980:2.
61. M. Walker, 1980:35.
62. Hay, 1987:284-285.
63. Cash, 1941; Altman, 1982.

APPENDIX

Research Methods, Methodological Issues, and Participant Data

Facts do not organize themselves into concepts and theories just be being looked at; indeed, except within the framework of concepts and theories, there are no scientific facts but only chaos. There is an inescapable a priori element in all scientific work. Questions must be asked before answers can be given. The questions are all expressions of our interest in the world; they are at bottom valuations.

Gunnar Myrdal, *Objectivity in Social Science Research*[1]

Research, as Myrdal correctly noted, is about values. The choice of topics, research questions, methodological designs, data analysis methods and interpretations reflect the values of the researcher and the social scientific community at some point in time. Research, too, is political. Not only are projects funded (or not funded) on the basis of ideological agendas, but the purposes for which the research is conducted and the beneficiaries of such research also fall within the political domain.[2]

Acknowledging the importance of values and politics in conducting social science research, this section discusses several methodological issues including sampling methods and reliability of responses. The second part of this section displays a variety of data in both aggregate and disaggregate forms. The display of these data in

431

a variety of tables and figures provides the reader with an opportunity to test the adequacy of my interpretations as well as to explore hypotheses which I may not have considered.

QUESTIONS OF METHOD

The process of collecting qualitative data is somewhat different from more conventional social science research methodology.[3] The qualitative inquirer does not have a set of null hypotheses to reject. Although general questions are posed at the outset of this type of inquiry, *a-priori* hypotheses and pre-selected data collection methods to test them are not part of qualitative inquiry. The qualitative inquirer begins with general questions and, *as data are collected and analyzed*, develops and refines specific research hypotheses and further data collection strategies.

I began my work by talking informally with members of the lesbian and gay community in South Carolina about their experiences. During this time, I reviewed the literature on homosexuality and research designs. Based upon this preliminary work, in the autumn of 1986, I began interviewing self-identified Southern gay men and lesbians who had attended high school within the past 10 years. Participants were sought through community associations, friendship networks, newspaper advertisements, and gay-owned businesses throughout South Carolina.

During the next year and a half, I interviewed 36 individuals. I purposively constructed a diverse participant pool with respect to race, gender, and educational background. Consequently, some persons who expressed an interest in participating were politely turned down and individuals in under-represented categories were actively recruited. Each of the 36 persons in this study participated in a three-hour research session consisting of an open-ended, audiotaped interview and the administration of two standardized questionnaires.[4] Participants were assured of confidentiality and anonymity.

Americans' fondness for generalizations, ranging from oft-quoted quips of Benjamin Franklin to assuring assertions of Ronald Reagan, and our fetish for numbers, ranging from IQ to sports statistics, appears unabated. For those who share this belief, interviewing more people and seeking even greater diversity might have been desirable. One hundred interviews *might* have been better than 36. Interviews with a gay Cherokee man, a black lesbian fluent in Gullah growing up on the sea islands, and a white lesbian Debutante may well have provided additional insight. The power of qualitative data, however, lies not in the number of people interviewed but in the researcher's ability to know a few people well. The test of qualitative inquiry is not its unearthing of a seemingly endless multitude of unique individuals but illuminating the lives of a few well chosen individuals. The idiographic often provides greater insight than the nomothetic.

Some qualities of the human experience transcend culture, region, and even time. These include joy and sorrow, hope and fear, hate and love, courage and timidity, shallowness and self-understanding. These human qualities, whether conveyed through the poetry of Allen Ginsberg or Audre Lorde or the ethnography of Marvin Harris or Evelyn Hooker, I believe are more enduring and heart-felt than statistics or generalizations of fleeting interest.

This study raises other methodological issues. One is sampling. Researcher Stephen Morin has written, "[T]here is no such thing as a representative sample of lesbians and gay men. Researchers are sampling what is essentially a hidden or invisible population. Therefore, when homosexual samples are used, expanded subject descriptions that permit adequate replication are needed."[5] In this study, 26 of the participants are white, one-half are female, and two-thirds had attended or were attending college at the time of the interview. Ages of these 36 lesbians and gay men ranged from 18 to 28; the average was 23. One-third of these participants' parents had been divorced. Five were the only child; the average number of siblings of the participants was three. All but four were native-born South Carolinians. All but six had attended public schools throughout their elementary and secondary education. The families of most of these participants had belonged to fundamentalist religious groups—the vast majority (20) being Southern Baptists. Two of these participants have aristocratic backgrounds; eight were members of families who were below the poverty line or classified as the working poor. The majority had middle-class family backgrounds. Seventy percent had attended college or were attending college at the time of the interview. Finally, 17 had labelled themselves "homosexual" prior to their eighteenth birthday, and 80 percent did not begin to feel good about their sexual identity until after this age. As Morin has suggested, I provide detailed descriptions of the participants through thumbnail portraits displayed in the second section of this chapter.

Sampling a homosexual population is certainly difficult. Despite the recent advances in gay and lesbian research and methodology, there are no reliable demographic data.[6] This lack of data attests to the social prejudice rampant in the heterosexual community and the self-imposed silence of many homosexual-identified men and women. Since this study's sample was drawn exclusively from a Southern population, generalizations beyond the South are certainly unwarranted. Within the South itself, this sample of rich and poor, black and white, rural and urban Southerners is probably reflective of this region's youthful gay and lesbian population.

Another important methodological issue is the reliability of responses provided by the young adult participants about their experiences while growing up and attending school. Data gathered through retrospective studies are, of course, subject to distortion due to the passage of time and the changing mindset of the respondent. These historical and personal biases were addressed in several ways.

First, the complimentary use of interview techniques and survey instruments resurrected a variety of feelings, attitudes, and meanings held during high school. Participants responded first to a general set of survey questions about events and activities common to high school life (e.g., involvement in school clubs and association with particular types of students). The completion of these items required participants mentally to place themselves back into their high school years. During the subsequent interview, questions about these experiences generated reflective and detailed responses. Following these two phases, participants were then asked to complete a second questionnaire which inquired into their attitudes and feelings held during high school. Through participants' immersion in this research session and the layering of surveys and interviews during the session, the historical bias was minimized.

Second, if sexuality is an important component of an adolescent's life, which was one of the working hypotheses of this study, then the richness and accuracy of memories tied to that component should be greater than memories of the more mundane aspects of everyday school life. Memories of social activities and poignant events are often more readily recalled than those classroom lessons which are never carried over into adult life. Data gathered during this study supported this position. Many of the participants became visibly moved as they recalled their struggle with their sexual identities.

Third, there was a brief gap in time between many of the participants' present age and their high school experience (mean age of participants was 23). This gap is important because, as other researchers have noted:

> Even reports from young people themselves can be inaccurate, made on the basis of defenses that do not allow them to be objective. In other words, it is often easier for persons to be objective about their pasts only after they have survived them and are in a position to view them more dispassionately.[7]

There is, however, little doubt that interviews with these participants a decade from now would reveal differing interpretations and constructions of these events. The issue is not how closely their reported biographies as adults correspond to those they might have reported as adolescents but how these participants make personal meaning of these experiences. The construction of identities, not the description of growing up is at the heart of *Growing Up Gay in the South*.

There was another reason for not drawing upon a sample of homosexual-identified adolescents. It is probable that only a small number of high school students have acquired a homosexual identity and that fewer of them have adjusted to it. Certainly, those from whom the data would be gathered would not be a representative sample. Some researchers report that those who "come out" early differ in many important ways from those who adopt a homosexual identity in later life.[8] They tend to be less educated, have a greater likelihood of professional referrals (judicial, psychological, medical), and have more interest in emotional intimacy. Given this obvious sampling bias, a preferable method is to gain information from respondents who are somewhat older.[9]

Data gathered during this study clearly demonstrate that a broad spectrum of sexual populations exists within the school setting: first, those who openly identify themselves as lesbian and gay, second, those who privately acknowledge (e.g., to close friends) their homosexual feelings; third, those who personally acknowledge but tell no one about these feelings; fourth, those who have same-sex feelings but choose to repress or deny them; fifth, those who occasionally engage in homosexual activities but identify themselves as heterosexual; and, sixth those who have had no sexual contact with or physical attraction toward members of the same gender. Clearly, had this sample been drawn exclusively from adolescent homosexual students, only the first two groups would have been selected. Such a sample would certainly have skewed data analyses and interpretations.

DATA PRESENTATION

Thumbnail Portraits

The richness and depth of data collected through qualitative methods far outdistance those collected through simple empirical tools. This very richness and depth, however, makes reporting of data cumbersome and lessens the likelihood of readers coming to alternative conclusions. In order to compensate for this weakness, thumbnail portraits are provided for the 36 participants in this study. Table 1 describes the demographic characteristics of each participant. The ages of participants' first sexual experiences and significant homoerotic events, together with their sexual identity pattern code, are presented in Table 2. Finally, Table 3 notes a variety of psychosocial behaviors reported by these participants during their high school years.

By examining these data the reader may be able to explore patterns in *Growing Up Gay in the South* as well as provide alternative explanations to those noted in the commentaries. To facilitate this process, the book's index includes names of all the participants with

TABLE 1

Demograhic Data of Participants

Participant	Age	Race	Gender	Educ[*]	SES[**]	Siblings	Family Church	Divorced Parents?	Father[***] Relations	Mother Relations
ALSTON	25	W	M	HS	2	2b, 2a	S. Baptist	N	distant	close
AUDREY	20	W	M	CS	4	6b, 1a	S. Baptist	N	distant	close
BRANDON	23	W	M	CG	2	0b, 2a	S. Baptist	N	distant	close
BRETT	19	W	M	CS	4	1b, 1s	Lutheran	N	distant	close
CARLTON	23	W	M	CS	5	1b, 1s	S. Baptist	N	dependent	distant
CORY	21	W	M	HS	5	1b, 1s	None	Y	close	distant
DARLA	21	W	F	HS	5	0b, 0s	None	Y	incestuous	close
DREW	21	W	M	CS	5	2b, 2s	Lutheran	N	distant	close
ELISA	20	W	F	CS	2	0b, 0s	S. Baptist	N	distant	distant
EVERETTA	23	W	F	HS	4	3b, 2s	S. Baptist	Y	distant	distant
FAWN	26	W	F	CS	4	1b, 0s	S. Baptist	N	distant	close
FRANKLIN	18	B	M	CS	2	1b, 0s	S. Baptist	Y	distant	close
GEORGINA	18	W	F	CS	5	1b, 1s	S. Baptist	N	distant	distant
GRANT	22	B	M	CS	4	0b, 0s	Afr. Meth.	N	distant	close
HENRY III	22	W	M	CG	7	1b, 0s	Episcopal	N	close	close
HEYWARD	25	B	M	CG	4	2b, 3s	Afr. Meth	Y	distant	distant
IRWIN	24	B	M	CG	2	1b, 0s	Jeh. Witness	Y	died at 6	close
ISAIAH	28	W	M	CG	4	0b, 0s	S. Baptist	N	close	close
JACKSON	26	W	M	CG	3	3b, 0s	Methodist	Y	distant	close
JACOB	26	B	M	CG	4	2b, 2s	S. Baptist	Y	distant	close
KEVIN	25	W	M	CG	7	2b, 0s	Epsicopal	N	distant	distant
KIMBERLY	19	B	F	CS	5	2b, 0s	S. Baptist	N	distant	close
LENORA	21	B	F	CS	3	1b, 1s	S. Baptist	N	distant	close
'LIZABETH	19	W	F	CS	4	0b, 0s	Catholic	N	distant	close
MALCOLM	27	B	M	HG	1	5b, 5s	Jeh Witness	Y	distant	close
MARIAN	24	W	F	CG	5	2b, 1s	Catholic	Y	close	distant
NATHANIEL	18	B	M	HS	5	4b, 1s	S. Baptist	N	distant	close

TABLE 1 (continued)

Participant	Age	Race	Gender	Educ*	SES**	Siblings	Family Church	Divorced Parents?	Father*** Relations	Mother Relations
NORMA	24	W	F	CS	2	1b, 0s	S. Baptist	Y	incestuous	distant
OBIE	19	B	F	HS	4	1b, 1s	Jeh Witness	N	distant	close
OLIVIA	23	W	F	CS	5	1b, 0s	S. Baptist	N	distant	close
PHILLIP	20	W	M	CS	4	1b, 0s	S. Baptist	N	distant	close
ROYCE	29	W	M	CG	6	1b, 2s	S. Baptist	N	distant	close
STEVE	29	W	M	HG	2	2b, 0s	Lutheran	Y	left at 1	died at 1
TERRY	22	W	M	HG	3	8b, 1s	Catholic	N	distant	close
VINCE	23	W	M	HG	3	1b, 1s	S. Baptist	Y	distant	close
WILLIAM	27	W	M	HG	5	1b, 1s	S. Baptist	Y	close	close

*coded as follows: HS: Not completed high school; HG: high school graduate; CS: college student; CG: college graduate
**coded as follows: (1) below poverty line (2) lower class (3)lower-middle class (4) middle-class (5) upper-middle class (6) upper class (7) old family aristocrat
***Mother/Father relationships determined by the Interviewer. "Closeness" and "distance" are defined within the context of the specific parent-child relationship described by the interviewee.

page numbers listed when that person is discussed or quoted within the text.

Milestones in Acquiring a Homosexual Identity

The process of acquiring a homosexual identity is said to gradually culminate in early adulthood with each participant "coming out" to parents, siblings, or friends.[10] First, however, homosexual-identified youth confront their own sexual feelings and fantasies *and* identify those feelings, fantasies, and themselves as "homosexual." As detailed in the previous section, there are idiosyncratic differences among participants in this study. Generally, though, a considerable amount of time passed between the initial awareness of same-sex attraction and disclosure to others coupled with self-acceptance of their sexual identities. During this interval, most of these lesbians and gay men experienced a variety of milestones.

Table 4 represents a chronology of these milestones reported by

TABLE 2

Ages of First
Sexual Activities and Experiences

Participant	Sexual Identity Pattern	Feelings of Attraction	Erotic Feelings	Homo. Behav.	Homo. Identity	Hetero. Behav.	Come out to Parent	Feeling Positive Sexually
ALSTON	ABEI	10	15	14	15	--	17	17
AUDREY	AEBI	10	16	17	18	14	19	19
BRANDON	AEIB	10	14	19	16	--	--	22
BRETT	AEBI	13	17	17	17	--	19	19
CARLTON	AEBI	7	9	10	14	19	21	20
CORY	BEAI	17	7	7	18	16	17	18
DARLA	AEBI	4	11	18	18	12	18	18
DREW	AEIB	5	13	21	19	--	--	21
ELISA	AEIB	5	13	24	13	18	--	24
EVERETTA	AEBI	6	10	11	16	11	--	18
FAWN	AEBI	10	10	17	19	13	20	20
FRANKLIN	AEIB	6	6	14	14	14	18	18
GEORGINA	AEBI	6	12	14	17	12	--	17
GRANT	BAEI	12	12	7	19	--	--	19
HENRY III	ABEI	6	20	19	20	--	20	20
HEYWARD	BAEI	13	13	12	20	--	--	20
IRWIN	AEBI	4	14	14	18	18	19	14
ISAIAH	AEBI	4	13	17	19	--	24	24
JACKSON	AEBI	13	13	16	19	16	23	22
JACOB	AEBI	10	12	12	16	--	--	18
KEVIN	AEIB	10	12	24	23	17	--	24
KIMBERLY	AEBX	8	18	18	--	--	--	19
LENORA	AEIB	13	16	17	16	15	17	20
'LIZABETH	AEIX	6	6	--	18	7	19	19
MALCOLM	AEBI	3	3	4	5	4	24	21
MARIAN	AEBI	20	20	20	21	--	20	21

TABLE 2 (continued)

Participant	Sexual Identity Pattern	Feelings of Attraction	Erotic Feelings	Homo. Behav.	Homo. Identity	Hetero. Behav.	Come out to Parent	Feeling Positive Sexually
NATHAN	AEBX	11	13	13	--	13	--	16
NORMA	AEBI	21	21	21	22	8	22	22
OBIE	AEBI	13	13	13	16	--	--	19
OLIVIA	AEBI	6	10	15	15	12	20	20
PHILLIP	AEBI	11	11	11	16	--	18	16
ROYCE	AEBI	12	12	12	16	19	--	17
STEVE	AEBI	13	13	13	16	--	--	20
TERRY	ABEI	7	12	9	16	17	--	16
VINCE	AEBI	4	9	9	13	14	20	21
WILLIAM	AEBI	11	18	18	22	19	--	23

these participants. Table 4 also lists the number of persons experiencing each milestone, the range of ages among these participants, and the number of individuals for whom each milestone occurred at 18 years of age or later. These mean ages are similar to those reported by other researchers with samples of similar age and gender groups.[11]

As indicated in Table 4, the average gap between non-erotic same-sex attraction and feeling positive about one's homosexual identity is 10 years. These 14 milestones reflect various stages posited by developmental theorists. An abbreviated description of these models, provided by one scholar,[12] collapses these milestones into four generic stages. Stage One, *first awareness of one's homosexual feelings*, is reflected in the first three milestones. In this stage, individuals acknowledge same-sex feelings and identify their sense of difference as sexual in nature. For participants in this study, these milestones occurred, on average, between 9.5 and 12.6 years of age. The actual range in age that participants experienced these milestones varied widely. For example, at the age of six, Everetta first felt same-sex attraction toward Louise to whom she would

TABLE 3

Psycho-Social Behaviors During High School

Participant	Homo Friends	Hetero Dating	Homo Dating	Hetero Steady	Homo Steady	Feel Isolated	Reg Use Drugs/ Alcoh.	Consider Suicide	Harassed
ALSTON	Y	Y	N	Y	Y	Y	Y	Y	Y
AUDREY	N	Y	N	N	N	Y	N	Y	Y
BRANDON	Y	Y	N	Y	N	Y	N	Y	Y
BRETT	Y	Y	N	Y	N	N	N	Y	Y
CARLTON	N	N	N	N	N	Y	N	Y	Y
CORY	Y	Y	Y	N	Y	N	Y	N	Y
DARLA	N	Y	N	Y	N	Y	Y	Y	Y
DREW	N	Y	N	Y	N	Y	N	Y	Y
ELISA	N	Y	N	Y	N	Y	Y	Y	Y
EVERETTA	Y	Y	N	Y	N	Y	Y	Y	Y
FAWN	Y	Y	N	Y	N	Y	N	Y	Y
FRANKLIN	Y	Y	N	N	N	Y	N	Y	Y
GEORGINA	Y	Y	Y	Y	Y	N	Y	Y	Y
GRANT	N	Y	N	N	N	N	Y	Y	Y
HENRY III	N	N	N	N	N	Y	N	Y	Y
HEYWARD	N	Y	N	Y	N	N	Y	N	Y
IRWIN	Y	Y	Y	N	Y	N	N	N	Y
ISAIAH	N	Y	N	Y	N	Y	N	N	Y
JACKSON	N	Y	N	Y	N	Y	N	N	N
JACOB	Y	Y	Y	N	N	N	N	N	N
KEVIN	N	Y	N	N	N	Y	N	Y	Y
KIMBERLY	Y	Y	N	Y	N	N	N	N	N
LENORA	N	Y	Y	Y	Y	Y	Y	Y	Y
'LIZABETH	N	Y	N	Y	N	Y	N	Y	Y
MALCOLM	Y	Y	N	Y	N	Y	N	Y	Y
MARIAN	N	Y	N	Y	N	Y	N	B	N

TABLE 3 (continued)

Participant	Homo Friends	Hetero Dating	Homo Dating	Hetero Steady	Homo Steady	Feel Isolated	Reg Use Drugs/ Alcoh.	Consider Suicide	Harassed
NATHANIEL	Y	Y	Y	Y	Y	N	Y	N	Y
NORMA JEAN	N	Y	N	Y	N	Y	N	Y	Y
OBIE	Y	N	Y	N	Y	N	N	Y	Y
OLIVIA	N	Y	N	Y	Y	Y	N	Y	N
PHILLIP	N	Y	N	Y	N	Y	N	Y	Y
ROYCE	N	N	Y	N	Y	N	Y	Y	Y
STEVE	Y	N	Y	N	Y	N	N	N	N
TERRY	Y	Y	N	Y	N	N	Y	N	Y
VINCE	N	Y	N	Y	N	N	N	N	N
WILLIAM	N	Y	N	N	N	N	Y	Y	N

write love notes. By the time she was 10, Everetta began experiencing homoerotic feelings. Although Cory remembers experiencing erotic feelings with his babysitter's boyfriend during elementary school, he did not feel attracted to another male until his experience with Winston at the age of 17.

Testing and exploration, Stage Two, is the exploration of sexual options and exposure to homosexual relations while bracketing a heterosexual identification. During this stage, a person's ability to interact within a sexual environment is developed. On the average, these milestone occurred between the ages of 13.8 and 14.7. Again, great variation existed. Olivia first engaged in same-sex behavior with Kris at the age of 15. She had already engaged in heterosexual behavior three years earlier. Though Kevin had long been aware of his homosexual feelings, he did not engage in homosexual behavior until the age of 24. Seven years earlier he had had a sexual experience with a woman.

Identity acceptance, marks the entrance into the homosexual community as participants identify themselves as lesbian or gay. The principal task during this stage is to achieve self-acceptance through interaction with others who have similar sexual interests. Self-acceptance does not imply that individuals feel good about their sexual identities; they are simply acknowledged. This stage

TABLE 4

Milestones for Southern Lesbian and Gay Youth

EVENT	N	GROUP MEAN	AGE RANGE	N 18+
Stage One				
Non-erotic awareness of same sex attraction	35	9.5	3-21	2
Exposure to fag jokes/derrogatory comment	36	10.6	4-16	0
Erotic Awareness of same sex attractions	36	12.6	3-21	5
Stage Two				
Opposite Sex Experiences	21	13.8	4-19	4
Same sex experiences	35	14.7	4-24	10
Stage Three				
Reading material supportive of homosexuality	35	17.1	11-22	18
Learning about homosexuality in history	31	17.1	9-24	15
Self-designation as "homosexual"	34	17.1	5-23	17
Finding someone comfortable to talk about homosexuality	36	18.2	13-24	20
Finding a supportive teacher	18	18.9	14-23	13
First attendance at a social gathering of lesbians/gay men	33	19.2	14-25	27
Stage Four				
Beginning to feel positive about being "gay"	36	19.5	14-24	29
Initial dislosure to close friends	28	19.6	16-25	23
Initial disclosure to a parent	20	19.9	17-26	17

corresponds to six milestones cited in Table 4. The average age represented by this stage is 17.1 through 19.2. All but two (Kimberly and Nathaniel) had identified themselves as "homosexual" at the time this study was conducted. Again, the actual range in ages of participants reporting these events was wide. Royce first labelled himself as "homosexual" at the age of 16. He was not exposed to material supportive of being gay and did not find a supportive teacher until his freshmen year in college. These same events did not occur in Norma Jean's life until she was in her early twenties.

Finally, Stage Four represents *identity integration* wherein a person internalizes a positive homosexual identity. The last three milestones illustrate experiences common during this stage. This stage, on average, begins at about 19 and extends into adulthood where other stages should be experienced. Vince disclosed his homosexuality to his mother when he was 20; Darla "came out" at the age of 18; Kevin, Royce, Everetta, Jacob, and Obie have yet to disclose their sexual identities to their parents, though all have "come out" to some of their heterosexual friends.

Though stage development theory provides a useful conceptual framework for thinking about the biographies of these sexual rebels; as a predictive device, it has limited utility. In her intensive interviews with 14 women over a one-year period, Joan Sophie concluded that stage development theories do not account for individual variation. "As soon as more specificity was introduced," she writes, "the theory was inaccurate in accounting for development in various individuals."[13] Even a cursory analysis of the thumbnail portraits provided in this chapter substantiates Sophie's point. More importantly, these milestones, as British sociologist Kenneth Plummer underscores, tell us little about the *sexual meanings* assigned to these acts by individuals:

> Nearly all the studies, for example, that we have of childhood and sexualization simply tell us the age at which a child committed a first act, and other observable, external facts that are easily capable of being quantified. But while it may be well established that children play with their genitals, have orgasms, and conjure up copulatory fantasies, we cannot automatically assume that such activity represents a sexual meaning to the child.[14]

The meanings assigned to these activities reflect the cultural as well as psychological state wherein the individual dwells at any particular time. Thus, the meaning of a same-sex experience for a Southern black child at 10 is not only different for a Anglo child of that age but will be very different from the meanings that either assign to them 15 years later. Therefore, the insights provided in the biographies of these sexual rebels are critical for a holistic understanding of the construction of sexual identity.

Table 5 provides an opportunity to match chapter biographies with a variety of psychosexual experiences and feelings held by these participants during high school. These are divided into seven broad areas: peer support; adult support; peer pressure; social-sexual activities; coping behaviors; personal feelings; and gay/lesbian involvement. Table 5 also notes the percentage of the total sample that recalled such experiences and feelings.

Differences as well as similarities in the formation of sexual identities among individuals were observed on the basis of their gender or race. For example, there were commonalities in identity construction between the males and females of this study. As Table 6 indicates, similarities generally existed in the *order of the four stages* among males and females as they acquired homosexual identities. For example, both genders were likely to engage in same-sex experiences prior to identifying themselves as lesbian or gay. Although the time gap between these two events was much more pronounced in the males (3.3 years) than the females (.3 years), the only significant difference between males and females existed in the order of several milestones *within* a particular stage. The most profound difference was in Stage Two. Females experienced heterosexual activity at an average age of 11.3 (before erotic awareness of same-sex attraction in Stage One); males, on average, experienced their first heterosexual activity four years later. Males were also much more likely to experiment with homosexual activity *prior* to engaging in heterosexual behavior. Women in this study had the opposite order of experiences. The span of time between these first heterosexual and homosexual encounters was also significantly different for males and females. On average, about two years passed before males, familiar with homosexual behavior, engaged in heterosexual activity. In contrast, nearly six years elapsed, on average, between female heterosexual and homosexual experiences.

As illustrated in Table 6, African-Americans experienced Stages Two through Four at an earlier age than their white peers. Blacks passed every milestone, with the exception of experiencing nonerotic homosexual feelings, the first hearing of "fag" jokes, and

TABLE 5

High School Experiences and Feelings

Experience/Feeling	Per Cent "Yes"	Chapter Portraits Answering "Yes
Peer Support		
Would liked to have had friends of my same sex who were gay/lesbian*	.92	2, 4, 5, 6, 7, 8, 9 10, 11, 12, 13, 14
Friends of same sex who I knew were gay/lesbian	.46	3, 6, 7, 8, 9, 10, 11, 14
Suspected friends of same sex who were gay/lesbian	.78	2, 3, 5, 6, 7, 8, 9 10, 11, 12, 13, 14
Friends of opposite sex who were gay/lesbian	.33	3, 7, 8, 10, 11, 14
Suspected friends of opposite sex who were gay/lesbian	.59	3, 5, 6, 7, 8, 10, 11, 13, 14
Part of support group that placed a positive value on being gay/lesbian	.06	8
Isolated from other homosexual persons	.70	2, 3, 5, 8, 9, 10, 11, 12, 13, 14
Adult Support		
Would like to have had an "openly gay" teacher*	.78	2, 5, 6, 7, 8, 9 11, 12, 13, 14
Knew a teacher who was lesbian or gay	.39	3, 7, 8, 9, 10, 14
Suspected a teacher of being lesbian/gay	.86	2, 3, 4, 5, 6, 7, 8, 9 10, 11, 13, 14
Class with teacher who was lesbian/gay	.23	7, 8, 9
Class with teacher suspected of being lesbian/gay	.63	5, 6, 7, 8, 10, 11, 13
Teachers discussed homosexuality/gay issues	.14	3
Teachers had negative attitudes about homosexuality	.73	7, 8, 9, 10, 11, 13
Would have liked to have known an "understanding adult" to talk about my sexual orientation*	.94	2, 3, 5, 6, 7, 8, 9, 10, 11, 12, 13, 14
Talked to teacher about my sexual orientation	.17	7, 8, 11, 14
Guidance counselors well informed about homosexuality	.15	9, 11
Talked to guidance counselor about my sexual orientation	.06	8, 11
Felt comfortable talking to guidance counselor about my sexual orientation*	.06	8, 11
Received support of guidance counselor for being gay/lesbian	.08	3, 8, 11

Experience/Feeling	Per Cent "Yes"	Chapter Portraits Answering "Yes
Adult Support (cont'd)		
Received support of minister for being gay/lesbian	.08	8
Read books/articles positive about homosexuality	.44	3, 6, 7, 8, 9 10, 11, 13
Received counseling/therapy to "turn straight"	.11	11
I would have liked for my parents to have known I had gay friends	.38	7, 10, 13, 14
Peer Pressure		
Did not care if my friends knew that I was attracted to members of my sex*	.09	7, 11
Peer group aware that I had homosexual friends	.36	6, 7, 8, 9
Homosexuality considered an alternate lifestyle in school	.15	3, 8
Classmates displayed negative attitudes about homosexuality	.97	2, 3, 4, 5, 6, 7, 8, 9 10, 11, 12, 13, 14
Fearful of being harassed**	.56	3, 4, 10, 11, 12, 13
Afraid of being harassed if I "came out" in school*	.81	2, 5, 7, 9, 10 11, 12, 13, 14
Kids picked on me very often.***	.54	4, 7, 11, 13, 14
Harassed because I was "different"	.77	3, 4, 5, 7, 8, 9, 10, 11, 12, 13, 14
Attempt to pass for "straight"**	.64	2, 3, 4, 6, 11, 12, 13, 14
Openly disagreed with a "fag" joke	.19	6, 7, 8, 13
Social-Sexual Activities		
Rarely thought about sexuality	.28	2, 4, 5, 9
Dated members of opposite sex	.86	2, 3, 4, 6, 8, 9, 10, 11, 12, 13, 14
Went "steady" with opposite sex person	.64	2, 3, 4, 8, 10, 11, 12, 14
Engaged in heterosexual activity	.44	2, 3, 4, 8, 9, 11, 12
Dated members of same sex	.25	5, 7, 8, 9, 10, 12
Went "steady" with person of same sex	.28	5, 7, 9, 10, 12
Had a same sex lover	.31	5, 7, 9, 10, 12, 14

TABLE 5 (continued)

Experience/Feeling	Per Cent "Yes"	Chapter Portraits Answering "Yes
Sexual advances made my member of same sex	.54	3, 5, 6, 7, 8, 9, 10, 11, 14
Engaged in homosexual activity	.67	2, 3, 5, 6, 7, 8, 9, 10, 11, 12, 13, 14
"Cruised" a public place	.31	3, 5, 11

Coping Behaviors

Experience/Feeling	Per Cent "Yes"	Chapter Portraits Answering "Yes
School work negatively affected by sexual orientation	.40	3, 13, 14
Performed poorly on tests**	.14	10, 14
Worked up to my ability in school**	.41	2, 5, 6, 12
I was proud of my school work.***	.54	2, 3, 5, 6, 12
Recognized for outstanding school achievements**	.47	2, 5, 6, 12
Disciplined by school officials**	.14	9, 11
Regularly used alcohol or illegal drugs	.41	5, 8, 9, 10, 11
I used alcohol or drugs to deal with my sexual orientation*	.17	2, 5, 11
Sometimes contemplated suicide	.63	3, 4, 5, 7, 11, 13, 14
Attempted suicide	.11	7, 11

Personal Feelings

Experience/Feeling	Per Cent "Yes"	Chapter Portraits Answering "Yes
It was pretty tough to be me.***	.81	2, 3, 4, 5, 6, 8, 10, 11, 12, 13, 14
Things were all mixed up in my life.***	.64	3, 4, 7, 10, 11, 12, 13, 14
I wished that I was "straight."*	.46	2, 3, 7, 11, 12
I felt depressed whenever I thought a lot about being a "homosexual."*	.40	3, 12
I felt ashamed for being attracted to members of my same sex.*	.40	2, 3, 12
I felt bad whenever I heard a "fag" joke.*	.51	3, 6, 7, 12, 14
I was afraid people would discover I was gay/lesbian.**	.57	2. 3, 11, 12, 13, 14
I felt isolated.**	.61	3, 4, 10, 11, 12, 13
I felt inferior to others.**	.36	4, 7, 11

Experience/Feeling	Per Cent "Yes"	Chapter Portraits Answering "Yes"
I had a low opinion of myself.***	.54	3, 4, 7, 11, 13, 14
I felt anger.**	.33	3, 4, 10, 11
I felt sadness.**	.46	3, 7, 10, 11, 13
I often wished I was someone else.***	.63	3, 5, 7, 8, 10, 11, 13, 14
I was a lot of fun to be with.***	.72	2, 3, 5, 6, 8, 9, 10, 12, 14
I felt happy.**	.53	2, 5, 6, 8, 9, 10, 14
I felt romantic love.**	.17	3, 5, 9, 13
I was popular with people my age.***	.58	2, 3, 5, 6, 8, 9, 12
Things usually didn't bother me.***	.39	2, 3, 6, 8, 9
My family usually considered my feelings.***	.58	5, 6, 10, 12, 13
My family understood me.***	.33	6
I got upset easily at home.***	.50	3, 5, 7, 11, 13, 14
There were many times when I would have liked to have left home.***	.67	3, 4, 5, 7, 8, 9, 10 11, 13, 14

Gay/Lesbian Involvement

Attend meeting of lesbians/gay persons	.03	----
Join lesbian/gay organization	.03	----
Visit a gay/lesbian bar	.33	5, 6, 8, 9, 10
Donated money to a gay/lesbian cause	.08	8, 10
Participated in an AIDS support group	.06	----

*Five item Likert response set with strongly Agree and Agree coded as "Yes."
**Five item response set ranging from never to always. Very frequently and always were coded as "Yes."
***Response set "like me" "unlike me" coded as "yes," and "no."

going to a homosexual social gathering, at an earlier age. African-Americans, for example, experience homoerotic feelings, on average, nearly a year earlier than Anglo-Americans. In Stage Two, black participants were much more likely to engage in homosexual and heterosexual behaviors at an earlier age. On average, the Afri-

TABLE 6

Milestone for Lesbian and Gay Youth

EVENT	MALE	FEMALE	WHITE	BLACK
Stage One				
Non-erotic awareness of same sex attraction	9.2	10.2	9.3	9.5
Exposure to fag jokes/derrogatory comments	10.4	11.0	10.4	11.2
Erotic Awareness of same sex attractions	12.4	13.3	12.9	12.0
Stage Two				
Opposite Sex Experiences	15.4	11.3	14.2	12.8
Same sex experiences	13.6	17.1	15.6	12.5
Stage Three				
Reading material supportive of homosexuality	16.6	18.0	17.7	15.4
Learning about homosexuality in history	16.3	18.5	17.9	15.3
Self-designation as "homosexual"	16.9	17.4	17.5	15.5
Finding someone comfortable to talk about homosexuality	18.5	17.5	18.6	17.2
Finding a supportive teacher	18.4	19.3	19.3	16.3
First attendance at a social gathering of lesbians/gay men	19.1	19.5	18.3	19.5
Stage Four				
Beginning to feel positive about being "gay"	19.4	19.8	19.9	18.4
Initial dislosure to close friends	19.7	19.5	19.9	18.4
Initial disclosure to a parent	20.1	19.4	19.9	19.5

can-Americans first engaged in homosexual activity three years earlier than their white counterparts and participated in heterosexual activity one and one-half years earlier. In Stage Three, black lesbians and gay-identified men were exposed to material supportive of homosexuality at a much earlier age (15.4 versus 17.7) and first labelled themselves as "homosexual," on average, two years earlier than their white peers. Racial differences during Stage Four, identity integration, were less marked.

Dimensions of Homosexual Identity

Another way of examining the construction of sexual identities among these sexual rebels is through data collected from the Klein Sexual Orientation Grid.[15] Each of the 36 participants completed this instrument which includes seven dimensions: sexual attraction and fantasy, social and emotional preference, and sexual behavior, self-identification, and lifestyle. According to Professor Klein, sexual identity is the constellation of these seven dimensions.

Each dimension is placed on an interval scale with continuous graduations between exclusively heterosexual (score of 1) and exclusively homosexual (score of 7).[16] The individual scores for each of these seven dimensions are additive. This sum represents the person's sexual identity at a particular moment time. Thus, these scores are developmental snapshots of gay and lesbian identities. Three "snapshots" were taken as participants placed themselves along these seven continua at three moments in time: their high school years, the present, and their ideal world. Table 7 lists these Southerners' mean scores and standard deviations along the seven dimensions during these three points in time.

As Table 7 illustrates, participants scored in the homosexual

TABLE 7

Mean Scores and Standard Deviations
of Seven Dimensions for
Participants' Past, Present, and Ideal Sexual Identities

Dimension	Past Score/Std. Deviation	Present Score/Std. Devision	Ideal Score/Std. Deviation
Sexual Attraction	5.7/1.1	6.3/.8	5.1/2.2
Sexual Behavior	5.1/2.3	6.6/1.0	5.5/2.2
Sexual Fantasy	5.7/1.6	6.3/1.3	5.4/1.9
Emotional Preference	4.5/1.9	5.7/1.3	5.3/1.7
Social Preference	3.7/1.6	4.7/1.1	4.6/ .9
Sexual Identification	4.0/2.1	6.3/1.1	5.3/2.1
Sexual Lifestyle	2.1/1.3	4.9/1.1	4.7/1.1

range (score of 5.5 or higher) in feelings of sexual attraction and their sexual fantasies but the most public dimension (sexual lifestyle) was decidedly heterosexual. As adults in their early twenties, these participants were more homosexually oriented on every dimension with five of these being in the predominantly homosexual range. Interestingly, these participants were still not "open" with regard to sexual lifestyle with a score placing them in the bisexual range (score range > 2.5 and < 5.5). Finally, when asked to think about their ideal situation, participants' average scores were less homosexually-oriented on every dimension. Sexual attraction, behavior, and identification all fell into the bisexual range.

These aggregate data, however, cloud much of the variation evidenced in this study. Of much greater interest is the changing perspectives held by individual participants. Table 8 lists the high school, present, and ideal sexual identity scores for each of these sexual rebels. The differences between participants' high school and present sexual identity scores as well as their present and ideal scores also are listed in Table 8.

In reviewing participants' responses, one interesting point of analysis is participant movement *from high school to the present time*. This temporal change in sexual identification is calculated by subtracting present score from past score. The more positive the number the greater the relative movement toward a homosexual identity. Several findings are worthy of comment. First, at the time participants were high school students every person, with the exception of Norma Jean, had a bisexual or homosexual identity (score of 2.5 or higher). Second, at the time of the interview, 27 (including Norma Jean) expressed a homosexual identity (score of 5.5 or higher). Norma Jean demonstrated the greatest change between high school and the present. Audrey, Henry III, Jackson, Kevin, Kimberly, Malcolm, Marian, and Royce also showed significant movement toward homosexuality. Carlton and Obie were the only two participants who reflected an incremental movement toward heterosexuality.

Each point in Figure 1 represents a participant. Along the X-axis is the sexual identity scores of participants' high school pasts.[17] The Y-axis represents present sexual identity scores of these persons.

TABLE 8

	NAME	KSOG PAST	KSOG PRESENT	PR/PA	KSOG IDEAL	ID/PR
1	'LIZABETH	4.00	4.83	0.83	5.00	0.17
2	ALSTON	5.00	5.71	0.71	5.71	0.00
3	AUDREY	3.33	6.17	2.84	2.50	-3.67
4	BRANDON	4.83	6.29	1.45	2.00	-4.29
5	BRETT	4.00	5.71	1.71	5.29	-0.43
6	CARLTON	4.14	3.86	-0.29	2.14	-1.71
7	CORY	5.28	6.43	1.15	6.00	-0.43
8	DARLA	4.43	6.00	1.57	6.29	0.29
9	DREW	4.33	5.71	1.38	2.43	-3.29
10	ELISA	4.92	6.00	1.08	6.29	0.29
11	EVERETTA	4.86	6.29	1.43	6.14	-0.14
12	FAWN	4.80	6.00	1.20	5.40	-0.60
13	FRANKLIN	5.00	5.71	0.71	6.14	0.43
14	GEORGINA	3.86	5.43	1.57	6.00	0.57
15	GRANT	4.71	5.71	1.00	6.29	0.58
16	HENRY III	3.83	6.43	2.60	6.57	0.14
17	HEYWARD	4.57	6.14	1.57	6.14	0.00
18	IRWIN	4.71	5.29	0.57	5.71	0.43
19	ISIAH	4.71	5.86	1.14	5.86	0.00
20	JACKSON	4.14	6.43	2.29	4.00	-2.43
21	JACOB	6.14	6.57	0.43	6.57	0.00
22	KEVIN	3.42	6.43	3.01	4.43	-2.00
23	KIMBERLY	3.50	5.71	2.21	5.14	-0.57
24	LENORA	4.29	5.71	1.43	5.57	-0.14
25	MALCOLM	2.71	5.43	2.71	3.14	-2.29
26	MARIAN	4.00	6.00	2.00	6.00	0.00
27	NATHANIEL	3.14	4.14	1.00	3.43	-0.71
28	NORMA JEAN	1.86	5.86	4.00	6.43	0.57
29	OBIE	5.43	5.29	-0.14	4.00	-1.29
30	OLIVIA	3.57	4.57	1.00	3.00	-1.57
31	PHILLIP	4.86	6.43	1.57	6.43	0.00
32	ROYCE	4.29	6.29	2.00	5.43	-0.86
33	STEVE	5.86	6.71	0.86	7.00	0.29
34	TERRY	4.71	6.43	1.71	6.29	-0.14
35	VINCE	5.29	6.29	1.00	4.00	-2.29
36	WILLIAM	3.67	5.43	1.76	5.29	-0.14

The number adjacent to that point corresponds to the participant's name cited in Table 8.

Scores may fall within one of nine distinctive domains:

Domain I: Past-Heterosexual, Present-Heterosexual (The All American)
Both scores between 1 and 2.5. No participant fell into this cell.

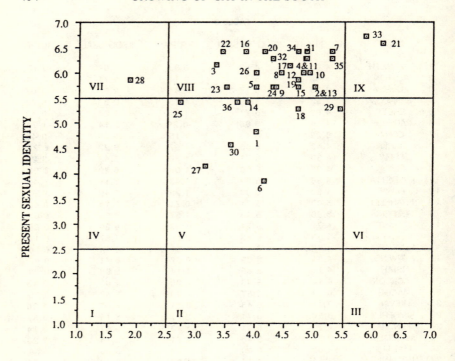

HIGH SCHOOL SEXUAL IDENTITY

FIGURE 1. Participants' past and present sexual identities

Domain II: Past-Bisexual, Present-Heterosexual (The Experimenter)
Past score between 2.5 and 5.5; present score between 2.5 and 5.5. No participant was in this domain.

Domain III: Past-Homosexual, Present-Heterosexual (The Saved)
Past score between 5.5 and 7; present score between 1 and 3. No participant fell into this cell.

Domain IV: Past-Heterosexual, Present-Bisexual (The Curious)
Past score between 1 and 2.5; present score between 2.5 and 5.5. No participant fell into this domain.

Domain V: Past-Bisexual, Present-Bisexual (AC/DC)

Scores between 2.5 and 5.5. Nine participants fell into this cell. Carlton, the most centrist person in this cell, simply proclaims, "I like both sexes." Five of these nine persons are near the boundary separating those whose present identity is homosexual or bisexual. Two of these participants, Malcolm and Obie, are at opposite corners. At this time, both have a similar sexual identity; during their high school years, Malcolm was closer to a heterosexual identity and Obie was closer to a homosexual identity. Though Malcolm was more attracted to men, he dated and eventually married Surlina. Obie, engaging in exclusively homosexual relationships with high school girls such as Connie, enjoyed spending time with men such as Paul. Since high school, Malcolm has traveled a considerable distance along the continuum of sexual identification; Obie has traveled little.

Domain VI: Past-Homosexual, Present-Bisexual (The Recovering)

Past score between 5.5 and 7; present score between 2.5 and 5.5. No participant fell into this cell.

Domain VII: Past-Heterosexual, Present-Homosexual (The Converted)

Past score between 1 and 2.5; present score between 5.5 and 7. One participant, Norma Jean, fell into this domain. With the exception of preferring the social company of women, she was very opposite-sex oriented during high school though she refused to have sexual intercourse with her boyfriend, Marty. Following the death of David and support from Charmaine, she now engages in exclusive homosexual behavior and identifies herself as lesbian.

Domain VIII: Past-Bisexual, Present-Homosexual (The Discreditable)[18]

Past score between 2.5 and 5.5; present score between 5.5 and 7. Two-thirds (24) of the participants were in this cell. These include Alston, Darla, Cory, Everetta, Kevin, Royce, and Vince. The most centrist person within this domain is Marian. Though Marian identified herself as "straight" and engaged in a heterosexual lifestyle during high school, her sexual fantasies were more bisexual and her emotional and social preference was for women. This contrasts sharply with her present identity as a lesbian who has enjoyed a monogamous relationship with her female lover for the past three years.

Domain IX: Past-Homosexual, Present-Homosexual (The Discredited)

Scores between 5.5 and 7.5. Two participants, Jacob and Steve, fell into this domain. Jacob identified himself as gay at the age of 16, though he hid his homosexual identity from family and friends, he engaged in exclusive same-sex behavior. Steve did not label himself gay until he was 18, however, since he had returned to complete the three remaining years of high school when he was 17, he had a homosexual identification as a high school student. Both men have been unchanging in their homosexual identification.

The 36 participants occupied four of the nine possible domains. This is in contrast to plotting participants sexual identity scores *from the present time to their ideal state* where six domains were occupied.

Referring back to Table 8, it is noteworthy that *20 participants underscored an interest in lessening their homosexual identity*. Some, like Everetta, indicated relatively little movement ($-.14$) while others, like Brandon, evidenced substantial movement (-4.29). More males than females expressed this sentiment, and males were significantly more likely to desire a more marked movement toward heterosexual identity. Thus, the total number of participants desiring a predominantly homosexual identity (score of 5.5 or higher) dwindled from the present state of 27 to 19 and included Jacob, Norma Jean, Cory, and Phillip. Those expressing an interest in bisexuality, however, increased from 6 to 14. These included Brett, Malcolm, Obie, Royce, and Vince. Finally, three participants, Brandon, Carlton, and Drew, desired a heterosexual identity.

These relationships are depicted in Figure 2. Again, each point represents a participant whose number corresponds to those in Ta-

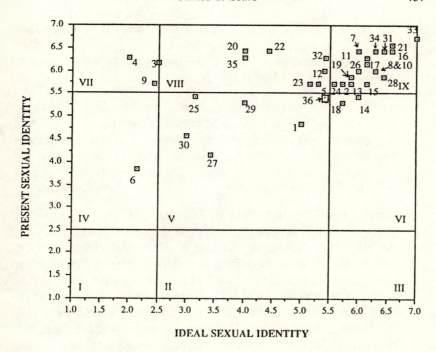

FIGURE 2. Participants' ideal and present sexual identities

ble 8. Along the X-axis are participants' ideal sexual identity scores and along the Y-axis are their present scores on sexual identity.

Scores may fall within one of nine distinctive domains:

Domain I: Ideal-Heterosexual, Present-Heterosexual (The All American)
    Both scores between 1 and 2.5. No participant fell into this cell.

Domain II: Ideal-Bisexual, Present-Heterosexual (The Broad-Minded)
    Ideal score between 2.5 and 5.5; present score between 2.5 and 5.5. No participant was in this domain.

Domain III: Ideal-Homosexual, Present-Heterosexual (The Tormented)

Ideal score between 5.5 and 7; present score between 1 and 3. No participant fell into this cell.

Domain IV: Ideal-Heterosexual, Present-Bisexual (The Coveting)

Ideal score between 1 and 2.5; present score between 2.5 and 5.5 One participant fell into this domain. Carlton, indicated a bisexual identity during high school and, at the time of his interview, preferred to be physically and emotionally drawn only to the opposite gender.

Domain V: Ideal-Bisexual, Present-Bisexual (AC/DC)

Scores between 2.5 and 5.5. Six participants fell into this cell. All of these, 'Lizabeth, Malcolm, Nathaniel, Obie, Olivia, and William, were also in this cell in Figure 1. Thus, their past, present, and ideal sexual identities fall into the bisexual range. The reasons for this, however, vary with each participant. The movement between past and ideal identities is also interesting. William and 'Lizabeth moved toward a more homosexual identity while Obie moved toward a more bisexual identity.

Domain VI: Ideal-Homosexual, Present-Bisexual (The Changeling)

Ideal score between 5.5 and 7; present score between 2.5 and 5.5. Two participants fell into this cell. Both Georgina and Irwin had recorded bisexual identities in high school as well as the present time but expressed a preference for homosexual identities.

Domain VII: Ideal-Heterosexual, Present-Homosexual (The Damned)

Ideal score between 1 and 2.5; present score between 5.5 and 7. Two participants, Brandon and Drew, fell into this domain. Both expressed disdain for their homosexual lifestyle and erotic preference for men. Brandon simply considered himself a "lost soul," while Drew's sense of inferiority and isolation led him to desire a heterosexual identity.

Domain VIII: Ideal-Bisexual, Present-Homosexual (The Searching)
  Ideal score between 2.5 and 5.5; present score between 5.5
  and 7. Eight of the participants were in this cell, though only
  three, Jackson, Kevin, and Vince, fell into a centrist position.
  All three of these men have had heterosexual experiences and
  would prefer to adopt a bisexual identity. Audrey contrasts
  sharply with the other four participants who fall on the opposite ends of the ideal spectrum. Brett, Fawn, Kimberly, and
  Royce are very close to the homosexual end of this spectrum
  while Audrey, who has always expressed a desire to "fit in"
  and "raise a family," falls on the heterosexual end.

*Domain IX: Ideal-Homosexual, Present-Homosexual (The Commu-
  nity)*
  Scores between 5.5 and 7.5. Seventeen participants fell into
  this domain — the vast majority of them moving from Domain
  VIII (Figure 1) as they entered into adulthood. These included
  Alston, Cory, Everetta, Phillip, and Terry. Two of them,
  Steve and Jacob, have continued to remain in this cell during
  all three time periods. And one, Norma Jean moved from a
  past heterosexual identity to an ideal homosexual identity.

Differences also were found between these sexual rebels' high
school, present, and ideal sexual identities vis-à-vis their gender
and race. For example, significant differences were found between
males and female participants during their high school years on five
of the seven dimensions of sexual identity. These differences are
listed in Table 9.

During their high school years, lesbians were more likely to report experiencing bisexual fantasies and were more likely to have
been sexually attracted to both sexes. Females in this study, though,
were more likely to report an emotional closeness with members of
their same gender during high school and to have spent more time in
same-sex socializing. Males, on the other hand, were more likely to
report engaging in homosexual activity, fantasizing about members
of the same sex, and being sexually attracted to males during high
school. Lesbians and gay men in this study did not significantly

TABLE 9
Male and Female Mean Scores of Seven Dimensions
For Participants' Past, Present, and Ideal Sexual Identities

High School

Dimension	Male Mean/SD	Female Mean/SD	t-value	p
Sexual Attraction	6.0/ .7	4.9/1.4	2.3	<.05
Sexual Behavior	5.6/2.2	3.7/2.3	1.9	<.01
Sexual Fantasy	6.1/1.3	4.8/1.9	2.4	<.001 ·
Emotional Preference	4.0/1.8	5.4/1.9	-2.1	<.001
Social Preference	3.3/1.4	4.4/1.8	-2.2	<.001
Sexual Identification	4.3/2.2	3.5/1.9	---	---
Sexual Lifestyle	2.1/1.4	2.0/1.1	---	---

Present

Dimension	Male Mean/SD	Female Mean/SD	t-value	p
Sexual Attraction	6.3/ .8	6.2/ .6	---	---
Sexual Behavior	6.7/1.0	6.4/1.0	---	---
Sexual Fantasy	6.5/ .8	5.7/1.8	1.6	<.05
Emotional Preference	5.6/1.2	5.9/1.5	---	---
Social Preference	4.8/1.0	4.7/1.4	---	---
Sexual Identification	6.3/1.2	6.2/ .9	---	---
Sexual Lifestyle	5.0/1.0	4.7/1.3	---	---

Ideal

Dimension	Male Mean/SD	Female Mean/SD	t-value	p
Sexual Attraction	4.9/2.3	5.4/2.0	---	---
Sexual Behavior	5.3/2.4	5.8/1.9	---	---
Sexual Fantasy	5.1/2.3	6.0/1.0	-1.6	<.001
Emotional Preference	5.0/1.8	5.9/1.2	-1.7	<.001
Social Preference	4.6/ .9	4.7/ .9	---	---
Sexual Identification	5.0/2.2	5.7/2.0	---	---
Sexual Lifestyle	4.8/1.2	4.5/ .9	---	---

differ on their *public* lifestyle or their sexual identity adopted during high school.

As noted in Table 9, the differences between these males and females generally disappeared along these dimensions as they entered adulthood. However, between their high school years and the present time women in this study were much more likely to identify themselves as homosexual. At the time of the interviews, gender differences were evident on only one dimension: gay men were still more likely to report having mostly homosexual fantasies than females.

Finally, when comparing participants' present sexual identities to that of their ideal, males were more likely to desire bisexual fantasies and to engage in mixed sex socializing than their female counterparts. Of particular interest are the significant changes among males on most of these dimensions. Generally, males moved much more readily to the bisexual end of the spectrum when thinking about their ideal sexual identity than females. And, on three of the seven dimensions females remained the same or increased their desire for a homosexual identity. Graphically, these differences are represented in Figure 2.

Fewer differences were found between black and white participants. As indicated in Table 10, African-Americans differed from their Anglo counterparts on three of the seven dimensions of sexual identity held during high school. White lesbian and gay youth were significantly more attracted to members of their same sex and more likely to have experienced same-sex fantasies. Whites, however, were more likely to have adopted a *heterosexual* lifestyle during high school than were the black participants.

By the time these participants had entered early adulthood, differences in homosexual fantasies, attraction, and lifestyle had disappeared. Differences, however, emerged on two other dimensions of sexual identity: social preferences and sexual identification. During the time of their interviews, white participants were more likely to socialize with the same sex than the black lesbians and gay men in this study; white lesbians and gay men scored themselves somewhat higher on their identification as homosexual than their African-American peers. Finally, in comparing the aggregate scores on

TABLE 10
Black and White Mean Scores of Seven Dimensions
For Participants' Past, Present, and Ideal Sexual Identities

High School

Dimension	White Mean/SD	Black Mean/SD	t-value	p
Sexual Attraction	5.9/1.0	5.1/1.1	2.0	<.001
Sexual Behavior	4.8/2.4	5.5/2.1	---	---
Sexual Fantasy	5.9/1.5	5.1/1.7	1.3	<.10
Emotional Preference	4.6/1.8	4.4/2.2	---	---
Social Preference	3.7/1.7	3.5/1.3	---	---
Sexual Identification	3.8/2.3	4.5/1.7	---	---
Sexual Lifestyle	1.7/1.0	3.0/1.6	-2.4	<.001

Present

Dimension	White Mean/SD	Black Mean/SD	t-value	p
Sexual Attraction	6.4/ .6	6.0/1.1	---	---
Sexual Behavior	6.5/1.0	6.7/ .9	---	---
Sexual Fantasy	6.3/1.4	6.2/ .9	---	---
Emotional Preference	5.8/1.1	5.4/1.7	---	---
Social Preference	4.9/1.2	4.3/ .8	1.7	<.001
Sexual Identification	6.4/1.0	5.8/1.1	1.6	<.01
Sexual Lifestyle	5.0/1.2	4.6/1.0	---	---

Ideal

Dimension	White Mean/SD	Black Mean/SD	t-value	p
Sexual Attraction	5.0/2.2	5.3/2.3	---	---
Sexual Behavior	5.4/2.4	5.7/1.9	---	---
Sexual Fantasy	5.5/2.0	5.2/1.9	---	---
Emotional Preference	5.3/1.6	5.3/2.1	---	---
Social Preference	4.6/ .9	4.7/ .9	---	---
Sexual Identification	5.2/2.4	5.3/1.4	---	---
Sexual Lifestyle	4.6/1.2	5.0/ .9	---	---

these seven dimensions, white participants scored significantly ($p < .05$, $t = 1.4$) higher on the homosexual identification scale than blacks. Both groups, however, were in the homosexual range. The average African-American participant score was 5.6; their white counterparts' scores averaged 5.9. No differences were found in these two groups' ideal sexual identities.

REFERENCE NOTES

1. Myrdal, 1969:9.
2. For an elaboration of this argument, see Sears, Marshall and Otis-Wilborn, 1986.
3. Substantial scholarship has been produced that critically examines conventional social science research (Bernstein, 1983; Bredo and Feinberg, 1982; Giddens, 1976; Habermas, 1971; Rorty, 1982). Conventional social science inquiry, as Kenneth Plummer (1981:213) concludes in a review of research into homosexuality, "lacks a concern with meaning and intention, is overtly behaviouristic, usually provides 'absolute truths' rather than relative [perspective-based] ones, conceals values behind a mask of objectivity, views facts as unproblematic and favours methodological exactitude over theoretical understanding." For a more in depth discussion of the use of qualitative inquiry in social science research, its unique assumptions, and approaches to data collection, see: Glaser and Strauss, 1967; Guba and Lincoln, 1981; Miles and Huberman, 1984; Yin, 1984.
4. Information about the attitudinal instruments, copies of the questionnaires, and questions asked during the interviews are provided in preliminary reports (Sears, 1987; 1988a).
5. Morin, 1977:636.
6. Bell, Weinberg and Hammersmith, 1981; Harry, 1982.
7. Bell, Weinberg and Hammersmith, 1981:6.
8. "Coming out" is widely used within the gay and lesbian sub-culture to connote a person who has accepted a homosexual identity and disclosed it to others. According to some researchers, "the phenomenological event of self-definition seems to have stronger relationships with attitudes than does the behavioral event of coming out" (Harry and DeVall, 1978:69). See, also: Harry, 1982; Troiden, 1979.
9. Harry, 1986.
10. According to Coleman (1981/82), individuals enter this stage when they first acknowledge their homosexual feelings. Once these feelings have been acknowledged and identified, then the next developmental step is disclosure to non-gay friends and family members. A number of scholars have developed theoretical models of homosexual identity formation (Cass, 1979; Coleman, 1981/82;

Hencken and O'Dowd, 1977; Plummer, 1975; Schafer, 1976). Based upon developmental theories of Erikson (1956) and Sullivan (1974), these models are linear and predicated on the assumption that specific developmental tasks must be completed prior to advancement into the next stage.

11. Bell, Weinberg and Hammersmith, 1982; Coleman, 1981/82; Fisher, 1983; Kimmel, 1979; Minton and Macdonald, 1983/84; Raphael, 1974; Riddle and Morin, 1977; Sophie, 1985; Sophie, 1986; Spada, 1979; Spaulding, 1982; Troiden, 1979; Troiden and Goode, 1980; Weinberg, 1983.

12. Sophie, 1986.

13. Sophie, 1986:50.

14. Plummer, 1975:210.

15. Klein, Sepekoff and Wolf, 1985.

16. Specifically the scale is read as follows for the first five dimensions: 1 (other sex only); 2 (other sex mostly); 3 (other sex somewhat more); 4 (both sexes equally); 5 (same sex somewhat more); 6 (same sex mostly); and 7 (same sex only). For the last two dimensions (identification and lifestyle) the scale reads as follows: 1 (heterosexual only); 2 (heterosexual mostly); 3 (heterosexual somewhat); 4 (heterosexual-homosexual equally); 5 (homosexual somewhat more); 6 (homosexual mostly); and, 7 (homosexual only).

17. High school past was defined by the participant as *either* his or her overall feelings during the four years or his or her feelings during a particularly memorable high school year.

18. The terms "discreditable" and "discredited" are defined in Erving Goffman's ground-breaking book, *Stigma*. The discredited individual "assumes his differentness is known about already or is evident on the spot," whereas the discreditable individual assumes "it is neither known about by those present nor immediately perceivable by them" (Goffman, 1986:4).

References

Abbott, M. (1967). *The Freedman's Bureau in South Carolina, 1865-1872*. Chapel Hill: University of North Carolina Press.

Abbott, S. (1983). *Womenfolks: Growing up down South*. New Haven, CT: Ticknor & Fields.

Abbott, S., & Love, B. (1971). Is women's liberation a lesbian plot? In V. Gornick & B. Moran (Eds.), *Woman in sexist society*. (pp. 601-621). New York: Mentor.

Abbott, S., & Love, B. (1972). *Sappho was a right on woman: A liberated view of lesbianism*. New York: Stein & Day.

Abramson, P. (1984). *Sarah: A sexual biography*. Albany: State University of New York Press.

Adam, B. (1986). Age, structure, and sexuality: Reflections on the anthropological evidence on homosexual relations. In E. Blackwood (Ed.), *The many faces of homosexuality—Anthropological approaches to homosexual behavior*. (pp. 19-33). New York: Harrington Park Press.

Adam, B. (1987). *The rise of a gay liberation movement*. Boston: Twayne.

Aguero, J., Bloch, L., & Byrne, D. (1984). The relationships among sexual beliefs, attitudes, experience, and homophobia. *Journal of Homosexuality*, *10*(1/2), 95-107.

Akers, J., & Conaway, C. (1979). Female homosexual behavior in *Macaca mulatta*. *Archives of Sexual Behavior*, *8*, 63-80.

Alcoff, L. (1988). Cultural feminism versus post-structuralism: The identity crisis in feminist theory. *Signs*, *13*(3), 405-436.

Aldridge, D. (1980). Black female suicides: Is the excitement justified? In L. F. Rodgers-Rose (Ed.), *The black woman*. (pp. 273-284). Beverly Hills: Sage.

Alfred, R. (1982, March 18). Will the real clone please stand up? *Advocate*, *338* (pp. 22-23).

Allen, B. (1987). Youth suicide. *Adolescence*, *22*(86), 271-289.

Altman, D. (1971). *Homosexual: Oppression and liberation*. New York: Outerbridge & Dienstfrey.

Altman, D. (1982). *The homosexualization of America, the Americanization of the homosexual*. New York: St. Martin's Press.

Alyson, S. (1980). *Young, gay and proud*. Boston: Alyson.

Anderson, C. (1981). The effect of a workshop on attitudes of female nursing students toward male homosexuality. *Journal of Homosexuality*, *7*(1), 57-69.

Anderson, S., & Henderson, D. (1985). Working with lesbian alcoholics. *Social Work*, *30*, 518-525.

Apple, M. (Ed). (1982a). *Cultural and economic reproduction in education: Essays on class, ideology and the state*. Boston: Routledge & Kegan Paul.

Apple, M. (1982b). *Education and power*. Boston: Routledge & Kegan Paul.

Apple, M., & Weiss, L. (Eds). (1983). *Ideology and practice in schooling*. Philadelphia: Temple University Press.

Aptheker, B. (1982). *Woman's legacy: Essays on race, sex, and class in American history*. Amherst: University of Massachusetts Press.

Archer, S., & Waterman, A. (1983). Identity in early adolescence. *Journal of Early Adolescence*, *3*(3), 203-214.

Aries, P. (1962). *Centuries of childhood*. New York: Random House.

Ashley, D. (1978, May 28). Teen clubs changing. *Columbia Record*, 1C-2C.

Associated Press. (1987a, March 5). S.C. senator proposes club legislation. *The State*, 15A.

Associated Press. (1987b, October 12). State's black voter turnout below average. *The State*, 12A.

Atkinson, M., & Boyles, J. (1985). The shakey pedestal: Southern ladies yesterday and today. *Southern Studies*, *24*(4), 398-406.

Babchuk, N., & Ballweg, J. (1972). Black family structure and primary relations. *Phylon*, *33*(4), 334-347.

Baer, H. (1984). *The black spiritual movement: A religious response to racism*. Knoxville: University of Tennessee Press.

Baetz, R. (1980). *Lesbian crossroads: Personal stories of lesbian struggles and triumphs*. New York: Morrow.

Bailey, K. (1964). *Southern white protestants*. New York: Harper & Row.

Baker, D. (1980). *A survey of attitudes and knowledge about homosexuality among secondary school teachers in training*. Unpublished masters thesis, Southern Methodist University, Dallas, TX. ERIC No. ED204693.

Baker, L. (1983). *The Percys of Mississippi: Politics and literature in the New South*. Baton Rouge: Louisiana State University Press.

Baker, R. (1966). *The first Southern Baptists*. Nashville, TN: Broadman.

Baker, R. (1968). *Drag: A history of female impersonation on the stage*. London: Triton.

Baker, R. (1974). *The Southern Baptist Convention and its people, 1607-1972*. Nashville, TN: Broadman.

Baker, S. (1980). Biological influences on human sex and gender. *Signs*, 6(1), 80-96.

Baker, T., Steed, R., & Moreland, L. (Eds). (1983). *Religion and politics in the South: Mass and elite perspectives*. New York: Praeger.

Baldwin, J. (1953). *Go tell it on the mountain*. New York: Dial.

Baldwin, J. (1963). *Nobody knows my name*. New York: Dial.

Baldwin, J. (1979). *Just above my head*. New York: Dial.

Baldwin, L. (1983). *"Invisible" strands in African Methodism: A history of the African Union Methodist Protestant and Union American Methodist Episcopal churches, 1805-1980*. Metuchen, NJ: Scarecrow.

Ball, S. (1981). *Beachside comprehensive*. Cambridge, England: Cambridge University Press.

Baraka, A. (1971). *Raise race rays raze: Essays since 1965*. New York: Random House.

Barnhart, E. (1975). Friends and lovers in a lesbian counterculture community. In N. Glazer-Malbin (Ed.), *Old family, new family*. (pp. 90-115). New York: Van Nostrand.

Barrett, M. (1980). *Women's oppression today: Problems in Marxist feminist analysis*. London: Verson.

Bartlett, D. (1977). A Biblical perspective on homosexuality. *Foundations: Baptist Journal of History and Theology*, *20*, 133-147.

Bartley, N. (Ed). (1988). *The evolution of Southern culture*. Athens: University of Georgia Press.

Bass, E., & Thorton, L. (Eds). (1983). *I never told anyone: Writings by women survivors of child sexual abuse*. New York: Harper & Row.

Bass-Hass, R. (1968). The lesbian dyad. *Journal of Sex Research*, *4*(2), 108-126.

Batchelor, E. (Ed). (1980). *Homosexuality and ethics*. New York: Pilgrim.

Bate, N. (1982, August 19). A gay magazine ahead of its day. *Advocate*, *349* (p. 41).

Bates, J., Bentler, P., & Thompson, S. (1979). Gender-deviant boys compared with normal and clinical control boys. *Journal of Abnormal Child Psychology*, *7*(3), 243-259.

Beam, J. (Ed). (1986). *In the life: A black gay anthology*. Boston: Alyson.

Beame, T. (1982a, April 1). From a black perspective: Racism (a conversation). *Advocate*, *339* (pp. 23-25).

Beame, T. (1982b, December 23). Mike Smith and *Black and White Men Together*. *Advocate*, *358* (pp. 21-22).

Beame, T. (1982c, July 8). Young, gifted, black and gay. *Advocate*, *346* (pp. 25-27, 55).

Beck, E. (Ed). (1982). *Nice Jewish girls: A lesbian anthology*. Watertown, MA: Persephone.

Beck-Fein, S., & Nuehring, E. (1975). Perspectives of gender-integrated gay community. *Homosexual Counseling Journal*, *2*(4), 150-163.

Bell, A., & Weinberg, M. (1978). *Homosexualities*. New York: Simon & Schuster.

Bell, A., Weinberg, M., & Hammersmith, S. (1981). *Sexual preference*. Bloomington: Indiana University Press.

Bell, A. (1971). *Dancing the gay lib blues: A year in the homosexual movement*. New York: Simon & Schuster.

Bellah, R. (1975). *The broken covenant: American civil religion in time of trial*. New York: Seabury.

Bene, E. (1965). On the genesis of female homosexuality. *British Journal of Psychiatry, 111*(478), 815-821.

Bennett, G. (1982). *The black church in American culture: An empirical study of black church members' perceptions of the black church in Albany, Georgia as a social change agent.* Unpublished doctoral dissertation, Bowling Green State University, Bowling Green, OH. *Dissertation Abstracts International, 44,* 284A.

Bennett, S., & Gibbs, J. (1980). Racism and classism in the lesbian community: Towards the building of a radical autonomous lesbian movement. In J. Gibbs & S. Bennett (Eds.), *Top Ranking: A collection of articles on racism and classism in the lesbian community.* (pp. 1-31). New York: February 3 Press.

Bentson, M. (1969). The political economy of women's liberation. *Monthly Review, 21*(4), 13-27.

Bernard, L., & Epstein, D. (1978). Androgyny scores of matched homosexual and heterosexual males. *Journal of Homosexuality, 4*(2), 169-178.

Bernstein, B. (1977). *Class, codes and control, Volume 3: Towards a theory of educational transmissions.* London: Routledge & Kegan Paul.

Bernstein, R. (1983). *Beyond objectivism and relativism.* Chicago: University of Chicago Press.

Berry, M., & Blassingame, J. (1982). *Long memory: The black experience in America.* New York: Oxford University Press.

Berry, S. (1982, December 9). Up the social ladder: Cutting the upper crust. *Advocate, 357* (pp. 27, 29).

Bethel, E. (1981). *Promiseland: A century of life in a Negro community.* Philadelphia: Temple University Press.

Bieber, I., Dain, H., Dince, P., Drellich, M., Grand, H., Gundlach, R., Kremer, M., Rifkin, A., Wilbur, C., and Bieber, T. (1962). *Homosexuality: A psychoanalytical study.* New York: Basic Books.

Bieber, I. (1976). A discussion of "Homosexuality: The ethical challenge." *Journal of Consulting and Clinical Psychology, 44,* 163-166.

Billingsley, A. (1968). *Black families in white America.* Englewood Cliffs, NJ: Prentice-Hall.

Billingsley, A. (1976). The evolution of the black family. In National Urban League (Ed.), *Black perspectives on the Bicentennial*. New York: Author.

Billingham, R., & Hockenberry, S. (1987). Gender conformity, masturbation fantasy, infatuation, and sexual orientation. *Journal of Sex Research*, *23*(3), 368-374.

Birchard, R. (1977). Metropolitan Community Church: Its development and significance. *Foundations: Baptist Journal of History and Theology*, *20*(2), 127-132.

Birke, L. (1982). From sin to sickness: Hormonal theories of lesbianism. In R. Hubbard (Ed.), *Biological woman – The convenient myth*. (pp. 71-90). Cambridge, MA: Schenkman.

Birke, L. (1981). Is homosexuality hormonally determined? *Journal of Homosexuality*, *6*(4), 35-49.

Blachford, G. (1981). Male dominance and the gay world. In K. Plummer (Ed.), *The making of the modern homosexual*. (pp. 184-210). Totowa, NJ: Barnes & Noble.

Black Scholar. (1979). The black sexism debate. [Special issue]. *Black Scholar*, *10*(8/9).

Blackwell, J. (1975). *The black community*. New York: Dodd, Mead.

Blackwelder, J. (1979). Southern white fundamentalists and the civil rights movement. *Phylon*, *40*(4), 334-341.

Blackwood, E. (1986). Breaking the mirror: The construction of lesbianism and the anthropological discourse on homosexuality. In E. Blackwood (Ed.), *The many faces of homosexuality – Anthropological approaches to homosexual behavior*. (pp. 1-17). New York: Harrington Park Press.

Blackwood, E. (1984a). Sexuality and gender in certain Native American tribes. *Signs*, *10*(1), 27-42.

Blackwood, E. (1984b). *Cross-cultural dimensions of lesbian relations*. Unpublished master thesis, San Francisco State University, San Francisco, CA.

Blanchard, R., McConkey, J., Roper, V., and Skiner, B. (1983). Measuring physical aggressiveness in heterosexual, homosexual, and transsexual males. *Archives of Sexual Behavior*, *12*(6), 511-524.

Blassingame, J. (1971). *The slave community*. New York: Oxford University Press.

Bolton, S. (1982). *Southern Anglicanism: The Church of England in colonial South Carolina*. Westport, CT: Greenwood Press.

Boney, F. (1984). *Southerners all*. Macon, GA: Mercer.

Bossard, J., & Boll, E. (1950). *Ritual in family living: A contemporary study*. Philadelphia, PA: University of Pennsylvania Press.

Boswell, J. (1980). *Christianity, social tolerance, and homosexuality*. Chicago: University of Chicago Press.

Botting, H., & Botting, G. (1984). *The Orwellian world of Jehovah's Witnesses*. Toronto, Canada: University of Toronto Press.

Bourdieu, P., & Passeron, J. (1977). *Reproduction in education, society and culture*. Beverly Hills: Sage.

Bowles, S., & Gintis, H. (1976). *Schooling in capitalist America*. New York: David McKay.

Brandes, S. (1981). Male sexual ideology in an Andalusian town. In S. Ortner & H. Whitehead (Eds.), *Sexual meanings: The cultural construction of gender and sexuality*. (pp. 192-239). Cambridge, England: Cambridge University Press.

Braungart, R., & Braungart, M. (1988). From yippies to yuppies: Twenty years of freshman attitudes. *Public Opinion*, *11*(3), 53-57.

Bredo, E., & Feinberg, W. (Eds). (1982). *Knowledge and values in social and educational research*. Philadelphia: Temple University Press.

Brick, B. (1979). Judaism in the gay community. In B. Berzon & R. Leighton (Eds.), *Positively gay*. (pp. 79-87). Milbrae, CA: Celestial Arts.

Bronski, M. (1984). *Culture clash: The making of gay sensibility*. Boston: South End.

Broverman, I., Vogel, S., Broverman, D., Clarkson, F., and Rosenkratz, P. (1972). Sex-role stereotypes: A current appraisal. *Journal of Social Issues*, *28*(2), 59-78.

Brown, L. (1987). Lesbians, weight, and eating: New analyses and perspectives. In Boston Lesbian Psychologies Collective (Ed.), In *Lesbian psychologies: Exploration and challenges*. (pp. 294-309). Urbana: University of Illinois Press.

Brown, R. M. (1970). The woman-identified woman. *Ladder*, *14*(11-12), 6-8.

Browning, C. (1984). Changing theories of lesbianism: Challenging the stereotypes. In T. Darty & S. Potter (Eds.), *Women-identified women*. (pp. 11-29). Palo Alto, CA: Mayfield.

Browning, C. (1987). Therapeutic issues and intervention strategies with young adult lesbian clients: A developmental approach. *Journal of Homosexuality*, *14*(1/2), 45-52.

Buhrich, N., & McConaghy, N. (1978). Parental relationships during childhood in homosexuality, transvestism and transsexualism. *Australian and New Zealand Journal of Psychiatry*, *12*, 103-108.

Buhrich, N., & McConaghy, N. (1979). Tests of gender feelings and behavior in homosexuality, transvestism, and transsexualism. *Journal of Clinical Psychology*, *35*(1), 187-191.

Bulkin, E., Pratt, M., & Smith, B. (1984). *Yours in struggle: Three feminist perspectives on anti-semitism and racism*. Brooklyn, NY: Long Haul.

Bullough, V. (1976). *Sex, society, and history*. New York: Science History.

Burgess, A., & Holmstrom, L. (1979). *Rape: Crisis and recovery*. Bowie, MD: Brady.

Butts, J. (1981, April). Is homosexuality a threat to the black family? *Ebony* (pp. 138-140, 142-144).

Califia, P. (1979). Lesbian sexuality. *Journal of Homosexuality*, *4*(3), 255-266.

Caplan, P. (Ed). (1987). *The cultural construction of sexuality*. London: Tavistock.

Carby, H. (1986). It jus be's dat way sometime: The sexual politics of women's blues. *Radical America*, *20*(4), 9-24.

Carlson, D. (1980/81). Making student types. *Interchange*, *11*(2), 11-29.

Carnoy, M., & Levin, H. (1985). *Schooling and work in the democratic state*. Stanford: Stanford University Press.

Carrier, J. (1986). Childhood cross-gender behavior and adult homosexuality. *Archives of Sexual Behavior*, *15*(1), 89-93.

Carrier, J. (1980). Homosexual behavior in cross-cultural perspective. In Judd Marmor (Ed.), *Homosexual behavior: A modern reappraisal.* (pp. 100-122). New York: Basic.

Carrington, C. (1980). Depression in black women: A theoretical appraisal. In L. Rodgers-Rose (Ed.), *The black woman.* (pp. 265-271). Beverly Hills: Sage.

Cash, W. (1941). *The mind of the South.* New York: Knopf.

Cass, V. (1979). Homosexual identity formation: A theoretical model. *Journal of Homosexuality, 4*(3), 219-235.

Castells, M., & Murphy, K. (1982). Cultural identity and urban structure: The spatial organization of San Francisco's gay community. In N. Fainstein & S. Fainstein (Eds.), *Urban policy under capitalism.* (pp. 237-259). Beverly Hills: Sage.

Cather, W. (1936). The novel demeuble. *Not under forty.* (pp. 43-51). New York: Knopf.

Cauthern, C. (1979). 900 black lesbians. *Off Our Backs, 9*(6), 12.

Cauthern, C. (1980). Black lesbians and the gay liberation movement. In J. Gibbs & S. Bennett (Eds.), *Top ranking: A collection of articles on racism and classism in the lesbian community.* (pp. 42-43). New York: February 3 Press.

Cavin, S. (1985). *Lesbian origins.* San Francisco: Ism.

Cheal, D. (1988). The ritualization of family ties. *American Behavioral Scientist, 31*(6), 632-643.

Cherow-O'Leary, R. (1987). *The state-by-state guide to women's legal rights.* New York: McGraw-Hill.

Chesbro, J. (Ed) (1981). *Gayspeak: Gay male and lesbian communication.* New York: Pilgrim.

Chodorow, N. (1978). *The reproduction of mothering: Psychoanalysis and the sociology of gender.* Berkeley: University of California Press.

Cicourel, A., Jennings, K., Jennings, S., Leiter, K., MacKay, R., Mehan, H., Roth, D. (1974). *Language use and school performance.* New York: Academic Press.

Circourel, A., & Kitsuse, J. (1963). *The educational decision makers.* Indianapolis: Bobbs-Merrill.

Clark, K. (1956). *The nude: A study of ideal art.* Princeton, NJ: Princeton University Press.

Clarke, C. (1983). The failure to transform: Homophobia in the black community. In B. Smith (Ed.), *Home girls: A black femi-*

nist anthology. (pp. 197-208). New York: Kitchen Table: Women of Color Press.

Cleaver, E. (1968). *Soul on ice*. New York: McGraw Hill.

Cole, R. (1970, September 30). Collision in San Francisco. *Advocate, 43* (pp. 1-2, 6-7, 12).

Coleman, E. (1981/82). Developmental stages of the coming out process. *Journal of Homosexuality, 7*(2/3), 31-43.

Coleman, J. (1961). *Adolescent society: The social life of the teenager and its impact on education*. New York: Free Press.

Coleman, M. (1986). Nontraditional boys: A minority in need of reassessment. *Child Welfare, 65*(3), 252-259.

Coles, R. (1967). *Children of crisis*. Boston: Little, Brown, and Company.

Coles, R. (1971). *Migrants, sharecroppers, and mountaineers*. Boston: Little, Brown, and Company.

Coles, R., & Stokes, G. (1985). *Sex and the American teenager*. New York: Harper & Row.

Collins, A., & Sussewell, D. (1986). The Afro-American woman's emerging selves. *Journal of Black Psychology, 13*(1), 1-11.

Colsanto, D. (1988). Black attitudes. *Public Opinion, 10*(5), 45-49.

Combahee River Collective. (1982). A black feminist statement. In G. Hull, P. Scott, & B. Smith (Eds.), *But some of us are brave: Black women's studies*. (pp. 13-22). New York: Feminist Press.

Cone, J. (1988). Black religious thought. In C. Lippy & P. Williams (Eds.), *Encyclopedia of the American religious experience: Studies of traditions and movements, Volume II*. (pp. 1173-1187). New York: Scribner.

Cone, J. (1984). *For my people: Black theology and the black church*. Maryknoll, NY: Orbis.

Conroy, P. (1976). *The great Santini*. Boston: Houghton Mifflin.

Cook, A. T. (1988). *And God loves each one: A resource for dialogue about the church and homosexuality*. Nashville, TN: Reconciling Congregation Program.

Cooper, A. (1969). *A voice from the South*. New York: Negro University Press.

Corbett, M. (1982). *Political tolerance in America: Freedom and equality in public attitudes*. New York: Longman.

Corbett, M. (1988). Changes in noneconomic political attitudes of southern and northern youth, 1970s to 1980s. *Journal of Youth and Adolescence*, *17*(3), 197-210.

Cornwell, A. (1978). Three for the price of one: Notes from a gay black feminist. In K. Jay and A. Young (Eds.), *Lavender culture*. (pp. 466-476). New York: Jove.

Cornwell, A. (1983). *Black lesbian in white America*. Tallahassee, FL: Naiad.

Cory, D., & LeRoy, J. (1963). *The homosexual in his society*. New York: Citadel.

Cotton, W. (1975). Social and sexual relationships of lesbians. *Journal of Sex Research*, *11*(2), 139-148.

Crew, L. (1978). Honey, Let's talk about the Queen's English. *Gai Saber*, *1*(3), 240-243.

Culler, J. (1982). *On deconstructionism*. Ithaca, NY: Cornell University Press.

Curb, R., & Manahan, N. (Eds). (1985). Lesbian nuns: Breaking the silence. Tallahassee, FL: Naiad.

Current, R. (1983). *Northernizing the South*. Athens: University of Georgia Press.

Cusick, P. (1983). *The egalitarian ideal and the American high school*. New York: Longman.

Daly, M. (1973). *Beyond God the father: Toward a philosophy of women's liberation*. Boston: Beacon Press.

Daly, M. (1984). *Pure lust: Elementary feminist philosophy*. Boston: Beacon Press.

Daniel, R. (1980). *Fatal flowers: On sin, sex, and suicide in the Deep South*. New York: Holt, Rinehart and Winston.

Dank, B. (1971). Coming out in the gay world. *Psychiatry*, *34*(2), 180-197.

Darsey, J. (1981a). From "commies" and "queers" to "gay is good." In J. Chesbro (Ed.), *Gayspeak: Gay male and lesbian communication*. (pp. 224-247). New York: Pilgrim.

Darsey, J. (1981b). "Gayspeak": A response. In J. Chesbro (Ed.), *Gayspeak: Gay male and lesbian communication*. (pp. 58-67). New York: Pilgrim.

Davenport, W. (1965). Sexual patterns and their regulation in a society of the Southwest Pacific. In F. Beach (Ed.), *Sex and behavior*. (pp. 164-207). New York: Wiley.

Davidson, C. (1972). *Biracial politics*. Baton Rouge: Louisiana State University Press.

Davis, A. (1970). Sexual assaults in the Philadelphia prison system. In J. Gagnon, & W. Simon (Eds.), *The sexual scene*. (pp. 107-124). Chicago: Aldine.

Davis, M. (Ed) (1982). *Contributions of black women to America. Volumes I and II*. Columbia, SC: Kenday.

Davison, G., & Wilson, G. (1973). Attitudes of behavior therapists toward homosexuality. *Behavior Therapy*, *4*(5), 686-696.

Davison, K., Brierly, H., & Smith, C. (1971). A male monozygotic twinship discordant for homosexuality. *British Journal of Psychology*, *118*(547), 675-682.

de Beauvoir, S. (1952) *The second sex*. New York: Knopf.

de Young, M. (1982). *The sexual victimization of children*. Jefferson, NC: McFarland.

DeCecco, J. (Ed). (1988). *Gay relationships*. New York: The Haworth Press.

DeCecco, J. (1981, October 29). Pleasure and queers. *Advocate*, *329* (pp. 20-23).

D'Emilio, J. (1983). *Sexual politics, sexual communities: The making of a homosexual minority in the United States, 1940-1970*. Chicago: University of Chicago Press.

D'Emilio, J., & Freedman, E. (1988). *Intimate matters: A history of sexuality in America*. New York: Harper & Row.

Denis, A. (1967). *Taboo*. New York: Putnam.

Denniston, R. (1980). Ambisexuality in animals. In J. Marmor (Ed.), *Homosexual behavior: A modern reappraisal*. (pp. 25-40). New York: Basic.

Deutsch, H. (1945). *Psychology of women*. New York: Grune & Stratton.

Dewey, J. (1916). *Democracy and education*. New York: Macmillan.

Diamond, D., & Wilsnack, S. (1978). Alcohol abuse among lesbians: A descriptive study. *Journal of Homosexuality*, *4(2)*, 123-142.

Dimen, M. (1984). Politically correct? Politically incorrect? In C.

Vance (Ed.), *Pleasure and danger*. (pp. 138-148). Boston: Routledge & Kegan Paul.

Donovan, J. (1985). *Feminist theory: The intellectual traditions of American feminism*. New York: Ungar.

Dörner, G. (1976). *Hormones and brain differentiation*. Amsterdam: Elsevier.

Dörner, G., Rohde, W., Stahl, F., Krell, L. and Wolf-Günther, M. (1975). A neuroendocrine predisposition for homosexuality in men. *Archives of Sexual Behavior*, *4*(1), 1-8.

Dressler, J. (1978). Gay teachers: A disesteemed minority in an overly esteemed profession. *Rutgers Camden Law Review*, *9*(3), 399-445.

Dressler, J. (1985). Survey of school principals regarding alleged homosexual teachers in the classroom: How likely (really) is discharge? *University of Dayton Law Review*, *10*(3), 599-620.

Dreyfus, H., & Rabinow, P. (1983). *Michael Foucault: Beyond structuralism and hermeneutics*. Chicago: University of Chicago Press.

DuBay, W. (1987). *Gay identity: The self under ban*. Jefferson, NC: McFarland.

Duberman, M. (1986). *About time*. New York: Gay Press.

Duberman, M. (1980/81). ''Writhing bedfellows'': 1826 Two young men from antebellum South Carolina's ruling elite share ''extravagant delight.'' *Journal of Homosexuality*, *6*(1/2), 85-101.

DuBois, W. (1967). *The Philadelphia Negro*. New York: Schocken. (Original work published in 1899).

Dunbar, J., Brown, M., & Vourinen, S. (1973). Attitudes toward homosexuality among Brazilian and Canadian college students. *Journal of Social Psychology*, *90*(2), 173-183.

Duncan, B., & Duncan, O. (1978). *Sex typing and social roles*. New York: Academic.

Durant, T., & Louden, J. (1986). The black middle class in America: Historical and contemporary perspectives. *Phylon*, *47*(4), 253-263.

Durell, A. (1984). At home. In B. Galloway (Ed.), *Discrimination against gay people in modern Britain*. (pp. 1-18). London: Routledge & Kegan Paul.

Dutile, F. (1986). *Sex, schools and the law*. Springfield, IL: Thomas.

Ebert, A. (1980, April). Lea Hopkins: Just different. *Essence, 10* (pp. 88-89 +).

The Economist. (1982 January 23). Business brief: The homosexual economy. *The Economist*, 73-74.

Egerton, J. (1974). *The Americanization of Dixie: The Southernization of America*. New York: Harper's Magazine Press.

Eggleston, J. (1977). *The sociology of the school curriculum*. Boston: Routledge & Kegan Paul.

Eighmy, J. (1972). *Churches in cultural captivity*. Knoxville, TN: The University of Tennessee Press.

Eisenstein, Z. (Ed.). (1979). *Capitalist patriarchy and the case for socialist feminism*. New York: Monthly Review.

Elkins, S. (1968). *Slavery: A problem in American institutional and intellectual life*. Chicago: University of Chicago Press.

England, M. (1980). *The Bible and homosexuality*. San Francisco: Metropolitan Community Church.

Engram, E. (1982). *Science, myth, reality: The black family in one-half century of research*. Westport, CT: Greenwood.

Erickson, F. (1975). Gatekeeping and the melting pot: Interaction in counseling encounters. *Harvard Educational Review, 45(1)*, 44-70.

Erikson, E. (1956). The problem of ego identity. *Journal of the American Psychoanalytic Association*, *4*, 56-121.

Erikson, E. (1968). *Identity, youth, and crisis*. New York: Norton.

Escoffier, J. (1985). Sexual revolution and the politics of gay identity. *Socialist Review*, *82-83*, 119-153.

Evans, R. (1969). Childhood parental relationships of homosexual men. *Journal of Consulting Psychology*, *33*(2), 129-135.

Everhart, R. (1983). *Reading, writing and resistance*. Boston: Routledge & Kegan Paul.

Eysenck, H. (1986). *Decline and fall of the Freudian empire*. New York: Viking.

Faderman, L. (1984). The "new gay" lesbians. *Journal of Homosexuality*, *10*(3/4), 85-95.

Fanon, F. (1967). *Black skin, white masks*. New York: Grove.

Farganis, S. (1986). *Social reconstruction of the feminine character*. Totowa, NJ: Rowman & Littlefield.

Faust, D. (1982). *James Henry Hammond and the Old South: A design for mastery*. Baton Rouge: Louisiana State University Press.

Fausto-Sterling, A. (1985). *Myths of gender. Biological theories about women and men*. New York: Basic.

Fay, R., Turner, C., Klassen, A., & Gaganon, J. (1989, January 20). Prevalence and pattern of same-gender sexual contact among men. *Science, 243*(4889), 338-349.

Feinberg, A. (1981). *Sex and the pulpit*. Toronto, Canada: Methuen.

Fields, W. (1983). Jordan's stormy banks: Religion in a changing South. In J. Boles (Ed.), *Dixie dateline: A journalist portrait of the contemporary South*. (pp. 65-79). Houston, TX: Rice University Studies.

Finger, F. (1975). Changes in sex practices and beliefs of male college students during 30 years. *Journal of Sex Research, 11*(4), 304-317.

Finkelhor, D. (1986). *A sourcebook on childhood sexual abuse*. Beverly Hills: Sage.

Finkelhor, D., & Hotaling, G. (1984). Sexual abuse in the national incidence study of child abuse and neglect: An appraisal. *Child Abuse and Neglect, 8*(1), 23-33.

Fischer, T. (1982). *A study of educators' attitudes toward homosexuality*. Unpublished doctoral dissertation, University of Virginia, Charlottesville, VA. *Dissertation Abstracts International 43*, 10, 3294A.

Fisher, E. (1983). *An investigation of the process of identification and disclosure of the sexual preference of lesbians*. Unpublished doctoral dissertation, University of Pittsburgh, Pittsburgh, PA. *Dissertation Abstracts International 44*, 8, 173.

Fisher, S. (1965). A note on male homosexuality and the role of women in ancient Greece. In J. Marmore (Ed.), *Sexual inversion: The multiple roots of homosexuality*. (pp. 165-172). New York: Basic.

Fishman, J. (1934). *Sex in prison*. New York: National Library Press.

Fitzgerald, F. (1986). *Cities on a hill*. New York: Simon & Schuster.

Fladung, T. (1987, October 18). S.C. battles for defense dollars. *The State*, 1G, 7G.

Flynt, W. (1979). *Dixie's forgotten people: The South's poor whites*. Bloomington: Indiana University Press.

Fogarty, E. (1980). *Passing as straight: A phenomenological analysis of the experience of the lesbian who is professionally employed*. Unpublished doctoral dissertation, University of Pittsburgh, Pittsburgh, PA. *Dissertation Abstracts International* 41, 6, 2384B.

Fogel, W., & Engerman, S. (1974). *Time on the cross*. Boston: Little, Brown and Company.

Ford, C., & Beach, F. (1951). *Patterns of sexual behavior*. New York: Harper & Row.

Foreman, A. (1977). *Femininity as alienation: Women and the family in Marxism and psychoanalysis*. London: Pluto.

Forgey, D. (1975). The institution of the Berdache among the North American Plains Indians. *Journal of Sex Research*, *11(1)*, 1-15.

Fort, J., Steiner, C., & Conrad, F. (1971). Attitudes of mental health professionals toward homosexuality and its treatment. *Psychological Reports*, *29*(2), 347-350.

Fortunato, J. (1982). *Embracing the exile: Healing journeys of gay Christians*. New York: Seabury.

Foster, J. (1975). *Sex variant women in literature: An historical and quantitative survey*. New York: Vantage Press.

Foucault, M. (1978). *The history of sexuality: Vol 1: An introduction*. New York: Pantheon.

Franklin II, C. (1984). Black male-black female conflict: Individually caused and culturally nurtured. *Journal of Black Studies*, *15*(2), 139-154.

Fraser, W., Saunders, R., & Wakelyn, J. (1985). *The web of social relations: Women, family and education*. Athens: University of Georgia Press.

Frazier, E. F. (1925). Durham: Capital of the black middle class. In A. Locke (Ed.), *The new Negro*. (pp. 333-340). New York: Boni.

Frazier, E. F. (1932). *The free Negro family*. Nashville: Fisk University Press.

Frazier, E. F. (1939). *The Negro family in the United States*. Chicago: University of Chicago Press.

Frazier, E. F. (1949). *The Negro in the United States*. New York: Macmillan.

Frazier, E. F. (1964). *The Negro church in America*. New York: Schocken.

Frazier, E. F. (1968). *On race relations: Selected writings*. (G. Franklin, Ed.) Chicago: University of Chicago Press.

Frazier, E. F. (1957a). *Black bourgeoisie*. New York: Collier.

Frazier, E. F. (1957b). The Negro middle class and desegregation. *Social Problems*, *4*, 291-301.

Frazier, J. (1913). *The Golden Bough*. New York: Macmillan.

Freedman, M. (1971). *Homosexuality and psychological function*. Belmont, CA: Brooks/Cole.

Freud, S. (1922). *Group psychology and the analysis of the ego*. In James Strachey (Trans.), New York: Liveright.

Freud, S. (1963a). The passing of the Oedipus Complex. In P. Rieff (Ed.), *Sexuality and the power of love*. (pp. 176-182). New York: Collier. (Original work published in 1924).

Freud, S. (1963b). The psychogenesis of a case of homosexuality in a woman. In P. Rieff (Ed.), *Sexuality and the power of love*. (pp. 133-159). New York: Collier. (Original work published in 1920).

Freud, S. (1963c). Some psychological consequences of the anatomical distinction between the sexes. In P. Rieff (Ed.), *Sexuality and the power of love*. (pp. 183-193). New York: Collier. (Original work published in 1925).

Freud, S. (1964). *Leonardo da Vinci and a memory of childhood*. Alan Tyson (Trans.), New York: Norton.

Freund, K., & Blanchard, R. (1983). Is the distant relationship of fathers and homosexual sons related to the sons' erotic preference for male partners, or to the son's atypical gender identity, or both? *Journal of Homosexuality*, *9*(1), 7-25.

Freund, K., Nagler, E., Langewin, R., Zajac, A., & Steiner, B. (1974). Measuring feminine gender identity in homosexual males. *Archives of Sexual Behavior*, *3*(3), 249-260.

Furnish, V. (1979). *The moral teaching of Paul: Selected issues*. Nashville: Abingdon.

Fyfe, B. (1983). "Homophobia" or homosexual bias reconsidered. *Archives of Sexual Behavior, 12*(6), 549-554.

Gagnon, J., & Simon, W. (1973). *Sexual conduct*. Chicago: Aldine.

Garfinkle, E., & Morin, S. (1978). Psychologists' attitudes toward homosexual psychotherapy clients. *Journal of Social Issues, 34*(3), 101-112.

Garrett, D. (1986). Creating ourselves: An open letter. In J. Beam (Ed.), *In the life: A black gay anthology*. (pp. 93-103). Boston: Alyson.

Gartrell, N. (1982). Hormones and homosexuality. In W. Paul et al. (Eds.), *Homosexuality: Social, psychological and biological issues*. (pp. 169-183). Beverly Hills: Sage.

Gartrell, N., Kraemer, H., & Brodie, H. (1974). Psychiatrists' attitudes toward female homosexuality. *Journal of Nervous and Mental Diseases, 159*(2), 141-144.

Gathorne-Hardy, J. (1978). *The old school tie: The phenomenon of the English public school*. New York: Viking.

Gaustad, E. (1980). *Baptists, the Bible, church order and the churches: Essays from "Foundations, a Baptist Journal of History and Theology."* New York: Arno.

Gay Teachers' Group (1978). *Open + positive: An account of how John Warburton came out at school and the consequences*. London: Gay Teachers' Group.

Gay Teachers' Group (1987). *School's out*. London: Biddles.

Geertz, C. (1973). *The interpretation of culture*. New York: Basic Books.

Geist, V. (1971). *Mountain sheep*. Chicago: University of Chicago Press.

Genovese, E. (1974). *Roll, Jordan, roll: The world the slaves made*. New York: Pantheon.

Genovese, E., & Fox-Genovese, E. (1988). The religious ideals of southern slave society. In N. Bartley (Ed.), *The evolution of southern culture*. (pp. 14-27). Athens: University of Georgia Press.

Gentry, C. (1986a). Social distance regarding male and female homosexuals. *Journal of Social Psychology*, *127*(2), 199-208.

Gentry, C. (1986b). Development of scales measuring social distance toward male and female homosexuals. *Journal of Homosexuality*, *13*(1), 75-82.

George, C. (1973). *Segregated Sabbaths: Richard Allen and the emergence of independent black churches, 1760-1840*. New York: Oxford University Press.

Gerard, K., & Hekma, G. (1989). *The pursuit of sodomy: Male homosexuality in Renaissance and Enlightenment Europe*. New York: Harrington Park Press.

Gerstner, J. (1978). *The teachings of the Jehovah's Witnesses*. Grand Rapids, MI: Baker.

Giallombardo, R. (1966). *Society of women*. New York: Wiley.

Gibbons, S., Wylie, M., Echterling, L., & French, J. (1986). Patterns of alcohol use among rural and small-town adolescents. *Adolescence*, *21*(84), 887-900.

Gibson, P. (1983). Gay and lesbian youth suicide. In *National Conference on Prevention and Interventions in Youth Suicide*. Oakland, CA: U.S. Department of Health and Human Services, National Institute of Mental Health, Task Force on Youth Suicide.

Giddens, A. (1976). *New rules of the sociological method*. New York: Basic Books.

Giddings, P. (1984). *When and where I enter: The impact of black women on race and sex in America*. New York: Morrow.

Giroux, H. (1988). *Teachers as intellectuals: Toward a critical pedagogy of learning*. Boston: Bergin & Garvey.

Giroux, H. (1983). *Theory and resistance in education*. South Hadley, MA: Bergin & Garvey.

Gladue, B., Green, R., and Hellman, R. (1984, September 9). Neuroendocrine response to estrogen and sexual orientation. *Science*, *225* (pp. 1496-1499).

Glaser, B., & Strauss, A. (1969). *The discovery of grounded theory: Strategies for qualitative research*. Chicago: Aldine.

Glassner, B., & Owen, C. (1979). Variations in attitudes toward homosexuality. *Cornell Journal of Social Relations*, *11*, 161-176.

Glenbard East *Echo* (1987). *Voices of conflict: Teenagers themselves*. New York: Adama.

Glenn, A., & Russell, R. (1986). Heterosexual bias among counselor trainees. *Counselor Education and Supervision*, *25*(3), 222-229.

Goffman, E. (1986). *Stigma: Notes on the management of spoiled identity*. New York: Touchtone.

Goldfoot, D., Loon, H., Groeneveld, W., and Slob, A. (1980). Behavioral and physiological evidence of sexual climax in the female stump-tailed macaque (*Macaca arctuides*). *Science*, 208, (pp. 1477-1479).

Goldstein, B., & Oldham, J. (1979). *Children at work: A study of socialization*. New Brunswick, NJ: Transaction Books.

Goldstein, M. (1982). Some tolerant attitudes toward female homosexuality throughout history. *Journal of Psychohistory*, *9*(4), 437-460.

Gooch, B. (1984, May 15). Cursing the San Remo. *Advocate*, *394* (pp. 26-30).

Goode, E., & Troiden, R. (1979). Heterosexual and homosexual activity among gay males. *Deviant Behavior*, *1*(37), 37-55.

Goodwin, J. (1984). *More man than you'll ever be: Gay folklore and acculturation*. Unpublished doctoral dissertation, Indiana University, Bloomington, IN. *Dissertation Abstracts International* 46, 1, 200A.

Gottlieb, D. (1977). *The gay tapes: A candid discussion about male homosexuality*. New York: Stein & Day.

Gouldner, A. (1971). *The coming crisis in sociology*. New York: Avon.

Grahn, J. (1984). *Another mother tongue: Gay words, gay worlds*. Boston: Beacon Press.

Grahn, J. (1985). *The highest apple: Sappho and the lesbian poetic tradition*. San Francisco: Spinsters' Ink.

Gramick, J. (1984). Developing a lesbian identity. In T. Darty & S. Potter (Eds.), *Women-identified women*. (pp. 31-44). Palo Alto, CA: Mayfield.

Grant, J. (1982). Black women and the church. In G. Hull, P. Scott & B. Smith (Eds.), *All the women are white, all the blacks are men. But some of us are brave: Black women's studies*. (pp. 141-152). Old Westbury, NY: Feminist Press.

Green, M. (1983). *Black women composers: A genesis*. Boston: Twayne.

Green, R. (1969). Childhood cross-gender identification. In R. Green & J. Money (Eds.), *Transexualism and sex reassignment*. (pp. 25-35). Baltimore, MD: Johns Hopkins University Press.

Green, R. (1973). Twenty-five boys with atypical gender identity. In J. Aubin & J. Money (Eds.), *Contemporary sexual behavior. Critical issues in the 1970s*. (pp. 351-358). Baltimore: The Johns Hopkins University Press.

Green, R. (1974). *Sexual identity conflict in children and adults*. New York: Basic Books.

Green, R. (1976). One-hundred ten feminine and masculine boys: Behavioral contrasts and demographic similarities. *Archives of Sexual Behavior*, 5(5), 425-446.

Green, R. (1987). *The "sissy boy syndrome" and the development of homosexuality*. New Haven, CT: Yale University Press.

Green, R., & Money, J. (1966). Stage-acting, role-taking, and effeminate impersonation during boyhood. *Archives of General Psychiatry*, 15(11), 535-538.

Greenberg, D. (1988). *The construction of homosexuality*. Chicago: University of Chicago Press.

Greer, G. (1970). *The female eunuch*. New York: McGraw-Hill.

Grellert, E. (1982a). Childhood play behavior of heterosexual and homosexual men. *Psychological Reports*, 51(2), 607-610.

Grellert, E., Newcomb, M., & Bentler, P. (1982b). Childhood play activities of male and female homosexuals and heterosexuals. *Archives of Sexual Behavior*, 11(6), 451-478.

Grier, B., & Reid, C. (Eds). (1976). *Lesbian lives: Biographies of women from The Ladder*. Oakland, CA: Diana Press.

Griffin, P. (1989) *Using participatory research to empower gay and lesbian educators*. Paper presented at the American Educational Research Association. San Francisco.

Griffin, S. (1980). *Woman and nature: The roaring inside her*. New York: Harper.

Grindal, B. (1982). The religious interpretation of experience in a rural black community. In R. Hall & C. Stack (Eds.), *Holding on to the land and the Lord*. (pp. 89-101). Athens: University of Georgia Press.

Groves, P. (1985). Coming out. *Women and therapy*, *4*(2), 17-22.

Guba, E., & Lincoln, Y. (1981). *Effective evaluation*. San Francisco: Jossey-Bass.

Guest, C. (1986). *The debutante's guide to life*. New York: Fawcett.

Gumaer, J. (1987). Understanding and counseling gay men: A developmental perspective. *Journal of Counseling and Development*, *66*(3), 144-146.

Gundlach, R. (1977). Sexual molestation and rape reported by homosexual and heterosexual women. *Journal of Homosexuality*, *2*(4), 367-384.

Gundlach, R., & Reiss, B. (1968). Self and sexual identity in the female: A study of female homosexuals. In B. Reiss (Ed.), *New directions in mental health*. New York: Grune & Stratton.

Gurdjieff, G. I. (1950). *All and everything*. New York: Harcourt/Brace.

Gutman, H. (1976). *The black family in slavery and freedom, 1750-1925*. New York: Pantheon.

Gutman, H. (1975). Persistent myths about the Afro-American family. *Journal of Interdisciplinary History*, *6*(2), 181-210.

Guttmacher Institute. (1986). *United States and cross-national trends in teenage sexuality and fertility behavior*. New York: Alan Guttmacher Institute.

Haas, A. (1979). *Teenage sexuality: A survey of teenage sexual behavior*. New York: Macmillan.

Habermas, J. (1971). *Knowledge and human interests*. Boston: Beacon Press.

Hall, R. (1983, June 23). Historian Jonathan Katz: A new documentary for a new minority question. *Advocate*, 370 (pp. 37 +).

Halleck, S., & Hersko, M. (1962). Homosexual behavior in a correctional institution for adolescent girls. *American Journal of Orthopsychiatry*, *32*(5), 911-917.

Halloran, J. (1979). *Understanding homosexual persons*. Hicksville, NY: Exposition.

Hammersmith, S. (1987). A sociological approach to counseling homosexual clients and their families. *Journal of Homosexuality*, *14*(1/2), 173-190.

Hampson, J., & Hampson, J. (1961). The ontogenesis of sexual behavior in man. In W. Young (Ed.), *Sex and internal secretions*. (pp. 1401-1432). Baltimore, MD: Williams & Williams.

Hansen, E., Forrester, M., and Bird, F. (1966). *The Tenderloin ghetto: The young reject our society*. San Francisco: Glade Urban Center.

Hansen, K. (1977). Gaylord v. Tacoma School District No. 10: Homosexuality held immoral for purposes of teacher discharge. *Wilamette Law Journal*, *14*, 101-114.

Harbeck, K. (1989). *The homosexual educator: Past history/future prospects*. Paper presented at the American Educational Research Association. San Francisco.

Harbeck, K. (1987). *Personal freedoms/public constraints: An analysis of the controversy over the employment of homosexuals as teachers. Volumes I and II*. Unpublished doctoral dissertation, Stanford University, Palo Alto, CA. *Dissertation Abstracts International* 48, 7, 1862A.

Harlan, S. et al. (1981). *Male and female adolescent prostitution: Huckleberry House Sexual Minority Youth Services Project*. Washington, DC: Dept. of Health and Human Services.

Harley, S., & Terborg-Penn, R. (Eds). (1978). *The Afro-American woman*. Port Washington, NY: Kennikat.

Harrell, D. (1971). *White sects and Black men in the recent South*. Nashville, TN: Vanderbilt University Press.

Harrell, D. (Ed). (1981). *Varieties of Southern evangelicalism*. Macon, GA: Mercer University Press.

Harris, W. (1976). Work and family in black Atlanta. *Journal of Social History*, *9*(3), 319-330.

Harrison, B. (1978). *Visions of glory*. New York, NY: Simon & Schuster.

Harrison, D. (1978). Black women in the blues tradition. In S. Harley & R. Terborg-Penn (Eds.), *The Afro-American woman: Struggles and images*. (pp. 58-73). Port Washington, NY: Kennikat.

Harry, J. (1983). *Adolescent sexuality: Masculinity-femininity, and educational attainment*. ERIC Document No. 237395.

Harry, J. (1985). Defeminization and social class. *Archives of Sexual Behavior*, *14*(1), 1-12.

Harry, J. (1982). *Gay children grow up*. New York: Praeger.

Harry, J. (1986). Sampling gay men. *Journal of Sex Research*, *22*(1), 21-34.

Harry, J. (1984). Sexual orientation as destiny. *Journal of Homosexuality*, *10*(3/4), 111-124.

Harry, J., & DeVall, W. (1978). *The social organization of gay males*. New York: Praeger.

Hart, J. (1984). Therapeutic implications of viewing sexual identity in terms of essentialist and constructionist theories. In J. DeCecco (Ed.), *Gay personality and sexual labeling*. (pp. 39-51). New York: Harrington Park Press.

Hartmann, H. (1981). The unhappy marriage of Marxism and feminism. In L. Sargent (Ed.), *Women and revolution: A discussion of the unhappy marriage of Marxism and feminism*. Boston: South End Press.

Harvard Medical School (1986). *Adolescent suicide: Understanding and responding*. Boston: Harvard Medical School.

Hatterer, L. (1970). *Changing homosexuality in the male: Treatment for men troubled by homosexuality*. New York: McGraw-Hill.

Hawkey, E. (1983). Southern conservatism 1956-1976. In T. Baker, R. Steed, & L. Moreland (Eds.), *Religion and politics in the South*. (pp. 48-72). New York: Praeger.

Hawkins, J. (1976). Lesbianism and alcoholism. In M. Greenblatt & M. Schuckit (Eds.), *Alcoholism problems in women and children*. (pp. 137-153). New York: Grune and Stratton.

Hay, H. (1987). A separate people whose time has come. In M. Thompson (Ed.), *Gay spirit: Myth and meaning*. (pp. 279-291). New York: St. Martin's Press.

Hayes, J. (1976). Gayspeak. *Quarterly Journal of Speech*, *62*(3), 256-266.

Hayes, J. (1981). Lesbians, gay men, and their "languages." In J. Chesbro (Ed.), *Gayspeak: Gay male and lesbian communication*. (pp. 28-42). New York: Pilgrim.

Haynes, S., & Oziel, L. (1976). Homosexuality: Behaviors and attitudes. *Archives of Sexual Behavior*, *5*(4), 283-289.

Hays, B. & Steely, J. (1981). *The Baptist way of life*. Macon, GA: Mercer University Press.

Hechinger, G., & Hechinger, F. (1978, March). Should homosexuals be allowed to teach? *McCall's, 105* (pp. 100, 160-163).

Hedblom, J. (1973). Dimensions of lesbian sexual experience. *Archives of Sexual Behavior, 2*, 329-341.

Hedstrom, J. (1982). *Evangelical program in the United States, 1945-1980: The morphology of establishment, progressive, and radical platforms*. Unpublished doctoral dissertation, Vanderbilt University, Nashville, TN. *Dissertation Abstracts International* 44, 1, 196A.

Heilbrun, A., & Thompson, N. (1977). Sex-role identity and male and female homosexuality. *Sex Roles, 3*(1), 65-79.

Hellman, R., Green, R., Gray, J., & Williams, K. (1981). Childhood sexual identity, childhood religiosity, and 'homophobia' as influences in the development of transsexualism, homosexuality, and heterosexuality. *Archives of General Psychiatry, 38(8)*, 910-915.

Hemmons, W. M. (1980). The women's liberation movement: Understanding black women's attitudes. In L. F. Rodgers-Rose (Ed.), *The black woman*. (pp. 285-299). Beverly Hills: Sage.

Hencken, J. (1982). Homosexuality and psychoanalysis: Toward a mutual understanding. In W. Paul, J. Weinrich, J. Gonsiorek & M. Hotvedt (Eds.), *Homosexuality: Social, psychological, and biological issues*. (pp. 121-147). Beverly Hills: Sage.

Hencken, J. (1984). Conceptualizations of homosexual behavior which preclude homosexual self-labeling. In J. DeCecco (Ed.), *Gay personality and sexual labeling*. (pp. 53-63). New York: Harrington Park Press.

Hencken, J., & O'Dowd, W. (1977). Coming out as an aspect of identity formation. *Gai Saber, 1*, 18-26.

Hendin, H. (1978). Suicide: The psychosocial dimension. *Suicide and Life-Threatening Behavior, 8(2)*, 99-117.

Henning, H. (1936). *Columbia: Capital city of South Carolina*. Columbia, SC: Bryan.

Herek, G. (1984). Beyond "homophobia": A social psychological perspective on attitudes toward lesbians and gay men. *Journal of Homosexuality, 10*(1/2), 1-18.

Herek, G. (1986). On heterosexual masculinity: Some physical consequences of the social construction of gender and sexuality. *American Behavioral Scientist, 29*(5), 563-577.

Hernton, C. (1985). The sexual mountain and black women writers. *Black Scholar, 16*(4), 2-11.

Heron, A. (1983). *One high school student in ten*. Boston: Alyson.

Herskovits, M. (1967). *Dahomey*. Evanston, IL: Northwestern University Press.

Hess, E. (1983). Feminist and lesbian development: Parallels and divergencies. *Journal of Humanistic Psychology, 23*(1), 67-78.

Hetrick, E., & Martin, A. D. (1987). Developmental issues and their resolution for gay and lesbian adolescents. *Journal of Homosexuality, 14*(1/2), 25-43.

Higgs, R., & Manning, A. (Eds). (1975). *Voices from the hills: Selected readings of Southern Appalachia*. New York: Ungar.

Hill, C. (1977). Anthropological studies in the American South: Review and directions. *Current Anthropology, 18(2)*, 309-314.

Hill, E. (1985). *The family secret: A personal account of incest*. New York: Dell.

Hill, R. (1972). *The strengths of black families*. New York: Emerson.

Hill, S. (1967). *Southern churches in crisis*. New York: Holt, Rinehart and Winston.

Hill, S. (1972). The South's two cultures. In S. Hill (Ed.), *Religion and the solid South*. (pp. 24-26). Nashville, TN: Abingdon.

Hill, S. (1980). *The South and the North in American religion*. Athens: University of Georgia Press.

Hill, S. (1983a). *On Jordan's stormy banks: Religion in the South*. Macon, GA: Mercer University Press.

Hill, S. (Ed). (1983b) *Religion in the southern states: A historical study*. Macon, GA: Mercer University Press.

Hill, S. (1988). The South. In C. Lippy & P. Williams (Eds.), *Encyclopedia of the American religious experience: Studies of traditions and movements, Volume III*. (pp. 1493-1508). New York: Scribner.

Hill, S. (1987). *Churches in cultural captivity: A history of the social attitudes of Southern Baptist*. Knoxville, TN: University of Tennessee Press.

Hill, S. (Ed). (1988). *Varieties of southern religious experience*. Baton Rouge: Louisiana State University Press.

Hite, S. (1981). *The Hite Report on male sexuality*. New York: Knopf.

Hockenberry, S., & Billingham, R. (1987). Sexual orientation and boyhood gender conformity: Development of the boyhood gender conformity scale. *Archives of Sexual Behavior*, *16*(6), 475-487.

Hocquenghem, G. (1978). *Homosexual desire*. London: Allison & Busby.

Hodges, H. (1973). *Conflict and consensus*. New York: Harper & Row.

Hoffman, M. (1972). The male prostitute. *Sexual Behavior*, *2*, 16-21.

Hong, S. (1983). Sex, religion and factor analytically derived attitudes towards homosexuality. *Australian Journal of Sex, Marriage, and Family*, *4*(3), 142-150.

Hood, E. (1983). Black women, white women: Separate paths to liberation. *Black Scholar*, *14*(3-4), 26-37.

Hooks, B. (1981). *Ain't I a woman*. Boston: South End Press.

Horkheimer, M. (1972). *Critical theory*. New York: Herder & Herder.

Horner, T. (1978). *Jonathan loved David: Homosexuality in Biblical times*. Philadelphia: Westminster.

Hoult, T. (1983-84). Human sexuality in biological perspective: Theoretical and methodological considerations. *Journal of Homosexuality*, *9*(2/3), 137-155.

Hrdy, S. (1975). *Male and female strategies of reproduction among the languars of Abu*. Unpublished doctoral dissertation, Harvard University, Cambridge.

Hudson, W. (1979). *Baptists in transition: Individualism and Christian responsibility*. Valley Forge, PA: Judson.

Hudson, W., & Ricketts, W. (1980). A strategy for the measurement of homophobia. *Journal of Homosexuality*, *5*(4), 357-372.

Hughes, L. (1958). *The Langston Hughes reader*. New York: Braziller.

Huguley, S. (1987, April 12). Study in black and white: Economics of housing. *The State*, 1A, 16A.

Hull, G. (1983). Poem. In B. Smith (Ed.), *Home girls: A black feminist anthology.* (pp. lvii-lviii). New York: Women of Color Press.

Hull, G., Scott, P., & Smith, B. (Eds). (1982). *But some of us are brave: Black women's studies.* New York: Feminist Press.

Humphreys, L. (1970). *Tearoom trade.* Hawthorn, NY: Aldine.

Humphreys, L. (1972). *Out of the closets: The sociology of homosexual liberation.* Englewood Cliffs, NJ: Prentice-Hall.

Humphreys, L. (1979). Exodus and identity: The emerging gay culture. In M. Levine (Ed.), *Gay men: The sociology of male homosexuality.* (pp. 134-147). New York: Harper & Row.

Hundley, D. (1979). *Social relations in our southern states.* Baton Rouge: Louisiana State University Press.

Hunt, C., & Hunt, M. (1977, June 24). Female-female pairing in western gulls in Southern California (*Larus occidentalis*). *Science*, (196), 1466-1467.

Hunter, K. (1968). *The soul brothers and sister Lou.* New York: Scribners.

Hurn, C. (1978). *The limits and possibilities of schooling.* Boston: Allyn & Bacon.

Hyman, H., & Reed, J. (1969). Black matriarchy reconsidered: Evidence from secondary analysis of sample surveys. *Public Opinion Quarterly*, *33*(3), 346-354.

Imperato-McGinley, J., Peterson, R., Gautier, T., & Sturla, E. (1979). Androgens and the evolution of the male-gender identity among male pseudohermaphrodites with 5a-reductase deficiency. *New England Journal of Medicine*, (300), 1233-1237.

Irigaray, L. (1985). *This sex which is not one.* Ithaca, NY: Cornell University Press.

Irwin, P., & Thompson, N. (1977). Acceptance of the rights of homosexuals: A social profile. *Journal of Homosexuality*, *3*(2), 107-121.

Issac, R. (1982). *The transformation of Virginia.* Chapel Hill: University of North Carolina Press.

Jandt, F., & Darsey, J. (1981). Coming out as a communicative process. In J. Chesbro (Ed.), *Gayspeak: Gay male and lesbian communication.* (pp. 12-27). New York: Pilgrim.

Jay, K., & Young, A. (1979). *The gay report.* New York: Summit.

Jelen, T. (1982). Sources of political intolerance: The case of the American South. L. Moreland, T. Baker, & R. Steel (Eds.), *Contemporary southern political attitudes and behavior*. (pp. 73-91). New York: Praeger.

Jencks, C. (1972). *Inequality: A reassessment of the effect of family and schooling in America*. New York: Basic Books.

Johnson, C. (1967). *Growing up in the black belt: Negro youth in the rural South*. New York: Schocken.

Johnson, C. (1969). *Shadow of the plantation* [1934]. Chicago: University of Chicago Press. (Original work published in 1934).

Johnson, J. (1981). *Influence of assimilation on the psychosocial adjustment of black homosexual men*. Unpublished doctoral dissertation, California School of Professional Psychology, Berkeley, CA. *Dissertation Abstracts International 42*, 11, 4620B.

Johnson, L. (1981). Perspectives on black family empirical research: 1965-1978. In H. McAdoo (Ed.), *Black families*. (pp. 87-102). Beverly Hills: Sage.

Johnston, L., Bachman, J., & O'Malley, P. (1981). *Highlights from student drug use in America, 1975-1981*. Rockville, MD: National Institute on Drug Abuse.

Jones, J. (1982). My mother was much of a woman: Black women, work, and the family under slavery. *Feminist Studies*, *8*(2), 255-269.

Jones, L. (1984). South Carolina. In S. Hill (Ed.), *Encyclopedia of religion in the South*. (pp. 704-720). Macon, GA: Mercer University Press.

Joseph, G. (1981). Black mothers and daughters: Their roles and functions in American society. In G. Joseph & J. Lewis (Eds.), *Common differences: Conflict in black and white feminist perspectives*. (pp. 75-126). New York: Anchor.

Joseph, G., & Lewis, J. (1981). *Common differences: Conflicts in black and white feminist perspectives*. New York: Anchor.

Jung, C. (1955). *The secret of the golden flower*. New York: Wehman.

Kagan, J. (1964). The acquisition and significance of sex-typing and sex-role identification. In M. Hoffman & L. Hoffman (Eds.), *Review of child development research*. (pp. 137-168). New York: Sage.

Kandel, D., Teriman, D., Faust, R., & Single, E. (1976). Adolescent involvement in legal and illegal drug use: A multiple classification analysis. *Social Forces, 55*, 438-458.

Katz, J. (1976). *Gay American history: Lesbians and gay men in the U.S.A. – A documentary*. New York: Crowell.

Katz, J. (1983a). *Gay/lesbian almanac: A new documentary*. New York: Harper & Row.

Kelsey, G. (1973). *Social ethics among Southern Baptists, 1917-1969*. Metuchen, NJ: Scarecrow.

Kenyon, F. (1968). Studies in female homosexuality: IV – social and psychiatric aspects; V – sexual development, attitudes, and experiences. *British Journal of Psychiatry, 114*(11), 1337-1350.

Kerr, P. (1988, July 10). The American drug problem takes on 2 faces. *New York Times*, 5E.

Key, V. O. (1949). *Southern politics in state and nation*. New York: Knopf.

Kim, C. (1977). *An Asian anthropologist in the South*. Knoxville, TN: University of Tennessee Press.

Kimmel, D. (1979). Heterosexism revisited. *Contemporary Psychology, 24*(6), 495-496.

King, F. (1975). *Southern ladies and gentlemen*. New York: Stein & Day.

King, J. (1964). *History of South Carolina Baptists*. Columbia, SC: General Board of the South Carolina Baptist Convention.

King, N. (1976). *The hidden curriculum and the socialization of kindergarten children*. Unpublished doctoral dissertation, University of Wisconsin, Madison. *Dissertation Abstracts International* 37, 11, 6927A.

Kinsey, A., Pomeroy, W., & Martin, C. (1948). *Sexual behavior in the human male*. Philadelphia: Saunders.

Kinsey, A., Pomeroy, W., Martin, C., & Gebhard, P. (1953). *Sexual behavior in the human female*. Philadelphia: Saunders.

Kinsman, G. (1987). *The regulation of desire*. Montreal: Black Rose.

Kirby, J. (1986). *Media-made Dixie*. Athens: University of Georgia Press.

Kitzinger, C. (1987). *The social construction of lesbianism*. London: Sage.

Klein, C. (1986). *Counseling our own: The lesbian/gay subculture meets the mental health system*. Seattle, WA: Consulting Services Northwest.

Klein, F., Sepekoff, B., & Wolf, T. (1985). Sexual orientation: A multi-variable dynamic process. *Journal of Homosexuality*, *11*(1/2), 35-49.

Kleinberg, S. (1987). The new masculinity of gay men and beyond. In F. Abbott (Ed.), *New men, new minds: Breaking male tradition*. (pp. 120-138). Freedom, CA: Crossing Press.

Klintworth, G. (1962). A pair of male monozygotic twins discordant for homosexuality. *Journal of Nervous and Mental Disease*, *135*, 113-125.

Kooden, H. et al. (1979). *Removing the stigma: Final report of the Board of Social and Ethical Responsibility for Psychology's Task Force on the Status of Lesbian and Gay Male Psychologists*. Washington, DC: American Psychological Association.

Kopkind, A. (1985, June 1). Gay city on the hill: Once upon a time in the West. *Nation*, (pp. 667-672).

Kremer, M., & Rifkin, A. (1969). The early development of homosexuality: A study of adolescent lesbians. *American Journal of Psychiatry*, *126*(1), 91-96.

Krieger, S. (1982). Lesbian identity and community: Recent social science literature. *Signs*, *8*(11), 91-108.

Krieger, S. (1983). *The mirror dance: Identity in a women's community*. Philadelphia: Temple University Press.

Kristeva, J. (1980). Women can never be defined. M. August (Trans.) In E. Marks, & I. Courtivron de (Eds.), *New French feminism*. (pp. 137-141). New York: Schocken.

Kristeva, J. (1981). Women's time. A. Jardines (Trans.). *Signs*, *7*(1), 13-15.

Krody, N. (1977). An open lesbian looks at the church. *Foundations: Baptist Journal of History and Theology*, *20*(2), 148-162.

Kronus, S. (1971). *The black middle class*. Columbus, OH: Merrill.

Krysiak, G. (1987). Very silent and gay minority. *School Counselor*, *34*(4), 304-307.

Kus, R. (1988). Alcoholism and non-acceptance of gay self: The critical link. *Journal of Homosexuality*, *15*(1/2), 25-41.

Laermer, R. (1985, February 5). The televised gay: How we're pictured on the tube. *Advocate, 413* (pp. 15-20).

Lance, H. (1989). The Bible and homosexuality. *American Baptist Quarterly, 8*(2), 140-151.

Lance, L. (1987). The effects of interaction with gay persons on attitudes toward homosexuality. *Human Relations, 40*(6), 329-336.

Landry, B. (1987). *The new black middle class*. Berkeley: University of California Press.

Langton, K. (1967). Peer group and school and the political socialization process. *American Political Science Review, 61*(3), 751-758.

Langton, K., & Jennings, M. (1968). Political socialization and the high school civics curriculum in the United States. *American Political Science Review, 62*(3), 852-867.

Larsen, K., Reed, M., & Hoffman, S. (1980). Attitudes of heterosexuals toward homosexuality: A Likert type scale and construct validity. *Journal of Sex Research, 16*(3), 245-257.

Larson, P. (1982). Gay male relationships. In W. Paul et al. (Eds.), *Homosexuality: Social, psychological and biological issues*. (pp. 219-232). Beverly Hills: Sage.

LaTorre, R., & Wendenburg, K. (1983). Psychological characteristics of bisexual, heterosexual, and homosexual women. *Journal of Homosexuality, 9*(1), 87-97.

Laurentis de, T. (1984). *Alice doesn't*. Bloomington, IN: Indiana University Press.

Lauritsen, J., & Thorstad, D. (1974). *The early homosexual rights movement (1864-1935)*. New York: Times Change Press.

Laws, J., & Schwartz, P. (1977). *Sexual scripts: The social construction of female sexuality*. New York: Holt, Rinehart & Winston.

LeBlanc, C. (1987, March 5). Wildewood, Spring Valley open clubs for high school matches. *The State*, 1A, 14A.

Lebovitz, P. (1972). Feminine behavior in boys: Aspects of its outcome. *American Journal of Psychiatry, 128*(10), 1283-1289.

Lee, J. (1979). The gay connection. *Urban Life, 8*(2), 175-198.

Legman, G. (1950). Fathers and sons. In G. Hamilton & G. Legman (Eds.), *On the cause of homosexuality: Two essays, the second in reply to the first.* (pp. 17-31). New York: Breaking Point.

Legman, G. (1941). The language of homosexuality: An American glossary. In G. Henry (Ed.), *Sex variants.* (pp. 1147-1178). New York: Hoeber.

Lehne, G. (1976). Homophobia among men. In D. David, & R. Brannon (Eds.), *The forty-nine percent majority: The male sex role.* (pp. 66-88). Reading, MA: Addison-Wesley.

Lerner, G. (1972). *Black women in white America: A documentary history.* New York: Pantheon.

Lerner, G. (1986). *The creation of patriarchy.* New York: Oxford University Press.

Lesselier, C. (1987). Social categorizations and construction of a lesbian subject. *Feminist Issues, 7*(1), 89-94.

Levin, J. (1983). *Reflections on the American homosexual rights movement.* New York: Gay Academic Union.

Levine, M. (1979). Gay ghetto. In M. Levine (Ed.), *Gay men: The sociology of male homosexuality.* (pp. 182-204). New York: Harper & Row.

Levi-Strauss, C. (1969). *The elementary structures of kinship.* Boston: Beacon Press.

Levitt, E., & Klassen, A. (1974). Public attitudes toward homosexuality. *Journal of Homosexuality, 1,* 29-43.

Lewis, C., Saghir, M., & Robins, E. (1982). Drinking patterns in homosexual and heterosexual women. *Journal of Clinical Psychiatry, 43*(7), 277-279.

Lewis, D. (1975). The black family: Socialization and sex roles. *Phylon, 36*(3), 221-237.

Licata, S. (1978). *Gay power: A history of the American gay movement, 1908-1974.* Unpublished doctoral dissertation, University of Southern California, Los Angeles. *Dissertation Abstracts International* 39, 1, 407A.

Licata, S. (1980/81). The homosexual rights movement in the United States: A traditionally overlooked area of American history. *Journal of Homosexuality, 6*(1/2), 161-189.

Lieb, S. (1981). *Mother of the blues: A study of Ma Rainey.* Amherst: University of Massachusetts Press.

Lincoln, C. E. (1974). *Black church since Frazier*. New York: Schocken.

Lincoln, C. E. (1985). The black heritage in religion in the South. In C. Wilson (Ed.), *Religion in the South*. (pp. 35-57). Jackson: University Press of Mississippi.

Lipman-Blumen, J. (1972). How ideology shapes women's lives. *Scientific American*, *226*(1), 34-42.

Lippy, C., & Williams, P. (Eds). (1988). *Encyclopedia of the American religious experience: Studies of traditions and movement*. New York, NY: Scribner.

Litt, E. (1963). Civic education norms and political indoctrination. *American Sociological Review*, *28*(1), 69-75.

Lockard, D. (1986). The lesbian community: An anthropological approach. In E. Blackwood (Ed.), *The many faces of homosexuality: Anthropological approaches to homosexual behaviors*. (pp. 83-95). New York: Harrington Park Press.

Lockwood, D. (1980). *Prison sexual violence*. New York: Elsevier.

Lockwood, R. (1974). Gay on gay. *Journal of Clinical Child Psychology*, *3*(3/4), 16-17.

Lohrenz, L., Connelly, J., Coyne, L., & Spare, K. (1978). Alcohol problems in several Midwestern homosexual communities. *Journal of Studies on Alcohol*, *39*(11), 1959-1963.

Lorde, A. (1978). *The black unicorn*. New York: Norton.

Loveland, A. (1980). *Southern Evangelicals and the social order, 1800-1860*. Baton Rouge: Louisiana State University Press.

Lowe, J. (1978). Civil rights—homosexual teacher dismissal: A deviant decision—Gaylord v. Tacoma School District No. 10. *Washington Law Review*, *53*(499), 499-510.

Lynn, D. (1961). Sex differences in identification development. *Sociometry*, *24*, 372-383.

MacDonald, A. (1974). The importance of sex-role to gay liberation. *Homosexual Counseling Journal*, *1*(4), 169-180.

MacDonald, A. (1976). Homophobia: Its roots and meanings. *Homosexual Counseling Journal*, *3*(1), 23-33.

MacDonald, A., & Games, R. (1974). Some characteristics of those who hold positive and negative attitudes toward homosexuals. *Journal of Homosexuality*, *1*(1), 9-27.

Macdonald, J. (1975). The quality of everyday life in the schools. In J. Macdonald & E. Zaret (Eds.), *Schools in search for meaning*. (pp. 78-94). Washington, DC: Association for Supervision and Curriculum Development.

Mader, D. (1978). *Men and boys: An anthology*. New York: Coltsfoot.

Mallen, C. A. (1983). Sex role stereotypes, gender identity and parental relationships in male homosexuals and heterosexuals. *Journal of Homosexuality*, 9(1), 55-74.

Malyon, A. (1982). Psychotherapeutic implications of internalized homophobia in gay men. In J. Gonsiorek (Ed.), *Homosexuality and psychotherapy: A practitioner's handbook of affirmative models*. (pp. 59-69). New York: Haworth Press.

Manis, A. (1987). *Southern civil religions in conflict: Black and white Baptists and civil rights, 1947-1957*. Athens: University of Georgia Press.

Mannion, K. (1976). Female homosexuality: A comprehensive review of theory and research. *Journal Supplement Abstract Service — Catalogue of Selected Documents in Psychiatry*, 6(MS 1247).

Manosevitz, M. (1970). Early sexual behavior in adult homosexual and heterosexual males. *Journal of Abnormal Psychology*, 76(1), 396-402.

Margolies, L., Becker, M., & Jackson-Brewer, K. (1987). Internalized homophobia: Identifying and treating the oppressor within. In Boston Lesbian Psychologies Collective (Ed.), *Lesbian psychologies: Explorations and challenges*. (pp. 229-241). Urbana: University of Illinois Press.

Maris, R. (1985). The adolescent suicide problem. *Suicide and Life-Threatening Behavior*, 15(2), 91-109.

Marotta, T. (1981). *The politics of homosexuality: How lesbians and gay men have made themselves a political and social force in modern America*. Boston: Houghton Mifflin.

Marsden, G. (1980). *Fundamentalism and American culture: The shaping of twentieth century evangelicalism, 1870-1925*. New York: Oxford University Press.

Martin, A. D. (1982). Learning to hide: The socialization of the gay adolescent. In S. Feinstein & J. Looney (Eds.), *Adolescent psy-*

chiatry: Developmental and clinical studies. (pp. 52-65). Chicago: University of Chicago Press.

Martin, A. D., & Hetrick, E. (1988). The stigmatization of gay and lesbian adolescents. *Journal of Homosexuality*, *15*(1-2), 163-185.

Martin, B. (1982). Feminism, criticism, and Foucault. *New German Critique*, *27*(2), 3-30.

Martin, N., & Dixon, P. (1986). Adolescent suicide. *School Counselor*, *33*(4), 265-270.

Marty, M. (1970). *Righteous empire: The protestant experience in America*. New York: Dial.

Marty, M. (1981). *The public church: Mainline-Evangelical-Catholic*. New York: Crossroad.

Mass, L. (1986, May 26). Insight into gender and roles: (Some) boys will be boys. *Advocate*, *473*, 54, 56.

Mathews, D. (1977). *Religion and the old South*. Chicago: University of Chicago Press.

Mathews, D., & Prothro, J. (1966). *Negroes and the new southern politics*. New York: Harcourt, Brace & World.

Maxwell, J. (1968). Rural negro father participation in family activities. *Rural Sociology*, *33*(1), 80-83.

May, E. (1974). Counselors', psychologists', and homosexuals' philosophies of human nature and attitudes toward homosexual behavior. *Homosexual Counseling Journal*, *1*(1), 3-25.

Mayfield, C. *Growing up southern: Southern Exposure looks at childhood, then and now*. New York: Pantheon.

McAdoo, H. (Ed). (1981). *Black families*. Beverly Hills: Sage.

McBridge, A., & Hebb, D. (1948). Behavior of the captive bottlenose dolphin. *Journal of Comparitive and Physicological Psychology*, 41, 111-123.

McCarthy, T. (1978). *The critical theory of Jurgen Habermas*. Cambridge: Massachusetts Institute of Technology Press.

McCoy, S., & Hicks, M. (1979). A psychological retrospective on power in the contemporary lesbian-feminist community. *Frontiers*, 4(3), 65-69.

McCray, C. (1980). The black woman and family roles. In L. Rodgers-Rose (Ed.), *The black woman*. (pp. 67-78). Beverly Hills: Sage.

McCullers, C. (1940). *The heart is a lonely hunter*. Boston: Houghton-Mifflin.

McDermott, R. (1977). Social relations as contexts for learning in school. *Harvard Educational Review*, 47, 198-213.

McDonald, G. (1981). Misrepresentation, liberalism, and heterosexual bias in introductory psychology textbooks. *Journal of Homosexuality*, 6(3), 45-59.

McDonald, G. (1982). Individual differences in the coming out process for gay men. *Journal of Homosexuality*, 8(1), 47-60.

McDonald, G., & Moore, R. (1978). Sex-role self concepts of homosexual men and their attitudes toward both women and male homosexuality. *Journal of Homosexuality*, 4(1), 3-14.

McKern, S. (1979). *Redneck mothers, good ol' girls and other Southern bells: A celebration of the women of Dixie*. New York: Viking.

McNaught, B. (1981). *A disturbed peace: Selected writings of an Irish Catholic homosexual*. Washington, DC: Dignity.

McNeill, J. (1976). *The church and the homosexual*. Kansas City, KS: Sheed, Andrews & McMeel.

McNeill, J. (1988). *Taking a chance on God: Liberating theology for gays, lesbians, and their lovers, families, and friends*. Boston: Beacon Press.

McRobbie, A. (1978). Working class girls and the culture of femininity. In Women Studies Group (Ed.), *Women take issue*. (pp. 96-108). London: Hutchinson.

McWhirter, D., & Mattison, A. (1984). *The male couple: How relationships develop*. Englewood Cliffs, NJ: Prentice-Hall.

Mead, M. (1935). *Sex and temperament in three different societies*. New York: Morrow.

Mehan, H. (1978). Structuring school structure. *Harvard Educational Review*, 48(1), 32-64.

Meiselman, K. (1978). *Incest: A psychological study of causes and effects with treatment recommendations*. San Francisco: Jossey-Bass.

Mesnikoff, A., Rainer, J., Kolb, L., & Carr, A. (1963). Intrafamilial determinants of divergent sexual behavior in twins. *American Journal of Psychiatry*, 119 February, 732-738.

Miles, M., & Huberman, A. (1984). *Qualitative data analysis: A sourcebook of new methods*. Beverly Hills: Sage.

Miller, J., Mucklow, B., Jacobsen, R., & Bigner, J. (1980). Comparison of family relationships: Homosexual versus heterosexual women. *Psychological Reports, 46*(3), 1127-1132.

Miller, J. (1982). People, berdaches, and left-handed bears: Human variation in Native Americans. *Journal of Anthropology Research, 38*(3), 274-287.

Miller, J. (1990). Teachers as curriculum creators. In J. Sears & J. Marshall (Eds.), *Teaching and thinking about curriculum: Critical inquiries*. New York: Teachers College Press.

Miller, N. (1989). *In search of gay America: Women and men in a time of change*. New York: Atlantic Monthly Press.

Millett, K. (1970). *Sexual politics*. New York: Avon.

Millham, J., San Miguel, C., & Kellogg, R. (1976). A factor-analytic conceptualization of attitudes toward male and female homosexuals. *Journal of Homosexuality, 2*(1), 3-10.

Millic, J., & Crowne, D. (1986). Recalled parent-child relations and need for approval of homosexual and heterosexual men. *Archives of Sexual Behavior, 15*(3), 239-246.

Minnigerode, F. (1976). Attitudes toward homosexuality: Feminist attitudes and sexual conservatism. *Sex Roles: A Journal of Research, 2*(4), 347-352.

Minton, H., & MacDonald, G. (1983/84). Homosexual identity formation as a developmental process. *Journal of Homosexuality, 9*(2/3), 91-104.

Mitchell, H. (1975). *Black belief: Folk beliefs of blacks in America and West Africa*. New York: Harper & Row.

Mitchell, J., & Rose, J. (1982). *Feminine sexuality: Jacques Lacan and Ecole Freudienne*. New York: Norton.

Money, J. (1970). Matched pairs of hermaphrodites: Behavioral biology of sexual differentiating chromosomes to gender identity. *Engineering and Science, 33*, 34-39.

Money, J. (1980). Genetic and chromosomal aspects of homosexuality. In J. Marmor (Ed.), *Homosexual behavior: A modern reappraisal*. (pp. 59-72). New York: Basic.

Money, J. (1987). Sin, sickness, or status? Homosexual gender identity and psychoneuroendocrinology. *American Psychologist*, *42*(4), 384-399.

Money, J., & Dalery, J. (1976). Latrogenic homosexuality: Gender identity in seven 46, XX chromosomal females with hyperadrenocortical hermaphroditism born with a penis, three reared as boys, four reared as girls. *Journal of Homosexuality*, *1*(4), 357-371.

Money, J., Devore, H., & Norman, B. (1986). Gender identity and gender transposition: Longitudinal study of 32 male hermaphrodites assigned as girls. *Journal of Sex and Marital Therapy*, *12*(3), 165-181.

Money, J., & Ehrhardt, A. (1972). *Man and woman, boy and girl: Differentiation and dimorphism of gender identity from conception to maturity*. Baltimore: Johns Hopkins University Press.

Money, J., Hampson, J., & Hampson, J. (1955). Hermaphroditism: Recommendations concerning assignment of sex, change of sex, and psychologic management. *Johns Hopkins Hospital Bulletin*, *97*, 284-300.

Money, J., & Russo, A. (1979). Homosexual outcome of discordant gender activity. Role in childhood: Longitudinal follow-up. *Journal of Pediatric Psychology*, *4*(1), 29-49.

Monk, F. (1987, March 8). Exclusionary clubs raise larger issues. *The State*, 1A, 5A.

Moraga, C., & Anzaldua, G. (Eds). (1981). *This bridge called my back: Writings by radical women of color*. Watertown, MA: Persephone Press.

Morgan, G. (1980). Homophobia. *It comes with the plumbing*. Lyrics and music by G. Morgan. KC 102449. Bellingham, WA: Nexus Records.

Morin, S. (1974). Educational programs as a means of changing attitudes toward gay people. *Homosexual Counseling Journal*, *1*(4), 160-165.

Morin, S. (1977). Heterosexual bias in psychological research on lesbianism and male homosexuality. *American Psychologist*, *32*(8), 629-637.

Morin, S., & Garfinkle, E. (1978). Male homophobia. *Journal of Social Issues*, *34*(1), 29-47.

Morris, V. C. (1966). *Existentialism in education: What it means*. New York: Harper & Row.

Morrison, T. (1974). *Sula*. New York: Bantam.

Moses, A. E., & Buckner, J. (1982). The special problems of rural gay clients. In A. E. Moses & R. Hawkins (Eds.), *Counseling lesbian women and gay men*. (pp. 173-180). St. Louis: Mosby.

Moses, A. E., & Hawkins, R. (1982). Lesbians' and gay men's relationships. In A. E. Moses & R. Hawkins (Eds.), *Counseling lesbian women and gay men*. (pp. 123-166). St. Louis: Mosby.

Moses, W. (1982). *Black Messiahs and Uncle Toms: Social literary manipulations of religious myths*. University Park: Pennsylvania State University Press.

Mowrer, O. (1953). *Psychotherapy: Theory and research*. New York: Ronald Press.

Moynihan, D. (1965). *The Negro family: The case for national action*. Washington, DC: Government Printing Office.

Munroe, R., Whiting, J., & Holly, D. (1969). Institutionalized male transvestism and sex distinctions. *American Anthropologist, 71*(1), 86-91.

Murdock, G. (1937). Comparative data on the division of labour by sex. *Social Forces, 15*(4), 551-553.

Murphy, J. (1971). *Homosexual liberation: A personal view*. New York: Praeger.

Murphy, L. (1988). *Perverts by official order: The campaign against homosexuals by the United States Navy*. New York: Haworth Press.

Myrdal, G. (1969). *Objectivity in social research*. New York: Pantheon.

Myron, N., & Bunch, C. (1974). *Women remembered: A collection of biographies from the "Furies."* Baltimore: Diana Press.

Napier, T., Carter, T., & Pratt, M. (1981). Correlates of alcohol and marijuana use among rural high school students. *Rural Sociology, 46*(2), 319-332.

Nardi, P. (1982). Alcohol treatment and the non-traditional 'family' structures of gays and lesbians. *Journal of Alcohol and Drug Education, 27*, 83-89.

Naylor, G. (1983). *The women of Brewster Place*. New York: Penguin.

Near, H. (1978). Put away. *Imagine my surprise*. Lyrics by H. Near, music by J. Langley. San Francisco: Redwood Records.

Nelson, J. (1980). Gayness and homosexuality: Issues for the church. In E. Batchelor (Ed.), *Homosexuality and ethics*. (pp. 186-210). New York: Pilgrim Press.

Neverdon-Morton, C. (1978). The black woman's struggle for equality in the South, 1895-1925. In S. Harley & R. Terborg-Penn (Eds.), *The Afro-American woman: Struggles and images*. (pp. 43-57). Port Washington, NY: Kennikat.

Newcomb, M. (1980). *The development of a measurement device that allows the retrospective personality assessment of mother relative to father, and validation of this instrument on heterosexuals, homosexuals, and male transvestites*. Unpublished doctoral dissertation, University of California, Los Angeles. *Dissertation Abstracts International* 40, 9, 4497B.

Newcomb, T. (1966). The general nature of peer group influence. In T. Newcomb & E. Wilson (Eds.), *College peer groups*. (pp. 2-16). Chicago: Aldine.

Newman, B., & Newman, P. (1975). *Development through life*. Chicago: Dorsey.

Newman, F., & Oliver, D. (1967). Education and community. *Harvard Educational Review*, *37*(1), 61-106.

Newton, D. (1979). Representations of homosexuality in health science textbooks. *Journal of Homosexuality*, *4*(3), 247-253.

Newton, E. (1979). *Mother camp: Female impersonators in America*. Chicago: University of Chicago Press.

Nickeson, S. (1980). *A comparison of gay and heterosexual teachers on professional and personal dimensions*. Unpublished doctoral dissertation, University of Florida, Gainesville, FL. *Dissertation Abstracts International* 41, 9, 3956A.

Nicol, M. (1957). *Psychological commentaries, Volume 1*. London: Vincent Street.

Nicoloff, L., & Stiglitz, E. (1987). Lesbian alcoholism: Etiology, treatment, and recovery. In Boston Lesbian Psychologies Collective (Ed.), *Lesbian psychologies*. (pp. 283-293). Urbana: University of Illinois Press.

Nielsen, L. (1987). *Adolescent psychology*. New York: Holt, Rinehart and Winston.

Niethammer, C. (1977). *Daughters of the earth: The lives and legends of American Indian women*. New York: Collier-Macmillan.

Noble, E. (1978). *Third special report to the U.S. Congress on alcohol and health*. Rockville, MD: National Institute on Alcohol and Alcoholism.

Norse, H. (1984, October 2). Of time and Tennessee Williams. *Advocate, 404* (pp. 38-41).

Nunn, C., Crockett, H., & Williams, J. (1978). *Tolerance for nonconformity*. San Francisco: Jossey-Bass.

Nyberg, K., & Alston, J. (1977). Homosexual labeling by university youths. *Adolescence, 12*(48), 541-546.

Oakely, A. (1972). *Sex, gender and society*. New York: Harper & Row.

Oakes, J. (1985). *Keeping track: How schools structure inequality*. New Haven, CT: Yale University Press.

O'Connor, F. (1969). *Mystery and manners: Occasional prose*. S. and R. Fitzgerald, (Eds.). New York: Farrar, Straus & Giroux.

Ogbu, J. (1978). *Minority education and caste: The American system in cross-cultural perspective*. New York: Academic Press.

Olson, M. (1987). A study of gay and lesbian teachers. *Journal of Homosexuality, 13*(4), 73-81.

Oshana, M. (1985). *Women of color: A filmography of minority and third world women*. New York: Garland.

Owens, L. (1971). *Saints of clay: The story of South Carolina Baptists*. Columbia, SC: Bryan.

Owens, L. (1976). *The species of property: Slave life and culture in the Old South*. New York: Oxford University Press.

Owens, V. (1980). *The total image: Or, selling Jesus in the modern age*. Grand Rapids, MI: Eerdmans.

Owsley, L. (1949). *Plain folk of the Old South*. Baton Rouge: Louisiana State University Press.

Padgug, R. (1987). More than the story of a virus: Gay history, gay communities, and AIDS. *Radical America, 21*(2/3), 35-42.

Page, L. (1987, April 14). Realtors say housing law won't stop discrimination. *The State*, 16A.

Parker, N. (1964). Homosexuality in twins: A report on three discordant pairs. *British Journal of Psychiatry, 110*, 489-495.

Parkhurst, J. (1938). The Black Mammy in the plantation household. *Journal of Negro History*, *23*(3), 349-369.

Passaro, J. (1987). Conceptualizations of gender: An example from Nicaragua. *Feminist Issues*, *7*(2), 49-60.

Pauly, I., & Goldstein, S. (1970). Physicians' attitudes in treating male homosexuals. *Medical Aspects of Human Sexuality*, *4*, 26-45.

Payne, D. (1969). *History of the African Methodist Episcopal Church*. New York: Arno Press. (Original work published in 1891).

Pennington, S. (1981). *But Lord, they're gay*. Hawthorne, CA: Lambda Christian Fellowship.

Penton, M. (1985). *Apocalypse delayed*. Toronto, Ontario: University of Toronto Press.

Percy, W. (1973). *Lanterns on the levee: Reflections of a planter's son*. Baton Rouge: Louisiana State University Press.

Percy, W. (1990, March 22). [Personal Communication to James T. Sears].

Perry, T. (1972). *The Lord is my shepherd and He knows I'm gay*. Los Angeles: Nash.

Persell, C. (1977). *Education and inequality*. New York: Free Press.

Pillard, R. (1974). Incidence of teenage homosexual behavior. *Medical Aspects of Human Sexuality*, *8*(4), 192.

Pittenger, N. (1967). *Time for consent*. London: SCM.

Plummer, K. (1975). *Sexual stigma: An interactionist perspective*. London: Routledge & Kegan Paul.

Plummer, K. (1981). *The making of the modern homosexual*. London: Hutchinson.

Pomeroy, W. (1972). *Dr. Kinsey and the Institute for Sex Research*. New York: Harper & Row.

Ponse, B. (1978). *Identities in the lesbian world: The social construction of self*. Westport, CT: Greenwood.

Ponse, B. (1980). Finding self in the lesbian community. In M. Kirkpatrick (Ed.), *Women's sexual development*. (pp. 181-200). New York: Plenum.

Poole, K. (1972). The etiology of gender identity and the lesbian. *Journal of Social Psychology*, *87*(5), 51-57.

Potter, S., & Darty, T. (1981). Social work and the invisible minority: An exploration of lesbianism. *Social Work*, *26*(3), 187-192.

Powell, A., Farrar, E., & Cohen, D. (1985). *The shopping mall high school: Winners and losers in the educational market place*. Boston: Houghton Mifflin.

Price, J. (1982). High school students' attitudes toward homosexuality. *Journal of School Health*, *52*(8), 469-474.

Propper, A. (1978). Lesbianism in female and coed correctional institutions. *Journal of Homosexuality*, *3*(3), 265-274.

Puterbaugh, G. (1984). Born gay? Hand preference and sex preference. *Cabirion*, *10*, 12-18.

Quinn, B., Anderson, H., Bradley, M., Guetting, P., & Shriver, P. (1982). *Churches and church membership in the United States, 1980*. Atlanta: Glenmary Research Center.

Raboteau, A. (1988). Black Christianity in North America. In C. Lippy & P. Williams (Eds.), *Encyclopedia of the American religious experience: Studies of traditions and movements, Volume I*. (pp. 635-648). New York: Scribner.

Raboteau, A. (1978). *Slave religion: The "invisible institution" in the antebellum South*. New York: Oxford University Press.

Raphael, S. (1974). *Coming out: The emergence of the movement lesbian*. Unpublished doctoral dissertation, Case Western Reserve University, Cleveland, OH. *Dissertation Abstracts International* 35, 8, 5536A.

Rausch, F. (1974). Gay liberation and the public schools. In National Organization of Legal Problems (Ed.), *Current trends in school law*. (pp. 25-42). Topeka, KS: National Organization of Legal Problems.

Rawick, G. (1972). *The American slave: A composite autobiography—sunup to sundown*. Westport, CT: Greenwood.

Real, J. (1983, August 4). Dragtime: "Dressing up" down South. *Advocate*, *373* (pp. 46-50).

Rebecca, M., Hefner, R., & Oleshansky, B. (1976). A model of sex-role transcendence. *Journal of Social Issues*, *32*(3), 197-206.

Rechy, J. (1984, March 24). The ghettoization of gay art. *Advocate*, *390* (pp. 26-29).

Reed, J. (1972). *The enduring South*. Chapel Hill: University of North Carolina Press.

Reed, J. (1986). *Southern folk, plain and fancy: Native white social types*. Athens: University of Georgia Press.

Reiss, A. (1961). The social integration of queers and peers. *Social Problems, 9*(2), 102-119.

Remafedi, G. (1987a). Male homosexuality: The adolescent's perspective. *Pediatrics, 79*(3), 326-330.

Remafedi, G. (1987b). Adolescent homosexuality: Psychosocial and medical implications. *Pediatrics, 79*(3), 331-337.

Rich, A. (1980). Compulsory heterosexuality and lesbian existence. *Signs, 5*(4), 631-660.

Rich, C., Fowler, R., Young, D., & Blenkush, M. (1986). San Diego suicide study: Comparison of gay to straight males. *Suicide and Life-Threatening Behavior, 16*(4), 448-457.

Richardson, D. (1981a). Lesbian identities. In J. Hart & D. Richardson (Eds.), *The theory and practice of homosexuality*. (pp. 111-124). Boston: Routledge & Kegan Paul.

Richardson, D. (1981b). Theoretical perspectives on homosexuality. In J. Hart & D. Richardson (Eds.), *The theory and practice of homosexuality*. (pp. 5-37). Boston: Routledge & Kegan Paul.

Richardson, H. (1976). *Dark salvation: The story of Methodism as it developed among blacks in America*. Garden City, NY: Anchor.

Rickgarn, R. (1987). Youth suicide: Update on a continuing health issue. *Educational Horizons, 65*(3), 128-129.

Riddiough, C. (1981). Socialism, feminism and gay/lesbian liberation. In L. Sargent (Ed.) *Women and revolution: A discussion of the unhappy marriage of Marxism and feminism*. (pp. 71-89). Boston: South End Press.

Riddle, D. (1978). Relating to children: Gays as role models. *Journal of Social Issues, 34*(3), 38-58.

Riddle, D., & Morin, S. (1977). Removing the stigma. *APA Monitor, 16*(1), 53.

Rist, R. (1970). Social class and teacher expectations: The self-fulfilling prophecy in ghetto education. *Harvard Educational Review, 40*(3), 411-451.

Rist, R. (1973). *The urban school: A factory for failure*. Cambridge: MIT Press.

Roberts, G. D. (1971). *Liberation and reconciliation: A black theology*. Philadelphia: Westminster Press.

Roberts, J. (1981). *Black lesbians: An annotated bibliography*. Tallahassee, FL: Naiad Press.

Rodgers, B. (1972). *The queen's vernacular: A gay lexicon*. San Francisco: Straight Arrow.

Roebuck, J., & Hickson, M. (1982). *The southern redneck: A phenomenological study*. New York: Praeger.

Roesler, T., & Deishler, R. (1972). Youthful male homosexuality. *Journal of the American Medical Association, 219*(8), 1018-1023.

Rofes, E. (1983). *I thought people like that killed themselves*. San Francisco: Grey Fox Press.

Rofes, E. (1985). *Socrates, Plato, and guys like me: Confessions of a gay schoolteacher*. Boston: Alyson.

Romanovsky, R. (1984). Paint by numbers. *I thought you'd be taller*. Lyrics and music by R. Romanovsky. San Francisco: Bodacious Records.

Romanovsky, R. (1986). Carnival people. *Trouble in Paradise*. Lyrics and music by R. Romanovsky. Berkeley, CA: Fresh Fruit Records.

Rorty, R. (1982). *Consequences of pragmatism*. Minneapolis: University of Minnesota Press.

Roscoe, W. (1987). Living the tradition: Gay American Indians. In M. Thompson (Ed.), *Gay spirit*. (pp. 69-77). New York: St. Martin's.

Roscoe, W. (1988). We 'Wha and Klah: The American Indian berdache as artist and priest. *American Indian Quarterly, 12*(2), 127-150.

Rosenbaum, J. (1976). *Making inequality: The hidden curriculum of high school tracking*. New York: Wiley.

Rosenthal, R., & Jacobson, L. (1968). *Pygmalion in the classroom*. New York: Holt, Rinehart and Winston.

Ross, M. (1980). Retrospective distortion in homosexual research. *Archives of Sexual Behavior, 9*(6), 523-531.

Ross, M. (1983). Homosexuality and social sex roles: A re-evaluation. *Journal of Homosexuality, 9*(1), 1-6.

Ross-Reynolds, G., & Hardy, B. (1985). Crisis counseling for disparate adolescent sexual dilemmas: Pregnancy and homosexuality. *School Psychology Review*, *14*(3), 300-312.

Rubin, G. (1975). The traffice in women: Notes on the "political economy" of sex. In R. Reiter (Ed.), *Toward an anthropology of women.* (pp. 157-210). New York: Monthly Review Press.

Rugg, H. (Ed.) (1939). *Democracy and the curriculum: The life and program of the American school.* New York: Appleton-Century.

Rule, J. (1975). *Lesbian images.* Garden City, NY: Doubleday.

Ruse, M. (1988). *Homosexuality: A philosophical inquiry.* New York: Blackwell.

Russo, A. (1982). *Power and influence in the homosexual community: A study of three California cities.* Unpublished doctoral dissertation, Claremont Graduate School, Claremont, CA. *Dissertation Abstracts International* 43, 2, 561B.

Russo, V. (1979). Camp. In M. Levine (Ed.), *Gay men: The sociology of male homosexuality.* (pp. 205-210). New York: Harper & Row.

Russo, V. (1981, April). When it comes to gay money gay lib takes care of the pennies: Will big business take care of the pounds? *Gay News*, (212), 16-17.

Saghir, M., & Robins, E. (1973). *Male and female homosexuality.* Baltimore: Williams & Watkins.

Sang, B. (1978). Lesbian research: A critical evaluation. In G. Vida (Ed.), *Our right to love; A lesbian resource book.* (pp. 80-85). Englewood Cliffs, NJ: Prentice-Hall.

Sauds, S., & Guth, J. (1981). White clergymen in southern politics. In M. Black & J. Reed (Eds.), *Perspectives on the American South.* New York: Gordon & Braach.

Saunders, J., & Valente, S. (1987). Suicide risk among gay men and lesbians. *Death Studies*, *11*(1), 1-23.

Savin-Williams, R. (1987). An ethnological perspective on homosexuality during adolescence. *Journal of Adolescent Research*, *2*(1), 283-302.

Schafer, S. (1976). Sexual and social problems of lesbians. *Journal of Sex Research*, *12*(1), 50-69.

Schneider, M., & Tremble, B. (1986a). Training service providers to work with gay or lesbian adolescents: A workshop. *Journal of Counseling and Development*, *65*(2), 98-99.

Schneider, M., & Tremble, B. (1986b). Gay or straight: Working with the confused adolescent. *Journal of Homosexuality*, 71-82.

Schneider, W. (1987). Homosexuals: Is AIDS changing attitudes? *Public Opinion*, *10*(2), 6-7, 59.

Schneider, W., & Lewis, I. (1984). The straight story on homosexuality and gay rights. *Public Opinion*, *7*(1), 16-20, 59-60.

Schofield, M. (1965). *Sociological aspects of homosexuality*. London: Longmans, Green.

Schuettinger, R. (Ed). (1970). *The conservative tradition in European thought*. New York: Putman.

Schultz, A. (1970). *Alfred Schultz on phenomenology and social relations*. Chicago: University of Chicago Press.

Scott, A. (1970). *The Southern lady: From pedestal to politics, 1830-1930*. Chicago: University of Chicago Press.

Scroggs, R. (1983). *The New Testament and homosexuality: Contextual background for contemporary debate*. Philadelphia: Fortress.

Seajay, C. (1980). The class and the closet. In J. Gibbs, & S. Bennett (Eds.), *Top ranking: A collection of articles on racism and classicism in the lesbian community*. (pp. 119-133). New York: February 3 Press.

Sears, J. (1983). Sexuality: Taking off the masks. *Changing Schools*, *11*, 12-13.

Sears, J. (1987). Peering into the well of loneliness: The responsibility of educators to gay and lesbian youth. In A. Molnar (Ed.), *Social issues and education: Challenge and responsibility*. (pp. 79-100). Alexandria, VA: Association for Supervision and Curriculum Development.

Sears, J. (1988a). *Attitudes, experiences, and feelings of guidance counselors about working with homosexual students*. Paper presented at the American Educational Research Association. New Orleans: ERIC Document No. 296 210.

Sears, J. (1988b). Growing up gay: Is anyone there to listen? *American School Counselors Association Newsletter*, *4*, 4, 7.

Sears, J. (1988c). *Developing a sense of difference among gay and lesbian children in the Deep South*. Paper Presented at the 9th

Annual Curriculum Theory Conference. Dayton, OH: ERIC Document No. ED 288 126.

Sears, J. (1989a). *Personal feelings and professional attitudes of prospective teachers toward homosexuality and homosexual students: Research findings and curriculum recommendations*. Paper presented at the 1989 American Educational Research Association. San Francisco. ERIC Document No. 312 222.

Sears, J. (1989b). The impact of gender and race on growing up lesbian and gay in the South. *NWSA Journal, 1*(3), 422-457.

Sears, J. (1989c). Counseling sexual minorities: An interview with Virginia Uribe. *Empathy, 1*(2), 1, 8.

Sears, J. (In press). *Sexuality and the curriculum*. New York: Teachers College Press.

Sears, J., Marshall, J., & Otis-Wilborn, A. (1986). *Conducting qualitative research in higher education*. Paper presented at the First International Conference on the Freshman Year Experience. Newcastle, England. ERIC Document No. 272 107.

Seattle Institute for Child Advocacy (1985). *Talking about touching: A personal safety curriculum*. Seattle, WA: Seattle Institute for Child Advocacy.

Segrest, M. (1985). *My mama's dead squirrel: Lesbian essays on southern culture*. Ithaca, NY: Firebrand.

Selzer, R., & Smith, R. (1985). Race and ideology: A research note measuring liberalism and conservatism in Black America. *Phylon, 46*(2), 98-105.

Sernett, M. (Ed). (1985). *Afro-American religious history: A documentary witness*. Durham, NC: Duke University Press.

Sewell, W. (1971). Inequality of opportunity for higher education. *American Sociological Review, 36*(5), 793-809.

Sewell, W., & Hauser, R. (Eds). (1976). *Schooling and achievement in American society*. New York: Academic Press.

Sgroi, S. (1982). *Handbook of clinical intervention in child sexual abuse*. Lexington, MA: Lexington.

Shange, N. (1977). *For colored girls*. New York: Emerson Hall.

Shavelson, E., Biaggio, M., Cross, H., & Lehman, R. (1980). Lesbian women's perceptions of their parent-child relationships. *Journal of Homosexuality, 5*(3), 205-215.

Shepherd, G. (1987). Rank, gender, and homosexuality: Mombasa as a key to understanding sexual options. In P. Caplan (Ed.), *The cultural construction of sexuality*. (pp. 240-270). London: Tavistock.

Sherrill, R. (1968). *Gothic politics in the deep South*. New York: Grossman.

Shively, M., & DeCecco, J. (1977). Components of sexual identity. *Journal of Homosexuality, 3*(1), 41-48.

Shockley, A. (1984). The black lesbian in American literature. In T. Darty & S. Potter (Eds.), *Women-identified women*. (pp. 267-275). Palo Alto, CA: Mayfield.

Shortridge, J. (1977). A new regionalization of American religion. *Journal of the Scientific Study of Religion*, 16, 143-153.

Shostak, M. (1981). *The life and worlds of a Kung woman*. Cambridge, MA: Harvard University Press.

Siegelman, M. (1974). Parental background of male homosexuals and heterosexuals. *Archives of Sexual Behavior, 3*(1), 3-18.

Siegelman, M. (1981). Parental backgrounds of homosexual and heterosexual men: A cross national replication. *Archives of Sexual Behavior, 10*(6), 505-513.

Silverstein, C. (1981). *Man to man: Gay couples in America*. New York: Quill.

Simari, C., & Baskin, D. (1982). Incestuous experiences within homosexual populations. *Archives of Sexual Behavior, 11*(4), 329-344.

Simkins, F., & Woody, R. (1932). *South Carolina during Reconstruction*. Chapel Hill: University of North Carolina Press.

Simon, W., & Gagnon, J. (1967). Femininity in the lesbian community. *Social Problems, 15*(2), 212-221.

Simon, W., & Gagnon, J. (1973). *Sexual conduct: The social sources of human sexuality*. Chicago: Aldine.

Simon, W., & Gagnon, J. (1986). Sexual scripts: Permanence and change. *Archives of Sexual Behavior, 15*(2), 97-120.

Sipova, I., & Brzek, A. (1983). Parental and interpersonal relationships of transsexual and masculine and feminine homosexual men. *Journal of Homosexuality, 9*(1), 75-85.

Slater, B. (1988). Essential issues in working with lesbian and gay male youths. *Professional Psychology: Research and Practice, 19*(2), 226-235.

Smith, B. (Ed). (1983). *Home girls: A black feminist anthology*. New York: Kitchen Table: Women of Color Press.

Smith, B. (1982). Racism and women's studies. In G. Hull, P. Scott, & B. Smith (Ed.), *But some of us are brave: Black women's studies*. (pp. 48-51). New York: Feminist Press.

Smith, D. (1985). *An ethnographic interview study of homosexual teachers' perspectives*. Unpublished doctoral dissertation, State University of New York at Albany, Albany, NY, *Dissertation Abstracts International* 46, 1, 66A.

Smith, K., & Crawford, S. (1986). Suicide behavior among "normal" high school students. *Suicide and Life-Threatening Behavior*, *16*(3), 313-325.

Smith, L. (1949). *Killers of the dream*. New York: Norton.

Smith, M. (1986). By the year 2000. In J. Beam (Ed.), *In the life: A black gay anthology*. (pp. 224-229). Boston: Alyson.

Smith, S. (1985). *Myth, media, and the southern mind*. Fayetteville, AR: University of Arkansas Press.

Snead, E. (1988, May 8). Wedding 'belles.' *The State*, 4E.

Soares, J. (1979). Black and gay. In M. Levine (Ed.), *Gay men: The sociology of male homosexuality*. (pp. 263-274). New York: Harper & Row.

Sontag, S. (1978). Notes on "Camp." In S. Sontag, *Against interpretation and other essays*. (pp. 275-292). New York: Octagon.

Sophie, J. (1986). A critical examination of stage theories of lesbian identity development. *Journal of Homosexuality*, *12*(2), 39-51.

Sophie, J. (1985). *Stress, social network and sexual orientation identity change in women*. Unpublished doctoral dissertation, New York University, New York. *Dissertation Abstracts International* 45, 9, 3051B.

Sorensen, R. (1973). *Adolescent sexuality in contemporary America*. New York: World.

South Carolina Comprehensive Health Education Act. (1988). *SC Code of Laws*, 59-32-10 through 59-32-90.

South Carolina Division of Research & Statistical Services (1990). *South Carolina statistical abstract*, 1990. Columbia, SC: Author.

Spada, J. (1979). *The Spada report*. New York: Signet.

Spaulding, E. (1982). *The formation of lesbian identity during the "coming out" process*. Unpublished doctoral dissertation, Smith College School for Social Work, Northampton, MA. *Dissertation Abstracts International* 43, 6, 2106A.

Sprague, G. (1983, August 18). Chicago past: A rich gay history. *Advocate*, *374* (pp. 28-31, 58-59).

Stabiner, K. (1982, May 3). Tapping the homosexual market. *New York Times*, 34+.

Stambolian, G. (1984). A black man. In G. Stambolian (Ed.), *Male fantasies—gay realities*. (pp. 129-145). New York: Sea Horse.

Stanley, J. (1970). Homosexual slang. *American Speech*, *45*(1/2), 45-49.

Stanley, J., & Wolfe, S. (1980). *The coming out stories*. Watertown, MA: Persephone.

Staples, R. (1987). Social structure and black family life: An analysis of current trends. *Journal of Black Studies*, *17*(3), 267-286.

Stark, R., & Bainbridge, W. (1985). *The future of religion: Secularization, revival and cult formation*. Berkeley: University of California Press.

Stark, R., & Glock, C. (1968). *American piety: The nature of religious commitment*. Berkeley: University of California Press.

Starzecpyzel, E. (1987). The Persephone complex. In Boston Lesbian Psychologies Collective (Ed.), *Lesbian psychologies: Explorations and challenges*. (pp. 261-282). Urbana: University of Illinois Press.

Stember, C. (1978). *Sexual racism*. New York: Harper & Row.

Stephan, W. (1973). Parental relationships and early social experiences of activist male homosexuals and male heterosexuals. *Journal of Abnormal Psychology*, *82*(3), 506-513.

Sterling, D. (1979). *Black fore-mothers: Three lives*. Old Westbury, NY: Feminist Press.

Sterling, D. (Ed). (1984). *We are your sisters: Black women in the nineteenth century*. New York: Norton.

Stevenson, W. (1968). *The inside story of Jehovah's Witnesses*. New York: Hart.

Stoller, R. (1976). Two feminized male American Indians. *Archives of Sexual Behavior*, *5*(6), 529-538.

Stone, C. (1981, Sept. 3). The semantics of gay. *Advocate, 325* (pp. 20-22).

Storms, M. (1978). Attitudes toward homosexuality and femininity in men. *Journal of Homosexuality, 3*(3), 257-263.

Stouffer, S. (1955). *Communism, conformity, and civil liberties.* New York: Doubleday.

Strong, S. (1946). Negro-white relationships as reflected in social types. *American Journal of Sociology, 52*(1), 23-30.

Strother, D. (1986). Suicide among the young. *Phi Delta Kappan, 67*(10), 756-759.

Stuart, B. (1987, October 18). Single-member plan could help Barnwell. *The State*, 1B, 8B.

Sullivan, H. (1974). *The interpersonal theory of psychiatry.* New York: Norton.

Sykes, G. (1958). *The society of captives: A study of a maximum security prison.* Princeton, NJ: Princeton University Press.

Symonds, M. (1969). Homosexuality in adolescence. *Pennsylvania Psychiatric Quarterly, 9*(2), 15-24.

Talamini, J. (1982). *Boys will be girls: The hidden world of the heterosexual male transvestite.* Landham, MD: University Press of America.

Tanner, D. (1978). *The lesbian community.* Lexington, MA: Lexington.

Tate, A. (1977). *The fathers and other fiction.* Baton Rouge: Louisiana State University Press.

Taub, D., & Leger, R. (1984). Argot and the creation of social types in a young gay community. *Human Relations, 37*(3), 181-189.

Taylor, A. (1983). Conceptions of masculinity and femininity as a basis for stereotypes of male and female homosexuals. *Journal of Homosexuality, 9*(1), 37-53.

Taylor, A. (1976). *Travail and triumph: Black life and culture in the South since the Civil War.* Westport, CT: Greenwood.

Taylor, W. (1961). *Cavalier and Yankee: The Old South and American national character.* New York: Braziller.

Teal, D. (1971). *The gay militants.* New York: Stein & Day.

Teeter, R. (1988). The travails of 19th-century urban youth as a precondition to the invention of modern adolescence. *Adolescence*, *23*(89), 15-18.

TenHouten, W. (1970). The black family: Myth and reality. *Psychiatry*, *33*(2), 145-173.

Terborg-Penn, R. (1978). Discrimination against Afro-American women in the woman's movement, 1830-1920. In S. Harley & R. Terborg-Penn (Eds.), *The Afro-American woman: Struggles and images*. (pp. 17-27). Port Washington, NY: Kennikat.

Thayer, J. (1980). The berdache of the northern plains: A socioreligious perspective. *Journal of Anthropological Research*, *36*(3), 292-293.

Thomas, W., & Zaniecki, F. (1927). *The Polish peasant in Europe and America*. New York: Dove.

Thompson, G., & Fishburn, W. (1977). Attitudes toward homosexuality among graduate counseling students. *Counselor Education and Supervision*, *17*(2), 121-130.

Thompson, M. (1983, October 13). Sociobiologist James Weinrich: Probing the puzzle of homosexual behavior. *Advocate*, *378* (pp. 47-48 +).

Thompson, N., Schwartz, D., McCandless, B., & Edwards, D. (1973). Parent-child relationships and sexual identity in male and female homosexuals and heterosexuals. *Journal of Consulting and Clinical Psychology*, *43*(1), 120-127.

Tindall, G. (1967). *The emergence of the new South, 1913-1945*. Baton Rouge: Louisiana State University Press.

Tinney, J. (1986). Why a gay black church? In J. Beam (Ed.), *In the life: A black gay anthology*. (pp. 70-86). Boston: Alyson.

Townsend, L. (1935). *South Carolina Baptists, 1670-1805*. Florence, SC: Florence Printing Co.

Trenchard, L. (Ed). (1984). *Talking about young lesbians*. London: London Gay Teenage Group.

Trenchard, L., & Hugh, W. (1984). *Something to tell you . . . the experiences and needs of young lesbians and gay men in London*. London: London Gay Teenage Group.

Trivers, R. (1976). Sexual selection and resource-accuing abilities in *Anolis garmani*. *Evolution 30*(2), 253-269.

Troiden, R. (1979). Becoming a homosexual: A model of gay identity acquisition. *Psychiatry*, *42*(4), 362-373.

Troiden, R., & Goode, E. (1980). Variables related to the acquisition of a gay identity. *Journal of Homosexuality*, 5(4), 383-392.

Tucker, S. (1982). The power of naming. *Christopher Street*, 58 (pp. 60-63).

Tuten, J. (1987, October 18). Election changes opening political office doors for Blacks. *The State*, 1B, 9B.

Tyson, P. (1982). A developmental line of gender identity, gender role, and choice of love object. *Journal of the American Psychoanalytic Association*, 30, 61-86.

Valentine, F. (1980). *A historical study of Southern Baptist and race relations, 1917-1947*. New York: Arno. (Originally published in 1949).

Van Dyck, P. (1984). A critique of Dörner's analysis of hormonal data from bisexual males. *Journal of Sex Research*, 20(4), 412-414.

Van Wyk, P., & Geist, C. (1984). Psychosocial development of heterosexual, bisexual, and homosexual behavior. *Archives of Sexual Behavior*, 13(6), 505-544.

Vance, B., & Green, V. (1984). Lesbian identities. *Psychology of Women Quarterly*, 8(3), 293-307.

Vander Mey, B., & Neff, R. (1986). *Incest as child abuse: Research and implications*. New York: Praeger.

Vining, D. (1982, March 18). Signs and shibboleths. *Advocate*, 338 (pp. 24-27).

Wade-Gayles, G. (1980). She who is black and mother: In sociology and fiction, 1940-1970. In L. Rodgers-Rose (Ed.), *The black woman*. (pp. 89-106). Beverly Hills: Sage.

Walker, A. (1982). *The color purple*. New York: Harcourt Brace and Jovanovich.

Walker, C. (1981). *A rock in a weary land: The African Methodist Episcopal Church during the Civil War and Reconstruction*. Baton Rouge: Louisiana State University Press.

Walker, M. (1980). *Visionary love: A spirit book of gay mythology and trans-mutational faerie*. San Francisco: Treeroots Press.

Walker, S., & Barton, L. (Ed). (1983). *Gender, class and education*. Sussex, England: Falmer.

Wallace, D. (1917). *Historical background of religion in South Carolina*. Florence, SC: Greenville Historical Society.

Wallace, M. (1978). *Black macho and the myth of the superwoman*. New York: Dial.

Wallerstein, I. (1988). What can one mean by southern culture? In N. Bartley (Ed.), *The evolution of southern culture*. (pp. 1-13). Athens: University of Georgia Press.

Walter, D. (1989, April 11). Choosing to be gay. *Advocate*, *522* (p. 23).

Wamble, H. (1976). Baptists in the South. In J. Wood, Jr. (Ed.), *Baptists and the American experience*. (pp. 279-304). Valley Forge, PA: Judson.

Warren, C. (1974). *Identity and community in the gay world*. New York: Wiley.

Washington, J. (1964). *Black religion*. Boston: Beacon.

Washington, J. (1984). *Black sects and cults*. Landham, MD: University Press of America.

Weathers, B. (1980). Alcoholism and the lesbian community. In C. Eddy, & J. Ford (Eds.), *Alcoholism in women*. (pp. 142-149). Dubuque, IA: Kendall-Hunt.

Weber, M. (1946). From Max Weber: Essays in sociology. H. Gerth, & C. W. Mills (Eds. & Trans.), New York: Oxford University Press.

Wechsler, H. (1976). Alcohol intoxication and drug use among teenagers. *Journal of Studies on Alcohol*, *37*(11), 1672-1677.

Weeks, J. (1981). Discourse, desire and sexual deviance. In K. Plummer (Ed.), *The making of the modern homosexual*. (pp. 76-111). London: Hutchinson.

Weeks, J. (1987). Questions of identity. In P. Caplan (Ed.), *The cultural construction of sexuality*. (pp. 31-51). London: Tavistock.

Wein, G. (1982). Gay kids say the darndest things. *Christopher Street*, *61*, 18-26.

Weinberg, G. (1972). *Society and the healthy homosexual*. New York: St. Martin's Press.

Weinberg, M., & Williams, C. (1974). *Male homosexuals: Their problems and adaptations*. New York: Oxford University Press.

Weinberg, T. (1984). Biology, ideology, and reification of developmental stages in the study of homosexual identities. *Journal of Homosexuality*, *10*(3/4), 77-84.

Weinberg, T. (1983). *Gay men, gay selves: The social construction of homosexual identities*. New York: Irvington.

Weinberg, T. (1978). On "doing" and "being" gay: Sexual behavior and homosexual male self-identity. *Journal of Homosexuality*, *4*(2), 143-156.

Weinrich, J. (1980). Homosexual behavior in animals. In R. Forleo & W. Pasini (Eds.), *Medical sexology*. Littleton, MA: PSG Publishing.

Weisberg, D. (1985). *Children of the night: A study of adolescent prostitution*. Lexington, MA: Lexington Books.

Weiss, A., & Schiller, G. (1988). *Before Stonewall*. Tallahassee, FL: Naiad Press.

Welch, S., & Combs, M. (1985). Intra-racial differences in attitudes of blacks: Class cleavages or consensus? *Phylon*, *46*(2), 91-97.

Wellman, M. (1984). The school counselor's role in the communication of suicidal ideation by adolescents. *School Counselor*, *32*(2), 104-109.

Wesberry, J. (1966). *Baptists in South Carolina before the War Between the States*. Columbia, SC: Bryan. (Original published in 1935).

West, W. (1977). Public tolerance of homosexual behavior. *Cornell Journal of Social Relations*, *12*(1), 25-36.

Whalen, W. (1962). *Armageddon around the corner*. New York: John Day.

Whitam, F. (1977a). The homosexual role: A reconsideration. *Journal of Sex Research*, *13*(1), 1-11.

Whitam, F. (1977b). Childhood indicators of male homosexuality. *Archives of Sexual Behavior*, *6*(2), 89-96.

Whitam, F. (1980). The prehomosexual male child in three societies: The United States, Guatemala, Brazil. *Archives of Sexual Behavior*, *9*(2), 87-99.

Whitam, F., & Zent, M. (1984). A cross-cultural assessment of early cross-gender behavior and familial factors in male homosexuality. *Archives of Sexual Behavior*, *13*(5), 427-439.

White, E. (1983). *States of desire: Travels in gay America*. New York: Dutton.

White, L., & Brinkerhoff, D. (1981). The sexual division of labor: Evidence from childhood. *Social Forces, 60*(1), 170-181.

White, R., & Hopkins, H. (1976). *The social gospel: Religion and reform in changing America*. Philadelphia: Temple University Press.

Whitehead, H. (1981). The bow and the burden strap: A new look at institutionalized homosexuality in native North Americans. In S. Ortner & H. Whitehead (Eds.), *Sexual meanings: The cultural construction of gender and sexuality*. (pp. 80-115). Cambridge, MA: Cambridge University Press.

Wiggins, W. (1973). Jack Johnson as a bad nigger: The folklore of his life. In R. Christman & N. Hare (Eds.), *Contemporary black thought*. (pp. 53-70). Indianapolis: Bobbs-Merrill.

Wilde, O. (1926). *The picture of Dorian Gray*. New York: Modern Library.

Wilde, O. (1972). The critic as artist. In *The works of Oscar Wilde: Intentions*. (pp. 107-237). New York: AMS. (Original published in 1909).

Wilkins, T. (1970). *Cherokee tragedy*. New York: Macmillan.

Williams, C. (1961). *The southern mountaineer in fact and fiction*. Unpublished doctoral dissertation, New York University, New York. *Dissertation Abstracts International 27*, 6, 1797A.

Williams, T. (1955). *Cat on a hot tin roof*. New York: New Directions.

Williams, W. (1986). *The spirit and the flesh*. Boston: Beacon.

Willie, C. (1981a). Dominance in the family: The black and white experience. *Journal of Black Psychology, 7*(2), 91-97.

Willie, C. (1981b). *A new look at black families*. Bayside, NY: General Hall.

Willis, P. (1977). *Learning to labour: How working class kids get working class jobs*. Westmead, England: Saxon House.

Wilmore, G. (1972). *Black religion and black radicalism*. Garden City, NY: Doubleday.

Wilson, C. (Ed). (1985). *Religion in the South*. Jackson: University Press of Mississippi.

Wolf, D. (1979). *The lesbian community*. Berkeley: University of California Press.

Wood, R. (1987). Raging bull: The homosexual subtext in film. In

M. Koufman (Ed.), *Beyond patriarchy*. (pp. 266-276). Toronto, Ontario: Oxford University Press.

Wooden, W., & Parker, J. (1982). *Men behind bars*. New York: Plenum.

Woods, S. (1989). *Describing the experience of lesbian physical educators: A phenomenological study*. Paper presented at the American Educational Research Association. San Francisco.

Woodson, C. (1918). *A century of Negro migration*. Washington, DC: Association for the Study of Negro Life History.

Woodson, C. (1972). *The history of the Negro church*. New York: Associated Press.

Wrate, R., & Gulens, V. (1986). A systems approach to child effeminacy and the prevention of adolescent transexualism. *Journal of Adolescence*, *9*, 215-229.

Wright, R. (1966). *Black boy: A record of childhood and youth*. New York: Harper & Row.

Wright, R. (1940). *Native son*. New York: Harper & Row.

Wyatt, G. (1985). The sexual abuse of Afro-American and white American women in childhood. *Child Abuse and Neglect*, *9*(4), 507-519.

Wyatt, G., Peters, S., & Guthrie, D. (1988). Kinsey revisited part I: Comparison of the sexual socialization and sexual behavior of white women over 30 years. *Archives of Sexual Behavior*, *17*(3), 201-239.

Wyatt-Brown, B. (1982). *Southern honor: Ethics and behavior in the Old South*. New York: Oxford University Press.

Wyatt-Brown, B. (1988). The evolution of hero's honor in the southern literary tradition. In N. Bartley (Ed.), *Evolution of southern culture*. (pp. 108-130). Athens: University of Georgia Press.

Yance, N. (1978). *Religion southern style: Southern Baptists and society in historical perspective*. Danville, IL: Association of Baptist Professors of Religion.

Yearwood, L., & Weinberg, T. (1979). Black organizations, gay organizations: Sociological parallels. In M. Levine (Ed.), *The sociology of male homosexuality*. (pp. 301-316). New York: Harper & Row.

Yin, R. (1984). *Case study research*. Beverly Hills: Sage.

Young, M., & Whertvine, J. (1982). Attitudes of heterosexual students toward homosexual behavior. *Psychological Reports*, *51*(2), 673-674.

Young, T. (1985). Adolescent suicide. *High School Journal*, *69*(1), 55-59.

Young, V. (1970). Family and childhood in a southern Negro community. *American Anthropologist*, *72*(2), 269-288.

Zaretsky, E. (1976). *Capitalism, the family and personal life*. New York: Harper & Row.

Zelnick, M., & Shah, F. (1983). First intercourse among young Americans. *Family Planning Perspectives*, 15(2), 64-70.

Ziebold, T., & Mongeon, J. (1982). Introduction: Alcoholism and the homosexual community. In T. Ziebold & J. Mongeon (Ed.), *Gay and sober*. (pp. 3-7). New York: Harrington Park Press.

Zollar, A. (1985). *A member of the family: Strategies of black family continuity*. Chicago: Nelson-Hall.

Zuger, B. (1966). Effeminate behavior present in boys from early childhood. I. The clinical syndrome and follow-up studies. *Journal of Pediatrics*, *19*(6), 1098-1107.

Zuger, B. (1970). The role of familial factors in persistent effeminate behavior in boys. *American Journal of Psychiatry*, *126*(8), 151-154.

Zuger, B. (1976). Monozygotic twins discordant for homosexuality: Report of a pair and significance of the phenomenon. *Comprehensive Psychiatry*, *17*(5), 661-669.

Zuger, B. (1978). Effeminate behavior present in boys from childhood: Ten additional years of follow-up. *Comprehensive Psychiatry*, *19*(4), 363-369.

Zuger, B. (1984). Early effeminate behavior in boys: Outcome and significance for homosexuality. *Journal of Nervous and Mental Disease*, *172*(2), 90-97.

Subject Index

Name Index

"With the mind of the scholar and the heart of the native son, Sears presents the complex and diverse experience of growing up gay, lesbian, and bisexual in the South while providing an analysis which I, a long-time Northerner, found TRULY ILLUMINATING. Included is a series of vivid portraits exhibiting a cross-section of southerners who, by dint of their sexuality, are branded as rebels. In reality, though, they are heroes all."
Warren J. Blumenfeld, MEd, Executive Board Member, Gay, Lesbian, and Bisexual Speakers Bureau, Boston, Massachusetts; Instructor, Cambridge Center for Adult Education, Cambridge, Massachusetts; Co-author (with Diane Raymond) of *Looking at Gay and Lesbian Life* (Philosophical Library, Inc., 1988); Co-producer of *Pink Triangles* (Cambridge Documentary Films)

"This book PROMISES TO HEAL, ENLIGHTEN, AND PROVOKE DISCUSSION. The 'coming out' stories are both comforting and unsettling. Analysis of the influence of religion and culture expands our understanding of the great diversity within the gay and lesbian community. Sears' thoughts on the development of identities encourages much-needed debate."
Brian McNaught, Gloucester, Massachusetts; Author of *On Being Gay—Thoughts on Family, Faith and Love*

"This is AN IMPORTANT PORTRAIT OF YOUNG GAY LIVES, honoring both their uniqueness and singularities while underlining their social importance. Sears succeeds in recreating the specificity of individual lives while linking them to contemporary political and gender issues. It is a fine piece of work."
William F. Pinar, PhD, Professor and Chair, Department of Curriculum and Instruction, Louisiana State University, Baton Rouge, Louisiana

"A wonderful contribution to the body of information on gay and lesbian youth. It takes the reader on a journey that few authors have been willing to make. [It] will make you laugh and cry—but most of all it will grip you with its candid blending of scientific research and matter-of-fact narratives. . . . there is a universal quality that makes this book WORTHWHILE FOR ALL READERS."
Virginia Uribe, PhD, Founder, Project 10, Los Angeles Unified School District, Los Angeles, California

"SHOULD BE ESSENTIAL READING for all educators concerned with the issues of sexual identity, gender, and voice. This is a book that combines pedagogy in the broader sense of reconstructing how voices both speak and are shaped around the issue of growing up gay, lesbian, and bisexual in the South. It is a book that combines narrative and theory with a politics that is essential to rethinking how subjectivities are constructed in gendered terms. This is a book of courage and hope. Its scholarship is impeccable and its vision refreshing. Moreover, it is elegant in its style. A must for educators."
Henry A. Giroux, PhD, Professor, Department of Educational Leadership, Miami University, Oxford, Ohio